For Errol

Associate yourselves, O ye people, and ye shall be broken in pieces; and give ear, all ye of far countries; gird yourselves, and ye shall be broken in pieces.

—ISAIAH 8:9

CONTENTS

PART III

DEATH AND REBIRTH

A NOTE ON DATES,
NAMES, TRANSLATION, AND
TRANSLITERATION

Until the Bolsheviks switched over to the Gregorian calendar in 1918, Russia followed the Julian, which was thirteen days behind by 1914. The Ottoman Empire traditionally used a modified version of the Islamic lunar calendar, with years dated from the time of Muhammad's exodus from Mecca (*hejira*) in AD 622—although it switched over to the Julian version of solar calendar dates in the nineteenth century (except for Muslim religious holidays, which still, to this day, are dated by the old lunar calendar). To keep things simple, I have used Gregorian dates consistently throughout the text, with the exception of certain major pre-1918 dates in Russian history, which Russian history buffs may know by the "old" dates, in which case I have given both dates with a slash, as in March 1/14, 1917, where *1* is the Julian and *14* the Gregorian date.

For Russian-language words, I have employed a simplified Library of Congress transliteration system throughout, with the exception of commonly used spellings of famous surnames (e.g., Yudenich, not Iudenich; Trotsky, not Trotskii). I have also left out "soft" and "hard" signs from the main text, so as not to burden the reader.

With regard to Turkish spellings, I have generally rendered the "c" phonetically as "dj" (as in *Djavid* and *Djemal*) and used the dotless ı where appropriate (it sounds a bit like "uh") to differentiate from the Turkish "i," which sounds like "ee." Likewise, I have tried to properly render ş (sh) and ç (ch) to help readers puzzle out pronunciations, even if these letters are really post-1928 concoctions of Atatürk's language reforms. With Arabic names, I have used the most widely known Western variants (thus Hussein, not *al-Husayn ibn 'Ali al-Hashimi,* and Ibn Saud, not *'Abd al-Aziz ibn 'Abd al-Rahman al-Saud*). It is impossible to be consistent in all these things; may common sense prevail.

With apologies to any Turkish readers, I have referred to the Ottoman capital consistently as Constantinople, not Istanbul, unless referring to the present-day city, because it was so called by contemporaries, including Ottoman government officials. Likewise, I have followed the transition in nomenclature from St. Petersburg to Petrograd after Russia went to war with Germany in 1914 (luckily, we do not have to reckon with "Leningrad" in the bounds of this narrative). With "lesser" cities and other place-names, I have used the contemporary form, affixing the current equivalent in parentheses, thus "Adrianople (Edirne)" and "Üsküp (Skopje)." Antique geographic terms used by Europeans but not by the Ottomans, such as Palestine, Cilicia, and Mesopotamia, I have generally deployed in the manner they were used in diplomatic gamesmanship (which is to say without precise territorial definition, as there was not any). The maps should, in any case, help readers clear up these vexatious questions to the extent this is possible.

All translations from the French, German, Russian, and Turkish, unless otherwise noted, are my own.

LIST OF MAPS

INTRODUCTION: THE SYKES-PICOT MYTH AND THE MODERN MIDDLE EAST

NINETY-TWO YEARS AFTER its dissolution by Mustafa Kemal Atatürk, the Ottoman Empire is in the news again. Scarcely a day goes by without some media mention of the contested legacy of the First World War in the Middle East, with borders drawn then being redrawn now in the wake of the Syrian civil war and the rise of the Islamic State of Iraq, Syria, and the Levant (or whatever its latest territorial iteration). "Is It the End of Sykes-Picot?" asked Patrick Cockburn in the *London Review of Books*, assuming that his readers will have heard of the two men who (it is said) negotiated the agreement to partition the Ottoman Empire between Britain and France.[1] As the war's centennial arrived in 2014, "Sykes-Picot" moved beyond historical trivia to the realm of cliché, a shorthand explanation for the latest upheaval in the Middle East that rolls easily off every tongue.

From the ubiquity of media reference to them, one might suppose that Sir Mark Sykes and Georges Picot were the only actors of consequence on the Ottoman theater in the First World War, and Britain and France the only relevant parties to the disposition of Ottoman territory, reaching agreement on the subject in (so Google or Wikipedia informs us) *anno domini* 1916. As glibly summarized by the Claude Rains character in David Lean's classic film *Lawrence of Arabia*, the gist of the traditional story is that "Mark Sykes [was] a British civil servant. Monsieur Picot [was] a French civil servant. Mr. Sykes and Monsieur Picot met and they agreed that, after the war, France and England would share the [Ottoman] empire, including Arabia."[2]

The popular resonance of the Sykes-Picot legend is not difficult to understand. In our postcolonial age, imperialism and long-dead imperialists are easy targets on whom one can safely assign blame for current problems. Sykes and Picot are stand-ins for the sins of Britain and France, whose centuries-long project of colonial expansion reached its final apogee with the planting of the Union Jack and the French tricolor in the Arab Middle East, where it all (by a kind of poetic justice, some would say) began to go horribly wrong. Britain's backing of Zionism in the Balfour Declaration of 1917 was, in this dramatic tale of hubris followed by nemesis, a step too far, which awakened Arabs from a centuries-long slumber to rise up against the latter-day Crusaders—Europeans and Israelis alike—who had seized their lands. The more recent rise of pan-Islamic movements such as the Muslim Brotherhood, Hamas, Hezbollah, al-Qaeda, and the Islamic State—groups that all strive to erase artificial, European-imposed state boundaries—now appears to be putting the final nails in the coffin of Sykes-Picot.

It is a seductive story, simple, compact, elegant, and easy to understand. But the Claude Rains summary of Sykes-Picot bears little resemblance to the history on which it is ostensibly based. The partition of the Ottoman Empire was not settled bilaterally by two British and French diplomats in 1916, but rather at a multinational peace conference in Lausanne, Switzerland, in 1923, following a conflict that had lasted nearly twelve years going back to the Italian invasion of Ottoman Tripoli (Libya) in 1911 and the two Balkan Wars of 1912–13. Neither Sykes nor Picot played any role worth mentioning at Lausanne, at which the dominant figure looming over the proceedings was Mustafa Kemal, the Turkish nationalist whose armies had just defeated Greece and (by extension) Britain in yet another war lasting from 1919 through 1922. Even in 1916, the year ostensibly defined for the ages by their secret partition agreement, Sykes and Picot played second and third fiddle, respectively, to a Russian foreign minister, Sergei Sazonov, who was the real driving force behind the carve-up of the Ottoman Empire, a Russian project par excellence, and recognized as such by the British and French when they were first asked to sign off on Russian partition plans as early as March–April 1915. None of the most notorious post-Ottoman borders—those separating Palestine from (Trans) Jordan and Syria, or Syria from Iraq, or Iraq from Kuwait—were drawn by Sykes and Picot in 1916. Even the boundaries they did sketch out that year, such as those that were to separate the British, French, and Russian zones in Mesopotamia and Persia, were jettisoned after the war (Mosul in northern Iraq, most famously, was originally assigned to the French, until the British decided they wanted its oil fields). After the Russians signed a separate peace with the Germans at Brest-Litovsk in 1918, the entire zone assigned to Russia in 1916 was taken away and thereafter expunged from historical memory. To replace the departed Russians, the United States (in a long-forgotten episode of American history) was enjoined to take up the broadest Ottoman mandates, encompassing much of present-day Turkey—only for Congress to balk on ratifying the postwar treaties. With the United States and Communist Russia bowing out of the game, Italy and Greece were invited to claim their share of the Ottoman carcass, only for both to later sign away their territorial gains to Mustafa Kemal entirely without reference to the Sykes-Picot Agreement. Nor was there so much as a mention in the 1916 partition agreement of the Saudi dynasty, which, following its conquest of the Islamic holy cities of Mecca and Medina, has ruled formerly Ottoman Arabia since 1924.

The Ottoman Empire had endured for more than six centuries before it was finally broken against the anvil of the First World War. From 1517 to 1924 (but for a brief interregnum from 1802 to 1813 when Wahhabi insurgents had taken over), the sultans had ruled over the Islamic holy places of Arabia, granting them legitimacy, in the eyes of the Muslim faithful, as caliphs of Islam. The Ottoman sultans gave their millions of subjects, in turn, a common identity and pride in belonging to a great empire, pride held above all by Muslims but also shared, to some extent, by the empire's large Jewish and Christian minorities, who depended on the sultan for protection. A great deal more was therefore at stake in the Ottoman wars of 1911–23 than the mere disposition of real estate.

Journalists are not wrong to search out the roots of today's Middle Eastern problems in early twentieth-century history. But the real historical record is richer and far more dramatic than the myth. We must move beyond the Sykes-Picot myth if we are to understand the impact of the First World War on this vast region, on which it left physical traces from Gallipoli to Erzurum to Gaza to Baghdad. The Ottoman fronts stretched across three continents and three oceans, embroiling not only Britain and France but all the other

European Great Powers (and a few smaller ones)—and, of course, the Ottomans themselves.

So far from a sideshow to the First World War, the Ottoman theater was central to both the outbreak of European war in 1914 and the peace settlement that truly ended it. The War of the Ottoman Succession, as we might call the broader conflict stretching from 1911 to 1923, was an epic struggle, as seen in the larger-than-life figures it made famous—Ismail Enver, Ahmed Djemal, and Mehmed Talât, the three "Young Turk" triumvirs; Kaiser Wilhelm II, Admiral Wilhelm Souchon, and Otto Liman von Sanders on the German side; Kitchener, Churchill, T. E. Lawrence, and Lloyd George in Britain; Sergei Sazonov, Grand Duke Nicholas, Nikolai Yudenich, and Alexander Kolchak in Russia; Sherif Hussein of Mecca and his sons Feisal and Abdullah, along with Ibn Saud, in Arabia; Eleftherios Venizelos and King Constantine in Greece; and not least Kâzım Karabekir, Ismet Inönü, and Mustafa Kemal as fathers of the Republic of Turkey. It was not Sykes and Picot but these far greater men who forged the modern Middle East in the crucible of war. A century later, with the opening of the last archives of the period, their story can be told in full.

THE
OTTOMAN
ENDGAME

SEPTEMBER 7, 1876

FROM EVERY CORNER OF THE EMPIRE they came to witness the ceremony. The streets were aglow with the colorful costumes of the empire—red conical fezzes with black silk tassels, white turbans, Arab-style keffiyehs, alongside the elegant formal wear of European diplomats. Witnesses claimed that a hundred thousand souls lined the waterfront, craning to catch a glimpse of the sovereign-to-be as he was rowed in his white-and-gold *caïque* from the Bosphorus past the teeming multitudes on the Galata Bridge. After docking on the Golden Horn, the thirty-four-year-old heir mounted his white charger and rode through the Imperial Guard to Eyüp mosque, the most sacred in the empire, built by Mehmet the Conqueror after the fall of Constantinople in 1453. Here, beneath the silver shrine to the Prophet's standard bearer, who fell during the Arab siege of the city in 670, Abdul Hamid II was girded with the Sword of Osman, empowering him as the thirty-fourth sultan of the empire and (following the conquest of the holy places in 1517) twenty-sixth Ottoman caliph of the Islamic faithful.

While most observers agreed that the new sultan conducted himself with great dignity during the proceedings, there were discordant notes that seemed to bode poorly for his reign. Physically, Abdul Hamid was so unprepossessing that the Sword of Osman seemed to dwarf his slight frame. The much taller *Sheikh-ul-Islam* who invested him with the sword had to bend over sharply in order to kiss the sultan on the left shoulder, as required by tradition. Other portentous incidents transpired elsewhere in the city, where crowding on the Galata Bridge caused it to partially collapse nearly four feet, and to very nearly sink into the Golden Horn. Just a stone's throw away, a cable snapped in the underground funicular tram linking the quay with Pera, the European quarter up on the hill.[1]

More ominous still was the news from Europe. The previous October, then-sultan Abdul Aziz, bankrupted by the compounding interest on his own palace extravagances, had suspended payments on Ottoman bond coupons, a default that had alienated thousands of bondholders, of whom a large and vocal number were to be found in Paris and London. When a Christian uprising spread across Ottoman-ruled territory in the Balkans, the government (generally called the Sublime Porte) thus found itself bereft of sympathy. It tried to douse the flames of Balkan unrest, sending in irregular Circassians (the Bashi-Bazouks) in part because pay to the regular army was in arrears. By summer 1876, stories of horrendous atrocities had spread across Europe. Coming out of retirement to chastise the British government of Benjamin Disraeli for its indifference, the former prime minister William Ewart Gladstone worked himself into a state of high moral dudgeon in a soon-to-be world-famous pamphlet denouncing the *Bulgarian Horrors*, which hit newsstands even as Abdul Hamid was being girded at Eyüp. While Disraeli, condemning both sides as "equally terrible and atrocious," dismissed Bashi-Bazouk horror stories as "coffee-house babble,"* Gladstone saw in them proof that Turks were "the one great anti-human specimen of humanity," who should be "clear[ed] out from the province they have desolated and profaned . . . bag and baggage."[2]

Gladstone said nothing that pan-Slavist propagandists, many on the tsarist Russian payroll, had not already been saying for months. But he said it with the full fury of English parliamentary eloquence, raising the frightful prospect for Abdul Hamid II that Great Britain, Turkey's traditional protector against Russian encroachment, would do nothing to help her if the tsarist armies intervened in the Balkans, as looked increasingly likely as volunteers boarded train after train in Moscow that summer, hoping—like Tolstoy's Vronsky in *Anna Karenina*—to strike a blow for Slavdom. With (unofficial)

---

* Disraeli later said that he had been "mistaken" in dismissing atrocity stories from Bulgaria. The Ottoman government itself admitted the Bashi-Bazouks were responsible for 6,000 civilian deaths; Europeans estimated 12,000. Still, in a sense his description was apt. Written before serious investigation of the events in Bulgaria had been carried out, Gladstone's famous pamphlet was based on the "reporting" of Edwin Pears, a Constantinople lawyer who did not even travel to Bulgaria: he simply passed on stories fed to him by American missionaries at Robert College, told to them by their Bulgarian Christian students. Not "coffee-house babble," but gossip, nonetheless.

Russian encouragement, Serbia had declared war on Turkey in June, placing her army under the command of Russian general Mikhail Grigorievich Chernyaev, recent conqueror of Tashkent. Montenegro had then piled on too. Adding insult to injury, none other than Lord Stratford Canning, the now-retired longtime ambassador to the Porte who had almost single-handedly brought Britain into the Crimean War on the Ottoman side, publicly endorsed Gladstone's anti-Turkish stance in a letter to the London *Times*—indeed, Gladstone had dedicated the *Bulgarian Horrors* to Canning. In an especially embittering touch, Canning was the first foreigner Abdul Hamid, while a sickly and lonely young child, had met, three decades ago, in a chance encounter in the Topkapı Palace gardens—in fact, Canning was the first adult of any nationality to have treated the boy with genuine kindness, such that the future sultan remembered the incident decades later. If Russia's ambitions to partition the Ottoman Empire—first broached by Tsar Nicholas I in 1853 in conversation with the British ambassador when he called it the "Sick Man" (of Europe)—now had the tacit support of Abdul Hamid's hero and Britain's most notorious Turcophile, there would seem to be little hope for the empire's survival.

Still, despite the litany of disturbing news pouring into the capital, Abdul Hamid had reasons for guarded optimism as he left the Eyüp mosque. He had already achieved more than his immediate predecessor, Murad V. Although hailed by large and enthusiastic crowds as the "Great Reformer" after the violent deposition of Abdul Aziz in May, Murad had never mustered the strength to face the public in an accession ceremony. During his years in the *kafes*, or gilded confinement, endured by all heirs to the throne, Murad had developed a fatal taste (on a heavily chaperoned trip to Paris) for champagne laced with brandy. Already shaky, within days of his ascension Murad learned that the deposed Abdul Aziz had committed suicide, slashing both wrists with a pair of scissors (a difficult trick, leading to rumors of foul play). Learning of his predecessor's fate, Murad fainted. When he came to, he fell into a violent fit of vomiting. As if this were not enough, on June 15, to enact vengeance for the "martyred" Abdul Aziz, a young Circassian officer, whose sister Nesrin had been the late sultan's harem favorite, blasted his way into a cabinet meeting, murdering the conspirator who had deposed him—War Minister Hüseyin Avni, along with the foreign minister, Raşid Pasha. Small wonder Murad was a gibbering wreck (diagnosed with "monomania of the suicidal type"), unable to receive the Sword of Osman, meet ambassadors, or carry out any other duties of a sultan. Simply by making it through the girding ceremony unscathed, Abdul Hamid had done much to restore public confidence in the embattled empire.

True, the young sultan was an enigma, an unknown quantity even to his advisers. Until the terrible summer of 1876—known to Turks ever after as the "year of three Sultans"—reformist politicians, led by the great constitutionalist Midhat Pasha, along with Christian minorities and scheming European statesmen, had invested their hopes in the handsome and charming Murad, believing him to be sympathetic to Western liberal values (or at least malleable enough to embrace them upon prodding). Abdul Hamid, by contrast, was painfully shy, socially awkward, and odd-looking. His hook nose was so striking that many Turks believed his mother, Pirimujgan, to be secretly Armenian or Jewish (she was in fact the usual Circassian slave dancing girl, briefly a favorite of Sultan Abdul Mecid, before she succumbed to consumption, dying at twenty-six, when her son was only seven). Abdul Hamid, raised by a foster mother and neglected by his father as unpromising, had suffered through a childhood and *kafes* confinement even lonelier than the norm, his only companions harem women and palace eunuchs. Not unnaturally, his relations with women were generally warmer than with men. Abdul Hamid had been taken into confidence at a young age by Pertevniyal, the *Valide Sultana* (harem mother) of the martyred Abdul Aziz, who, in her pre-harem days, had been a gossipy bath attendant, which kept her close to the pulse of public opinion. The future sultan had even carried on an affair with an "infidel," Flora Cordier, a Belgian glove-seller from Pera, who acquainted him with European views of the empire. In the months before his accession, Abdul Hamid had also strolled frequently through the gardens of Therapia with a certain Mr. Thomson, a British trader friendly with Her Majesty's ambassador Sir Henry Elliott, who acquainted the future sultan with Westminster procedure (Abdul Hamid requested that parliamentary Blue Books be translated into Ottoman for him). Although he was relatively unknown both inside the empire and abroad, few modern sultans had ascended the throne better informed about the world outside the palace than Abdul Hamid II.[3]

This is not to say, however, that the new sultan was a westernizing liberal in the notional mold of Murad. Midhat Pasha, who had already begun drafting a historic constitution for the Ottoman Empire, had been devastated when Murad proved unable to be the vehicle for his reforms—although curiously it was Midhat who convinced the cabinet to press for Murad's deposition, despite never having met Abdul Hamid and knowing next to nothing about him. As insurance against any revival of traditional sultanic authority, Midhat Pasha, after being deputized to sound out the young heir, had tried to tie Abdul Hamid's hands by making his accession conditional on the continued incapacity of Murad V—offering him a regency, that is, not a full-on sultanate. Abdul Hamid, understandably reluctant to rule with a half-mad pretender hovering behind his throne, refused. Negotiations then proceeded, in the course of which Midhat Pasha extracted a promise that Abdul Hamid would promulgate a constitution "without delay." The heir, for his part, insisted on a formal and permanent deposition of Murad V, on the grounds of confirmed insanity, documented by unimpeachable medical records. On this basis, a deal was struck—a deal that left the young sultan suspicious of Midhat Pasha and the constitutionalists, and unwilling to countenance further meddling in his prerogatives.

Despite the intrigues swirling around his accession, there were sound reasons for the confident air Abdul Hamid assumed at Eyüp. Having lived through two wrenching depositions already that summer, no one in the capital wished to endure a third. In the Balkans, the worst news seemed to be over, even if Gladstone's fiery pamphlet implied that new atrocities were around the corner. After much fanfare about how the Serbs would destroy the Ottoman army of "old, fat Abdul Kerim," the Russian-commanded Serbian offensive against Turkey had bogged down quickly, before swinging into reverse in early August, when the Turks captured the gateway to the Morava Valley leading to the heart of Serbia. On September 1, the day after Murad's deposition and thus the first official day of Abdul Hamid II's reign, the Serbs and their Russian commander were decisively defeated at Deligrad. By the time the new sultan was girded at Eyüp, Serbia had asked for an armistice, and Ottoman diplomats were drawing up triumphant peace terms to be imposed on Belgrade that would include disarmament, occupation of fortresses, and an indemnity.[4] The conqueror of Tashkent had been routed, Serbia humiliated, and the Turks were rolling north into Europe again.

With the sultan astride his white steed, "bridled in gold," the imperial retinue, led by the *Sheikh-ul-Islam* carrying the green banner of the Prophet, crossed the Golden Horn at the second bridge and rode past the ruined walls of Byzantine Blachernae, the Greek quarter of Phanar and the Orthodox patriarchate, before winding its way into the narrow streets of old Muslim Stambul. At last the procession reached the Sublime Porte, where foreign diplomats, seated upon an "estrade of honor," paid homage to Abdul Hamid II as sovereign of the Ottoman Empire, ruler of the Black and White Seas, along with lands stretching from the Danube Principalities to the Persian Gulf, the North African Maghreb to the Transcaucasus. On the streets, the people shouted in acclamation, "*Padişahım çok yaşa!* [Long live the sultan!]."

PART I

THE

SICK MAN

OF EUROPE

CHAPTER 1

THE SICK PATIENT

What can you expect of us, the children of slaves,
brought up by eunuchs?

—ABDUL HAMID II,
to a British friend, prior to his accession as sultan in 1876

Our state is the strongest state. For you are trying to cause
its collapse from the outside, and we from the inside,
but still it does not collapse.

—FUAD PASHA,
Ottoman grand vizier and foreign minister,
to a Western ambassador

FOR A TERMINALLY ILL PATIENT, the Sick Man of Europe took a long time to die. Dating the onset of Ottoman decline is one of the great intellectual parlor games of modern history. Did it begin, as a popular Turkish explanation would have it, with the fateful decision of Suleyman the Magnificent to put his capable son and heir, Mustafa, to death in 1553, consigning the empire to an endless succession of incompetent sultans? Or could the key moment have come even earlier, with the first of the soon-to-be-notorious Capitulations signed with France in 1536, conceding to French subjects trading privileges of the kind that, by the early twentieth century, had evolved into an entire system granting Europeans extraterritorial legal status in the empire? Was it the Ottoman failure to take Vienna during the first siege, in 1529, or the second, in 1683? Was it the crushing Treaty of Karlowitz (1699), marking the first loss of Ottoman conquered territory in Europe? Or the still more devastating Treaty of Küçük Kaynarca (1774), which heralded the Russian advance south? Napoleon's invasion of Egypt in 1798, which demonstrated the crushing superiority of European arms? The humiliating defeats against the armies of the Egyptian pretender, Mohammad Ali, which forced Turkey to turn to her archenemy Russia for protection in 1833? Or was it the Ottoman Empire's strange victory in the Crimean War (1853–56), which turned her into a financial dependent of her powerful allies, Britain and France?

The broad sweep of events used to mark the stages of degeneration suggests, at the least, that the question is not easily answered, if it is the right question to be asking. As Gibbon famously said of Rome, rather than inquiring why the Ottoman Empire was destroyed, "we should rather be surprised that it had subsisted so long."[1] Other empires fared far worse under the European onslaught, from the Aztecs and Incas in the Americas to the Mughal dynasty in India, the Manchus in China, the Qajar Shahs of Persia, and the entire continent of Africa. True, the Ottoman sultans, as supreme princes, or caliphs, of the entire Islamic world since the conquest of the holy places of the Hejaz region of western Saudi Arabia in 1517, measured themselves by a higher standard than those of regional empires like the Aztecs or Incas. Even so, Turkey's location, straddling the Near East from the forests of European Rumeli through Asia Minor to the desert sands of Arabia and Persia, with the ancient cities of Palestine, Syria, and Mesopotamia in between, was if anything a greater temptation to European predators than lands farther afield. The plight of the empire's substantial Christian minority, nearly a third of the population, was a perennial excuse for Western intervention; indeed, the Crimean War was literally fought over disputed Orthodox and Latin "protection rights" for churches in Jerusalem and Bethlehem. As the unification of Italy and Germany brought ethno-nationalism to the fore later in the nineteenth century, the Ottomans had to reckon further with irredentist movements from the myriad subject nations of the empire: Serbs, Romanians, Bulgarians, Macedonians, Albanians, and Greeks in Europe; Armenians, Kurds, Arabs, and yet more Greeks in Asiatic Turkey. Motivated by the sister callings of Christian Orthodoxy and pan-Slavism, the Russians alone had invaded Turkey five times in the century preceding the accession of Abdul Hamid II to the throne in 1876—and they would do so again the very next year. Considering that the empire's tsarist Russian nemesis could field armies drawing on a rapidly growing population base already more than four times larger than the Ottoman, the real wonder is that Turkey, in 1877, was still fighting.

Part of the explanation lies in geography. Not unlike her great northern antagonist, the sprawling Ottoman Empire was difficult to defend—but harder still to conquer. What "General Winter" was for Russia against would-be conquerors, mountains, deserts, and fortified waterways were for Turkey. Since the empire's high-water mark of expansion under Suleyman, the easily traversable border areas—the Hungarian plain, the Danube Principalities (modern Romania), the Crimea, the Caucasian Black Sea littoral—had fallen, leaving behind a much more defensible frontier.* In the Crimean War, the Russians had gotten bogged down on the Danube even before the French and British had intervened (and Austria had forced them to withdraw from the Principalities, on pain of intervention). This great river was guarded by the fortresses of Silistria, Rustchuk, and Vidin, with heavily garrisoned forts at Varna, Shumla, and Plevna awaiting in the hinterland beyond it. Next came the Balkan Mountains, impassable but for the heavily fortified Shipka Pass. If an invading army forced the pass, it would still have to reduce the great fortress defenses of Adrianople (Edirne) before approaching Constantinople across the lengthy plains of Thrace. Little wonder not even the Russians had made it this far yet (except by invitation, in 1833).

The empire's prime strategic location also conferred diplomatic advantages. Each time an invading power threatened a key imperial choke point—the French in Egypt in 1798, the Egyptians at Kütahya, en route for the Bosphorus, in 1833, Russia crossing the Danube in 1853—the Ottomans were able to raise a countercoalition among powers anxious not to see an ambitious rival inherit the crown jewels of the empire. The Crimean War itself was something of a triumph of Ottoman diplomacy. The empire's embrace of liberal reform in the Tanzimat era (inaugurated by the so-called Rescript of the

---

* It is true that the "Romanian" principalities of Wallachia and Moldavia remained under Ottoman suzerainty until 1878, but they had been absorbed into a Russian protectorate as early as the Treaty of Adrianople (Edirne) in 1829. The empire's real European frontier against Russia was the river Danube.

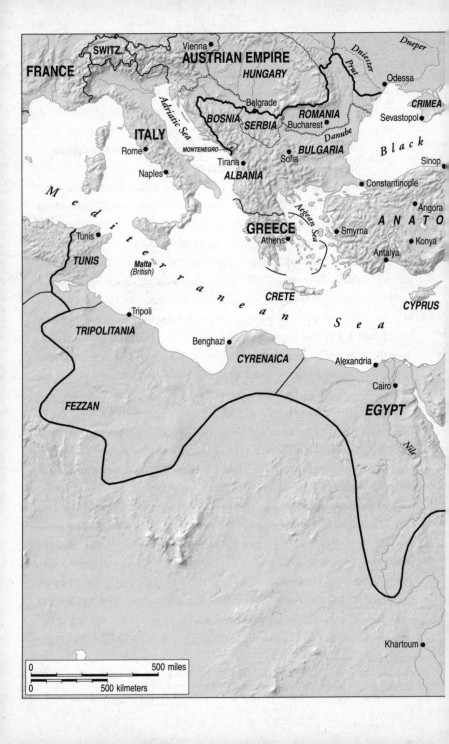

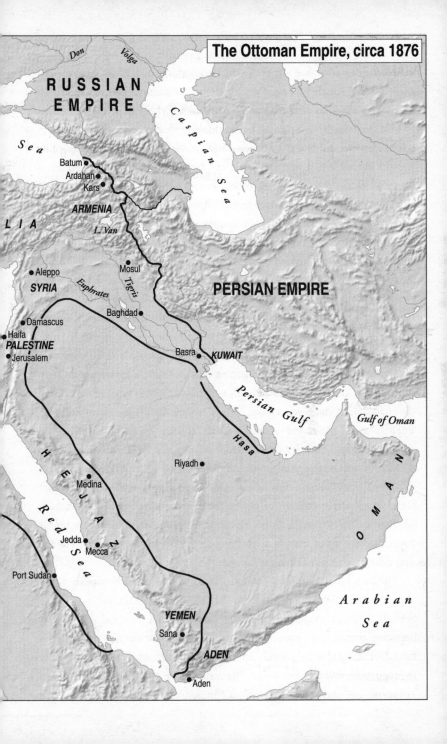

The Ottoman Empire, circa 1876

RUSSIAN EMPIRE

Don

Volga

Caspian Sea

Sea

Batum
Ardahan
Kars

ARMENIA

L. Van

LIA

Aleppo

Mosul

PERSIAN EMPIRE

SYRIA

Euphrates

Tigris

Damascus

Baghdad

Haifa

PALESTINE

Jerusalem

Basra

KUWAIT

Persian Gulf

Gulf of Oman

Hasa

Riyadh

*H
E
J
A
Z*

Red Sea

Medina

*O
M
A
N*

Jedda
Mecca

Port Sudan

YEMEN

Arabian

Sea

Sana

ADEN

Aden

Rose Bower (*Hatt-ı-Şerif*) in 1839, which took the first tentative steps toward granting civic equality for non-Muslims) won her such sympathy from France and Britain that they declared war against Russia on her behalf in 1854 (joined by Piedmont-Sardinia, a coming power that piggybacked on the crisis to unify Italy). However futile the war seemed in retrospect to Western (especially British) chroniclers, it won the Ottomans formal admission in the Treaty of Paris (1856) to "the advantages of the Public Law and System of Europe," along with a tripartite guarantee from Britain, France, and Austria "guaranteeing joint and several defense of Ottoman independence and integrity."[2]

This diplomatic triumph, of course, came at a tremendous cost, beginning with nearly 120,000 Turkish casualties. The "advantages of the Public Law" mostly meant access to Western bond markets (first and foremost, to pay down the costs of the war), a two-edged sword that, sped along by extravagant spending on the new Dolmabahçe Palace, led directly to the Ottoman default of 1875. And the famous *Hatt-ı-Hümayun*, or Reform Edict, of 1856, issued even while foreign troops still blanketed Constantinople, was so obviously shaped by growing European influence that it aroused more resentment than appreciation among Ottoman Muslims, many of whom were not sure why they had fought and died in a war so as to forfeit their legal supremacy over Christians, and—in one of the most notable reforms—to allow church bells to ring in Constantinople for the first time in centuries. Especially after British opinion of the Ottomans began to sour after the war, the Ottoman "victory" in 1856 appeared increasingly hollow. One can understand the bitterness that seeps into a recent official history of the conflict prepared by the Turkish General Staff, in which the authors lament that "those who appeared to be our friends were not our friends . . . in this war Turkey lost its treasury. For the first time it became indebted to Europe."[3]

The increasingly perilous entanglement of finance and European diplomacy was brought home painfully in the Balkan crisis of the 1870s. The suspension of bond coupon payments in October 1875 cost the empire any lingering sympathy in France and Britain, even while the financial crunch forced Sultan Abdul Aziz to rely on the Circassian Bashi-Bazouks, instead of the regular army, to restore order. The resulting Bulgarian atrocities isolated Turkey still further, and only dramatic measures, such as the deposition of two sultans at the hands of conspiring reformers, seemed to offer a way out of the impasse. Midhat Pasha's constitution of 1876 represented, in theory, the capstone of Tanzimat liberal reform. In foreign policy terms, the constitution was a last desperate throw of the dice to ward off an impending European partition of the empire.

The diplomatic drama ratcheted up quickly following the girding of Abdul Hamid II with the Sword of Osman. In late October 1876, the Ottoman armies destroyed what remained of the Serbian army at Djunis, opening the path through the Morava Valley to Belgrade. On the strategic principle of "heads we win, tails you lose," Russia then moved to bail out her floundering Serbian ally, issuing an ultimatum on October 31 to the effect that Turkey must agree to an armistice, on pain of Russia severing diplomatic relations with her. Two weeks later, Tsar Alexander II ordered the mobilization of six corps of the Russian Imperial Army, along with reserves—some 550,000 men in all.[4] With war fever spreading through St. Petersburg and Constantinople alike, with Gladstone's polemic pamphlet rousing public opinion against Turkey in England and (in subsidized translation) Russia, with the powers demanding to hold a conference in the Ottoman capital at the tip of the Russian bayonet to force Balkan reforms, negotiations over the first-ever constitution for the Ottoman Empire reached the critical final stage.

Although the young sultan had promised to promulgate a constitution as the price of his throne, Abdul Hamid had no intention of ruling as a limited constitutional monarch, much less a figurehead beholden to a European-style parliamentary regime. The sharpening of the Balkan crisis hardened his stance still further. In mid-December, even as European diplomats were descending on Constantinople to draw up terms for a partition of Ottoman Europe, Abdul Hamid endorsed a controversial new clause granting the sultan the power to exile "dangerous" political opponents. Additionally, the sultan retained the untrammeled power to appoint, and depose, cabinet ministers, and to convoke, and prorogue, a new bicameral parliament to be elected by popular vote. While other elements of the constitution—relating to *Osmanlılık*, or the equality of Ottoman subjects (including non-Muslims) in civil liberties, and penal and tax law, along with the right of petition and the security of property and home against seizure—were liberal enough, ultimate sovereignty was still invested in the sultan-caliph, Abdul Hamid, who clearly did not intend to dilute his own power—certainly not in the face of outside pressure from the European powers. Nor was the sultan, or any of his advisers, willing to accept a partition of Ottoman Europe: Article 1 of the constitution expressly stated that the empire "can at no time and for no cause whatever be divided."[5]

As if to emphasize the point, the constitution was formally promulgated at the Sublime Porte in the afternoon of December 23, 1876, even as, in the nearby Admiralty building on the Golden Horn, European diplomats convened the first meeting of the Constantinople Conference, meant to determine the fate of the empire. One hundred and one guns boomed to announce the onset of the first Ottoman constitutional era, or *Meşrutiyet*, loudly enough to interrupt the conference. The Ottoman delegate, Foreign Minister Safvet Pasha, then helpfully explained (in his poor, halting French) that the constitutional salute meant the delegates could now go home. The invitation to disperse was ignored. Unimpressed by a gesture they saw as too little, too late, the powers insisted on proceeding with the program for redrawing the map of the Balkans.*

While the Turks had some hopes that Disraeli's envoy, Lord Salisbury, would summon up some of the old Tory Russophobia to damp down the tsar's demands, these were dashed quickly. Before the conference, Salisbury had already concluded that the Crimean War had been a "deplorable mistake," and that this time "the Turk's teeth must be drawn even if he be allowed to live."[6] After he arrived in Constantinople in early December, Salisbury was taken in by the formidable Russian ambassador, Count Nikolai Ignatiev, and his beautiful wife. The Ignatievs manipulated him so effectively that an open breach developed between Salisbury and Britain's ambassador, Sir Henry Elliott—who was himself closer to Disraeli's Russophobic line (Salisbury thought that Elliott had "gone native"). Salisbury also took an immediate dislike to Midhat Pasha, now grand vizier, and Abdul Hamid, whom he dismissed as "a poor frightened man with a very long nose and a short threadpaper body."[7] With Salisbury all but endorsing Gladstone's Russophile line at the

---

* Least impressed of all was, predictably, Gladstone, who, on hearing the news, harrumphed sarcastically in his diary, "Turkish constitution!!!"

conference, there was no one strong enough to water down the terms dictated to the Porte, which included autonomy for Bosnia-Herzegovina under outside protection, an autonomous Bulgaria in two halves occupied by an international gendarmerie, and an independent Principality of Montenegro.*

To almost no one's surprise, Abdul Hamid rejected these humiliating terms on January 20, 1877, paving the way for the tsar's armies to achieve by force what the powers had failed to achieve by diplomacy. Making sure not to repeat the mistakes that led to Russia's encirclement in the Crimean War, tsarist diplomats negotiated, with Otto von Bismarck's mediation from Berlin, a pledge of neutrality from Vienna (the price was Russian support for an Austrian protectorate over Bosnia-Herzegovina), and free passage for tsarist troops across the Danube Principalities (in exchange for gold shipped to Bucharest and Russian backing for an independent Romania).[8] In a sense, the Ottoman Empire had reverted back to the pre-Tanzimat isolation of the 1820s, when the European powers had come together to support the Greeks in their war of independence. Four decades of liberal reform had won the Turks little lasting sympathy in the Western capitals; even Britain's traditional Russophobic Turcophilia had curdled into contempt. Although the sultan and his advisers retained some hope that Prime Minister Disraeli, unlike his unfriendly diplomatic envoy, might come around and dispatch the British fleet if the Russians threatened the capital, until that happened the Turks, unlike in 1853–56, would have to fight this war on their own.

Despite the unpromising diplomatic circumstances, Abdul Hamid's decision to resist was not senseless. Because the sultan had embraced the constitution, he was enjoying something of a honeymoon with his subjects. The overbearing behavior of the Europeans at the Constantinople conference had alienated nearly everyone in the capital, even the Christian minorities, who were more interested in their new rights, especially that of electing representatives to the empire's first-ever parliament. Representation in the capital itself would be split equally between Muslims (five deputies) and non-Muslims (two Greeks, two Armenians, and a Jew). Ottoman Greeks, an influential

---

* It is true that the Russians' desired "Big Bulgaria" was divided in two at this conference, as it would be again two years later at the Berlin Congress. But this owed more to general European, and especially Austrian, opposition, than to any great effort on Salisbury's part.

minority in much of the Balkans, had no wish for a greater Bulgaria to emerge under Russian tutelage. Many Turkish Armenians, for their part, were frustrated by the hue and cry over Bulgarian Christians, which had drowned out sympathy in Europe for their own plight. Midhat Pasha became the first grand vizier to honor the Greek and Armenian patriarchs by calling on them: they greeted him as "the resuscitator of the Ottoman Empire." The historic Ottoman parliamentary elections, held in February–March 1877 even as tsarist troops were gearing up to invade the empire, had the effect of uniting the country behind the sultan in war fever against the Russian bully. On March 19, 1877, all the notables of Constantinople gathered in the throne room of Dolmabahçe Palace to inaugurate the first-ever Ottoman parliament, with 115 deputies (of which 67 were Muslim, 44 Christian, and 4 Jewish), comprising some fourteen different nationalities. There was one European ambassador notable in his absence: Count Ignatiev. On April 24, 1877, Russia declared war, aiming for, in the words of General Obruchev, architect of her invasion plan, "the full, irrevocable decision of the eastern question, the unconditional destruction of Turkish rule in the Balkan peninsula."[9]

With six months to prepare for the onslaught, the Turks were ready. The Ottoman riverine fleet had near-total control of the Danube, and the Black Sea was almost uncontested, as the Russians had been forbidden to build ships or maintain ports on the littoral by the 1856 Treaty of Paris (although they had "cheated" by floating a small striking force in the Sea of Azov, which was then quietly expanded into the Black Sea under cover of the Franco-Prussian War in 1870–71). While the Ottoman navy was not terribly strong on the Black Sea itself, the fact that it operated freely there forced Russia to keep 73,000 troops in reserve, guarding Russia's southern coastline. Buttressing the Danube fortresses, Bulgaria had been flooded with nearly 180,000 Turkish troops, most of them armed with the new Peabody-Martini rifles, sighted in at 1,800 paces and greatly superior to the Russians' mixed bag of Krnkas, Berdans, and Karlés, with only the Berdan accurate as far as 1,500 paces (the Russians' weapons were furthermore not interchangeable, meaning that ammunition for one rifle would not work for the others). In artillery, too, the Ottomans had the advantage, having equipped their Balkan armies with the latest steel breech-loaders from Krupp.[10] Judging by the order of

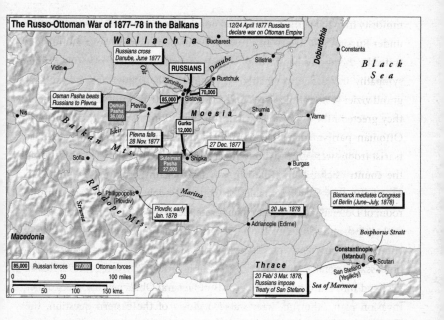

The Russo-Ottoman War of 1877–78 in the Balkans

12/24 April 1877 Russians declare war on Ottoman Empire

Wallachia — Bucharest

Russians cross Danube, June 1877

Vidin

RUSSIANS — Danube — Silistria

Zimnitsa — Rustchuk

Osman Pasha beats Russians to Plevna

85,000 — Sistova

Osman Pasha 36,000 — Plevna

Moesia — Shumla

Nis

Gurko 12,000

Plevna falls 28 Nov. 1877

Balkan Mts. — Iskir

Süleyman Pasha 27,000 — Shipka

27 Dec. 1877

Sofia

Rhodope Mts. — Srumia

Phillippopolis (Plovdiv)

Maritsa

Plovdiv, early Jan. 1878

Varna

Burgas

Bismarck mediates Congress of Berlin (June–July, 1878)

20 Jan. 1878

Adrianople (Edirne)

Constanta

Black Sea

Doburdzhia

Bosphorus Strait

Constantinople (Istanbul) — Scutari

San Stefano (Yeşilköy)

Macedonia

Thrace

20 Feb/ 3 Mar. 1878, Russians impose Treaty of San Stefano

Sea of Marmora

85,000 Russian forces   27,000 Ottoman forces

0 — 50 — 100 miles
0 — 50 — 100 — 150 kms.

battle, there was no reason for Abdul Hamid to expect that the Russians would make it any closer to Constantinople than they had in 1854.

Obruchev's campaign was, however, audaciously conceived and, for the most part, executed. After the spring floods had subsided, Russian sappers would secure a crossing point on the Danube between Zimnitsa and Sistova (Shishtov) by mining the river on both sides, to neutralize the Ottoman river fleet. This was achieved on the night of June 27–28, 1877, at the cost of about eight hundred Russian casualties. Obruchev had then insisted that the first army, 120,000 strong, should head straight for the Shipka Pass and, once through it, Constantinople, leaving a second army behind to deal with Ottoman fortresses on its flanks and rear. But Grand Duke Nikolai Nikolaevich, a prince of the blood given the command, chose instead to split his forces into three main columns, with the stronger two sent sideways to reduce Ruschuk and Plevna, while only a small spearhead of 12,000 men, under Y. V. Gurko, raced ahead to Shipka. Although Gurko reached and held the pass, the Ottomans, under Süleyman Pasha, brought up reinforcements and placed his men under siege. Farther north, a relieving force of 36,000 men under Osman

Pasha, outraced the Russians to Plevna and entrenched themselves in the fortress city, enabling the Turks to repel bloody Russian offensives all through summer and fall. In the end the Russians won Plevna only by surrounding it (with the help of Romanian troops, keen to win their independence), cutting off Osman Pasha's supply lines and starving him out. Winning the honorific of "Gazi," Osman Pasha went down fighting, his horse shot out from under him. He surrendered on December 10, 1877.

Thus far, the clash of arms had been fairly evenly matched. The Russians had performed better in the Caucasus, taking Ardahan in May and Kars in November. And yet everyone knew the Balkans were the main theater of the war, with Bulgaria—and possibly Constantinople itself, known to the covetous Russians as Tsargrad—its object. Even after Gazi Osman Pasha's capitulation, the situation seemed far from dire for the Turks. The Russians, now that their troops freed up from Plevna could and did relieve Gurko at Shipka Pass, might well push on through the mountains—but in winter, through the snows and ice? Surely, with the military odds narrowing and the prospect of British naval intervention in case his armies reached the Thracian plain—Disraeli had ordered the Mediterranean fleet to Besika Bay, at the mouth of the Dardanelles, as soon as Russian troops had crossed the Danube in late June—it seemed that the tsar would prefer to negotiate some favorable peace settlement based on his great victory at Plevna instead.

The Russians now surprised everyone. Even as diplomats in Vienna, Berlin, and London began gearing up for another partition conference, the generals resolved to push on. As Grand Duke Nikolai Nikolaevich, commander in chief, told Tsar Alexander II, "We must go to the centre, to Tsargrad, and there finish the holy cause you have started."[11] After breaking enemy resistance in the Shipka Pass on December 27, 1877, and taking thirty thousand Turks prisoner, Gurko doubled back west and descended the Balkan Mountains above Sofia, occupying that city on January 4, 1878. The Russians then raced ahead to Philippopolis (Plovdiv), which fell on January 17. Three days later, with the Ottoman armies disintegrating, a Russian cavalry force entered Adrianople (Edirne), encountering little resistance. By January 24, 1878, advance units had reached San Stefano (Yeşilköy, site of today's Istanbul Atatürk Airport), on the shores of the Sea of Marmara, just six miles from the city gates.* After centuries of trying, the Russians had at last reached Constantinople. Would they claim their prize?

Not if the British had a say in the matter. Despite all the mischief wrought by Gladstone's pamphleteering and Salisbury's intrigues, Disraeli was still prime minister, and he was not about to miss an opportunity to stand up to the Russians—not with crowds of English patriots waving the *Ottoman* flag in Trafalgar Square, singing the popular new tune "We don't want to fight, but by jingo if we do . . . The Russians shall not have Constantinople!" Buoyed by the revival of popular Russophobia, Disraeli stood down his cabinet critics, and, on January 23, 1878, ordered the fleet to proceed through the Dardanelles.† Faced with the likelihood of British intervention, on January 30, 1878, Grand Duke Nikolai Nikolaevich accepted Abdul Hamid's request for an armistice.[12]

By a miracle, the Sick Man of Europe had been saved on his deathbed. Except that it was not really a miracle. Like clockwork, the empire's traditional strategic advantages had resurfaced when they were most desperately needed. The geography of the Balkans had not, quite, prevented the Russians from nearing the capital this time, but it ensured that when they did, they were too exhausted and disease-ridden to fight. By spring 1878, more than half of the troops at San Stefano had gone down with fever, even as the Turks were quietly regrouping, raising nearly 100,000 men to defend the capital if the armistice was broken. The very threat to Constantinople, meanwhile, had reawakened the ghost of British Russophobia from the dead, with public opinion rapidly veering 180 degrees from Gladstone's anti-Turkish hysteria to jingoistic war fever against Russia.‡ As if to celebrate his deliverance, Abdul

---

* The Russians later built a memorial church (*Aya Stefanos*) in San Stefano to memorialize the heroic advance to the shores of the Sea of Marmara and to bury soldiers who died in the campaign. Consecrated by Grand Duke Nicholas and the Greek Orthodox patriarch on December 18, 1898, it was demolished by Turkish troops in November 1914, after Russia declared war on the Ottoman Empire.

† Facing bitter cabinet opposition, Disraeli was forced temporarily, on receipt of favorable news of Russia's peace terms regarding the Ottoman Straits (which later turned out to be erroneous), to rescind the orders to the fleet. By the time the fleet had turned around, however, the Russians had learned it was coming, which made the point just as well as if the orders had not been rescinded. On February 8, the British fleet passed through the Dardanelles again, this time to stay.

‡ Literally, in that the term "jingoism" was born of this crisis ("by jingo if we do").

Hamid prorogued the parliament indefinitely on February 14, 1878, as was his constitutional right.

True, the empire's delivery owing to outside naval intervention was not what the sultan had wanted. In its own way, the British fleet anchored just south of Constantinople at Prinkipo island (Büyükada) was just as much a threat to Abdul Hamid's throne as the Russian troops encamped outside the city.* Still, it was the Russians who drew up terms for a diktat peace at San Stefano, ratified by the sultan under duress on March 3, 1878, creating a "Big Bulgaria," under Russian occupation, an enlarged Serbia and Montenegro, a war indemnity of 1.4 billion rubles (although only 40 million Turkish pounds, or about 400 million rubles, was to be paid in cash), huge Russian gains in Anatolia, and the right of passage for Russian warships through the Ottoman Straits.[13] But, as Abdul Hamid knew, with the British fleet at Prinkipo, and the other powers anxious about Russian gains, the treaty could not endure.

The resulting Congress of Berlin (June–July 1878) hosted by Bismarck was, on the surface, a humiliating affair for the Ottomans. Although the Russians' "Big Bulgaria" was broken up, with a new province called Eastern Rumelia placed back under full Turkish control and a rump "Bulgaria" still under nominal Ottoman suzerainty, and tsarist warships denied the right of access to the Straits, Turkey still lost the provinces of Kars, Ardahan, and Batum to Russia, and any remaining claim on a Montenegro now doubled in size, or on Romania or Serbia, both now fully independent. Austria-Hungary, upon prior agreement, was also given the right to occupy and administer Bosnia-Herzegovina, and Britain gained a protectorate over Cyprus. Although the Russians' war indemnity was reduced to manageable size ("not more than 26,750,000 francs"), and the newly independent states were enjoined to pay their share of the Ottoman debt, European financial influence would now be all but absolute, with a new Debt Commission established to oversee the collection of Turkish customs, tariffs, and tolls so as to pay the empire's creditors. Most onerous of all, Article 61 established European oversight of Ottoman internal affairs, stipulating that the "Sublime Porte undertakes to carry out, without further delay, the ameliorations and reforms demanded by

---

* On March 30, the tsar offered to "protect" Constantinople in case the British tried to occupy it.

local requirements in the provinces inhabited by Armenians, and to guarantee their security against the Circassians and Kurds. It will periodically make known the steps taken to this effect to the powers, who will superintend their application." Capturing the spirit of the affair, at one point Bismarck remarked, upon hearing his pet canine growl at an unfortunate diplomat, "The dog has not finished his training. He does not know whom to bite. If he did know what to do, he would have bitten the Turks."[14]

Still, not all the news was bad for Abdul Hamid and the Ottomans. The empire had survived, and had been spared the worst. In some ways the Treaty of Berlin infuriated the Russians, deprived of what they viewed as the spoils of a hard-earned victory, more than the Turks, who could not have expected very much. Indeed Russia was nearly bankrupted by the war, having spent a billion rubles and incurred 200,000 casualties, in order to "liberate" Balkan Slavs, even while populist-nihilist-terrorist opposition to the tsarist autocracy was growing at home, culminating in the assassination of Alexander II in March 1881. Despite the territorial losses of 1878, and the creeping European control over his pocketbook confirmed by the Muharrem Agreement of 1881, which established the Ottoman Public Debt Commission (*Düyün-u Umumiye Komisyonu*), Abdul Hamid was himself safer than ever on his throne—not least because the financial reforms imposed by European bankers raised public revenues by over 40 percent and capped annual debt service payments at a manageable level, improving the regime's financial position considerably. The loss of Egypt to British occupation in 1882 after the khedivial regime defaulted on its debts proved, in similar fashion, a backhanded blessing, as Cairo more reliably paid Constantinople the tribute (£665,000 annually) necessary to underwrite new loans for Abdul Hamid. Like Egypt, the other newly independent or semi-independent provinces—Bulgaria, Cyprus, and Montenegro—were forced to pay down their share of old Ottoman obligations, routed through the Debt Commission. British and French bondholders, having been burned badly in 1875, wanted to make sure the sultan could pay down his bonds—as did even the Russians, hoping to salvage scraps of their hoped-for war indemnity. In this way the European powers, in their own financial interest, began nursing the Sick Man back to health.[15]

Taking the lead in this endeavor was Imperial Germany. Notwithstanding

Bismarck's famous disinterest—before the Reichstag in December 1876 he had declared the entirety of the Ottoman Empire "not worth the bones of a Pomeranian grenadier"—there were good reasons for Germany to assume the burden of unofficial protector-of-Turkey-against-Russian-encroachment, now that Britain was cooling on the role (especially after Gladstone returned to power in 1880). With impeccable timing, Bismarck responded to the British move into Egypt in 1882 by sending a military mission, under General-Major Otto Kaehler, to train the Ottoman army and appointing a higher-level ambassador to the Ottoman Empire, Joseph Maria von Radowitz (a former state secretary who had been ambassador to Russia during the Balkan crisis). Even as Bismarck was quietly reassuring St. Petersburg, in a "very secret" protocol of the Reinsurance Treaty (ratified in 1887), that Germany would remain neutral if Russia tried to seize Constantinople and the Straits, he was authorizing German officers, working with state-of-the-art imported German artillery (Krupp, Mauser & Lowe, and Schichau), to revamp Ottoman shore defenses on the Bosphorus and Dardanelles, and on land, where a new line of fortifications at Çatalca defended the approaches from Thrace. With German instructors dominating the Harbiye War Academy, and an energetic officer-on-the-make, Colmar Freiherr von der Goltz Pasha, taking over the military mission after Kaehler's death in 1885, the Ottoman army was fully reorganized on the Prussian/German model, divided into seven military districts, each assigned a numbered army and its own section of reserves (*redif*), ready to be absorbed into the active army in wartime.[16] Meanwhile, German railway engineers were extending the Orient Express railway into Asia Minor, reaching Ankara in 1892, with plans to reach all the way to Baghdad.

The German-Ottoman relationship, nurtured quietly by Bismarck, blossomed into public maturity under Kaiser Wilhelm II after he forced the Iron Chancellor into retirement in 1890. At the impressionable age of thirty, the kaiser had been received with elaborate ceremony at Yıldız Palace by Abdul Hamid in 1889—a trip Bismarck had opposed, for fear of alarming the Russians. When the sultan told his young fellow sovereign, with an air of conspiracy, that his "visit would make [the] powers very nervous," it was music to Wilhelm's ears. Years later, the kaiser could still recall every detail of the trip (not least the lubricious dancing of the sultan's Circassian slave girls).[17]

The burgeoning ties with Germany paid off handsomely in the next major crisis to face the Ottoman Empire. Inspired—although ultimately disappointed—by the halfhearted endorsement of their plight in the Berlin Treaty of 1878, Ottoman Armenians had begun organizing opposition groups, advocating "freedom" (the *Dashnaksutiun*, or Dashnaks) and "independence" (the Hunchakian Revolutionary Party, or Hunchaks). Beginning in Erzurum in 1890, violent incidents rocked eastern Turkey, as several Ottoman government officials were assassinated, leading to reprisals against Armenians. Faced with what appeared to be a rebel movement, Abdul Hamid responded the next year by organizing Hamidiye regiments of irregular Kurdish tribesmen (most of whom needed little incentive to target Armenians). The crisis made international headlines in 1894, when an Armenian uprising in Sassun, near Van, led to the massacre of hundreds (or thousands) of civilians.* The slow-burning civil war spread to Bitlis, Zeytun, Erzurum, Trabzon, and finally Constantinople, when, following the capture of the Imperial Ottoman Bank by Armenian revolutionaries, populist Muslim mobs rampaged through the streets, killing Armenians. No one knows for sure how many Armenians perished between 1894 and 1896, but it was a substantial number, and it certainly dwarfed the much smaller number of Muslim victims (around 1,000). The true number is probably in between the official Ottoman estimate of 13,432 and higher contemporary figures, whether European Commission reports (38,000 "Christian," i.e., mostly Armenian, deaths in the provinces, then 5,000–6,000 in the capital in August 1896) or a widely cited Armenian figure of 100,000. A leading demographer recently analyzed the hopelessly clashing data sets and came to no firm conclusion whatever.[18]

Once again, ethno-religious unrest involving a Christian minority had provoked unwanted attention from Europe. But whereas in 1877, Russia was able to count on the neutrality, at least, of the other powers, in case she intervened on behalf of the Armenians, this time Abdul Hamid had a friend and patron in tow. As the hue and cry against anti-Armenian atrocities grew to a

---

* Initial Armenian claims, passed on by the British consul at Erzurum, suggested as many as 10,000 civilians had perished in Sassun. The consul who reported this figure later revised it down to 900. A joint commission of inquiry sent to Sassun to investigate, composed of five Ottoman officials and the French, British, and Russian consuls, registered 263 deaths, with another 12 children being orphaned.

feverous pitch in fall 1896—with Lord Salisbury, now prime minister, reprising Gladstone's tune with only a bit less moralistic fervor—there was one European statesman conspicuously absent from the chorus. While privately, Kaiser Wilhelm II harbored doubts as to Abdul Hamid's political future, in public he made the most dramatic gesture possible, sending his friend a signed family portrait to celebrate his birthday on September 22, 1896, even as other Europeans were denouncing the sultan as "Abdul the Damned" and "the monster of Yıldız."[19]

More important than this symbolic gesture was the German role in strengthening the Ottoman military. True, the Kurdish Hamidiye regiments, modeled more on the Cossacks on the Russian side of the border than the Prussian army, had not distinguished themselves fighting Armenian partisans in eastern Turkey any more than had the Circassians in Bulgaria, with "Hamidiye" now replacing "Bashi-Bazouk" as a European byword for civilian atrocities. But the German-reformed regular army was soon given a chance to prove its worth, when, in January–February 1897, an uprising of Greek Christians on the island of Crete reached crisis stage. Although rooted in the same explosive nexus of ethno-religious antagonism as the Armenian troubles, the Cretan rebels had close links, via the nationalist society Ethnike Hetairia, to mainland Greece. With some ten thousand Greek volunteers embarking at Salamis and Piraeus to fight for the Cretan cause, on February 2, 1897, a Greek colonel, Timoleon Vassos, speaking for the islanders, proclaimed *Eunosis*, or Cretan union with Greece. Not wishing to be outdone, in March some 2,600 Greek partisans on the mainland crossed the border into Ottoman Macedonia, hoping to spark a general Greek uprising against the sultan. On April 10, Crown Prince Constantine led a force of the regular Greek army across the Turkish border, toward Janina. Fighting was already under way in both Crete and Macedonia when, on April 17, 1897, the Ottoman Empire declared war.

The Turks were ready. Under Marshal Ibrahim Ethem Pasha, the Macedonian army had carried out a methodical, German-style mobilization, with each disciplined infantry unit equipped with smokeless repeating Mauser rifles, easily superior to the Greeks' single-shot French Gras models. After repulsing Greek attacks at Janina and the Melluna Pass, Ethem Pasha led his main force into Greek Thessaly, routing the Greeks at Tirnovo and Larissa (Yenişehir), before the Greeks, under Colonel Konstantinos Smolenskis, rallied some 40,000 soldiers to defend the Thessalian hub of Domokos (Dömeke) against 45,000 Ottoman troops. After heavy fighting, Smolenskis was forced to pull back again, this time for a last stand at the legendary coastal pass of Thermopylae (though with considerably more men than the three hundred Spartans who had tried to hold off Xerxes). Before it came to that, the Russians intervened to force an armistice on the Ottomans, signed on May 19, 1897. The Thirty Days' War had been short, sharp—and a triumph for Turkey.[20]

In a flash, Abdul Hamid had dispelled the portents of doom surrounding the Ottoman Empire. Just months previously, the powers had been gearing up for another conference, with the Armenian massacres an excuse to put the empire through another partition; now they were begging the sultan to be magnanimous in victory. Having reversed the military humiliation of 1877–78, and knowing—this time—that it was best to stop before the Russians intervened, Abdul Hamid saw no reason to push his luck. While demanding that Greece pay a war indemnity, he made no claims on Greek Thessaly, aside from "rationalizing" the border line by incorporating about twenty villages into Turkey. Crete was given autonomy akin to Bulgaria's, under Ottoman suzerainty, and an occupation force of Russian, British, French, and Italian troops were sent to the island to keep the peace between Muslims and the Greek Christian majority.[21]

Although the war was a failure in terms of territorial gains and losses, the Ottomans—and Abdul Hamid himself—had regained the far more precious commodity of prestige. As if to beatify the beleaguered sultan's reputation, Wilhelm II paid him an even more grandiose state visit in October 1898, which culminated in the kaiser's notorious tribute before the tomb of Saladin in Damascus. "May the Sultan," Wilhelm declaimed, "and his 300 million Muslim subjects scattered around the earth, who venerate him as their caliph, be assured that the German Kaiser will be their friend for all time."[22]

Although the kaiser was known for this kind of bombast, his praise for Abdul Hamid was no mere rhetorical flourish. Germany's new ambassador, Baron Adolf Marschall von Bieberstein—soon known as the Giant of the Bosphorus—threw his considerable weight behind the sultan. Although a formal German-Ottoman alliance was never signed, a series of deals was agreed on in 1898–99 that amounted to a kind of strategic partnership. In exchange for granting the Berlin-Baghdad Railway concession, the sultan demanded that Berlin share intelligence on revolutionary opponents of his regime. The Germans, for their part, were given excavation rights on lands through which the railway would pass, including historical artifacts and also copper- and coal-mining grants.[23]

The railway concession itself, signed on December 23, 1899, represented a considerable German investment in the kaiser's friend. While the deal was misinterpreted in most of Europe's capitals as a kind of mortgaging of the Ottoman Empire to Berlin, the terms were actually tailor-made for the extension of sultanic authority into the more loosely controlled regions of the empire, such as the Kurdish and Armenian areas of the southeast, and the Bedouin-bandit-dominated deserts of Syria and Mesopotamia. The Germans, through the offices of Deutsche Bank, had pledged to raise all necessary capital—beginning with a deposit of 200,000 Turkish lira in the Ottoman Treasury—and to finish construction within eight years. Meanwhile, in a clause personally negotiated by Abdul Hamid, the Ottoman government, "on its side," reserved "the power of using, whenever it may desire to do so, its right of buying up the line from Konya to Baghdad and Basra." In supplementary negotiations, the German Baghdad Railway Company further promised to construct telegraph poles at sixty-five-meter (seventy-one-yard) intervals along the entire line, to set aside 4 million francs for building Ottoman military installations nearby, and, in case of war, to put at the sultan's disposal the railway's "entire rolling stock, or such as might be necessary, for the transportation of officers and men of the army, navy, police, and gendarmerie, together with any and all equipment."[24]

Of course, the Germans still had to actually *build* the railway, which turned out to be far more difficult—and expensive—than anyone expected. German banks were nowhere near as well capitalized as the French and British ones that still dominated Ottoman trade, and it was a devilish business for the Porte to pay down German railway bonds under the oversight of the French-dominated Debt Commission, which controlled most forms of public revenue in the empire. The Taurus range in southeastern Anatolia was a logistical nightmare, which would require extensive—and expensive—blasting; in the end some three dozen tunnels were needed. Progress was halting at first, and then stopped completely in 1905 when the Ottoman government ran out of money again, even before the line reached the Taurus range.

Still, the German investment in Abdul Hamid and his regime was too serious to be abandoned easily. Even as the Baghdad Railway was bogged down in financial difficulty, another German-led railway project was making tremendous progress, in part because it was financed independently of the European bond market. Under head engineer Heinrich August Meissner Pasha, construction had begun in 1901 on a Hejaz railway running from Damascus to Medina. This line, designed to speed up travel for Hajj pilgrims, was paid for almost entirely by popular subscription among Muslims, to the tune of 75 million francs. By 1908, the line had reached Medina, with plans to extend it to Mecca, and thereby allow Muslim pilgrims to come in by way of Ottoman ports and avoid the British-dominated route from Egypt across the Red Sea entirely.[25]

In a way, the Hejaz line embodied the German-Ottoman partnership even better than did the Berlin-Baghdad project. The kaiser, after all, had declared himself the "friend for all time" of the sultan-caliph and his *Muslim* subjects, which gave political point to the Hejaz railway. Abdul Hamid had himself begun to promote pan-Islam as a means of uniting his empire, printing thousands of copies of the Koran for free distribution to Ottoman Muslims, demanding that officials address him as "The Shelter of the Caliphate" (*Hilâfetpenâh*), paying for mosque restoration out of his "Privy Purse," scrupulously observing Islamic religious festivals, and promoting more Muslim Arabs to high imperial positions than had any sultan in centuries. Yıldız Palace, which Abdul Hamid rarely left except for Friday prayers at the nearby Hamidiye Mosque, became a sort of "Muslim Vatican," to which the global Sunni *umma*, or community of believers, increasingly paid homage.[26]

Pan-Islam also made for good internal politics, at a time when the percentage of Muslims in the empire—and in Constantinople itself—was increasing steadily. As Ottoman power receded on the empire's borders, a great demographic backwash was under way, as the tide of Islamic advance into the Balkans, the Caucasus, and the southern Russia rimlands was reversed by increasingly assertive Christian peoples. Each of the wars of the nineteenth century had provided a spur to this process. In the wake of the Crimean War, some 300,000 Muslim Crimean Tatars had fled to Anatolia, followed shortly in the 1860s by over a million Circassians and Abkhazians from the north Caucasus (this later wave also reflected the defeat, in 1859, of the Avar "Lion of Daghestan," Imam Shamil, whose Murid warriors had fought on the Ottoman side against Russia, although many Chechens and Abkhazians carried on the resistance until 1862). The Russo-Ottoman war of 1877–78, and the subsequent partition at the Congress of Berlin, resulted in the forced migration of some 90,000 Turks and 40,000 Laz Muslims from the Caucasian territories forfeited to Russia, even while 20,000 Armenian Christians fled in the opposite direction, to Russia. Farther west, the numbers were higher still, with 150,000 Crimean Tatars leaving Russia for Turkey, 120,000 Bosniaks (Bosnian Muslims) fleeing their homes, some 600,000 Turkish Muslims leaving the "Romanian" Principalities, and nearly 200,000 Bulgarian Christians leaving Ottoman territory to enter the new, quasi-independent Bulgarian statelet. Little wonder that in the first modern census conducted in the Ottoman Empire, begun in 1881 and completed in 1893, this famously multidenominational empire was beginning to show a serious list toward Islam, with 12.5 million Muslims out of an overall population of 17.4 million, or about 72 percent. The trend continued after 1900, with the Muslim proportion of the Ottoman population reaching nearly 75 percent of a population of 21 million, by 1906. Constantinople itself, after briefly seeing the emergence of a Christian majority in the heyday of the Tanzimat in midcentury, had reverted to a Muslim-majority city by 1897, as it remains, to an even greater extreme, today.[27]

Respectable opinion in Europe, of course, looked deeply askance at the Hamidian embrace of pan-Islam—and at Kaiser Wilhelm II's uncritical endorsement of it. And yet, the more Western liberals, and his own opponents—most now living in exile—excoriated the sultan as "Abdul the Damned," the more plots to depose him (both real, as in 1876 and 1896, and imaginary, most of the rest of the time) were revealed by his own and German spies—and the more he began to conflate his own personal survival with the fate of the Ottoman Empire. Abdul Hamid's paranoid fear of assassination was legendary. It was said he carried a pistol at all times and did not allow the army to train with live ammunition—this was the high era of anarchism, after all (seven heads of state, including the Russian tsar and the U.S. president, were assassinated between 1881 and 1908). By the early 1900s, Yıldız had been turned into a survivalist compound, with its own farm, stables, and workshops spread out over the sprawling grounds. The "Muslim Vatican" was surrounded by unscalable encircling walls and guarded by seven thousand Imperial Guard troops under the command of Gazi Osman Pasha, hero of Plevna.[28]

Unattractive as Abdul Hamid's regime was to Western sensibilities, under his rule the Ottoman Empire was arguably in a stronger strategic position than it had been in decades. Railways, telegraphs, and paved all-weather roads were beginning to unite the empire, improving communications with provincial authorities while giving a solid spur to internal trade. By the turn of the twentieth century, over 800 kilometers of new roads were being laid every year, and another 450 kilometers repaired. While the empire still ran a large trade deficit with Europe in manufactured goods, Ottoman exports of foodstuffs, cotton, silk, carpets, tiles, and glass, along with coal and certain increasingly strategic metals like chrome, borax, and manganese, were booming in turn. Despite his reputation for Islamic obscurantism, Abdul Hamid (a speaker of French and devotee of Italian opera himself) was quietly supporting the expansion of European-style education in the empire. Eighteen new professional colleges were established during his reign, teaching subjects like French, composition, geography, statistics, economics, and commercial, civil, and international law. Funded by revenues specially set aside from a new Assistance Surtax (*Iane Vergisi*) levied by the sultan since 1883, hundreds of new state schools were being built across the empire, along with new public libraries serving an increasingly literate urban population. The number of students attending secondary schools with a secular curriculum doubled in the last three decades of the nineteenth century, suggesting that the Hamidian era may have represented more a "culmination of the Tanzimat" than a repudiation of it.[29]

Meanwhile, although the powers continued to pry into Ottoman minority affairs, Abdul Hamid, relying on his German patrons and his own diplomatic skills, was able to keep new partition plans at bay. The sultan was more than Machiavellian enough to play the Balkan states off one another. Autonomous Bulgaria, after its absorption of Eastern Rumelia in 1885, was emerging as a regional bully, above all in Macedonia, where the Bulgarian Macedonian-Adrianople Revolutionary Committee (BMARC), founded in 1893, pressed irredentist claims (this is the organization that would evolve into the better-known Internal Macedonian Revolutionary Organization, or IMRO, still an essentially Bulgarian affair though the new name concealed this better). Quietly, Abdul Hamid acquiesced in Greek rebel activity in the province so as to weaken Bulgarian influence. Negotiations were under way between the Porte, Greece, Serbia, and Romania to forge a general anti-Bulgarian alliance.[30]

Meanwhile, the very vitriol directed at the sultan by the Western press commended him all the more to the kaiser and his German advisers as an ally. After the collapse of Bismarck's system, Germany had, since 1892, faced a Franco-Russian military alliance. Britain and France had reached an *entente cordiale* over African colonial questions in 1904. With French encouragement, in 1907 London and Petersburg then put Great Game tensions to bed by dividing Persia, Afghanistan, and Tibet into spheres of influence in an Anglo-Russian Accord. Spurred to action by the threat of encirclement by a Triple Entente, Ambassador Marschall and Abdul Hamid renegotiated a far-reaching railway agreement in spring 1908, which provided new revenue sources to help the Germans begin blasting the Taurus Mountains. The burgeoning partnership saw its physical manifestation in Haydarpasha Station, the great German-built flagship of the Baghdad Railway, nearing completion on the Asian shore of the Bosphorus.

With a powerful new ally in tow, the Sick Man of Europe, given up for dead at the onset of Abdul Hamid's reign three decades previously, now appeared to be in full-on convalescence. Outside the gated fortress walls of Yıldız, however, others, unconfident of recovery, were sharpening their scalpels. Like so many patients under the knife, the Ottoman Empire could only hope that the cure was better than the disease.

CHAPTER 2

RADICAL SURGERY: THE YOUNG TURKS

*The memory is so intense that to this day, I cannot think of it unmoved.
I think of it as a final embrace of love between the simple peoples of Turkey
before they should be led to exterminate each other for the political
advantage of foreign powers or their own leaders.*

—HALIDÉ EDIB,
Memoirs[1]

*When Muslims learn that the [newly installed] Caliph is powerless,
and is only the puppet of people who are more or less estranged from Islam,
then a major crisis will be unavoidable.*

—BARON MARSCHALL,
German ambassador to the Ottoman Empire,
October 1909[2]

FROM THE DISTANCE OF A CENTURY, pictures capturing the euphoric crowds in Constantinople in July 1908 appear at once inspiring and profoundly depressing. Can the peoples of this simmering ethno-religious cauldron of a country—Muslims and Christians, Balkan Serbs, Croats, Bosniaks and Albanians, Turks and Greeks, Circassians, Tatars, Armenians and Kurds, Arabs and Jews—really have believed that a few French words (*liberté, fraternité, égalité*) would submerge their differences, reverse the Ottoman Empire's centuries-old stagnation and decline, and bring Turkey into the sunlit uplands of modern constitutional democracy?

Like all revolutionaries, the men and women of 1908 were truly united only in what they opposed: the tyranny (*İstibdat*) of the "monster of Yıldız." Armenian activists blamed Abdul Hamid for the creation of the Hamidiye regiments, the massacres of 1894–96, and much else besides. Bulgarians resented the sultan's stubborn claim of suzerainty over their country, even if Abdul Hamid had quietly acquiesced in the absorption of Turkish "Eastern Rumelia" into Bulgaria in 1885. Many Ottoman Greeks were still smarting from the humiliation of Greece in the 1897 war. Journalists chafed under the strict censorship regime the sultan had imposed, even as dissidents and exiles despised his secret police, which (with help from German intelligence) spied on them. Educated women, like many Christians and Jews, resented the Hamidian revival of Islam, which threatened to snuff out any progress toward civic equality gained in the Tanzimat era (the sultan had, on several occasions, decreed that women not leave home unveiled, or unaccompanied by males—although these instructions were widely ignored).[3] Above all, ambitious Turkish military officers and politicians blamed the sultan for eviscerating the constitution of 1876, sidelining the parliament and Sublime Porte bureaucracy, and ruling by arbitrary decrees from Yıldız.

If anything, it was Abdul Hamid's own coreligionists and blood relations who seemed to despise him the most. Few Christians could have improved on the rhetoric of Ahmed Rıza, former director of state education in Bursa, founder of the Committee of Union and Progress (*Ittihad ve Terakki Cemiyeti*, or CUP), and editor (from 1895) of the bilingual French-Ottoman journal *Meşveret* (*Consultation*), in which pages the sultan was variously described (as a legal complaint filed by Abdul Hamid's lawyers later noted) as "cheat, hangman, scourge of God, bloody majesty, bloody despot, degenerate tyrant, disgrace of the Mussulmans, wolf guarding the sheepfold," and of course, "red Sultan." Murad Bey, a Circassian Muslim who published a rival opposition organ, *Mizan* (*Scale*), was no less colorful in his indictments of a "reigning family . . . degraded by the debauches of the Seraglio."[4] Not to be outdone, "Damad" Mahmud Pasha, the sultan's brother-in-law, who "fled" to Paris in 1899, told a sympathetic reporter from *Le Matin* that "the whole

Ottoman Empire is a prison. Abdul Hamid keeps us all in prison, from Sultan Murad V to the lowliest member of the *ulema* in Istanbul." To a Fleet Street hack, Mahmud was more colorful still, informing readers of the London *Standard* that the monster of Yıldız had "annihilated thousands of human beings—Muslims and Christians."[5]

Of course, we should be suspicious of testimony coming from royal pretenders like Mahmud Pasha. As one of Germany's pro-Hamidian papers, *Der Bund*, sarcastically observed, had the wayward prince's hatred for his brother-in-law been genuine, he might have turned down his annual retainer of three million Swiss francs.[6] Like Rıza, Murad Bey, and the other "Young Turk" exiles, Mahmud believed that, given the chance, he could rule better than their sovereign. And yet these howls of agony in the face of oppression ring somewhat hollow when we consider that all of the main opposition figures lived quite comfortably abroad. Had the sultan's autocracy really been up to snuff, *Meşveret* and *Mizan* would never have found such a wide readership, nor their editors fame and influence.

Viewed objectively, the vigorous political activity of Hamidian exiles suggests that the sultan's "tyranny" was considerably softer than they claimed. Abdul Hamid, it is true, did do away with at least one dangerous opposition figure—Midhat Pasha, the very man who had helped put him in power. Tried and convicted in 1881 (on the testimony of the sultan-mother, Pertevniyal) for the murder of Abdul Aziz in 1876, the former grand vizier was exiled to Taif, east of Mecca, and reportedly strangled to death in May 1883. But, despite uncovering a real CUP plot to depose him at the height of the Armenian crisis in September 1896—a plot involving some 350 conspirators in the Ottoman army and civil service—Abdul Hamid had not executed his opponents for treason, but simply exiled them to distant provinces (Libya for the most dangerous, Mesopotamia, Syria, and Arabia for others).* The entire phenomenon of Ottoman exile politics is inconceivable without the sultan's surprising leniency in 1896, which created an international cadre of elite enemies.[7]

---

* In that the historic *Hatt-ı-Şerif* of 1839 expressly guaranteed Ottoman subjects security of life and property against the whims of sultans, one could see here more evidence that the Hamidian era was as much a "culmination" of the Tanzimat as a repudiation of it.

There is an intriguing parallel here with the experience of Russian revolutionary exiles in the same era. Despite what Bolshevik propaganda would have us believe about the butchery of "bloody Nicholas," the last of the tsars oversaw a remarkably humane sort of police state by later Soviet standards. Socialists convicted of acts of treason during the Russian Revolution of 1905, such as Leon Trotsky, were serenaded by cheering crowds tossing flowers at them as they boarded well-equipped trains—Trotsky's carried his personal library—for Siberia (Lenin, a late arrival to the 1905 Revolution, was denied the honor of internal exile, although he left Russia again in 1907). Trotsky found Siberia mildly disagreeable enough to escape on foot, later surfacing in Europe's capitals, where he continued his fight against "Bloody Nicholas" in comfort. Likewise, most of the Young Turk "men of 1896," inconvenienced by internal Turkish exile, decided they preferred the salons of Paris or Geneva to the deserts of Asiatic Turkey. For neither the first nor the last time, these autocratic sovereigns helped summon a mortal enemy into being by virtue of their own clemency.

There was always a flexible dynamic of give-and-take between Abdul Hamid and his opponents. Some of them, he realized, were ambitious men who really did resent exile, and could be made use of. The Circassian Murad Bey, for example, after years of intriguing against the sultan from Cairo and Geneva, was lured back to Constantinople in August 1897 to join the State Council. His journal *Mizan* was never the same. Two more of the original founders of the CUP, Abdullah Cevdet and İshak Süküti, who (unlike those exiled earlier, such as Murad and Rıza) had personally participated in the 1896 plot, sought to fill the void created by Murad's defection by publishing a new journal in Geneva, *Osmanlı*—until they, too, accepted state sinecures in 1899. No one was happier than Ahmed Rıza, whose opposition journal *Meşveret* now had no real rival in the Ottoman exile community.

There is something curious, if not downright suspicious, about the enduring strength of Ahmed Rıza's position in the Young Turk movement. This fervent Francophile, born of a Bavarian mother and an English-speaking father, had scarcely pretended to an interest in returning home since moving permanently to Geneva in 1895. Early issues of *Meşveret*, smuggled into the empire by way of the European embassies' post offices, carried the positivist credo of Auguste Comte on the masthead, and used the Western calendar for dating, as if Rıza, a staunch secularist, feminist, and borderline atheist, did not wish to conceal his fundamental hostility to the religion of his birth. (As a younger Rıza had written to his sister while visiting Paris, "Were I a woman, I would embrace atheism and never become a Muslim. Imagine a religion that imposes laws always beneficial to men but hazardous to women such as permitting my husband to have three additional wives and as many concubines as he wishes, houris awaiting him in heaven, while I cover my head and face as a miller's horse . . . keep this religion far away from me.") Rıza was so pure in his positivism that he insisted the CUP slogan should be "Order (İntizam) and Progress," not "Union and Progress." As Arif Bey Oğlu, one of Rıza's fellow exiles in Geneva, complained in a private letter, "If Istanbul publishes this among the already uneducated public, the little sympathy which exists in our favor will be ruined." Worse than this was Rıza's stubborn personality and domineering attitude. As Oğlu concluded his complaint, "Since we have refused to accept [Ottoman dynastic] rule, why should we conform to the will of Ahmed Rıza?" As if sensing that Rıza's prickly personality was an asset allowing him to divide and conquer his opponents, the sultan made no offer to entice him back to Turkey, even while quietly buying off Rıza's rivals. Abdul Hamid was usually a step ahead of his opponents.

With Rıza unable to unite the factions of the CUP, for a time it looked like Damad Mahmud Pasha would himself take over the movement. And yet Mahmud's health was slowly failing, in part because of his exhausting travel schedule. As a fugitive royal harboring clear intent to depose a sitting sovereign, he was having trouble finding a country willing to allow him to reside permanently (even Swiss patience, it turned out, had limits). Seeking to force matters while he was still capable of doing so, Mahmud issued an appeal from Cairo, inviting Ottoman exiles—including also Armenian groups such as the Dashnaks and Hunchaks, along with Greek, Albanian, Jewish, Arab, and even Albanian opponents of the sultan—to attend a Congress of Ottoman Liberals in Paris in February 1902. And yet Mahmud was too weak to lead the conference himself (he died less than a year after it met, in January 1903), so the initiative fell to his son, Prince Sabahaddin.

Seizing the moment, Sabahaddin staked his own claim to leadership. A man of real, if conventional, eloquence, Sabahaddin had fully imbibed European ideas of social equality and religious tolerance, alongside a roseate view of the Ottoman past in which these values were believed to have been uniformly practiced—until mercilessly thrust aside by the tyrant of Yıldız. "From its début to its constitution," he told the forty-seven multi-ethnic, multi-faith delegates in Paris, "the Ottoman Empire has never failed to respect the language, the customs, the religion of all the various peoples over whose destinies it presided." Never, that is, until Abdul Hamid had come to the throne, unleashing on his people "a regime of oppression, the sole source of the misdeeds which are committed in the Empire and which inspire the indignation of the whole of humanity." In order to restore to Ottoman subjects "the full enjoyment of their rights recognized by the Imperial *Hatts* [decrees] and consecrated by international treaties," Sabahaddin proposed that the delegates unite to overthrow the sultan (presumably, although he did not specify this, so that his father, or he himself, could assume the throne).

To these sentiments, few Ottoman exiles could object. And yet the *means* by which Prince Sabahaddin wished them to topple the tyrant of Yildiz could not have been more controversial. As if determined to forfeit his own ascendancy in the movement, Sabahaddin added an important rider to the majority resolutions, which established a "permanent committee" to lobby the European signatories of the Treaties of Paris (1856) and Berlin (1878) "in order to obtain their moral concurrence and a benevolent action on their part," with the aim of "putting into execution of the international agreements stipulating internal order in Turkey." The reference to the Treaty of Berlin clearly pointed to Article 61, which had established European oversight of "the ameliorations and reforms demanded by local requirements in the provinces inhabited by Armenians, and to guarantee their security against the Circassians and Kurds." Playing to the crowd in Paris—a crowd in which Armenians were prominent—Sabahaddin had gone on record advocating European intervention on behalf of Christian minorities in the Ottoman Empire, as if wishing to reprise the Crimean War. Nothing could have been more fatal to his standing among Turks and other Ottoman Muslims.

The first to realize this was, predictably, Ahmed Rıza. Despite his own reputation for Western-style secularism, Rıza was too clever a politician to endorse European meddling in Ottoman internal affairs. In a minority dissent to Sabahaddin's resolution, Rıza pointed out that "the Powers are guided by self-interest and that this self-interest is not always in accord with that of our country." While expressing hopes that a reformed Ottoman government could, in line with the principles "of liberty and of justice," satisfy the "legitimate desires of the Armenians," along with that of "all the peoples of the empire," Rıza and his supporters "rejected entirely an action which infringes the independence of the Ottoman Empire."[8]

In this way a powerful cleavage was opened up in the Ottoman exile movement, just at the moment when it seemed to be coalescing into a serious force. With the death of Damad Mahmud Pasha in 1903, Sahabaddin was left as the undisputed spokesman of Ottoman "Liberals," with the support of most of the Christian minority groups, even as Ahmed Rıza spoke for the "unionist" faction dominated by Turks and Muslims. True to his promises in Paris, Sabahaddin petitioned the powers for help in overthrowing the Hamidian regime. In ecumenical fashion, he even petitioned the Vatican in March 1906 for an audience with Pope Pius X to discuss the plight of Catholics in the Ottoman Empire. Mostly, though, Sabahaddin focused on England, hoping to summon back the old liberal Turcophilia of the Tanzimat era. "With the triumph of Liberal ideas in Turkey," he wrote to Foreign Secretary Sir Edward Grey in August 1906, "the great moral influence which Constantinople possesses over Islam at large is destined to assume an intellectual character. Such an influence would then serve as a powerful agent of reconciliation between East and West."[9]

With his liberal rival begging for British intervention and intriguing with the pope, it was not difficult for Ahmed Rıza to pose as the authentic Ottoman voice of opposition. Positivist he may have been, but Rıza was a patriot too—patriot enough to go on the warpath against exile backsliders who advocated the dismemberment of the empire. Although he accepted an invitation from the Dashnaks to stage a reconciliation with Prince Sabahaddin at a new Paris Congress in December 1907, Rıza insisted that the delegates confirm the inviolability of the empire, including the rights of the sultanate—and the caliphate, implying that Muslims would still enjoy symbolic primacy (even if not superior legal status). While the majority resolution worked up by the

Dashnaks and liberals emphasized the need for "passive resistance" against the sultan (e.g., the refusal to pay taxes), "unarmed resistance" (such as public employee strikes), and "armed resistance to acts of oppression" (vaguer but clearly implying minority sedition), Rıza insisted, in another dissent, that "we are met not to commit follies and crimes or to create a pretext for the intervention of the Powers, but to realize a noble aim . . . by revolutionary means which suit the temper of our compatriots."[10]

Abdul Hamid would have been pleased. Even in asserting the common goal of overthrowing his regime by force, his opponents were still parsing the fine points as to tactics. He was now in the thirty-second year of his reign, surpassing Mahmud II (1808–1839) as the longest-lasting sultan since the seventeenth century. Murad, the sultan's half-mad half brother, had died in 1904, the year after his brother-in-law, Mahmud, succumbed: there was thus no plausible pretender to disturb his repose. True, there were periodic assassination scares: an attempted stabbing in summer 1904, a carriage dynamited while Abdul Hamid was at prayer at Hamidiye Mosque in 1905. On one occasion, an earthquake felled the gargantuan four-ton chandelier of Dolmabahçe Palace while the sultan was sitting on his throne, receiving a foreign delegation. By now used to such frights, Abdul Hamid was so unperturbed he did not even stand.[11]

Still, the sultan was not infallible. If it was not too difficult a trick to keep exiled politicians and pretenders quarreling among themselves, the spread of dissent through his army was more serious. Abdul Hamid had always had a difficult relationship with the armed forces, in large part because of the budgetary axe. To keep European creditors at bay, beginning in the 1880s the sultan had pared down the army bureaucracy. Judging from the 1897 war with Greece, the German-inspired rationalization of the Ottoman army had been fairly successful—but it left behind a large and growing class of disgruntled graduates of the service academies, unable to receive the cushy staff commissions they believed were owed them. The Ottoman navy was even worse off, as it was last in line for expenditure. Abdul Hamid's fear of assassination had deleterious effects on both services—just as army recruits were not allowed to train with live ammunition, Turkish naval vessels were not allowed to be armed while in port (nor did the sultan allow them to venture into the

Bosphorus, lest they turn their guns on Yıldız). After the turn of the twentieth century, military pay was almost chronically in arrears, which had a catastrophic impact on morale in the officer corps.[12]

The trouble brewing was most serious in the Third Army in Macedonia,

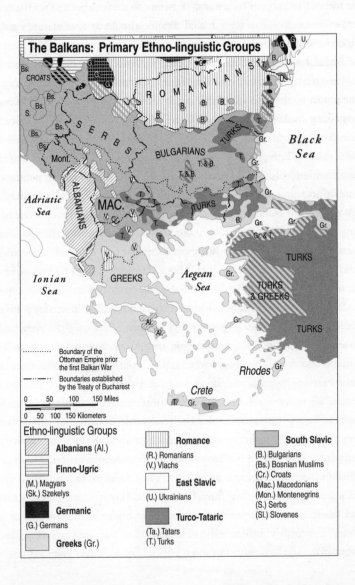

The Balkans: Primary Ethno-linguistic Groups

.... Boundary of the
Ottoman Empire prior
the first Balkan War

– – – – Boundaries established
by the Treaty of Bucharest

0   50   100   150 Miles

0 50 100 150 Kilometers

Ethno-linguistic Groups

Albanians (Al.)	Romance	South Slavic
Finno-Ugric	(R.) Romanians	(B.) Bulgarians
(M.) Magyars	(V.) Vlachs	(Bs.) Bosnian Muslims
(Sk.) Szekelys	East Slavic	(Cr.) Croats
Germanic	(U.) Ukrainians	(Mac.) Macedonians
(G.) Germans	Turco-Tataric	(Mon.) Montenegrins
Greeks (Gr.)	(Ta.) Tatars	(S.) Serbs
	(T.) Turks	(Sl.) Slovenes

the Ottoman region stretching from Thrace to Albania, in between the Aegean Sea to the south, the Šar Mountains to the north, and Lake Ohrid in the west, marking the boundary with Albania. Much of this territory had been assigned to the "Big Bulgaria" the Russians had tried to create in the short-lived San Stefano Treaty of 1878, before being returned to the Ottomans in the Treaty of Berlin with a kind of special autonomous status, granted under Article 23. In part to stave off a unified movement for Macedonian independence, after the turn of the century Abdul Hamid had split Macedonia into three provinces (Salonica, Monastir, and Kosovo). Macedonia was a microcosm of the Balkan ethnic cauldron, with the Bulgarians the largest group but substantial minorities of Greeks, Serbs, "Macedonians" or Macedo-Slavs (who, according to chauvinists in the previous three groups, did not really exist), Vlachs (related to Romanians and mostly Orthodox), Turkish and Albanian Muslims, Albanian Christians, and a large Jewish population centered in Salonica (Thessaloniki). With the European powers looking on with a mixture of horror and greedy encouragement, Greece, Serbia, and semi-independent Bulgaria all pressed historico-irredentist claims on Macedonia, with the Bulgarians the most forceful. The Internal Macedonian Revolutionary Organization, or IMRO (formerly BMARC), founded in Salonica by Gotse Delchev in 1893, is often described as the prototypical modern terrorist organization. Confusingly, it advocated "Macedonia for the Macedonians," although it was mostly a Bulgarian affair. By the early 1900s, Macedonia was a byword for intrigue and political terrorism, plagued by periodic assaults on mosques and churches, politically motivated train and postal carriage holdups, and ransomed kidnappings.

In 1903, tensions ratcheted up to the most dangerous level yet. In April, a group of young Bulgarian anarchist "assassins" (not, apparently, affiliated with the IMRO) launched an uprising in Salonica with the aim of soliciting European intervention, in the style of the Bosnian-Bulgarian uprisings of 1876, but in a more targeted, twentieth-century terrorist fashion, blowing up water and electricity plants, tunneling under and then dynamiting an Ottoman bank office, and attempting (although failing) to fire a post office and natural gas facility, before self-destructing in a hail of some sixty bombs tossed in a shoot-out with Ottoman police. The assassins received just the response they wanted from the sultan, who yet again dispatched Circassian irregulars (the Bashi-Bazouks) to mop up resistance in the city, leading to a more generalized wave of popular Muslim retaliation against Christians that summer, which spread to Kosovo, ensnaring the Russian consul in Üsküp (Skopje), who fell victim to a mob lynching in mid-August. In an eerie echo of the earlier Bulgarian crisis, Russia dispatched its Black Sea Fleet to the Bosphorus, pursuant to forcing through a reform program that would include an international gendarmerie to keep order in Macedonia. Acting as a battering ram for Russia and the powers, the IMRO then struck in force, mustering (the government claimed) some 26,000 heavily armed guerrillas in a coordinated attack on Ottoman army positions in Kruševo and Smilovo (both of which fell), the rail lines around Üsküp, and in Thrace, focusing on Adrianople (Edirne). The uprising was by now serious enough that the regular Ottoman army was called on to crush the rebels, and it did so with relish, recapturing Kruševo and Smilovo, securing the railways and Edirne, and mopping up the last serious IMRO resistance by the second week of September. The death toll, comprising some 5,300 Turks and 6,000 Macedonians, was not historically high by Balkan standards. But hundreds of villages were burned to the ground, leaving over 70,000 Macedonians homeless, with another 30,000 or so fleeing to Bulgaria. The casualties included Gotse Delchev, founder of the IMRO, himself.[13]

The powers seized on the violence to force through a sweeping new reform program at Mürzteg (October 9, 1903), cosigned by Russian tsar Nicholas II and Franz Josef I of Austria-Hungary. The centerpiece was an international gendarmerie to police Macedonia, similar to the one dispatched to Crete in 1897. Once again, the powers had determined to intervene after an Ottoman *victory*—in part to deaden its impact. It is not hard to imagine the resentment of Turkish officers in the Third Army, who had just put down a large-scale irredentist rebellion in less than three weeks, when they learned that they must now obey the dictates of European officers sent to keep them in line. Ostensibly, the Europeans were there because the Ottomans were not strong enough to provide law and order in Macedonia—and yet what had the army just proved, if not that it was perfectly capable of doing so (if at great human cost)?

What galled many of the Turks even more was that the French, British, Russian, Austro-Hungarian, and Italian officers with whom they now rubbed shoulders in Salonica (the Germans alone, owing to the kaiser's cultivation of Abdul Hamid and their own role training the Ottoman army, declined to participate) were far more sharply turned out than they, not least because they could afford to be. Since Mahmud II had suppressed the Janissaries in 1826, the Ottoman army had been thoroughly westernized down to dress and drill—but Western costumes and equipment, along with the social rituals surrounding their use, were *expensive*. Never well paid, Turkish officers and enlisted men alike were hit hard by the pinch of another Ottoman budget crisis in 1906, which stopped construction on the Baghdad Railway cold, and left army pay months in arrears. By year's end mutinies had broken out across the empire, for the simple reason that no one was being paid—not even the officers, who protested alongside their men. Next year, the protests became nearly universal, with something like seventeen mutinies occurring over the twelve months from July 1907 to July 1908. Most of them petered out as soon as the sultan came up with the back pay.[14]

In Macedonia, mutinous sentiment was more serious. In the Third Army, general dissatisfaction over poor pay blended together with resentment at the lavishly outfitted European officers, and the general air of Balkan conspiracy. Gotse Delchev and the IMRO may or may not have been the "first" terrorist group—they were certainly aware of the activities of the Dashnaks in eastern Turkey in the early 1890s, and the pan-Slavist intrigues that erupted in Bulgaria in the 1870s—but their example certainly influenced other irredentist movements, most famously the Serbian network that evolved into the Black Hand. It was perhaps only natural that Turkish soldiers targeted by IMRO conspirators seeking to destroy the Ottoman Empire would borrow their techniques in order to save it.

A whiff of legend still surrounds the spread of revolutionary sentiment through the Third Army in Macedonia in the years before 1908. The "Young Turk" conspiracy has variously been ascribed to the Bektashi dervish order of the now-defunct Janissaries, Freemasonry, offshoots of the Italian Carbonari, and the covert influence of the *Dönme*, or crypto-Jewish Muslims believed to have clung to their faith after their spiritual leader, Sabbatai Zevi, publicly converted to Islam in 1666 (*Dönme* were numerous in Salonica). Whatever the truth about its ultimate inspiration, there is no doubt that cloak-and-dagger-style army "cells" existed, in which each new initiate, after being conducted into a secret meeting place blindfolded, would swear a loyalty oath (on "the sword and the Koran"), vowing to obey orders from the revolutionary committee, up to and including killing or suffering death. Each new member would learn the names of no more than a handful of others, with meetings of more than five people strictly forbidden.[15]

In practice, not everyone followed such discretion. One of Mustafa Kemal's officer friends, Ömer Naci, like him a card-carrying member of the Ottoman Freedom Society (*Osmanlı Hürriyet Cemiyeti*), as the movement was called before 1907, published his revolutionary musings in a Salonica children's journal, leading to an order for his arrest.[16] Naci was alerted in time for him to flee to Paris in March 1907, where he met Ahmed Rıza (whose "unionist" program sounded far more appealing to army officers than did Sabahaddin's encouragement of European meddling in the empire). In September, the Ottoman Freedom Society was renamed the Committee of Union and Progress (henceforth CUP), in a kind of fusion with Rıza's exile movement. All this was supposed to be secret, but Paris meetings of disgruntled Turkish officers with famous exile politicians, not to mention the increasingly open discussions of politics in the cafés of Salonica, were hard to hide from the sultan's spy network. As Mustafa Kemal recalled of the scene of the time, "Revolutionaries were sitting at one table . . . I noticed that they were drinking *rakı* and beer. Their talk was most patriotic. They spoke of making a revolution. The revolution, they said, needed great men. Everyone wanted to be a great man."[17] Little wonder that the German liaison officer in charge of training the Ottoman army, Goltz Pasha, noted a dangerous politicization of the Third Army in a report to Kaiser Wilhelm II as early as December 11, 1907.[18]

By spring 1908, rumors of some kind of conspiracy were widespread enough that the sultan began sending accredited agents to investigate. Things were coming to a head in Macedonia, not least because of an upcoming summit between the British king Edward VII and Tsar Nicholas II on June 8–10. If the worst fears of Turkish nationalists came true, the two sovereigns,

pursuant to the Anglo-Russian Accord of 1907 delimiting spheres of influ-
ence in Asia, would bury the final Great Game hatchet by agreeing to a partition of what remained of Ottoman Europe. Adding to these fears, Russia's
Black Sea Fleet was conducting menacing maneuvers along Turkey's Black
Sea coast. With a sense of apocalypse in the air, on June 11, 1908, Nazım Bey,
a former police chief appointed by Abdul Hamid as central commandant of
Salonica, was shot by unknown assailants shortly before he was to return to
Constantinople with his report, reputedly on the orders of Ismail Enver Bey, a
young CUP officer. The sultan responded by sending an official commission
to investigate, whereupon Enver fled into the mountains on June 25–26. He
was shortly followed by a higher-ranking Albanian CUP conspirator, Adju-
tant Major Ahmed Niyazi Bey, accompanied by some two hundred armed
soldier-followers. On July 7, General Şemşi Pasha, sent in by the sultan to
crush the burgeoning mutiny in the Third Army, was gunned down in broad
daylight in the streets of Monastir by a CUP officer, Lieutenant Arıf. Troops
sent from Anatolia to finish the job instead went over to the revolution. In the
days that followed, CUP committees across Macedonia began declaring the
reinstatement of the constitution, going so far as to wire this demand formally to Yıldız Palace. The Third Army was in open mutiny against the
sultan.[19]

Abdul Hamid now played a masterstroke. With the word "constitution"
being invoked far and wide as a kind of talisman of revolution, the sultan
simply appropriated the term himself. On the night of July 23–24, 1908,
Abdul Hamid announced the recall of the parliament, in effect reinstating
the constitution. Imperial decrees then followed on August 1 and 3, abolish-
ing the secret police and its prerogatives for searches and seizures, eliminating preemptive censorship, and requiring the publication of an annual budget.
The special tribunals established in Macedonia to snuff out CUP activity
were dissolved; a general amnesty for political prisoners was proclaimed, and
extended to nonpolitical prisoners who had served more than two-thirds of
their sentence. The CUP revolution had succeeded, it seemed, without a shot
being fired—its aims endorsed by none other than Abdul Hamid. The Bloody
Sultan, by stealing the revolutionaries' thunder, had saved his throne.[20]

It is important to recall the sequence of events in summer 1908 precisely, because they were so badly misunderstood outside the country. European journalists mostly noticed the euphoric, multi-ethnic crowds chanting French revolutionary slogans—*Egalité! Liberté! Justice! Fraternité!* And yet these crowds did not materialize until *after* the sultan had announced the recall of the parliament; they cannot have played any role in driving events. Until Abdul Hamid's preemptive move, no one in the capital, nor anywhere else in the empire outside Macedonia, had the slightest idea that any kind of revolution was afoot—nor were most people clear on what, exactly, was meant by the reinstatement of the constitution.

An idea of the popular disconnect between rhetoric and reality was captured in a famous exchange between Dr. Riza Tewfik, a future CUP deputy, and a crowd of Kurdish porters. "Tell us what constitution means!" the porters shouted. Dr. Tewfik replied, "Constitution is such a great thing that those who do not know it are donkeys." "We are donkeys!" the porters roared back. "Your fathers also did not know it. Say that you are the sons of donkeys." "We are the sons of donkeys," the porters shouted back, although whether with enthusiasm or bewildered sarcasm is unknown. Another aspiring politician with a long red beard, less practiced in the arts of persuasion, promised his would-be constituents that "I have a beloved wife and five children. I swear that I am ready to cut them to pieces for the sacred cause as I would have done for His Majesty."* Listeners could only surmise which "sacred cause" it was meant to espouse: the sultan, the constitution, or the CUP and its platform.[21] Judging from the best-informed observers, the most popular slogan heard on the streets in the last days of July 1908 was "Long live the sultan! [*Padişahım çok yaşa!*]." Many Turks were seen proudly carrying portraits of Abdul Hamid.[22]

The confusion was not confined to the public. Before the sultan preempted their conspiracy to overthrow him, CUP leaders had not settled on a political program, beyond the goals of restoring the constitution and holding elections. Did CUP army officers want to run for office themselves? Elect puppet candidates, who would take orders from the CUP? Try to infiltrate the

---

* As the feminist Halidé Edib, a neighbor of the speaker, mused after hearing this threat, "I wondered why he did not cut himself rather than his wife and children."

government, purge the palace and Sublime Porte bureaucracies of Hamidian loyalists, and rule by secret decrees? Or simply dissolve into the background now that the victory seemed to be won, and allow electoral democracy to take its course?

Not surprisingly, the CUP approach mixed together a bit of everything. True to the movement's origins in secret cells, soon after the sultan's climb-down the CUP dispatched a Committee of Seven to Constantinople to negotiate with the palace, including three future notables: Staff Major Djemal Bey, an ambitious postal official named Talât Bey, and Mehmed Djavid Bey, an economist, former bank clerk, and newspaper editor from Salonica (Enver and Ahmed Niyazi Bey were still in hiding). Quietly, the Committee of Seven exercised pressure on Abdul Hamid to reform the government and ensure that the parliamentary elections would be freely conducted. On the surface, this peculiar arrangement functioned reasonably well, as the sultan stream-lined the bureaucracy and reduced state salaries—except for the army, which was now given priority. In the parliamentary elections, it was determined, all taxpaying males twenty-five years or older could vote for deputies who them-selves were required to know Turkish. True to the "unionist" position of the CUP, there would be no ethnic quotas, but no discrimination either (in prac-tice representation ended up split more or less proportionally among the empire's ethno-religious groups). The CUP would make no effort to stifle other parties from contesting the elections, scheduled to begin in late October—although the existence of the Committee of Seven suggested to many opponents, not least the "Liberal Union" followers of Prince Sabahad-din (whose cause was now taken up inside Constantinople by the Circassian turncoat Mizancı Murad), that they were pulling strings behind the scenes.[23]

The period between the July revolution and the fall elections was a time of great expectations for Ottoman reformers, liberals, and minorities. Inevita-bly, the period acquired a rose-tinted glow in folk memory. Halidé Edib, daughter of a palace secretary who had attended the American College for Girls in Üsküdar, was spurred to a life in letters by the events of 1908, which she witnessed firsthand. Nothing inspired her more than the celebratory atmosphere of the parliamentary poll. "Masses of people," she recalled, followed the election urns, decked in flowers and flags. In carriages sat the Moslem and Christian priests [*sic*], hand in hand. Christian and Moslem maidens, dressed in white, locked in childish embrace, passed on, while the crowd that followed sang enthusiastically, "O country, O mother, be thou joyful and happy to-day." The memory is so intense that to this day I cannot think of it unmoved.[24]

The jubilation of democracy aborning was tempered, however, by sobering news from the empire's borderlands. Even as election fever began to spread through the capital in September and October, Turkey's traditional enemies began maneuvering for position. Since the Crimean War, Austria-Hungary and Russia had eyed one another warily in the Balkans, with only Bismarck's mediation preventing a major breach during the crisis of 1875–78. Kaiser Wilhelm II's support for the Hamidian regime, by helping to throw Russia into the arms of France, had effectively ended the old *Dreikaiserbund* of the three Eastern emperors, but this did not mean that the other two could not team up together against the Ottomans, as the tsar and Emperor Franz Josef I had done in 1903 over Macedonia (it helped that Russia was, at the time, focused mostly on her rivalry with Japan in the Far East). With the sultan's hold on power tottering after the July revolution, negotiations between Vienna and St. Petersburg began over yet another diplomatic move at Turkey's expense. The idea, hashed out at the Buchlau country estate of the Habsburg foreign minister, Baron Alois Lexa von Aehrenthal, with his Russian counterpart, Alexander Izvolsky, was for Russia to go along with Austria's formal annexation of Bosnia-Herzegovina in exchange for Austrian support for revising the Berlin Treaty so as to allow Russian warships access to the Ottoman Straits.

The final timing of Aehrenthal's announcement was still up in the air when another diplomatic bombshell detonated in Constantinople. In late September, Abdul Hamid's long-serving foreign minister, Ahmet Tevfik Pasha, invited European diplomats to dinner—with the notable exception of the Bulgarian *agent diplomatique*, the slight signifying the sultan's refusal to brook any notion that Bulgaria was independent of Ottoman rule. On

October 5, Prince Ferdinand, hitherto merely governor of an Ottoman vilayet, or province, decided to test the mettle of a diminished Abdul Hamid by proclaiming himself tsar of an independent Bulgaria. As if offended by being thus upstaged, next day Austria announced the annexation of Bosnia-Herzegovina, Aehrenthal adding helpfully that he had received Russia's prior endorsement of it. Not to be outdone, Crete then declared *Enosis*, or union, with mainland Greece.

Ottoman diplomats were able, in time, to dampen these blows by negotiating financial compensation and safeguards for the rights of Muslims in lost territories. And yet there was no hiding the humiliation. Compounding the shock, Turkey's Christian neighbors had piled on her during the Islamic holy month of Ramadan, as if intentionally to enrage the Muslim faithful. In these circumstances, it is surprising that religious minorities did as well as they did in the November elections, with 23 Greek deputies, 12 Armenians, 5 Jews, 4 Bulgarians, 3 Serbs, and 1 Vlach as against 142 Turks, 60 Arabs, and 25 Albanians. If anyone could be said to have "won" the elections, it was the CUP, with 60 deputies expressing allegiance to the committee, and the only other organized party, the Liberal Union, netting barely a handful. In recognition of his role in the movement, Ahmed Rıza was elected president of the Chamber when the body convened in the parliament building next to Hagia Sofia. Abdul Hamid himself opened the first session, as if to beatify the revolutionary conspiracy meant to topple him. He had suspended the parliament, the sultan explained as if in apology, in order to complete the work of modernizing the empire. This work done, deputies could help him stand up to the powers and restore Ottoman prestige.[25]

The CUP ascendancy was, however, more fragile than it seemed. Opposition was already growing in the capital to this shadowy movement rumored to be running the government, even if no one knew just how it was doing it (the CUP had as yet obtained no cabinet positions). Ahmed Rıza, as president of the Chamber, was in the curiously exposed position of holding no real power, but being the public face of a reputedly secularist party, and parliament, which many Muslims resented for undermining the authority of a sultan still broadly popular among the faithful. Only in February 1909 did the CUP take a direct hand in governance, engineering a no-confidence vote in the grand vizier, Mehmed Kâmil Pasha (an old Hamidian stalwart first appointed to this post in 1885), and appointing a loyal committee man, Hüseyin Hilmi, in his stead. For better or worse, the CUP—and its most famous politician, Ahmed Rıza—could now be blamed for anything that went wrong.

It did not help matters for Turkish secularists that the elections seemed to bring in their wake not only the diplomatic humiliations endured during Ramadan, but the appearance of more and more assertive unveiled women, like Halidé Edib, in the streets. Ahmed Rıza, long rumored to be an atheist and a closet feminist, was hardly the man to reassure the faithful that the traditional privileges of Muslims would be observed under the new regime. The unionist Rıza, owing to his feud with Prince Sabahaddin, was a lightning rod for the liberals too. He was, in short, the worst possible choice to unite the public behind the CUP. With almost painful inevitability, Rıza emerged over the winter as the embodiment of everything ordinary Muslims detested about secularism and European-style politics more broadly. While liberals were themselves outraged by what they saw as CUP abuse of its power, soon it was the *hocas* and *imams* who were making the running, uniting behind an opposition vehicle called the Society of Islamic Unity (*Ittihad-ı Muhammedi Cemiyeti*), founded by a Bektashi, Hafız Derviş Vahdeti.

By spring, the Society of Islamic Unity, through its main organ, the newspaper *Volkan*, was calling openly for the restoration of Sharia law—to turn the political clock back not only to 1907, that is, but all the way to 1838, before the reforms of the Tanzimat. A mass meeting of Muslims was held in the Hagia Sofia mosque on April 3, the birthday of the Prophet. Several days later, Hasan Fehmi, editor of the liberal paper *Serbestî* (*Freedom*), known for its vitriolic attacks on the CUP, was murdered in broad daylight on the Galata Bridge, the assailant disappearing into the crowd before his identity could be established. Ottoman liberals, including many Christians, now took to the streets to protest against the government, alongside growing numbers of Muslim theological students (*softas*) with whom they had little in common other than an all-pervasive resentment of the CUP. Adding a crucial armed element to the burgeoning opposition were young noncommissioned officers in the First Army (known as regimentals, or *alayli*), who resented the arrogance of CUP men in the army, who tended to be educated graduates of the academies (*mektepli*, or "schooled"). Revolutions make for strange bedfellows, and this banding together of an anti-CUP coalition of liberal secularists, Sharia-spouting *softas*, and disgruntled subalterns was stranger than most.[26]

The gathering storm of opposition finally burst on the night of April 12–13, 1909.* The driving political element seems to have been the *softas*, although the forceful arm was provided by about three thousand *alayli* soldiers, including Hamidian loyalists from the Taksim barracks, who marched into the old city and surrounded the parliament. While there does not seem to have been any concerted political program behind the march, the demands of the *softas* and mutineers were announced in full-throated shouts: the restoration of "the sharia law of the illustrious Mohammed," the end of CUP control of the army, the restoration of Abdul Hamid's prerogatives as sultan, and the handing over of Ahmed Rıza—so he could be replaced by a "true Muslim" (and presumably lynched). When no answer was forthcoming from the Chamber, the armed mob invaded the parliament. Terrified deputies ran for their lives; two were killed, apparently on false recognition (one was thought to be Ahmed Rıza, the second the editor of the CUP newspaper, *Tanin*). The CUP grand vizier, Hüseyin Hilmi, rushed to Yıldız Palace to tender his resignation. Rıza himself somehow escaped and went into hiding, holed up under German protection in a Baghdad Railway Company building.[27]

It was a moment of truth for Turkey—and for Abdul Hamid. While no conclusive evidence has emerged that the sultan organized or supported the mob assault on parliament, he was clearly its immediate beneficiary. Grateful for what appeared to be good fortune, Abdul Hamid accepted the resignation of Hüseyin Hilmi and the entire cabinet. Tevfik Pasha, Abdul Hamid's loyal long-serving foreign minister, was made grand vizier. Hamidian loyalists took over the army and naval ministries, with the aim of restoring the influence of *alayli* officers. A non-CUP deputy, Ismail Kemal, was elected president of the Chamber, and Mizancı Murad offered the new government the full support of the Liberal Union. Buoyed by what appeared to be a genuine

---

* Because the Julian calendar then used by the Ottoman Empire was thirteen days behind the Gregorian, this episode is known in Turkish history as the *Otuz bir mart vakası*, or March 31 incident.

popular clamor for the return of traditional sultanic authority, on April 15, the restoration of Sharia law was wired to every regional governor, as if to obliterate the Tanzimat from memory. Muslim mobs began to appear in the streets of provincial towns. In Adana, the CUP's call to restore parliamentary authority led to clashes between Armenian groups favorable to the revolution and the local, pro-Hamidian army garrison, producing the worst massacres since 1896: some twenty thousand died, the vast majority (though not all of them) Armenians.* In the capital itself, a kind of terror descended, with CUP ministers assassinated and their newspaper offices sacked. Foreign observers must have been suffering from whiplash: Turkey had gone from Hamidian despotism to constitutionalism and back again, all in less than nine months.[28]

Retribution was not long in coming. Having survived in power for nearly thirty-three years, Abdul Hamid may have overestimated his own political acumen in reading the situation in April 1909. He may also have suffered from poor intelligence, not least because his old spy chief, Izzet Pasha, had skipped town in early August 1908, after hiding out from the then-anti-Hamidian mob in the German embassy (the Germans' similar sheltering of the anti-Hamidian scapegoat Ahmed Rıza eight months later being a curious reflection of their enduring influence in Constantinople, whichever faction held sway).[29] Whatever the reason, the sultan overplayed his hand badly. By crushing the CUP so openly, he could not but unite the powerful cells of the Third Army in Macedonia against him, along with the entire class of educated *mektepli* officers. Under the leadership of General Mahmud Shevket Pasha, with support from younger *mektepli* officers like Enver Bey and Mustafa Kemal, a new Action Army (*Hareket Ordusu*) was formed to march on the capital. On April 22, the commanders met with deposed parliamentary deputies and other political notables outside the city gates at Yeşilköy—where the Russians had stopped their advance in 1878. They agreed that the sultan must be deposed, although they would not announce this until the city was secured.

---

* Again the figures clash hopelessly. An initial Ottoman claim that more Muslims were killed in Adana (1,900) than Armenians (1,500) was believed by almost no one. Armenian claims of as many as 30,000 Christian deaths were likewise rapidly dismissed as too high. An Ottoman commission of inquiry later conceded that Christian civilian victims outnumbered Muslim ones, the latter including gendarmes and soldiers (by 4,196 to 1,487), but this figure is generally dismissed as low. There seems to be a rough scholarly consensus that 20,000 is the best estimate for deaths in the Adana riots of 1909, with all but 1,000 to 2,000 of the victims Armenian Christians.

On April 24, the Action Army stormed into the capital. Abdul Hamid, realizing too late what he was up against, ordered his troops not to resist, but many chose to anyway. The fighting lasted on through the day, with major engagements in Taksim,* Fatih, and the old Sublime Porte in Stambul, before Guard troops made a last stand at Yıldız, fortified by the sultan into an armed compound for precisely such a contingency. But the stand did not last long. By nightfall, the overmatched Guard troops gave in. The Action Army cut off the electricity, plunging Yildiz into darkness. Servants were seen fleeing the palace, "carrying bundles of linen and jewels." Abdul Hamid's sons fled, seeking refuge in the palaces of their married sisters. The palace eunuchs and ladies, it was said, fell into hysterics. At last, as one of the sultan's daughters recalled, "in the great palace there were only women."[30]

On April 25, General Shevket Pasha imposed martial law on Constantinople amid terrible scenes as pro-Hamidian soldiers and officials were executed in public view. Two days later the reconvened parliament decreed the deposition of Abdul Hamid II, in favor of his brother, Mehmed Reshad (who would rule as Mehmed V). As if to taunt the man they were humiliating, the CUP decided to exile Abdul Hamid to Salonica, epicenter of the political conspiracy that had destroyed his regime. This time, unlike in July 1908, there would be no backsliding, no restoration. Shevket Pasha took over command of all forces in the capital, and was appointed inspector of the First, Second, and Third Armies, just in case Hamidian sentiment reared its head again. The CUP was in power, this time in earnest.[31]

The position of the new regime, however, remained precarious. Diplomatically speaking, the humiliations of October 1908 were compounded by a creeping estrangement from Imperial Germany, whose support had given crucial strategic ballast to the Hamidian regime. Not even Baron Marschall, the Giant of the Bosphorus, could stanch the blow to German-Turkish relations struck by Austria-Hungary's annexation of Bosnia-Herzegovina, especially after Russia acquiesced in it in March 1909 owing to pressure from

---

* In a powerful echo of the dramatic events of April 1909, it was Prime Minister Recep Tayyip Erdoğan's decision to rebuild the old Taksim barracks in place of the tree-lined Gezi Park (coming on top of new Islam-inspired restrictions on dress and alcohol sales) that sparked the "Turkish Spring" Gezi Park demonstrations of May–June 2013. It was not lost on Turks on either side of the struggle that the pro-Hamidian (read: Islamist), anti-CUP (read: anti-secularist) mutiny of March 31, 1909, had begun in Taksim.

Berlin, bringing to an end this dangerous First Bosnian Crisis, as it later came to be called. The Germans, for their part, were perturbed not only by the treatment of the kaiser's friend Abdul Hamid, but by a series of strikes that all but halted construction on the Baghdad Railway. While elements of the old strategic partnership between Berlin and Constantinople, such as the Goltz military mission, were, in time, restored, the spirit of the thing had been lost. "Hajji" Wilhelm had fallen for Abdul Hamid expressly *because* of the traditional Islamic prerogatives of the Ottoman sultanate (and caliphate), which seemed to offer Germany a way to undermine her colonial rivals. Now that the Young Turks had done away with both him and his pan-Islamic policies, the kaiser had no cause for pro-Ottoman enthusiasm.

Domestically, the CUP position was murkier still. Martial law was hardly an encouraging slogan for a new era of popular government. In a seemingly adroit political move, Enver Bey organized a public funeral for fifty unidentified men felled in the capital on April 24. He reminded the crowds, as if to heal the gaping political wounds of the revolution, counterrevolution, and counter-counterrevolution, that here were "Moslems and Christians lying side by side." In the new CUP era, he promised, Ottoman citizens would all be "fellow-patriots who know no distinction of race or creed."[32] Yet by emphasizing the rights of religious minorities, Enver was implicitly conceding that the CUP, just as Muslim critics had asserted, did *not* believe in Sharia law. After the violation of the sultan-caliph by the Action Army—which had literally invaded the sacred precinct of the Imperial Harem—it appeared to many pious Muslims that the Young Turks were not Muslims at all, but were maybe even *Dönme*, or crypto-Jews. As Ambassador Marschall noted in an October 1909 dispatch, "When Muslims learn that the [newly installed] Caliph is powerless, and is only the puppet of people who are more or less estranged from Islam, a major crisis will be unavoidable." For this reason, CUP leaders needed to watch their mouths. "Since the catastrophe of 13 April," he observed, "the [Young Turks] have become more careful. Women's emancipation is being put to the side, and once again Sharia law is spoken of. Nevertheless, strict Muslims regard the whole [CUP] regime with deep mistrust, if not with outright hostility."[33]

Whether out of conviction, opportunism, or simple fear, the Young Turks gradually abandoned their positivist credos in the years after 1909 to make their peace with the majority Muslims of the land they now ruled. By the time of the CUP congress of April 1911, party leaders were speaking openly of Sharia law, and publicly denouncing members, such as the Salonica sophisticate and financier Djavid Bey, suspected of Jewish-*Dönme* connections. The CUP platform approved by 180 delegates on April 22, 1911, was, as Ambassador Marschall informed Berlin with a note of approval, "of a strong Islamic-reactionary character."[34] After all the *Sturm und Drang* of the revolution, it was as if Abdul Hamid had never left his throne.

Reforms in the Ottoman army, meanwhile, after being thrown off-kilter during the upheaval of 1908–9, took on a much more serious aspect after the *mektepli* officers had established their ascendancy with the counter-counterrevolution of April 24, 1909. A law passed on June 26, 1909, established maximum ages for various officer grades, in order to clear out "dead wood" (meaning *alayli*, or less educated, officers, who also tended to be older) and open spots for the promotion of ambitious *mektepli* men. On August 7, 1909, the Law for the Purge of Military Ranks was passed, establishing new educational requirements for commissions, with much the same intent. Longer-term reforms, some of which had already been in the works in the late Hamidian era, were also accelerated. The most significant of these was the introduction of a proper corps structure, with each corps, comprising three infantry divisions, under the command of a lieutenant general (a rank previously unknown in the Ottoman army, as was the corps). Following the ideas of Goltz Pasha, who had devoted intense study to the lessons of the Russo-Japanese War of 1904–5, the Ottomans also streamlined infantry divisions on a "triangular" basis, reducing the total number of battalions in each from sixteen to nine, divided up into three infantry regiments matched by three corresponding artillery battalions, alongside a rifle battalion (each division would also have its own musical band). The idea was to make each division more flexible, allowing regiments to be rotated into and out of the front lines, and to enable much closer tactical coordination between artillery and infantry. Reserve units (the *redif*) were also reorganized into proper army corps, each of them given artillery components to improve their striking power.

It would take years for these measures to mature fully. New mobilization and campaign plans needed to be drawn up, and staff for corps-level head-quarters created nearly from scratch. Key matériel shortages in the army remained in everything from rifles and cannons to pack animals and medical supplies. Nevertheless, signs of progress were visible in maneuvers staged in Macedonia over the winter of 1909–10, which were observed with considerable pride by Goltz Pasha. In October 1910, the revamped Second Army (now covering the Balkan fronts) put more than sixty thousand men into the field for simulated combat operations, deeply impressing the military attachés who had come out from Constantinople to observe. Seventy-five years after the suppression of the Janissaries, it appeared the Ottomans had finally created the Western-style army of Mahmud's dreams, even if there were many kinks left to iron out.[35]

Pleased by the CUP's reactionary turn toward pan-Islam, and impressed by Ottoman military reforms, Germany began renewing its strategic investment in the empire. In a popular pan-German primer by the Turcologist Ernst Jäckh, Turkey was sold to prospective German officers, engineers, and salesmen as *Der aufsteigende Halbmond* (The Rising Crescent). In December 1910, Deutsche Bank fronted a major new loan of 160 million francs, intended to underwrite the next stage of construction on the Baghdad Railway. Krupp signed hundreds of millions of marks of new Ottoman contracts for guns and shells. In June 1912, the German firm F. H. Schmidt began a major renovation of the Third Army barracks at Üsküp, in the heart of contested Macedonia, intended to be the strategic linchpin of Ottoman Europe. Having evidently forgotten and forgiven the Young Turk deposition of his friend in Yıldız Palace, Kaiser Wilhelm II was ready, it appeared, to go all in again.[36]

It had taken some time, but the empire seemed finally to have emerged from the turmoil of the Young Turk Revolution. The patient, though nearly killed by the shock of surgery, had recovered much, if not all, of his former strength. This was all to the good, for the Ottoman Empire was about to be tested again.

CHAPTER 3

THE JACKALS POUNCE

If war breaks out, the Powers declare that they will not allow any
modification of the territorial status quo [in the Balkans].

—Declaration by the Great Powers of Europe to the Ottoman Empire
and the Balkan League, October 10, 1912[1]

His Imperial Majesty the Sultan cedes to Their Majesties, the Allied Sovereigns,
all the territories of his Empire on the continent of Europe west of a line drawn
from Enos on the Aegean Sea to Midia on the Black Sea, with the exception
of Albania. The exact line of the frontier shall be determined by
a commission appointed by the Powers.

—Treaty of Peace Between Turkey and the Balkan Allies,
signed at London, May 30, 1913[2]

WITH THE SUPPRESSION OF the pro-Hamidian counterrevolution in April 1909, the Young Turks had eliminated their most serious rivals for influence in the Ottoman army and bought some time for its modernization. In the international environment of the early twentieth century, however, time between crises was usually in short supply. The CUP had itself precipitated the last one with the July 1908 revolution, which had spurred Bulgaria and Austria-Herzegovina to aggressive action, followed in short order by Crete and Greece. The First Bosnian Crisis had very nearly plunged Europe into war, with both Austria-Hungary and Russia on hair-trigger alert all winter, before the threat of German intervention prompted the tsarist regime to back down, in part to avoid a repeat of Russia's own revolution, which had followed the war with Japan in 1905. By winter 1909, when the CUP's military reforms began to grow serious, international tensions had begun, fitfully, to dissipate.

The year 1910 brought a kind of Indian summer of old Europe, a moment when it seemed the worst was past. The naval race between Britain and Germany, which had stepped into high gear with the launching of HMS *Dreadnought* in 1906, was slowing down at last, mostly because the Germans were falling decisively behind. Germany's new chancellor, Theobald von Bethmann Hollweg, was determined on rapprochement with London, to the extent of wishing to exit the naval race altogether by sacrificing Germany's high seas fleet (although he did not have the backing of the kaiser, nor that of Naval Minister Alfred von Tirpitz, for doing so). With Russia's foreign minister Izvolsky, humiliated in the First Bosnian Crisis, forced to resign his position, his successor, Sergei Sazonov, took a generally softer line so as to forestall another diplomatic crisis from breaking out while Russia was still recovering her strength from the Revolution of 1905. In fall 1910, Sazonov worked out the essentials of a deal with Berlin, which would see Russia allow the extension of the German-built Baghdad Railway from Mesopotamia to the Persian border, in exchange for a German promise not to countenance further "aggressive dispositions" by Vienna in the Balkans.* The general spirit of international reconciliation was visible in the London funeral of King Edward VII of England in May 1910, memorably chronicled by Barbara Tuchman in *The Guns of August*, which brought all the crowned heads of Europe together in one place for what proved to be the last time.[3]

It was not destined to last. Just as the violent conclusion of the Young Turk Revolution in April 1909 had left deep wounds in Ottoman political culture, the First Bosnian Crisis had left behind several ticking diplomatic time bombs that were going to explode at one time or another. The most obvious of these related to Russian and Serbian resentment of the Austrian annexation of Bosnia-Herzegovina. Izvolsky, after resigning as Russian foreign minister,

---

* While the deal was not formally ratified until September 1911 in Potsdam, the terms had been ironed out by Russian and German diplomats by November 1910.

was given the consolation prize of the embassy in Paris, from which post he plotted his revenge against the Austro-Germans. In Serbia, indignation was nearly universal, finding voice first in the semi-secret society known as *Narodna Odbrana*, or National Defense, formed to overturn the annexation, and then in the still more secret terrorist organization known as *Ujedinjenje ili smrt*, "Union or Death," or colloquially, the Black Hand.

There was more. In order to cushion the diplomatic blow of the annexation, Aehrenthal had dropped various hints that Vienna might allow interested powers compensation—and not just the Russians, with his hollow promise to help them revise the Straits Convention. The principle of "compensation" originally dated to the Berlin Congress of 1884–85, when European spheres of influence were established for carving up Africa into colonies. By applying it to the Balkans, Aehrenthal had, in effect, brought the dark arts of Europe's African imperialism into Ottoman Europe. To compensate Turkey for losing sovereign control of Bosnia-Herzegovina, Aehrenthal had "offered" to withdraw Austrian troops from the Sanjak of Novi Pazar, a province extending out from Bosnia-Herzegovina between Serbia and Montenegro (which had been created largely to keep those countries apart). Far from welcoming this "gift," Ottoman strategists recognized it as a booby prize, as the salient was virtually indefensible. By withdrawing her troops from this precariously perched Ottoman province, Austria-Hungary had all but invited Serbia and Montenegro to invade it whenever they saw a favorable opportunity for doing so.

No less dangerous were Aehrenthal's maneuvers to placate Rome. Italy, unified only in 1861 and like Germany a latecomer to the game of empire, was a "parvenu" power, jealous of the more established states and keen to establish her position. Although Italy had been roped into Bismarck's alliance system in 1882 as a member of a Triple Alliance alongside Berlin and Vienna, Austria-Hungary and Italy were natural rivals in the Balkans and along the Adriatic coastline more generally. Italy scarcely bothered to disguise her designs on Austrian Trieste and the South Tyrol. Italian opinion was nearly as enraged as Russian by the annexation of Bosnia-Herzegovina—indeed Izvolsky, in one of his last initiatives before resigning in 1910, tried to rope Rome into a bilateral security agreement with St. Petersburg on the basis of shared enmity with

Vienna. In exchange for Italian support for revising the Straits Convention in Russia's favor, Izvolsky recognized the Italian "right" to develop influence in Ottoman Tripolitania and Cyrenaica, comprising modern-day Libya. Italy had already secured assurances on Libya from Germany (relating to their mutual defensive alliance against France) and London (in exchange for Italian support of Britain's occupation of Egypt). Aehrenthal himself had dropped a hint, before the Bosnian annexation, that Vienna might support Italian claims in Tripoli in exchange for accepting the annexation.[4] In this way the diplomatic shenanigans surrounding Austria-Hungary's annexation of Bosnia-Herzegovina helped to strengthen both Russia's designs on the Ottoman Straits and Italy's claims on the last Ottoman stronghold in Africa. While Russia still faced strong resistance to her Straits ambitions in Berlin and London, Libya was weaker on Europe's radar. Only a pretext—some new diplomatic crisis—would be needed to prompt an Italian move into Tripoli. It was not long in coming.

Europe's short-lived Indian summer expired in spring 1911 with a Franco-German showdown over Morocco. In March 1905, Kaiser Wilhelm II had visited the Moroccan sultan, Abdul Aziz, in Tangier, the German idea being to break the budding Anglo-French colonial entente of 1904 by forcing Paris into a provocative revision of Morocco's independent status (the German bluff in this "First Moroccan Crisis" did not work). Six years later, the new Moroccan sultan, Abdul Hafid, threatened by a tribal rebellion, asked Paris to send troops to defend his throne. This time, the Germans sent not the kaiser but a powerful battleship, SMS *Panther*, which dropped anchor at the Atlantic port of Agadir on July 1, 1911. A serious war scare developed between Paris and Berlin, and the British Admiralty began looking seriously, for the first time, into plans for going to war against Germany alongside France. Fortunately for the peace of Europe, cooler heads prevailed, and a face-saving compromise was arranged, with France ceding to Germany two more or less worthless river basins in the Congo in exchange for her recognition of a formal French protectorate over Morocco.

The Ottomans were not so lucky. With the European press focusing on the Germans and Agadir, Italy's new foreign minister, Antonino San Giuliano, seized on the French move to press Italy's claim for "compensation" in North

Africa. With France and Germany at loggerheads over Morocco, the British on war alert against Berlin, Russia preoccupied with the Straits question, and her allies in Germany and Austria in no position to object after the Bosnian annexation, San Giuliano had timed his move perfectly. The only power with a serious objection to an Italian occupation of Tripolitania and Cyrenaica was the Ottoman Empire itself, but this opposition was exactly what he was counting on. When the CUP government, in its post–April 1909 mode of assertive Ottoman Muslim nationalism, refused Italy's (probably cynical) demand for a new concession to renovate the harbor of Tripoli, Rome had just the excuse it needed. On September 23, 1911, San Giuliano sent a formal protest to the Sublime Porte that Italian nationals were being mistreated in Tripoli. Several days later, an ultimatum followed: the Ottoman government must agree within twenty-four hours to an Italian occupation of both Tripoli and Cyrenaica. At 2:30 p.m. on September 29, 1911, the ultimatum expired. Italy and the Ottoman Empire were at war.

If there is a single conflict that exemplifies the *reductio ad absurdum* of European imperialism, it is surely this one. The two North African provinces were thinly populated outside of a handful of port towns on the Mediterranean (Tobruk, Derna, and Benghazi in Cyrenaica, the province abutting Egypt; Tripoli in Tripolitania, on the west, next to Tunisia). The area was a mere afterthought in the Ottoman Empire, itself the weakest member of the Concert of Europe. Oil had not yet been discovered there. The land was 90 percent desert, with a primitive economy dominated by the fanatical Bedouin tribes of the Sanussi order, whose lifestyle was essentially untouched by the modern world. The Ottomans held on to the provinces for mostly sentimental reasons, with this last outpost in Africa enabling the symbolic claim of an "empire on three continents." Britain and France had left Libya alone as genuinely worthless even as they carved up the rest of North Africa.

Still, the Ottoman garrison put up surprising resistance. In all there were about 15,000 regular troops defending the two provinces, divided into four infantry and one mostly Arab cavalry regiment, with one field artillery battalion and some fixed gun batteries along the coast. Against these defenses the Italians deployed a vastly superior navy transporting an initial amphibious force of 34,000. On October 3, the Italians began shelling Tripoli. Next day, they landed 1,700 marines to occupy the city, meeting little serious resistance. More troops were landed at Tobruk, again mostly unopposed. By mid-October, some 20,000 Italian troops had been landed at Tripoli and Tobruk. From the latter, Cyrenaican, port the Italians began fanning out along the coast. Derna was taken, only to be surrounded by Turkish and Arab troops, who encamped outside the town. The first major setback was at Benghazi on October 23, when the Italians finally encountered the main Ottoman forces. Fierce fighting ensued in the outskirts of the town. The Italians now had a real war on their hands.

Seizing the opportunity to make a name for themselves, ambitious Ottoman officers asked for commissions in Libya. Enver Bey, promoted to lieutenant colonel, arrived first and was soon given overall command in Cyrenaica. Mustafa Kemal, promoted to major and given nominal command in Tripoli, came in by way of Egyptian Alexandria, accompanied by his old CUP friend Ömer Naci. Kemal never made it to Tripoli, absorbing himself instead in the fighting around Tobruk and then Derna. With the Italians controlling the ports, backed by naval guns, Kemal and Enver worked together with Sanussi sheikhs and Arab irregulars to pin them down before they could reach the interior of Cyrenaica. To the extent that Italy had to pour more and more men into the theater, ultimately some 140,000, simply to hold the coast, these guerrilla tactics succeeded. But they failed to dislodge the Italians.

Although few knew it at the time, the Italo-Turkish or Tripolitanian war (*Trablusgarp savaşi*), as it came to be called, marked a kind of watershed in military history. In one sense, it was the last of the nineteenth-century wars of European colonial expansion; in another, it was the first modern, guerrilla-style war to dislodge a colonial power, with the costs of simply holding on mounting so rapidly as nearly to bankrupt the occupying power (Italy spent more than a billion lira on the conflict, outrunning initial cost estimates by 500 percent). In the Benghazi suburbs, Turks and Arabs dug lines of trenches, in what would become a classic defensive tactic to dampen the impact of enemy fire. The war also saw the first use of offensive airpower, with Italian dirigibles bombing Ottoman positions, though to little effect.

More significantly in the short run, the war brought painfully home to the Ottoman high command the strategic dimension of naval power. With the superior Italian fleet—seven times as large as the Ottomans' in tonnage—preventing communications across the Mediterranean (Mustafa Kemal was forced to travel incognito to Alexandria on a Russian warship, disguised as a journalist), there was really no way the Ottomans could win the war. Although struggling to subdue Cyrenaica, the Italian navy routed the inferior Ottomans in several engagements at Kunfuda Bay in the Red Sea (January 1912) and at Beirut in the eastern Mediterranean (February 1912). Frustrated by the continued resistance in North Africa, the Italians moved into the Aegean, occupying the twelve Dodecanese islands abutting Turkey's southwestern coastline (including Rhodes). On April 18, 1912, the Italians began shelling the outer forts of the Dardanelles, aiming to break through to the Sea of Marmara and threaten Constantinople itself. The Ottomans, lacking any remaining naval capacity in the Aegean or Mediterranean, did the only thing they could: close the Dardanelles to *all* ships, laying extensive lines of mines and stretching steel chains across the water.

The strategic consequences of the Ottoman-Italian showdown at the Straits were serious. Russia, with her only warm-water lifeline to the world economy cut off, went into a panic. Roughly half of Russia's export trade was routed via the Ottoman Straits linking her Black Sea ports to the Mediterranean, including oil, manganese, and 90 percent of her grain, which accounted for the bulk of her hard currency earnings. Through the Dardanelles, in the other direction, flowed the imported components needed for Russian industry. Under the impact of the Ottoman closure of the Straits during the Tripolitanian war in summer 1912, the volume of Russia's Black Sea exports for that year dropped by one-third, and revenue likewise. Heavy industry in Ukraine nearly ground to a halt. Russia's balance-of-payments surplus plummeted almost to zero between 1911 and 1913, threatening the entire fabric of her rapidly industrializing economy. Little wonder the Russian government convened a series of crisis meetings in winter 1912–13 to develop contingency plans for any renewed closure of the Straits—including a crash dreadnought-building program in the Black Sea and plans for amphibious landings at the Bosphorus. The Ottomans, for their part, placed orders with British shipyards for state-of-the-art dreadnoughts they hoped could help them stave off further threats to the Straits, whether coming from Italy, Russia, or any other power. Greece, too, placed dreadnought orders, hoping not to be left behind by the Ottomans. Italy's move into Tripoli and Cyrenaica had, in this way, brought the dreadnought-building race into the eastern Mediterranean, with all of its manifold dangers.[5]

By exposing Ottoman weakness, the Tripolitanian war also spurred the empire's other enemies to action. It had taken all the skill of Hamidian diplomats to stave off a Balkan coalition from developing to carve up what remained of Ottoman Europe. The perennial trouble in Macedonia, to be sure, had helped, in the negative sense that Greeks and Bulgarians had remained mostly at each other's throats over the prospect of who might take over the Ottoman provinces of Monastir and Salonica, even while Serbian irredentists hungrily eyed Kosovo and particularly Üsküp (Skopje). But, despite the conflicting interests of the three rising Balkan powers over Macedonia, and between Serbia and Montenegro over the Sanjak of Novi Pazar, the Christian states of the Balkans shared the much larger common interest in destroying Ottoman power in Europe. Only two things were needed to bring them together: an outside power willing and able to broker an agreement between them, and a *casus belli*.

The Tripolitanian war provided both. Despite their own interests in the Ottoman Straits, Russian statesmen had always had qualms about upsetting the delicate equilibrium in the Balkans. Owing to Russian support of their independence movements and to ties of religion (Orthodoxy) and/or Slavic ethnicity, Serbia, Bulgaria, Greece, and Montenegro were all, to one extent or another, Russian client states. And yet client states were known to get into trouble. The last thing Russian statesmen wanted was an ambitious young power on the make, like Bulgaria or Serbia, to break out into the Thracian plain and conquer Constantinople without Russian help.* From the strategic perspective, it was better for Russia to have a weak and pliable Ottoman government sitting astride the Straits, to ensure access for her imports and exports (if not also her warships, for which prospect she would need the other European powers to revise the Berlin Treaty).

Weak, but not too weak. The problem exposed in spring-summer 1912,

---

* "Tsar" Ferdinand of Bulgaria was said to have a full-on Byzantine emperor's regalia hanging in his closet, ready to wear for just such an occasion.

when the Ottomans were forced to close the Straits, was that the very help-lessness of the Ottomans in the face of outside aggression could be just as damaging to Russian interests as a strong power inheriting the Straits. Short of a Russian amphibious strike to seize Constantinople, for which operational plans (although long in development, and now given top priority) remained premature, there was no ideal solution to Russia's Straits problem. But the Tripolitanian war forced the issue squarely onto the table. With the Ottoman Empire under threat of forcible partition, the status quo at the Straits no lon-ger seemed tenable for Russia—or at least, it was not safe enough for her to go out of her way to prop it up any longer.

The coalition of Bulgaria-Serbia-Greece-Montenegro that emerged in 1912 came as a surprise to many European diplomats familiar with the peren-nial squabbling of these land-hungry, irredentist Balkan rivals. Russian dip-lomats, above all the passionate pan-Slavist minister to Belgrade, Nikolai Hartwig, clearly helped to knock heads together, particularly stubborn Ser-bian and Bulgarian heads. But many of the key decisions seem to have been made independently of Great Power influence, as growing Ottoman dis-comfiture in Tripoli—and in Albania, plagued by uprisings all through spring and summer 1912, which ultimately drew in 50,000 Ottoman troops—produced a kind of infectious regional spirit of opportunism among the empire's land-hungry neighbors. The first agreement was made between Bul-garia and Serbia in March 1912. Reduced to its essentials, it was a gangster pact, dividing up Ottoman Macedonia, with the Serbs getting all the land north of the Šar Mountains, and everything east of the Struma River and the Rhodope Mountains assigned to Bulgaria (although this still left much of Monastir and Salonica unassigned). A military convention soon followed, with each power promising to put at least 100,000 men in the field against the Ottomans. In May, Greece and Bulgaria came to terms, although not over territorial war aims, promising only that, in case of war with Turkey, they would "undertake to assist each other with all their armed forces, and not to conclude peace except by joint agreement." Finally, Montenegro, eyeing Novi Pazar and the Albanian coastal hub of Scutari, came to a series of verbal agreements with Serbia over these territories. On October 6, 1912, Serbia and Montenegro agreed to declare war on the Ottoman Empire by October 14 at the latest. Two days later, Montenegro, presumably to get a head start on her larger partner Serbia, declared war. Nine days later, after a perfunctory ultimatum expired, Bulgaria, Greece, and Serbia followed suit. The war for Ottoman Europe was on.[6]

The Balkan jackals had chosen their moment well. While none of the outside powers overtly supported the coalition—even the Russians had their doubts, with Sazonov getting cold feet at the last moment*—none had come out against it either. Austria-Hungary had no desire to see Serbia expand, but Germany's state secretary Alfred von Kiderlen-Wächter, not wanting to risk another confrontation with Russia over her ally's Balkan "adventures," had quietly warned Vienna that Berlin would do nothing to block Belgrade.[7]

The Ottoman government, too, was in disarray, owing to a kind of coup d'état carried out in July 1912 by a group of "Savior Officers" (*Halaskâr Zabitan Grubu*) aimed, paradoxically, at getting the army (or at least, uppity CUP *mektepli* officers), out of politics. The cabinet was forced to resign, and on August 5, Sultan Mehmed V announced new fall elections—during which the main CUP organ, *Tanin*, would be banned from publication. A caretaker cabinet was formed under the retired general, "ghazi" Ahmed Muhtar Pasha, who devoted his energy to peacemaking. The grand vizier brokered an agreement with Albanian rebels on September 4, 1912, and then with Italy in mid-October (the Ottomans agreed to withdraw from Cyrenaica and Tripoli, in exchange for Italy returning the Dodecanese islands—the latter part of the agreement was not carried out). After Montenegro's declaration of war on October 8 and the tripartite ultimatum that followed, Ahmed Muhtar Pasha sought to come to terms with the Balkan coalition as well. Some units in the First Army, covering Thrace, were even demobilized as a conciliatory gesture, although the effect on the enemy (especially Bulgaria) was more like waving a red flag before a bull. This pacific gesture was the last straw for deposed CUP politicians and officers, who rallied popular opposition to the grand vizier's peace policy. With loud pro-war demonstrators surrounding the Sublime Porte, Ahmed Muhtar Pasha gave in on October 17, declaring war on the

---

* Hartwig, in Belgrade, had no such qualms. In early October, he told Serbia to go ahead and attack Turkey, and not worry about "foolish Sazonov."

Balkan League (although clearly under duress—the grand vizier resigned twelve days later). The Balkan war thus began against the backdrop of virtual civil war in the Ottoman capital.[8]

In spite of the empire's dire strategic outlook, most European military experts and diplomats expected the Ottomans to defeat the raggle-taggle coalition arrayed against them. The Turks had beaten Greece badly in 1897, after all, as they had Serbia and Montenegro in 1876—before Russia had come to their aid. Bulgaria was a wild card, but her army had never been tested before, whereas the Turks had just fought a major war against Italy, and had fought serious campaigns against rebels in Macedonia as recently as 1903. Demographically, the Balkan coalition was dwarfed by the Ottoman Empire's overall population of 24 million, with the populations of Bulgaria (4.3 million), Serbia (3 million), Greece (2.67 million), and Montenegro (250,000) together amounting to only 10 million. Europeans in Constantinople, as the French military attaché reported to Paris, were "convinced of Ottoman superiority . . . the disparity between the two camps, in population, military effectives, resources of every kind, was considerable." Only if we appreciate the general expectation of a Turkish *victory* can we make sense of the curious declaration lodged by the powers in each of the belligerent capitals on October 10, 1912, that "they will not allow any modification of the territorial status quo."[9] If the Balkan League surprised everyone and won, of course, then all territorial bets would be off.

The soon-to-be-notorious European status quo declaration was based, as the conventional wisdom so often is, on faulty intelligence. In reality, the balance of forces strongly favored the Balkan coalition. While the Ottoman army was indeed larger overall and could *potentially* put an army of nearly 600,000 in the field in Thrace and Macedonia, the Tripolitanian diversion curtailed available Turkish strength considerably. Bulgaria's peacetime army had only some 62,000 men, but these were buttressed by over 300,000 trained reservists. When fully mobilized, Bulgaria could field an army of over 350,000 men, enough alone to outnumber scattered Ottoman forces in Europe (let alone just in Thrace, where the main Bulgarian thrust would be directed). Serbia's peacetime army boasted 168,000 actives and almost as many reserves. Fully mobilized, she could put about 230,000 men into the field. Greece could contribute another 200,000 troops to the coalition. More important, with the underequipped, half-modernized Ottoman navy in flux (the office of naval minister changed hands nine times between 1908 and 1911), the substantial Greek fleet, boasting sixteen destroyers, nineteen torpedo boats, a submarine, and a fast armored cruiser, the *Georgios Averov*, ensured that the Balkan coalition could prevent the Ottomans from routing significant reinforcements across the Aegean from Anatolia. Even tiny Montenegro could put 44,500 men into the field, giving the Balkan League a striking force of some 800,000, while the Ottomans would be able to muster only about 315,000 effectives (200,000 in Macedonia, and 115,000 in Thrace).[10]

Above all, the coalition forces had the advantage of timing. The Ottoman government was in meltdown, its army in disarray. Many of the best Ottoman officers found themselves on the wrong continent, with the Italian and now the Greek fleet blocking their return path. To the end of his life, Mustafa Kemal could only lament the cruel twist of fate that saw him marooned in Africa while his ancestral home in Salonica (where his mother still lived) came under attack by the combined armies of Greece and Bulgaria. His decision to volunteer for a guerrilla war in the Libyan desert, he later wrote with the benefit of hindsight, had been "precipitate and pointless." Kemal, accompanied by a hundred or so fellow officers, returned by way of Marseille (from Alexandria), Bucharest (by train), by river steamer to Constanţa, and then across the Black Sea to the Bosphorus. The roundabout journey took over a month, with Kemal arriving in Turkey only in late November, and reaching the front on December 1. Enver, who feared political fallout in the empire's Arab provinces if he staged a mass withdrawal of Ottoman troops from Cyrenaica, stayed on even longer in the desert, returning to Constantinople only on December 20, 1912.[11]

As if sensing weakness and distraction in the enemy, the aggressors pounced quickly. Bulgaria launched an immediate offensive into Thrace, hoping to emulate the Russian breakthrough of 1877–78, which had opened the way to Constantinople. And yet the Bulgarians had a considerable advantage over the Russians, in that the main Ottoman fortresses in Thrace, at Adrianople (Edirne) and Kırk Kilise (Lozengrad), were not thousands but scarcely fifty miles from the Bulgarian frontier, with no natural barriers between them. Two Ottoman mistakes also helped the Bulgarian commanders. First, following the political logic of Bulgarian irredentism, which had always targeted Macedonia (not Thrace), the Ottoman high command expected the main Bulgarian thrust to go south and west, not southeast—this is why more than two-thirds of available Turkish strength was assigned to the Second Army in Macedonia, whereas the Bulgarians themselves had chosen to throw the vast majority of their forces into Thrace. Second, Abdullah Pasha, commander of the Ottoman First Army, following the instructions of War Minister Nazim Pasha, ordered his troops forward on October 21, not realizing that enemy forces outnumbered his (hoping to envelop three divisions, Abdullah Pasha encountered eight instead). Next day, the opposing armies clashed along a thirty-six-mile front between Adrianople and Kırk Kilise. By October 24, the baffled Turks were in full-scale retreat, with dozens of artillery pieces abandoned and many soldiers dropping their rifles in panic. Abdullah Pasha was able to regroup and make a stand on October 29 at a new defensive line between Lüleburgaz and Pinarhisar, in a seesaw battle that lasted four days, with both sides inflicting about 20,000 casualties. By November 2, the overmatched Turks, having lost another forty-five field guns, were retreating again, this time for the Çatalca lines, just 40 kilometers, or 25 miles, from the capital. While the Turks were still holding out in the great fortress of Adrianople, the rout was on, after only two weeks of war.[12]

Things looked little better in Macedonia. On October 24, the day the Bulgarians won Kırk Kilise, the Serbian First Army, more than 100,000 strong, defeated the 58,000-man Vardar army of Zeki Pasha at Kumanovo, opening the path to Bitola and Monastir. Farther west, the Serbian Third Army rolled up Kosovo and took Üsküp (Skopje), the base the Germans had been renovating for the Ottomans (who would later claim, in court, that they need not pay down the construction costs of a Turkish army base now occupied by Serbia).[13] By early November 1912, the Serbs had crossed into mostly Muslim Albania, wreaking terrible destruction in their path. Meanwhile, Greece's Army of Thessaly, commanded, as in 1897, by Crown Prince (now King) Constantine, had surprised the Turks by advancing straight toward Salonica via the heavily fortified Sarantaporos Pass, which fell on October 22, and Yanitsa (Yenije Vardar), which succumbed on November 2. On November 7, the

Greeks reached Salonica, even as a Bulgarian rifle division approached the city from the north (about twenty-four hours behind the Greeks). While negotiations began, on November 8, 1912, the deposed Sultan Abdul Hamid II, to escape the clutches of vengeful Greeks or Bulgarians, boarded a German warship for Constantinople. That night, at 8:00 p.m., the Ottoman commander, Hasan Tahsin Pasha, agreed to surrender Salonica to the Greeks, who offered more generous terms than the Bulgarians (these included freedom of movement for Ottoman officers, and soldiers, provided they turned over their arms, and a Greek promise not to arrest municipal officials and staff). Less than three weeks after it began, the Balkan war seemed to be all over but the shouting.[14]

There remained, however, much shouting to be done. Everywhere the advance of the Balkan armies was accompanied by atrocities against Muslim civilians. As a British diplomat observed in Thrace, "The track of the invading Bulgarian army is marked by 80 miles of ruined villages."[15] Constantinople witnessed a "traffic jam of ox-carts," with Muslim families pouring in from Macedonia and Thrace, sitting "weary and emaciated on the straw." Old Stambul was a refugee camp, the Hagia Sofia a cholera infirmary. In Pera, the German embassy was turned into a hospital. Wounded Ottoman soldiers "staggered up the hill past the Pera Palace hotel, to the sound of waltzes being played within." Tales of wholesale massacres of Balkan Muslims were spread through the bazaars, exaggerated only slightly in the telling.[16] Such stories gave Turkish Muslim troops ample motivation to fight on.

The Ottoman First and Second Armies, although defeated, were still in the field. Many key fortresses had held (including Adrianople in Thrace, Janina in Epirus, and the Çatalca lines defending Constantinople). The Greeks' rush to Salonica had allowed the Ottomans to reinforce the Bitola area, slowing down the Serbian advance (and then, after they withdrew from Bitola, to resist the Serbs as they advanced toward the Adriatic coast). Albania was turned into a kind of western rear base for the retreating Vardar army, which the empire might barter for Macedonian territory farther east. Montenegro's own offensive had bogged down in a lengthy siege of Scutari, with Serbia plucking most of the territorial fruit in Novi Pazar and Kosovo, including the town of Prizren, which had been one of Montenegro's key objectives.

Territorial Changes Resulting from the First and Second Balkan Wars

1 Territory gained by Montenegro
2 Territory gained by Serbia
3 Territory gained by Greece
4 Territory gained by Bularia
5 Territory lost by Bulgaria to Romania

━━━ Boundary of the Ottoman Empire prior to the Balkan Wars

········· Former boundaries

—··—··— Boundaries established by the Treaty of Bucharest

0 50 100 150 miles
0 50 100 150 kilometers

As the Prizren spat showed, even in victory the Balkan states were fated to fall out over the carcass of Ottoman Europe. Greece and Bulgaria had both made an armed claim on Salonica. Bulgaria had done the most strategic damage with her powerful thrust into Thrace, which grand strategic triumph had, in effect, cost her a fair share in the carve-up of Macedonia, with Serbia getting most of Kosovo and Monastir and Greece, Salonica.

Despite the initial disaster of defeat, that is, the Ottoman Empire stood poised for a rebound, if the Sublime Porte could work some of its old diplomatic magic to divide its enemies. But none of Turkey's traditional allies had a real dog in the fight. Britain had never displayed much interest in the Balkans. France, under the premiership and Foreign Ministry of the bellicose nationalist Raymond Poincaré (whose ascendancy was confirmed in his election as president in January 1913), was so firmly pro-Russian as to be almost more Serbophile than the government in Petersburg (regarding a prospective Austro-Hungarian intervention against Serbia, on November 17, 1912, Poincaré told Ambassador Izvolsky that "if Russia goes to war, France also will go to war").[17] Germany, a more recent Ottoman partner, had cooled in her diplomatic support, in large part because her sovereign still resented the Young Turks' treatment of his friend Abdul Hamid (the kaiser's loyalties in the present conflict were complicated further by the fact that his sister Sophie was queen of Greece). Even though the Ottoman army was trained by German officers and fought with German weapons, Kaiser Wilhelm II declared his policy to be one of "free fight and no favor."[18]

If any power had a strategic interest in cutting the Balkan League down to size, it should have been Austria-Hungary, plagued by her own irredentist problems with Slavic minorities (especially the Serbs of Bosnia-Herzegovina). But mistrust between Vienna and the Sublime Porte was still rampant in the wake of the Bosnian annexation. Despite a shared concern with Serbian aggrandizement, Austrian and Ottoman interests did not really align in the Balkans, as shown by the earlier Austrian withdrawal from Novi Pazar, which had just encouraged Serbian and Montenegrin aggression. As soon as it became clear that the Turks were losing, the new Habsburg foreign minister, Leopold von Berchtold, renounced his "status quo" declaration of October 10, 1912, in favor of a new line, laid down on October 30, accepting Serbia's enlargement, provided it did not include Albania—especially the Adriatic harbor town of Durazzo (Dürres). He also suggested that postwar Serbia be invited to enter a "close economic union" with Austria-Hungary.[19] With Berchtold taking this feeble a stance on Serbian aggression, the Ottomans could hope for little succor in Vienna.

All the same, there was a serious European war scare in November–

December 1912, not over the prospect of an Ottoman collapse, but of Serbian absorption of Albania. On November 17, Serbia's Third Army reached the Adriatic coast at Alessio, about fifty miles north of Durazzo. While resistance continued among Muslim Albanian irregulars to the north and Ottoman troops to the south, it appeared that Serbia was about to win its coveted port on the Adriatic, crossing the one (though rather blurry) "red line" Berchtold had laid down in Vienna. In response, Austria-Hungary took a serious step on November 21, mobilizing the IV, VII, and VIII Army Corps facing Serbia in Bosnia-Herzegovina and Dalmatia and, as insurance against possible Russian intervention, the I, X, and XI Army Corps in Galicia. In response the next day, Russia's war minister, V. A. Sukhomlinov, wrote up orders for a "partial" mobilization of Russia's military districts of Warsaw (roughly, Russian Poland) and Kiev (Ukraine), facing Austria-Hungary, and Odessa (from which an amphibious operation in Constantinople might be launched). Tsar Nicholas II convened the Council of Ministers on November 23. The conservative chairman, V. N. Kokovtsov, argued that mobilizing the Warsaw district would force the Germans to mobilize too (likely true—the kaiser himself had promised Emperor Franz Josef I the day before that Germany would not leave her ally in the lurch if Russia mobilized), plunging Europe into war. Sazonov, who did not himself believe it was in Russia's interest for Serbia to indulge Great Power pretensions by expanding to the Adriatic, went along with Kokovtsov, thus narrowly averting what might well have been the Great War—of 1912.[20]

Europe had dodged a bullet, but the war scare was not yet over. Even as the powers, following the arrangement of an armistice between Bulgaria and the Ottomans on December 3, geared up for a mediation conference in London, Kaiser Wilhelm II convened a crown council on December 8, 1912, eerily similar to the one the Russians had held. Although unaware of how close the Russians had come to mobilizing, the Germans remained concerned that the Balkan war would embroil the powers in a general European conflagration. Speaking for the army, Chief of the General Staff Helmuth von Moltke ("the Younger") argued that time was not on the side of Germany and Austria-Hungary, since Russia was believed to be growing stronger every year. European war was, in his view, "unavoidable, and the sooner the better."[21] But

Moltke was overruled by Chancellor Bethmann, Naval Secretary Tirpitz (who realized the German fleet was completely overmatched by Britain), and Kaiser Wilhelm II, who found the idea of going to war to block Serbian access to the Adriatic Sea "nonsense" (annoyed with Austrian adventuring in the Balkans, the kaiser would ironically prove to be more pro-Serbian on the Albanian question than Russia's foreign minister).[22]

If the lack of a sharply defined conflict between the two alliance blocs over Serbia's future borders helped stave off a European conflagration, it did not help the Ottomans, who were effectively isolated as two parallel "London" conferences convened on December 16–17, 1912 (one involving the belligerents, and the other a meeting of the six signatory powers of the 1878 Treaty of Berlin, hoping to adjudicate the Serbian-Albanian question to prevent the conflict from embroiling Austria-Hungary and Russia). Seeing the military situation as hopeless, the Ottoman representative, Reshid Pasha, declared himself willing to accept the loss of Macedonia, but not Adrianople and Thrace (he also objected to the Greek claim on the four Aegean islands guarding the mouth of the Dardanelles—Samothrace, Imbros, Lemnos, and Tenedos). Further, the Ottomans insisted that Albania be granted autonomy, under supervision of the powers (i.e., that it not be ruled by Serbia). It was a sensible posture, which split the difference on Greek war aims (conceding Salonica but not the Aegean islands), gave something to Serbia but enlisted the outside powers against her in Albania, and left the Bulgarian delegate, Dr. Stoyan Danev, sputtering in rage. The Bulgarians, despite doing the bulk of the damage to the Ottoman armies and threatening Constantinople itself, had lost the race to Salonica to Greece by a day and were now threatened with the loss of Turkish Thrace, most of which they had won under arms. But the Ottomans insisted that they must hold on to Adrianople, which, as the first European capital of the empire, predating the conquest of Constantinople, had more than strategic value. As one Ottoman diplomat told Dr. Danev, "Adrianople is a window into our harem."[23] For now, with the Ottoman garrison holding out, the window remained closed. But it was only a matter of time before the frustrated Bulgarians would try to pry it open.

Aghast at the hypocrisy of the powers with their bogus "status quo" declaration and fearful that Reshid Pasha would sign away the store in London, a

General Edmund Allenby, commander of Egyptian Expeditionary Force, enters Jerusalem, December 1917

Statue of General Sir Frederick Stanley Maude, conqueror of Baghdad in March 1917

Ahmet Tevfik Pasha,
last grand vizier of the Ottoman Empire

Mehmed (Reshad) V,
Ottoman sultan,
1909–1918

Mehmed (Vahdettin) VI, last sultan of the Ottoman Empire, 1918–1922

Constantine I, king of Greece,
1913–1917 and 1920–1922

Eleftherios Venizelos,
prime minister of Greece,
1910–1915, 1917–1920

Mustafa Kemal in 1918

Turkish nationalists at Sivas, 1919. Second to fourth from left:
Rauf (Orbay), Bekir Sami (Kunduh), Mustafa Kemal.

The Battle of Sakarya, August–September 1922. Mustafa Kemal is fourth from left.

Halidé Edib,
Turkish novelist, nationalist,
and feminist leader (1884–1964)

Mustafa Kemal and his wife, Latife Hanım, 1923.

Winston Churchill, T. E. Lawrence,
and Emir Abdullah of Transjordan
in Jerusalem, 1921

David Lloyd George, prime minister of
the United Kingdom, 1916–1922

group of CUP officers began plotting a coup to restart the war. The animus of the CUP was directed primarily at the Liberal Union government of Mehmed Kâmil Pasha, who had become grand vizier again after Ahmed Muhtar Pasha's resignation (the same Kâmil who had served loyally under Abdul Hamid, most recently in 1908–9). Kâmil, who had once been governor of Cyprus, was believed to have good English connections, which, in the current situation, spoke against him. It is not hard to see where the conspirators' motivation came from. Enver Bey and many of his fellow plotters had arrived in Constantinople from the Cyrenaican desert only on December 20. Having missed the entire war, they were not in the mood for a quiet surrender.

On January 17, 1913, with the Ottomans and the Balkan League still at a standoff in London, the powers issued a collective warning to the Sublime Porte—backed by an implied threat of Russian intervention—not to resume hostilities, the upshot of which was that the Ottomans would have to give up both Adrianople (to Bulgaria) and the Aegean islands (to Greece). Facing an impossible decision, Kâmil's cabinet convened a Grand Council of leading religious, civil, judicial, and military officials to cushion the political fallout. On January 22, the verdict came in: by 69–1, the Ottoman dignitaries voted for peace even at the price of surrendering Adrianople. Next day, Enver, accompanied by Talât, Djemal, and about fifty officers, led a raid on the Sublime Porte. Displaying the old conspiratorial skills from Salonica, Enver's men had cut the telephone line and arranged for CUP loyalists to be on guard duty. There was little resistance as they ran up the stairs crying "Death to Kâmil Pasha!" The grand vizier, by agreeing to resign, was spared this fate, although the minister of war, Nazım Pasha, and Kâmil's aide-de-camp, Captain Kibrisli, were not so lucky. Enver appointed Mahmud Shevket Pasha, commander of the Action Army, which had overthrown Abdul Hamid in April 1909, as grand vizier and minister of war. On January 30, 1913, the new cabinet, with three CUP ministers, offered to cede the western half of Thrace (but not Adrianople or the Aegean islands). On February 3, the Balkan League rejected the Ottoman offer, and the Bulgarians resumed the bombardment of Adrianople and the Çatalca lines. Boasting that he would work "36 hours a day," Enver guaranteed victory.[24]

In the short run, Enver's coup backfired badly. On February 7–8, 1913, a bold Ottoman amphibious strike at Bulair, at the northern tip of the Gallipoli Peninsula (though south, i.e., to the rear, of the Bulgarian position facing the Çatalca lines), began promisingly but ran aground quickly as the entrenched Bulgarians unleashed murderous bursts of machine-gun fire on the advancing Turks, who lost some six thousand men before the attack was called off.[25] Another amphibious landing farther south on the European side of the Sea of Marmara, at Sharkoi, was foiled by the Bulgarians on February 10. Three days later, Serbian heavy siege guns arrived outside Adrianople. On March 20 the final assault began, with Serbian units assisting the Bulgarians. On March 26, 1913, with stores of food inside the city running out (the bread ration had been cut to 450 grams a day) and Bulgarian cavalry breaking into the city, Mehmet Sükrü Pasha, commander of the Ottoman garrison, surrendered Adrianople. On April 15, the Bulgarians agreed to an armistice at Çatalca.

In Albania, meanwhile, the Ottoman VI Corps, under Djavid Pasha, was ground down by the pincer advance of the Serbs from the north and Greeks from the south. The Greek army stormed Janina on March 6, the last serious Ottoman stronghold in Epirus. Seven days later, Scutari fell to the Montenegrins (although the Ottoman commander, Esad Pasha, surrendered mostly to deny the city to Serbia and/or Austria-Hungary, which had enjoined the powers—excepting Russia—to dispatch warships to the Montenegrin coast; the "victorious" Montenegrins allowed the Turks to leave with their weapons).

The renewal of the fighting had won the Ottomans nothing, and cost them another 6,000 dead and 18,000 wounded (at Bulair), 33,000 casualties including prisoners (at Janina), and 15,000 killed and 60,000 prisoners (at Adrianople). The Treaty of London, signed by all the belligerents on May 30, 1913, saw Ottoman Europe—but for the sliver of land behind the Enos-Midia line and the Gallipoli Peninsula—pass into the history books.[26] By prolonging the struggle, however, Enver's coup undoubtedly helped to exacerbate the divisions between the Balkan states (and the powers, still meeting in London), thus paving the way for what would become the Second Balkan War. Bulgarian and Greek troops had already exchanged hostile fire in March, at Nigrita to the northeast of Salonica. Serbs and Bulgarians, likewise, were skirmishing in eastern Macedonia. Seeking common cause, Serbs and Greeks had begun to collude against the Bulgarians, with Serbia supporting the Greek claim on Salonica in exchange for Greek support for the Serbian position in western Macedonia and Albania. On June 1, 1913, Athens and Belgrade signed a formal alliance, pledging to keep the Bulgarians out of Macedonia. Romania, having stayed neutral in the Balkan war, sensed which way the wind was blowing and demanded that Bulgaria cede her the Danubian fortress city of Silistria (Bulgaria agreed to this under Russian pressure on May 8, 1913). Feeling misused and abused by his allies, Bulgaria's prime minister, Ivan Geshov, resigned in May, to be replaced by Dr. Danev, the Bulgarian delegate to London, who had firsthand knowledge of the machinations of his "allies" and motivation to avenge them. Danev, a Russophile, angled for Russian support. But the Russians had been terrified by the advance of Bulgarian troops to the Sea of Marmara, which suggested that "Tsar" Ferdinand's plans to conquer Constantinople and the Straits were not idle. As Sazonov told Danev bluntly on June 24, 1913, "Do not expect anything from us."[27] The Bulgarians were on their own.

On the night of June 29–30, 1913, the Bulgarian Fourth Army, facing the Serbs along the Bregalnitsa and Zletovska Rivers in eastern Macedonia, north of Salonica, went on the attack. Commanded by Mihail Savov, the Bulgarian forces were able to cross the Zletovska, with his left flank reaching the Vardar River. Prime Minister Danev, from Sofia, disowned the offensive and called on Mihail Savov to resign—only to be overruled by Ferdinand. The resulting confusion gave the Serbs several days in which to prepare a counterattack, even while the Greek Army of Thessaly went on the offensive (beginning with the small Bulgarian battalion in Salonica, which was wiped out). Montenegro declared war, too, although her intervention was rapidly rendered moot when Romania declared war on Bulgaria on July 10, crossing the Danube with a force of nearly 250,000 troops and seizing Dobruja without meeting any resistance. Romanian cavalry roamed freely through northern Bulgaria, taking Varna on the Black Sea coast, then heading back inland, taking the town of Vrzhdebna, only seven miles from Sofia, on July 23, 1913. With little hope of victory, Danev resigned, and Ferdinand appealed to Italy and Russia to mediate.

Relishing the turnabout, the Ottomans seized on Bulgaria's comeuppance to make a strike of their own. On June 11, the grand vizier and war minister, Mahmud Shevket Pasha, had been gunned down in his car at Bayazit Square in Constantinople, reputedly by anti-CUP agents of the Liberal Union. Another CUP coup, of sorts, followed, with Djemal Pasha, commander of troops in the capital, declaring martial law; sixteen Liberal Union members were then arrested and convicted for the crime (including Prince Sabahaddin, *in absentia*). A committee man, Said Halim Pasha (grandson of Mohammad Ali, the Egyptian khedive-reformer) was appointed grand vizier, and four more CUP ministers were named to the cabinet, including Talât, as minister of internal affairs. The man of the hour, though, was Enver Bey, who convinced the cabinet to renew the war with Bulgaria, and set off for the front.

On July 12, 1913, the Çatalca Army crossed the Enos-Midia line en route to Adrianople—where, reconnaissance showed, only a token Bulgarian occupation force remained. On the morning of July 22, Enver, with dramatic flair, joined the lead cavalry unit, which entered the city. At 10:30 a.m., he wired the capital: "Now, I have entered Edirne [Adrianople]. The Bulgarians are retreating . . . I have taken artillery and equipment." Meeting no resistance, the Turks continued marching west until August 2, ultimately pushing the border with Bulgaria back a full 200 kilometers (124 miles) in the Treaty of Constantinople, signed on September 30, 1913.

The Balkan Wars had cost the Ottoman Empire 340,000 casualties (50,000 killed, 100,000 wounded, 75,000 from disease, and 115,000 prisoner), Macedonia, four Aegean islands, and control of Albania (although negotiations still continued on its future status).[28] Another 400,000 Balkan Muslims had been expelled or fled east to Turkey, with the influx of these bitter refugees exacerbating ethnic tensions in the empire: some 200,000 Orthodox Christians, mostly Greeks from Thrace, Smyrna (Izmir), and the Aegean region, were expelled westward in turn.[29] In the final reckoning, though, the Ottomans had won back a measure of imperial pride—and Enver the honorific *ghazi*, as the (re)conqueror of Edirne.

Enver's victory also helped to entrench the CUP in power. In both January and June, the committee's leaders had chosen to fight on while their opponents were ranged on the side of peace. Fairly or unfairly, the Liberal Union was now tainted with the June assassination of the grand vizier, which had seemed expressly designed to keep the empire out of the Second Balkan War—a war which had ended in triumph for Turkey.

At first furtively, then all but openly, a ruling triumvirate began to emerge in Constantinople behind the government of Grand Vizier Said Halim Pasha, with Djemal Bey serving as military governor of the capital, Talât Bey as interior minister, and Enver (now) Pasha, named war minister on January 4, 1914, at the tender age of thirty-two. Questionable as their methods may have been, the CUP men had learned a valuable lesson in all the turmoil since 1908: the importance of continuity. Turnover in the government ministries, navy, and army—in the sultanate itself—had only encouraged Turkey's enemies to strike. The Ottoman Empire had a new government now, and it seemed to be here to stay.

CHAPTER 4

SEARCHING FOR AN ALLY

A strong Ottoman state must form an alliance with Germany
and take a defensive position against the Russian and Balkan Slavs;
this is the foundation of any sound policy.

—ABDURRAHMAN CAMI BAYKUT,
founder of the Turkish National Constitution Party,
April 1914[1]

ON ANY OBJECTIVE EVALUATION, the Italian and Balkan wars had been a catastrophe for the Ottoman Empire and its subjects. The territorial losses were not only strategically damaging but humiliating, with Turkey's adversaries all but cackling as they counted up their winnings, even as the Great Powers connived in the carve-up. The human suffering was beyond reckoning, with battlefield and civilian casualty counts giving only a small glimpse of the devastation wrought upon whole peoples and communities. Ethnic cleansing had come to the Balkans with a vengeance, with hundreds of thousands of Muslims displaced from ancestral homes, and Anatolian and Thracian Turks now seeking to avenge them by persecuting local Christians. Compounding the sense of imperial doom, in Asiatic Turkey unity among the empire's Muslim peoples, cultivated so carefully by Abdul Hamid, was fracturing. Seizing on the empire's discomfiture in Europe, a number of important Kurdish tribal chieftains in southeastern Anatolia and northern Mesopotamia declared fealty to the Russian empire. Secret societies of Arab nationalists began conspiring in Damascus, even as British intrigues with Sherif Hussein of Mecca stepped into high gear. Most ominously of all, a powerful new "brotherhood," or *Ikhwan*, in Arabia between the fanatical Muslim tribes of al-Saud and al-Wahhab, already entrenched (since 1902) at Riyadh, conquered the oases of the Hasa region in 1913 (known today as the Eastern Province of Saudi Arabia), dealing a serious blow to Ottoman influence and prestige in the heartland of Islam in the face of the Saudi-Wahhabi ascendancy. By fall 1913, all the evils of the modern age seemed to have been unleashed in the tottering Ottoman Empire, which had lost 40 percent of its territory in the preceding five years. The Sick Patient, abandoned for dead by the Great Powers, surely could not survive much longer.[2]

And yet the patient himself was not willing to give in without a fight. Dubious though it might have seemed on its own terms, Enver's "triumph" at Adrianople was just enough to give the Young Turks a glimmer of hope. Invigorated by this deathbed miracle, CUP thinkers and their critics alike took on a tone of surprising optimism in the months after the Second Balkan War, writing popular screeds with titles like "Turkey, Awake!" (*Türkiye Uyan*), the idea being that the Turkish nation, like her Balkan Christian enemies, had now "awoken after centuries of slumber."[3] Not surprisingly, in view of the fact that so many Young Turk intellectuals had spent time in France or knew French, the new mood of revanchist patriotism in Constantinople mirrored the *réveil national* spirit emerging in France at the same time (France's own "awakening" being inspired by the strong stand taken against the Germans in the Moroccan crisis of 1911, and manifested in the election of the nationalist Raymond Poincaré to the presidency and the passage of the Three-Year Service Law expanding the size of the peacetime army, both occurring in 1913). While it is impossible to gauge the popular impact of the intellectual turn toward assertive (and exclusive) Turkish nationalism on the country's mostly illiterate Muslim subjects, there is no denying that this mood took hold of Ottoman politicians and policymakers. As Halil Bey, Speaker of the Chamber of Deputies, admonished his fellow parliamentarians in a rousing speech on May 19, 1914, Turks must not "forget the cradle of our freedom and our constitution: our beloved Salonica, verdant Monastir, Kosovo . . . the entire beautiful Rumeli," nor "the memories of our brothers and sisters who have remained on the other side of our borders and who must be saved."[4]

Translated into policy, this meant Turkey needed to arm herself, and quickly. The empire desperately needed new warships, to enable the Ottoman fleet to contest, and hopefully control, the Aegean approaches to the Dardanelles against the Greeks and/or Italians—and to guard the Black Sea approaches to the Bosphorus against the Russians. A number of dreadnought orders had therefore been placed with British shipyards, of which two were confirmed by the end of the Balkan Wars: the *Sultan Osman I* (originally contracted to Brazil as the *Rio de Janeiro*), launched on January 22, 1913, which would mount more (12-inch) guns than any ship ever afloat—fourteen of them—and the *Reshadieh*, a generation more advanced still, launched on September 3, 1913, which would mount 13.5-inch (343 mm) guns. A British naval mission to Turkey, headed by the formidable Admiral Arthur Limpus, was helping to train "skeleton crews" to man these dreadnoughts as soon as they arrived, fully fitted out, in the Sea of Marmara sometime in spring or summer 1914—with Turkish officers now being required to learn English and spend two years in England to complete their training. On top of this, the Ottoman naval command placed orders for three cruisers in Italy, two German submarines, and six French minesweepers—and new Krupp guns for the shore batteries guarding the Dardanelles. While it would take months for all these ships and guns to arrive, the scale of Ottoman naval orders in fall-winter 1913 was substantial enough to set alarm bells ringing in St. Petersburg—and in Athens, where a nasty diplomatic wrangle was under way with Constantinople over the future disposition of the Aegean islands.[5]

Critical as naval power had shown itself in the wars of 1911–13, in some ways diplomacy loomed even larger. Despite all the inevitable postmortems about the poor performance of half-reformed Ottoman armies in the field, the basic fact was that they were simply outnumbered and outgunned in the European theater. Given naval control of the Aegean—if, say, the Ottoman dreadnoughts had arrived in 1912, instead of, as projected, 1914— reinforcements from North Africa or Anatolia might have remedied this deficiency up to a point. Even assuming naval dominance, however, the dispatch of hundreds of thousands of troops to the Balkans would have taken far more time than the Ottomans had. After all, the decisive battle at Kırk Kilise, which had opened up the Thracian plain to the Bulgarians, had occurred less than a week after war was declared. The importance of diplomacy was borne out inarguably in the Second Balkan War, when the Ottomans were able to reverse the decision in Thrace in the First not because of any tactical innovations or improvements in the army, but simply because the enemy coalition had fractured. Bulgaria's resentment of her grasping rivals had, in effect, neutralized the threat she posed to Ottoman Thrace. If this resentment ratcheted up a step further, Sofia might even be turned into Turkey's ally.

The harsher diplomatic lesson of the Italian and Balkan wars was that, thumping Turkish nationalist rhetoric aside, the Ottoman Empire was simply not strong enough to survive intact without at least one Great Power patron able to veto collective action against her. Abdul Hamid II had understood this, which is why he had craftily cultivated the kaiser's friendship. German patronage, or at least implied support, had enabled him to survive the Armenian crisis of 1896, the Greek war of 1897, and the Macedonian crisis of 1903, without any loss of territory. By contrast, when the Great Powers acted in unison, as with the ultimatum of January 17, 1913, demanding that the Ottomans accept the Balkan League's terms of partition, there was little the empire could do in response but sputter in frustration or fight against hopeless military odds (the Turks had done both). Whether or not the Germans would revert back to the more robust partnership of the Hamidian era, or the British rediscover their old Tanzimat enthusiasm, the Ottomans needed *someone* to back them. By spring of 1914, Ottoman diplomats had approached each of the European powers in turn with entreaties for a bilateral alliance, although none of them had yet agreed to terms.

Still, despite the apparent isolation of an empire that had just lost two major wars (and "won" a third without really fighting), there were signs of better diplomatic things to come. Britain, to be sure, was a lost cause, owing not only to Ottoman resentment of her occupation of Egypt and the Persian Gulf States, but to the condescending attitude of her diplomats (under the influence of the anti-Semitic embassy dragoman, Gerald Fitzmaurice, the Foreign Office had adopted the view that the Young Turks were crypto-Jewish internationalists, not to be trusted).*6 But with the Germans, things were

---

* So thoroughgoing was this prejudice that the British embassy conspired to get Djavid Bey, the finance minister (falsely) rumored to be Jewish, sacked from his post. In reality, Djavid was the most passionate Anglophile in the Ottoman government!

looking up. Reluctant though Berlin was to sign a formal alliance treaty, German and Ottoman interests were converging again in the wake of the Balkan Wars—although oddly not in the Balkans themselves, where the kaiser continued favoring Greek and Serbian claims on Albanian territory over Ottoman (enraging Austro-Hungarian emperor Franz Josef I, with whom Wilhelm was not close).

What was bringing Germany and Turkey together, rather, was a shared fear of the growth of Russian power. Russia's population was exploding, having grown by forty million just since 1900. Her economy was expanding by nearly 10 percent annually. Alongside the passage of France's Three-Year Service Law, 1913 had seen the enactment of Russia's Great Programme, which envisioned the expansion of her peacetime army to 2.2 million men, roughly triple the size of Germany's, and the speeding up of her mobilization to the point where, by 1917, she would be only three days behind Germany in military readiness, thus invalidating German strategic doctrine for a two-front war against France and Russia. In February 1914, Russia had convened a naval planning conference, which, parallel to the army's Great Programme, envisioned a massive expansion of the Black Sea Fleet (including the construction of four new dreadnoughts), with the goal of making it strong enough to easily seize Constantinople and the Ottoman Straits by force by 1917. This plan was ratified by Tsar Nicholas II on April 5, 1914.[7] While not all these details were known outside Russia, the trend line was clear enough, and not only in Berlin. As Abdurrahman Cami (Baykut), a leading CUP strategist, argued in the pages of *Tanin* on April 30, 1914, "The Slavic world is growing more rapidly than its neighbors . . . a strong Ottoman state must form an alliance with Germany and take a defensive position against the Russian and Balkan Slavs."[8]

Two diplomatic crises helped to strengthen the still-unofficial German-Ottoman partnership over the winter of 1913–14. The first surrounded a renewed push for an Armenian reform program, launched by A. A. Neratov, Russia's vice minister for foreign affairs, on June 2, 1913, during the brief respite in between the two Balkan Wars. All fall and winter, Russia's ambassador to the Ottoman Empire, M. N. Girs, piggybacking on Ottoman weakness exposed in the First Balkan War, had worked to unite the

European diplomatic community of Constantinople behind a plan to appoint a European governor and an international gendarmerie to oversee reforms in the six "Armenian" provinces of eastern Turkey (which would be united as one administrative district), similar to the model used for Crete in 1897 and Macedonia in 1903. Only one ambassador resisted: Hans von Wangenheim, Germany's new giant of the Bosphorus, who kept the Turks informed of everything the Russians were up to. Viewing the campaign as essentially a Russian plot, Wangenheim demanded that Girs personally insist that the Turks agree to controversial points, such as the appointment of European inspectors, so that the Germans themselves could escape Turkish opprobrium. As Girs complained to Wangenheim on October 17, 1913, "It would be dangerous if we alone had to make this demand, as then all of Turkey's exasperation would fall exclusively on us [Russians]." The final terms of the reform agreement ratified on February 8, 1914, did not (due to German insistence) even mention "Armenians" or "Armenian provinces," as both the Russians and Armenian activists pointedly complained.[9]

The second crisis, which rapidly became intertwined with the first, was sparked by the arrival of a new German military mission of forty-two officers headed by Otto Liman von Sanders on December 14, 1913. The German mission had been requested back in the spring, against the backdrop of Turkey's defeat in the First Balkan War, by General Mahmud Muhtar Pasha, the Ottoman ambassador in Berlin. While it was no secret that Enver favored the idea of closer military cooperation with Germany, the initiative predated his ascendancy (Adrianople was retaken only in late July). As early as April 1913, Mahmud Shevket Pasha, Ottoman grand vizier and war minister (until he was assassinated in June), had told Ambassador Wangenheim that he was "counting on Germany" to reorganize the Ottoman army after the Balkan Wars. Talât was thinking on the same lines. As the interior minister told the U.S. ambassador, Henry Morgenthau, he had already concluded that Turkey must "decide herself for Germany and either swim with the Germans or go under."[10]

The German Reform Mission (*Heyet-i Islahiye Reisi*) headed by Liman von Sanders was therefore far more politically significant than a mere technical support team, however much Liman himself would later protest otherwise. When Sultan Mehmed V named Liman commander of the Ottoman First Army Corps on December 4, 1913, this gave effective command of the Bosphorus defenses to a German national. With the Russians already on high alert over the Straits owing to the closure of summer 1912, the Bulgarian threat to Constantinople in the First Balkan War (which had even prompted Sazonov, on October 26, 1912, to request that the tsar give command of the Black Sea Fleet to Ambassador Girs in Constantinople), and Russia's own, increasingly detailed contingency plans for seizing them, the news of Liman's appointment struck Russian policymakers like a thunderclap. The two months that followed witnessed a serious war scare between Berlin and St. Petersburg, with the Armenian reform negotiations lending added frisson to the "Liman affair." Russian troops massed on the Caucasian border, and Sazonov considered the idea of occupying East Bayazit or Erzurum as bargaining chips. In a memorandum sent to Tsar Nicholas II on January 6, 1914, Russia's foreign minister mooted the idea of a general partition of the Ottoman Empire, with Britain landing troops at Smyrna (Izmir), France at Beirut, and the Russians at the Black Sea port of Trabzon.[11] At an emergency meeting of the Russian Council of Ministers held one week later, Sazonov and Russia's military chiefs openly discussed whether to risk provoking a European war over Liman's appointment, with only Chairman Kokovtsov (reprising his role as the voice of caution from November 1912) ruling out the military option. Before it came to that, a diplomatic compromise was arranged on January 15, 1914, which saw Liman promoted to marshal and inspector general of the entire Ottoman army, rendering him "overqualified" to command the corps guarding the Straits defenses.[12]

Together with the resolution of the Armenian reform campaign several weeks later, the German-Russian climbdown over Liman's appointment ended the European war scare. But this was little comfort to the Ottoman government. The reform campaign and the Liman affair had nakedly exposed Russia's ambitions to partition the empire—ambitions no longer camouflaged, as they had been in 1912–13, through her Balkan clients. Just in case the Turks had not gotten the message from the Armenian reform campaign, in January 1914 Sazonov called in Turhan Pasha, the Ottoman ambassador in St. Petersburg, "more than once" to warn him that if another "massacre" of

Armenians occurred in eastern Turkey, Russia would intervene.[13] Only German resistance in the form of Wangenheim's stubbornness, it seemed, had prevented Sazonov and Girs from roping the other European powers into supporting a *de facto* Russian protectorate over the six provinces of eastern Turkey.

The Liman mission itself was equally important to the empire's prospects for survival. To be sure, the Germans did not know everything. At least some of the Ottoman army's disastrous performance in the First Balkan War could in fact be traced to the doctrine of "envelopment and annihilation" preached by German officers already in Turkey before 1912 (although this, in turn, reflected the prevailing European fashion for finding the enemy's flanks through offensive élan, which none of the general staffs had yet outgrown, despite contrary evidence about the power of entrenched defenders emerging from the Russo-Japanese, Tripolitanian, and Balkan wars). Absent effective coordination with artillery, frontal infantry assaults had proved disastrous in Thrace and Macedonia. Like so many battlefield disasters, however, these were salutary, in that the Ottomans had speeded up their learning curve. The Liman mission would, the Turks hoped, speed it up still further. Enver Pasha, who had been posted as military attaché in Berlin in 1909 and spoke good German, was fully devoted to "Germanizing" the officer corps. Encouraged by the German assistant chief to the Ottoman General Staff, Colonel Fritz Bronsart von Schellendorf (with whom he was much closer than he was with Liman), following his promotion to war minister, Enver "retired" more than 1,000 *alayli*, or regimental officers, including 2 field marshals, 3 lieutenant generals, 30 major generals, 95 brigadiers, and 184 colonels, paving the way for the rapid advancement of younger officers who had proved their worth in the Balkan Wars.[14]

On April 7, 1914, just two days after Russia's tsar approved a naval building program aiming at facilitating the conquest of Constantinople and the Straits, the Turkish General Staff approved a new Primary Campaign Plan aimed at shoring up the Ottoman Empire against the Russian threat. Discarding offensive strategy as counterproductive, the new posture emphasized flexible strategic defense in Thrace (where the First Army deployed nine divisions in the I, II, and III Corps), though allowing for the possibility of conducting "limited attacks" against the Russians in the Caucasus under favorable conditions (the Third Army, headquartered at Erzurum, comprised nine divisions in the IX, X, and XI Corps, plus two cavalry brigades for border surveillance).[15] Although shortages of all kinds still plagued the army following the Italian and Balkan wars, morale was surprisingly robust, at least in the streamlined officer corps. With Liman and Bronsart helping Enver to implement the new, corps-level operations training, there was every reason to believe that the Ottoman army, given time to recover, would dramatically improve its battlefield performance in the next conflict.

By June 1914, war clouds were beginning to darken the air over Constantinople again. Enraged over rumors of mistreatment of Greeks in the Aegean region, and terrified that the arrival of the *Sultan Osman I* and *Reshadieh* in Ottoman waters, expected within weeks, would allow Turkey to reverse the verdict of the Balkan Wars in the Aegean, Greek nationalists were banging war drums in Athens. On June 12, a formal Greek note of protest, lodged with the Sublime Porte, called ominously for an immediate end to the persecution of Greek Orthodox subjects in Asia Minor, along with the restoration of confiscated property. The Ottoman government replied that, while it would address Greek complaints, the real blame for the unrest lay with the Balkan League for displacing Muslim refugees into Turkey. Viewing war as imminent, Turkish diplomats were trying to hammer out terms of an Ottoman-Bulgarian alliance directed against Athens. Russia's diplomats, meanwhile, were furiously trying to stave off a Third Balkan War, lest the Straits be closed yet again.[16] With the dreadnought *Sultan Osman I* expected to enter the Sea of Marmara in July, it seemed to most European diplomats in Athens and Constantinople that only days remained before Greece (to preempt the Ottoman dreadnoughts)—or Turkey (after the first one arrived)—would launch the Third Balkan War. Compelling as the unfolding Greek-Turkish drama was, however, a team of Serbian conspirators in Belgrade was determined not to be upstaged.

PART II

THE WAR OF 1914: TURKEY PLAYS ITS HAND

CHAPTER 5

MANNA FROM MARS:
THE ARRIVAL OF SMS *GOEBEN*

---

*[I resolved] to force the Turks, even against their will, to spread the war
to the Black Sea against their ancient enemy, Russia.*

—ADMIRAL WILHELM SOUCHON,
commander of the German dreadnought SMS *Goeben*[1]

ON JUNE 28, 1914, Archduke Franz Ferdinand and his wife, the Duchess of
Hohenberg, were murdered by an assassin of Serbian nationality named
Gavrilo Princip as the heir to the Habsburg throne of Austria-Hungary conducted a royal progress through the Bosnian capital of Sarajevo. At least one
other assassin, also of Serbian nationality (although like Princip, a Bosnian
and therefore an Austro-Hungarian subject), had evidently been involved in
the plot, throwing a fuse-bomb at the royal motorcade about an hour before
the fatal shots were fired (in fact, there were seven plotters in all, as would
later be discovered). Proclaiming that the "threads of the conspiracy came
together at Belgrade," the hitherto hesitant Habsburg foreign minister Berchtold, after receiving a "blank cheque" of diplomatic support from Berlin, drew
up a sharply worded forty-eight-hour ultimatum to Serbia, which was delivered in Belgrade on July 23. When Serbia, having received its own "blank
cheque" from Russia, herself having been assured of French backing for a
strong line against Austria-Hungary, refused full compliance with Berchtold's terms two days later, Europe's military doomsday machine cranked
methodically into motion. Serbia and Austria-Hungary mobilized against

one another, even as a secret Russian pre-mobilization began in support of Serbia, directed not only against Austria-Hungary but also her German ally. When Tsar Nicholas II decreed Russian general mobilization on July 30, 1914, it seemed only a miracle could avert a European war that would bring in its wake—in the tsar's own words from the night before, when he had agonized over the decision—"monstrous slaughter."[2]

Considering the centrality of Ottoman affairs in the First Bosnian Crisis of 1908–9, the Tripolitanian war of 1911–12, and the Balkan Wars of 1912–13, it is curious that, at first glance, Turkey played so little a role in the July crisis of 1914. As recently as the third week of June, the diplomatic chatter in Europe had been focused on the threat of a Third Balkan War between Greece and the Ottoman Empire. But the Sarajevo incident, and resulting diplomatic showdown between the Great Powers, seemed to overwhelm all the recent drama in the Balkans, rendering both Turkey and Greece mere afterthoughts in the Great Power capitals as the countdown to war began.

If we look more closely, however, we can see hints that the Ottoman question remained central to Great Power strategy as the July crisis reached its terrible climax, especially in St. Petersburg and Berlin. As early as June 30, just two days after Sarajevo, Russia's foreign minister demanded up-to-date information from the Naval Ministry regarding the war-readiness of Russia's Black Sea Fleet. Sazonov had himself chaired the February planning conference at which Russia's military service chiefs had vowed to speed up the arrival of the first "echelon" of amphibious troops dispatched to Constantinople (comprising about 30,000 men, or roughly an army corps, including one division's artillery component) from mobilization day (M) + 10 to M + 5. As the foreign minister later recalled in his memoirs, the reason for urgency was that everyone present "considered an offensive against Constantinople inevitable, should European war break out." On June 15, 1914, with tensions between Turkey and Greece peaking, Ambassador Girs had warned Sazonov that Russia must be prepared to launch "immediate counter measures" to seize the Straits if a Third Balkan War broke out. Now, after Sarajevo, with a broader European war appearing possible if not likely, Sazonov asked Russia's naval minister, I. K. Grigorevich (the "K" stood, appropriately, for the patronymic *Konstantino*vich), in a "very secret and urgent request," whether the first Russian troops could now be put ashore at the Bosphorus within "four or five days" of mobilization.[3]

In Berlin, meanwhile, the still undeclared partnership with the Sublime Porte acquired an importance beyond price once the extent of Germany's diplomatic isolation began to come into focus toward the end of July. On Friday, July 24, the day after Austria-Hungary dispatched her ultimatum to Serbia, Kaiser Wilhelm II ordered his ambassador in Constantinople, Wangenheim, to reopen alliance talks. The first Ottoman draft for a bilateral military agreement was wired to Berlin on Tuesday, July 28, only to be drowned out in the clamor over Austria-Hungary's declaration of war on Serbia, announced at noon that day. On Friday, July 31, with Russia's general mobilization under way and signs that Britain was leaning toward belligerence against Germany, things looked so desperate in Berlin that Chancellor Bethmann Hollweg took time to wire to Constantinople, asking Wangenheim whether Turkey, in exchange for Germany signing her draft alliance treaty, was prepared to "undertake some action worthy of the name against Russia."[4] On Saturday, August 1, after Germany's ultimatum asking Russia to cease mobilizing had expired, Bethmann's resistance crumbled further: now he would sign the Ottoman treaty simply on Liman's assurance that Turkey's army was "battle-ready," with no guarantee of action against Russia.[5]

Meanwhile, Russian statesmen were gearing up for an armed clash with Turkey, which they assumed would follow immediately on the outbreak of war in Europe. On July 27, two days after Serbia rejected Vienna's ultimatum but one day before Austria-Hungary declared war on her, Russia's chief of army staff, N. N. Yanushkevitch, issued top secret orders to Nikolai Yudenich, chief of staff at Russia's Caucasian Army command in Tiflis, to mobilize against the Ottoman Empire.[6] That same day, Girs sent a top secret memorandum to Sazonov warning that if Russia backed down against the Austro-Germans in Europe, it would signal such dangerous weakness in Constantinople and across the Near East that "[we] might be forced to take the initiative ourselves in waging war [against Turkey]."[7] On July 29, even as Tsar Nicholas II was hesitating, Hamlet-like, over whether to issue the final, irreversible order for general mobilization (he actually did issue it around 9:00 p.m., only to change his mind and rescind the order less than an hour later), Yanushkevitch was assuring Yudenich that he should proceed with the mobilization of the Caucasian Army according to variant 4, for a European war in which "Turkey does not *at first* take part."[8] On July 30, after the tsar had finally overcome his scruples and given the fateful general mobilization order, Sazonov wired urgently to his ambassador in London, Count Benckendorff, that he intervene to cut off the imminent handover of the dreadnoughts *Sultan Osman I* and *Reshadieh* to the Ottoman Empire (Turkish crews were in fact scheduled to take them over on August 2). Back in May, Benckendorff had requested to His Majesty's foreign secretary, Sir Edward Grey—very, very carefully—that this be done, only for Grey and the First Lord of the Admiralty, Winston Churchill, to object on the grounds that Britain's government did not have the right to interfere in private business contracts. Now, with European war about to break out in a matter of days, if not hours, Sazonov could not afford to stall any longer. "These ships," he insisted that Benckendorff admonish Churchill and Grey, "must be retained in England."[9]

As if reading Sazonov's mind (although in fact knowing nothing of the latest Russian request, which had not yet reached him), Winston Churchill now injected himself into the story with one of his most controversial actions in a career full of them. On Friday, July 31, with Russia's general mobilization under way (although he apparently did not know this either) and Germany about to issue her ultimatum to St. Petersburg, the First Lord of the Admiralty ordered English naval crews to board the dreadnoughts *Sultan Osman I* and *Reshadieh*, so as to prevent Turkish crews from raising the Ottoman flag. With this flagrantly illegal act, Churchill bought Britain added insurance against the German High Seas Fleet in the war that now seemed unavoidable (to him, at least). He also, entirely unwittingly, fulfilled one of Russia's primary strategic objectives—denying the Ottoman navy its lusted-for dreadnoughts, with which she might seize control of the Black Sea from her—while offering a priceless gift to hawks in the Ottoman government, not to mention German leaders trying desperately to bring Turkey into the war.[10]

Enver Pasha was not a man to let an opportunity like this slip by. With German chancellor Bethmann's terms for signing a formal alliance with Turkey having softened, in his increasing desperation, from a promise of "action worthy of the name" against Russia on Friday, July 31, to Turkey merely being "battle-ready" by the following afternoon, the Ottoman war minister decided to split the difference. Saturday morning, Enver learned that British crews had forcibly commandeered the two Ottoman dreadnoughts (although Churchill's action had not yet been endorsed by the British cabinet, nor announced publicly). Thinking fast, on Saturday afternoon Enver promised Ambassador Wangenheim that in exchange for a generous alliance treaty, he would turn over to Germany the *Sultan Osman I* (the idea was to dock it at a German port on the North Sea—though how it would evade the massive British fleet en route was left unsaid, as was the fact that the ship, as Enver knew, was no longer his to dispose of!)[11]

After comparing this offer to Bethmann's latest instruction that he insist only that Turkey show herself "battle-ready," Wangenheim decided that Enver had met the chancellor's terms. At 4:00 p.m. on Sunday, August 2, 1914, the ambassador therefore wrote his signature alongside that of Said Halim Pasha, the Ottoman grand vizier and foreign minister, on a secret bilateral defense treaty, valid until December 31, 1918, in which Turkey promised to join Germany if the latter went to war with Russia on behalf of Austria-Hungary, in exchange for a promise by which "Germany obligates itself, by force of arms if need be, to defend Ottoman territory in case it should be threatened."[*][12] Wangenheim also promised to expedite to Berlin Enver's urgent request that Germany's Mediterranean squadron, composed of SMS *Goeben* and her support cruiser, the *Breslau*, be ordered to Constantinople. Unaware that he had been deceived by the Ottoman war minister into signing a devious treaty on false pretenses, Wangenheim wholeheartedly seconded Enver's idea, pointing out helpfully to Berlin that "with the *Goeben*, even an [Ottoman] landing on Russian territory would be possible." On hearing the news, Liman von Sanders then issued mobilization orders for the German officers in his military mission to the Ottoman army, now seventy-one strong.[13]

Not unreasonably, Liman, along with Moltke at the German army

---

[*] This treaty, drafted by Ottoman diplomats, was ingeniously worded such that it obliged the Ottoman Empire to declare war on Russia only if Germany had gone to war with her according to the terms of her own alliance with Austria-Hungary. Since Berlin, owing to Bethmann's misguided emphasis on legal niceties, had declared war on Russia first, the *casus foederis* did not technically apply to Turkey (nor to Austria-Hungary, for that matter). Realizing this, the Habsburg foreign minister, Leopold von Berchtold, dithered and delayed until heavy pressure from Berlin at last forced Austria-Hungary, on August 6, 1914, to declare war on Russia.

command and Grand Marshal Tirpitz at the Admiralty, concluded that Wangenheim had won a binding pledge from Enver that the Ottoman Empire would shortly enter the war against Russia. This erroneous belief was bolstered by the fact that Enver had decreed Ottoman general mobilization against Russia on Saturday, August 1 (an order confirmed by the Turkish cabinet on Sunday), and then ordered, on Monday, August 3 (though without cabinet authorization), the mining of the northern entrance to the Bosphorus and the southern entrance to the Dardanelles.[14] Moltke, with his hair-trigger mobilization plan, requiring a lightning advance on Paris, already falling behind schedule owing to Russia's secret early mobilization and Belgium's decision to resist the German violation of her territory, began bombarding Wangenheim with requests for prompt Ottoman intervention against Russia—and, he hoped, Britain and France as well.[15] Once a state of war between France and Germany was confirmed on Monday afternoon, August 3, it became imperative for the German Admiralty to find a safe anchorage for SMS *Goeben* and the *Breslau* before Britain declared war and the superior Allied Mediterranean fleet blew them out of the water. Disinclined to look Churchill's gift horse in the mouth and believing in Enver's promises, Tirpitz ordered Souchon, in the small hours of Tuesday, August 4, 1914, to proceed forthwith to the Ottoman capital.[16]

Admiral Wilhelm Souchon had been born for this moment. The idea of sending his powerful warship into the Bosphorus to contest Russian control of the Black Sea was not a new one. In fact Souchon had docked there back in the first week of May, making such a strong impression in the Ottoman capital that CUP leaders like Cami Baykut began openly clamoring for the *Goeben* to be impressed into Ottoman service. The warm welcome Souchon had received in Constantinople provided a striking contrast to his reception in other Mediterranean ports of call, where the long-dominant British fleet was in the habit of docking the minute he left in order to erase any positive impression he made (or as the kaiser liked to say, to "spit in the soup"). The Russians knew all about Souchon too. In the wake of the Liman affair in January, Sazonov had lodged warnings in Berlin that the *Goeben* must not be impressed into Ottoman service. With Russia's Black Sea Fleet still two years or more away from launching its first operational dreadnought, the arrival of *any* dreadnought-class vessel in Ottoman territorial waters threatened to tip the naval balance on the Black Sea in Turkey's favor, rendering well-nigh impossible any Russian amphibious strike on the Bosphorus.[17]

When Souchon decoded his orders from Berlin just past 3:00 a.m. on Tuesday, August 4, 1914, he was approaching the French Algerian port of Philippeville, where colonial troops were embarking for the western front. Having learned at 6:00 p.m. on Monday, while steaming southwestward from Sicily, of the German declaration of war on France, he was at last nearing his target and could already, as he later recalled, "taste that moment of fire so ardently desired by us all!" Disregarding Tirpitz's summons to Constantinople—for now—Souchon continued on course for Philippeville. Just past 6:00 a.m., SMS *Goeben* opened fire on the French troopships while the *Breslau* shelled the nearby port of Bone. Although the shelling did not cause significant casualties or great physical damage to either the troopships or the port, the German attack concerned the French fleet commander, Vice Admiral Augustin Boué de Lapeyrère, enough that he ordered his squadron to form escort convoys, a laborious process that would take several days. By thus delaying the dispatch of French Algerian soldiers to the front, Souchon had succeeded in his object. Satisfied, he withdrew his ships and turned back toward Sicily, hoping to coal there before proceeding to Constantinople, some 1,200 miles (2,000 kilometers) distant.[18]

Now the hard part began. While the panic he had sowed at Philippeville and Bone had dissuaded the French commander from pursuing him, Souchon had still to reckon with the British Mediterranean fleet, headed by three large battle cruisers, the imposingly named *Inflexible*, *Indomitable*, and *Indefatigable*, all of the "Invincible" type launched in 1907. While none of the three was current dreadnought class—each displaced only 18,000 tons, compared with the 23,000 tons of SMS *Goeben* (itself just barely registering as a last-generation dreadnought)—the British battle cruisers mounted eight 12-inch guns and could make 25 or 26 knots, as fast as all but the latest dreadnoughts. In theory, the *Goeben*, launched in 1911 and mounting ten 11-inch guns, could run its 5,200-horsepower engines, at full thrust, to a speed of 28 or 29 knots. But, as Souchon (although not his British pursuers) was painfully aware, with three of his twenty-four boilers out of action and others leaking, his ship was incapable of such a feat. On Monday, August 3, Churchill, by way of Admiral Sir Berkeley Milne, commander of Britain's Mediterranean fleet, had ordered HMS *Indomitable* and HMS *Indefatigable* to hunt down SMS *Goeben* and then "follow and shadow her wherever she goes." At 10:32 a.m. on Tuesday, August 4, following the shelling of Philippeville and Bone, the lookouts on the *Indomitable*, proceeding toward Algeria in a belated attempt to repulse Souchon's attack, caught sight of the *Breslau* off the starboard bow, "steering to eastward at high speed." Within seconds, the *Goeben* was spotted off the port bow—bearing almost directly at the *Indomitable*. Both ships were in firing range, but, as Britain and Germany were not yet at war, Captain Kennedy, commander of the *Indomitable*, could do little but turn to starboard, cutting off Souchon's attempted pass and forcing him to diverge slightly from his course. Souchon had dodged his first bullet.[19]

He was not safe yet, however. With *Indefatigable* joining the chase, the mood at the British Admiralty was ebullient. Churchill, who, owing to a garbled transmission, mistakenly thought Souchon was heading *southwest*, toward Algeria, wired just past noon that Admiral Milne was to "hold" the German ships and to engage them if they "attacked French transports," after giving "fair warning." Even this somewhat equivocal order, however, was rescinded two hours later, after Churchill was rebuked in the cabinet: now Milne was to hold his fire until war was declared on Germany. Adding uncertainty to these confusing orders, back on July 31, Churchill had instructed Milne to "husband your force at the outset" and that it must "not at this stage be brought to action against superior forces." Unaware of the difficulties Souchon was having with his boilers, Churchill and his fleet commanders still thought of her as the fastest, most powerful ship in the Mediterranean. Milne therefore had every reason for caution.[20]

Whether or not the British were authorized to engage him, Souchon could not afford to be complacent. Hoping to outrun the *Indomitable* and *Indefatigable* to Messina, the nearest "neutral" port on the leeward side of Sicily, Souchon ran his boilers at full capacity all afternoon, nearly killing his stokers in the process but inching the *Goeben* up to nearly 23 knots and slowly distancing himself from his pursuers. At around 4:00 p.m., the British warships fell out of firing range. At 4:35 p.m., with a thick fog descending, the

Goeben and *Breslau* disappeared from Milne's view off the Sicilian coast. By the time Britain's ultimatum to Germany (demanding that she evacuate Belgian territory) expired without a positive reply at midnight (11:00 p.m. London time), creating the state of war that would finally have allowed the British to fire, Souchon was well out of range, approaching the neutral waters of the Straits of Messina. Under the laws of neutrality, after docking at Messina, he would have only twenty-four hours in port.[21]

A furious diplomatic struggle now began over the fate of SMS *Goeben*. To begin with, Souchon was enraged that the Italian authorities were "shameless enough in their treachery" to put him on the clock, despite Italy being nominally a member of the Triple Alliance alongside Germany and Austria-Hungary. Showing where the true sympathies in the country already lay, the port authorities even refused him coal. Souchon had to waste precious time wiring the Foreign Ministry in Rome to overcome local obstruction. With no other German warships in the Mediterranean, the only chance for an escort lay with the Austrian Adriatic fleet at Pola. But Souchon's plea that she "come and fetch *Goeben* and *Breslau* from Messina as soon as possible," wired to the Austrian Admiralty at 2:00 a.m. on August 5, went nowhere. Admiral Milne had posted British warships at both entrances to the Straits of Messina, observing the "six mile" rule of neutrality, but ready to fire as soon as Souchon's ships breached the limit. The Austrians saw nothing to gain from risking an engagement, not least because Austria-Hungary and Britain were not yet at war. Adding to Souchon's frustration was a cryptic message from Tirpitz in Berlin, wired on Wednesday, August 5, but deciphered only at 11:00 a.m. on Thursday, that "at the present time [your] arrival in Constantinople not yet possible, for political reasons."[22]

Undeterred by these bad tidings, Souchon pressed his men to the limit of their powers. With no hope of rescue, the *Goeben* and *Breslau* would need enough coal to race through what he could only assume was a heavy British screen. So Souchon pressed every hand available into the effort, exhorted on by "music in the form of martial airs, extra rations, stirring speeches, the example of those officers who worked with them, and my own encouragements." On the quay, Sicilian touts hawked souvenirs and postcards to the Germans who, as in the old Roman gladiatorial salute, were "about to die."

On and on Souchon's men labored, with dozens of men collapsing from exhaustion or sunstroke in the August heat. When one stoker fell, he was hustled belowdecks and another was pressed into his place. Other coalers, beginning to slip, were "plied with cool drinks and baths." But time was short, and only 1,580 tons of coal could be loaded onto the *Goeben*, and 495 tons onto the *Breslau*, before the last man standing collapsed Thursday afternoon, August 6. It was not enough to reach the Dardanelles. But it would have to do. Souchon gave his men a much-needed rest and ordered them to prepare for departure at 5:00 p.m.[23]

Although Ottoman permission to enter the Dardanelles had been withdrawn, Souchon did have one other option. After rounding the boot of Italy, he could head up the Adriatic to hole up at Pola with the Austrian fleet—the same one that had refused to rescue him. But doing this would have consigned Souchon, and his beloved *Goeben*, to a passive war "waiting on events," penned in by the superior British fleet. Accepting such a fate would have gone against every grain of his stubborn, irascible character. And so Souchon decided, entirely of his own volition, "not to waver from my duty to break out

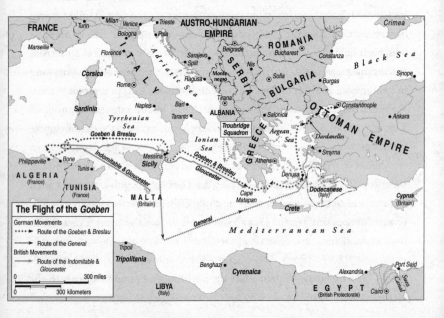

into the eastern Mediterranean . . . hoping that I could later reach Constanti-nople and thereby be able to bring the war into the Black Sea."[24]

Souchon's plan, though foolhardy, was not entirely senseless. Expecting to be followed anyway, he made sure to depart before nightfall, so that the Brit-ish spotters would see him heading northward up the Adriatic. Once dark-ness fell and he—hopefully—fell out of enemy sight, he would "make a wide turn to starboard, surreptitiously"—heading east toward the Greek islands, where a German collier was waiting at Cape Malea to resupply the *Goeben* and *Breslau* with enough coal for the onward journey to Constantinople. Still, Souchon knew that he would need to continue his run of good luck if he was to evade his pursuers.

His British opponents proved more than obliging.* At the Admiralty, Winston Churchill was so little clued in to the importance of Constantinople that he had commandeered the powerful dreadnoughts Ottoman strategists had been dreaming of for years—for the purchase of which a public subscrip-tion had been opened, to great popular fanfare. Neither Churchill nor Admi-ral Milne so much as suspected the possibility that Souchon might make a dash for the Dardanelles. Milne was so certain the *Goeben* would head west, for Gibraltar and the open waters of the Atlantic, that he posted only a single light cruiser, the *Gloucester*, at the eastern entrance to the Straits of Messina (although he did have a squadron commanded by Rear Admiral Sir Ernest Troubridge guarding the Adriatic in case Souchon headed for Pola, consisting of four armored battle cruisers, with eight destroyers held in reserve).[25]

When Souchon exited the Straits of Messina early on the evening of Thursday, August 6, the inferior *Gloucester* could do little more than follow at a safe distance, radioing the German position (whenever Souchon did not succeed in jamming it) to Admiral Milne, who passed it on to the Adriatic squadron. Troubridge, in ideal position to intercept Souchon, set out south-ward just after midnight, hoping to engage the *Goeben* and *Breslau* before first light at dawn. When, around 4:00 a.m., he had still not found them,

---

* In his memoirs Souchon claims that he was all but counting on British sloth and passivity, saying he had an "instinct that the English admirals of today would not challenge me unless they succeeded in bringing about the full superiority of all their concentrated forces." While this remark has the sound of hindsight—by the time he wrote this, Souchon obviously knew how tentative the British pursuit had been—his boldness at the time was entirely consistent with such a belief.

Troubridge had second thoughts. His destroyers, sent off to coal, had still not come up. Fearing that all four of his (slightly) inferior battle cruisers could be blown out of the water by the guns of SMS *Goeben* in a daylight encounter, and with Churchill's orders not to engage "superior forces" echoing in his ear, Troubridge called off the chase. Souchon had escaped another bullet.*[26]

Lucky in his principal antagonists, Souchon had still to reckon with Captain Howard Kelly, commander of the *Gloucester*, an Irishman nearly as stubborn as he. In a classic illustration of the importance of temperament in the fluid situation of combat, Kelly was just as determined to exceed his orders as Troubridge was to shirk them. After learning that his Adriatic squadron had broken off the chase, Milne had wired Kelly, at 5:30 a.m. on Friday, August 7, that he was "to drop astern and avoid capture." Displaying irascibility worthy of the man he was chasing, Kelly refused to pull back, even though Troubridge had left him utterly exposed to the *Goeben*'s superior guns. At midday on Friday, Souchon, unable to outrun the *Gloucester* in the *Goeben* owing to his leaking boilers (and the inferior coal loaded at Brindisi, which caused his ships to belch black smoke), ordered the *Breslau* to draw his pursuer away, figuring that the British captain would prefer to follow a ship more his size. By 1:30 p.m., the *Goeben* had begun to distance herself, although the *Gloucester* had closed to 11,500 yards behind the *Breslau*. At 1:35 p.m., Kelly ordered his six-inch fore guns to fire from the bow. At least one hit was scored (although it did little damage). The *Breslau* fired back a series of ranging shots, which missed, but threw up a tremendous spray all around the *Gloucester*. Souchon, aboard the *Goeben*, now reversed course and fired off a torpedo salvo at the *Gloucester* from long range, which likewise missed. As if terrified that his renegade captain might actually damage a German ship, Milne now ordered Kelly to back off, ordering that he not proceed past Cape Matapan into the Aegean, lest he risk an ambush in the Greek islands. Souchon had escaped once again.†[27]

---

* Rear Admiral Troubridge was later censured and tried by court-martial for failing to chase the *Goeben*, "an enemy then flying." As the fault clearly lay as much with Churchill and Milne for failing to clarify his instructions, Troubridge was honorably acquitted—although he was never again given a seagoing command.

† Although something of a dud, this engagement was well remembered—if only because it was witnessed by passengers on an Italian steamer, on which the daughter of Henry Morgenthau, U.S. ambassador to the Ottoman Empire, was traveling en route to Constantinople. (After arriving, Morgenthau's daughter was debriefed on the

Meanwhile, the political struggle in Constantinople was heating up. In the initial rush of enthusiasm after the conclusion of the German alliance treaty on August 2 and Wangenheim's promise to send him the *Goeben*, Enver had not only mined the upper Bosphorus but ordered the requisitioning of Russian merchandise in Ottoman ports, including oil and grain. Once Said Halim Pasha got wind of this on Wednesday, August 5, however, he objected to the illegal requisitions just as furiously as the Russian embassy did. The grand vizier was concerned, in the first instance, that no agreement with Bulgaria had been reached to ensure the safety of Thrace in case Turkey and Russia went to war. But he was hardly in a rush to come to terms with Sofia. Playing a subtler game than his young, headstrong war minister, Said Halim Pasha reasoned that, with SMS *Goeben* and *Breslau* surrounded by hostile squadrons patrolling the Mediterranean, Souchon really had nowhere else to go but Constantinople. While the Germans were coaling at Brindisi, the grand vizier decided to put the squeeze on. Before the Ottoman government would allow Souchon's ships free passage through the Dardanelles, he informed Ambassador Wangenheim on Wednesday, August 5, Germany must satisfy six conditions, including support for the abolition of the Capitulations—the holy grail of Ottoman diplomacy for decades—and firm pledges to help Turkey recover Aegean islands from Greece and to expand her Caucasian border eastward so as to "place Turkey into direct contact with the Muslims of Russia." It was this piece of diplomatic blackmail that lay behind the cryptic wire Souchon had received from Tirpitz on Brindisi, informing him that his arrival in Constantinople was not yet advisable for "political reasons." Under duress, and not wishing to jeopardize Souchon's precarious position still further, Wangenheim agreed on Thursday, August 6.[28]

Souchon, unaware of these negotiations and knowing only that matters in Constantinople remained murky, made his rendezvous at Cape Malea on Friday evening, August 7, with his collier, the *Bogadir*, which had adopted Greek disguise to evade detection. A second collier, the *General*, had also rejoined him after setting off in a separate direction from Messina. Had he known that

---

battle by Ambassador Wangenheim; his six-year-old granddaughter, Barbara, who also witnessed it, chronicled it fifty years later in her best-selling history *The Guns of August*.)

the supercautious Admiral Milne had called off British pursuit, Souchon might have coaled his ships right at Cape Malea. Instead he ordered his colliers to follow him deeper into the Aegean until they found a deserted coastline that seemed safe from enemy view, off the island of Denusa. All weekend on Saturday and Sunday, August 8–9, 1914, the *Goeben* and *Breslau* took on coal while keeping a steam up, in case they would be forced to depart on short notice. A special lookout post was erected at the highest point on the island to keep watch for the British. Souchon was now less than two hundred miles from the mouth of the Dardanelles, a distance he could cover in a day's steaming—if permission to enter was granted. But he could not risk wiring Constantinople, because a signal strong enough to reach the Ottoman capital would betray his position to the British fleet. With the political situation still unclear, Souchon once again chose the boldest course of action, dispatching the *General* Saturday night to the Ottoman port of Smyrna (Izmir) to transmit the following message to Captain Hans Humann, German naval liaison at the Ottoman Admiralty:

> Urgent military necessity requires an attack on the enemy in the Black Sea. Go to any length possible to arrange for me to pass through Straits immediately with the permission of the Turkish government, without formal approval if necessary.[29]

Back in Constantinople, Ottoman negotiators, with their negotiating leverage vis-à-vis the Germans increasing by the day, were thoroughly enjoying themselves. Even Enver, despite his earlier rashness, was cottoning to the game. On Wednesday, August 5, the same day the grand vizier was putting the screws on Ambassador Wangenheim, while Souchon was torturing his stokers in the Sicilian heat, the Russian military attaché in Constantinople, Generalmajor M. N. Leontiev, called on Enver at the Ottoman War Ministry. What the war minister told him was astonishing. In exchange for Russia signing a five- or ten-year defensive alliance with the Ottoman Empire and helping to broker a new Balkan settlement at the expense of Vienna (the idea was for Turkey to regain western Thrace from Bulgaria and several Aegean islands from Greece, with Greece compensated with Albania, and

Bulgaria given parts of Macedonia by Serbia, who would herself win Bosnia-Herzegovina), Enver promised to withdraw the IX and XI Corps of the Ottoman Third Army from eastern Turkey, so as to allow Russia to send the Army of the Caucasus to reinforce her European fronts against Austria and Germany. The day such a treaty was signed, this supposedly Germanophile Ottoman war minister promised Leontiev, he would expel Liman von Sanders and the entire German military mission from Turkey.[30]

To this day it is not known how serious Enver's trial balloon for a Russian-Ottoman alliance was. It does not seem to have originated with the Ottoman Foreign Ministry, although Said Halim Pasha eagerly took up Enver's idea as soon as he heard of it, as did Talât, at the Interior Ministry (notably, in that Talât had himself traveled to Livadia, on the Crimea, back in May, accompanied by Ambassador Girs, to propose something broadly similar to Tsar Nicholas II). All weekend from Friday, August 7, to Sunday, August 9, 1914, even as Admiral Souchon, holed up at Denusa, was desperately waiting for permission to enter the Dardanelles, a series of increasingly detailed alliance talks proceeded in Constantinople between Ottoman diplomats and Ambassador Girs, with Leontiev meeting Enver on the side. Whether or not Enver's offer had been made in good faith, it was certainly so taken by Girs and Leontiev, who both recommended that Sazonov take up the Ottoman proposal.[31]

On Sunday, matters came to a head. At about noon, Admiral Milne, after delaying pursuit once again owing to an erroneous report that Austria had declared war on England (thus threatening, in very theoretical theory, to descend on the Adriatic and cut his squadron off from Malta), resumed chasing the *Goeben* with his three main battle cruisers (although he would not actually reach the Aegean until nearly midnight). Souchon's urgent request, wired to Humann from Smyrna early Sunday morning and decoded in Constantinople around the same time Milne was renewing pursuit, drove home to the Ottoman government that time was running out on the *Goeben*. Still the grand vizier stalled, fobbing off Ambassador Wangenheim with a story about an impending Ottoman-Greek-Romanian neutrality pact which must not be prejudiced by the arrival of an armed German warship. Although Said Halim Pasha did not, for obvious reasons, mention this, alliance talks with Russia were also nearing their climax on Sunday—Ambassador Girs sent two urgent wires to Sazonov this day requesting that he sign immediately (alas, Sazonov received his own urgent message this afternoon, from Yanushkevitch at Russian military headquarters, advising that alliance talks with Turkey must be cut off before they were leaked to the press, lest they be interpreted across the Near East "as a sign of [Russian] weakness"). In order to keep his options open a little longer, Said Halim Pasha suggested to Ambassador Wangenheim that Souchon be allowed into the Dardanelles—but only if the *Goeben* was disarmed and converted into an "Ottoman" ship "by means of a fictitious sale."[32] It was not, exactly, an invitation. But it was all Souchon was going to get.

At 1:00 a.m. on Monday morning, August 10, 1914, the *General*, from Smyrna, wired the following message to the *Goeben*: "Enter and demand surrender of the Dardanelles forts." Two hours later, while he was still mulling over this strange instruction, Souchon picked up wireless signals from the British squadron, entering the Aegean in force. At 6:00 a.m., having received no clarification of his instructions, he decided he could wait no longer, setting off for the Dardanelles. Toward noon, when he was about halfway there, Souchon decoded another wire, sent overnight from the Admiralty in Berlin: "It is of the greatest importance, that the *Goeben* enter the Dardanelles as soon as possible. Acknowledge." Neither this nor the transmission from Smyrna specified that permission to enter had been granted by the Ottoman government, for the excellent reason that it had not, in fact, been given. Souchon could only guess what this meant: was he to force his way in or simply put on a show of doing so in order to give the Turks an excuse for letting him in? At any rate, he would soon find out, as, on current course, he would reach his destination by nightfall.[33]

In a week of mounting tension, the afternoon of Monday, August 10, was the most dramatic yet. At 4:00 p.m., steaming at a steady 18 knots toward the Dardanelles, Souchon sighted Tenedos and Imbros. The fate of SMS *Goeben* and the *Breslau*, along with the German campaign to force the Ottomans to honor the terms of the August 2 alliance treaty and enter the war against Russia, now depended on the reaction of the southern shore batteries at Cape Helles and Kum Kale once Souchon's ships came into range. Would they fire? Having received no clear orders from the War Ministry, as soon as the

German ships were sighted approaching just past 7:00 p.m., the commander at the great fortress of Chanak (*Çanakkale*) wired Constantinople for instructions. Lieutenant Colonel Friedrich Freiherr Kress von Kressenstein, meeting with Enver at the War Ministry, recalled the conversation that followed. Enver initially refused to give an answer without first consulting the grand vizier, but Kress pressed hard for a decision. Enver then fell silent for what seemed to Kress like an eternity. At last he said, "They should be allowed to enter." Kress was still not satisfied. "If English warships come in after the [*Goeben*]," he demanded to know, "will they be fired upon?" Again Enver hedged, protesting that he could not possibly decide a critical matter of war and peace without consulting the other ministers. But Kress insisted on an answer. "In that case," Enver replied at last, "yes." At 9:00 p.m., a Turkish torpedo boat sent out to meet the *Goeben* gave the long-awaited signal, "Follow me." With a sense of profound relief, Souchon followed the Turkish pilot through a safe channel of the well-mined Dardanelles into the Sea of Marmara.[34]

News of the arrival of SMS *Goeben* in Ottoman territorial waters was instantly telegraphed across Europe. Following a week that had seen Souchon narrowly escape the incompetent pursuit of a vastly superior British fleet, the coup was almost immediately recognized as a critical blow to the Entente position in Constantinople. To be sure, we have to be wary of the distortions of hindsight in accounts published long after the fact, which give off a strong whiff of literary license.* At the time, Milne and Churchill continued their borderline-farcical misreading of the situation, issuing orders that the Dardanelles be blockaded at the mouth in case Souchon tried to come *out*.[35] Prime Minister Herbert Henry Asquith, a bit more perceptively but still all but dripping with condescension, told the cabinet, "As we shall insist that the Goeben should be manned by a Turkish instead of a German crew, it doesn't much

---

* The most famous being Churchill's from *World Crisis*, in which he attributed to the *Goeben* "more slaughter, more misery and more ruin than has ever before been borne within the compass of a ship." Still, he had competition. Djemal Pasha, in his memoirs, has Enver telling him that night, "A son has been born to us." Ambassador Morgenthau, in his colorful but often unreliable memoir *Secrets of the Bosphorus*, has Ambassador Wangenheim waving around the telegram announcing Souchon's arrival "with all the enthusiasm of a college boy whose football team has won a victory."

matter: as the Turkish sailors cannot navigate her—except on to rocks or mines."[36]

British insouciance aside, there is no mistaking the critical nature of Enver's decision to let in the German ships and block entry to British and (by implication) French warships—a decision confirmed at 10:00 p.m. in a wire from Humann to the German Admiralty in Berlin. For good measure, Ottoman shore batteries allowed in two German civilian support ships Tuesday morning, including the *General* (fresh in from Smyrna) and the *Rodosto*, even while the growing armada of British and French vessels arriving in Besika Bay to watch the Dardanelles could only drop anchor and wait.*[37]

Whether or not the Ottomans had entered the war, they had clearly breached the laws of neutrality—and let a very powerful wolf into the diplomatic sheepfold at the Sublime Porte. As Souchon wired Tirpitz on August 12, 1914, "The Turkish government has welcomed the *Goeben* and *Breslau* with enthusiasm. Collaborative work with the Ottoman fleet is proceeding. I intend to begin operations in the Black Sea as soon as possible. Please send ammunition immediately. There is enough coal here."[38] With or without Turkish permission, Souchon was ready to bring the war into the Black Sea against Russia.

---

* Of course, they could have fired on the German vessels, and it is a bit strange that they did not. All manner of theories have been offered to explain Milne's passive behavior in August 1914, including a recent one, proffered by Geoffrey Miller in *Superior Force: The Conspiracy Behind the Escape of* Goeben *and* Breslau (1996), that a clique in Athens, possibly involving Rear Admiral Mark Kerr, head of the British naval mission to Greece, helped suppress evidence of the *Goeben*'s movements from Churchill and Milne. But as Miller unfolds his gripping narrative, it becomes clear that any such conspiracy was confined to Athens: garbled intelligence, faulty thinking, and sheer incompetence more than adequately explain Milne's failure to stop the *Goeben*.

CHAPTER 6

THE BATTLE FOR OTTOMAN BELLIGERENCE

If I were to encounter the Russian fleet, or a good portion thereof,
in favorable conditions, then I would not, so to speak, prevent
the cannons from going off by themselves.

—"OTTOMAN VICE ADMIRAL" WILHELM SOUCHON,
commander of the formerly German dreadnought SMS *Goeben*,
interpreting his orders from Ottoman war minister Enver Pasha,
October 25, 1914[1]

SOUCHON'S ARRIVAL IN THE SEA OF MARMARA on the night of August 10, 1914, was a great coup for the German cause in Constantinople, but it was not necessarily a welcome one to the Ottoman government. Even Enver, despite his Germanophile sympathies, had hesitated at the last minute when confronted with Souchon's *fait accompli*, which gave the lie to the war minister's ongoing alliance talks with the Russian military attaché. Said Halim Pasha, for his part, was a master of the diplomatic arts, who, given another week or two to put the squeeze on Wangenheim, might have succeeded in getting the Germans to promise to restore the empire's borders under Suleyman the Magnificent. The moment of maximum Ottoman leverage over the Germans had passed as quickly as it had come, with Said Halim Pasha's subtlety smothered by Souchon's stubborn will.

The diplomatic game, however, was far from over. Inevitably, the Entente ambassadors demanded that the German warships be forced to depart

Ottoman waters within twenty-four hours, or be disarmed. The grand vizier, as we have seen, had already planned his response. On Tuesday, August 11, Said Halim Pasha publicly announced that the Ottoman government had "bought" the *Goeben* and *Breslau* for eighty million marks (although in fact no money changed hands): they would be renamed *Yavuz Sultan Selim* and the *Midilli* and incorporated into the Ottoman navy, thus rendering null and void Entente complaints about Turkey docking a belligerent warship.* In an inspired touch, Said Halim Pasha added that the "purchase" of the *Goeben* was expressly conceived as retaliation for the British detention of the *Sultan Osman I.* [2] This had two welcome effects: it helped to stoke popular resentment of the British in Constantinople, even while wrong-footing the Germans. For how, as Wangenheim complained to Berlin, could Germany disavow the phony "sale" of her warships, a gesture already wildly popular with the Turkish public?[3]

The British could only blame themselves, of course, for the foul stench created by the commandeering of the Ottoman dreadnoughts. While Churchill would ultimately take the lion's share of the blame for alienating Turkish opinion, he had company. Mr. H. Beaumont, the embassy official charged with the unpleasant duty of assuaging the Ottoman government about the loss of their dreadnoughts, complained to Sir Edward Grey back on August 6, 1914, that Ottoman naval minister Djemal Pasha was "acting like a spoiled child in regard to the detention of the *Sultan Osman I.*" Djemal, it seems, had the gall not only to demand compensation, but to threaten cancellation of the Vickers-Armstrong contract "for the organization and reconstruction of the Ottoman dockyards at Constantinople," for the presumably trivial reason that the dreadnoughts meant to dock there no longer belonged to Turkey. Churchill, for his part, minuted on this report that there should be "no hurry" in compensating the Turks: "They may join the Germans, in which case we shall save our money. Negotiate and temporise." Four days later, when the impending arrival of the *Goeben* threatened to undermine Britain's already shaky position at the Porte, Beaumont did soften his tone somewhat, noting

---

* *Yavuz Sultan Selim* was named for Selim I, called "the Grim" in English, who conquered Egypt and Arabia, including the holy places, in 1517. Notorious for Sunni sectarianism, Selim the Grim was said to have butchered thousands of Shiites (mostly Alevis) in the province of Rum. His name carries strong echoes today. In 2013, it was announced that the Turkish government would name the third Bosphorus suspension bridge after him, to the passionate displeasure of Turkish Alevis, which added political heft to the Gezi Park protests in Istanbul.

in his report to London that, while the *Sultan Osman I* had been financed by new loans, money for the *Reshadieh* had been raised by "popular conscription, mostly in small sums, so that millions of Muslim contributors are personally interested in her fate." The "loss of these ships," he now noticed, was "deeply felt and widely resented," such that it might behoove Britain to promise compensation: the Turks were asking for £15 million.*[4] Next day, Said Halim Pasha beat London to the pass with his own form of compensation—the German warships—ensuring that Turkish opinion would never forgive Britain for Churchill's insult.

The Turks had more unpleasant surprises in store for the British embassy. On Saturday, August 15, Djemal Pasha ordered Souchon to steam north for the capital and prepare "to raise the Turkish flag" upon command. On Sunday, the dreadnought formerly known as SMS *Goeben* dropped anchor alongside her support cruiser in the Bosphorus, near the entrance to the Golden Horn. In a grand public ceremony, the naval minister denounced by Beaumont as a "spoiled child" proudly took the *Yavuz Sultan Selim* and *Midilli* into Ottoman service. While a token detachment of Turkish sailors had climbed aboard, the real nature of the handover was made plain to all when Souchon and his German officers ostentatiously put on fezzes and ran up the Ottoman colors. (Souchon, for his part, noted in his ship's log that night, "The ships remain, self-evidently, German.")[5]

Officially neutral though Turkey remained, the signs for the Entente—and particularly for Russia—were ominous. On August 12, a series of mines were laid at the mouth of the Bosphorus and Dardanelles, and the lighthouses were closed down; all incoming ships now required permits and guidance from pilot ships.[6] Belying the pose that Souchon's warships had been neutralized, Enver and Djemal requested that the German Admiralty send state-of-the-art mines, along with a team of officers, engineers, and technicians to replace the British naval mission and revamp Ottoman shore defenses at the Bosphorus and Dardanelles. Souchon gladly forwarded this request to

---

* Contrary to a claim widely parroted in the Turkish press, the ships were not paid for in full. The Ottoman government was still on the hook for two years of quarterly payments averaging £846,400 each on the *Reshadieh*, with the last quarterly payment falling due in June 1916. Still, millions had been raised—including a payment of £1.25 million in December 1913 and a final installment of £700,000, just days before Churchill's requisition.

Tirpitz, who agreed to send a special *Sonderkommando* headed by the formidable Admiral Guido von Usedom, consisting of naval officers, artillerists, engineers, torpedo and mine-laying experts, and hundreds of trained German cadets, along with mines, minesweepers, torpedoes, and other technical equipment. The first *Sonderkommando* detachment left for Constantinople as early as August 18.[7]

It seemed that the Germans had won a great diplomatic victory, with Ottoman belligerence sure to follow. On August 17, after news of the "transfer" of the ships into Ottoman service had reached London, Churchill proposed to the War Cabinet, "in his most bellicose mood," that Admiral Milne's squadron be authorized to send "a torpedo flotilla thro' the Dardanelles to threaten and if necessary to sink the *Goeben* and her consort."* But opinion in the cabinet was sharply opposed to this proposal, owing partly to concerns about the possible effect on Muslim opinion in Egypt and India, but also because of its source: many blamed Churchill for angering Turkey in the first place by commandeering her dreadnoughts.[8] Russian foreign minister Sazonov, for his part, had already authorized Admiral Andrei Eberhart, commander of Russia's Black Sea Fleet, to "pursue all measures in his power to prevent [the *Goeben* and *Breslau*] from entering the Black Sea and to annihilate them, even if this means we must violate Turkish territorial waters."[9] Now that Souchon had command of two "Turkish" warships with the apparent connivance of the Ottoman government, it seemed there was nothing that could stop him from carrying the world war into the Black Sea against Russia, just as he had vowed to do.

Said Halim Pasha, however, was not about to let Souchon force Turkey into the war before she was ready. Although he could no longer win concessions out of Wangenheim over the *Goeben*'s safe arrival, he could still lever Souchon over permission to operate in the Black Sea. It was not only Souchon who was raring to go. General Liman had already begun negotiations with Enver over the idea of landing Ottoman troops on Russia's Black Sea coast

---

* Somewhat incongruously, after his proposal was rejected, Churchill proposed to Grey that the British government offer Turkey compensation of £1,000 for every day the *Sultan Osman I* was impounded—provided, of course, that she expel from her territory every "last German officer and man belonging to the 'Goeben' and 'Breslau.'"

near Odessa, to threaten the flank of Russia's Eighth Army, just entering the final throes of its mobilization against Austria-Hungary in East Galicia. Tirpitz, at the Admiralty, proposed to the Ottoman military attaché in Berlin, Cemil Bey, that Souchon could steam off into the Black Sea to shell Russian targets, with other Ottoman warships firing rounds in the air in a kind of fake protest at his departure from the Bosphorus. Catching the spirit, Kaiser Wilhelm II wrote to Wangenheim on August 18 that absolutely "any [form] of Ottoman action is welcome."[10] But Said Halim Pasha was firm, informing Souchon on August 17, 1914, by way of Wangenheim, that no sorties would be permitted, in any form.[11]

Frustration in the German camp was mounting. Wangenheim had all but signed away the store to Turkey in the August 2, 1914, alliance treaty and in his concessions-under-blackmail on August 6, getting nothing in return other than tacit agreement to let the *Goeben* and *Breslau* enter the Dardanelles—only for them to be impounded by the Ottomans in the Bosphorus and forbidden from further action. So far from declaring war on Russia, Said Halim Pasha and Enver had been quietly courting her instead, seeing what terms St. Petersburg might give Turkey to stay out of the war. Djavid Bey, the Francophile (and Anglophile, although the British embassy, because of Fitzmaurice, didn't know this) Ottoman minister of finance, visited all three of the Entente ambassadors at their summer houses in Therapia (Tarabya) in mid-August to see what bribes they might offer for Ottoman neutrality. Even Djemal succeeded in charming Britain's ambassador, Sir Louis Mallet, who reported to Grey on August 20 that an agreement to keep Turkey out of the war might be possible.[12] On August 19, Said Halim Pasha's strongest argument for Turkey staying neutral was voided when the grand vizier signed a "treaty of alliance and friendship" with Bulgaria—yet there was still no declaration of war. Little wonder General Liman, infuriated by Ottoman duplicity, was overheard saying he would challenge Enver and Djemal to duels. Before it came to that, Liman, whose relations with Ambassador Wangenheim were cool (Wangenheim had snubbed him by refusing to meet him at Sirkeci station when he arrived in Turkey the previous December), wrote directly to Kaiser Wilhelm II on August 19, requesting that he and his fellow officers in the German Reform Mission be allowed to return to Germany.[13]

It is easy to sympathize with Liman's exasperation, even if his threat to resign was probably hollow. Out of one side of his mouth, Enver was asking that Tirpitz send Turkey hundreds of naval experts and specialist equipment to shore up her fleet and shore defenses, and feeding Wangenheim with happy talk about imminent Ottoman intervention, which, he promised on August 19, would shortly be followed by "a pan-Islamic revolution" in French North Africa, the Russian Caucasus, British Egypt, and India. Out of the other side of his mouth, Enver told Wangenheim the very next day that, despite signing a treaty with Sofia, the time was still not ripe for Turkey to enter the war: the war minister even threatened to demobilize the Ottoman army if the Germans kept pressuring him to intervene. Enver knew exactly what he was doing. Islamic holy war against Germany's enemies had been a pet idea of Kaiser Wilhelm II ever since he had proclaimed himself the "friend for all time" of the Muslim world before the tomb of Saladin in Damascus in 1898. "Hajji" Wilhelm was never going to let Liman leave his post, much less fight a duel with the Ottoman war minister. "I expect cooperation with Enver," Kaiser Wilhelm II admonished the head of the German Reform Mission, "to whom you are to convey my full trust and to pass on my greetings."[14]

Liman was not the only German driven crazy by Turkish delaying tactics. Admiral Souchon, after evading enemy pursuit from one end of the Mediterranean to the other, was hardly content to sit by and wait on events. Had he wanted to do that, he would have holed up with the Austrians at Pola, rather than running the British gauntlet. Colorful as its naval history was in premodern galley warfare—most famously in the Ottoman siege of Constantinople in 1453, when Mehmet the Conqueror had ships carried overland from the Bosphorus to the Golden Horn to outflank the Byzantine naval boom—the Ottoman capital was not the place for an enormous dreadnought, displacing 23,000 tons, to stage maneuvers. Bottled up in the Bosphorus at Istinye (site of today's new U.S. consulate), Souchon could not test his leaking boilers, fire his guns, or keep his men sharp. To maintain morale, he did drop anchor one day below the Russian embassy, whereupon his "officers and men lined the deck . . . all solemnly removed their fezzes and put on German caps." The band then played "Deutschland über Alles" and "Die Wacht am Rhein," with the German sailors "singing loudly to the accompaniment," before putting their fezzes back on.[15]

Taunting the Russians must have helped soothe Souchon's nerves a little. But he had not risked his skin in a mad dash for the Dardanelles in order to make jokes. On the twenty-fifth, Admiral Usedom pulled into Sirkeci station, accompanied by fifteen naval officers and nearly three hundred naval artillerists, the bulk of whom were sent down to the Dardanelles to work on the shore batteries. The first week of September, another four hundred Germans arrived in Constantinople to join Usedom's *Sonderkommando*. Not unnaturally, Moltke, at the German high command, believed that the diversion of seven hundred skilled men from the main European fronts, at a time of heavy fighting, would be sufficient evidence of good faith on the Germans' part to get Turkey to live up to its alliance obligations. The great Battle of Tannenberg, when Samsonov's Russian Second Army was destroyed in East Prussia, was engaged and won August 26–30, even as the Austro-Hungarian armies were reeling under the Russian offensive in Galicia (Lemberg/Lvov fell on September 2) and German armies in the West were marching southwest toward Paris after the bloody Battle of the Frontiers, each successive day bringing them nearer the limits of their endurance. As the German chief of staff reminded Wangenheim and Liman with a hint of understatement on September 4, 1914, even as the Franco-British defenders were regrouping east of Paris for what might be the decisive battle of the war, it would be "desirable" for the Ottoman Empire to stage a diversionary strike soon, whether by landing troops on Russia's Black Sea coast or threatening British Egypt at Suez. Three days later, with the Battle of the Marne under way, Chancellor Bethmann Hollweg exhorted Wangenheim to impress upon the Turks the urgency of "exploit[ing] every possibility to break the resistance of England." To this end, the ambassador was authorized to offer Enver all the "weapons and ammunition" he requested for a Suez offensive.[16]

Smelling desperation at the German high command, Enver and Said Halim Pasha decided it was time to put the squeeze on yet again. On Tuesday, September 8, 1914, the Ottoman war minister lodged a request with Wangenheim that the Germans send him "at least 6 rapid-firing field batteries with adequate munition," ideally 105 mm howitzers, with 8,000 shells each. Hans

Humann, the German naval attaché who was Enver's principal confidant, requested that Berlin front some 1.35 million Turkish pounds (about $8 million, or some $800 million in today's terms) to finance a Suez operation.[17] Enver moreover hinted that the Germans could ignore the grand vizier's conciliatory stance toward the Entente, as Said Halim Pasha was "no longer in charge of the situation." This would have come as news to the grand vizier, who immediately upstaged the war minister by publicly announcing the abolition of all remaining Capitulations enjoyed by the European powers (including Germany), encompassing everything from trade concessions and legal immunities to the right to collect customs and tolls. Wangenheim had, in theory, agreed to accept this back on August 6, but that was under duress, when Souchon had been trapped at Brindisi. When he heard Said Halim Pasha's latest surprise, the German ambassador was so angry that he threatened, Liman-style, to leave Constantinople. Although Wangenheim backed down from this threat, he did team up with the other European ambassadors—including those representing countries with whom Germany was at war—to issue a joint communiqué to the Sublime Porte protesting the move. But of course the Germans could do little but go along.[18]

In Enver's case, at least, it was not only opportunism that lay behind his demands. While his own preference was for the Suez operation favored by the German high command—for which he had requested the 105 mm howitzers— the Ottoman war minister also realized that putting it together would take far too long for it to affect the climactic Battle of the Marne on the western front by diverting away British strength. The eastern front, closer to Constantinople, was another matter. Simply letting Souchon operate in the Black Sea could put a scare into the Russians, and possibly tip neutrals like Romania and Bulgaria toward the Central Powers—and it would cost the Ottomans nothing. Quietly, and apparently without the knowledge of either Djemal or the other ministers, Enver told Souchon at some point over the weekend of September 12–13 that he could exit the Bosphorus for training maneuvers in the Black Sea. Souchon got straight to work, preparing to stage his first serious maneuvers in over a month on Tuesday, September 15. But on Monday, Djemal, catching wind of Souchon's preparations, issued a direct order forbidding the German admiral from leaving the Bosphorus, in rather sharp tones, saying that doing so would constitute a "political act" and therefore required full Ottoman cabinet authorization. Souchon was enraged at Djemal's "shameless" veto over his freedom of action, which contradicted Enver's verbal orders. The Ottoman war minister, he wrote in his log that night with a note of defiance, "was fully in understanding with my plans for Black Sea exercises, and they *will* take place."[19]

Behind the scenes, a battle royal was shaping up inside the Ottoman cabinet, and the Committee of Union and Progress more generally, over Souchon. Inside the committee, a German spy reported on Tuesday, September 15, Enver's pro-German stance had an overall majority, but the minority against included not only Djavid Bey, the finance minister, but influential senior figures like Dr. Nazım, Şakir Bachreddin, and Bedri Bey, the chief of the Ottoman police in the capital.[20] On Wednesday, September 16, some kind of confrontation took place in the cabinet, at which Enver's case for unleashing Souchon was shot down (if Enver indeed made this case; the record is unclear).[21] At any rate, Enver himself told Souchon during a naval review before the sultan at Pendik on Thursday, September 17, that permission for his German warships to operate in the Black Sea was "withdrawn until further notice."[22]

Souchon was not, however, a man easily discouraged. On Friday, September 18, the German admiral went ashore and personally berated Said Halim Pasha for the "faithless and indecisive behavior" of the Ottoman government. If the Sublime Porte did not give him permission to operate in the Black Sea, Souchon threatened to take matters into his own hands and "behave as dictated by the conscience of a military officer." Said Halim Pasha, no less stubborn in his own way than Souchon, refused to buckle. And so the admiral went back to Enver on Saturday morning, demanding that, if not the *Goeben*, then at least his consort, the *Breslau* (he refused to call it by its new name, *Midilli*), and several Ottoman destroyers, be permitted to stage practice exercises near the mouth of the Bosphorus—ostensibly remaining near Ottoman territorial waters so as not to alarm the Russians, but in fact with the intention of engaging Russian vessels if they encountered them. Enver promised to do what he could.[23]

That afternoon, the central committee of the CUP, forty-nine strong, convened to discuss Souchon's status, and the question of war and peace more generally. The political lines remained roughly the same as they had all month, with Enver speaking for the war party, opposed by Djavid Bey and senior figures such as Dr. Nazım, who wanted to disarm the German warships and demobilize the Ottoman army as a conciliatory gesture to the Entente (Djavid also noted that the government had run out of money to pay its soldiers). This time, though, Enver had prepared an ambush, instructing his supporters, who constituted a strong majority, to shout down Djavid and force a quick vote on demobilization, which the finance minister lost. Enver then convened a Ministerial Council with the grand vizier Saturday night, at which he revealed a new political weapon: Abbas Hilmi II, the khedive and thus nominal ruler of Egypt (under the British aegis), who had conveniently been summering on the Bosphorus when the world war broke out, far from Cairo and thus outside Britain's control. The khedive read out a fiery speech, vowing to do everything in his power to help the Ottoman Empire "liberate" Egypt from its English occupiers. Although the grand vizier still wanted to avoid provoking Britain near the Egyptian border, he did quietly authorize Enver to order troop concentrations to proceed in Sivas and Erzurum, facing the Russian front, and agreed that Souchon's ships should be allowed access to the Black Sea for training, so long as it was for "non-belligerent purposes." And so it came about that on Sunday, September 20, 1914, the *Breslau* finally entered the Black Sea, if only for a few hours (the *Goeben* remained anchored in the Bosphorus).[24]

The grand vizier was playing a subtle game. On Monday, the French and Russian ambassadors, Maurice Bompard and M. N. Girs, called on Said Halim Pasha to protest Souchon's small Sunday Black Sea sortie as a violation of Ottoman neutrality. The grand vizier's response was clever. Noting the absence of Britain's ambassador, Sir Louis Mallet (which may have been only accidental), Said Halim Pasha told Bompard and Girs that "the Germans are independent and can do what they like. If [the *Goeben* and *Breslau*] are here, it is not our fault. You should ask the English why they let them come here." Although implicitly confessing here that the "sale" of the ships to the Ottoman Empire was phony, Said Halim Pasha had also established a kind of plausible deniability for Souchon's actions, while shifting French and Russian animus toward their ally's naval incompetence, which had put them in this pickle. To confuse everyone still further, the grand vizier consented to a one-year appointment for Souchon as a vice admiral in the Ottoman navy, ostensibly a kind of independent status as head of a naval reform mission, akin to Liman's army commission. But when Souchon was formally invested with his new rank by Naval Minister Djemal on Thursday, September 24, he was required to swear an oath not to involve Turkish ships in belligerent action without proper authorization from the Ottoman high command. Entente observers trying to divine Souchon's real operational status, and Turkish intentions at the Sublime Porte, must have been spinning in circles. Even when apparently backed into a corner by the bellicosity of Enver and Souchon, the grand vizier had a way of turning things around to his own—and Turkey's—advantage.[25]

With German war matériel pouring into Sirkeci station every day, with Souchon staging his first maneuvers in the Black Sea—maneuvers closely observed by the Russian fleet—it seemed to Bompard and Girs that it was only a matter of days before Turkey took the plunge into war.[26] The prospect of Ottoman belligerence was by no means entirely unwelcome to Russia or her French ally. Back on August 11, the day after Souchon had arrived in the Sea of Marmara, Gaston Doumergue, a former French premier, had told Russia's ambassador to France, Alexander Izvolsky, that any diplomatic promises made to guarantee Ottoman territory in order to keep Turkey out of the war "need not disturb [Russia's claim] on the Straits at the end of the war."[27] Ambassador Girs, for his part, suggested to Sazonov as early as July 27 that Russia could even "take the initiative herself" against Turkey (although this was before the Goeben had arrived, ending in one fell stroke Russian naval dominance of the Black Sea and rendering all but impossible a Russian amphibious landing at the Bosphorus). When Girs reported the first rumors that Souchon was going to be allowed to exit the Bosphorus in late August, A. V. Krivoshein, the powerful Russian minister of agriculture, remarked to the British ambassador to Russia, Sir George Buchanan, that he "personally would be glad if the Turks declared war on Russia, as then the Turkish question would be finally settled." After his frustrating encounter with the grand vizier, Girs himself started talking openly about "settling accounts" with the Turks.[28]

The German position, however, was weaker than it appeared. The Entente victory at the Marne had destroyed any chance Germany had of winning the war quickly. On the eastern front, meanwhile, the beleaguered Austro-Hungarian army had already lost 350,000 men, with the Russians carrying all before them in Austrian Galicia, pushing the Habsburg armies back 150 miles along a broad front. In St. Petersburg, a program of annexation was being hashed out for Austrian Galicia and Prussian Posen and Silesia, in its way just as ambitious as the notorious September Programme to seize Belgium, Antwerp, and the Longwy-Briey iron-ore fields of northern France being worked out simultaneously in Berlin.[29] As Cemil Bey, the Ottoman military attaché in Berlin, reported to Enver on September 24, 1914, the same day Souchon was made a vice admiral of the Ottoman navy, "Originally [German] calls for our participation stemmed from their wish to find an ally. Now they feel the need for our support in the light of ever-increasing difficulties. They put more hope in us than in Romania or Bulgaria."[30] The asking price for Ottoman belligerence was going up.

Back in London, unaware of how much difficulty the Germans were having with the Turks, Churchill was losing patience. Since Souchon's arrival, a naval standoff had developed parallel to the diplomatic one, with a British squadron patrolling Besika Bay near the mouth of the Dardanelles, unable to come in owing to Ottoman hostility and unable to fire on the shore batteries owing to Ottoman neutrality. Admiral Limpus, marooned on the wrong side of the standoff in Constantinople, wrote to Churchill on August 26, 1914, that while he was striving awkwardly to maintain a posture of neutrality in the capital, Ottoman belligerence might not be the worst thing. If Turkey came in, he advised, the Royal Navy could easily "foment Arabian and Persian Gulf troubles" against her, while encouraging Greek amphibious operations "between Smyrna and the Dardanelles." If the Turkish defenses "on the Gallipoli peninsula" were knocked out, Limpus promised, it would "annihilate the remaining power of Turkey."[31]

Five days after Churchill received this bellicose advice, the Admiralty and

War Office began drawing up operational plans in case the Ottomans entered the war. By cabinet vote on September 2, Britain's Mediterranean squadron was given authorization to fire on Turkish vessels exiting the Straits if they were accompanying the *Goeben* or *Breslau*. Churchill, proactive as always, took this further on his own initiative. On Friday, September 25, the First Lord of the Admiralty authorized the new Mediterranean squadron commander, Admiral Sackville Carden (Milne had been recalled in disgrace following the debacle with the *Goeben*), to use his own discretion as to whether to allow Turkish warships to leave the Dardanelles.* On Sunday, September 27, Carden stopped a Turkish torpedo boat and ordered it to turn back. Enver, hearing the news, ordered Admiral Usedom, in charge of the Straits defenses, to close the passage to *all* vessels, laying mines, steel cable, and antisubmarine nets across the mouth of the Dardanelles. It was an act of war in all but name, which cut off Russia's only year-round, warm-water access to world markets at a time— unlike in 1912, when this had been done the first time—when she was at war.[32]

Souchon, Usedom, and the Germans had been demanding the closure of the Dardanelles to foreign ships for weeks. Finally, it seemed, Enver had delivered on his promises. And yet still no declaration of war came from the Sublime Porte. The ambiguous Ottoman posture was infuriating not only to the Germans but also to Churchill, who was angling for a fight at the Dardanelles but had no support in the cabinet for declaring war. But the larger-than-life war minister, Field Marshal Horatio Kitchener, whose outsized reputation as the "Conqueror of Khartoum" meant that other members of the War Cabinet were afraid to oppose his word, remained adamant that the initiative must be left to Turkey to start the war, so as not to antagonize Britain's millions of Muslim subjects in Egypt and India.[33]

In St. Petersburg, meanwhile, it was now expected, following Souchon's appointment as an Ottoman vice admiral on September 24, that the *Goeben* and *Breslau* would shortly strike at Russian positions in the Black Sea. But the Russians, no less than Kitchener, wanted to carefully manage Turkey's *terms*

---

* Churchill's own preference was to give the squadron command to Admiral Limpus, head of the British naval mission to the Ottoman Empire, who knew the Dardanelles defenses intimately (and possessed, as we have just seen, the requisite bellicosity of spirit). He was overruled in the War Cabinet, however, on the grounds that a Limpus appointment "from inside" would be seen in Constantinople as yet another Churchillian provocation.

of entry into the war (Russia had millions of Muslim subjects to worry about, too, from the Crimea and the Caucasus to Central Asia). The Sublime Porte would demand every last concession out of Berlin before going in. Russia and Britain, for their part, had to let the Ottomans take the initiative, so as to begin the war in the most favorable political conditions possible. For this reason, Ambassador Girs informed Sazonov in early October, Russia should welcome Souchon's upcoming "sneak attack," which would give Russia a *casus belli* to "liquidate the Straits question once and for all."[34]

Girs had good reason to suspect by this point that the Ottoman decision for war had already been made. With paid informants attending Ottoman cabinet meetings, the Russian ambassador was arguably the best-informed man in Constantinople. As early as October 4, 1914, Girs reported to St. Petersburg that Djemal, the naval minister, had been won over to the war party, joining Enver, Interior Minister Talât, and Halil Bey, Speaker of the Ottoman Chamber of Deputies.[35] Said Halim Pasha still claimed, publicly, to be aloof from the war party, but his opposition was far less firm than Djavid Bey's—in fact, it was the supposedly neutral grand vizier who had candidly and confidently told Girs's informant, on October 2, that Souchon would "annihilate Russia's fleet."[36] All that the Turks needed to take the plunge, Girs informed Sazonov, was the German gold expected as part of her terms of entry.[37]

Girs was on the money, as indeed the Germans would have to be if they wanted Turkey to declare war on Russia. The Turkish army had been mobilized for two months, draining the Ottoman treasury nearly dry. Even the officers, Enver told his friend Captain Humann on October 3, 1914, were on half pay. Moreover, the call-up of nearly half a million soldiers in August had disrupted the late summer harvest and wreaked havoc with the economy. There was simply no way, Enver impressed upon the Germans, that the empire could fight a Great Power war without full-on German subvention of its costs.[38]

In a sense, the idea of German material support for the Ottoman war effort had been implicit in the August 1914 alliance treaty itself, and in the dispatch of officers and equipment to Constantinople in September. Arthur Zimmermann, the undersecretary of state at the German Foreign Office, had even proposed a straight cash-for-belligerence deal as early as September 10, only for the Germans to balk over Ottoman delaying tactics. On October 1, Mahmud Muhtar, the Ottoman ambassador in Berlin, formally requested a loan of 5 million Turkish pounds, the equivalent of $25 million or some $2.5 billion today. The German Foreign Office was not opposed to the idea, but Zimmermann and State Secretary Gottlieb von Jagow insisted, sensibly, that any loan deal come with an ironclad guarantee of Ottoman belligerence. This Mahmud Muhtar could not yet give. Nevertheless, Zimmermann and Jagow demanded that Deutsche Bank get together the funds necessary, in gold. Critically, the funds would be deposited directly in the Ottoman grand vizierate, so as to bypass Djavid Bey and the Finance Ministry (the Germans, like Girs, were already confident that Said Halim Pasha's studied posture of neutrality was just for show).[39] Showing how serious the Germans were, Jagow informed Wangenheim that the five million Turkish pounds was only the upfront offer for securing Ottoman belligerence: once Turkey was in the war, Berlin was prepared to loan her as much as one hundred million.[40]

With Berlin authorizing the dispatch of German gold to subvene Turkey's war effort on October 1, 1914, the countdown to war had begun. As early as Thursday evening, October 8, Enver and Talât promised Wangenheim that Souchon would soon be granted permission for a "sneak attack" on Russia's naval forces in the Black Sea, prior to a declaration of war and possibly as early as Sunday, October 11. Although the German ambassador had misgivings himself about the wisdom of a "premature" Turkish attack in the Black Sea, the idea was received ecstatically in Berlin by Jagow and Bethmann. So on Sunday morning, October 11, 1914, Wangenheim invited Enver, Djemal, Talât, and Halil over for a breakfast meeting. Enver assured the ambassador that he now had an unshakable majority on the committee. Still, before unleashing Souchon, he insisted that the first two payments of one million Turkish pounds be physically present in Constantinople. This ruled out an attack on Monday. But Enver's proposed terms of entry for the Germans were, this time, explicit, including not only a promise that Souchon be allowed to strike, but that the Ottoman army would begin preparing for immediate offensives against British Egypt and the Russians in the Caucasus. Finally, as soon as Russia took Souchon's bait and declared war on Turkey, "His Majesty

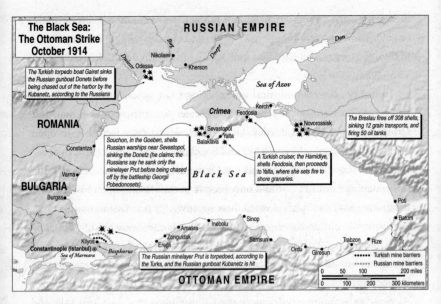

The Black Sea: The Ottoman Strike October 1914

RUSSIAN EMPIRE

The Turkish torpedo boat Gairet sinks the Russian gunboat Donets before being chased out of the harbor by the Kubanetz, according to the Russians

The Breslau fires off 308 shells, sinking 12 grain transports, and firing 50 oil tanks

Souchon, in the Goeben, shells Russian warships near Sevastopol, sinking the Donetz (he claims; the Russians say he sank only the minelayer Prut before being chased off by the battleship Georgii Pobedonosets).

A Turkish cruiser, the Hamidiye, shells Feodosia, then proceeds to Yalta, where she sets fire to shore granaries.

The Russian minelayer Prut is torpedoed, according to the Turks, and the Russian gunboat Kubanetz is hit

OTTOMAN EMPIRE

•••••• Turkish mine barriers
•••••• Russian mine barriers

the Sultan will declare holy war against the enemies of Germany, Austria-Hungary, and the Ottoman Empire." Just in case the Germans had any doubts that Enver was serious, the grand vizier—who, to maintain his useful reputation for neutrality, had not attended the breakfast—quietly reassured them on Monday, October 12, by way of Austria-Hungary's ambassador, Johann Markgraf von Pallavicini, that he did not really object to a surprise naval attack on Russia.[41]

A strange waiting game now began. The first shipment of one million pounds in gold arrived, via rail, in Sirkeci station on Friday, October 16. Once report of its safe receipt reached Berlin, the Germans sent off another installment on Saturday. As soon as the second shipment arrived, Ambassador Girs reported to Sazonov on Monday, October 19, Souchon would be authorized to strike. On Tuesday, Sazonov sent a top secret wire to Russian naval command at Sevastopol to expect Souchon's attack imminently. On Wednesday, October 21—the day the second German gold shipment arrived—Admiral Ketlinskii, from Sevastopol, wired back to Sazonov that the Black Sea Fleet was "completely ready." To ensure the maximum political effect inside Russia and on neutral countries, all of Russia's naval and port officers along the Black Sea littoral were given special instructions not to fire first if and when they might be engaged by Ottoman warships. In one final message sent on Sunday, October 25, Girs informed Sazonov that Souchon would exit the Bosphorus on Thursday, October 29.[42]

In fact the German admiral was working more quickly than this. Enver had given Souchon and his fellow officers sealed orders (in both German and Ottoman Turkish) on Saturday, October 24, which they were not to open until the fleet was in the Black Sea and Souchon received telegraphic instructions from the Ottoman Admiralty at Okmeidan to do so. Theoretically, the "Ottoman vice admiral" would only receive permission to open his orders if the grand vizier and cabinet voted their approval. (If permission was granted, they were then to destroy these orders as soon as they were read.)[43] On Sunday, October 25, Enver told the German naval attaché, Captain Humann, that he did not yet have Ottoman cabinet approval—but he added that it was fine if Souchon, on his own authority, "might serve up a fait accompli for them." As Souchon mischievously interpreted Enver's orders, "So I will take the whole [Ottoman] fleet into the Black Sea as soon as possible for exercises. If I were to encounter the Russian fleet, or a good portion thereof, in favorable conditions, then I would not, so to speak, prevent the cannons from going off by themselves."[44]

On Tuesday, October 27—two days in advance of Girs's prediction—Souchon steamed out of the Bosphorus in the dreadnought formerly known as *Goeben*, accompanied by the cruiser formerly known as *Breslau* and a number of lesser Ottoman warships. Ostensibly it was a simple training exercise, although the Russians, like the Germans and Turks, knew this was a cover story. Adding one final twist of Ottoman duplicity to the drama, Enver never did wire Souchon as to whether or not he was to open his sealed orders (which contained a list of Russian naval targets). And so the "Ottoman vice admiral" was left to his own devices. Just as he had vowed to do back in August, Souchon took the war into the Black Sea, with or without Turkish permission. Toward midnight on October 28, 1914, Ottoman warships opened fire on the Russian minelayer *Prut* and a gunboat, the *Kubanetz*, near the outer approaches to the Bosphorus (so Ottoman and German sources claim; the Russians insist more credibly that the *Prut* was torpedoed the following day along the Crimean coast, near Kherson, and that the *Kubanetz* was attacked in port at Odessa). The *Goeben*, accompanied by several Turkish destroyers, steamed for Sevastopol, while the *Breslau* made for Novorossisk. In the early morning hours of Friday, October 29, Souchon scored hits on five Russian warships near Sevastopol and Kerch, sinking the *Donetz* (he claims; the Russians say he sank only the minelayer *Prut*, though with 710 mines aboard, before being chased off by the battleship *Georgii Pobedonosets*). A Turkish cruiser, the *Hamidiye*, shelled Feodosia, then proceeded to Yalta, where she set fire to shore granaries. The *Breslau* fired off 308 shells at Novorossisk, sinking about a dozen grain transports, and setting fifty oil tanks ablaze. According to Russian sources, the Turkish torpedo boat *Gairet* sank the gunboat *Donetz* at Odessa before being chased out of the harbor by the *Kubanetz*. The action on October 29 was clearly substantial, although the strategic impact of Souchon's attack was less than he had hoped, with only one Russian warship and a minelayer sunk outright (though a half dozen other warships sustained damage, some from running over new mines laid by the *Breslau*).[45]

Confusing the diplomatic picture was the fact that no declaration of war had been issued. Was Souchon, then, acting as a free agent on Germany's behalf, or had he been authorized by the Sublime Porte (or by rogue elements in the Ottoman government, meaning Enver)? In a sense, both things were true, and neither. Enver's orders *had* specified Russian shore targets, but these had not been cleared with the cabinet (nor did Enver himself give final authorization for the orders to be opened). The fact was that not even Souchon himself knew whether he had Turkish support for the attacks. To the Germans' consternation, the early signals coming from the Ottoman cabinet suggested that the grand vizier might try to disown Souchon rather than declare war. Even now, with two million pounds of German gold in hand, with an unambiguous act of war committed against Russia by an "Ottoman vice admiral" in command of the Turkish fleet, the grand vizier was stalling for time. Improbably, the Ottoman government published a communiqué on Saturday, October 30, claiming that *Russia* had fired first in the Black Sea and protesting formally to the Russian Imperial Government. This was too much for Ambassador Girs, who asked Said Halim Pasha for his passports, but was told to wait until the cabinet met. Enver, cunningly, went along with the grand vizier's new propaganda line, filing an official report on the engagements of October 28–29 which claimed that the Russian minelayer *Prut*, guided by officers who had served on the Russian ambassadorial yacht and so knew the channel intimately, had been laying mines outside the Bosphorus to bottle in the Ottoman fleet: so all Souchon had done was stage a breakout into the open sea after being unjustly fired upon by the Russians. Considering that six different Russian ports on the other side of the Black Sea had been shelled by at least half a dozen Ottoman warships, Enver's story was evidently nonsense, but it had just enough resemblance to the truth (Souchon had indeed sunk the *Prut*, although almost certainly nowhere near the Bosphorus) to give the attack some diplomatic cover.[46]

On Sunday, October 31, 1914, the CUP convened its twenty-seven most senior officials to discuss the attacks. Now that war was truly imminent, Enver's supposedly crushing pro-interventionist majority softened to about 17–10. The grand vizier and Djavid Bey, joined by the ministers of trade, labor, and the postal service, all threatened to resign in protest at Souchon's action. To soothe tempers, Said Halim Pasha suggested that a note of apology be delivered to the Russian government. When the Germans got wind of this, Captain Humann was deputized to warn his friend Enver that Germany could easily sign a separate peace with St. Petersburg on the basis of partitioning Turkey. Enver, to reassure the Germans, inserted a phrase in the Ottoman "apology," handed over to Girs on November 1, 1914, expressing regret for the "hostile act, provoked by the Russian fleet."[47]

By this point in the "will she or won't she?" drama over Ottoman belligerence, an honest man would have had a hard time stomaching the duplicity at the Sublime Porte. Entente bribe offers to keep Turkey out of the war had been shown to be insincere when the European ambassadors protested the abolition of the Capitulations in September—though no more insincere than Wangenheim's ultimately rescinded promise to accept their abolition, granted under duress back in August. Britain, protesting every warlike act committed by Souchon or Enver, was nonetheless blockading the Dardanelles, no less an act of war by any reasonable definition than the sealing off of the waterway by the Turks. Russia's ambassador, Girs, had spent weeks rehearsing his "shocked, shocked!" response to the attack he had repeatedly warned Sazonov and the Black Sea Fleet command was soon coming. Said Halim Pasha was a model of pacifism when meeting with the British, French, and Russian ambassadors, and itching to "annihilate Russia's fleet" when speaking to the Germans and Austrians. Enver, a useful battering ram for the subtler grand vizier, kept dangling Ottoman belligerence before the Germans only to snatch it away at the last minute—even after they had paid the money he said was required to bring Turkey into the war.

Buried deep in these layers of deception and duplicity was a very simple truth. The war was going to happen, because nearly everyone in a position to influence events wanted it to. So little did the diplomatic niceties over Souchon's attack concern the British government that Churchill, on Sunday, October 31, wired all ships of His Majesty's Royal Navy (including Admiral Carden's Mediterranean squadron) to "commence hostilities at once against Turkey."[48] Sazonov, receiving Enver's cynical "apology," replied with equal cynicism that Russia would accept it, provided that Enver immediately expel from Turkish soil every last member of the German military missions in Turkey—by now numbering about 2,000 men. Russia's foreign minister knew perfectly well that Enver could not do this, as indeed Enver informed Girs he would not. On November 2, 1914, Tsar Nicholas II informed his subjects in an official proclamation, "with complete serenity," that Russia "takes on this new enemy, this ancient oppressor of the Christian faith and of all Slavic nations."[49]

As for Ottoman leaders, despite all the gnashing of teeth rumored to be taking place in the committee and cabinet, the war was finally accepted as Turkey's unavoidable fate, or *kismet*. Said Halim Pasha, slippery to the end, had only been bluffing about resigning over Souchon's attack: not only did he *not* resign, but he signed off on Enver's fraudulent apology to Russia, knowing perfectly well how the Russians would receive it. Djavid Bey alone, in the end, had offered serious resistance in the cabinet, mooting a proposal, during the November 1 cabinet meeting, to expel the German military mission—the only gesture, he knew, which might avert war. But the motion was swatted down by Enver and Djemal on the grounds that "the armed forces could not function without German specialists." Djavid's desire for peace was genuine, but even so, he waited until November 5 to resign from the government—four days too late to make any difference.[50] In the end, the Ottoman government was no less "serene" than the tsar in its decision to go to war. On November 10, 1914, Sultan Mehmed Reshad V declared war on Russia and her French and British allies (along with Belgium, Serbia, and Montenegro). Four days later, the *Sheikh-ul-Islam*, Ürgüplü Hayri Efendi, presented the sultan with the Sword of the Prophet at Fatih mosque to sanctify the conflict as an "Islamic holy war," or jihad, against the Entente powers. The fate of the Ottoman Empire, stretching from Europe to the Caucasus, the Black Sea to the Persian Gulf, would be settled by the clash of arms.

CHAPTER 7

BASRA, SARIKAMIŞ, AND SUEZ

Success [in battle] does not come from the appearance or kit of the soldiers,
but from valor and brave hearts.

—ENVER PASHA,
Ottoman war minister and acting commander in chief
of the Ottoman Third Army, to his men on December 20, 1914[1]

THE ONSET OF HOSTILITIES in November 1914 found the Ottoman Empire fully mobilized, but woefully unprepared for a Great Power conflict. The campaign plan of April 1914 had been partially updated after the European War broke out in August by Enver and his German chief of staff, Bronsart von Schellendorf, but it still bore the imprint of the "last war." Fully seven of twelve Ottoman army corps were concentrated in European Thrace and along the Asian coast of the Sea of Marmara and the Aegean, as if Turkey was preparing to fight a Third Balkan War against Greece (as indeed she had been doing until the July crisis). Only three corps were mobilized on the Caucasian frontier against Russia, and just two in Syria/Palestine facing British Egypt—despite the fact that Germany had demanded immediate offensives on both fronts as part of the terms for Turkey's entry into the war. Making early offensives still more problematic, all but one of the twelve Ottoman army corps were at less than full strength after the losses of 1911–13. The IX, X, and XI Corps, facing Russia, lacked everything from officers and men to rifles, rounds, artillery and shells, uniforms, horses, wagons, and oxcarts.

In Mesopotamia (modern Iraq), shortages were more serious still. Pursuant to the two planned offensives demanded by the Germans, the Ottoman

General Staff had pulled back its two main Mesopotamian army corps. The XII Corps, garrisoned at Mosul, was now sent to Syria to join in the planned assault on the Suez Canal, while XIII Corps, based in Baghdad, was sent to Erzurum to help spearhead the planned offensive against Russia. Left behind to guard Mesopotamia was a token Turkish force of 160 lightly armed men on Abadan island, 350 men (and four 87 mm cannons) in the fortress on the al-Fao peninsula (which housed a critical telegraph station), and a strategic reserve at Basra, sixty-nine miles upstream from the Persian Gulf, consisting of 4,700 riflemen, 18 field guns, and 3 machine-gun batteries.[2]

Considering that London had been a strategic partner of sorts until her occupation of Egypt in 1882, the lack of a serious Ottoman defense plan for Mesopotamia against the British threat was understandable. But it was still a critical oversight. Someone at the Ottoman high command—Enver, Bronsart, or Liman—should have known better than to trust Britain's public posture of desperation to keep the Ottomans out of the war.* For in fact the Royal Navy, with nearly uncontested control of the eastern Mediterranean, the Aegean, the Indian Ocean, the Persian Gulf, and the Red Sea, was perfectly positioned and well prepared for war with Turkey from the day it broke out—indeed before war was formally declared. Churchill, as we have seen, issued orders as early as October 31, 1914, for his naval commanders to commence hostilities against Turkey. Wasting no time, two British destroyers "destroyed a large Turkish yacht" entering the Gulf of Smyrna (Izmir) on November 1—four days before war was declared. On November 3, still two days prior to a British declaration of war, Churchill recalled matter-of-factly in *World Crisis*, Admiral Carden, commanding the Mediterranean squadron blockading the Dardanelles since September, "shelled the batteries on the European side at Sedd[ul] Bahr and Cape Helles" from long range (13,000 yards), even while French battleships "fired at the Asiatic batteries at Kum Kal[e] and Or[h]anie."[3]

Nowhere were Churchill's orders received with more alacrity than at the head of the Persian Gulf, where a small British riverine armada of armored

---

* As Churchill wrote to Sir Edward Grey on September 23, 1914, even before the incident that led the Ottomans to close the Dardanelles, "We are suffering very seriously from Turkish hostility . . . I am not suggesting that we should take aggressive action against Turkey or declare war on her ourselves, but we ought from now on to make arrangements with the Balkan states . . . without regard to the interests or integrity of Turkey."

sloops, river tugs, paddle steamers, and amphibious landing craft was assembling at the mouth of the Shatt-al-Arab delta guarding the approaches to Basra and southern Mesopotamia. A substantial British-Indian expeditionary force already lay in wait nearby at Bahrain, undergoing a crash course in "rowing, handling boats, and rehearsing landing operations." The very existence of this amphibious force, dispatched from Bombay on October 16 (the first troops landed at Bahrain on October 23, 1914), has much to tell us about British intentions toward Turkey prior to the outbreak of war.* The Anglo-Persian Oil Company (forerunner of today's BP) owned oil wells in "Arabistan," on the Persian side of the border, along with pipelines connecting the wellheads to the refinery on Abadan island (under nominal Ottoman suzerainty). Under Churchill's direction, the Royal Navy had begun transitioning from coal to faster, oil-fired engines in 1912, and the Abadan refinery had been expressly built to service it. Controlling the oil fields of Arabistan, the pipelines criss-crossed the border, and Abadan was therefore a strategic priority of the first order for London—and for Churchill.[4]

Token Turkish garrisons notwithstanding, the entire Gulf region, including southern Mesopotamia, was already part of the British Empire in all but name. Britain had secured navigation rights on Mesopotamia's rivers from the Sublime Porte as early as 1846. In 1903, then–Foreign Secretary Henry Petty-Fitzmaurice (better known as Lord Lansdowne) had announced "a sort of Monroe Doctrine for the Persian Gulf," declaring that encroachment by any other Power would be regarded as a "grave menace."[5] The waters of the Shatt-al-Arab delta, into which flow the shallow waters of the Tigris, Euphrates, and Karun Rivers before they reach the Gulf, were regularly patrolled by the Royal Navy in peacetime in order to protect the Indian trading dhows that serviced Basra (October–November, when the war was breaking out, was high season—when dates, the principal Mesopotamian export, were loaded). Farther upstream, British commercial paddle steamers plied the Euphrates and Tigris Rivers between Basra and Baghdad. The British consul general at Baghdad was something of an imperial proconsul already, overseeing most of

---

* The men had been told they were en route for France. But the commander, Brigadier General Walter Delamain, had been given sealed orders in Bombay ordering him to land at Bahrain instead.

the Shia pilgrim traffic from the Indian subcontinent and its funds (the salaries of the Shia grand mufti and his fellow clerics in holy Karbala were paid by the British consulate in Baghdad). Britain's consul general had a special swift "armed shallow draught yacht," the aptly named HMS *Comet*, for cruising the Tigris and Euphrates, which mounted ancient—but operational—Nordenfelt guns. The bridge of the *Comet* was surrounded by "light hardened steel armour," which accorded it protection from Bedouin snipers. This impressive vessel accorded Britain's consul far more prestige than was enjoyed by the Ottoman valis (governors) of the vilayets of Baghdad and Basra. Most of the Arab tribes received British protection, and the major local sheikhs, like the chieftain of Kuwait, a strategic port town near the mouth of the Shatt-al-Arab, were all on the imperial payroll.[6]

Until 1914, nominal Ottoman suzerainty over areas like southern Mesopotamia—and Egypt—had been a convenient and useful fiction for the Raj in Delhi. With upward of a hundred million potentially unruly Muslim subjects already in the Indian subcontinent, it did not behoove their British masters to remind them of the superiority they enjoyed elsewhere in the Islamic world. In this sense, the holy war proclaimed by the Ottoman sultan-caliph against the Entente powers was like calling Britain's bluff. For how could the perfidious English pretend to be friendly to Muslim interests when they were carving up the last remaining Islamic empire, province by province? The Foreign Office played along perfectly when, in December 1914, it declared Egypt a protectorate—thirty-two years after Britain had occupied it.

In southern Mesopotamia, the transfer of sovereignty following the outbreak of war between Turkey and Britain was just as rapid, although less bloodless. Following the removal of the two corps from the Ottoman Sixth Army in Mesopotamia, the Turkish garrison at Basra, commanded by Süleyman Askeri Bey, comprising the better part of the Thirty-Eighth Ottoman Infantry Division, was a bit under 5,000 strong (British intelligence overestimated it at 8,000), buttressed by the smaller forces downstream at Abadan and at al-Fao. The Turks did have a riverine gunboat, the *Marmaris*, displacing 420 tons, and four British-built Thornycroft motor patrol boats, capable of making ten or eleven knots. Against this, the British deployed an armada spearheaded by the armored sloops HMS *Espiègle* and *Odin*, each crewed by

120 men and displacing 1,070 tons, alongside the "armed screw" paddle steamers HMS *Dalhousie* and *Lawrence* and smaller armed tugs: HMS *Mashona, Miner, Lewis Pelly, Sirdar-i-Naphte, Carmsir* and *Shaitan* (Turkish for "devil"). Crowning the British Persian Gulf squadron was the pre-dreadnought battleship HMS *Ocean*, used to transport troops into the Gulf (although, with its heavy seagoing draft, it could not follow all the way up the Shatt-al-Arab, much less into the shallow waters of the Tigris and Euphrates), and HMS *Comet*, the consul's swift armored yacht, which (in another hint of Britain's intentions) had come down from Baghdad earlier in October, before the outbreak of war would have trapped her there. The expeditionary force from the Indian Army, commanded by Lieutenant General Sir A. A. Barrett, amounted to an entire division—the Sixth, or Poona, consisting of three full brigades, including the Sixteenth under General Walter Delamain. With the regional order of battle this lopsided in British favor, the outcome could not have been in doubt. Such, at any rate, was the conclusion of the sheikh of Kuwait, who sent over a white flag as early as November 4, 1914, offering his loyalty to Britain and thereby ensuring Kuwait's future as an "independent" kingdom.[7]

Nevertheless, the Turks put up a good fight. Realizing that his small fleet was outgunned, Süleyman Askeri Bey had commandeered a German merchant liner of the Hamburg Amerika Line, the *Ekbatana*, filled her with sand, and sunk her to block the Shatt-al-Arab waterway at the approaches to Basra. German and Turkish naval crews were rushed downstream from Baghdad to reinforce the crew of a German battle cruiser, SMS *Emden*, in case she broke through the British Gulf screen and made it to Basra. The *Emden*, with 4.1-inch guns, outranged even the largest sloops in the British squadron, and so she could have played a decisive role defending Basra. While Süleyman Askeri Bey's motor launches were speedy enough to get supplies to the men at al-Fao and Abadan before the British assault began, the longed-for *Emden* never arrived (pursued into the Indian Ocean by five fast British cruisers— including HMS *Gloucester*, which had bravely fired on the *Goeben* and *Breslau* in August—the *Emden* was finally scuttled on November 9, 1914, to avoid capture).[8]

The overmatched Ottoman fortress garrisons thus found themselves largely isolated when the main British assault began. At al-Fao, defended by only 350 Turks with four cannons, HMS *Odin* led the assault, opening fire from 5,500 yards just past 10:00 a.m. on November 6, 1914, before closing in to about a third this distance. The *Odin* did suffer "heavy rifle fire" from shore, but this petered out after less than an hour. By 11:00 a.m., British marines had landed ashore without opposition. At 2:00 p.m., they had secured the telegraph station. The Turks, having evacuated and taken their wounded with them, were nowhere to be seen. By the end of the day, six hundred British and Indian soldiers were onshore, including sappers and miners. The Union Jack flew above the fortress of al-Fao.

Resistance was fiercer at Abadan. Despite their smaller numbers, 160 lightly armed Turks defended this highly strategic position with ferocity. Süleyman Askeri Bey had ordered his men to dig trenches behind mud walls, camouflaged cleverly among the scrub and reeds of the riverbank. Just past noon on November 6, 1914, the Turks surprised HMS *Espiègle* as she approached Abadan with bursts of concealed rifle fire, scoring twenty or thirty hits on her hull and underworks, though failing to sink her. The British sloop returned fire with its 4-inch guns and several Maxim machine guns, only for most of the shells and bullets to strike without effect in the mud. Captain Wilfrid Nunn, commanding the *Espiègle*, then maneuvered into a position where he could hit the entrenched Turks with enfilading fire. He fired a shell into a small house that he had seen a dozen Turkish soldiers enter for refuge, and blanketed the mud shore trenches with shrapnel until at last no more fire was returned by the enemy. Some forty-six Turks were killed in this initial engagement, and it appeared the battle was won. But, although British marines were able to secure the Abadan refinery, the defenders regrouped inside the island's police station, guarded by a mud fort. A seesaw battle raged on for another three days, with the Turks holding out under siege.

Süleyman Askeri Bey now surprised the British invaders. From Basra, the Ottoman commander sent down reinforcements along both sides of the river, with the main detachment of about three hundred Turks and Arabs, under Sami Bey, pitching camp at a point opposite Mahommerah, on the Persian side of the border, which the British were using as a rear base and anchorage. Sami Bey ordered his men forward on November 10, and they made it within fifty yards of the British perimeter before they were pitched back by murderous fire, losing eighty men. Upriver, fierce fighting continued along the Shatt-al-Arab as the British sloops advanced. Süleyman Askeri Bey prepared to make a stand at the mud fort of Sahil, which, nearly five hundred yards from the western bank of the river, offered some strategic depth against an amphibious landing and the British riverine artillery. Some, but not enough. After British guns had found the range to pound the fort, marines waded ashore on November 17 and assaulted Sahil. The Ottomans were then routed in a confusing and bloody engagement, suffering some 800 casualties. British losses were heavy, too, with 4 officers and 50 men killed (21 British and 29 Indian), plus 17 officers and 414 men wounded. So far, the British forces had proved unstoppable, but it had been a heavy slog all the way.[9]

In Basra, the ongoing campaign downstream in the Shatt-al-Arab had been followed with a mixture of curiosity and trepidation. Subhi Bey, the Ottoman vali, had interned the British residents as a precautionary measure, including the consul. A volunteer with the American Red Cross Mission reported "grave rumors of a threatened massacre of Christians," but such a massacre never transpired (and the English prisoners appear to have been well treated). The rapidity of the British advance up the delta impressed the local Arabs, who had no compunction about switching sides once the mounting influx of wounded Turks and Arabs showed which way the battle was going. Although General Barrett was himself unsure how things stood owing to Britain's own heavy losses at the battle of Sahil, by November 20 news had reached him that the Turkish defenders (including not only Süleyman Askeri Bey but Subhi Bey, the vali, and his advisers) had fled from Basra, after freeing the British prisoners. Still, the British riverine fleet proceeded gingerly into town, slowed down by the presence of several scuttled vessels, including the German *Ekbatana*, which had nearly—but not quite—blocked the Shatt-al-Arab, and by the fear of enemy sniper fire from shore. Not until two days later were the British able to land safely in force and secure the town. On the afternoon of November 23, Captain Nunn of the *Espiègle* recalled,

General Sir A. Barrett made a ceremonial entry into the town at the head of the troops . . . the foreign consuls and notables were presented to the General by Mr. Bullard, who had recently been our Consul there, and a proclamation prepared by Sir Percy Cox in Arabic was then read by him on behalf of the G.O.C., and the Union Jack was hoisted on a flag-staff on a conspicuous house on the western side, and near the entrance of the Ashar creek. H.M.S. ESPIÈGLE firing a salute of thirty-one guns, the troops presenting arms, and three cheers given for the King.[10]

The fall of Basra was a serious blow for the Ottomans. The import trade of this prosperous city of sixty thousand, and the customs revenue that accrued from it, would now benefit the British Raj instead of the Ottoman sultan. Still, the lower Mesopotamian campaign was not over yet. Süleyman Askeri Bey, Subhi Bey, and what remained of the Ottoman Thirty-Eighth Division—several thousand strong—had fallen back to Qurna, another forty miles up the Shatt-al-Arab, at an angle in the river where the Tigris and Euphrates first meet. One of the traditional sites believed to be the model for the biblical Garden of Eden, Qurna was smaller than Basra—home to only two thousand people in 1914, and a small customhouse—but more strategic in its siting. Qurna marked the navigable limit for medium-draft vessels such as the British sloops (which drew about twelve feet) before they entered the Tigris and Euphrates, where the depth was usually under ten feet, often as low as four feet and, at certain points in the dry summer months, even shallower than this. Once Qurna was in British hands, the entire Shatt-al-Arab delta would be more or less secure (except for the odd Bedouin raid), and the Indian Army could safely load war matériel for any further push upriver toward Baghdad.

Seizing Qurna would not be easy, however. The Shatt-al-Arab grew shallower past Basra, and some of the British sloops began to run aground on the approach. Because the river bottom was mostly mud, running aground was not necessarily fatal for sloops, but it did leave them vulnerable to enemy fire as long as they were stuck. The retreating Turks had sunk yet another vessel, a small steel lighter, in a shallow area, to complicate passage. HMS *Odin* had its rudder disabled by the sunken ship, and had to be withdrawn from action. Shallower-draft tugs, like the portentously named HMS *Shaitan*, now joined

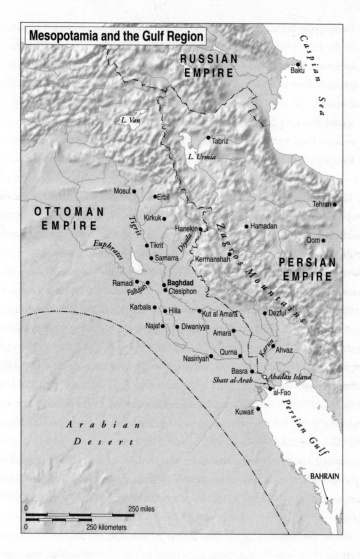

Mesopotamia and the Gulf Region

RUSSIAN EMPIRE

Caspian Sea

Baku

L. Van

Tabriz

L. Urmia

Mosul

Erbil

OTTOMAN EMPIRE

Tehran

Kirkuk

Hanekin

Hamadan

Tigris

Euphrates

Tikrit

Samarra

Diyala

Zagros Mountains

Kermanshah

Qom

PERSIAN EMPIRE

Ramadi

Fallujah

Baghdad

Ctesiphon

Karbala

Hilla

Kut al Amara

Dezful

Najaf

Diwaniyya

Amara

Karun

Nasiriyah

Qurna

Ahvaz

Basra

Shatt al-Arab

Abadan Island

al-Fao

Kuwait

Persian Gulf

Arabian Desert

BAHRAIN

0   250 miles

0   250 kilometers

the battle. On December 3, 1914, the first serious British probe of Qurna's defenses began, with troops landed ashore south of the city even as the main naval assault continued. Two small creeks, it was discovered, guarded Qurna, and the Turks had dug trenches among the date palms, from which they rained rifle fire down on the attackers. On the river, the Ottoman guns mercilessly pounded the British tugs, nearly sinking the flagship sloop, HMS *Espiègle*, and HMS *Miner*, which both ran to ground, escaping downstream only when high tide came on the evening of December 4. The probe had been costly: a British and an Indian officer killed along with three British soldiers and nineteen sepoys, with another sixty Indian troops wounded.[11]

After pausing for several days to regroup, the British began the main assault on December 7, 1914. This time, the sloops and tugs braved heavy fire to advance past Qurna into the Tigris, in order to land troops in the enemy's rear. The *Shaitan* "received a direct hit on the bridge," which killed her captain and wounded two other officers—but she did not sink. Risking another grounding, Commander Nunn once more threw HMS *Espiègle* into action, practically "dragging her through the mud" to offer covering fire for the landing troops. All afternoon, heavy fighting proceeded among the palm groves on the western bank of the Tigris (Qurna was on the eastern side), before word came in to the *Espiègle* at dusk that the main Ottoman force had fled north. This time, the report proved premature, as shellfire continued to pour down on the British sloops all night. On the morning of December 8, three Indian soldiers finally succeeded in crossing to the eastern side of the Tigris, securing the beach and allowing seventy marines to land that afternoon. At last, the British were able to outflank Qurna and "enfilade the northern defense." Just before midnight, a deputation of Turks came across to negotiate terms for Qurna's surrender—guaranteed by Subhi Bey, the Basra vali (Süleyman Askeri Bey, with a handful of top officers, had fled north aboard the *Marmaris*, whose smoke was seen upriver on the Tigris). In all, 45 Ottoman officers and 989 troops turned in their arms, which included Krupp guns and "a large quantity of rifles and ammunition." At 2:30 p.m. on December 9, 1914, the Union Jack was raised above Qurna.[12]

With the strategic outposts of Basra and Qurna, indeed the entire Shatt-al-Arab waterway, falling to Britain in the first month of the war, it seemed that Enver had paid a heavy price for privileging the Caucasian and Suez offensives. Still, there was a sense of the inevitable about the campaign. Even had the Ottoman XII and XIII Corps been left behind in Mesopotamia, they were both understrength and garrisoned much too far away—the former at Mosul and the latter at Baghdad—to affect the outcome in the Shatt-al-Arab, which the British had won mainly by virtue of naval superiority. So swift was the British victory that only a radically different deployment plan, such as the sending of XIII Corps down the Tigris from Baghdad before the war's outbreak, could really have made a difference. Baghdad, terminus of the (still uncompleted) railway from Berlin, was another story—but then, owing to the difficulty of pilotage on the Tigris and Euphrates, it was probably defensible even now, so long as Enver sent reinforcements to Mesopotamia in reasonable time. As it was, Süleyman Askeri Bey had done his bit, sinking two more steel lighters to block the Tigris above Qurna. The scuttled *Ekbatana*, too, continued to slow down British steamers delivering war matériel into Basra, until, months later, it had finally sunk far enough down into the mud to allow relatively free passage.[13]

Enver was, moreover, hardly alone in underestimating the importance of Abadan and the Shatt-al-Arab. The Germans, who initially hoped to gain control of the oil refinery themselves, dispatched a special team led by Captain Fritz Klein south from Baghdad in January 1915. Klein's highly skilled team of German officers, accompanied by two Turkish infantry regiments, was able to sabotage multiple stretches of the pipeline totaling twelve miles in all, depriving the Royal Navy of some 70 million gallons of oil before the damage was repaired in June. But Klein's small Turco-German force, although it remarkably evaded capture, failed utterly to threaten British control of the Gulf—not surprising, considering that the British already had 12,000 troops there.[14] In a more general sense, the Germans were responsible for the ordering of Ottoman priorities, as Berlin had demanded immediate offensives against Russia and Britain in exchange for fronting the money and gold which was to pay for Turkey's war. The Germans could hardly blame Enver for doing precisely what they had asked him to do.

There remains a certain air of mystery about Enver's Caucasian offensive of December 1914, because it so egregiously violated common sense. Even granted Enver's need to "please" the Germans by sending reinforcements to the Russian front, the timing, at the onset of winter, could not have been worse. It was one thing to push through a pass into a great lowland plain, like the Russians had done at Shipka in 1877–78 before racing along the Thracian flats to San Stefano. But in eastern Turkey, even the valley towns—such as

Erzurum, where the Ottoman Third Army was garrisoned—were 2,000 meters (nearly 7,000 feet) above sea level, whereas the mountains rose above 3,500 meters (12,000 feet). By December, the snows typically lay two meters deep in the *valleys*, and twice as deep in the mountains. Temperatures often dropped to minus 20 or 30 degrees Celsius (minus 4 to 22 degrees Fahrenheit). The frontline areas facing Russia were above the tree line, meaning no forest cover for attackers, nor wood to cook food or warm soldiers by campfires. All this was in addition to the woeful material state of the Third Army, which, Commander Hassan Izzet reported on November 29, 1914, was short 17,000 overcoats, 17,400 pairs of boots, 23,000 blankets, and 13,000 knapsacks.[15]

Against these unfavorable conditions for an offensive, Enver could reckon on some early tactical successes in the Caucasian theater. Belying their own posture of aggrieved shock at Souchon's naval attack, the Russians had launched an offensive against Turkey on November 2, 1914, the very day war was declared (or, according to some reports, even the day before), with a brigade commanded by General Bergmann crossing the Ottoman frontier south of Oltu, toward the Ottoman town of Hasankale, at the junction of the main road from Sarıkamış toward Erzurum. Bergmann's objective was to envelop Ottoman forces along the Sarıkamış-Erzurum road with I Caucasian Corps, commanded by General A. Z. Myshlayevskii. Taking personal charge of the battle, Hassan Izzet led a counterattack from the heights above Hasankale, driving Bergmann's brigade southeast to join Myshlayevskii east of Köprüköy, where the lines stabilized—with no Ottoman units enveloped. Farther north, a Russian offensive along the Black Sea coast from Batum was repulsed, with the aid of Ajari (Muslim Georgian) irregulars armed by the Ottomans. True, the new front at Köprüköy was twenty-five kilometers (fifteen miles) inside Turkey's frontier, but even so, Russian attacks had been firmly repelled, lending credence to Enver's belief that the Ottomans were capable of a successful offensive.[16]

On the Caucasian frontier, there was also an element of grand strategy involved, which appealed to Enver. Although sometimes dismissed as romantic "pan-Turkism"—the idea of a union of Turkic peoples stretching from Anatolia to Central Asia and Afghanistan—Enver's real objectives were more prosaic, although no less significant. At this civilizational fault line between the Muslim and Christian Orthodox worlds, the stakes of any war were high because of the minority populations behind the shifting front lines. Long before the Russo-Ottoman war was made official on November 2, 1914, covert agents from both sides had been fanning the flames of ethno-religious conflict in eastern Turkey and the Caucasus. Mostly, the Ottomans stirred up unrest among Caucasian Muslim groups—Tatars, Chechens, Circassians, Daghestanis, Avars, Ajaris, and Azeris. But there were Christians too: Germany, aside from promoting the idea of Ottoman Islamic holy war, had been cultivating Georgian resentment of Russia for years, and had agents on the ground in Tiflis. Enver himself had played a powerful role in developing the notorious Ottoman Special Organization (*Teşkilat-ı Mahsusa*) in charge of recruiting Caucasian Muslims into guerrilla units that could harass the Russians—as the Ajaris had done in November 1914 at Batum. The Ottoman high command even had a pet name for these volunteers: *Tavuk-Civciv* (loosely, "chicken-chicks"), the idea being that each "chicken" should hatch another fifty chicks ("chickens" and "eggs" also being operational code-speak for arms and ammunition).[17]

The Russians were playing the same dangerous game with Ottoman minorities. During the First Balkan War, Foreign Minister Sazonov had instructed Russian consuls in eastern Turkey to unify the querulous Kurds against the Ottoman government, winning a pledge of loyalty to the tsar from three major tribal leaders. Sheikh Mahmud, whose Kurds roamed northern Mesopotamia, had promised to put fifty thousand men under arms on Russia's behalf.[18] Lieutenant General Nikolai Yudenich, chief of staff of Russia's Caucasian Army in Tiflis, was arming Armenian volunteers on the Russian side of the Turkish border as early as August–September 1914, long before war was declared. By December 1914, no fewer than four Armenian volunteer battalions (*druzhiny*) had been formed to help augment Russia's frontline detachments, especially engaged in surveillance of Turkish troop movements.[19] On the Turkish side of the border, Russia's consul at Erzurum, A. A. Adamov, reported on November 1, 1914, as he was leaving Turkey on the outbreak of war, that Armenian partisan groups in Erzurum, Erzincan, Sivas, Mana

Hatun, and Kayseri had "hidden their weapons in secret storage caches" and were waiting anxiously for Russia's armies to arrive, so they could open them.[20]

Setting aside, for the moment, the politically explosive nature of these covert activities on either side of the Russo-Ottoman Caucasian border, there was a sense in which their very ubiquity began to influence strategic thinking. Without the hope that sedition behind Ottoman lines would break out, it is hard to see why Russia's Tiflis command risked an offensive in the first week of November 1914, with snows already beginning to fall, despite being understrength itself owing to the dispatch of two of three Caucasian Army corps to the European fronts against Germany and Austria-Hungary. I Corps, the only one left behind, was at best 150,000 strong, and that was only if one counted Cossack and Armenian volunteer *druzhiny* alongside the proper infantry force of 100,000 backed by 15,000 cavalry: superior to the Ottoman Third Army with its 75,000 regulars and 37,000 irregulars, but not decisively so. The Russians did have 256 guns, as against 168 in the Ottoman Third Army, but very few of these were brought up in the November 1914 offensive. Operating well inside Ottoman territory, along vulnerable supply lines, the Russians were lucky not to be routed.[21]

Enver should, that is, have had every reason for caution in December 1914, German demands for an early Caucasian offensive to relieve Russian pressure on Austrian Galicia notwithstanding. But caution was not in Enver's nature. Chided, in a notorious conversation on December 6, 1914, by Liman von Sanders—the German thought the idea of a winter offensive in the Caucasian mountains foolish—Enver replied that, once the Russians were beaten, he "contemplated marching through Afghanistan to India." This was just bombast, but even so, there is no denying Enver's boldness: he left the capital for Erzurum, accompanied by his German friend Bronsart von Schellendorf as chief of staff. Preceding them by several days was another member of Enver's Harbiye staff, the thirty-six-year-old Colonel Hafız Hakkı Bey, who was seen as more reliable than Hassan Izzet, who had already expressed doubts about the wisdom of a winter offensive. On December 19, Enver sacked Hassan Izzet and took over the Third Army command himself. Just as at Adrianople, Enver wanted to personally spearhead the reconquest of lost provinces, in this case Ardahan and Kars, seized by the Russians in the 1877 war.

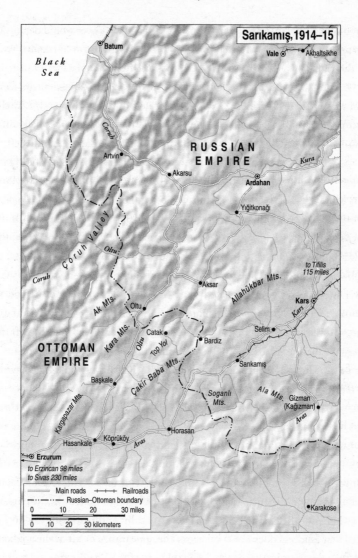

Enver's operational plan was simple—or at least, it would have been had it been carried out over flatlands in summer, rather than through mountain snows in high winter. Clearly influenced by the successful German Cannae-style envelopment of Samsonov's Russian Second Army at Tannenberg, the plan bore all the hallmarks of German thinking, probably by way of Bronsart and Major Felix Guse, the Third Army's chief of staff. Enver would deploy XI Corps, the weakest of his three corps, south of the Erzurum-Sarıkamış road on the right, in order to "pin" the Caucasian I Corps in place at Köprüköy, as IX and X Corps, on the left, pitched north and enveloped them from behind. On the extreme left, a special new detachment commanded by the German major Stange would attempt to isolate the Russian forces defending Batum, while securing the Çoruh Valley and seizing Ardahan. On the left, X Corps, led by Enver's trusted young commander Hafız Hakkı Bey, would race along the main road from Hasankale to seize Oltu, held only by a single Russian brigade (about eight thousand troops) under General Istomin, before pivoting eastward to cut off the Kars road east of Sarıkamış. In the middle, IX Corps would march along the reasonably flat elevated ridge (Top Yol) of the Çakir Baba Mountains toward Catak and Bardiz. Top Yol was exposed to high winds, but Enver hoped that this meant the snow cover would be shallower (and he reckoned, correctly, that the Russians would not defend it, although they did have an Armenian *druzhiny* watching it). Finally, IX and X Corps would seize Sarıkamış, the latter from behind, thereby cutting off the Russians' main road and railway communications from Kars: the Russians' I Caucasian Corps at Köprüköy, pinned down by XI Corps, would then have to surrender. The attack would begin on December 22. The Turks hoped to reach Sarıkamış by Christmas Day, not least because they carried only three days of supplies.

Enver was not unaware of the difficulties his men would face, nor that they were less than perfectly equipped for a serious winter campaign. After inspecting the assembled troops of the Third Army on December 20, 1914, he noted serious "deficiencies which would be difficult to remedy in the current situation." But he insisted, in a characteristically optimistic address to his men, that "success does not come from the appearance or kit of the soldiers, but from valor and brave hearts." The soldiers of the Third Army, he continued, should feel comforted (and warmed) by "the souls of your ancestors" buried on the Russian side of the border as they moved forward into the Caucasus. Above all, Enver told his men to remember that "God is always with you" as they carried out their historic mission to "rescue our brothers, who are waiting for us, from Russian oppression."[22]

Enver's great Caucasian offensive began reasonably well. The weather, to begin with, was mild by Caucasian standards, with no snow falling and decent visibility. On the morning of the second day, December 23, X Corps reached Oltu and quickly forced Istomin to retreat toward Ardahan, abandoning four guns. The IX Corps mastered the Top Yol (although its movement across it was reported to the Russian command by the Armenian observational *druzhiny*) and reached Bardiz on Christmas Eve. Stange's special detachment raced up the Çoruh Valley, wheeled east, and seized Ardahan on December 27, with Istomin's brigade cut off between Oltu and Ardahan, pursued from the south by Hafız Hakkı Bey (a mistake, in that this pursuit delayed X Corps from joining IX Corps at Bardiz). Thus far the Russians had done nothing but retreat. Only on the right wing was there resistance—and yet ironically not *enough* resistance: XI Corps failed to pin down the Russians at Köprüköy as planned. At noon on December 24, 1914, General Myshlayevskii ordered I Caucasian Corps to pull back from Köprüköy toward Sarıkamış, before himself getting shot during the retreat (though he survived the bullet wound).

On Christmas Day, the first advance units of Ottoman IX Corps reached the outskirts of Sarıkamış. But the mercury was now falling dramatically, and the troops were ill-equipped to deal with subzero temperatures: the men of IX Corps had actually been told to leave their greatcoats behind to lighten their burden as they marched across the frigid ridge of Top Yol. Moreover, X Corps was lagging behind, owing to Hafız Hakkı Bey's foolhardy pursuit of Istomin, which had not only wasted time (the bulk of X Corps reached Bardiz only on December 26) but increased his distance of march on Sarıkamış to nearly 75 kilometers (47 miles).* To make up time, X Corps had to scale the dangerous Allahükbar peaks at 3,000 meters (10,000 feet), piling simple exhaustion onto the perils of frostbite faced by its soldiers. So many men had already perished en route that Hafız Hakkı Bey issued an order for his officers to "collect rifles of the martyrs and wounded soldiers in order to remedy the deficiencies of other men."[23] Realizing that his soldiers were at the limit of

---

* The Turks may also have suffered from a kind of self-imposed "mirage" effect, in that their maps consistently underestimated the distances between mountain passes and towns, such that officers (and men listening to their exhortations) kept being unpleasantly surprised at not yet arriving at their next destination.

their endurance, Enver ordered IX Corps to wait for the arrival of its final division (the Seventeenth, which had straggled badly in the rear on Top Yol) before the attack on Sarıkamış began on December 27. Two days later, elements of X Corps joined the assault, which pitted 18,000 Turks against about 14,000 Russians. Advance units of X Corps raced up the road toward Kars, seizing the town of Selim and cutting off, temporarily, the main supply route to the east. If the Turks took Sarıkamış, the Russians' I Caucasian Corps would be cut off from Tiflis headquarters, in another famous victory that would have Enver's name on it.

The Battle of Sarıkamış, which raged through the day of December 29, 1914, and on into the night, marked a critical strategic moment in the first winter of the Great War. Judging by the chatter at Tiflis command, there was real fear of a crushing Ottoman victory, which would resound through the region, delivering a crippling blow to Russian prestige. General Myshlayevskii, not unlike Samsonov at Tannenberg, thought all was lost. Wounded on the retreat from Köprüköy on December 24–25, he had returned to Tiflis for treatment. Ironically, what pushed him over the edge was an intelligence coup: a Turkish divisional chief of staff had been captured by a Cossack patrol carrying an order from Enver, which laid out the ambitions of the Ottoman offensive—on paper—in blunt and terrifying grandeur. Removed now from the front, where he might have evaluated Enver's best-case scenario against hard facts on the ground, Myshlayevskii now spread panic in his wake through Kars, Yerevan, and Tiflis. Soon the rail stations were swarming with Russian and Georgian civilians, desperate to flee the upcoming orgy of Muslim vengeance massacres sure to follow a Turkish victory. "Situation critical," Tiflis command wired to Russian military headquarters (Stavka) at Baronivichi, near Brest-Litovsk, at 3:35 p.m. on December 30: "Sarıkamış cut off. Railway in Turkish hands. Three Turkish corps operating. The population is going over to the Turks. Recommend the evacuation of Ardebil and Azerbaijan. Evacuation of Tiflis to follow at 4:00 p.m." Minutes later, Tiflis command wired again: "Ardahan taken by the Turks! Have decided to begin partial evacuation of the entire Transcaucasus." At 3:31 p.m. on January 1, 1915, Tiflis command reported to Stavka that the evacuation of Tiflis had begun as planned. It was after reading these anguished reports from Tiflis describing the collapse of the Caucasian Army that Russia's commander in chief, Grand Duke Nicholas, lodged his fateful request with Britain's military attaché, Major General Sir John Hanbury-Williams, for a British diversionary strike against the Ottoman Empire, which would lead to the Dardanelles and Gallipoli campaigns of 1915.[24]

Never has the fog of war been foggier, with such long-lasting consequences, as at Sarıkamış. The battle, waged in subzero conditions, was brutal, with the Turks raining down shells from mountain guns from the shallow cover of "stone huts" in the hills above the town, being pounded in turn by Russian heavy guns, which Enver had assured his men the enemy did not have.* With ammunition stores running low, at around 10:00 p.m. lead troops from the Ottoman Seventeenth Division made a mad rush over the bridge of Sarıkamış-Çay and broke into the town with bayonet thrusts from its western flank. Briefly, about three hundred Turks overwhelmed the barracks of the Russian 156th Regiment, from which redoubt they made a kind of last stand as the Russians blasted their own barracks with artillery, with the few Turkish survivors surrendering at daybreak. By the morning of December 30, 1914, the Turks had fallen back from the "stone huts" above Sarıkamış, having lost six thousand men in battle, and from the cold, overnight. The danger to Sarıkamış—let alone to Kars or Tiflis farther east—had thus passed nearly twelve hours *before* the Caucasian Army command panicked into ordering a general evacuation.

Meanwhile, the Ottoman X Corps, Russian panic notwithstanding, never had cut the railway from Kars. Nor had the Muslim population of formerly Ottoman Kars, Ardahan, or Sarıkamış risen up to aid the Turks. On December 30, the Russians counterattacked IX Corps on the slopes above Sarıkamış and pushed the Turks all the way back to Bardiz. The X Corps, which had stretched itself out vulnerably north and east of Sarıkamış, began to pull back on January 1, only to be attacked on the retreat by a powerful Russian cavalry group of two divisions commanded by General N. N. Baratov (oddly enough,

---

* To be fair to Enver, back on Christmas Day, when he had *intended* to seize Sarıkamış, the Russians had only two field guns and two machine guns in the town. If Myshlayevskii had had his way, the town would have been evacuated entirely. But Yudenich, perceiving the vulnerability of Turkish supply lines through Bardiz, had overruled the shaken commander and poured in reinforcements every day. By December 29, when the decisive battle took place, the Russians had 34 guns in Sarıkamış, and nearly 50 machine guns.

Baratov's attack, long delayed, had been ordered by General Myshlayevskii shortly before his nerves had broken). The IX Corps was surrounded and surrendered en masse on January 4. Most of X Corps perished in the mountain snows of Allahükbar, with only some 2,500 survivors straggling back into Hasankale. With shorter lines to retrace, XI Corps fared better, staging a fighting retreat in the Aras area. Farther north, Stange's special detachment pulled back from Ardahan into the Çoruh Valley, where it would remain into March 1915. What remained of the Third Army withdrew behind the Köprüköy lines, where the offensive had started. Enver himself fell back to Erzurum—and then bade his staff officers farewell, Napoleon-style, before rushing back to Constantinople with Bronsart on January 9, 1915, to master the news cycle (i.e., to suppress news of the disaster that had befallen his troops). Far from a morale-crushing humiliation at Turkish hands, Sarıkamış had turned into a Turkish rout.

In all the Ottoman Third Army lost, by its own estimation, 30,000 dead and 7,000 wounded at Sarıkamış, or nearly half its effective fighting force. Some estimates go higher, noting that the Russians "found 30,000 frozen bodies around Sarıkamış alone," not counting another 27,000 Turkish prisoners taken alive. One recent military historian estimates that the Ottomans lost 47,000 men, though noting that the Russians, too, lost 28,000 dead, meaning nearly half of frontline troops on both sides perished.[25] Whatever the true number, it seems clear that the vast majority of the victims probably died from frostbite, hypothermia, or other cold-related causes rather than from enemy fire (after Christmas, temperatures never rose above minus 25 Celsius and fell as low as minus 40). Illustrating the deadly conditions faced by the men of Ottoman X Corps, Hafız Hakkı Bey himself succumbed to spotted typhus in early February 1915. The failure of an ambitious envelopment of the Russian Caucasian Army, in such conditions, was no badge of shame, as Enver had noted in his farewell message to the troops: they had fought bravely against "the weather and terrain, as well as the enemy." Still, despite strict press censorship inside Turkey, in the outside world there was no disguising the magnitude of Enver's defeat. It was a catastrophe.[26]

Considering the colossal scope of the Caucasian campaign and limited Ottoman resources, it is remarkable to recall that another major offensive campaign was under way to the south, almost simultaneously. In some ways the Suez offensive was more ambitious than Sarıkamış, as the goal was not simply to conquer a strategic region and draw off enemy forces, but to cleave the British Empire in two by severing the linchpin of its global communications. Because of the canal's critical importance, there would be almost no chance of catching the British entirely by surprise, other than at the local, tactical level of exactly which portion of the canal the Ottoman forces would strike. By the time London formally declared a protectorate over Egypt on December 18, 1914, the Egyptian Expeditionary Force (EEF), under Sir John Maxwell, numbered about seventy thousand troops. Although they were not all posted at Suez, as soon as there was any hint of an enemy attack coming across the Sinai peninsula, most could be rushed to the canal in a matter of hours. The British had a railway along the western side of the canal, meaning that reinforcements could easily be rushed north and south to any danger point (sensibly, the rail line was also pitched back some six kilometers, or three and a half miles, from the canal, such that only long-range heavy guns could damage it). On the eastern side the canal was defended by the Sinai desert itself, which, though lightly patrolled by British reconnaissance units, would require a march of 160 miles across ferociously hot and near-waterless territory. Simply to reach the Suez Canal, let alone cross or hold it, would be a real logistical achievement.

The Turks, however, had grounds for optimism. The XII Corps, from Mesopotamia, added two effective divisions to the main Syrian army being formed (the Fourth) at Damascus, Aleppo, and Homs. Two full-strength divisions from Thrace (the Eighth Rodosto Division) and the Aegean coast (the Tenth Infantry Division of Smyrna) were sent all the way to Palestine to join VIII Corps in the Suez attack. The Twenty-Second Infantry Division, based in the Hejaz, was also absorbed into VIII Corps. By December 1914, the Suez striking force mustering in Palestine numbered some fifty thousand men, including irregulars, and by all reports, morale was high.[27]

The real strength of VIII Corps, though, was its chief of staff, the formidable—and wonderfully named—Lieutenant Colonel Friedrich Kress von Kressenstein. At Kress's side was a brilliant German linguist, Curt Prüfer, who helped to smooth over communications problems in an army where most

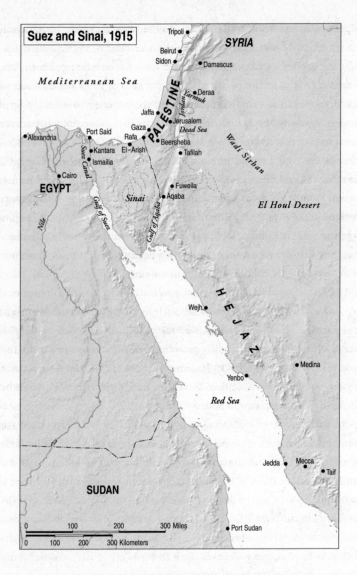

of the Turkish officers spoke neither Arabic nor German (meanwhile, the overall commander of the Fourth Army, Djemal Bey, spoke French but no German). Prüfer also put his linguistic skills to work recruiting Bedouin tribesmen, and mustering ten thousand camels for VIII Corps—a difficult and expensive business, as the British kept bidding up prices. Kress, for his part, achieved logistical wonders, turning Beersheba, at the southern tip of Palestine, into a forward supply dump, despite the lack of a rail connection from Jerusalem. Because both the northern, coastal route across Sinai and the southern route on the Red Sea littoral—the one used by Mecca pilgrims from Egypt—were in range of British naval guns, Kress sensibly chose a central desert crossing directly from Beersheba to Ismailia (over which the sand, on a limestone base, was also harder-packed and thus made for easier and safer going than the coastal routes). German sappers and engineers were sent ahead in small teams to dig wells at suitable intervals along the proposed central march route. With a better grasp of human limitations than Enver had shown at Sarıkamış, Kress stipulated that his men carry only fifteen kilograms of kit, so as not to exhaust themselves, and that they march only at night, when it was cooler (this would also help him evade aerial surveillance).

Kress and Djemal also believed they had a secret weapon at Suez, in the form of Muslim opinion in Egypt and North Africa more generally. While efforts to enlist the Egyptian khedive, Abbas Hilmi II, in the Suez campaign had run aground on mutual suspicions between him and the Young Turks (the grand vizier, Said Halim Pasha, was his cousin and a possible rival in any future Egypt), there was still good reason to believe that British rule was widely resented in Egypt and Sudan. German and Turkish agents were on the ground in Cairo, stirring up Muslim resentment of the infidel. A covert team led by Leo Frobenius was spreading terrible tales of English perfidy in the Red Sea and in Eritrea, with the aim of fomenting Islamic holy war against the British in Sudan. West of Egypt, meanwhile, the fanatical Muslims of the Sanussi order were still making trouble for the Italian occupiers, and there was hope the Germans and Turks could turn their fire against the British. Otto Mannesmann, sent to Tripoli under diplomatic cover, had been distributing holy war pamphlets ever since August 1914—using balloons to float them across the border into Egypt. The threat of a Sanussi incursion was taken seriously by the British consul general in Cairo, Milne Cheetham, along with the more general threat of a popular Muslim uprising if the Turks invaded Egypt in strength. Overestimating enemy strength, Gilbert Clayton, the head of military intelligence in Cairo, thought the Turks had an army of

100,000 in Palestine. If this was true and the Turks crossed the Suez Canal, the British were in trouble.[28]

The holy war fanfare also did much to buttress morale in the Turco-German camp as Kress prepared the ambitious Suez operation. A sacred green flag was carried in from Mecca, nearly setting off a riot when the flag bearer arrived in Jerusalem, as "every believing Muslim wanted to kiss the holy flag." A kind of holy war train then proceeded through the sacred city, bringing in its path, as Kress recalled, a mood of "indescribable jubilation and bright enthusiasm" in the "entire population." Lending credence to the holy war idea, volunteers had been enlisted from across the Muslim world: Druze from Lebanon, Kurdish cavalry units from Anatolia and Mesopotamia, Circassians from the Caucasus, and two thousand Muslim refugees from Tripoli, many of whom had fought the Italians. Djemal even brought a special company of Mevlevî whirling dervishes to Beersheba, complete with traditional conical hats (although they did not follow the army into the Sinai desert). To enhance the Islamic holy war atmosphere, those few Christians and Jews in VIII Corps were deliberately left behind at Beersheba (although Kress, Prüfer, and the German officers marched on). After the Muslim-and-German-only VIII Corps, some nineteen thousand strong, reached the oasis of Hafif el Auja, Djemal, in his resplendent Ottoman pasha's garb, walked among the men carrying the holy green banner from Mecca, enjoining each soldier to swear an oath on it. The Muslim army chaplains then read out "fiery speeches of such eloquence," Kress recalled, "that they made an impression even on the Germans, who understood not a word."[29]

Maintaining morale was no small feat, for the military odds facing VIII Corps were daunting. To reach Ismailia with sufficient striking power to win a bridgehead over the canal, VIII Corps had to carry water tanks for several long stretches between wells; two 15 cm (6-inch) howitzers for each of eight full artillery batteries, along with shells; heavy machine guns and ammunition stores; medical supplies; and not least boats and bridging materials, including heavy German steel pontoons. Thanks to Prüfer's heroics, Djemal and Kress did have twelve thousand camels to carry supplies, along with three hundred oxen and a thousand horses. But the men had to help, too, which is why everyone (except, it turned out, Djemal himself) was limited to fifteen kilograms of personal kit, which meant no portable beds to sleep on. Many of the Turkish soldiers lacked even shoes, treading the sands barefoot. Somehow, this force of nineteen thousand men and thirteen thousand pack animals, setting out from Beersheba on January 14, 1915, marching seven hours a night and resting during the hot days, reached its assembly area about ten kilometers northeast of the stretch of canal between Toussum and Serapeum on January 31. As Kress recalled the moment, "From atop a nearby sand dune we caught our first glimpse of the Suez Canal. Like a silver ribbon it wound itself through the white sand dunes, here and there widening out into a broad sea and then again disappearing from our sight."[30]

Reaching the canal in strength across the near-waterless wastes of the Sinai was a tremendous logistical achievement. And yet, despite all of Kress's precautions—avoiding the coastal routes, marching only at night—he failed to evade enemy surveillance. On the afternoon of February 2, 1915, even as Kress was making his final preparations for a nighttime assault on the canal, British military intelligence reported "a total enemy force of 19,000 and 16 guns now estimated within 4 to 12 miles from Suez Canal, extending from Kantara to Suez; additional force known to be pushing forward." In his final pre-battle communication, wired to Kitchener at 5:00 p.m. on February 2, Sir John Maxwell reported that "during the whole of today, General Wilson has been in contact with the enemy outside Ismailia. He expects to be attacked tonight and reports that the enemy are 6,000 to 8,000 strong and now entrenching." The British were ready.[31]

Tilting the odds still more heavily against Kress, a vicious sandstorm descended on the canal area that evening, forcing him to postpone his attack five hours from the original launch-time of 10:30 p.m. At 3:30 a.m. on February 3, the first column of Turkish troops began laying steel pontoons across the Suez Canal. By dawn, three of the bridging columns, amounting to about two Ottoman companies, had succeeded in crossing to the western side of the Suez Canal at Toussum and Ismailia—although it was a Pyrrhic victory, for the early morning light now exposed them to murderous British machine-gun fire. "The Turks," Maxwell reported to Kitchener on February 3, attempted to cross the canal South of Toussum during the night. They were allowed to approach and bring their bridging material right up to the bank, and a completely successful attack was delivered when it was observed that they had begun bridging operations. The Turks took to flight leaving in our hands the whole of the bridging material. Some of them were drowned and the bridging material is now being brought in. . . . 40 prisoners were captured.

At Ismailia, the Turks had a bit more luck initially, winning a defensible bridgehead by morning, but they were driven back there, too, with eight officers and 282 men taken prisoner. The shooting, one British officer put it a bit cruelly, resembled a "grouse drive."[32]

The battle was, in short, over almost as soon as it began. Gamely, the Turks held on to their western canal bridgehead at Ismailia until nearly 4:00 p.m. on February 3, even while Kress's howitzers, from the eastern bank, fired on British ships in the canal (doing serious damage to HMS *Hardinge*), along with British forts at Ferdan, Ismailia, Kantara, and Toussum. But by nightfall on February 4, Kress and Djemal had ordered a full retreat, first to the rear base ten kilometers behind the canal, and then all the way back to Beersheba and Gaza. In all, the British suffered more than 100 casualties at Suez, with 20 killed and about 90 wounded (the bulk of the losses borne by Indian soldiers).[33] Ottoman losses were much heavier, with 192 dead, 381 wounded, and 727 missing or captured (on the retreat, Djemal further lost 7,000 camels, which ruled out any new desert crossing for the near future).[34] Still, Maxwell refused to pursue the Turks across the Sinai desert, and the retreat, organized by the indomitable Kress, was conducted in good order, allowing VIII Corps to remain substantially intact as a fighting force—except for the Bedouin irregulars, who had fled as soon as the firing began. Although a clear British victory, Suez was no Sarıkamış: it was an Ottoman defeat, not a catastrophe.

Nevertheless, Suez had important strategic consequences. Concerned before the battle—as were Consul General Cheetham and Clayton at military intelligence—about the possible impact on Muslim opinion of a Turkish success, Maxwell could now crow over the crushing scale of his victory. "Reports which I have received," he wrote to Kitchener on February 18, 1915, "indicate that Turkish troops have withdrawn from the Canal and are returning to Jerusalem more or less demoralized. It is now common knowledge among the people of the country [i.e., Egypt] that the Turkish troops met with a reverse on the canal."[35] The tenor of British opinion in Cairo in the wake of Suez was captured in a letter from Aubrey Herbert to his friend and fellow Tory MP Sir Mark Sykes, in which Herbert passed on a sarcastic "intelligence" tip that "the Turks are to bring thousands of camels down to the Canal and then set a light to their hair. The camel, using its well known reasoning powers, will dash to the Canal to put the fire out . . . the Turks will [then] march over them." Back in London, Prime Minister Asquith, dripping with contempt, wrote to Venetia Stanley that "the Turks have been trying to throw a bridge across the Suez Canal & in that ingenious fashion to find a way into Egypt. The poor things & their would-be bridge were blown into smithereens, and they have retired into the desert."[36] Buoyed by their seemingly easy victories in the Shatt-al-Arab and Suez and believing the enemy to be reeling, British war planners now resolved to put an end to the Ottoman Empire, once and for all.

CHAPTER 8

DARDANELLES

The Dardanelles appeared to be the most suitable objective,
as an attack here could be made in co-operation with the Fleet. If successful,
it would re-establish communication with Russia; settle the Near Eastern question;
draw in Greece and, perhaps, Bulgaria and Roumania;
and release wheat and shipping now locked up in the Black Sea.

—FIELD MARSHAL HORATIO HERBERT KITCHENER "OF KHARTOUM,"
secretary of state for war, at British War Council held in the cabinet room in London,
January 7, 1915[1]

ON DECEMBER 30, 1914, the commander in chief of Russia's armies, Grand Duke Nicholas, summoned Britain's military attaché, Major General Sir John Hanbury-Williams, for an urgent audience at Stavka in Baranovichi. Reports were pouring in from Tiflis. The Turks, Nicholas told the Briton, had mustered an army of 100,000 and were advancing on all fronts: little wonder Tiflis command was preparing to evacuate the entire Transcaucasus. Pitching the panic high, the grand duke complained that Russia "had been forced to deprive the Caucasus of the better part of its troops to meet the common [German] threat as [desired] by our allies," thus opening the path for Enver's crushing Sarıkamış offensive. Reminding the British attaché about the fragility of civilian morale in Russia—there had been a wave of strikes in St. Petersburg in July 1914, shortly before the war's outbreak, which peaked during the week of the French presidential summit—Nicholas warned that any further losses sustained against Turkey, Russia's favorite old punching bag, could be fatal to her ability to stay in the war. And yet the "current upswing in enemy morale," he told

Hanbury-Williams, could be sharply reversed, as "there were many places in the Ottoman Empire where any force brought to bear could broadly compensate for Turkish victories in the Caucasus." As to where such force might be "brought to bear," Russia's commander in chief was unclear, but he suggested helpfully that it would be ideal if the Turks believed that "Constantinople was threatened." Laying it on thick, the grand duke at last remarked with a dose of self-pity that, if Russia's allies in France and Britain "believed differently, that the common interest was not imperiled by the Turks' exploitation of their victory in the Caucasus, then, well, so be it [*to pust' ne predprinimaiut nichego*]."[2]

In his not-so-subtle request for a British diversionary strike against the Ottoman Empire, Grand Duke Nicholas was pushing against an open door. Hanbury-Williams asked the Russian straightaway if a naval demonstration against Turkey would be helpful. The grand duke, Hanbury-Williams reported, "jumped at this idea gladly." Hanbury-Williams was then asked to expedite matters by traveling to Petrograd* in person, accompanied by Prince N. A. Kudashev, director of the diplomatic bureau at Stavka, to meet with Sazonov and Britain's ambassador, Sir George Buchanan. In this way the grand duke's passive-aggressive burbling was transformed into a full-blown strategic-diplomatic initiative, whereby Buchanan sent an urgent telegram to Sir Edward Grey on New Year's Day 1915, asking that Britain do *something* to relieve the terrible pressure Russia was facing on the Caucasian front. Grey, in turn, passed on the grand duke's apparently urgent request immediately to Kitchener and Churchill, who met on Saturday, January 2, 1915, to discuss how Britain might help. That same day, Kitchener wrote the commander of the British Expeditionary Force (BEF) in France, Sir John French, asking if troops could be spared for the Ottoman front. Learning from French that no "spare" troops were available, Kitchener then wrote back to Churchill later on Saturday that the only place in the Ottoman Empire where a "demonstration might have some effect in stopping reinforcements going East would be the Dardanelles—particularly if *as the grand duke says reports could be spread at the same time that Constantinople was threatened*."[3]

---

* As the Russian capital had been renamed after the outbreak of war with Germany: Peters*burg* being too obviously Germanic.

In the annals of inter-Allied wartime diplomacy, it is difficult to imagine communications more efficient than this. In three days, a fanciful wish-dream uttered by the Russian commander in chief at Stavka, in a far-off corner of eastern Europe, had been turned into a high-priority operational discussion in London between Britain's powerful secretary of state for war and her First Lord of the Admiralty. Of course, those same three days also saw the utter and total rout of the Turkish invaders at Sarıkamış, which fact should, presumably, have called into question the entire premise of the grand duke's request for a diversionary strike. Hanbury-Williams, in fact, reported to Kitchener the very next day (January 3, 1915) that "the position in Caucasus is at present somewhat better & the immediate danger of a bad reverse there seems to have passed." And yet it was already too late for a rethink. In much the same way newspapers often bury a retraction in the back pages after splashing the original, false story on the cover, Hanbury-Williams concluded this report by reaffirming to Kitchener that the Russians "will, I know, be much relieved if the Turkish pressure can be eased a bit."[4] And so Kitchener forged ahead with planning for a Dardanelles diversion.

Why did Kitchener jump so hard at the grand duke's request? Whether or not Russia's commander in chief knew it, not only the tone of his pitch, but also its timing, was perfect. Faced with a stalemate on the western front, where the Germans had fortified nearly impregnable elevated positions from Switzerland to the English Channel, the British War Cabinet was engaged in a vigorous and heated debate in the last week of December 1914 about where fronts might be fruitfully opened elsewhere. In his appropriately named Boxing Day Memorandum of December 28, 1914,* Maurice Hankey, secretary of the War Council, proposed that "Germany can perhaps be struck most effectively, and with the most lasting results on the peace of the world through her allies, and particularly through Turkey." Churchill, for his part, suggested, in a letter to Prime Minister Asquith on December 29 (i.e., before he learned of the grand duke's request), a Baltic diversion, to draw German strength away from the western front—although, after reading Hankey's memorandum, he,

---

* Boxing Day is the day after Christmas, when Britons traditionally passed out gifts (Christmas boxes) to the poor, which in a sense is what Hankey was proposing, to aid the "needy" Russians against the Ottomans.

too, began considering a strike against Turkey. So did Asquith, so long as whatever operation Britain came up with was "a diversion on a great & effective scale." Still, no one was clear on *where* to attack the Ottoman Empire: the chancellor of the exchequer, David Lloyd George, thought a landing in Syria, on the eastern Mediterranean littoral, would be best. It was only after receiving the bombshell from Stavka that the focus shifted to the Dardanelles. But everyone in the War Cabinet was already thinking about Turkey.[5]

Still, it remains somewhat curious that Kitchener settled on a Dardanelles operation so quickly, to the exclusion of other areas in the Ottoman Empire—not to mention the perfectly sensible option of doing nothing at all. The generals at Stavka knew as early as January 3, 1915, that the Turks were retreating from Sarıkamış. They had learned the full extent of their victory at Sarıkamış by mid-January 1915: two of three Ottoman army corps had been wiped out, and it was Enver, not the Russians, who was requesting urgent reinforcements.[6] Even setting aside the truth that the Russians were far from "needing" a diversionary strike, in a sense the British had *already* staged a diversionary strike against the Ottomans in the Shatt-al-Arab. Mesopotamia was, moreover, far closer to the Caucasus than the Dardanelles, and, with the Ottoman Sixth Army in disarray, offered the realistic prospect of joint British-Russian operations against Baghdad in the near future. By contrast, the only way Russia could participate in a Dardanelles operation, as Grand Duke Nicholas proposed in early January 1915, was by embarking a Siberian Corps from Vladivostok to the eastern Mediterranean by way of the Pacific and Indian Oceans (and the Red Sea and Suez Canal!).[7] More important still was the fact that after months of hard work by Guido von Usedom's *Sonderkommando* of naval defense specialists, the Dardanelles now constituted the single most fortified area of the Ottoman Empire. Analyzing the latest intelligence on Straits shore batteries—including in the Sea of Marmara, where the Princes Islands had been heavily fortified—the Russians had now ruled out an attack on the outer Bosphorus, though one had been seen as "more than feasible" as recently as July 1914. "The favorable moment for seizing the Straits," as Stavka concluded a study of the question in early 1915, "has been lost."[8]

Had British wartime intelligence on the Ottomans been as good as Russia's, Kitchener and Churchill would have concluded the same thing. The

Dardanelles defenses, vulnerable as recently as August 1914, were formidable by January 1915. Before Usedom arrived, the Dardanelles command had at its disposal twenty shore howitzers ranging from 15 to 28 cm (6- to 11-inch) caliber, mostly accurate only at short range, although the larger guns had an "extreme range" of 15 kilometers (9.3 miles). As the British knew, the main batteries were located at the southern tip of the Gallipoli Peninsula (Cape Helles, or Seddul Bahr, as the Turks called it) and at Kum Kale on the Asian shore opposite, with a second line of defense at the Narrows, at Kilid Bahr on the European side and the forts of Hamidiye and Chanak (Çanakkale) in Asia. What the British did not know was that Usedom and his 170 German gunnery experts had brought in heavy guns, including 355 mm (14-inch) Krupp monsters mounted south of Chanak. Many of the new mounted guns were cleverly camouflaged, while dummy batteries were erected elsewhere to draw off enemy fire. By year's end, there were enough guns that the Dardanelles (Çanakkale) command formed a third artillery battalion, to man a new "howitzer zone" behind the entry area at Kum Kale/Seddul Bahr, "responsible for the delivery of plunging fire on enemy ships." Both sides of the Straits were now blanketed with mobile gun batteries, with five on the European side and three on the Asian. Overall, by February 1915, the shore defenses consisted of 235 cannons, including 82 fixed and 230 mobile guns. On the water, eleven lines of mines—323 in all—had been laid below the Narrows, including state-of-the-art ones hauled all the way from Germany in very large courier bags (see map on p. 192).[9]

Above all, Usedom had succeeded in instilling a German-style culture of quiet discipline and confidence in the Turkish shore gunners, whose work ethic and ability to learn, in turn, impressed him. German noncommissioned officers were scattered throughout the peninsula, with at least one German serving in every Turkish gun crew. "The education of the Turkish gunners in the shore batteries," Usedom reported proudly to Kaiser Wilhelm II on December 18, 1914, has "been a great success. The last firing drills into the Straits demonstrated not only forward strides in accuracy but also in the direction of the batteries by Turkish officers, of whom a far greater number than was expected have proven themselves to be quick studies."[10] After touring the defenses in 1915, the U.S. ambassador, Henry Morgenthau, said that he had "the impression that he was in Germany . . . everywhere Germans were building buttresses with sacks of sand and in other ways strengthening the emplacements."[11]

Because those responsible for the Dardanelles campaign were later forced to defend themselves in front of an investigatory commission, we probably have more written evidence about their thinking in the debate-and-planning stage than for any battle ever fought. We can therefore assert, surprisingly but with considerable confidence, that the British Admiralty knew next to nothing of Usedom's work on the Dardanelles shore batteries as of January 1915, when the plans were set in motion. Even the vaunted "dissents" of naval gunnery experts such as Sir Henry Jackson, which were later endlessly hashed and rehashed to discredit the men behind the campaign, reflected more doctrinal skepticism about the strategic point of a naval-only campaign than any sort of accurate reckoning of the capability of the Ottoman shore batteries. "To arrive off Constantinople with depleted magazines and ships almost out of action from gun fire," Jackson wrote in a critical memorandum for Churchill on January 5, 1915, "would be a fatal error . . . even if [the Ottoman capital] surrendered, it could not be occupied and held without troops." The greatest Admiralty "skeptic" of January 1915, that is, still assumed the Dardanelles could be forced with naval power alone (if with fairly heavy losses, which might defeat its object)—he had nothing to say about mines, the caliber of the enemy guns, the positioning of shore batteries, the use of camouflage and "dummy" batteries, the deployment of mobile guns, or the intensive training the Turks had been receiving for months from Usedom's German experts. As for the even more notorious "silent" dissent of the First Sea Lord, Admiral John Arbuthnot "Jacky" Fisher ("I don't agree with one single step taken," Fisher wrote privately to Admiral Jellicoe on January 11, 1915, although he neglected to object to a Dardanelles offensive at either of the two War Councils held later that month), there is nothing in Fisher's erratic correspondence to suggest that he knew anything about the latest Ottoman dispositions at the Dardanelles.[12]

Churchill himself is the most interesting case of all. Initially cold to the entire idea of a Dardanelles campaign owing to his preference for a Baltic diversion, the mercurial First Lord of the Admiralty came over only gradually and for reasons that remain somewhat mysterious. On January 3, 1915, Churchill wired Admiral Carden, commander of the Mediterranean squadron, asking if he "consider[ed] the forcing of the Dardanelles by ships alone a practicable operation." The idea was not Churchill's, but rather that of Fisher. Fisher's rank and reputation loomed over the much younger civilian First Lord almost as menacingly as the persona of the imposing, larger-than-life "Conqueror of Khartoum," Lord Kitchener, who ruled the cabinet on army matters. Churchill had brought Fisher back as First Sea Lord at the start of the war, and had been tortured by him ever since. It seems to have been largely to show up Churchill, then attached to his Baltic scheme, that Fisher had first asked Churchill to look into "forcing" the Dardanelles back on January 3 (Kitchener, the day before, had spoken only of a "naval demonstration," combined with "reports being spread" that Constantinople was threatened). In a bind, Churchill called on Carden to resolve the dilemma. Somewhat to his surprise, Carden responded favorably on January 5, although with the caveat that he did not think the Dardanelles could be "rushed," although "they might be forced by extended operations with large number of ships." On January 11, Carden produced a four-point plan for a naval-only operation at the Dardanelles, which Churchill revealed to his colleagues at a War Council two days later, suddenly surprising everyone by embracing the idea.

Two factors seem to have tipped the balance for Churchill before the critical War Council of January 13, 1915. On January 7, the First Lord of the Admiralty learned from an intelligence report, correctly, that SMS *Goeben* had triggered two Russian mines near the Bosphorus on (appropriately for the Allies) Christmas Day and would be out of action until April. Second, Fisher, still in his gung-ho mood, had suggested on January 12 that while most of the attacking squadron would consist of older ships of the line, Britain's new super-dreadnought, the *Queen Elizabeth*, en route to Gibraltar for gun trials, could test out her new 15-inch (38 cm) guns in Turkey instead. As Churchill put it at the War Council, *Queen Elizabeth* could "conduct her trials against the Dardanelles forts, instead of against a target." Connecting the addition of the British super-dreadnought to the disarming of the German one, Churchill concluded his pitch like this: "Once the forts were reduced the minefields would be cleared, and the Fleet would proceed up to

Constantinople and destroy the *Goeben*. They would have *nothing to fear* from field guns or rifles, which would be *merely an inconvenience*."[13] If there is a single line in the documentary record that ensured Churchill would be scapegoated for his role in planning the Dardanelles campaign, this is surely it.

We must be careful, of course, in judging too harshly decisions taken in the heat of the moment, with imperfect information at hand, and with all the principals deeply involved in critical everyday matters elsewhere in the war—especially since few if any similar campaigns have ever been subject to such minute scrutiny. Nevertheless, it is abundantly clear that Churchill, Fisher, Kitchener, and the cabinet officials who listened to them grossly underestimated their Ottoman opponent. Just as they had heard what they wanted to hear in the grand duke's (vague) request for a diversionary strike, so did British policymakers believe what they wanted to believe about the enemy's dispositions—and fighting capacity. Carden's probing attack of November 3, 1914, on Seddul Bahr, though limited, had been unambiguously successful, as he had destroyed a large gun battery from long-enough range (about 16,000 meters)—killing its entire crew of five officers and sixty men—that the enemy was unable to return fire.[14] In mid-December, a British submarine had forced its way into the Straits and torpedoed a Turkish cruiser, *Messudieh*, sinking her within ten minutes.[15] Later in December, Captain Frank Larken, commanding HMS *Doris*, had subdued the minimal shore defenses of Alexandretta (Iskenderun) simply by showing up in port and getting the Ottoman vali to agree to dynamite two rail locomotives in lieu of bombardment, in a curious face-saving compromise (although Larken's attack failed to coerce Djemal into releasing British hostages held in Damascus, which was his real objective).[16] Finally, the news from Suez, which arrived in London on February 3, 1915, confirmed the general impression in the War Council that the Turks were soft.[17]

It is curious that so little attention, by contrast, was paid to the successful naval/amphibious campaign in the Shatt-al-Arab, which most clearly resembled the Dardanelles in operational terms. Abadan, al-Fao, Basra, and Qurna had all fallen, to be sure, but in southern Mesopotamia the Turks had sold their lives dearly, despite being massively outnumbered and outgunned. At

Abadan, the Ottoman defenders had constructed primitive but effective mud trenches, which the British naval guns were able to overwhelm only because the lay of the channel allowed them to enfilade them from the side. The battle of Sahil alone had cost the British-Indian expeditionary force nearly five hundred casualties, including fifty-four killed. Qurna was no picnic either, taking a whole week and costing the invaders another hundred casualties. Shatt-al-Arab was a British victory, to be sure: but it had been a bloody slog, requiring a month to secure a lightly fortified waterway that had been all but abandoned by the Ottomans since Enver was committed to his Caucasian and Suez offensives. More to the operational point, despite overwhelming naval superiority, the final British push at Qurna had required close coordination between naval fire and amphibious forces.

True, by the atrocious standards of the western front, Britain's casualties in the Shatt-al-Arab campaign were modest. And yet this was all the more reason for the campaign's relevance to British strategy in the Ottoman theater. A small but lethal riverine fleet, and a single infantry division, had secured the most important oil refinery in the British Empire, and pitched the Turks in a headlong retreat upriver toward Baghdad. News had then come in about developments on the Caucasian front, where it seemed the Turks, in part by denuding Mesopotamia of troops, had won a great victory over the Russians—only for the news to be happily revised, such that the Turks had suffered a catastrophic defeat instead! Without any deliberate efforts at coordination, the British and Russians had nevertheless struck a powerful one-two punch at the Ottoman Empire's southern and eastern defenses, at very little cost.

Had Churchill and Kitchener been thinking sequentially, in terms of regional and inter-Allied strategy, the logical move would have been the one Lloyd George had suggested during the late December brainstorming sessions, to strike next at the pivot of Turkey's Asian defenses along the "Syrian" coast.* In fact, Kitchener did float a trial balloon, during the January 7, 1915, War Council, of landing some thirty thousand to fifty thousand troops at

---

* In Ottoman times, the province of Syria also included Lebanon—that is, the eastern Mediterranean littoral above Palestine.

Alexandretta to "strike at Turkish communications" (although this was only a hypothetical, as Kitchener had himself stipulated that no troops were yet available).[18] The northeastern corner of the Mediterranean constituted a critical strategic choke point, with the Baghdad Railway running, for long stretches between Ceyhan and Dörtyol, less than ten kilometers from the coast, easily within range of British naval guns. From Cilicia, rail and road connections led northeast, toward the Ottoman Third Army at Erzurum fighting on the Caucasian front; south, toward the Ottoman Fourth Army in Damascus and Palestine; and southeast, toward the Ottoman Sixth Army in Baghdad. Were a British expeditionary force to secure this coastal area, it would cut off two Ottoman armies entirely (the Fourth and Sixth), while forcing the Third Army, already reeling after Sarıkamış, to rely on a single macadamized road from Sivas to Erzurum for all its supplies. By thus cleaving the Ottoman Empire in two, the British could have showed CUP leaders in Constantinople the terrible price they had paid for fighting alongside Germany. A separate peace with the Sublime Porte would certainly then have followed, with the Young Turks ruling over a rump Turkey shorn of its Arab provinces— more or less in its actual borders settled in 1923 (only without the eight subsequent years of carnage).*

Could it have been done? The episode with HMS *Doris* had shown the defenses of Alexandretta to be virtually nonexistent, and sparked considerable gossip in Cairo about the possibility of landing a larger force in Cilicia. The anchorage along the northeastern Mediterranean littoral was easy, and, unlike in the Straits, there were few mines to speak of. Troops landing ashore would encounter even lighter Turkish resistance than at the Shatt-al-Arab, with the slopes running from shore up to the nearby Amanus (Nur) and Taurus Mountains, shallower and easier to scale than those of the Gallipoli and Trojan peninsulas (see accompanying map). Most intriguing of all, the population of Cilicia was heavily Armenian, and therefore about as pro-Entente

---

* Of course, the postwar future of the Ottoman capital would still have to be decided. Without the Dardanelles campaign, however—along with the diplomatic agreements born of it—Russia would have had no cause for claiming Constantinople. Were it possible, following a decisive Cilician landing, to negotiate a deal allowing the Young Turks to remain in power in exchange for their giving up Mesopotamia, Syria, Palestine, and any claim on Egypt and opening the Straits to Russia, the Allies would surely have jumped at the chance.

in sympathy as could be imagined. Indeed, following the news of Larken's probe at Alexandretta, the idea of a British landing at Ceyhan or Alexandretta became something of an obsession for Armenian exiles in Cairo. Boghos Nubar Pasha, the Egyptian-born head of the Armenian National Delegation, which functioned as a kind of liaison Armenian government-in-embryo to the Entente powers, promised Sir John Maxwell on February 3, 1915, that, were the British to land troops in Cilicia, local Ottoman Armenians would offer them "perfect and total support."[19]

Eminently logical, the Cilician idea may have been too small-scale—too easy—to appeal to Kitchener and Churchill in their search for a grand move on the global chessboard. (Kitchener had described it, in his January 7, 1915, War Council hypothetical, as a "minor but useful operation.") Discussion of a possible landing at Alexandretta continued in the cabinet on through January and February, but only in the sense of a sideshow to the main action at the Dardanelles—a diversion within the diversion, or, in the worst-case scenario, a fallback option. As Maurice Hankey wrote to Arthur Balfour on

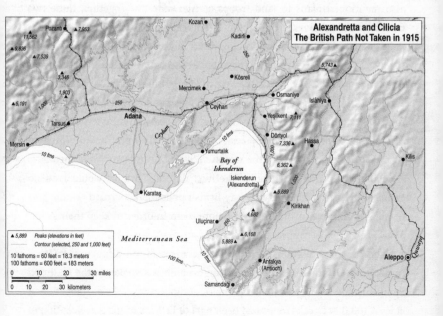

Alexandretta and Cilicia
The British Path Not Taken in 1915

▲ 5,889   Peaks (elevations in feet)
‒‒‒‒‒   Contour (selected, 250 and 1,000 feet)

10 fathoms = 60 feet = 18.3 meters
100 fathoms = 600 feet = 183 meters

0   10   20   30 miles
0 10 20   30 kilometers

Mediterranean Sea
Bay of Iskenderun

February 17, 1915, of the prospects of forcing the Dardanelles, "We may bring it off with the Navy, and, if we fail, we can pretend it was a feint & go to Smyrna or Alexandretta."[20]

In Churchill's case, part of the reason he neglected the Cilician option was political. A British landing there might easily upset the French, who had postwar designs on the region, and who were already sensitive over the highly charged business of which power would command the squadron attacking the Dardanelles. According to an agreement signed on August 6, 1914, pursuant to a prewar understanding negotiated in 1912, France was supposed to have the overall naval command in the Mediterranean, with Britain assuming responsibility for the North Sea, the Channel coast, and the Atlantic (including France's own northwestern coastline). In Besika Bay, Carden had already violated the spirit if not the letter of this agreement, assuming *de facto* command of the force blockading the Straits. Churchill, after the January 13 War Council, had informed the French naval attaché, the Comte de Saint-Seine, that while France was welcome to participate, Carden must have unfettered command in the planned Dardanelles offensive. Gingerly, Churchill also mentioned plans to land troops at Alexandretta. Together, these two Churchillian missives aroused the ire of France's naval minister, Victor Augagneur, who came to London to protest in person that France must have the naval command. To mollify the angry Frenchman, Churchill told Augagneur on January 26, 1915, that the French vice admiral in the Mediterranean, Émile Paul Amable Guépratte, could have command "in the Levant," including at Alexandretta—where any landing of troops would be left at France's discretion. To make absolutely certain that Churchill not "arouse [French] suspicions as to anything in the region of Syria," Sir Edward Grey then gave Augagneur a formal reassurance the next day that Britain would land no troops at Alexandretta.[21] In this way British policymakers ruled out the glittering Alexandrettine opportunity before them in order to keep their suspicious French allies happy.

The other obvious buttress to a Dardanelles operation, a concurrent Greek invasion of Ottoman Europe and/or an amphibious strike on the Gallipoli Peninsula, likewise fell afoul of diplomatic complications. The participation of at least 100,000 Greek troops had been part of Fisher's original conception of forcing the Dardanelles.[22] Back in November, the Greek prime minister, Eleftherios Venizelos, had declared himself "delighted to co-operate" in any British operation targeting the Dardanelles, although, as Greece was not at war, he was driving a hard bargain on her terms of entry. Uncertain about the fate of Serbia under the Austro-Hungarian assault and worried about his Bulgarian flank as well, Venizelos made it clear to London that he wanted British and French reinforcements to be landed at Salonica before he could risk deploying troops to Gallipoli. But even had the British met Greece's onerous terms, there remained the still larger stumbling block: that Russia's foreign minister, Sazonov, had firmly vetoed Greek participation. As Sir Edward Grey had to explain to his frustrated colleagues on numerous occasions in January and February, "the last thing the Russians wanted was to see anyone else making a triumphal entry into Constantinople."[23]

As for the Russians themselves, the complications were more frustrating still. The entire object of forcing the Dardanelles, as Kitchener had explained back on January 7, 1915, was to "re-establish communication with Russia . . . and release wheat and shipping now locked up in the Black Sea." It was therefore reasonable to expect that Russia would contribute *something* to the campaign, even if the Siberian Corps, as Grand Duke Nicholas was forced to admit, could not possibly arrive in time to take part. The quartermaster general who was really in charge under the grand duke's nominal command at Stavka, Yuri Danilov, had pointedly refused to spare any troops from the European fronts for an amphibious strike at the Bosphorus. Feeling bad about the whole business, which his own complaining had set in motion, the grand duke himself did tell Hanbury-Williams on January 24, 1915, that while he could not promise operational support for a Dardanelles campaign, he would "naturally use every endeavor, should opportunity present itself, to strengthen the hands of the Allies." True to his word, if with no great haste, the grand duke formally requested, on February 14, 1915, that Admiral Andrei Eberhart, commander of Russia's Black Sea Fleet, begin preparations for an assault on the Bosphorus—although Eberhart's enthusiasm was dampened by the latest Russian intelligence, which suggested that the Turks had 80,000 troops on the European side of the Bosphorus, with another 150,000 held in reserve. Russian promises to contribute arrived in London at regular intervals all through February and March 1915—but dates were never given. Secretly, the Russian Admiralty issued orders on February 17, 1915, *forbidding* the Black Sea Fleet from leaving Sevastopol "except in case of extreme emergency," as if deliberately to leave Russia's allies in the lurch at the Dardanelles.[24]

By mid-February 1915, when preparations were entering their final phase, Churchill must have been livid with frustration. Contrary to the claims later made by his critics, the First Lord of the Admiralty was by no means averse to the idea that ground troops should be involved. The reason he had originally asked Carden whether the Dardanelles could be forced "by ships alone" was that Kitchener had told him no troops were available. Churchill would have loved to have Russia's Siberian Corps at his disposal, or a Greek army of 100,000—but neither of these things was given him. On January 20, 1915, Churchill had formally requested, in a directive sent to Stavka, that Russia contribute both warships and troops to the Allied campaign at the Dardanelles—the idea being that the Russians commence their own amphibious assault on the Bosphorus "as soon as the outer Dardanelles forts are destroyed."[25] As late as January 28, 1915, when the new Sub-Committee on the Dardanelles Operation first met, Churchill pointed out that even if warships forced passage, "they cannot open these channels to merchant ships so long as the enemy is in possession of the shores." True, he did not press the point, and so planning at the Admiralty went ahead in February for a naval-only campaign, at least at the outset—even while "skeptics" like Fisher began compiling a written record opposing the idea (though never objecting in the War Council, when it mattered). But there was always a general idea that ground troops would be involved at some point, whether the Twenty-Ninth Division from England, the Russians, or Australian and New Zealand troops (about 39,000) freed up from Egypt now that the Turco-German Suez Canal offensive had been repulsed. At a War Council held in London on February 19, 1915, the very day Carden began bombarding the outer Dardanelles forts, Churchill in fact expressed grave disappointment when he learned that Kitchener did not want to send the Twenty-Ninth Division to support Carden. "We should never forgive ourselves," the First Lord of the Admiralty told his colleagues, "if this promising operation failed owing to insufficient military support at the critical moment." Kitchener, however, had now decided that the Commonwealth troops in Egypt would be enough (although it was still unclear when they would be available, and for what purpose). The secretary of state for war's "final" decision on February 19 was that he would agree to send the Twenty-Ninth Division in "case of necessity," but that he "did not want to send it just yet." Privately, Kitchener offered Churchill the following, not entirely reassuring, reassurance: "You get through! I will find the men."[26]

So what were these "men" to do, if and when they became available, and if and when Carden's squadron succeeded in forcing its way through the Narrows? Clearly, as critics have pointed out ever since, the doctrinal conception of the Dardanelles campaign was still in flux when the naval bombardment began. At some level, there was an element of wishful, almost magical thinking involved. Churchill may or may not have really told Kitchener, as Sir Arthur George later told the Dardanelles Commission, that the campaign would be won nearly alone by the super-dreadnought *Queen Elizabeth* with her "astounding effectiveness" and "marvelous potentialities." But he had invoked her 15-inch guns as a knockdown argument in the War Council back in January, and he did insist on numerous occasions that the fleet could get through on its own (although repeatedly insisting that the channel could be fully secured only with ground troops). As for Kitchener, he changed his mind more often than anyone else, now denying that any troops were available, now allowing that the Twenty-Ninth Division was, or again was not, now suggesting that the Australian and New Zealand units in Egypt should be used instead. To confuse everyone still further, Kitchener insisted, on February 19, 1915, that an amphibious operation at Alexandretta was preferable, after all, to the Dardanelles (this, on the day the naval bombardment of the outer Dardanelles forts began).*[27]

---

* Somewhat surprisingly, considering that he was known as the biggest thorn in Churchill's side, Jacky Fisher, hauled in by the Dardanelles investigatory commission in 1916, blamed Kitchener far more fervently than Churchill for the failure to properly coordinate the assault at the Dardanelles with ground troops. He was "convinced that Kitchener . . . knew in [his] heart that the men could have been freed for my plan on January 3rd, only [he] had this extraordinary idea of England being invaded—one of those astounding things you cannot get out of some people's heads." Fisher blamed Kitchener for "vacillation, indecision, procrastination; there was no imagination or audacity."

Churchill, by contrast, Fisher saluted, in spite of their differences. "I know Mr. Churchill," he told his interrogators. "He is magnificent, he is like a bull dog and will go on."

Still, it must be admitted that Kitchener, unlike Churchill, did see the strategic potential of the Cilician option—even if he was just as vacillating and indecisive about it as Fisher suggested. Had Kitchener 1) pushed from early January for troops to be made available, and 2) insisted consistently on Alexandretta, the Ottoman

Why, with the issue of ground troops still unresolved, did the British go ahead with the naval assault when they did? Part of the answer seems to be that Churchill wanted to get through as quickly as possible, before SMS *Goeben* was repaired (i.e., before early to mid-April). The enormous armada assembling in Mudros Bay, off the now-Greek island of Lemnos, grew more vulnerable every day it remained idle, as it presented something of a sitting target for enemy submarines. Whether or not ground troops were available, British naval power remained considerable, and there was always the chance that a really powerful attack would induce panic in the enemy. In Constantinople, wild rumors had been circulating all winter about the upcoming British assault on the Dardanelles. According to both the U.S. ambassador, Morgenthau, and the Austro-Hungarian ambassador, Johann Markgraf von Pallavicini, the Ottoman government began preparing special trains as early as the first week of January 1915 to evacuate the sultan and his Young Turk ministers, and the Ottoman state archives and gold reserves, to Ankara and Konya, respectively. Even the presumably well-informed German ambassador, Wangenheim, was worried enough that he had Morgenthau "store several cases of his valuables in the American Embassy."[28]

The British Foreign Office had learned of these rumors, and it is not an exaggeration to say that they factored into the final decision to strike. Sir Edward Grey, at the January 28 War Council, volunteered that he "thought that the Turks would be paralysed with fear when they heard that the forts were being destroyed one by one."[29] So far from denying that he held this opinion under interrogation by the later inquiry, Grey affirmed that it had indeed been his belief that a "revolution" would break out at Constantinople— although he confessed that he had not bothered to ask Sir Louis Mallet, Britain's ambassador, for his opinion on the subject. His source, rather, was Kitchener, who, Grey improbably remarked, "had as much experience as anybody . . . as to Turkish psychology."* Grey was not alone. "We were always

---

Empire would likely have been cleaved in two in 1915 and the entire world war would have turned out very differently.

* In one of the more revealing exchanges at the Dardanelles Commission hearings, Grey was incredulously asked, "I do not think he [Kitchener] had any experience of the Turks at Constantinople?" To which Grey replied, "Of course, Sir Louis Mallet had not been there very long" (Grey's idea being apparently that Kitchener's opinion of

given to understand," as Carden's successor, Admiral John de Robeck, recalled under questioning, "that there would have been a revolution in Constantinople if we had arrived there with the fleet." Sir John French, apprised of the latest plans in mid-February 1915, said that "we are promised a military rising and ultimate revolution on the fall of the first forts." Or as Captain William Reginald Hall, head of British naval intelligence and therefore Churchill's (and the cabinet's) principal source on enemy dispositions, put it, "the general impression that we had from our agents there, who were in a good position to know, was that the Turkish population generally in Constantinople were in the habit of going on their housetops and looking for the British fleet to arrive and relieve them from oppression; and that we had from many sources."[30]

What were Hall's sources? Contrary to his suggestion that he had honeycombed Constantinople with British agents, in fact Hall's information came from two emissaries he had sent to Athens on February 1, 1915, neither of high rank. The "mastermind" (if that is the right word) of the Hall operation was a railway engineer called George Griffin Eady, who had acted as a technical adviser to the British embassy. Eady's only claim to influence was that he had met with the grand vizier shortly before relations were broken off. Said Halim Pasha had, predictably, told him what he wanted to hear—that he was against the war party and friendly to Great Britain. Eady's assistant, Edwin Whittall, claimed to have access to the interior minister because his nephew had worked for the grand rabbi of Constantinople, who knew Talât.[31] Hall apparently told these two agents that Churchill had authorized him to use "funds on an extraordinary scale if necessary," offering £3 million or £4 million to "purchase" passage through the Dardanelles. Without saying which of these Young Turk leaders was involved, Hall later insisted, under interrogation, that some "high personage in Constantinople sent down another very high personage with no delay at all to meet our agents. They got into touch with high people in Constantinople on the 29th January [1915], and by the 15th February we were at close grips on the whole subject." Once this rather vague information was passed on to him at the Admiralty, Churchill, and

---

the popular mood in Constantinople, though based on no knowledge of the city worth mentioning, was more valuable than Ambassador Mallet's, based on real but limited experience of it).

through him the entire British War Cabinet, became convinced there was "readiness" on the part of Ottoman officials to negotiating a deal to open the Dardanelles.[32]

Incredible as the notion of the Young Turks agreeing to surrender the Ottoman Empire for a bribe of a few million pounds seems today, some such idea does seem to have been lodged in Churchill's fertile imagination as the Dardanelles campaign commenced. At the first session of a weeks-long grilling by the Dardanelles Commission in fall 1916, Churchill brought up the HMS *Doris* episode of December 1914, reminding everyone that Captain Larken had more or less talked his way into Alexandretta and gotten the Turks to dynamite their own rail line, after which "everybody seemed very pleased." This "incident," Churchill continued almost in a vein of self-accusation, "helped to form the opinion in our mind as to the degree of resistance which might in all circumstances be expected from Turkey . . . I must say that it was always in my mind that we were not dealing with a thoroughly efficient military power, and that it was quite possible that we could get into parley with them."[33]

Here, then, is where things stood as the Dardanelles assault began on February 19, 1915. On Kitchener's insistence, no ground troops were immediately available to land ashore concurrently with a Franco-British naval attack on the forts, although some might later be made available, in numbers unknown and for purposes still undefined. The Greeks had expressed interest in participating, then blown cold. Given the inducement of a strong naval campaign they might blow hot again, but hopefully not *too* hot, or it might alarm the Russians. Still, a Goldilocks-like threat of Greek intervention—not too hot or cold, just warm enough—might spur the Russians in a constructive way to get their act together, although there was little firm idea in London as to when the Russians would be ready to strike at the Bosphorus, or in what strength. There was a certain, apparently universal expectation in the British War Council that panic would break out in Constantinople following a serious attack on the Dardanelles, triggering some kind of a pro-Entente coup d'état; or that a bribe of substantial size, reaching the pockets of Young Turk leaders, might achieve similar results. In essence, then: Churchill, Grey, and Kitchener would make things up as they went along.

Considering the muddled thinking that lay behind it, the Dardanelles campaign did not begin badly. At 9:51 a.m. on February 19, 1915—the anniversary of the first and only forcing of the Dardanelles by naval power alone, by Admiral Duckworth in 1807—HMS *Cornwallis* opened fire from long range against Kum Kale and the adjacent fort of Orhanie. Another British warship, probably the *Vengeance* (commanded by Admiral de Robeck), then began shelling Seddul Bahr, also from long range. Carden's squadron, twelve strong (including the French pre-dreadnought battleships *Suffren*, the flagship commanded by Guépratte, and *Bouvet*), then began to close in. The Turkish guns, outranged, had not yet returned fire. But there was no way for Carden, de Robeck, and Guépratte to know what this meant, as they were much too far away to observe the effect of their initial bombardment.

The results, it would later emerge, had been minimal. While the ships were in motion, naval fire was inaccurate, especially from long range. Warned by the boom of British guns against Kum Kale and Orhanie, the batteries on the European side at Seddul Bahr had taken cover outside their forts, such that only three men had been lightly wounded there. After Carden's squadron closed to six thousand yards at 2:00 p.m., the guns boomed again, this time doing more damage to the forts of Seddul Bahr and Kum Kale. Just past 4:00 p.m., two 15 cm shells struck an observation post above Orhanie, killing the German officer commanding the battery, Lieutenant Woermann, along with his Turkish translator and telephone operator. It was the only real coup of the day's bombardment, for twenty minutes later the shore batteries, now ranged in, opened fire on the Allied squadron. Undeterred by Woermann's death, his second-in-command, Vice Sergeant Gunner Joerss, took over the Orhanie guns and poured down heavy fire on the attacking vessels, which immediately pulled into reverse. By 5:00 p.m., with his ships dangerously silhouetted by the setting sun, Carden called off the attack and withdrew. Observing the damage at Hamidie and Kum Kale that evening, Admiral Usedom noted an atmosphere in the batteries of "cold-blooded calm and composure." As if to confirm their brotherhood-in-arms, exactly two Germans and two Turks had been killed. The Allies had no significant losses, other than the 139 shells fired off to little effect.[34]

A strange phony war now descended on the Aegean Sea, as poor weather precluded Carden from attacking for the next five days. Carden had achieved little and lost the element of surprise. Still, the pause allowed British and French diplomats time to work on the Greeks and Russians, to see if either rival claimant of Constantinople wanted to get in on the action. On February 23, 1915, France formally requested that Russia begin her assault on the Bosphorus simultaneously with the Allied Dardanelles offensive. On February 25, Ambassador Benckendorff, in London, passed on Grey's identical request to Sazonov, who forwarded both requests to Stavka (although not until February 28). Even before receiving these belated messages, Grand Duke Nicholas had renewed, on both February 19 and 23, his earlier request that Eberhart prepare to strike at the Bosphorus: Stavka was now willing to give him one full army corps (the Caucasian V), about thirty thousand to forty thousand men. But Eberhart, in possession of much better intelligence on Bosphorus mines and shore batteries than the British had on the Dardanelles, continued dragging his feet into March.[35]

In Athens, meanwhile, the British minister, Sir F. E. H. Elliott, reported on February 28, 1915, that the Dardanelles attack had been discussed "with intense interest" and noted "a rapidly growing feeling that the capture of Constantinople ought not to take place without Greek co-operation." To beat the tardy Russians to the pass, next day Venizelos offered to send three Greek divisions to the Gallipoli Peninsula, going so far as to threaten to resign if King Constantine (a known Germanophile—his wife, Sophie, was the sister of Kaiser Wilhelm II) opposed him. Horrified, Russian diplomats informed Elliott on March 3, 1915, that Greek participation in the Dardanelles campaign was absolutely out of the question.[36] To justify Russia's anti-Greek veto, on March 1 Sazonov did coax a vow out of Eberhart that the Black Sea Fleet had been ordered "ready to steam" for the Bosphorus. On March 3—the same day the Russian veto was slammed down in Athens—Sazonov informed Britain's ambassador, Sir George Buchanan, that the V Caucasian Army Corps (freed up owing to the Turkish rout at Sarıkamış, although Buchanan and the British missed the irony) was being groomed for imminent departure for the Bosphorus, although the idea was that it would embark only after an Allied breakthrough. Eberhart walked back even this conditional promise, informing Stavka (which then passed on the news slowly—it took over a week to reach London) that V Corps would not be ready for another "two or three weeks." Russia would begin a "serious Bosphorus attack," Eberhart informed her co-belligerents, only after Carden's squadron had broken through the Dardanelles and "annihilated the Turkish fleet."[37]

It was an agonizing dilemma for the Allies. Greece had made, by far, the better offer: three divisions available to land on the Gallipoli Peninsula, giving immediate help to Carden's squadron at the Dardanelles. All the Russians were promising was an outright ban on Greek help, and a nebulous promise to assault the Bosphorus in the near future. The Russians, indeed, were all but explicitly promising *not* to help Carden, by making their own participation conditional on his having already destroyed the enemy fleet. Small wonder Churchill, sensing that his own career was increasingly tied up with the chancy Dardanelles campaign, was exasperated with the Russians. As he wrote Grey on Saturday, March 6, 1915:

> I beseech you at this crisis not to make a mistake in falling below the level of events. Half-hearted measures will ruin all—& a million men will die through prolongation of the war. Our fleet is forcing the Dardanelles. No armies can reach Constantinople but those which we invite . . . Tell the Russians that we will meet them in a generous and sympathetic spirit about Constantinople. But no impediment must be placed in the way of Greek co-operation—I am *so* afraid of your losing Greece, & yet paying all the future into Russia's hands. If Russia prevents Greece helping, I will do my utmost to oppose her having Constantinople.*[38]

Prime Minister Asquith was thinking along similar lines, writing to Venetia Stanley the same day that "the diplomatic sky begins to darken. Russia, despite all our remonstrations & remonstrances, declines absolutely to allow

---

* Curiously, Churchill never sent this letter, ostensibly because, before he could give it to Grey, news arrived that King Constantine had opposed Venizelos's proposal, and the Greek cabinet had resigned. But there were other good reasons he kept it to himself at the time (although he published it later). Russia's diplomatic offensive to have her claim on Constantinople recognized by her allies was ratcheting up into high gear: it would not do to go on record against something the cabinet was already inclined to give her.

Greece to take any part in the Dardanelles business, or the subsequent advance on Constantinople."[39]

The Russians were playing a weak hand very well. Even while Asquith and Churchill were muttering in frustration over Russian intransigeance, Russia's foreign minister called in Maurice Paléologue, France's ambassador to Russia, on March 5, 1915. Sazonov informed Paléologue that Russia, in exchange for possibly helping her struggling Allies occupy Constantinople once they had already defeated the common enemy for her, would accept no less than the "permanent incorporation" into the Russian empire of "Constantinople, the western bank of the Bosphorus, the Sea of Marmara and the Dardanelles, along with the Thracian plain as far as the Enos-Midia lines." If France did not agree to this (it is notable that Sazonov was already confident that Britain would), he warned Paléologue, "the consequences would be incalculable": the foreign minister would "offer his immediate resignation." Although Sazonov did not say who would replace him, the implication, Paléologue reported to Paris, was clear: Sergei Witte would be recalled—the greatest Germanophile in Petersburg. Russia must have Constantinople, her foreign minister was threatening implicitly, or she would sign a separate peace with the Germans.[40]

Sazonov's timing for this stunning diplomatic *démarche*, like that of the grand duke when he first requested British help, was exquisite. After the weather finally turned, Carden had resumed the Allied assault on the Dardanelles forts with a seven-hour barrage on February 25, 1915. Although Carden's guns seriously damaged the batteries at Kum Kale and Seddul Bahr (though not Hamidie), enemy casualties remained minimal. For the first time doubt began to creep in among the British naval gunners. Commander Worsley Gibson, aboard HMS *Albion*, noted that many of the forts were encased with earthworks, which made them nearly impregnable to low-trajectory fire. One of the batteries, Gibson reported, "stuck to it jolly well and not until we'd sent two windmills up into the air like a pack of cards, most humorous to watch, and planted several beauties right on top of them did they retire." But the Turks then came right back, and recommenced firing. Only after the British landed small demolition parties ashore were they able to knock out the guns at Kum Kale and Seddul Bahr (their crews having fled), destroying forty-eight Ottoman guns before reembarking, having suffered only nine casualties. With the outer fortress guns silenced, the entrance to the Straits could now be swept. Getting through the mouth was a Pyrrhic victory, however, as this brought the squadron into the teeth of the concealed and mobile howitzer battalions, with their "plunging fire." Safe from the demolished outer guns, Allied minesweepers were sitting ducks for the mobile howitzers. Nighttime sweeping was impossible, as the Turks deployed searchlights. On March 3, 1915—the day the Greeks tried to come in, and the Russians vetoed the idea—the British tried again to land four hundred marines ashore at Kum Kale and Seddul Bahr, only to meet fierce resistance, suffering seventy casualties—nearly twice as many as the Turks, who lost six dead and forty-one wounded. The Turks, moreover, had captured valuable intelligence from the fallen British marines, giving an idea of Allied intentions.[41] British seaplanes, trying to spot the naval guns to target, were strafed by rifle fire. On March 5, Ottoman howitzers took out the wardroom and the crew's washrooms aboard HMS *Agamemnon*. On the sixth, even the vaunted super-dreadnought *Queen Elizabeth* was hit by howitzers, forcing her to pull back to 20,000 yards (18.3 kilometers). These unexpected coups of Turkish gunnery spooked Carden, who complained to Churchill that his ships were facing "very destructive" fire.[42] As if sensing his Allies' discomfiture in the Dardanelles,* Sazonov now squeezed them, hard.[43]

It worked. In a positively heroic diplomatic performance waged during the critical days that saw Carden's Dardanelles assault bog down, Sazonov reminded Stavka of Churchill's urgent request for a diversionary strike at the Bosphorus with the hint that it would "not be desirable if Tsargrad were taken without us" (March 1 and 5)[44]; laid down Russia's terms in case the Young Turks decided to surrender bilaterally to St. Petersburg (March 2 and 3)[45]; distributed a formal aide-mémoire outlining Russia's postwar claim on Constantinople and the Straits for her ambassadors in Paris and London (March 4)[46]; blackmailed Paléologue into recommending to Paris that

---

* The Russians had excellent intelligence on Ottoman dispositions, from their own agents and Austrian cable traffic (they had broken the codes). On March 5, 1915, the Russian Foreign Office decoded a message from the Austrian minister in Sofia: the Dardanelles forts were holding strong. A summary, forwarded to Sazonov on March 16, reported that Carden had run into "serious difficulties." So Sazonov knew what was going on in the Dardanelles.

Russia's claims be indulged, lest she sign a separate peace with Germany (March 5–6)[47]; ordered Stavka and the Russian Admiralty to formulate a plan for occupying Constantinople, dividing the city up into three zones, with the Russians in Stambul, the French taking Pera (Beyoğlu), and the British Kadıköy, on the Asian side (March 7)[48]; won Paléologue's endorsement of Russia's claims in principle, in order to forestall his threatened resignation (March 8)[49]; and finally, on March 12, won the full endorsement, by Sir Edward Grey, of Russia's postwar claim on Constantinople and the Straits.

This historic decision, which ultimately led to the partition of the Ottoman Empire between the Entente powers, bears closer scrutiny. Swallowing Sazonov's lure, Grey argued in the War Council on March 10, 1915, that Britain must agree to Russia's every demand so as to deprive a would-be Germanophile government of the argument that "it had always been British policy to keep Russia out of Constantinople and the Straits . . . of course it was our policy still." Churchill, less naive, insisted that Grey's endorsement of Russia's claims be made conditional on a victorious conclusion to the war, and that Britain herself "realize the desiderata" Sazonov had vaguely alluded to as a share of the Ottoman spoils. In this way Britain's government was enjoined to stake its own claims to the Ottoman inheritance, and not subtly. As Asquith noted in his report of the historic March 10, 1915, War Council to Venetia Stanley, in their grasping alongside Russia and France for "a substantial share of the carcase of the Turk," the level of discussion in the War Council rapidly descended to "that of a gang of buccaneers." Paléologue, in Petersburg, held out for another month, winning from Sazonov a promise to humor France's claims in Syria and the Levant, along with guarantees of France's financial claims (France, holding the bulk of the Ottoman public debt, was less keen on destroying the regime which owed it than Britain, which held little Turkish debt, or Russia, which held almost none at all). Still, Sazonov's triumph was complete: the partition of the Ottoman Empire was now formal Allied policy, with Russia getting her great prize.[50]

While the fate of the postwar Ottoman "carcass" was being greedily discussed in Petrograd, Paris, and London, Admiral Carden's nerves were breaking under the strain of fire from the shore batteries of the supposedly moribund enemy. By the time the British cabinet endorsed Russia's claims on

Constantinople, Carden had already concluded that the "slow reduction" of the forts was not working. As he informed Churchill on March 11, 1915, the squadron's "operations are now greatly retarded by concealed batteries of howitzers . . . their effects are now as formidable as the heavy guns in the permanent batteries." Opinion on the best course of action was sharply divided, but everyone was agreed that the current course was not working. Churchill thought the time had come to abandon "caution and deliberate methods" in favor of a concentrated effort to "overwhelm the forts at the Narrows at decisive range by the fire of the largest number of guns, great and small, that can be brought to bear on them." Carden, in his reply, agreed that "vigorous sustained action was necessary for success," although he seemed vague on whether or not this meant he could go through alone or whether ground troops were needed. Admiral de Robeck, second-in-command, remarked on March 13, 1915, that "a heavy concerted bombardment and rush through the Dardanelles was to be considered." This was similar to Churchill's position, except that the First Lord was still waiting anxiously for the ground troops Kitchener had promised to send to Lemnos, ideally to participate in the final push (or following it, depending on when they arrived). Sir Henry Jackson thought the enemy's artillery must first be "cleared," which meant landing troops, at least on the European (Gallipoli) side, where the Turks' concealed batteries were strongest. Kitchener was, as ever, in no rush, content to let the navy continue to pound the Dardanelles forts until the Twenty-Ninth Division arrived in theater to spearhead the army's contribution to the campaign in some as-yet-unspecified way.[51]

With the decisive moment at the Dardanelles—it was hoped—approaching, and the Russians pressing for a decision on the postwar status of Constantinople, Britain's leaders finally began hashing out the role of ground troops in the operation. At the War Council on March 10, 1915, Kitchener at last agreed to dispatch the Twenty-Ninth Division, although it would take another six days before it would put out to sea (and take longer still for it to reach Lemnos). Because this was the only coherent and fully trained division involved, the Australian and New Zealand units assembling on Lemnos would have to wait for it before they could do anything. Relying a bit too heavily on the good faith of Grand Duke Nicholas, Kitchener also informed everyone that no fewer than 47,600 Russian troops were available, although he was vague on when or where they would arrive, and what they would do when they got there. Finally, Kitchener settled on the man who would take command of the armed forces at the Dardanelles: Sir Ian Standish Monteith Hamilton, the general then commanding Britain's Home Army. Still, prevaricating to the end, Kitchener waited two days before confirming Hamilton's appointment, and then insisted—over Churchill's strong objection—that Hamilton remain in London "until we have thoroughly studied the situation with which he may be confronted." In his usual cryptic style, Kitchener admonished Churchill, "More haste less speed."[52]

Historians can be grateful for the delay, for Hamilton left behind a record of the resulting conversation of March 12, 1915, which gives us a precious glimpse into the mind of Britain's larger-than-life oracle of military affairs at the transitional moment of the Dardanelles campaign, when the army took a hand. Called into the War Office to accept his historic new command, Hamilton knew little about the region, and Kitchener did little to enlighten him. The map Hamilton was shown of the enemy shore defenses was years out of date, and "of very little use." As to logistics and supplying troops after they landed on enemy territory, Hamilton later confessed, "To be quite frank my mind was a complete blank as to all these things. For all I knew the place was flowing with milk and honey." To put Hamilton's mind at ease, Kitchener reassured him, somewhat illogically, that "he hoped I would not have to land at all; if I did land the fact that I had a powerful Fleet at my back would influence my choice of time and place." Less helpfully still, Kitchener advised his new commander of ground troops that what he really needed were submarines: "Were a submarine to pop up alongside the town of Gallipoli, he said, and to wave the Union Jack three times, the whole Turkish garrison on the Peninsula would take to their heels and make tracks as fast as they could for the north side of the lines of Bulair." And so, in Kitchener's conception at this point, Hamilton was *not* to land on the Gallipoli Peninsula, but somewhere north of it, once the Turks had abandoned the Dardanelles out of terror of British ships (or submarines). This, naturally, brought Kitchener to the point: where British troops should be sent. Pulling out a large-scale relief map of the entire Straits area, Kitchener, Hamilton recalled, turned to me and asked me where I should land. I was a little dazed still and bewildered, having been told only half an hour previously that I was to go there at all, but having been in Constantinople, after a moment's reflection I hazarded the opinion that we might make a rush for the Chataldja lines [land on the European side of the Sea of Marmara, below the city] and get behind them from the south before the Turks from Adrianople and Thrace could get back. Lord Kitchener said he thought that was too risky a procedure, and that in his opinion the best plan would be to land on the Asiatic side of the Bosphorus [at Kadıköy] . . . [where] I would be able to *join hands with a Russian corps who were going to co-operate with me and be under my orders.*

As to when Hamilton was to land to meet the hoped-for Russian army corps, Kitchener was noncommittal, emphasizing only that he should wait until "all the British military forces detailed for the expedition should be assembled so that their full weight can be thrown in." It was possible, Kitchener admitted, that the fleet would "fail to get through" on its own, in which case Hamilton could use "the full weight" of his men to secure the Gallipoli Peninsula, prior to conquering Constantinople. But it was more likely, Kitchener believed, that the enemy would surrender long before this became necessary, which would argue for his preferred deployment on the Asiatic side of the Bosphorus. "When it was a question of garrisoning Constantinople," Hamilton recalls Kitchener telling him, "I should find both the Russians and the French troublesome people to deal with, and that I must be very careful." In fact, it would be best if Hamilton "let the Russians and French hold Constantinople, keeping my own troops to guard the railway line and Adrianople"—so that they might be "free to go up the Danube," to threaten the Balkan underbelly of the Central Powers. So as not to tempt the fates (or make the Russians jealous), Kitchener even crossed out his original name for Hamilton's new army (Expeditionary Force to Constantinople), designating its object as simply "Mediterranean" instead. Having thus outlined Hamilton's simultaneously grandiose and nebulous orders, Kitchener "clinched the matter by saying he thought there was no great hustle." And so Hamilton stayed in London another day, departing only on the evening of March 13, 1915, arriving in Mudros Harbor (by way of Marseille) four days later.[53]

In Kitchener's defense, he was not the only one succumbing to illusions in March 1915. Sir Edward Grey, putting too much stock in every rumor of an impending revolution in Constantinople—reports being assiduously spread by the U.S. ambassador, Henry Morgenthau, until he was taken on a tour of the Dardanelles forts by Enver—had already dispatched a diplomatic envoy, Gerald Fitzmaurice, the former first dragoman of the embassy in Turkey, to Athens, to take charge of the surrender negotiations.[54] Churchill was obsessing over (greatly exaggerated) reports that "the Turkish forts" were "short of ammunition," and of the resulting (entirely imaginary) collapse of morale in the Turco-German camp, with "desponding reports and appeals" being sent to Germany for resupply. Brimming with confidence, Churchill informed Carden on March 13 that "200 or 300 casualties would be a moderate price to pay for sweeping up as far as the Narrows."[55] While Carden and de Robeck, the men actually facing the enemy's concealed howitzers and mines, were less sanguine, expectation of an imminent breakthrough was well-nigh universal in London. As Maurice Hankey recalled, the operating assumption of the War Council during the critical March 10 session was "that the naval attack was going to succeed," with troops (including the Russian corps) being required only for "subsequent operations"—that is, "in time for the attack on Constantinople."[56]

By the time Hamilton arrived, the mood at Mudros was improving. True, the men he was to command had not yet assembled—the Twenty-Ninth Division had embarked only the previous day from England—but even so, the army was finally taking a hand, and the Admiralty had abandoned Carden's piecemeal strategy of reducing the enemy's defenses one fort at a time. Carden himself, who had come to symbolize the ineffectual nature of the Dardanelles campaign, had resigned his command for reasons of health the day before, leaving de Robeck, a much stronger personality, in charge. "In entrusting to you with great confidence," Churchill wired his new squadron commander on the morning of March 17, 1915, "I presume you . . . consider, after separate and independent judgement, that the immediate operations proposed are wise and practicable." De Robeck replied forthwith that he was "in full agreement" and that "operations will proceed to-morrow, weather permit-ting." He further noted that General Hamilton had arrived, and that his interview with the new army commander had been "entirely satisfactory." The British were ready for the final push to the Narrows.[57]

So, too, unfortunately for Churchill and de Robeck, were the Turks and Germans. Inside the Allied fleet, Carden's collapse was chalked up to a weak constitution, but he may also have begun to perceive better than the men around him just what he was up against. Since the Allied assault had begun on February 19, the Ottoman high command had been rushing all available reinforcements to Dardanelles fortress command, including not only men but also artillery and mines. With SMS *Goeben* still under repair, a number of her guns were stripped and sent to augment the shore batteries; likewise the guns of the Ottoman cruiser *Medjedieh*. With their own intelligence suggesting—correctly—that the Russians remained gun-shy about helping their allies with a diversionary attack, the Ottomans meanwhile began qui-etly stripping the Bosphorus defenses to reinforce the Dardanelles. Under cover of night on March 5–6, 1915, two mobile 15 cm (6-inch) howitzer bat-teries (of four guns each) were transferred south from the Bosphorus, fol-lowed shortly by heavy guns of 22 cm (8.7-inch), 24 cm (9.45-inch), and 355 mm (14-inch) caliber. Under Usedom's direction, an observation post was set up on the highest mountain peak at Maitos, offering an excellent view of Besika Bay and the mouth of the Straits. Most critically of all, on March 7, 10, and 11 a Turkish team aboard the *Nusret*, commanded by Major Nazım Emin and advised by a German expert, marine engineer Reeder, succeeded in lay-ing new lines of mines below the Narrows under cover of darkness. The Dar-danelles defenses were strengthening by the day, even as the British attacks seemed to be tapering off into nothingness. On March 17, 1915, the same day Hamilton was arriving and de Robeck was receiving his final go-order from Churchill, Usedom reported to Berlin that

> for the last eight days a notable change has been evident. Entire days go
> past, when owing to poor weather nothing is undertaken by the enemy. A
> feeble fire on the outer forts, followed by the appearance of a few ships at
> the entrance [to the Straits] are the only signs of the existence of an enemy

fleet. The overall impression is of a random undertaking, devoid of any plan, which raises the hope that maybe the enemy's plan has already been wrecked.[58]

If the British were confident, morale in the Turco-German camp was positively ebullient.

The weather looked promising at dawn on the morning of March 18, 1915, although it took a few hours before the morning fog dissipated over the Dardanelles. At 11:25 a.m., the *Queen Elizabeth* opened fire on the Narrows forts from 14,400 yards with her 15-inch guns, followed in rapid succession by the

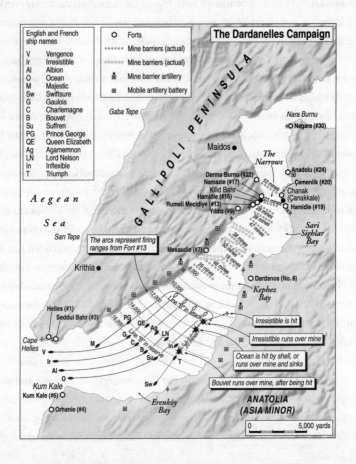

The Dardanelles Campaign

English and French ship names

V	Vengence
Ir	Irresistible
Al	Albion
O	Ocean
M	Majestic
Sw	Swiftsure
G	Gaulois
C	Charlemagne
B	Bouvet
Su	Suffren
PG	Prince George
QE	Queen Elizabeth
Ag	Agamemnon
LN	Lord Nelson
In	Inflexible
T	Triumph

○ Forts
••••• Mine barriers (actual)
○○○○○ Mine barriers (actual)
⚓ Mine barrier artillery
⊡ Mobile artillery battery

GALLIPOLI PENINSULA

Gaba Tepe

Aegean Sea

San Tepe

Maidos ●

Nara Burnu
⚓○ Nagara (#30)

The Narrows

Anadolu (#24)
Çemenlik (#20)

Derma Burnu (#22)
Namazie (#17)
Kilid Bahr
Hamidie (#16)
Rumeli Mecidiye (#13)
Yıldız (#9)

Chanak (Çanakkale)
○ Hamidie (#19)

Sari Sighlar Bay

The arcs represent firing ranges from Fort #13

Messudie (#7)

Krithia ●

○ Dardanos (No. 8)
Kephez Bay

Helles (#1)
Seddul Bahr (#3)

Cape Helles
V
Ir
Al
O

Kum Kale
Kum Kale (#6) ○

○ Orhanie (#4)

Erenköy Bay

PG QE Ag LN
G C
B
Su
In
T

Sw

Line 'B' in attack
Line 'B' in reserve

Irresistible is hit
Irresistible runs over mine
Ocean is hit by shell, or runs over mine and sinks
Bouvet runs over mine, after being hit

ANATOLIA (ASIA MINOR)

0   5,000 yards

modern battle cruisers *Agamemnon*, *Lord Nelson*, and *Inflexible*. For nearly half an hour the big battleships had the field to themselves, as they were still out of enemy range. At about 11:50 a.m., British spotters noted a "particularly heavy explosion" at the fortress of Chanak on the Asian side of the Narrows. An American journalist with the Associated Press, George Schreiner, who observed the action from a town near Kilid Bahr on the European side, was nearly taken out by a flying boulder dislodged from the earth. "The air," he recalled after picking himself up off the ground, "was thick with pulverized mortar and powder gases . . . over the forts and towns of Ischanak Kalessi hung a thick cloud of smoke, and the Kilid Bahr position was completely enveloped in thick powder fumes," with "howling, whining, shrieking, whistling fragments of steel and other matter." Everywhere buildings and houses were crumbling to the ground, "as if their foundations had been torn out from under them." Most of the damage, however, had been done to the town— not the batteries. Only direct strikes could take out fortified gun emplacements encased in earthworks, and such strikes were few and far between with long-range naval gunnery.[59]

Just past noon de Robeck sent in the French squadron, commanded by Vice Admiral Guépratte, to see what they could do from shorter range. Guépratte obliged with his usual dash, sending the *Gaulois*, *Charlemagne*, *Bouvet*, and *Suffren* up the Straits, right into the teeth of the Narrows defenses. Now the guns were booming on both sides, with the channel all but choked in smoke and rocked with one detonation after another. At 1:20 p.m., the *Bouvet* came within range of the Hamidie battery, which rained down fire on the French ship. At 1:50 p.m., Hamidie scored two direct hits from a 355 mm Krupp gun, causing an immense explosion, with a "column of smoke shot up from her decks into the sky." The *Bouvet*, listing to her side, then ran over a mine, capsized, and sank within minutes, with her captain, Rageot, and most of her crew of 639 Frenchmen drowning with her. An eerie calm then descended, as both sides observed the carnage in the water. At around 3:00 p.m., the firing began again, more intense than before. The *Gaulois* and *Suffren* were badly damaged by Turkish guns and had to withdraw; the *Gaulois* eventually ran aground on the beach of a small island in Besika Bay. At 4:00 p.m., de Robeck sent in his four main minesweepers, hoping to clear the

Narrows before another battleship sank, but they came immediately into the plunging fire of the Turkish howitzers and all four turned back in panic. Toward 4:00 p.m., the *Irresistible* had come in range of the deadly Krupp monster gun at Hamidie, which hit her fore-bridge and set it on fire. At 4:09 p.m., de Robeck observed that the *Irresistible* "had a list to starboard": she had raised a green flag, indicating a serious hit on that side. Though having passed out of range of Hamidie, she then drifted into range of the Rumeli Mecidiye Fort, which rained down shells on her. All the officers could do was evacuate wounded men onto the swift destroyer *Wear*, which pulled up alongside, and prepare for possible towing. At 4:11 p.m., the *Inflexible*, hitherto undamaged, ran over a mine and immediately began to list, down by the bows, in more serious trouble even than the *Irresistible*. Twenty-seven men aboard the *Inflexible* were killed in the explosion, and the ship's electric lights failed—along with its ventilator fans, with the men belowdecks nearly suffocating from the heat as they struggled to close the watertight doors. *Inflexible*, at least, was near enough the mouth to limp away from the battle: the *Irresistible*, having pressed up the Asian shoreline into the teeth of enemy fire, was not. Trying to salvage something from the burning, de Robeck sent in HMS *Ocean* to tow his wounded battle cruiser—only for *Ocean*, too, to suffer a huge explosion at 6:05 p.m.,* leaving both ships helpless under enemy fire at short range. Schreiner, from shore, witnessed the "coup de grâce" that sank the *Irresistible*:

From one of the forts on the European shore came the flash of a gun, followed by a detonation and a long, hollow rumble in the air. The men about me seemed to hold their breaths as I counted to 21—the shell landed in the water, a little to the left of the "Irresistible." "Short," said somebody in Turkish. Another flash, another crash, another shriek. Again I counted—this time [to] 19. And then no water spout. From the deck of the "Irresistible" rose the red flare of an exploding shell. A third shot. Again

---

* In keeping with their general unwillingness to credit enemy gunnery, British accounts claim that HMS *Ocean* ran over a mine. Turkish sources insist that the ship was sunk by a shell from the Rumeli Mecidiye Fort, possibly fired by a heroic corporal, Seyit, who, after his battery's auto-reloading gear was knocked out, loaded the fatal shell by hand. This story has a ring of implausibility about it. But German sources, too, suggest the *Ocean* was felled by shore guns and not mines. Usedom, in his report, insists on it.

an explosion on deck. Fort Dardanos began to fire. Miss—miss—miss—hit—miss—hit—hit—miss—hit, was the order of the results achieved . . . by 7:30 p.m. the "Irresistible" had shown that names mean nothing under certain conditions—she lay at the bottom of the sea where once Achilles disembarked his troops to make war upon Priam of Troy.[60]

De Robeck was now just as spooked as Carden before him. What on earth was he up against? Unaware of the mine-laying the Turks had carried out under cover of night on March 7, 10, and 11, and unwilling in any case to give much credit to enemy gunnery, de Robeck believed the Turks must have played some kind of trick, sending floating mines downstream from the Narrows. In his report wired to London the evening of March 18, de Robeck informed Churchill that the "plan of attack must be reconsidered and means found to deal with floating mines." Although wholly mistaken, this was a common opinion in the fleet. Roger Keyes, who had commanded the mine-sweepers (though it was not him who told them to withdraw in panic) and been put aboard the *Wear* by de Robeck in the forlorn mission to rescue the *Irresistible*, was sent out later that night to hunt for the *Ocean* and *Irresistible*, only to come up empty, as both had sunk. Improbably, Keyes recalled being overcome by "a most indelible impression that we were in the presence of a beaten foe . . . it only remained for us to organize a proper sweeping force and devise some means of dealing with the drifting mines to reap the fruit of our efforts." Back at the Admiralty, Churchill was far from discouraged, wiring de Robeck on March 20 that he must not "encourage enemy by an apparent suspension of the operations." As the First Lord wrote to de Robeck three days later, intelligence reports suggested that the Dardanelles "forts are short of ammunition and supply of mines is limited . . . all your preparations for renewing attack should go forward."* And yet this telegram of March 23, 1915, was never sent. De Robeck, after meeting with Hamilton on March 22, decided it was time to call off the naval-only campaign until the army could

---

* Churchill was probably referring to a message from Kaiser Wilhelm II to Usedom, decoded by British Admiralty cryptographers on March 12 but handed to him only on March 19, to the effect that the ammunition stores Usedom had requested were on their way. It seems likely that Churchill interpreted this message to mean that Usedom was desperate to receive stores exhausted during the previous day's battle, whereas in fact the kaiser was merely responding to an ordinary request for resupply.

first demolish the forts and batteries onshore. Churchill made his case for continuing the sweeping before the War Council, convincing Kitchener, at least—only to run into opposition from Fisher and Jackson at the Admiralty. With the fleet commander and two ranking admirals strongly opposed, Prime Minister Asquith sided against the First Lord of the Admiralty, in a decision Churchill would rue for the rest of his life.[61]

Was Churchill right? On the issue of enemy ammunition running out, his case was plausible—but exaggerated. Only 9 of 176 Ottoman shore guns had been put out of action, and in general the damage to the forts, Usedom concluded after inspecting them, was "minimal." It is true that the modern heavy guns that had done the heaviest damage against the British battle cruisers on March 18 did not have great stores in reserve: there were only 271 shells left for the five 355 mm (14-inch) Krupp guns, or about 54 apiece, and between 30 and 58 shells apiece for the more numerous 22 and 24 cm (roughly 9-inch) guns. Most of the howitzer batteries, however, retained ample stores, with about 130 rounds left for each 15 cm (6-inch) howitzer and 150 shells for each "plunging" mine defense gun. About 24,000 shells remained in reserve overall at Dardanelles command, the Ottoman batteries having expended a total of only about 2,250 on March 18. Most important, nine full lines of mines still lay intact, and it was these lethal underwater explosives, and not mythical "floating mines," that truly guarded the Narrows.[62]

As for Churchill's notion that enemy morale was about to crack, this one flies so powerfully in the face of logic that it is remarkable historians have ever given it credence. Doubtless believing the rumors about panic in Constantinople—which were *partly* true (the Sublime Porte archives, gold reserves, and important Islamic relics had indeed been evacuated to Asia Minor, although most government officials had stayed on)—Keyes and Churchill seem to have applied them to the shore batteries without thinking things through from the enemy's perspective. The Turks and Germans, after all, had just witnessed three enemy battleships sink to the bottom of the Straits under their fire from shore; the crippling of the modern, near-dreadnought-class battle cruiser *Inflexible*; and the rout of the entire French squadron. Over six hundred men had perished on the *Bouvet* alone, with the British suffering another sixty casualties. By contrast, only three Germans had been killed and fourteen wounded, with Turkish losses scarcely higher, at twenty-six killed and fifty-two wounded—a reasonable price to pay for knocking out fully a third of the invading enemy fleet (six out of eighteen ships).

Little wonder the mood in the Turco-German camp after the great battle at the Narrows was glowing. As the American George Schreiner, surrounded by jubilant Turks celebrating their victory, wrote a friend the day after the battle, "to get within good range of the Turkish guns was to court destruction. For artillery marksmanship the eighteenth of March should remain a red letter day in the history of Turkey and the world."* Souchon, from Ottoman naval headquarters at Okmeidan, wrote to his wife, Violet, "Here there is great euphoria in victory (*Siegesfreude*)." Noting that the *Bouvet*, the *Irresistible*, and the *Ocean* had sunk, three other ships had limped away, and that Turkish and German losses in the great battle of the Narrows had been "minimal," Souchon had never felt better about his achievement in helping bring Turkey into the war. "Hopefully," he signed off his letter with a note of *Schadenfreude*, "the English will come back!"[63] Souchon's wish was soon granted.

---

* Not surprisingly, March 18 is indeed a state holiday in modern Turkey—*Çanakkale deniz zaferi*, or Naval Triumph at the Dardanelles Day.

CHAPTER 9

GALLIPOLI

Such actions as the storming of the Seddul Bahr position . . . must live in history
for ever; innumerable deeds of heroism and daring were performed;
the gallantry and absolute contempt for death displayed alone
made these operations possible.

—ADMIRAL JOHN DE ROBECK,
"Landing of Army on the Gallipoli Peninsula, April 25–26, 1915"[1]

I don't order you to attack. I order you to die. By the time we are dead,
other units and commanders will have come up to take our place.

—MUSTAFA KEMAL,
recalling and possibly embellishing his orders to the Fifty-Seventh Regiment
at Ari Burnu on April 25, 1915[2]

AS THE SMOKE CLEARED over the Dardanelles following the great clash of
March 18, another uneasy pause descended on the Aegean. Winds had picked
up to gale force on the morning after the battle, and the generally foul weather
had continued on for an entire week. With visibility poor, surveillance flights
ceased on both sides (the Turks did have several planes at Chanak, on the
Asian side, although they rarely contested the skies when the British planes
were active). After clenching together tightly during the life-and-death struggle at the Narrows, the belligerents thus began to slowly lose sight of one
another each day the Allied fleet failed to return to action. Although the
mood at Ottoman Dardanelles command remained confident, Usedom and

his Turkish counterpart, Djevad Bey, could not be entirely certain whether the Allied naval assault had been called off, or whether the enemy was simply waiting for the weather to clear.

In every sense other than uncertainty about enemy intentions, the pause was welcome to the Turco-Germans. Damage to any forts lightly hit on March 18 was swiftly repaired, beginning with the 355 mm Krupp gun batteries, which were all brought to full battle readiness. Earthworks at all of the key batteries were fortified up to a height of nearly ten feet (two to three meters), with new lines of sandbags ringing the gun emplacements. With arms shipments from Germany still being held up because of Balkan complications— Serbia, still fighting, cut off both the Orient Express rail connection to Constantinople and the Danube River; Romania refused to allow weapons through, even when bribed—Usedom improvised other methods of resupply, having mines withdrawn from Smyrna and Trabzon, and stripping yet more guns from the Bosphorus batteries facing the Russians. If Souchon's wish came true and the Allied navy came back, Dardanelles command was more than ready to meet them.[3]

The nature of the likely confrontation, however, was changing rapidly owing to decisions taken on both sides, in almost uncanny chronological parallel. On March 22, on board the *Queen Elizabeth*, de Robeck huddled with General Hamilton, Hamilton's chief of staff, Major General Walter Braithwaite, and the commander of the Australian and New Zealand Army Corps (ANZAC) forces assembling on Lemnos, Lieutenant General Sir William Riddell Birdwood. Polemics have raged ever since about who said precisely what, but we can safely assert that first, de Robeck agreed to let the army take a direct hand by landing troops on the Gallipoli Peninsula, and second, the most aggressive course of action (favored by Birdwood), which would have seen a limited Anzac landing right away, probably at the upper "neck" of the peninsula at Bulair, in order to draw off Turkish forces from the Narrows and enable the naval assault to resume, was ruled out in favor of a joint army-naval assault on the lower half of the peninsula, which would clearly require the participation of all available troops—including the Twenty-Ninth Division from England, which had not yet arrived. On March 23, Hamilton wired Kitchener that he needed his full army group to assemble before he would act, which would put off any serious landing until mid-April at the earliest. The very next day, Enver Pasha called Liman von Sanders into the Ottoman War Ministry in Constantinople and offered the German general command of the new Ottoman Fifth Army group created to coordinate the overall defense of the Dardanelles area against an amphibious landing by the enemy, headquartered at the town of Gallipoli. On both sides, the army men had arrived, preparing for a land battle that now seemed unavoidable. Usedom, Churchill, and de Robeck had not bowed out of the Dardanelles drama, but they would now have to share the stage with Liman, Hamilton, Birdwood, and their subordinate officers and infantrymen.[4]

To be sure, Enver Pasha did not know all the details of the shake-up in British policy when he swallowed his pride and appointed a German commander, but he had a pretty good idea of the general drift. The assembly of troops and troop transports on Lemnos, the heavy naval traffic back and forth from Alexandria, and not least the long pause in naval operations after March 18, all suggested something of what was in the works. So, too, did mushrooming reports from Turkish informants, who were all over the Aegean. A curious and little-known aspect of the intelligence war surrounding the Dardanelles campaign is that although the British, in winter 1915, more or less took over the harbors and ports of the Aegean islands of Lemnos and Imbros—which had both been recently seized by Greece after the Balkan Wars—they did not expel the Greek administrators and take over governance themselves until September. What this meant in practice was that the still-numerous Turkish population was free to observe and report whatever they saw, with no censorship to speak of. Ottoman intelligence was not perfect, but by the end of March, Enver knew that a large army of French and English soldiers—he guessed about forty thousand and fifty thousand, respectively—was massing in the Aegean islands, and it was presumably not there on vacation.[5]

The most interesting wild card in the strategic picture was the Russian factor. Usedom had been quietly confident all along that the Russians would leave their allies in the lurch at the Dardanelles, which is why he asked Okmeidan to strip the Bosphorus defenses. And yet, by the end of March 1915, there were the first real signs of activity coming from the north. On

March 25, de Robeck wired Russia's Black Sea Fleet commander, Admiral Eberhart, that "any kind of demonstration by your fleet alongside our attack at the Dardanelles would be a powerful help. I will notify you [of our plans] in four days."[6] Perhaps ashamed not to have given any such help during the great Battle of the Narrows, on March 28 Eberhart made his first sortie to the Bosphorus, firing off about 120 shells at the defensive works surrounding the lighthouse at Rumelifener, blowing up some houses but otherwise achieving little. Next day, Eberhart, under growing pressure from Sazonov, finally agreed to formally subordinate himself to de Robeck's naval command. On March 30, the Russians shelled the Turkish Black Sea ports of Zonguldak, Kozlu, Ereğli, and Kilimli, which supplied Constantinople with coal, though again doing little damage.[7]

Were these halfhearted Russian attacks probes, feints, or mere gestures of solidarity with Russia's allies? No one in Constantinople could be sure. But Liman, suddenly responsible for the most important army command in the Ottoman Empire and a very cautious man by temperament, was inclined to think the worst. As he inspected the latest Gallipoli shore defenses aboard a swift motorboat with the Austro-Hungarian military attaché, Joseph Pomiankowski, in April 1915, Liman confessed that his greatest worry was that another Franco-British strike at the Dardanelles would be "followed by a Russian landing at the Bosphorus." The forces at his disposal, Liman told Pomiankowski, "would not be sufficient to defend both sides of the Straits." Pomiankowski was more sanguine, reminding this onetime general of cavalry that the Russian fleet had less experience than the British when it came to amphibious operations, and fewer transport ships too. More to the point, he informed Liman that SMS *Goeben*, having waited out the British naval campaign in the Dardanelles safely at Constantinople while under repair, had rearmed and relaunched into the Black Sea on April 1, 1915, and the Russians "had no ship which could match it." The opportune time for a strike at the Bosphorus had come and gone, and all the Russians had done was fire off a few shells at the lighthouse.[8]

The reappearance of the *Goeben*, just as Churchill had feared, had indeed altered the strategic equation. Admiral Souchon, after letting Usedom have the glory at the Dardanelles, was now throwing his weight around again. On

April 1, the *Goeben* and the *Breslau* steamed along the western coastline, reminding Bulgaria and Romania (both still neutral) who really ruled the Black Sea. On April 2, Souchon all but taunted Eberhart, steaming along Russia's Black Sea coast and sinking two heavy Russian steamers between Sevastopol and Odessa. Whether or not Eberhart sincerely intended to put himself under de Robeck's orders and coordinate a Bosphorus assault with the next Franco-British attack on the Dardanelles, he would be unable to do so now, for the simple reason that Souchon was jamming his signals. On April 8, 1915, Eberhart informed de Robeck (by way of Kudashev at Stavka, Sazonov in Petrograd, Ambassador Benckendorff in London, and Churchill at the Admiralty) that interference from the *Goeben* would, unfortunately, make it impossible for him to communicate directly with de Robeck, and thus follow the latter's orders.[9]

With the Russian threat to the Bosphorus neutralized by Souchon's intimidation of Eberhart, Liman could set to work with greater equanimity fortifying the coastal defenses of the Gallipoli Peninsula. But his task was still formidable. Many of the Turkish troops, he found, had grown stiff in the forts and garrison, and needed exercise. But staging daytime maneuvers was dangerous, as "hostile ships were cruising everywhere and firing on any detachment that became visible." To Liman's surprise and consternation, British naval guns "fired even on such single horsemen or pedestrians as they caught sight of."* Most drilling, therefore, had to be done at night, along with fortification. With communications with Constantinople difficult—the nearest railhead, at Uzun Köprü, was a seven days' march from Gallipoli, and roads on the peninsula were almost nonexistent—Liman had to work mostly with whatever materials were at hand. Such barbed wire as could be found was stretched underwater to impede beach-landing; when it gave out, the Turks ripped "fence and wire" out of the ground from nearby farms. Torpedo heads were stripped off Turkish vessels to serve as improvised land mines. With shovels lacking, trenches were dug with farm tools and bayonets. Hospital beds were prepared in the town of Gallipoli—a thousand by early April,

---

* This was no exaggeration. Lieutenant Robert Blackie, commander of the battleship *Triumph*, recalled that his general brief in April 1915 was "occasionally putting a salvo into any place where we saw the Turk making fresh trenches." Doing Blackie one better, a British destroyer, the *Scorpion*, signaled memorably, "Have just fired 6 rounds at a camel but the beggar is still grazing peacefully."

which was hardly sufficient but a good start. Liman had no way of knowing when the Allied assault was coming—"If only the English will give me eight days!" he said upon arriving in Gallipoli on March 27—and so every night in April 1915 his men stood on high alert.[10]

On April 17, Liman caught the first hint of an impending enemy strike when the British submarine E 15, commanded by Captain T. S. Brodie, ran aground on a sandbank near Kephez Point. Brodie had been trying to break through into the Sea of Marmara, only to strike a Turkish underwater net, which knocked him off course—and beached him in the worst possible spot, directly under the gunners of the Dardanos battery, who could not believe their luck and rained down shells on the sub. Brodie himself, who had climbed up the conning tower, was killed by a direct hit, along with seven others, before the rest of the crew waved the white flag of surrender. The Turks' run of luck continued, as one of the officers who surrendered, Lieutenant Clarence Edward Stanhope Palmer, formerly British vice consul at Chanak, was an intelligence officer on de Robeck's staff (after the war broke out, Palmer had fled to Athens and volunteered for service). Palmer was questioned by both Usedom and Colonel Djevad Bey, his Turkish counterpart at Dardanelles fortress command. After Djevad threatened to execute him as a spy, Palmer agreed to share information about British plans. Cleverly, Palmer mixed together accurate intelligence—such as the presence of two other British submarines, E 11 and E 14, in the Aegean, and the fact that General Hamilton was commanding the Allied landing force, with landings planned at both Cape Helles (Seddul Bahr) and Gaba Tepe (Kabatepe)—with inaccurate: he overestimated the number of troops Hamilton had by 25,000 and suggested that the plan to land at Cape Helles had been abandoned, with the new British idea being to land the main force at Bulair. As for the date planned for the landing, Palmer pleaded ignorance.[11]

The Palmer intelligence coup, like the Ottoman staff plan captured by the Russians at Sarıkamış, had serious consequences. Although he denied any connection in his memoirs, there is evidence suggesting that Liman was taken in by Palmer's disinformation about Bulair. There were really only four possible landing places on the western and southern side of the Gallipoli Peninsula (those on the eastern side, facing the heavily mined Straits and the shore guns on the Asian side, were ruled out): the southern tip at Cape Helles (Seddul Bahr); Gaba Tepe (Kabatepe), about halfway up on the western side; Suvla Bay, a bit farther north in an outcropping jutting out into the Aegean; and the northeastern neck, at Bulair. Wherever Hamilton landed his main forces, there would likely be feints at the other sites. So the first move was obvious: Liman held his best division (the Nineteenth, commanded by Mustafa Kemal, the only division to fight in the Balkan Wars and remain fully intact) in reserve near Maidos (Maitos) and the Narrows, on the "leeward" side of the Gallipoli Peninsula, which could reinforce whichever point was threatened. Still, it mattered greatly where Liman deployed his other five divisions. Two, the Third and the Eleventh, had to remain in Asia, to defend the fortress guns of the "Trojan" side of the Straits against capture, but their task was reasonably straightforward, as the only places where Allied naval guns could cover landing troops were in Besika Bay near Kum Kale. That left three divisions, of which at least one, the Ninth, had to defend the southern shore of Cape Helles, which was such an obvious target, exposed to naval fire on all three sides. So a sensible precaution would have been to assign at least one full division to patrol the nearly adjacent landing areas of Gaba Tepe and Suvla Bay, and one up at Bulair. Instead Liman deployed the bulk of *both* remaining divisions, the Fifth and Seventh, north to Bulair, leaving only a single regiment (the Twenty-Seventh, part of the Ninth Division) to guard Gaba Tepe (although it was very well entrenched there). Whether or not the German commander was unduly influenced by Palmer's revelations, his heavy focus on Bulair is undeniable.[12]

It was also sensible. Not unlike the glittering Alexandrettine option rejected for the heavily fortified Dardanelles back in February, Bulair all but beckoned to be attacked—as Birdwood had seen in the critical March 22 conference on the *Queen Elizabeth*. At its northern tip, the Gallipoli Peninsula is only about three and a half miles (five kilometers) wide. True, the waters of Bulair were mined and the marshy landing area was fortified with trenches and barbed wire, but then this was true of most of the other landing areas too. Most strikingly, the terrain was largely flat, shorn of the steep bluffs that adorned most of the peninsula's western and southern coastlines. As Liman noted, "If the enemy occupied the narrow ridges between the Gulf of Saros and the Sea of Marmara, the [Ottoman] Fifth Army would be cut off from every land communication and the communications by water become endangered as soon as British long range [naval] guns, assisted at night by search lights, commanded this narrow part of the Sea of Marmara."[13] Liman himself, along with Kemal and all the other top commanders of the Fifth Army, would be marooned helplessly down on the peninsula, having no choice but to come north and try to break out—fighting a battle on terrain that the British could choose. True, there were possible drawbacks. If an Allied beachhead was established at Bulair and troops fanned out across the neck of the Gallipoli Peninsula, the Turks could also route reinforcements from the First Army, in Thrace, to attack the enemy from the north. This was one of Hamilton's main concerns in rejecting Bulair and deciding on a feint there instead. And yet in a sense Liman himself made the point moot by concentrating so many troops at Bulair that it became almost unthinkable for the British to land there. As Hamilton recalled almost in awe, "We managed a pretty close peep at the coast and lines of Bulair, where I was startled to see the ramifications and extent of the spider's web of deep, narrow trenches. My staff agreed that they must have taken 10,000 men a month's hard work from dark to dawn."[14]

By the third week of April 1915, there was real trepidation on both sides about the collision that everyone knew was coming. The terror of British naval gunfire kept most Ottoman troops, along with civilians, from moving about during the day, even as furious efforts on the beach fortifications were carried out every night. On Tenedos, Greek sympathizers had "uprooted a vineyard" to clear space for a cement runway eight hundred yards long, from which pilots were flying regular sorties over the Gallipoli Peninsula. On April 22, British warplanes raided Maidos, near Kemal's headquarters opposite the Narrows, dropping seven 100-pound bombs, which set much of the town on fire. And yet the overflights had the effect of frightening the pilots, too, as they were able to observe, and sometimes photograph, the fortifications at the intended landing places at Cape Helles and north of Gaba Tepe. Air Commodore Charles Rumney Samson met regularly with Hamilton to discuss his aerial findings, and these were not encouraging. On April 15, Hamilton wired Kitchener to express his concern about enemy entrenchments and barbed wire on the landing beaches. Privately, Hamilton told Samson that he feared casualties as high as 50 percent in the initial landings (although he did not confide this fear to his men, nor to Kitchener).[15] Despite his outward show of calm, Liman, too, was filled with foreboding, knowing that however well dug in the defenders were, "all of these stretches of coast and the country in the rear" would be "deluged with a frightful fire from the large caliber naval guns of the British."[16]

We should not forget, meanwhile, that there was still an entirely reasonable expectation on both sides that the Russians were finally going to take a hand in the campaign to win them the great prize of Constantinople. In mid-April, with his troops (most of whom had been sent to Alexandria for reorganization and training) finally battle-ready and the weather improving, Hamilton fixed April 23—St. George's Day—as the day for the Gallipoli landings. On April 18, Sazonov, passing on de Robeck's "orders" to the Russian Black Sea Fleet, informed Eberhart that he should begin embarking his troop transports so that "they can be sent to Turkey quickly." On April 20, Sazonov correctly informed Eberhart that the landings were slated for the twenty-third, and requested that the admiral "coordinate his operations with that [of Russia's allies]."[17] If Eberhart had followed these orders and landed troops at the Bosphorus on April 23, 1915, even as the Allied armada landed 75,000 troops on both sides of the Dardanelles, Liman and Enver would have had some very quick thinking to do.

Another bout of foul weather descended on the Aegean on April 21, postponing Hamilton's plan by several days (as it would take two days for the full loading of the troop transports and their dispatch to the landing beaches). When the skies finally cleared on the morning of April 23—when it had originally been hoped to land the troops onshore—Hamilton ordered the loading to begin. It was an immense logistical undertaking, requiring close coordination between the army and navy on the transports and intricate planning as to supply. Soldiers were to carry three days' provisions, with replacements (including, crucially, large barricoes of drinking water) dumped onshore after the beaches, hopefully, were secured. Each man carried two pounds each of beef and biscuit, a full water bottle, and 200 rounds of rifle ammunition. Every landing party was also required to haul ashore specialized kit such as hemp coil, rope, yarn, picks, shovels, axes, and crowbars, along with lanterns, signal lamps, telescopes, Morse flags, and a megaphone. The most famous innovation was the use of a converted collier, the *River Clyde*, as a kind of "Trojan horse," which would beach itself at Cape Helles as if by accident while stowing two thousand troops in her hull (a steam hopper and three wooden lighters, stored aboard, were then to be thrust forward as landing bridges). With fair weather holding on April 23 and 24, the embarkation proceeded almost perfectly. As Hamilton recalled, "No hitch of any kind occurred . . . the successful marshalling of nearly 100 merchant ships without mishap or accident and strictly in accordance with the time-table, reflects very high credit on the combined Naval and Military staffs."[18]

Hamilton's final plan for the landings, endlessly questioned ever since, was not a bad one. With surprise at more than the local, tactical level clearly impossible, the goal was to land (and feint) in as many places as possible to keep the enemy commanders guessing as to where the main attack was directed. Hamilton's strongest division, the Twenty-Ninth, commanded by Aylmer Hunter-Weston, had the most important task, landing at five different beaches at Cape Helles, with the objective of capturing the commanding heights of Achi Baba (Alçı Tepe) above the landing zone. The Anzac troops, under Birdwood, would land at Brighton Beach, just north of Gaba Tepe, hoping to push eastward from there to capture the heights of the Sari Bair range, which would then open a field of artillery fire on the Narrows, before wheeling south to entrap the Turkish forces defending Cape Helles. French forces would land on the Asian side to capture and silence the guns of Kum Kale (which could reach the Helles landing zone, though barely). Finally, a serious naval feint at Bulair was intended to draw off Liman's reserves to the north, allowing the Anzacs and Hunter-Weston's main force to capture the peninsular heights before reinforcements could be rushed in.

The only serious disagreement in the British army command in the days before April 25 concerned whether to land at dusk or dawn. Hamilton favored night landings, "seeing that, although we should lose the backing of the guns of the Fleet, troops would run less danger of having to sit helpless in their boats under a well directed fire from the shore." Hunter-Weston argued that it would simply be too difficult to coordinate beach landings without light to see by, especially at Cape Helles, where tugs would have to fight the strong current coming out of the Dardanelles and avoid hitting rocks. Predictably, de Robeck and the naval officers sided with Hunter-Weston, and so daybreak (around 4:30 or 5:00 a.m. on most beaches) it would be. "The night of the 24th-25th," de Robeck recalled, "was calm and very clear, with a brilliant moon." With the moon not fully setting until nearly 8:00 a.m., the landings could thus be carried out in conditions of decent visibility.[19]

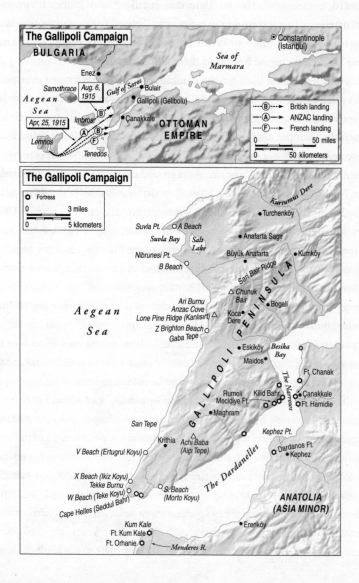

Decent visibility was, of course, a two-edged sword, just as Hamilton had feared. Sentries from the Turkish Twenty-Sixth Regiment defending Cape Helles, commanded by Major Mahmut Sabri, alerted the Ottoman command as early as 3:20 a.m. that an enemy armada was approaching. The British naval bombardment of the Helles forts began at 4:30 a.m., which telegraphed pretty clearly that a landing was imminent. Toward 6:00 a.m., the first landing tugs began coming ashore at X beach (Ikiz Koyu), W beach (Teke Koyu), and V beach (Ertugrul Koyu). At about 400 meters (1,312 feet), Turkish gunners began firing on the tugs with machine guns and light artillery. Ottoman riflemen, to conserve ammunition, were told to wait until the enemy had closed to 40 meters (131 feet) before opening fire. The action was furious and confusing, but the story was much the same across Cape Helles: British troops sustaining horrendous casualties as they clambered ashore, often even before they left their ships. On V beach, the men who came in on tugs (as opposed to the "lucky" ones on the *River Clyde*), Captain Guy Geddes of the Royal Munster Fusiliers recalled, "were literally slaughtered like rats in a trap."[20] Those on the *River Clyde*, which beached in shallow waters off V beach at 6:22 a.m., were initially spared the same fate, only for the landing bridges to fail to deploy as planned (the steam hopper stalled, then was struck by a gust of wind which took her off course). The only way from the *River Clyde* to shore (other than by swimming with a full pack) was across a narrow line of rocks strafed by Turkish rifle fire. By midday, the gangways of this would-be Trojan horse were "jammed with dead and dying." The morning's action on V beach was encapsulated in the fate of the men aboard a cutter poled to shore by a sailor from the *Lord Nelson*, who, "when he turned to beckon his passengers to the shore, found that they were no longer alive."[21] The action on W beach was much the same. By nightfall, the British forces, despite tall odds, had won precarious beachheads everywhere. As de Robeck reported to Churchill, the storming of Cape Helles "must live in history for ever . . . the gallantry and absolute contempt for death displayed alone made the operations possible."[22]

Heroism on the Turkish side was no less evident. What looked, to British observers like de Robeck, like a lopsided struggle in which the enemy had all the advantage of elevation and entrenched defensive position was of course perceived quite differently in the Ottoman camp. The naval bombardment, which had been designed to knock out the Turkish gun batteries of Cape Helles before the army landed, had evidently failed to achieve its object—but this did not make the shelling any less terrifying to the Turks onshore. As a German lieutenant observed, "The battlefield presented a grand and awful spectacle. The point of the peninsula was surrounded by a circle of war ships and transports. The ships' guns ... maintained a terrible fire against the Turkish lines." The British battleships, moreover, anchored far enough back that Ottoman field artillery at Cape Helles, frustratingly, could not fire back at them (although, unbeknownst to the Turks at the time, this was a crucial enemy mistake, as the naval guns were not accurate enough at such long range to offer effective "covering fire" to the landing troops).[23] Nor did the Turks have heavy machine guns, as the British suspected: it was accurate rifle fire that produced the slaughter.[24] Major Mahmut Sabri, who as commander of the Twenty-Sixth Regiment had local responsibility for Cape Helles, certainly had the tactical advantage over the invaders as to position and terrain, but before reinforcements were sent him on April 27, his men were outnumbered something like 10–1 by the British landing forces (in battalion terms, the British advantage was 12–1, although not all of the British battalions made it ashore intact). X beach, when the first British troops landed at 6:15 a.m., was defended by only nine Turkish soldiers before reinforcements arrived.[25] With multiple landings under way at once, there was confusion about enemy intentions at both regimental (Major Sabri) and divisional (Colonel Halil Sami) levels, confusion compounded at the top by Liman's uncertainty about whether the main thrust was still coming at Bulair—indeed he remained there all day on April 25, unwilling to abandon this crucial position until he had seen the British warships depart with his own eyes.[26]

At beaches where the Turkish defenses were less formidable, meanwhile, Allied landings on April 25 were almost wholly successful. On S beach (Morto Koyu) on the eastern side of Cape Helles, guarded by only a single Turkish platoon, the South Wales Borderers, along with marines and sailors from the *Cornwallis* (who landed without authorization on orders of its commander, Captain Alexander Davidson), sustained only sixty-three casualties—to the chagrin of the men of V beach, who were denied covering fire from the *Cornwallis* all morning. At Y beach on the far western side of Cape Helles, the

King's Own Scottish Borderers landed nearly unopposed at 5:00 a.m. and scaled the heights above the beach. By midmorning, nearly two thousand troops had come ashore, the landing being effected so easily that most of them seemed not to know what to do next. In a soon-to-be-infamous cock-up, Colonel Koe and Colonel Matthews squabbled over who had the command (Hamilton had not given clear orders to this effect), and received no answer when they sent messages to Hunter-Weston asking for instructions. In this way valuable time was lost: the men did not entrench on the heights above Y beach, nor did they move south to aid the men being butchered on V, W, and X beaches—the Turkish lines were only an hour's march away. Instead, the "men sat down to smoke and brew themselves a cup of morning tea." Hamilton, observing the "peaceful bivouac" at Y beach aboard the *Queen Elizabeth*, wired Hunter-Weston to ask whether he wished to disembark more troops there, only to receive (two hours later) an anguished refusal to pull back any strength from the bloody landing beaches farther south.[27]

The French landing was similarly successful, although it was never intended by Hamilton as more than a diversion. Although the first French troops, commanded by General Albert d'Amade, did not wade ashore on the Asian side of the Straits until nearly 9:30 a.m., d'Amade chose a beach, just north of Kum Kale, that was nearly undefended. By 11:15 a.m., the French invaders, some three thousand strong and covered by naval fire from the *Henri IV*, had secured both the town and fort of Kum Kale, although confusing skirmishing continued through the day (most, but not all, of the surrounded Turkish garrison surrendered, with five hundred prisoners taken in the first twenty-four hours, even as some units resisted). Whether or not there was ever any intention of testing Liman's reserves, which stood in wait behind the Menderes River, the point was made moot by French naval artillery, which knocked out the only bridge. Hamilton seems to have briefly considered letting d'Amade have a shot, before ordering the French to reembark on April 26, 1915, to join the main assault at Cape Helles.[28]

Somewhere in the middle on the success scale were the Anzac landings near Gaba Tepe on Z beach. To this day, controversy rages about where, exactly, the main force was supposed to land, as Birdwood's transports missed the target by somewhere between a few hundred yards and two miles to the north. This is hardly surprising in that the maps of Gallipoli provided by the British Admiralty were of poor accuracy and did not even go as far up the peninsula as Gaba Tepe.[29] Contrary to what was implied in the polemics of the "wrong beach" business, however, Ottoman evidence suggests that, had the Anzacs landed on Brighton Beach as intended, they would have been directly under the six main guns of Gaba Tepe, while also being strafed with fire from Ottoman Fifth Company (of the Twenty-Seventh Regiment), dug in above the beach: it was a "pre-planned killing zone" like V beach down at Helles.[30] Anzac Cove, where they did land, was sheltered by the cliffs above, which allowed the landing troops to establish a beachhead and even advance inland, into the scrubby wastes of Ari Burnu, where they finally encountered serious resistance. Much was amiss at Anzac Cove, of course. There were serious problems with the offloading and great confusion about where exactly the men were and where they were supposed to go. Nevertheless, the fact remains that the landing was far more successful than at any of the main Helles beaches.

There was considerable confusion on the Turkish side about the Anzac sector, too, which suggests that Hamilton's conception of multiple landings at many spots had real merit. Apparently Turkish sentries reported hearing noises offshore as early as 2:30 a.m., but they were not acted on, as it was not yet clear which landing sites were real and which feints. Mustafa Kemal, at Nineteenth Division headquarters at Bogali, heard firing from the west about dawn, and received a message reporting enemy activity at Ari Burnu from Colonel Halil Sami, whose Ninth Division had responsibility, at 6:30 a.m. Kemal set out across the peninsula on horseback, reaching the high point of Chunuk Bair (Conk Bayırı) at around 9:40 a.m.

A famous scene was then enacted. Kemal, still waiting for his main force (the Fifty-Seventh Regiment, plus a cavalry company and mountain battery) to arrive, encountered Turks from the Twenty-Seventh Regiment, who, having failed to dislodge the Anzacs from the cove, were retreating. "Why are you running away?" he asked, to be told that the men were out of ammunition. Kemal then ordered them to "fix bayonets and lie down." When his

Fifty-Seventh Regiment arrived from Bigali, Kemal then, according to legend, told his troops, "I don't order you to attack. I order you to die."* Crucially, Halil Sami unselfishly agreed to subordinate his Twenty-Seventh Regiment to Kemal, enabling the energetic young officer to direct a blistering counterattack in the early afternoon, pushing the Anzac troops back toward the beaches. Kemal's triumph was not absolute. There were notorious problems with the Seventy-Seventh Regiment, composed mostly of Arab conscripts, who all but melted away during the day's fighting. And his thrust failed to "throw the enemy into the sea," as every Turkish commander hoped to do. Still, the fighting at Ari Burnu on April 25 was a clear Turkish victory. Morale plunged in the Anzac camp, to the point where the two main division commanders, Major General W. T. Bridges and Major General Sir Alexander Godley, advocated an immediate evacuation from Anzac Cove. Birdwood referred the request to Hamilton, who discussed the idea with his senior aides and officers. Instead, the men were told "they must stick it" and advised to "dig, dig, dig."[31]

It had been a dramatic day of fighting, though maddeningly inconclusive. Postmortem analysis of the Gallipoli landings on April 25, 1915, began almost immediately and has continued ever since. Clearly, the British fleet could and should have offered closer naval support to the landing forces on V and W beaches, as was done far more effectively at S and X and Y beaches, Kum Kale, and Anzac Cove. It was partly for fear of strafing landing parties with "friendly fire" that the naval guns stayed largely silent after the initial bombardment, but this, in turn, reflected the poor decision to anchor at long range, where accuracy was questionable. The men being slaughtered on V beach suffered from the decision of Davidson, aboard the *Cornwallis*, to muck about on S beach all morning when he could have done far more good at V beach next door. All kinds of things went wrong at Anzac Cove, although things might have been far worse if troops had landed on Brighton Beach as intended, which rather moots the argument. The French landings at Kum

---

* Clearly, at least some of this story was later embellished to burnish the Kemal legend. Nevertheless, there are bits and pieces of truth in it. An order in Kemal's name, later found on the body of a Turkish soldier of the Fifty-Seventh Regiment—which was indeed nearly wiped out in subsequent fighting—read, a bit less elegantly, "I do not expect that any of us would not rather die than repeat the shameful story of the Balkan war. But if there are such men among us, we should at once lay hands upon them and set them up in line to be shot!"

Kale, or the successful British ones at S and Y beaches, could have been reinforced, with landing forces pulled back from the carnage on V, X, and W
(thereby reinforcing success, rather than failure). On the Ottoman side, most
of the argument surrounds the failure, by Halil Sami, to reinforce the Helles
beaches more rapidly, forgoing the chance to capitalize on British distress and
thrust the invaders back into the Aegean Sea. The Twenty-Fifth Regiment of
Halil Sami's Ninth Division, poised in strategic reserve fifteen kilometers (9.3
miles) northeast of Helles in a position that would have allowed him to reinforce either Ari Burnu or the south, was held back until nearly 6:30 p.m., by
which time the British landing forces at Helles, though suffering terribly, had
won beachheads. Even Kemal has come in for criticism for his handling of the
largely Arab Seventy-Seventh Regiment, which had been temporarily diverted
south owing to a false rumor of an Allied landing at Kum Tepe, to the south
of Gaba Tepe. Liman has been raked over the coals for mistakenly reinforcing
Bulair: he ordered the Fifth Division to deploy there as late as April 26, long
after it should have been apparent that the British naval attack there was a
feint.[32]

   Still, while any of these alternative decisions, made in the heat of a complex unfolding battle, might have altered local outcomes, the pattern of the
campaign as a whole was largely decided by the balance of forces in theater.
Like the action on the western front, Gallipoli was almost fated to be a stalemate once the dust had settled after the initial clashes. The Allies could really
only have won a decisive advantage by winning the heights of Sari Bair or
Achi Baba on the first day, which feat, in turn, would only have been possible
if the Turks had panicked utterly. Kemal's achievement at Chunuk Bair was
real, but it was a matter of common sense and courage under pressure, not a
miracle. Conversely, the Turco-German defenders could only have "won"
Gallipoli by pushing the enemy landing forces back into the sea before they
could entrench themselves. With the balance of forces at Cape Helles and
Anzac Cove/Ari Burnu, in numbers of troops if not tactical position, strongly
in favor of the Allies, this was clearly impossible. In the end, the "what-ifs" of
the Gallipoli landings remain a bit fanciful. A Kemal-esque reaction from
Halil Sami to expel the enemy from Cape Helles would have required the
Twenty-Fifth Regiment to cover fifteen kilometers to the southern tip of the

peninsula, over uneven ground, in several hours (say, if helicopters had existed in 1915). Some kind of British reinforcement of Y beach, or at least clearer orders given the men there to move south and strike at the Turkish positions from the rear, is a bit more realistic, but would have required real-time field communications of a kind that did not exist in 1915, especially among officers just landed onshore with whatever kit they could carry (which did not tend to include wireless equipment that, at the time, weighed upward of six hundred pounds). The "straggling" on some of the landing beaches was a matter of much hand-wringing in the Allied command, but most of these men had never experienced combat before, and it is unrealistic to expect that all would have maintained perfect discipline under murderous fire. A fair assessment of the initial clash of April 25 must conclude that both sides performed reasonably well, given the difficult, multivariate tasks before them.

For the historian, the more interesting Gallipoli counterfactual relates to two dogs that did not bark: Greek and Russian participation. Of course, a contribution from Athens had been expressly ruled out by the Russians, and so the notion of a Greek army of 150,000 landing on Gallipoli, or sweeping across Thrace toward Constantinople, must be dismissed as impossible in the diplomatic circumstances. The Russians, however, *had* agreed to contribute a diversionary strike at the Bosphorus concurrently with the Gallipoli landings, as indeed they had also promised to do at the Dardanelles in February. Owing to excellent intelligence on Turkish shore dispositions, Admiral Eberhart remained gun-shy in February and March, at the very time he could have helped divert Ottoman strength northward from the Dardanelles.

There were sound reasons for Russia's reticence, however fatal her inaction proved to her Allies at Gallipoli. Enver, Liman, and Souchon were well aware of the ongoing naval buildup at Odessa, including the assembly of amphibious landing forces and troop transports. With the *Goeben* down for repairs from January until the end of March, Eberhart had been able to conduct probes along Turkey's Black Sea coast, regularly shelling the coal ports near Zonguldak. Every time there was even a hint of Russian action near the Bosphorus, though, Souchon staged a counter-sortie into the Black Sea to scare Eberhart off. After a sighting of Russian ships near the coast on March 15, Souchon ordered the *Breslau* and two torpedo boats to raid Russia's Black

Sea ports. Eberhart's halfhearted shelling of Rumelifener on March 28 prompted a stronger countermove, made possible by the newly repaired SMS *Goeben*. On March 31, Enver ordered Souchon to send the entire Ottoman fleet—including the *Goeben*—to menace Russia's Black Sea coast, with the principal objective being, in Enver's words, "to destroy as many transports as possible, in order to lessen the chance of a landing of troops [at the Bosphorus]."[33] The resulting sortie of April 1–3, which saw the *Mecidiye*, the *Hamidiye*, and a fleet of torpedo boats and minesweepers attack Odessa, even as the *Goeben* and *Breslau* steamed by Bulgaria and Romania before shelling Sevastopol, put such a scare into Eberhart that he did not venture across the Black Sea for the next three weeks. For good measure, the *Goeben* staged another intimidating steam-by at Odessa on April 11. It was thus with considerable anxiety that Eberhart received Sazonov's April 18 orders to stage a diversionary strike on the Bosphorus alongside the Allied Gallipoli landings slated for April 23.[34]

If the Russians were going to show up to claim their prize, it was now or never. The two-day weather delay gave Eberhart still more time to get his act together, although surely he should have been ready to go by the twenty-third. By the time the Allied troops waded ashore on the Gallipoli Peninsula under murderous enemy fire on the morning of April 25, 1915, nearly five weeks had passed since the climactic battle at the Narrows. The initial Dardanelles attack, when the Russians had been enjoined to mount a simultaneous Bosphorus attack, had transpired a month earlier still. Perhaps the most relevant date to recall is January 20, when Churchill had initially requested Russian participation in the upcoming campaign. Eberhart had thus had three months and five days to prepare for his moment of glory at the Bosphorus.* "Projectiles from our ships reached as far as Sariyer and Beykos," the Russian commander reported at the conclusion of his day's work on April 25. True, none of these shells did visible damage to "any populated areas" other than at Akbaba, a small, unfortified town on the Asian side of the Bosphorus. But then his ships had come under "heavy fire" from a Bosphorus fort, and one

---

* The delay was not accidental. After learning of the failure of the Allies at the Narrows on March 18, 1915, Stavka issued orders *forbidding* the dispatch of Caucasian troops by sea from Batumi, the idea being that, with the Turco-German fleet still a menace, it was safer to send them to Odessa by land. As with nearly every decision made at Stavka and the Russian Admiralty, the needs of Russia's allies were, at best, a secondary consideration.

ran over a mine and began to list, so it was understandable that he had had to turn back.[35] A week later, Eberhart returned to the Bosphorus with a larger force, comprising five battleships, three cruisers, eight destroyers, a single "aircraft carrier" platform (an ocean liner converted so as to carry five seaplanes), and four trawlers (including minesweepers). The next day after Eberhart's fleet was scared off into open sea by the hard-charging SMS Goeben on May 2, 1915, Eberhart's two longest-range warships, the Tri Svyatitelya and the Rostislav, ventured within range of land and fired off 132 six-inch (152 mm) shells at the forts at the outer mouth of the Bosphorus, and 39 larger-caliber 254 mm shells. Eberhart reported proudly that he had caused a "fantastic" explosion at the fort of Elmaz, although he was unable to ascertain further damage, as his seaplanes had not been able to observe the target area.[36] Souchon, unimpressed (Okmeidan reported that "only a few houses were destroyed"), ordered the Goeben, Breslau, and Hamidiye out into the Black Sea on May 6, 1915, to scare off further Russian attacks.[37]

Eberhart got the hint. Although preparations continued at Sevastopol and Odessa for the eventual dispatch of troops to Constantinople, Russia's Black Sea Fleet did not return to the Bosphorus all summer. On May 15, 1915, Eberhart informed de Robeck and Hamilton that he had assembled an expeditionary force, the V Caucasian Corps, under General Istomin, comprising some 40,000 men, including marines, cavalry, and medical corps. The French and British were to understand, however, that these troops were really "only a symbol of our participation in the conquest of Constantinople," as they could only possibly land there "once the Allies had arrived in Constantinople and the Turkish fleet"—presumably including the Goeben and Breslau—"had been destroyed." Once the Straits and "Tsargrad" had been won by Russia's allies, that is, she would be happy to claim her prize. And yet, as Eberhart signed off wistfully, if less than helpfully, "This moment will not likely occur in the near future."[38]

One can only imagine the reaction of the British, French, and Anzac grunts entrenched at Gallipoli if this message had been read out to them. Indeed, Sazonov began to feel a pang of guilt as the human price of Russia's no-show was coming into focus. On May 13, 1915, Russia's foreign minister lashed out at Eberhart and the generals at Stavka for failing to "provide the help from the Bosphorus that our allies counted on"—help he and the grand duke had expressly promised Churchill and Kitchener. The sufferings of Russia's brothers-in-arms, Sazonov wrote, "were greatly exacerbated, because the Turks were able to concentrate against them all of their strength." It would be "insupportable," he concluded this belated plea, "if Tsargrad, the most valuable prize that we might gain out of the present war, were conquered exclusively by the efforts of our allies, without our participation."[39]

Insupportable or not, the conquest of "Tsargrad" for Russia was exactly what those Allies were bleeding and dying for on the Gallipoli Peninsula, whether or not they knew it. It was an odd thing for a soldier from New Zealand or Australia to fight for, but then the Gallipoli campaign as a whole becomes odder the closer one looks at it. Perhaps by virtue of the absurdity of their being in Turkey in the first place—for what quarrel could there possibly be between antipodeans and Turks, separated from one another by two oceans and thousands of miles?—the Anzac front has always had a special place in Gallipoli lore. It was on the precarious beachhead of Anzac Cove on the night of April 25 that the first serious rethink of the campaign occurred. Some fifteen thousand men had been landed during the day. The Anzacs had made it farther inland than troops on any other front, and yet had been routed by Kemal and sent back down the slopes they had hopefully scaled just hours earlier. The initial taste of victory had soured into defeat, all in one dramatic day. As Birdwood informed Hamilton that night, his divisional generals "fear their men are thoroughly disorganized by shrapnel fire to which they have been subjected all day after exhaustion and gallant work in the morning . . . if we are to re-embark it must be at once."[40] The French had been re-embarked from Kum Kale, after all, as had (most of) the King's Own Scottish Borderers from Y beach. Why not withdraw the Anzacs too? Or why not, indeed, pull back the main landing force at Helles, which could be shipped back to Alexandria, refitted, and deployed (as per Kitchener's original wishes) to Alexandretta instead?

Far from a shocking display of unseemly panic, as Birdwood's message was initially read by Allied commanders,* his message to Hamilton was

---

* Birdwood's message later became notorious, but at the time, the request for an evacuation of Anzac Cove was successfully hushed up, being revealed to the public only with the publication of Hamilton's *Gallipoli Diary* in 1920.

marked by a flash of insight, a glimpse of the ultimate futility of the campaign. Try though the Anzacs mightily did to win higher ground in a series of desultory attacks at Ari Burnu, as the British and French did at the two "battles of Krithia" on April 28 and May 6–8, 1915, all the Allies could do was to move the front line forward a few hundred yards (in the harsh scrub of Ari Burnu) and a mile or two (above Helles). Nor did the Turks' own, equally desultory counterattacks succeed in dislodging the enemy. By the time the first series of battles were over on May 8, 1915, the Allies had suffered 20,000 casualties and the Turks 15,000. All that this horrific carnage had produced was a smaller-scale replica of the trench lines of the western front, with the Germans (alongside their Turkish hosts) yet again "enjoying" the high ground, with a better field of fire and slightly more sanitary living conditions, even though they were facing down an enemy far better supplied with munitions (in the case of Gallipoli these included naval guns, although they were ultimately neutralized by German submarines) and resolved to fight to the bitter end.

The outlines of the stalemate were grasped well enough by de Robeck, who, not as personally invested in the success of the army as Hamilton, was free to speak his mind. "General Hamilton informs me," de Robeck wrote to Churchill on May 10, 1915, "that the Army is checked, its advance on Achi Baba can only be carried out by a few yards at a time, and a condition of affairs approximate to that in Northern France is threatened." De Robeck, regretting that "the help which the Navy has been able to give the Army in its advance has not been as great as was anticipated," was willing to consider attempting another concerted push through the Narrows, if he thought it would help the army. And yet he was not sure what the point would be *even if* the fleet blasted its way through the Narrows. "From the vigour of the enemy's resistance," he reasoned, "it is improbable that the passage of the Fleet into the Marmora will be decisive and therefore it is equally probable that the Straits will be closed behind the Fleet." In a subtle reminder of his argument with Churchill over pushing on after March 18, de Robeck concluded that "the temper of the Turkish Army in the peninsula indicates that the forcing of the Dardanelles and subsequent appearance of the Fleet off Constantinople will not, of itself, prove decisive."[41]

So where did that leave the Allied armies? They could only dig in, just as Hamilton had advised the Anzacs. The one mercy of Gallipoli, as compared with the western front, was that, Turkey being the land of "bright sun," the trenches on both sides were drier. This was a mixed blessing. Instead of rooting around in mud, the men breathed in hot dust and suffered the agonies of heat exhaustion—compounded by the lack of trees to provide any shade. The mercury rose through May and June, on into the brutal Turkish summer, with every uptick in temperature bringing forth a riot of creatures crawling through the trenches: ants, lice, scorpions and centipedes, tarantulas. The ants could be useful—as they ate the lice—but there was no escape from the mosquitoes. Dysentery and diarrhea, spread by the flies, were rampant on both sides. The worst torment of all was the stench of dead bodies, and it was not accidental that the first signs of grudging respect between the enemies involved truces to bury the dead. Stories abound of "gifts" thrown across the lines, with Brits sharing their "bully beef" tins and the Turks their grapes and olives. Still, we must not romanticize what was, after all, one of the worst killing grounds of the First World War. As on the western front, for every story of fraternization at Gallipoli, there were dozens more of privates getting their heads blown off if they raised them above the parapet.[42]

Far from the decisive move on the chessboard Kitchener and Churchill had dreamed of, Gallipoli had turned into another stalemate. It had called forth great valor and heroism on both sides, along with all the attendant horrors of stationary warfare between evenly matched, well-entrenched enemies at close range. Absent some major new tactical innovation, or the dispatch of massive numbers of reserves that neither side had yet found, the stalemate looked like it would continue through the summer. The Ottoman Sick Man, it seemed, had won yet another stay of execution in the existential struggle at the Straits. On the other side of Asia Minor, however, the death agonies of the empire were calling forth a new kind of horror.

CHAPTER 10

MASSACRE IN TURKISH ARMENIA

There is no mercy east of the Hellespont!

—RAFAEL DE NOGALES,
Venezuelan soldier of fortune and commander of Ottoman forces
besieging Van in April–May 1915[1]

ALL BUT LOST IN THE DRAMA at Gallipoli was the original reason the British high command had sent troops there—to aid the "needy" Russians. Had there not been some urgent strategic imperative involved—something about a Russian collapse in the Caucasus? Of course, faced as they were with the terrible stalemate above the beaches—with all the thorny tactical problems involved in overwhelming a well-armed enemy entrenched on higher ground—it is easy to see why men such as Birdwood and Hamilton paid little attention to faraway developments on Turkey's eastern borderlands, which could have only an indirect impact on the Gallipoli front. Historians, however, have no such excuse. So let us at least try to unpack the tangled skein of cause and effect, to see how the Gallipoli landings affected the bitter struggle in eastern Turkey that had brought them forth in the first place.

The most tangible effect the British Dardanelles stratagem had on the Caucasian front was to draw off Russian troops raised in Tiflis so they could participate in the hoped-for occupation of Constantinople. To replace his own losses at Sarıkamış, Yudenich began assembling the new V Caucasian Corps in February 1915 out of the Third Caucasian Rifle Division and the First and Second Plastun Brigades. Scarcely had the Caucasian chief of staff put his new corps together, however, than orders came down from Stavka (courtesy of Sazonov, trying to accede to British requests) for the V Caucasian Corps to be sent to Odessa to prepare for amphibious operations at the Bosphorus. With his own generals insisting that no strength be diverted from the critical European fronts against the Austrians and Germans, Grand Duke Nicholas had been forced to lean on Yudenich instead. In this way the British Dardanelles and Gallipoli campaigns, originally conceived as a way of aiding Russian troops supposedly beleaguered on the Caucasian front, had the effect of depriving that very front of an entire army corps that might have allowed Yudenich to exploit his victory at Sarıkamış.

The weakening of the Russian position in the Caucasus was compounded, moreover, by the same panic in Tiflis that had called forth the Dardanelles "diversion" in the first place. On December 30, 1914, at the height of the scare spread by General Myshlayevskii (recently wounded on the retreat from Sarıkamış, and having captured a terrifying battle plan signed by Enver), Count I. I. Vorontsov-Dashkov, viceroy and commander in chief of Russia's Caucasian Army, ordered General T. G. Chernozubov to conduct a full-scale retreat of Russian forces from northern Persia, an order that, unlike the concurrent order to abandon Tiflis, was actually carried out. Vorontsov-Dashkov's order may have been enforced for political as much as strategic reasons: the presence of some twelve thousand Russian troops in "Persian Azerbaijan," where most had been encamped since 1908, was a major irritant in Anglo-Russian relations, and more irritating still to the semi-independent government of Ahmad Shah in Teheran, which understandably resented being occupied. Sir Walter Townley, His Majesty's consul in Teheran, had been hearing complaints for months about the depredations of Russian troops in northern Persia. He had repeatedly urged Sir Edward Grey to lean on the Russians to withdraw to "prevent, if possible, [Persian] Azerbaijan becoming a theater of war between Russia and Turkey." In the Sarıkamış panic, Vorontsov-Dashkov saw an opportunity to assuage British concerns, and so Chernozubov pulled back from Urmia province and Tabriz (which was supplied directly by rail from Tiflis)—although some Russian troops remained at Kazvin, north of Teheran, and at Resht and Enzeli on the Caspian.[2]

The curious upshot of these two related developments was to give the Ottoman Third Army renewed hope in the wake of Enver's catastrophic defeat in the snows—and, more to the strategic point, to shift the focus of action south, where the large-scale Russian withdrawal from northern Persia had all but invited an Ottoman incursion there. Indeed Sazonov, in deflecting Grey's requests to evacuate Persian Azerbaijan prior to Sarıkamış, had emphasized Russia's vulnerability on this southern front, where the low-lying valleys between Lake Urmia and Lake Van functioned as a kind of strategic cockpit, posing few serious obstacles to mobile armies. Enver's offensive had, if nothing else, proved just how difficult it was for armies to maneuver in the high mountains between Erzurum and Tiflis, in effect putting that front into deep freeze, where it should have remained all along. The much warmer valley lowlands of Urmia were ground zero in the Russo-Turkish espionage and propaganda wars over the loyalties of local Kurds, Armenians, and Assyrian, or Nestorian, Christians (a Semitic people still speaking a dialect of Eastern Aramaic with their own apostolic church dating to the first century AD), with agents smuggling weapons, propaganda, and people across the nebulous borders where the Ottoman, Russian, and Persian empires collided. Now this critical ethno-religious frontier cauldron, long simmering, would boil over under the strain of world war.

The first blow was struck by the Turks. In late January, Enver sent his uncle, Halil Bey, to Diarbakır, and then Van to command the reconstituted Ottoman Thirty-Sixth Division, augmented by new levies of Frontier Guards, Jandarma battalions, and irregular Kurdish cavalry units. It is noteworthy that Halil Bey, originally with the Sixth Army in Mesopotamia, had arrived in Erzurum too late to participate in Enver's anticipated victory at Sarıkamış: he was now to spearhead the Turkish conquest of Persian Azerbaijan instead.

Before Halil Bey's regular army arrived, however, the battle for Urmia was joined by forces closer to hand. Taking advantage of the Russian withdrawal, pro-Turkish Kurdish tribes began plundering the towns around Lake Urmia in early January, before moving north toward Dilman and Khoy. Hot on their heels was a sort of jihadist army of Muslim volunteers commanded by Ömer Naci Bey, an old Unionist conspirator of 1908 who now directed Enver's Special Organization, the *Teşkilat-ı Mahsusa*, in Mosul. Ömer Naci's volunteers stormed into Tabriz on January 14, 1915, burned down the Russian bank, and put the few remaining Russian officers and Cossacks to flight. With Halil Bey mustering his forces at Lake Van, and a Turco-German mission to enlist Persia and Afghanistan in Islamic holy war against the British Raj gathering strength in Baghdad, it seemed that danger on the Ottoman Empire's eastern borderlands had turned into opportunity. As Goltz Pasha, the longest-serving German officer in the Ottoman Empire, reported to the German high command on January 30, 1915, although the Turks had met setbacks at Sarıkamış, Suez, and Basra, "in Persia things are moving forward. Tabriz and Khoy are now in Turkish hands."[3]

It was a mirage. Thus far the fighting in Persian Azerbaijan had involved mostly irregulars and locals, with regular army units on both sides still being assembled behind the front lines. Ömer Naci's volunteers had made the running against spotty opposition at best. And, although the Russian V Caucasian Corps being assembled was destined for Odessa, Yudenich still had enough forces in Tiflis to contest Persian Azerbaijan as soon as he chose to. On the very day Goltz Pasha reported the capture of Tabriz, the city was stormed by Russian forces under General Chernozubov, advancing from Djoulfa. Khoy and Dilman, both taken by the Turks in January, were retaken

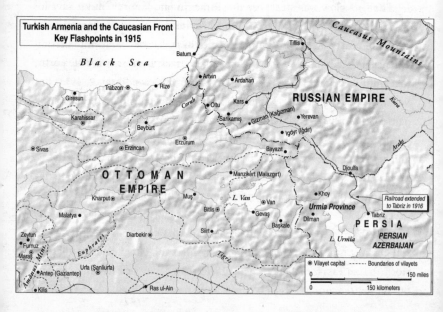

by the Russians in March. True, Enver's uncle had not yet arrived in Persian Azerbaijan with the main Ottoman striking force. By the time he did in mid-April 1915, however, the Russians were more than ready.

The battle of Dilman, which began on April 29, 1915, is not a household name in the historiography of the First World War. But it should be. After months of seesaw, tit-for-tat skirmishing between irregulars in the critical strategic underbelly of Persian Azerbaijan, Dilman saw the first serious engagement between regular Russian and Turkish troops, aided by "co-religionist" volunteers on both sides, which ratcheted up the stakes. Holding the city was a single Russian battalion, under General Nazarbekov, augmented by an Armenian volunteer *druzhiny* and six guns. Six more Russian battalions and two Cossack cavalry battalions were stationed in reserve four miles to the north, giving Nazarbekov a total force of about five thousand, still less than division strength though including a strong cavalry component. On the Ottoman side, Enver's uncle Halil Bey had a proper infantry division, the Thirty-Sixth, escorted by mounted Muslim Kurds. With more than ten thousand troops, Halil's striking force was considerably superior to the Russians' in numbers, although Nazarbekov had had two months to fortify a defensive position. Halil had been preparing his offensive for weeks, advancing methodically from Muş and Bitlis, around the southern shore of Lake Van, through the Ottoman frontier town of Başkale, and finally into Persian Azerbaijan. Halil now ordered his men to attack Russian lines in waves, directing five assaults on Dilman between April 29 and May 2, 1915. But Nazarbekov and his Russo-Armenian force were ready, as were the Cossacks, waiting in reserve in case Nazarbekov needed them. The Turks were routed. Leaving "nearly a thousand dead on the field," Halil Bey at last withdrew the Thirty-Sixth Ottoman Division back across the border toward Van.[4]

If we peel back to examine concurrent events on other Ottoman fronts, we can see why the little-known battle of Dilman mattered so greatly. On the other end of Asia Minor, the Allied assault on Gallipoli was heating up, between the initial landings of April 25 and the great battles of Krithia (April 28 and May 6–8) over the heights of Achi Baba. Dilman marked the farthest advance east for the advancing right flank of the Ottoman Third Army, its last real chance to salvage something from Enver's failed offensive at

Sarıkamış and put Yudenich and the Russians on their heels. Instead, Halil had repeated his nephew's mistake of overextension, forcing the Turkish right wing back in a pell-mell retreat and leaving the Russians in firm control of strategic Urmia, with the door now open for their advance on Ottoman Van, Bitlis, and Muş. Behind Ottoman lines, meanwhile, an Armenian rebellion against Ottoman authority had just erupted at Van, directly in the path opened up by the Russian victory at Dilman.*

The Armenian rebellion at Van was long in gestation. The leading Armenian revolutionary party–cum–paramilitary organization, the *Dashnaksutiun* (Dashnaks) had always been strong in this picturesque city nestled between snow-capped mountains and Lake Van. Aram Manukian Pasha, the local Dashnak strongman, was already a combat veteran, although interestingly his partisans had most recently seen action at the side of Ottoman troops, as both pursued Kurdish brigands away from Van in June 1913. Aram Pasha also met regularly with Russia's vice consul, S. Olferiev. Olferiev reported two key conclusions about Van to Sazonov in the months before the world war: first, the local Armenian population, previously somewhat ambiguous in its loyalties (and split between the other revolutionary parties—with the Hunchaks and the Armenakan competing with the Dashnaks), was now strongly "Russophile," with the Dashnaks, dominating the field, "completely on our [i.e., the Russian] side"; and second, Van was already "an armed camp . . . all the Armenian merchants are stockpiling guns in their stores."[5] Even the British consul, with no dog in the local fight, was reporting by 1914 that the Dashnaks had pushed the less extreme Armenian groups in Van to the side, and the party "has actively concerned itself with the secret importation of arms and their distribution amongst its followers . . . Mauser pistols are their favourite weapon; they are easily hidden and imported and can be used as a carbine, being sighted up to 1,000 metres." Strikingly, the British consul observed that "in Van it is said that the Armenians are now better armed than

---

* May 2, 1915, the date of Halil's withdrawal from Dilman, was also the day of the great German breakthrough at Gorlice-Tarnow, which punctured Russian lines in Austrian Galicia and paved the way for Russia's Great Retreat of 1915 that saw most of Russian Poland fall to the Central Powers. Critical as this battle was for the future course of the war in eastern Europe, though, its impact was felt only weeks later by the Caucasian Army—and later still by the Russian advance guard now approaching Van. It did not factor into Ottoman perceptions of the strategic situation at the time, as did Gallipoli, Dilman, and Van.

the Kurds."[6] The Russians, for their part, had been trying to smuggle weapons to the Armenians of Van all fall and winter, even while they were organizing Armenian volunteer *druzhiny* all along the Ottoman border, in towns like Oltu, Gizman (Kağızman), Igdyr (Iğdır), and Sarıkamış itself, where, as we saw, they played an important role in surveillance. By March 1915, there were four Russian-armed operational Armenian *druzhiny*, a thousand strong, at Bayazıt, on the Ottoman side of the border northeast of Lake Van.[7]

In the city of Van itself, armed clashes between Armenian partisans and government forces were reported as early as September 1914, even before Turkey had entered the world war. On September 24, 1914, Ottoman Third Army intelligence reported evidence that the Russians were smuggling weapons and ammunition across the border, and warned that any subjects caught smuggling "shall be immediately executed." The onset of war ratcheted tensions up still further, with reports of Armenian army draftees either resisting service or deserting to Russian lines. Behind Ottoman lines, incidents of sabotage—the cutting of telegraph wires, attacks on local officials and police barracks, fuse bomb detonations disturbing important road junctions—began occurring in December with numbing regularity, with the culprits, believed to be Armenian partisans, difficult to track down. On December 21, 1914, Ottoman officials reported that Armenian bands were in open revolt in the districts of Karçekan and Gevaş, both in Van province. January, February, and March 1915 saw rebel activity spread further, with incidents reported as far away as Erzincan, Sivas, and Cilicia, although the most serious ones were occurring nearer the front lines in Van, Bitlis, and Erzurum. Ottoman army intelligence was, by now, reporting (accurately) that Armenian *druzhiny* had been organized in Oltu, Gizman (Kağızman), and Sarıkamış—missing only Igdyr (Iğdır). On the Ottoman side of the border, "the pillaging and destroying of Muslim villages" by partisans had already begun. Mushrooming rebel activity portended, in the view of Ottoman army intelligence, a "catastrophe of unimaginable proportions."[8]

Fearful for the supply lines of the Third Army, and for its control of Turkish Armenia more generally, the Ottoman high command likely exaggerated the scale of the threat posed by this as-yet-uncoordinated rebellion (the commander in Van, for example, believed erroneously that the Russians had given machine guns and artillery to the Armenian *druzhiny*; this was untrue, although they were well supplied with rifles, pistols, and ammunition).[9] Before we dismiss its importance, however, we should take into account the fact that Russian reports on these same developments match Ottoman ones almost perfectly. Before leaving Erzurum at the onset of hostilities, the Russian consul there, A. A. Adamov, had reported that armed Armenian partisans—not only in Erzurum, but "also in all cities surrounding it, including Erzincan, Sivas, Mana Hatun and Kayseri, not to mention in the villages and rural areas"—were "awaiting with impatience the arrival of the Russian troops who will free them from the Turkish yoke." Sensibly, Adamov reported that these Turkish Armenians, having "hidden their weapons in secret storage caches . . . would not dare to take them up" until the moment was ripe—until, that is, "the Russians are right on their doorstep." Timing was therefore critical. "The slightest delay," Adamov warned Tiflis command, "in coming to aid [the Armenians] could lead to their complete destruction."[10] Catching the hint, Sazonov himself instructed Yudenich, on December 17, 1914, that "any order for an Armenian uprising must only be given after receiving prior agreement with the Foreign Ministry."[11]

Did the Russians ever give this agreement? In mid-February 1915, delegates from an Armenian revolutionary committee from Zeytun, in the mountains northwest of Cilicia, traveled to Tiflis and promised to "pounce on Turkish [army] communications" if they were given Russian arms and ammunition. Because this was as much a political as a military matter, Vorontsov-Dashkov stepped in to scotch the proposal. This suggests that Tiflis had not received Sazonov's blessing for aiding an Armenian rebellion behind Ottoman lines.[12]

Blessed or unblessed by Russian authorization, however, there is no doubt that Armenian rebel activity took on a serious aspect in spring 1915, even before the insurrection broke out at Van. The first week of April, a delegation of Hunchak revolutionaries proudly reported to Yudenich at Tiflis command that Armenian partisans were ready to rise "all over Cilicia," with three thousand separate armed cells operating in the region between Adana and Aleppo—the very region the British could easily have conquered had they chosen to land at Alexandretta instead of Gallipoli. At Maraş, Armenian army deserters, resisting arrest, killed six Ottoman gendarmes on March 12 and then fled to Zeytun, where, on March 23, they teamed up with another 150 or so Armenian rebels to attack an Ottoman weapons convoy and army barracks, inflicting several hundred casualties, before fleeing to the hills, accompanied by local Armenian civilians.[13] By mid-April, Russian military intelligence in Tiflis had received reports of "a general uprising in Cilicia" and "bloody clashes" between Armenians and government forces in Bitlis and Muş, not to mention "systematic slaughter in Erzurum . . . Zeytun and environs."[14] This Russian intelligence, in turn, corresponds almost perfectly to what is found in Ottoman military sources, which report uprisings across Cilicia in early April, though noting also the movement of armed Armenian partisan bands as far afield as Kilis (near Aleppo), Bayburt, Kayseri, Konya, and Sivas. Partisan activity was also reported near the particularly vulnerable Baghdad Railway mountain choke point at Pozantı.[15]

Alarming as these reports appeared, they were a mere prelude to the clash at Van, which reached its critical stage in the second week of April 1915. In the countryside surrounding the city, violence had been endemic all winter, though so far casualties were usually counted in single digits. March saw the first skirmishing between rebels and regular army units. The Ottoman Third Army command dispatched to Van a six-hundred-strong Jandarma battalion under Cevdet Bey, a hardened veteran of campaigning in Persian Azerbaijan. On March 25, 1915, Cevdet, eyeing not only rebel activity but also a possible Russian incursion from the east, requested a cannon and an infantry battalion.[16] Enver, recognizing the seriousness of the situation, sent in a trusted volunteer officer, the Venezuelan soldier of fortune Rafael de Nogales, to help Cevdet Bey defend the city—although by the time Nogales arrived, Van had already fallen to the rebels.*

Much remains unclear about the insurrection at Van, and there is little agreement even as to the dates. Russian sources (based on reports received from Armenian couriers) suggest that the Armenian Revolutionary Federation

---

* Nogales had originally volunteered to fight in the Belgian army because King Leopold II had befriended him as a boy. Neither Belgium (his first choice) nor France (his second), however, would allow Nogales to take a regular army commission without renouncing his Venezuelan citizenship. At a loose end, Nogales washed up in neutral Bulgaria, where he came to the attention of the Germans and Turks, who met his terms.

(ARF), the formal Dashnak-dominated rebel-government-in-embryo, had control of the city as early as April 15, 1915, although Ottoman sources date this to around April 18–20, when it was first reported that Armenian partisans had taken over the Akkilise Monastery and burned down the large Hamid Ağa army barracks—although the Turks still held the citadel. The fighting appears to have been a messy affair, with a general "sorting" into Muslim and Christian areas, followed by the erection of barricades. Armenian sources claim the rebels were forced into taking up arms by unprovoked shelling of Armenian neighborhoods. Whether or not this is true, local Armenians had every reason to fear the coming government onslaught, not least because inter-ethnic bloodletting had been escalating for weeks in the surrounding rural areas: Armenian couriers told Russian army intelligence that the Turks had already burned down a hundred Armenian villages in Van province, massacring their inhabitants.[17] Whoever fired first in the city itself, the larger story of Van province suggests that the uprising of mid-April 1915 was more climax than cause of the larger clash. The violence is, in any case, not difficult to *explain*: it was ethno-religious war of the most brutal kind, brought on by months of escalating rebel probes and attacks, government counterattacks, partisan hostage taking, savage government reprisals against Christian civilians (Armenians and Assyrians alike), summary executions of suspected rebels, the burning of whole villages. As Nogales recalled the terrible scene in Van, with some perplexity at his involvement in the middle of it:

Here I was . . . a *giaur* [gavur, or infidel], or dirty Christian dog, laying siege at the head of twelve thousand Turks to thirty-five thousand Armenians in their home town. I don't blame the Armenians a bit for having felt sore at me . . . the city and the castle were shrouded in a thick cloud of smoke. They had been shaken for over twenty days by the roar of cannons and the incessant rattle of musketry, which resembled from afar the low rumbling of a mighty cataract . . . it was a Danteesque scene. It reminded me of the ancient saying: "There is no mercy east of the Hellespont!"[18]

Granting Nogales a pinch of literary license, there is no reason to doubt the veracity of his general observations (although his combatant numbers are high). Contemporary sources disagree on the numbers engaged on each side. The best recent estimates of government forces, based on Ottoman archival sources, come out at around two thousand regular and Jandarma troops, plus maybe a thousand Kurdish irregulars, with Armenian partisans having nearly as many (if not slightly more) under arms. Both sides were evidently well armed, with not only rifles and pistols but explosives and incendiary devices. The Ottoman regulars did have artillery, which the partisans did not, although Armenian gunfire may have been more lethal, as the Dashnaks had acquired a stock of C-96 Mauser machine pistols before the war, which were nearly as effective as machine guns: "Instead of shooting one shot at a time they fire four, five, and sometimes six towards the same target." Even the semi-official Armenian chronicler of the battle, Haig Gossoian, inclined to underestimate the size of the rebel forces and arsenal for obvious reasons, claims that the Armenians of Van had ninety semiautomatic Mauser pistols with 13,500 rounds, in addition to rifles and revolvers.[19] There was clearly a real battle in Van, which saw the rebels hold out under a ferocious government onslaught for four weeks—long enough to deliver the city to the Russian Cossacks, who, accompanied by three thousand Armenian *druzhiny* volunteers, arrived on May 20, 1915, four days after Cevdet had ordered a general withdrawal, conceding the citadel to the Armenian rebels.

Whatever else it was, the insurrection at Van was a fine achievement in irregular warfare. The Armenian victors estimated that they had killed about 500 of the enemy (Turks and Kurds), while losing only 135 fighters themselves.[20] The ARF even succeeded in communicating with the Russian army during the siege, although (as the telegraph line had been cut) this was only in the form of couriers carrying messages sewn into the lining of the messengers' clothing. A typical message, dated May 12, 1915, stated that "we are expecting Russian help every day."* After restoring the telegraph line, Aram Manukian Pasha, on behalf of "the Armenians of Van," sent a formal telegram to Vorontsov-Dashkov on May 20, announcing the delivery of the city to Russia and boasting that Armenian volunteers had "defeated a month-long

---

* With clear intent to deceive, Sazonov later forwarded this message to Paris and London, with the word "Russian" deleted, so that it could be read as a plea for help from innocent civilians, rather than a treasonous communication with Turkey's wartime enemy.

siege by Turkish troops." Sending the viceroy birthday greetings, Aram Pasha passed on the gratitude of all Armenians for the "liberation of Armenia" and saluted "the victory of the Great Russian Army over all its enemies."[21] So far from wishing to hush up the connection between the insurrection at Van and the ongoing Russo-Ottoman war, *Mshak*, the leading Armenian newspaper in Tiflis, openly boasted that Armenian partisans had delivered Van to the Russians, as indeed they had.[22]

This ferocious battle behind Ottoman military lines was already in full swing when Halil Bey's effort to turn Russia's flank in northern Persia foundered at Dilman—even as the Allied troops were making their last furious efforts to win the heights on the Gallipoli Peninsula. Already smarting from the failures at Suez and Sarıkamış and the British advance up the Shatt-al-Arab, the Ottoman Empire was being pinched in three directions at once. The Fourth Army in Syria and the Sixth in Mesopotamia were both in danger of being cut off owing to partisan attacks in Cilicia. In the worst position of all, however, was the Third Army facing the Russians, who were advancing against a beaten and battered enemy on both the northern (Erzurum) and southern fronts (Dilman–Van). True, the Russian advance on Van had been slow—far too slow for civilians caught in the crossfire—but this was because Yudenich, with an eye on the restive nomads who roamed the region, had insisted that Nazarbekov make a good "show" with his mounted Cossack divisions (especially the Third Transbaikal Cossack Brigade), to overawe the Kurds and reestablish the prestige Russia had lost in northern Persia with her abrupt withdrawal in the wake of Sarıkamış. It worked, even if the methodical pace was not entirely to Yudenich's liking. By June, the Cossacks, accompanied by Armenian *druzhiny*, had secured the eastern, southern, and northern shores of Lake Van, pitching Halil Bey's Thirty-Sixth Division back to a defensive line east of Bitlis. The Turks were reeling.

At the Ottoman high command, the strategic meltdown in the east, coming on top of the Dardanelles and Gallipoli offensives, produced a perfect storm of paranoia. Already concerned about Greek sedition at Gallipoli—deportations of Greek Christians from the peninsula had begun in April 1915—the Young Turks now lashed out at the Armenians of the east, where, it seemed, a full-scale rebellion had broken out in the rear of the army. The idea that Armenian partisans were active behind the front lines with Russia is a matter of intense controversy (when it is not simply denied) today, but it was far from so at the time. U.S. ambassador Morgenthau, far from a pro-Ottoman apologist—indeed his later memoirs (composed after the United States had entered the war) are often cited by genocide scholars as strong evidence for the prosecution—reported to Washington on May 25, 1915:

> It would seem as if an Armenian insurrection to help the Russians had broken out at Van ... These insurgents are said to be in possession of a part of Van and to be conducting guerrilla warfare in a country where regular military operations are extremely difficult. To what extent they are organized or what successes they have gained it is impossible for me to say; *their numbers have been variously estimated* but *none puts them at less than ten thousand and twenty-five thousand is probably closer to the truth.*[23]

To this day it is not clear how many men Armenian revolutionary organizations were able to put under arms on Ottoman territory. Nor is it clear how their activities were coordinated with the Russians, aside from in exceptional cases such as Van, where written evidence exists (although even then it is inconclusive as to the full extent of coordination). The one thing we *can* say, with abundant and extremely well-documented confidence, is that the Armenian security threat on the Russian fronts (and in Cilicia, near the Baghdad Railway and other road choke points in army supply lines to Syria and Mesopotamia) was taken very seriously by the Ottoman high command and civilian government.[24]

In traditional narratives of the Armenian deportation campaign, the inaugurating event is usually dated to April 24–25, 1915 (the very night of the Gallipoli landings), with the arrest of some 180 Armenian notables, unarmed civilians all, in Constantinople. The latest research in Ottoman archives, however, suggests that the deportation campaign actually began several weeks earlier than this, with targeted "relocations" of Armenian nationals from Zeytun and Maraş (where the first serious Armenian uprisings had occurred) ordered on April 8, 1915. The archival work of Taner Akçam suggests a progressive "ramping up" of repression throughout April and May. The first escalation occurred on April 24, with the roundup of Armenians in the capital and two critical policy decrees. The first, issued by Interior Minister Talât to provincial and district governors, stipulated that Armenians suspected of enemy sympathies be denied travel documents. The second, more significant, was issued by Enver at the War Ministry (although he prepared the decree on Talât's instructions): it ordered the reduction of the Armenian share of the population in frontier districts to less than 10 percent, and recommended the removal of known "rebels" from frontline areas, along with the repopulation of these areas with Muslims. On May 2, 1915, two more significant decrees were issued. One ordered the confiscation of weapons held by non-Muslims in frontline areas (mostly in the east but also including Edirne, near the western Thracian frontier, several Black Sea ports, and Konya). The other decree ordered the removal of the *entire* Armenian population of the Lake Van area, in order that this "hotbed of rebellion [be] dispersed."[25]

Thus far, Ottoman Armenian deportation decrees had been somewhat ad hoc. Even the destination had not been decided yet. The earliest victims, from Zeytun and Maraş, were ordered to be sent to Konya (i.e., away from the front lines). In the Van province deportation decree of May 2, 1915, the idea was to send Armenians "to Russia or to disperse them into various places within the Anatolian interior"—where they would be scattered about to ensure that Armenian Christians would everywhere be outnumbered by Muslim neighbors.[26] On May 16, about thirty thousand Armenians were "removed" from the vicinity of Third Army headquarters at Hasankale (near Erzurum), with no more specific goal than forcing them westward and as far away from the Russian army as possible.[27]

Slowly, fitfully at first, the campaign began to acquire more systematic overtones. First the Zeytun and Maraş deportees, and then those from the Van area, were rerouted to "southeastern Aleppo, Der Zor [today's Dayr az Zawr], and Urfa." It was then determined that Urfa and Aleppo would not do: Armenian deportees would be sent farther southeast still, into the Syrian desert. By month's end, when Talât issued his infamous decree of May 31, 1915, on the "coercive circumstances necessitating the relocation and transfer of the Armenians" in the six eastern provinces away from frontline areas (they were also to be removed from anywhere within 25 kilometers [15.5 miles] of "the Baghdad railroad and other railroad links"), the primary destination of the deportees was the far-off and largely inhospitable Syrian desert province of Der Zor—implying strongly that the survival of the deportees was not Talât's first priority.[28] June and July saw a further escalation, when a new series of partisan uprisings behind Ottoman lines in Maraş and Zeytun (again), Gaziantep, Antioch (Antakya), and Urfa prompted the Third Army command to dispatch three entire divisions southward to Cilicia to put them down. The new insurrectionary wave also furnished Talât with the pretext to extend the Armenian deportation campaign beyond the eastern provinces, with new decrees targeting Samsun, Sivas, and Trabzon, as well as the Cilician-Mediterranean port cities of Mersin and Adana.

On paper, the Armenian deportations were never universally applicable or applied. Armenian civilians in Ankara, Smyrna (Izmir), and Constantinople were supposed to be spared, although we know that thousands there (not only the 180 notables arrested in April) were rounded up anyway. There were category exemptions, in theory, for Armenian Catholics and Protestants, women, children, the elderly, active-duty soldiers and their families, and irreplaceable artisans (such as those working on the Baghdad Railway as blacksmiths, locksmiths, mechanics, and stokers). Antalya was formally exempted because it had fewer Armenians than Mersin and Adana. Also in theory, deportees were to receive compensation for the homes and property they had left behind (if they were unable to cash them out before leaving to local Muslims at fire-sale prices): accounts were to be opened in their names with *Ziraat Bank* to "receive all deposits coming from rents or sales."[29]

Predictably, these provisions were honored largely in the breach. In practice, most Armenian deportees, traveling on foot, could take only what they could carry on their backs. Even if they survived the journey, they never did receive compensation for property they had left behind, most of which was seized by opportunistic neighbors or later nationalized.*[30] Talât's guidelines

---

* Adding insult to these considerable injuries, Armenian refugees who returned to their hometowns after the Russian conquest of much of eastern Turkey in 1916 were turned away if they did not possess "valid property deeds," which few, of course, still possessed.

and "exemptions" were often willfully disregarded by local officials and army officers who had been looking for an excuse to persecute "disloyal" Armenians for years. It was a measure of the confused nature of the orders that the Ottoman army convened more than a thousand courts-martial during the war against those "guilty of organizing or failing to prevent attacks" against Armenian civilians, and a number of officials would be executed for gross human rights abuses.[31] In Adana, the Ottoman vali openly defied an order from Talât to halt ongoing deportations, declaring "that the orders of the [Interior] ministry meant nothing to him; he alone was going to decide what to do with the local Armenians." So thorough was the cleansing of Adana (six thousand Armenians expelled, including those who had kept the streetlights working) that the entire city emptied out, including, in a richly deserved turnabout, the vengeful vali and his own family.[32]

By July 1915, it would have been obvious to everyone in Turkey that a large-scale campaign of violent ethnic cleansing was under way. Category exemptions to the deportation decrees (especially for women and children) were widely ignored, and there is no question that local governors, gendarmes, officers-in-charge, and Kurdish Hamidiye regiments committed horrible atrocities against Armenian civilians, whether because some resisted the deportations or because they were scapegoated for attacks launched nearby by armed partisans.* Having helped unleash Dante's inferno in Van, Rafael de Nogales was later haunted by scenes such as this, outside Siirt: "On a nearby slope, like snow on a mountain-side, lay thousands of half-nude and bleeding Armenian corpses, piled in heaps or interlaced in death's final embrace."[33] Those Armenians who made it as far as Syria, meanwhile, often succumbed to thirst or starvation in sight of the Baghdad Railway, on which few could afford passage. One traveler on the rail line said that he had seen with his own eyes "1,000 dead Armenians during the daylight hours of his

---

* The issue of resistance and reprisal is fraught, but it should be noted that Ottoman military sources give figures for the numbers of Armenians killed in clashes with government forces, accounted separately from the numbers deported to Syria. For example, the Ottoman military reports 6,500 Armenian combatants killed or missing in Trabzon province, 8,657 in Erzurum, and 89,500 (of 109,521 residents) in Bitlis province who "either died in the clashes, or ran away." These figures likely include Armenian civilians executed on (often spurious) charges of collaboration, along with armed partisans. To deny that *any* Armenian victims died in combat situations, however, is no longer tenable, now that Ottoman and Russian archives are open.

journey, lying by the railway at various points." The caravan roads, too, presented a terrible sight, with whole stretches "littered with decomposing bodies." Deportation to the Syrian desert province of Der Zor was a terrible fate, and was indeed fatal for hundreds of thousands of Ottoman Armenians, including women, children, and elderly civilians: casualties were particularly severe among those not strong enough to endure the journey. One scholar estimates that of roughly 800,000 Armenians deported from the eastern provinces, "only 500,000 made it to their designated settlement areas."[34] No one knows the true number of Armenians who perished in 1915, whether through starvation, thirst, disease, simple exhaustion, or at the hands of execution squads. A number of recent estimates, based on the latest demographic research, suggest that the figure is somewhere between 650,000 and 700,000 out of a prewar Armenian population of about 1.5 million, although some historians still go as high as a million deaths. The end result was clear: the extirpation of the Armenian population of "Turkish Armenia"—from areas in eastern Asia Minor and Cilicia where Armenians had lived for centuries.[35]

Following Turkey's entry into the cauldron of world war, the story of Ottoman Armenians was probably never going to have a happy ending. Nevertheless, a number of contingencies related to strategy and military events cry out for closer scrutiny. To begin with, there is the failure of the Russians to come to the aid of the Armenians before it was too late. In fairness to Yudenich and Vorontsov-Dashkov, though, we must consider that the terrible moment of reckoning for Ottoman Armenians coincided with Russia's own strategic crisis in Europe, with the Germano-Austrian breakthrough at Gorlice-Tarnow of May 2, 1915, opening the plains of Poland up to the enemy. Russia's Great Retreat of summer 1915 brought its own horror in its wake, producing an exodus of nearly two million civilian refugees, including more than 500,000 Jews expelled from frontline areas because they were suspected of pro-German sympathies. With a scorched-earth meltdown under way in Russian Poland that very nearly brought down the tsarist regime in 1915, it is not surprising that the Russian high command was less than fully focused on the fate of Ottoman Armenians.

To the extent the Russians *were* engaged in eastern Turkey, meanwhile, they undeniably helped the Armenian cause. Van was largely a bombed-out ruin when the Cossacks showed up on May 20, but the Armenians held the town. The insurrection may have been fatal to less well-armed Armenians elsewhere, but in Van it was the Muslim survivors who, having lost their homes (the Muslim quarter was razed), were forced onto the refugee trail with whatever they could carry on their backs, not the Christians.* In this sense the problem with the Van rebellion for Armenians was not that it happened, but that it did not spread quickly enough—or in closer coordination with the Russian army. True, the Russian advance from Dilman had been slow, but it had succeeded.

Returning to the shifting battle lines, the Armenians delivered Van to the Russians in May, just one episode in a complex unfolding story. Even as Djevdet was surrendering Van, the Ottoman Third Army was preparing a counterstroke, by training and deploying three new divisions from Erzurum to reinforce Halil Bey on the southern front. Unbeknownst to the Russians, who believed the enemy to be in disarray, by the end of June some eight strong Turkish infantry divisions, comprising nearly 70,000 troops in a new IX Corps under Abdul Kerim Pasha with the German major Guse as chief of staff, were assembling in their path of march. The Russian units moving around the northern shore of Lake Van, spearheaded by the First and Second Caucasian Cossack Divisions, General Trukhin's Second Transbaikal Cossack Brigade, parts of the Sixty-Sixth Infantry Division, and Armenian *druzhiny*, were more mobile than the Ottoman IX Corps standing in their path, but they were outnumbered nearly three to one, the total Russian force comprising fewer than three regular army divisions.

As if compelled by some law of geopolitical gravity, the opposing forces converged, in the second week of July 1915, on the plain of Manzikert (Malazgırt), where the Selçuk Turks, under Alp Arslan, had famously defeated the Byzantines in 1071, opening Asia Minor up to their advance.† In the

---

* By boat, across Lake Van to Tatvan and then overland to Bitlis. Some 700 of 1,200 Muslim refugees reached Bitlis alive (the rest either drowned in a storm or were captured by Armenian partisans onshore after being blown off course). The Muslim quarter of Van was put to the torch, along with Muslim villages nearby that had aided government forces.

† In 1064, Alp Arslan had conquered the Armenian capital of Ani, whereupon the prince of Kars, the last independent Armenian kingdom, handed over his "keys" to the Byzantine emperor in return for estates to the south, in the Taurus Mountains. And yet Armenian relations with the Byzantines were poor. Complicating any simplistic picture of a clash of civilizations, many Armenians actually fought on the Turkish side at Manzikert in 1071,

annals of the First World War, this battle is as little known as Dilman, although again it *should* be known. Engaged between July 12–15 and 20–26, 1915, Manzikert was a larger Dilman in reverse, with the overextended Russians rushing into a trap of their own making. After several weeks of savage fighting, on July 22–23 Abdul Kerim Pasha outflanked the Russian right wing. On July 26, the Russians evacuated the town of Manzikert itself and ordered a general withdrawal across the line. On August 4, the Russians evacuated the city of Van, then Van province entirely, pulling back across the border into Persian Azerbaijan.[36]

The impact of this Second Manzikert was immediate and terrible for Armenians left behind by the Russians. Vahakn Dadrian claims that 50,000 Armenians were put to death in retaliation for having delivered the city to the Russians in May.[37] Taner Akçam claims that the Ottoman forces "killed the city's entire Armenian population."[38] Lending documentary credence to such claims, Ottoman military files give a figure of 67,792 Armenians "recorded in registries" in Van province, while leaving blank estimates for numbers deported in 1915 and numbers killed in fighting. It seems clear that very few, if any, Armenians survived the Ottoman reconquest of this rebellious province from the Russians in early August 1915.[39]

Is there any way the Armenians of Van, not to mention those elsewhere in eastern Turkey and Cilicia, could have been saved? The Russians, as we have seen, certainly did their part to come to their aid in Van province, even if arriving a bit late in May and then making the cardinal mistake of overextending forward in June and July. But we must not forget Russia's fellow belligerents. Back in early February 1915, as we have seen, Boghos Nubar Pasha, on behalf of the Armenian National Delegation in Cairo, had proposed to Sir John Maxwell that the Armenians of Cilicia would offer "perfect and total support" if the British landed troops in Alexandretta. When the Armenian delegation from Zeytun petitioned the Russians for support later that month, Vorontsov-Dashkov had suggested to Sazonov that as Zeytun was far closer to the Cilician coastline than Tiflis, the British or French should try to get

---

although this did not convince the Selçuks to restore the lost Armenian kingdoms. The historical significance of Manzikert was, in any case, lost on few of the men who fought there in summer 1915.

arms to Armenian rebels there instead, by means of an amphibious landing or a covert weapons dump on the coast.[40] Kitchener and Churchill were far too committed to the upcoming Dardanelles and then Gallipoli adventures to take up these promising proposals, but they were never forgotten. On March 23, 1915, representatives of the Armenian National Defense Committee of America informed the British consul in Boston that preparations were under way "for the purpose of sending volunteers to Cilicia, where a large section of the Armenian population will unfurl the banner of insurrection against Turkish rule"—the idea being that the British supply these volunteers with arms. Again, nothing was done.[41]

Once word of the terrible fate of Armenian deportees began to spread in June and July, these appeals naturally took on a more urgent aspect. On July 10, 1915, the very day that the Battle of Manzikert was joined, U.S. ambassador Morgenthau reported that "because Armenian volunteers, many of them Russian subjects, have joined the Russian Army in the Caucasus and because some have been implicated in armed revolutionary movements and others have been helpful to Russians in their invasion of Van district, terrible vengeance is being taken."[42] Well aware of these developments, Sir Mark Sykes (who would famously help draw up the 1916 agreement to carve up the Ottoman Empire) was sent to Cairo in early July 1915 to investigate the possibility of aiding the Armenians of Cilicia. Sykes reported to Major General Charles Callwell on July 14 and 16, 1915, that Armenian rebels inside Turkey expected shortly to take Muş and that Armenian exiles in Egypt could raise six thousand volunteers for a Cilicia landing, if Britain supplied transports and weapons.[43] On July 20 and 22, as the climactic scenes were transpiring at Manzikert, Boghos Nubar Pasha again approached Sir John Maxwell, first with an appeal to his conscience ("the mass deportations will cause the annihilation of the Armenian population of the region if . . . protection is not extended to them soon") and then with a promise of armed collaboration, were the British to land in Cilicia:

Allow [the Armenian National Defense Committee] to state that the military campaign in question would require a force of 10,000 to 12,000 fighters to occupy Alexandretta, Mersin, and Adana (together with the defiles) and ensure the collaboration of 10,000 Armenian volunteers and the total Armenian population of the region . . . it would be possible to rely on the 25,000 Armenian insurgents in Cilicia and on the more to come from nearby provinces. This formidable force of close to 50,000 would even be able to advance well beyond the borders of Cilicia and thus become an asset for the Allies. It would be just the reiteration of an oft-repeated truth . . . that in Turkey only the Armenians of Armenia [i.e., Erzurum, Bitlis, and Van provinces] and Cilicia are the inhabitants with obvious insurrectional tendencies against Turkish rule.[44]

Boghos Nubar Pasha was, of course, hoping to convince Britain that Armenians were worthy co-combatants who deserved an independent state after the war. Before we dismiss his proposal as biased, however, it is noteworthy that Boghos Nubar Pasha's figure of armed Armenian insurgents (25,000) is the same one Morgenthau came up with at the same time, with no motivation to exaggerate. It also tracks closely with Russian military intelligence of "3,000 separate armed cells operating in the region between Adana and Aleppo" (at five to ten men per cell), and with Ottoman countermeasures: surely the rebels must have had at least 25,000 under arms to draw off three whole divisions from an active military front.

The more interesting figure, from the perspective of Gallipoli, was the "10,000 to 12,000 fighters" required to achieve a secure landing on the Cilician coastline, before meeting up with friendly Armenian rebels and civilians inland. Sykes had proposed, to the British War Office, that Armenians in Egypt would supply half this force (about six thousand), meaning that Britain need spare only six thousand of its own troops to secure Alexandretta and then fan out across Cilicia, where the heavily Armenian population (lately augmented by the massive influx of deportees, straggling along the caravan roads and the Baghdad Railway bed toward Syria) would greet them as liberators. Perhaps this figure was optimistic, and the Armenian volunteers from Egypt could not be reckoned as equal to trained British Tommies. To ensure success, Maxwell could have doubled the British contingent to twelve thousand soldiers, escorting six thousand armed Armenian volunteers across the Mediterranean to liberate their suffering Ottoman brethren. This still would have been *less than half the number of troops the British actually sent to reinforce the Anzac front on Gallipoli in early August 1915, against enemy defenses orders of magnitude stronger than any they might encounter at Alexandretta.**

Did the British not see that another golden opportunity lay before them in Alexandretta, less glittering perhaps than the one passed up earlier (as the Dardanelles disaster had already happened), but more urgent, not least on humanitarian grounds? If the headlong rush into the Dardanelles in February reflected a failure of strategic imagination, the new Anzac/Suvla landings represented also a failure of *moral* imagination. Britain and France, of course, bore no responsibility for the catastrophe that befell Turkish Armenians in 1915, except in the indirect sense that the Gallipoli landings had contributed to the atmosphere of paranoia in the Ottoman government in April–May, which furnished a pretext for the mass deportations. But in July 1915, it was not too late to do something to help. The deportation campaign was still spreading (it reached Mersin and Adana only in August). Most of the refugees had not yet arrived in the Syrian desert. While thousands of Armenians had already perished, many thousands more were still alive. True, a British landing in Cilicia might have led to a new wave of reprisals against Armenian civilians once the news reached the Ottoman Army Command. But this risk should have paled in comparison to the prospect of saving thousands of Armenian refugees now strung out across Cilicia, and the cutting off of further deportations to Syria†—where the Ottoman Fourth Army would itself have been cut off.

Moving back to the realm of strategy, a British-Armenian landing in Cilicia in July 1915 would have been the last straw for the Ottoman Third Army, which had already peeled most of its strength away from Erzurum to meet the Russian forces enveloping Lake Van and to suppress Armenian partisans in

---

* While it was true that Suvla Bay, where about 16,000 of these 25,000+ British troops were landed on August 6–7, 1915, was defended by only two Ottoman battalions, it is no less true that this landing was merely auxiliary to the main Anzac assault against the heavily fortified entrenchments of the Sari Bair heights, which was the real object of the offensive. Emphasis added.

† Cilician deportations from Mersin and Adana began long after these discussions took place—indeed it was ostensibly for fear that local Armenians would aid British landing parties that they were deported. Rather than provide the Ottoman government with a pretext to persecute these Armenians with lots of *talk* in Cairo about a Cilician landing, the British could have actually landed—and saved these Armenians before they were deported.

Cilicia, and would now have had to divert several more divisions south to fend off a British expeditionary army operating in extremely friendly country. Rather than a new Manzikert, which amounted to a final death sentence for the Christians of Turkey's eastern provinces (beginning with Van, after the Russians evacuated that city earlier won by Armenian arms), July and August 1915 might have seen the final rout of the Ottoman Third Army, paving the way for the historic restoration of an independent Armenia under British and Russian protection.

At least two Britons in Cairo saw the potential. Sir Henry McMahon—the British high commissioner in Egypt who was already knee-deep in schemes to entice Sherif Hussein of Mecca to lead an Arab revolt against the Ottomans—pointed out to the Foreign Office that an "unexpected descent" on Alexandretta could easily cut off the Ottoman armies in Arabia (thus making an Arab revolt moot), Mesopotamia (where British armies were engaged in a brutal slog up the Tigris, with the Ottoman Sixth Army waiting for them in Baghdad), Palestine, and Syria.[45] The other was T. E. Lawrence (later "of Arabia"), who, poring over his "massive sectioned map" of the Ottoman Empire in his office at the Savoy Hotel, became all but obsessed with Alexandretta in 1915 as the critical strategic crux-point where Syria and the other Arab provinces to the south could be cut off from the empire's Turkish Anatolian hub—and where a British landing force would be aided by the sympathetic Armenians of Cilicia to the north.[46] But Lawrence was a mere temporary second lieutenant interpreter in army intelligence, to whom nobody yet much listened. And McMahon, though a man of consequence, only proposed his own version of the Alexandretta idea in late September 1915—more than a month after the Anzac/Suvla Bay landings had effectively rendered it moot.

And so the British, instead of landing several divisions in scarcely defended Alexandretta to cleave the Ottoman Empire in two, aid their Russian allies fighting the Ottoman Third Army at Manzikert, and save thousands of Armenian civilian refugees, chose to reinforce failure by landing yet another 25,000 troops on Gallipoli to face the deadly fire of Turco-German forces entrenched on high ground. After beginning so well at Basra and Suez, 1915 had turned thoroughly sour for Britain in the Ottoman theater. It was about to get worse.

CHAPTER 11

A COLD WINTER
FOR THE BRITISH EMPIRE

The Turks were found in great strength and full of fight.

—Sir Ian Hamilton
to Lord Kitchener following the failure of the Anzac breakout,
August 17, 1915[1]

Nineteen fifteen was a depressing year for the Allied cause. The British, at least, had their moment of foolish optimism at the Dardanelles, after being buoyed by earlier victories against the Ottomans at the Shatt-al-Arab and Suez. For the French, the year brought mostly a painful reminder that, as Clemenceau liked to chide readers of his newspaper *La Justice*, "les allemands sont toujours à Noyon." At this bulge in the trench lines, a German salient thrust out within sixty miles of Paris, all but taunting the Allies into ordering suicidal attacks to break through on the flanks to envelop it. Even though the Germans transferred ten divisions to the eastern front in preparation for the May assault at Gorlice-Tarnow, Allied attacks in the west at Neuve-Chapelle (April), Arras/Ypres (May), and later at Loos/Champagne (September) came to nothing. Hopes entertained the previous winter that "the spring of 1915 would see the beginning of operations which would decisively clear French [and] Belgian . . . territory and carry our armies across the German frontier" had failed miserably, Churchill noted in a *Report Upon the General Military Situation* composed for the British War Council on June 18, 1915. "Out of approximately 19,500 square miles of France and Belgium in German hands," he remarked acidly, "we have recovered about 8."[2]

Italy's entry into the war on the side of Britain and France (i.e., against Austria-Hungary) on May 23, 1915, might have shored up plummeting Entente morale. But it came three weeks after Gorlice-Tarnow had pitched the Russians back from Austrian Galicia and thus given new life to the Habsburg cause—as did, paradoxically, Italy's very entry into the war, which finally gave the Austro-Hungarians an opponent they could defeat, unaided. Even in moral terms, the Allied propaganda claim to be fighting a "war for civilization," given a new fillip by the German use of poison gas at Ypres in April, was sullied when the British themselves deployed poison gas at Loos in September (it blew back in their faces).

Most painful of all was the stalemate on Gallipoli. Hoping to pivot around the hopeless western front with a bold strategic thrust to the rear of the Central Powers to aid the Russians, the Allied forces had instead succeeded only in re-creating the misery of France and Flanders, and this time without the excuse that they were facing Germans. True, the Ottoman Fifth Army was liberally supplied with German officers, but its men were mostly Turkish. Great Britain, ruler of the largest empire in recorded history and the world's preeminent naval power, was being taught a bitter lesson by the Sick Man of Europe. This sense of frustration and humiliation must help explain the deepening British commitment over the course of spring and summer to the Dardanelles and then Gallipoli offensives, in spite of mounting evidence of their futility. For how could the best brains of the Admiralty, army, War Council, and cabinet not come to grips with the Turks—who had, in recent years, been soundly beaten in the field by a ragtag Balkan coalition—and before that by Italy!

For the Central Powers, by contrast, the strategic picture was improving. There had been frightening moments for the Turks, to be sure, at Basra, Sarıkamış, and Suez. The fall of Van and the cascading Armenian uprisings had seemed to portend the final breakdown of Ottoman authority in eastern Turkey. The very brutality of the government response, however, along with the Russian reversal at Manzikert and the failure of the British to intervene in Cilicia, had brought about a recovery of Ottoman prestige in the East. The Sick Man had cheated death once again, though this was no consolation to

Ottoman Armenians, whose tantalizing moment of near triumph in the East had turned into a human catastrophe.

Still, as Clemenceau might have said, the fact remained that Allied expeditionary forces were still encamped on the Gallipoli Peninsula, just 300 kilometers (about 180 miles) from the Ottoman capital. The campaign was already a source of acrimony in the British high command, but it was not as if Britain herself was imperiled by it in the way Turkey was—or the way France was by the German salient at Noyon. The comparative safety of "island Britain" with her coalition allies was an old theme in early modern and modern warfare. But in 1915 the contrast was even more striking. Whether they were drawn from the British Isles or the Commonwealth, Tommies were fighting once again in *other people's countries*, either to defend them from invaders (France) or to win them for the empire (Mesopotamia and Gallipoli). Suez was the exception that proved this strange rule, and even there it was mostly British Indian soldiers defending British Egypt, rather than Britons defending Britain.

Britain's geographic isolation from the active fronts of the world war gave her flexibility, but with this luxury came the burden of choice. After Paris was saved at the Marne, France's overriding strategic goal was simple: expel the Germans from France. On the eastern front, Russia had maneuverability in 1914—only to see this evaporate at Gorlice-Tarnow, after which the only real question was how far to retreat. Italy's entry into the war opened yet another front, but the accident of geography meant that she and Austria-Hungary were destined to fight on a front all of 20 miles (32 kilometers) wide—on the only flatland between Trieste and the Alps. Erich von Falkenhayn, at German high command, did have some flexibility as to how he would apportion troops and munitions between the western and eastern fronts, plus Turkey. But, with Britain controlling the seas and communications with Constantinople difficult (Serbia was still in the war, cutting off the Orient Express railway and shelling the Danube River, and Romanian neutrality stood in the way of large-scale German arms shipments to Turkey), German options, too, were narrow. Only Britain had a free hand to decide where to send spare troops, and for what purpose. Only Britain, moreover, had significant numbers of spare troops to shift around the world, as the western front had been stabilized long before the "New Army" Kitchener was creating from scratch reached the field.

Where should they be sent? France was an obvious destination, but there seemed little hope that raw new recruits would do any better against the Germans than the more seasoned British Expeditionary Force had. As Churchill explained the problem to the War Council on June 18, 1915, "Numbers after a certain point do not count toward the solution of the problem in the western theatre," where "the power of the defensive . . . is a factor permanently superior to any preponderance of numbers likely to be acquired by either side."[3] Cilicia, as we have seen, was never seriously considered, though by all strategic and moral logic it surely should have been. After the decisive repulse of the Ottoman attack on Suez in February, Egypt seemed safe for the time being. Mesopotamia was a possibility, but it lay in the strategic purview of Delhi and the British Indian Army, not London and the New Army.

This left Gallipoli as the obvious destination. Responding, somewhat belatedly, to a request for reinforcements that Hamilton wired to London on May 18, 1915, the War Council resolved on June 7 "to reinforce Sir Ian Hamilton with the three remaining divisions of the First New Army with a view to an assault in the second week of July." Churchill and Kitchener then asked Hamilton, on June 11, where he wanted to deploy these new divisions, with their own preference being Bulair—with the aim of cutting off the Ottoman Fifth Army from Constantinople. Although Hamilton was not averse to the idea, it was overruled by de Robeck as too risky for the navy in view of shallow water and mines: Suvla Bay offered a much safer anchorage. To Churchill's frustration, a "starving" operation at Bulair was thus abandoned in favor of a "storming" one, with the idea being to use the new troops on the flank of a general breakout from Anzac Cove west toward the Narrows. Critical time was lost as this was being hashed out, with the landing date postponed until the first week of August. The extra weeks did allow two more territorial divisions to be assembled in reserve of the main landing force, but they also gave Liman more time to plan for an offensive he knew was coming, owing to the methodical and scarcely hidden concentration of troops on Lemnos.[4]

Although Liman knew some kind of landing was imminent, he of course did not know where it would come. The Allies could thus achieve real tactical surprise, with the added advantage that, unlike in April, the Allies already had troops ashore who could launch diversionary offensives to mask the landing. The final plan fixed for August 6, 1915, which Hamilton hammered out with his officers in late July, was both complex and elegant. Over the previous two days, nearly two full divisions had been quietly landed ashore at Anzac Cove under guise of ordinary shifting of men in and out of the line, in order to strengthen the main assault. Rumors were spread at Mytilene, on Lesbos island, about a landing on the Asian coast, while still more disinformation surrounded Bulair (where, it was remembered, Liman had held his reserves for too long in April). With the enemy hopefully in the dark about both the actual landing site (Suvla Bay) and the true objective (Chunuk Bair and the Sari Bair ridge more generally, en route to Maidos and the Narrows), a kind of creeping strategic barrage would then ensue, spreading up the Gallipoli Peninsula from south to north. The first feint was a bombardment of the Krithia trenches on the Helles front, to begin around 2:30 p.m. Three hours later, a bigger feint on the right wing of the Anzac front would open toward Lone Pine (Kanlısırt), a ridge on which Turks had cut down all trees but one. Here sappers had dug a tunnel some five hundred yards (457 meters) under the Turkish lines, from which "the Australians planned to issue forth like disturbed ants." Toward 9:30 p.m., Birdwood's principal attack would begin on the Anzac left flank, where "the Turkish outposts were to be rushed and an advance made in several columns up the precipitous ravines leading to Chunuk Bair." At 10:30 p.m., fresh New Army troops of the Eleventh Division would land at Suvla Bay under cover of darkness, followed by the Tenth Division at daybreak, with the Fifty-Third Division in reserve (the Fifty-Ninth Division had still not arrived, in yet another instance of War Office bungling that was later picked apart by the Dardanelles Commission). These landing forces, commanded by Lieutenant General Frederick Stopford, had what Hamilton deemed the "comparatively easy" task of advancing southwest from Suvla Bay "with the object of assisting Birdwood in the event of the other's attack being held up."[5]

On paper, it was a brilliant plan, with every chance of success if pursued with vigor and determination. An Anzac breakout across the peninsula could silence the shore guns of the Narrows, allowing the British to sweep the

Dardanelles mines and open a path for the fleet. In his inimitably lyrical way, Churchill explained the stakes in a July 1915 memorandum for the War Council:

> We are now on the eve of a most critical battle in the Gallipoli Peninsula. If we are successful, results of the greatest magnitude will follow, and the fall of Constantinople will dominate the whole character of the great war and throw all other events in the shade . . . we must get Bulgaria now . . . unless we can gain Bulgaria to our cause or attack Constantinople before the end of September without her . . . other circumstances will intervene in the Balkans [i.e., Bulgarian intervention against Serbia on the Germano-Austro-Turkish side] . . . and these circumstances may be fatal to the issue of the war and disastrous in a peculiar degree to Great Britain.[6]

Liman, less lyrically, agreed with Churchill about the possible strategic impact of a British breakout on Gallipoli in August 1915. With British naval guns dominating the Sea of Marmara, the German commander of the Ottoman Fifth Army wrote in his memoirs:

> The lines of Çatalca . . . which had saved the city in the Turko-Bulgarian war, would be of little value, because both flanks would have been under the fire of the enemy's fleets. A Russian landing would no doubt have coincided with the Anglo-French operations. At that time many reports from Bucharest and Athens mentioned the concentration of troops and ships in Odessa. Secure communication between the Western Powers and Russia would have been established and Turkey would have been split off from the Central Powers.[7]

Battles, alas, are not fought on paper, but on rough and often unpredictable terrain, by officers and men subject to all the limitations posed by nature. They are fought against opponents who may summon forth unexpected valor when they are pushed against the wall. The Turks had proved their fighting worth at the Dardanelles in March, on the Gallipoli beaches in April, at Krithia in May, and on the Anzac front all spring and summer. In view of this general picture of fortitude, the only really surprising thing about the battles of August 1915 is that the British officers planning the latest offensive seem to have been surprised by Turkish valor once again.

Great reputations were won and lost in the Anafarta battles, which have been endlessly dissected ever since. The decisions of the commanders clearly mattered, beginning with Hamilton's poor decision to appoint Stopford to command the landing troops—a man who combined the worst qualities of age (he was an old sixty-one) and inexperience (he had never led troops in battle). Stopford's laggardly advance forward from Suvla Bay was instantly legendary. The straggling of New Army troops on the beaches left Birdwood fully exposed on his left flank as his men clambered up the Sari Bair ridge under heavy Turkish fire, while giving Liman more than enough time to bring down his XVI Corps from Bulair to reinforce the defense in the Anzac sector. On the Turkish side, Anafarta is as important to the Atatürk legend as April 25. Famously, Liman gave Mustafa Kemal his first corps-level command, of the XVI, just before the climactic action took place on Sari Bair. More famously still, Kemal personally directed a blistering "six battalion" counterattack on August 10, 1915, which blasted the Anzacs off a desperately won corner of Chunuk Bair (Rhododendron Spur) and, subsequently, the entire Sari Bair ridge.[8]

Important as these command decisions were, it is hard to escape the conclusion that the Allied breakout failed in large part because the Turks simply fought better, with stronger motivation and more desperate courage. The backbiting on the British side was even nastier than in April, with Hamilton blaming Stopford and the other officers in the field for a "lack of energy and determination" (Hamilton then added, cruelly and unfairly, that "Stopford and his divisional Generals . . . have no heart" for further action, and were "in fact . . . not fit for it"). More unfairly still, Stopford himself blamed the "distinctly disappointing attacking qualities" of his own troops—blaming, in effect, Hamilton and Kitchener for having given him raw recruits with no "regular troops to set them a standard." While professing forgiveness of the shortcomings of men not only new to battle but physically drained and thirsty (there were endless problems with getting water ashore), Stopford nevertheless twisted the knife in by noting how unhelpful it was that, when encountering shrapnel fire, his poorly trained men tended to "bunch together and stand up instead of spreading out and lying down." Commander Worsley Gibson, who observed the straggling at Suvla Bay, directed blame back at the high command, noting sourly that "it was obvious . . . that a great mistake had been made in sending absolutely raw troops who'd never heard a shot fired in anger to do a difficult job like night landing under fire." By contrast, the battle-seasoned Anzacs at Lone Pine and Sari Bair performed, by all accounts, magnificently, advancing with reckless abandon—indeed the Australians held on at Lone Pine even after Kemal had retaken Chunuk Bair. All the same, the Allied forces were fought to a standstill by the Turks across the Anzac front, and no breakout ever seriously threatened. Unfair as Hamilton's scapegoating of his officers may have been, his final verdict on Anafarta has the ring of truth. "I had hoped," Hamilton concluded his postmortem to Kitchener on August 17, 1915, "that [Turkish] reinforcements would be of poor quality and not a match for ours but this is not the case, and unfortunately the Turks have temporarily gained the moral ascendancy over some of our new troops . . . We are up against a Turkish Army which is well commanded and fighting bravely."[9]

The butcher's bill for Anafarta was high on both sides, with the British suffering nearly 25,000 casualties in just four days (August 6–10, 1915), and the Turks about 20,000. At Sari Bair alone, the Anzacs took 12,500 casualties. One survivor of the battles remembered mostly an impression of "hot dusty swollen brown stinking corpses lying about everywhere."[10] Still more thousands of men were felled in August by dysentery, now reaching epidemic proportions. But the sacrifice was not the same on each side. The Turks had won a battle to defend their country and capital, in which a great commander enhanced an already lustrous reputation. All the Allies had gained for throwing away tens of thousands of men was to extend the Anzac trench lines northward by about 12 kilometers (7.5 miles).[11]

The strategic consequences of Anafarta, nevertheless, were serious, although they were not the consequences desired by the British. Instead of knocking Turkey out of the war in large part so the Balkan neutrals (Greece and Romania) would join the Allies, while convincing Bulgaria to stay neutral instead of invading Serbia, the British defeat had the opposite effect, just as Churchill had feared. Compounding the ill impression made by the fruitless Gallipoli offensive was the fact that it coincided with the last desperate convulsions of Russia's retreat in eastern Europe. Warsaw and Ivangorod fell on August 5, just prior to the Suvla Bay landings. Kovno fell just as Kemal was leading the great counterassault on Chunuk Bair. Even as the Anzacs were being repulsed all across the line at Sari Bair the next day, the great Russian fortress at Brest-Litovsk was captured by the Germans. In all, the Russians lost not only Poland but some 325,000 prisoners of war to the Germano-Austrian advance. Once the news of the latest British humiliation on Gallipoli reached Sofia in mid-August, one could therefore forgive "Tsar" Ferdinand of Bulgaria for concluding that the Germans had a good chance of winning the war.

The German high command, too, had waited for news from Gallipoli with bated breath. Pleased as he was with the fall of Russian Poland, Erich von Falkenhayn, Moltke's successor as chief of the General Staff, remained deeply concerned about Gallipoli, because of its importance for the Balkans. "If the Dardanelles were lost," he wrote in his memoirs, "no advantage that could be gained against the Russians was of any value." Since spring, German diplomats in Sofia had been trying to rope Bulgaria into the war, to knock Serbia out of the conflict and thereby open up an interrupted rail connection to Constantinople. German officers had been quietly inspecting the Danubian front all summer. Impressed by the Turkish victory at Anafarta, Ferdinand sent Lieutenant Colonel Gantschev to German military headquarters to hammer out terms of entry. Enver and the grand vizier, keen to expedite arms shipments to Gallipoli now that Serbia's defeat was in prospect, put up no objections to Bulgarian terms, which included the cession of Ottoman territory west of the Maritza River, along with Bulgarian control of the railway between Adrianople and Dedeagatch, so as to give Sofia a strategic buffer zone in western Thrace. With Austrian, German, Turkish, and Bulgarian interests aligning (though the Turks resented being forced to give up territory), negotiations were swift. On September 6, 1915, Falkenhayn, Gantschev, and Austria-Hungary chief of army staff Franz Conrad von Hötzendorf agreed that Germany and Austria-Hungary would muster six divisions each on the Serbian frontier within thirty days and Bulgaria four divisions against Serbia no later than five days after this (as Bulgaria was not yet at war, she was also enjoined to order general mobilization no later than September 21). In a show of how serious the Germans were, Falkenhayn gave the overall command to August von Mackensen, the hero of Gorlice-Tarnow who had been promoted to field marshal in June.[12]

In this way Serbia's fate was sealed, as the British themselves recognized as soon as they learned, in a devastating one-two punch, that Bulgaria had mobilized (September 25, 1915) and that Mackensen was on the Serbian frontier (October 4, 1915).[13] With nearly every spare Allied man, gun, and explosive thrown into the offensive at Champagne/Loos (which began on September 25), there was little Britain could do for Serbia other than lean on the Greeks to reprise the Second Balkan War by attacking Bulgaria. At Athens' request, the Allies did agree to rush two divisions to Salonica (for political symmetry, one French and one British). On short notice, the only place these troops could be found was, of course, Gallipoli. For Churchill, it was like a replay of the diplomatic nightmare of March, when Russia had vetoed Greek participation at the Dardanelles, lending ammunition to the Germanophile King Constantine in his struggle with pro-Entente prime minister Venizelos over foreign policy (the king had won that battle, forcing the prime minister to resign, only for Venizelos to triumph at the polls in August 1915 and return to office). But October was far more painful, in that it was not a Russian veto but the impression of Britain's own impotence that stayed Venizelos's hand. In order to lure Greece into the war against Bulgaria, Britain was forced to weaken her forces at the Dardanelles, just as King Constantine, along with Romania's leaders and everyone in the Balkans, was beginning to suspect the Turks might hold on there after all.

Mackensen was no more impressed with the British move into the Balkans than King Constantine. The first echelon of British troops began landing at Salonica on October 5–6, 1915—just as the Austro-German forces began bombarding Serbian positions. On October 7, as the British were scrambling to figure out how to convince either Greece or Romania to enter the war on the side of a bumbling ally that could not even beat the Turks, the Austro-Hungarian Third Army crossed the Danube between Kupinovo and Belgrade, and the left half of the German Eleventh Army crossed at Ram, with the right wing crossing one day later. On October 9, 1915, Belgrade fell to the Central Powers for the second time in the war, this time for good. Two days later, the Bulgarians invaded Serbia from the south, trapping the Serbian army in between two giant pincers, closing mercilessly. Skopje (Üsküb, the former linchpin of Ottoman defenses in Europe, renovated by the Germans before it fell to Serbia in the First Balkan War) was captured on October 22, with Nish, the second capital, falling the first week of November. What remained of the Serbian army now converged on Blackbird Field in Kosovo, staging a chaotic fighting retreat into the mountains of Albania. In less than a month, Serbia, whose survival was the original *casus belli* for Russia and her Allies, had been wiped from the map, before the Allied troops at Salonica had even reached the Serbian frontier.[14]

The crushing of Serbia was terrible news for Allied troops on Gallipoli, where another uneasy pause had descended on the peninsula after the blood-lust had been spent on Anafarta. By September, something like eight hundred sick men on the Allied side were being evacuated from the beaches every day, and the ones left behind to contend with dust and mosquitoes were hardly in a happier state. The "gains" of August, as one general sarcastically remarked, amounted to "five hundred acres of bad grazing ground" and "three sieges to contend with, instead of two." In early September there had been talk of re-inforcements from France—as many as four whole French divisions!—only for this to turn into another will-o'-the-wisp, postponed until November at the earliest, if at all. Hamilton himself concluded the game was up as soon as he saw the two divisions sent off to Salonica at the end of September. "At whose door," he wrote in his diary in early October 1915, "will history leave the blame for the helpless, hopeless fix we are left in—rotting with disease and told to take it easy."[15]

Not everyone was ready to give up. Churchill, fully in character, wanted to salvage something from the wreck. In a policy brief prepared for the War Council on October 5, 1915, just as Mackensen was readying to strike across the Danube, Churchill reminded his colleagues that it would take time for the Central Powers to subdue Serbia (in the event only a month), that even once German ammunition reached Constantinople by rail it "has still to be transported to the Gallipoli peninsula," and that even if, once regular resup-ply from Germany was established, "the artillery fire directed against our positions will increase in severity, that is no reason why our troops should not be able to maintain themselves." The men were entrenched (though Churchill admitted that conditions in the trenches could be considerably improved), the ground on each main front broken and uneven, which afforded Allied soldiers "innumerable opportunities of securing effective defilade." Colder fall and winter weather could improve the sanitary situation and lessen the desperate need for water, even if it would also require warmer clothing for the men. There was thus no reason "to doubt our ability to maintain ourselves, in spite of losses, for an almost indefinite period." Of course, as Churchill himself conceded, it was an open question "whether it was desirable to leave an army of these dimensions indefinitely to waste by fire and sickness on the Gallipoli Peninsula without hope of an offensive to relieve it." His own solution to this vexing problem was to give the Gallipoli expedition purpose, by finding some way for the army, or the navy, to break through. To this end, Churchill implored his colleagues on the War Council to "rouse themselves to effective and energetic action before it is too late."[16]

With the first cold snap of cold weather hitting the Aegean in early October 1915, it was getting late already. On October 11, Kitchener first broached the subject of withdrawal, asking Hamilton for an estimate of the casualties he expected might attend a full-on evacuation from Gallipoli. Horrified, Hamilton replied that "it would not be wise to reckon on getting out of Gallipoli with less loss than that of half the total force." As this was not the answer Kitchener (or anyone else in London) wanted to hear, Hamilton was promptly sacked. His replacement, General Sir Charles Monro, revised the estimated losses downward to about "thirty to forty percent," but with the crucial revision that he actually favored an evacuation. Disgusted with these depressing answers, Kitchener swung over to Churchill's side, summoning to London Captain Keyes (the same who had sided with Churchill in March, hoping to push on at the Dardanelles), to pitch a new plan to force the Straits in a naval assault in concert with a new landing at Bulair. Won over by Keyes's boldness, Kitchener wrote on November 3, "I absolutely refuse to sign orders for evacuation, which I think would be the gravest disaster and would condemn a large percentage of our men to death or imprisonment." Monro was relieved of his command and sent to Salonica. With de Robeck dead against the idea, Kitchener proposed to turn his naval command over to Admiral Sir Rosslyn Wemyss and give the Anzac sector commander, General Birdwood (who remained full of fight) overall command of the army. To spearhead the heroic final chapter of the saga, Kitchener set out for Gallipoli himself to inspect the battlefield for the first time.[17]

Kitchener's enthusiasm did not survive the visit. It was part of Churchill's continuing run of bad luck that Keyes was held up in London arranging for naval reinforcements and then failed to make his rendezvous with Kitchener in Marseille en route to the Aegean. When the minister of war arrived at Mudros, de Robeck was therefore able to pour cold water all over Keyes's ideas, unopposed. It may, however, simply have been the depressing sight of the endless, fruitless bivouacs onshore that, compounded by Kitchener's age and exhaustion from the trip, soured him on the idea of trying to force the Straits again. When Keyes finally caught up with him aboard the *Dartmouth* in the harbor of Salonica, the aging titan looked "weary and harassed." "Well, I have seen the place," Kitchener told Keyes. "It is an awful place and you will never get through." At the very cusp of action at the end of the campaign, Kitchener had developed the same cold feet as he had on February 19, at its beginning. He had the same flash of insight too. On the advice of McMahon and Maxwell from Cairo, Kitchener now decided that new reinforcements coming from England and France, along with divisions pulled from Gallipoli, should land at: Alexandretta.

Of course, this idea had gone nowhere in winter and spring, when it was most fresh and promising. In July, when a Cilician landing might have done the most immediate good, saving thousands of Armenian lives in addition to cutting off the Ottoman armies in Mesopotamia and Syria, it had seemed only a distraction from the front already opened up at Gallipoli. Now that yet another front had been opened at Salonica, Kitchener's latest brainstorm proved even less compelling to the War Council: with two precariously held beachheads in the east, why open a third? Then, too, winter was approaching, and the clock was ticking fast on the window of opportunity for a relatively painless withdrawal before German arms and ammunition began flooding in through the Balkans. With Keyes alone favoring a naval offensive against the advice of his superior officers and the generals—even Birdwood gave up after hearing the news from Serbia—evacuation seemed the only answer. On November 22, 1915, Kitchener cabled to the War Council that Suvla Bay and Anzac Cove should be evacuated, with the Helles front holding on for now (though presumably to follow in short order). He then returned to London to make the case. After another round of polemics and backbiting, the War Council, on December 7, resolved to evacuate Anzac and Suvla. The great Dardanelles adventure was drawing to a close.

As if to confirm final judgment on the Gallipoli campaign, a tremendous storm struck the peninsula in the last week of November, with sheets of rain pouring down for twenty-four hours, followed by "two days of snow and icy sleet." The shock was particularly severe at Anzac Cove, where many of the antipodean and Indian soldiers had never seen snow before. More serious was the fact that winter clothing had not arrived yet, and the waters were too rough for ships to come ashore. By November 30, 1915, some ten thousand men had been stricken with frostbite or hypothermia, or had simply frozen to death on the beaches. Whatever fighting spirit was left in the Allies was slowly seeping away in the wet and cold.

Of course, the evacuation itself, if conducted in such brutal conditions, would be no picnic. And yet, in another unexpected twist, the weather gods now smiled down on the Aegean. The month of December 1915 proved to be mild and mostly sunny, with the crisp, bracing air doing much to improve the health and temper of the men once they had finally warmed up. Those who went down sick, along with those rotated out of the front lines, were pleas-antly surprised to learn that they were not being sent back to the beaches, but were going home instead. It emerged that a gradual and secret withdrawal was under way, finally revealed to the men of Anzac and Suvla on December 12. An elaborate pretense was maintained, which included the propping up of "self-firing rifles" with kerosene tins, to keep up a spasmodic fire after each unit left. Millions of rounds of ammunition were thrown into the sea, along with hand grenades. By midnight on December 20, 1915, the evacuation of the two northern beachheads was complete, with almost total surprise achieved. The British and French troops at Helles followed in early January, with the evacuation interrupted only by a last-ditch Turkish offensive on January 7 at Gully Spur, which failed so spectacularly that Liman decided to hold back again, allowing the last 17,000 Allied soldiers to get away nearly unmolested. In a campaign now a byword for Allied futility, the evacuation proceeded almost flawlessly, with minimal casualties during the final embarkation.[18]

Having been warned by Hamilton and Monro that casualties would be 30–50 percent, the British were naturally relieved that the evacuation came off so well. But there was no disguising the magnitude of Britain's defeat. Casualties on the Allied side were reckoned at over a quarter-million men, with some 205,000 British dead or wounded and 47,000 French. The Turks lost as many or more, with estimates ranging from 190,000 to 350,000 casualties, but they had saved their capital from occupation, saved the beleaguered Ottoman Empire itself. Even if the Turco-German triumph at Gallipoli was a defensive one, involving no captured enemy territory, it still must be reckoned as one of the greatest victories of the First World War. As Liman reported to Enver on January 9, 1916, "God be thanked, the entire Gallipoli peninsula has been cleansed of the enemy." In his memoirs, Liman's carefully maintained tone of detachment at last gives way when he recalls the scene on the Helles beaches evacuated by the enemy:

> The booty at the south group was extraordinary. Wagon parks, automobile parks, mountains of arms, ammunition and entrenching tools were collected . . . most of the tent camps and barracks had been left standing, in part with all their equipment. Many hundreds of horses lay in rows, shot or poisoned, but quite a number of horses and mules were captured and turned over to the Turkish artillery . . . the immense booty of war material was used for the Turkish armies. Many ship loads of conserves, flour and wood were removed to Constantinople. What the ragged and insufficiently nourished Turkish soldiers took away, cannot be estimated.[19]

The news from farther east was no happier for the British War Council. Since early October, a high-level German delegation had been encamped in

Kabul, trying to enlist Afghanistan in a holy war to bring down the British Raj. Headed by a brilliant Bavarian artillery officer, Oskar von Niedermayer, the delegation also included a high-level German diplomat, Werner Otto von Hentig, empowered to negotiate terms of alliance, and two Indian revolutionary exile-pretenders, one Hindu (Prince Mahendra Pratap) and one Muslim (Mohammed Barakatullah). Niedermayer's team also carried elaborate imperial greetings to the emir from Kaiser Wilhelm II and the Ottoman sultan, Mehmed Reshad V; twenty-seven letters addressed to Indian princes rumored to be estranged from the Raj, each signed by Chancellor Bethmann Hollweg and "sumptuously bound in leather"; and ornate gifts for Emir Habibullah, the ruler of Afghanistan, and his retainers, which included "bejeweled gold watches, gold fountain pens, gold-topped canes, hand-ornamented rifles and pistols, binoculars, cameras, compasses, a cinema projector," and a dozen radio alarm clocks. Having evaded a British-Russian cordon set up to prevent them from crossing the Persian frontier, Niedermayer's men were now enjoying the hospitality of the Afghan emir as he contemplated whether or not to spearhead an invasion of British India through the Khyber Pass. Among the factors working on Habibullah's subtle mind that winter was the fate of the British expedition at Gallipoli.[20]

All year, British intelligence had picked up worrying portents of German- or Turkish-inspired plots against the Raj. In January, a mutiny brewing in the 130th Baluchi Regiment of the Indian Army was snuffed out in Bombay. February had seen a more serious mutiny of Indian sepoys in the Singapore garrison, which took the lives of forty-seven British officers before order was restored with the help of French, Russian, and Japanese warships. In June, a German spy named Vincent Kraft was arrested in Singapore. On interrogation, he confessed that he had been tasked with inciting a rebellion in Bengal, as suggested by the map he was carrying, which pinpointed possible landing spots for weapons dumps on the coast. Tipped off by Kraft, the British stepped up patrols of the South China Sea, the Straits of Malacca, and naval surveillance of the coastal areas near Burma and Bengal. At least one vessel carrying German-supplied weapons, the *Henry S.*, was captured and impounded in the Indian Ocean, and another one sunk at sea. The British were also able to root out German plans to incite a "Christmas Day" insurrection in Calcutta with a series of raids in mid-December 1915. While Niedermayer remained in the good graces of Emir Habibullah in Kabul, the threat of a coordinated invasion–cum–holy war uprising to topple the Raj had been scotched, for now.[21]

Terrifying as these far-flung plots seemed to leaders in Delhi and London as 1915 drew to a close, in many ways the news from Mesopotamia was far more serious. The year had begun promisingly enough for the British-Indian expeditionary army based at Basra. With naval passage above Qurna difficult owing to the shallow waters of the Tigris, the British had focused initially on fortifying their downstream positions and fending off Turco-German attacks on the oil pipelines of the Karun River region. In early March 1915, a force of about five thousand Turkish irregulars, accompanied by a small team of German officers and local Arabs from the Beni Lam tribe, crossed the Persian border to assault the British garrison at Ahwaz, only to be repulsed with ease after Brigadier General C. T. Robinson surprised them with a preemptive night attack. April saw an even more lopsided battle at Shaiba, southwest of Basra, where Süleyman Askeri Bey had mustered four thousand Turkish regulars, accompanied by about ten thousand Arab and Kurdish irregulars, to try to threaten the British left flank, guarded by about seven thousand Indian soldiers. In a series of fierce engagements between April 12 and 14, 1915, the Ottoman forces were routed, sustaining some six thousand casualties and seven hundred prisoners. It did not help the Ottoman cause that most of the Arabs and Kurds had fled before the firing started. Although several thousand Turkish men and officers were able to retreat north, their commander, Süleyman Askeri Bey—whether out of shame at another humiliating loss or a feeling of betrayal by the local Arab Muslim community he was defending—shot himself.[22]

For a time it had looked like British prestige might carry all before it in Mesopotamia. In the aftermath of Shaiba, the Beni Lam and most of the other tribes deserted the Ottoman cause. On April 23, General Charles Townshend arrived in Basra to take over the Sixth Poona Division, under the overall command of ranking general Sir John Nixon. Townshend was already a legend in the Indian Army after staring down a siege of the Chitral Fort on the Northwest Frontier back in 1895. Nixon ordered Townshend to resume the advance up the Tigris. At 5:00 a.m. on May 31, Townshend's force opened fire on the

Turkish position at Bahran, scattering the defenders back toward Amara, a town located at a bend where the al-Mscharra River fed into the Tigris, which—conveniently for the British riverine fleet—was nearly surrounded by water during the late spring high tide, with both the Tigris and al-Mscharra 300 meters (328 yards) wide. Townshend himself, accompanied by Sir Percy Cox and Captain Nunn, pursued the retreating Turks aboard the *Espiègle*, until it ran aground and they transferred to HMS *Comet*. They could not keep pace, however, with the shallowest-draft vessel, HMS *Shaitan*, commanded by Captain Mark Singleton with a crew of nine. Astonishingly, this advance guard of ten all but captured waterlogged Amara by itself, taking the surrender of 250 Turkish troops and 11 officers before Townshend arrived with the *Comet* to take prisoner another 128 Ottoman officers and 1,384 men with their weapons (including 12 field guns, 5 naval guns, and 2,718 rifles), with another 2,000 Turks retreating north. Townshend lost only 4 killed and 21 wounded. Little wonder Nixon, encouraged by the viceroy in Delhi, Charles Hardinge, directed Townshend to pursue the Turks up the Tigris and Euphrates Rivers in order to occupy Baghdad "before the Russians arrive anywhere near it."[23]

It was a fateful decision. Already there was grumbling among the men at the appalling conditions in Mesopotamia, the intense heat, the swarms of flies and mosquitoes. It was like Gallipoli, only hotter, more humid, and even less sanitary—like fighting and living in a muddy swamp. Compounding the discomfort were the periodic tribal raids, along with regular doses of deadly sniper fire from the flanks. It was true that more Arab tribesmen abandoned the Ottomans with every British victory, but this was a mixed blessing. Arab irregulars, often ineffective on the battlefield, could be deadly to stragglers, including—especially—those on their own side. British and German officers alike were horrified by Bedouin brutality in Mesopotamia. As General Sir Edmund Barrow observed, "The Amara Arabs, who at the beginning had greeted the [Ottoman] left wing advance with cheers, now set on the detachment, stripped, looted, and murdered them." Hans Lührs, a German officer active in the Karun region that spring, observed of the retreat from Ahwaz that "the Arabs stripped those fallen in action completely, leaving them naked and unburied." Viewing incidents like this was hardly reassuring to regular soldiers on either side.[24]

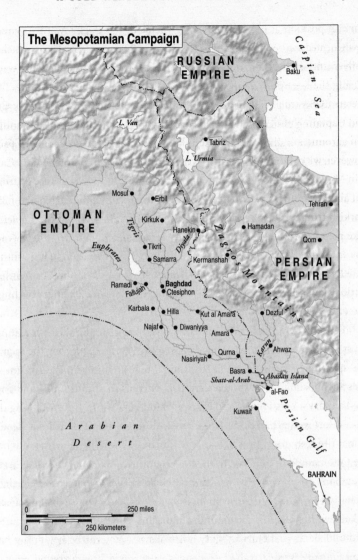

The Mesopotamian Campaign

In July, the British won another Pyrrhic victory on the Euphrates. To secure the northwestern approaches to Basra and to cover Townshend's left flank, an auxiliary force under Major General George Gorringe was sent up toward Nasiriyah, guided by the ubiquitous Captain Nunn aboard HMS *Sushan*. By now it was high summer, and daytime temperatures often topped

120 degrees Fahrenheit (49 degrees Celsius)—in the shade. As they neared Turkish positions along the creeks and canals guarding Nasiriyah, British Indian infantrymen had to "creep forward yard by yard, from sodden trench to sodden trench, [in] a moist swampy heat—eaten alive with insects." The first British assault, launched on July 14, went horribly wrong, with 120 of 400 men becoming casualties, with the vulture-like descent of Bedouin Arabs in the aftermath making it impossible to rescue the dead, who were simply abandoned in the water where they lay. With British understatement, Gorringe reported that his position had become "most unenviable." It was emblematic of the conditions of the Mesopotamian summer that the only reinforcements available downstream were some 350 men "sick but able to bear arms." Only when a small, cooling breeze came in on July 24 were Gorringe's soldiers able to muster the strength for a renewed attack. The battle of Nasiriyah was a brutal affair, with bayonet charges and close-order fighting that cost some 2,000 Turkish soldiers their lives, along with 400 British Indians. Basra was secure.[25]

Thus far the Indian Army was carrying all before it. But there was ample cause for concern. Politically, the creeping British occupation of Mesopotamia opened up a hornet's nest of problems. Annexations had not been cleared with Britain's allies. The French were already concerned about apparent British designs on Cilicia, part of France's "desiderata" from the Ottoman carcass. The Russians had made no claim on Baghdad, but they had not signed off on a British claim to it either. It was not clear whether conquered Arab territories would be annexed to the Raj or granted some kind of protectorate status akin to pre-1914 Egypt—and if the latter, who would have nominal sovereignty—Arab tribesmen? In logistical terms, the advance to Amara had already lengthened British communications lines up the Tigris nearly a hundred kilometers past Qurna—sixty miles of swampy scrub offering plenty of cover for snipers. Nasiriyah had extended river supply lines up the Euphrates by two hundred kilometers above Basra. Simply to keep the men supplied with bare subsistence provisions was difficult, and to keep them healthy was well-nigh impossible. Every bend in the river, every mud fort, every town the British conquered became a new target for snipers. Every battle left more wounded to send downriver for treatment, if they were lucky enough not to fall into the hands of rapacious Bedouins. And every mile Townshend's men advanced was a mile closer to the main Ottoman Sixth Army reserve at Baghdad, where the Turks were frantically calling up troops and scrambling up new gendarmerie battalions.

Undeterred by these daunting problems, Townshend pressed on up the Tigris toward the next strategic bend-in-the-river crux-point at Kut. Lying about 112 miles (180 kilometers) south of Baghdad by road (though 200 miles, or 322 kilometers, along the river), Kut bestrode the junction of the Tigris River and the Shatt-el-Hai; overland trade routes also crossed there. Owing to the grain trade it was a reasonably prosperous town by Ottoman Mesopotamian standards, home to some six thousand people, a military garrison, a customhouse, and "a few fairly well built houses with a quay," fringed with gardens and date palms. Nureddin Bey, who had taken over what remained of the Thirty-Eighth Ottoman Infantry Division along with part of the Thirty-Fifth, had assembled his forces about seven miles south of the city in a strong defensive position. Sunken boats blocked the river. Most impressive was what Townshend later described as "a line of earthworks, entrenchments and redoubts of the most modern type." Hidden pits had been dug, tapered down to enclose a "3-foot sharpened stake" at the bottom. The trenches were expertly camouflaged, such that British spotters could not recognize them at less than a hundred yards; some of the communications trenches were ten to twelve feet deep. There was, however, a gap of three hundred yards in the trenches, over drier ground where it had proved too difficult to dig.[26]

After careful and patient reconnaissance, Townshend was ready to strike. On September 27, 1915, the largest Mesopotamian battle yet was joined, with a furious British artillery barrage, followed by a frantic rush through the gap in the trenches masked by a feint on the river, where sappers laid a pontoon bridge as if to crown the main assault. It was another confusing and close-run affair, with real-time field communications failing utterly to keep abreast of developments. The gap in Ottoman lines turned out to be smaller than believed, and the main British thrust, under General Delamain, was nearly encircled, only to survive because of slow Turkish pursuit. In the end Nureddin Bey's men seem to have been ground down mostly by attrition, with morale plunging so quickly that ordering another retreat upriver was the only way to keep his men from surrendering en masse. As it was, the Turks lost 1,153 prisoners, with another 2,800 or so casualties. But the British suffered 1,233 casualties themselves, in what might have been taken as a warning.[27]

Should the Indian Army press on toward Baghdad? Townshend himself, concerned about both heavy casualties and precarious supply lines, would have preferred to dig in at Kut for the winter. But Nixon was raring to go, and he had the backing of Delhi, where pressure was building to salvage something out of this *annus horribilis* of the empire. In October 1915, it was clear that Gallipoli was a bust; Serbia was being overrun by the Central Powers; the Germans were making trouble in Kabul; and even neutral Persia seemed to be falling into the hands of the Turco-Germans, with rumors swirling around Teheran that Ahmad Shah, encouraged by the Germans, was about to "perform a *hejira*, or ceremonial exodus from the capital to the holy city of Qom," just as Muhammad had once tactically abandoned Mecca for Medina. To reverse this tide of woe, it seemed necessary to "strike a blow somewhere," as Viceroy Hardinge wrote to London, and this could be done "quite easily by striking at Baghdad." Nixon seconded the motion, informing Delhi and London that the expeditionary force faced a "demoralised" and "shaken" enemy. After much hand-wringing over whether or not to reinforce or restrain Nixon in Basra, on October 21, 1915, the War Council at last gave a sort of grudging green light to a "raid" on Baghdad (though not a permanent occupation—at least, not yet). With language uncannily similar to that used in the "gang of buccaneers" session of March 10 dividing up the "carcase of the Turk," Sir Edward Grey explained London's halfhearted endorsement of the conquest of Ottoman Baghdad to Maurice Hankey like this: "It was necessary to gain strength by eating *now*, even if it involved indigestion later on."[28]

For Townshend and his men, the indigestion came quickly. Far from "easy," the seizing of Baghdad would require a frontal assault on yet another strong Turkish defensive position at Ctesiphon (Salman Pak),* where Nureddin Bey had assembled about eighteen thousand regular troops, thirty-eight field guns, two lines of entrenchments, and a kind of final barricade of boats

---

* In Ottoman Turkish, the place was named after Muhammad's barber Salman (Suleiman) Pak, who is thought to be buried nearby.

Abdul Hamid II, Ottoman sultan, 1876–1909

Wilhelm II, emperor of Germany, 1888–1918

Colmar Freiherr von der Goltz Pasha,
adviser to Ottoman army, field marshal,
commander of Ottoman Sixth Army in Baghdad

Ismail Enver Pasha,
Ottoman war minister
and generalissimo

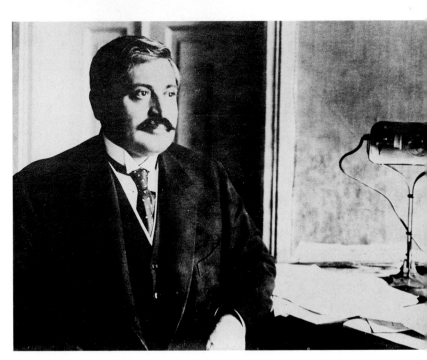

Talât Bey, Ottoman interior minister and grand vizier

Djemal Pasha,
Ottoman naval minister, Fourth
Army commander in Damascus, and
virtual dictator in wartime Syria

Otto Liman von Sanders, lieutenant general
and head of German Reform Mission to Turkey

Wilhelm Souchon,
German admiral, commander
of SMS *Goeben*, and vice admiral
of the Ottoman navy

SMS *Goeben*, incorporated into the Ottoman navy as the *Yavuz*
in August 1914, docked in Istinye, Constantinople

Winston Churchill, First Lord of the Admiralty, 1911–1915

Friedrich Freiherr Kress von Kressenstein, German lieutenant colonel directing Suez operations of Ottoman Fourth Army under Djemal

Turkish soldiers under German command at a Dardanelles shore battery

Horatio Herbert Kitchener
"of Khartoum," British field marshal
and secretary of state for war, 1914–1916

Herbert Henry Asquith,
prime minister of the United
Kingdom, 1908–1916

strung together. Enver's uncle Halil Bey had recently arrived in Baghdad to spearhead the defense under German field marshal Goltz Pasha, who had just been appointed commander of the Ottoman Sixth Army (although Goltz was still en route to Mesopotamia). At 8:00 a.m. on November 22, 1915, on a "bitterly cold morning" by Mesopotamian standards, Townshend, commanding some eleven thousand Indian Army regulars from the Poona Division, launched a three-column assault on the Turkish trench lines, with a fourth mobile "flying" column directed to outflank the enemy's left flank. With the middle or "B" column, consisting mostly of Gurkhas and Punjabis, taking the lead, Townshend's men succeeded in taking the first line of trenches and about eight guns, but were repulsed at the second line—suffering four thousand casualties in the first day, mostly wounded men whose evacuation turned into a logistical nightmare. On November 23, Townshend briefly resumed his attack, but the Turkish lines held. So brutal was the carnage that, on the morning of November 24, both sides began withdrawing to stronger defensive positions—until Halil and Nureddin Bey realized the enemy was retreating and they ordered their men to advance.[29]

Unlike Amara or Kut, Ctesiphon was not even a Pyrrhic victory for the British. Although the Turks had again lost more men overall—some 6,188 casualties of 18,000, as against 4,200 British killed or wounded out of 11,000 engaged—the British losses were both proportionately higher and much harder to recoup, including 130 British and 111 Indian Army officers. Moreover, this time the Turks were left in possession of the battlefield, with the invading enemy pitched back downriver. By December 1, 1915, the retreating Poona Division had reached the "dubious refuge" of Kut, where in October, Townshend had proposed to dig in for the winter before being overruled by Nixon, Delhi, and London. Unfortunately for Townshend and his men, the intervening battle at Ctesiphon had depleted their strength and morale, while costing precious time that might have been spent on defensive entrenchment. The retreat, meanwhile, was marred by difficulties on the river, where many of the vessels carrying weapons became trapped in the mud and had to be fired to prevent their falling into Turkish hands. Barges, remembered Captain Nunn, were "constantly grounding," which in turn tied up other river craft that were needed to tow them, especially in cases where the grounded tugs carried wounded men Townshend was loath to leave behind. Downriver, the news was no better, as supply lines ran all of five hundred miles (eight hundred kilometers) from Basra to Kut, which could be sabotaged at any point by Bedouins encouraged by news of the British retreat.[30]

Most ominous of all were the reports of Ottoman pursuit. By the end of November, British aerial surveillance reported "the advance of large columns of enemy estimated at 12,000 with guns, and a cavalry brigade." On December 8, Nureddin Bey opened an artillery bombardment on British positions at Kut from three sides. Although unable to break British resistance, the Turks easily outflanked Townshend's forces, completing the encirclement of Kut when they crossed and held the river a few miles downstream at Sheikh Saad. Just before the ring closed, Townshend was able to get his cavalry away, but he and his infantrymen—about 11,600 combatants in all, plus several thousand support staff—were now trapped inside the mud-walled city of Kut with only sixty days' rations, surrounded by Ottoman forces, which now outnumbered them—forces that would shortly be taken in hand by a legendary German field marshal and the uncle of the Ottoman war minister, whose own prestige would now be invested in the siege of Kut. It would be a cold winter in London.

CHAPTER 12

ERZURUM AND KUT

If the Russian army attacks you in strength, you can always withdraw towards Sivas.

—ENVER PASHA
to Ottoman Third Army commander Mehmed Kâmil Pasha,
January 1916[1]

ON THE CAUCASIAN AND PERSIAN FRONTS, a certain lull seemed to have descended after the fury of summer 1915, symbolized by the strange fate of the city of Van. Rocked all spring by ethnic bloodletting before it fell to the Russians in May, Van had then seen the exodus of its Muslim survivors—only to see a massacre of its Christians once the Ottomans, after Abdul Kerim Pasha's victory at Manzikert, retook the city in early August. After Abdul Kerim Pasha had repeated the Russian mistake of overextending his offensive into Urmia, the Russians had then retaken Van less than four weeks later, though this beautiful and much-contested city was by then little more than a ghost town. By November, Russian cavalry units were once again patrolling the southern shores of Lake Van and surveilling the approaches to Bitlis, as if the Ottoman victory at Manzikert and subsequent Armenian massacres had never happened.

Considering the drama transpiring elsewhere, it is unsurprising that eastern Turkey took on a lower strategic profile in fall 1915. The Russian retreat in Poland had so shaken the tsarist regime that Nicholas II took over the army command himself in September to rally the public behind the war. The hammering of Serbia following Bulgaria's entry into the war in October sealed the fate of the Allies on Gallipoli, leading to the withdrawal in

December–January. Even the Mesopotamian front had begun to eclipse the Caucasus in the eyes of the Ottoman high command, with Enver transferring two whole Third Army divisions (the Fifty-First and Fifty-Second) from Erzurum in time to contribute to the great Turkish victory at Ctesiphon in November. As for the divisions freed up following the British withdrawal from Gallipoli—some twenty-two in all—Enver surprised even his own allies by suggesting that seven of them be sent to aid the Austrians in Galicia (and possibly Italy), while also ordering preparations to begin for a second Suez Canal offensive in spring 1916. After all the sound and fury of Sarıkamış, Van, and Manzikert, it was as if the Caucasian front had been forgotten.

It had not been forgotten by the Russians, however. In a sign of the reshuffling of priorities to which Enver and the Germans should have paid closer attention, the Caucasian command was entrusted, on September 24, 1915, to Grand Duke Nicholas, lately deprived of overall command by the tsar. Even if his luster was diminished somewhat by the Great Retreat of 1915, a Romanov grand duke now had his own reputation on the line in the Caucasian theater, and would not take lightly to its neglect. Understandably, the generals at Stavka (now relocated farther east to Mogilev, as Baranovichi had fallen to the Germans) were loath to part with men or war matériel until the front lines had stabilized in eastern Europe. By November, however, Grand Duke Nicholas had brought his considerable weight to bear in provisioning a new fourteen-thousand-strong expeditionary force (eight thousand cavalry and six thousand infantry) to Persia, headed by cavalry general N. N. Baratov (hero of the pursuit after Sarıkamış). After Baratov's advance guard made a show of force on the Kazvin-Teheran road, with an implied threat to storm the capital, Ahmad Shah surrendered Teheran to the Russians on November 15, 1915, putting the German and Austrian consuls to flight. By February, Baratov's cavalry had cleared northern Persia of German and Turkish forces, restoring Russian prestige in Azerbaijan and threatening (in theory) to invade Mesopotamia from the east in relief of Townshend's men holding out under siege at Kut.[2]

Considerable as Baratov's achievements were, however, their real import was soon felt elsewhere. The Persian incursion served its own strategic purpose in clearing Azerbaijan of the enemy, but it also worked as important camouflage for a far more ambitious Russian offensive in eastern Turkey being quietly cooked up by Yudenich (although Grand Duke Nicholas had not yet been informed). Hoping to deal the Ottoman Third Army a decisive defeat before Enver could rush reinforcements in from Gallipoli—a process he estimated would take three months—Yudenich envisioned a sharp, surprise thrust to break through the Ottoman lines at Köprüköy defending the approaches to Erzurum, with the aim of a "partial annihilation" of the Third Army before it could be reinforced. In December 1915, Russian troop trains began to set off southward nearly every day from Tiflis toward Tabriz as if to reinforce Baratov, only to return each evening. To crown the ongoing *maskirovka*, or deception, Yudenich made a show of giving his officers and men holiday leave, with ostentatious preparations for a great Christmas feast. Then, even more than today, the Orthodox Christmas was a grand occasion, often stretching out for a week or more. The very scale of the Caucasian Army, now nearing 200,000 in strength with new recruits, meant that the festivities would be colossal in scale—offering a perfect opportunity for yet more camouflage, as supplies needed for a winter offensive could be and were shuffled nearer to the front in the guise of holiday preparation. Instead of noisemakers and liquor, Yudenich's logistics teams were actually distributing short fur coats (*polushubki*), cotton wool-lined trousers and gloves, felt boots, fur caps, and, in a special touch, two short logs per man (perfect for yuletide—or for lighting fires on the frigid wastes of Top Yol, where so many wood-deprived Turks had frozen to death during the Sarıkamış offensive). As tsarist Russia still used the Julian calendar, thirteen days behind the Gregorian, the revelry was expected to climax during the week of January 7–14, 1916 (Western style). It was on the fourth day of Orthodox Christmas—January 10—that Yudenich planned to strike.[3]

It was a measure of Yudenich's great skill at *maskirovka* that he succeeded in keeping these preparations secret even from the Caucasian commander in chief, who was brought in only on December 18/31, 1915. Yudenich needed to be careful, for he knew that the Caucasus had been receding in priority for months not only for the Ottomans, but for Stavka as well. After the disasters of 1915, Tsar Nicholas II and his chief of staff, General M. V. Alekseev, were keen to restore Russian initiative—and prestige—in Europe, eyeing a new offensive in Galicia against the weaker Austro-Hungarian armies. Considering that the Turks, in the wake of Sarıkamış and the more recent defeats near Lake Van, clearly posed no threat to the Russian position in the Caucasus, Alekseev saw no reason to leave a large force there and demanded, in early January 1916, that Tiflis send reinforcements to Poland. Predictably, Grand Duke Nicholas bristled at the prospect of depriving his new command of troops and importance. He now threw his weight behind Yudenich's proposed offensive.

Russian surprise was nearly total. When the attack began, the Ottoman Third Army commander, Mehmed Kâmil Pasha, was at the War Ministry in Constantinople while his German chief of staff, Guse, was on medical leave in Germany following a nasty bout of typhus. Clearly the Persian and holiday *maskirovka* had worked, lulling Erzurum command to sleep just when the Turks should have been on high alert. And yet it is an exaggeration to say that no one on the Turkish side was expecting a Russian offensive in the near future (if not quite this soon). The reason Mehmed Kâmil Pasha was in the capital was precisely to request reinforcements from Enver, in case the Russians tried to strike. So unconcerned was Enver, according to the Third Army commander, that he instructed Mehmed Kâmil Pasha simply to "withdraw to Sivas" if the Russians attacked.[4] Even had Enver wished to rush troops to Erzurum, there would have been no way of getting them there quickly. The Russian Black Sea Fleet, though wary of the *Goeben*, was more than strong enough to harass Turkey's Black Sea coastline, effectively ruling out the sea route to Trabzon. There was a rail connection from Constantinople to Ankara, but, as John Buchan's heroes discovered in his best-selling wartime thriller *Greenmantle*, it was over five hundred miles from the railhead there to Erzurum, over a single, heavily trafficked macadamized road on which most troops would march on foot, with guns and other equipment hauled slowly in animal-drawn wagons. Abdul Kerim Pasha, acting Third Army commander at Erzurum in Mehmed Kâmil Pasha's absence, would therefore have to do the best he could with what he had—about 74,000 infantrymen spread out across IX, X, and XI Corps, 77 machine guns, and 180 field artillery guns.[5]

It was nowhere near enough. While Yudenich had only a thin superiority in numbers (about 80,000 infantry counting the Armenian *druzhiny* units, as against 74,000 Ottoman rifles), he was able to throw the better part of 85 operational battalions, from II Turkestan Corps, I Caucasian Corps, and the Fourth Caucasian Rifle Division, into the Köprüköy offensive, supported by 230 field guns, with shells hauled by camels.[6] More important than any numerical advantage was the fact that Yudenich's careful preparations ensured that the Russian forces were far better equipped for Caucasian winter conditions than the Turks. This, along with the element of surprise, proved decisive.

The first stage of Yudenich's planned offensive began on the fourth day of Orthodox Christmas, January 10, 1916, when the II Turkestan Corps, led by General Przevalski, attacked the Ottoman left (north) wing between Lake Tortum and the Çakir Baba ridge, aiming to capture the heights of Karadağ (Black Mountain) and draw in Ottoman reinforcements from Hasankale, where Abdul Kerim Pasha maintained a strategic reserve, though it consisted of only six thousand men. Meeting stiff resistance, especially from Ottoman machine gunners, Turkestani troops failed to capture the heights during two days of bitter fighting. But Przevalski's attack succeeded in its main strategic objective, which was to direct Abdul Kerim Pasha's attention to the northern sector, to which he sent two divisions (the Thirty-First and Thirty-Fourth). Yudenich then confused the Turks further by unleashing I Caucasian Corps against the Ottoman right wing, in the Aras River basin. The fighting there was fiercer still, involving bayonet thrusts and advances into the teeth of heavy Ottoman machine-gun fire (the unfortunate *muzhiks* had apparently not been told their attack was a diversion). Thus far the Russians, attacking on both enemy wings over three bloody and inconclusive days, had seized little but a few advance trenches. Abdul Kerim Pasha, not entirely taken in, had concluded that at least one of the Russian attacks was a feint—likely the northern one, with the result that he now routed his strategic reserve to the south.

Yudenich now played his trump. Having concluded that the weakest link in the Köprüköy lines lay in the junction of the central and right wings along the Çakir Baba ridge, the Russian chief of staff had amassed his greatest striking power there against the Ottoman Thirty-Third and Thirty-Fourth

Divisions, a force of some 35,000 men comprising 42 battalions including the entirety of the Fourteenth, Fifteenth, and Sixteenth Caucasian Rifle Divisions, deploying twenty-six field guns and eight howitzers. So well had Yudenich camouflaged his intended breakthrough attack, slated for the fifth day of the ongoing offensive, that Abdul Kerim Pasha ordered his massively outnumbered Thirty-Third Division itself to attack on day four (January 13, 1916), not realizing that he was sending his men into the teeth of Yudenich's massed strength. The Turkish center was thus already softened up by Russian defensive fire before the main attack began on day five.

As dawn broke on January 1/14, 1916—Russian Orthodox New Year—the Russians opened "an intense artillery bombardment" against the Ottoman center between Karsin and Kalender. By 11:00 a.m., the main Turkish trenches at Maslahat were taken, and the overmatched Thirty-Third Ottoman Division, along with elements of the Ottoman Eighteenth, was pitched into retreat. By afternoon Russian advance columns were racing through the valley between the heights of Koziçan and Cilligül, capturing the critical junction at Hisar Dere, where good roads opened up south toward the Ottoman headquarters at Köprüköy. Farther south, the Russian left resumed the attack in the Aras River basin, making more headway now that the enemy was retreating in the center. On January 15, the Russians captured the section of the Çakir Baba ridge separating the central and northern sectors, opening up a long section of the same Top Yol on which so many Turks had frozen to death the previous winter. With their felt boots and fur coats and caps, the Russians had less trouble enduring the winter winds on the exposed ridge. Making steady, if unspectacular, progress, by day seven—January 16, 1916— the Russians had outflanked the Ottoman right wing on the Aras River, cutting off communications with Köprüköy headquarters. The rout was on.

Not all was lost for Abdul Kerim Pasha. Just as Enver had discovered at Sarıkamış, even the best-laid battle plans tend to break down when man meets nature, especially in high winter. Yudenich's predominantly Caucasian troops, buttressed by a Siberian Cossack division, were hardy enough, and they were about as well prepared for the cold as an early twentieth-century soldier could have hoped for. They were still human, however, and not even the toughest mountain *muzhik* was at his swiftest marching through snow-drifts. Sensing victory, Yudenich gave orders on the night of January 16–17 for his advance columns to wheel south so as to cut off an Ottoman retreat from the Aras front. Having concluded earlier that day that the battle was lost, Abdul Kerim Pasha had ordered a full retreat hours before Yudenich's command could take effect—and even then the Russian pursuit was far too slow to cut off the Turks. By the time Yudenich's Siberian Cossacks reached Hasankale on day nine—January 18, 1916—it was all but an open city, with only four rearguard battalions left behind to cover the Ottoman retreat. This was just the kind of battle Cossacks lived for, against enemy forces cut off and helpless. The Turks were annihilated at Hasankale, losing 1,000 dead, 1,500 prisoners, and all four of their guns. The Russians had broken the Köprüköy lines and captured Köprüköy itself. But, thanks to the quick thinking of Abdul Kerim Pasha, the main Ottoman forces had avoided the Russian net and drawn back to the safety of Erzurum, with its great fortress guarding a city already well defended by high mountains. The Turks had escaped to fight again.[7]

Nevertheless, Köprüköy was a clear Russian victory, the largest and most significant to date on the Caucasian front. The Ottoman Third Army, reeling ever since Sarıkamış, had lost another 22,000 casualties, including some 5,000 prisoners and a similar number of deserters in addition to 10,000 or so killed, wounded, or frozen to death in the snows. The XI Corps suffered losses equaling nearly 70 percent of its strength. True, Abdul Kerim Pasha's timely retreat had saved nearly 40,000 men, who could continue to the fight from the comparative safety of Erzurum. And he lost only 20 or 30 guns captured—a substantial number, but hardly fatal to an army that still had a defensive stronghold to fall back on. All this was true, but it was equally true that Yudenich had beaten the Turks soundly, on a front where the two sides were nearly equal in strength. Russian tactical superiority in the center was made possible only by conceding Ottoman superiority on the wings, masked by overaggressive feints. Yudenich's victory was made of strategic élan and superior staff work. As the Ottoman military postmortem concluded, the reason Russian losses—about 10,000 casualties—were lower than Turkish, despite entrenched defenders being at a dramatic advantage in this department in the First World War, was superior logistics: "The number of Russian casualties was less than Turkish since they had made their preparations for the winter."[8]

Yudenich now wished to repeat the same performance at Erzurum. Having failed to pursue fast enough to encircle or cut off Turkish detachments at Köprüköy, the Russian chief of staff did not want to give the enemy time to recover strength and morale. Captured Turkish men and officers were grumbling savagely about their incompetent commanders, lending credence to the view that the Third Army was broken as a serious fighting force, its morale shattered in the snows. Cossack patrols, Armenian sympathizers, and aerial surveillance (the Russians had about twenty planes in theater) were reporting that the retreating Turks had abandoned the approaches to Erzurum entirely, falling back inside the city's forts and entrenchments as if to make a last stand. All signs pointed to a demoralized enemy little capable of resisting a strong frontal attack. Such, at any rate, was the argument Yudenich put to Grand Duke Nicholas, only for him to punt the matter over to Stavka (the grand duke was worried about his ammunition stores, which would likely be exhausted in another offensive). Alekseev and the tsar, impressed that they had finally found a field commander worth his salt, gave Yudenich their full backing for renewing the offensive.

Storming Erzurum would not be easy. The city was the second most heavily fortified in the entire Ottoman Empire (after Adrianople), with three strong lines of forts, sixteen in all, blocking the valley coming in from Hasankale to the east, with two more "flanking groups" of fortresses blocking access 12 kilometers (7.5 miles) to the north and 5 kilometers (3 miles) to the south. Improvements in the city's fortifications had been overseen by a team of British engineers following the Russo-Turkish war of 1877–78, and then taken still further by German technical advisers beginning in the 1890s, who had built the southern forts on the mountain heights of Palandöken (today Turkey's premier alpine ski resort). The mountains provided another formidable obstacle to any attacker, with the Deve-Boyun ridge, dominating the central and northeastern approaches to the city, rising to 2,500 meters (8,200 feet), at which height a fortress had been raised to dominate the field of

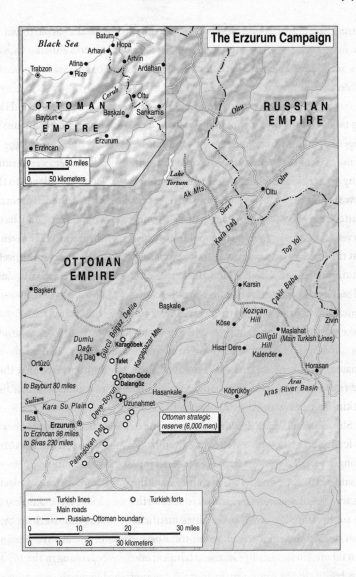

The Erzurum Campaign

Black Sea

Batum
Hopa
Arhavi
Atina
Trabzon
Rize
Artvin
Ardahan

OTTOMAN
Çoruh
Oltu

EMPIRE
Bayburt
Başkale
Sarıkamış

Erzurum

Erzincan

0   50 miles

0   50 kilometers

RUSSIAN
EMPIRE

Oltu

Lake
Tortum
Ak Mts.
Oltu

Sivri

Kara Dağ
Top Yol

OTTOMAN
EMPIRE

Başkent

Karsin

Çakir Baba

Başkale

Koziçan
Hill

Köse
Zivin

Cilligül
Hill

Maslahat
(Main Turkish Lines)

Dumlu
Dağı
Ağ Dağ

Güncü Boğaz Delila

Karagöbek

Hisar Dere
Kalender

Horasan

Ortüzü

Tafet
Kargapazar Mts.

to Bayburt 80 miles

Çoban-Dede
Dalangöz

Aras
Aras River Basin

Suliun

Deve-Boyun

Hasankale
Köprüköy

Kara Su Plain

Uzunahmet

Ilica

Erzurum

to Erzincan 98 miles
to Sivas 230 miles

Ottoman strategic
reserve (6,000 men)

Palandöken Dağ

Turkish lines   O   Turkish forts
Main roads
Russian–Ottoman boundary

0   10   20   30 miles

0   10   20   30 kilometers

fire on the ridge below. To the north of the city, Dumla Dağı rose to 2,963 meters (nearly 10,000 feet). In all, the Third Army, though now reduced to about 40,000 effectives, had 235 fixed or semi-fixed artillery guns at Erzurum, sprinkled liberally around the hilltop fortresses dominating the city's approaches and mounted atop the narrow mountain passes through which Yudenich's attackers would have to trudge in the winter snows; the Turks had another 112 mobile cannons, which ostensibly could be moved to reinforce any danger point. If they survived this gauntlet, the Russians would then have to contend with a final concentric ring of trenches and wire fields around the city itself, where well-concealed riflemen and machine-gun detachments were ready to rain fire upon them.

Formidable as it appeared on paper, there were considerable holes in the Turkish defense. Most of the Third Army's guns at Erzurum were fixed inside the forts, and these were not primarily of the heaviest modern caliber. None were larger than 150 mm (6 inches), and of these there were few. The bulk consisted of 87 mm, 80 mm, and 75 mm field guns, with a sprinkling of about forty 90 mm (3.5-inch) quick-firing Krupps. Several dozen Turkish machine guns had been left behind at Köprüköy; there were only about thirty-nine left at Erzurum. The Third Army had been reduced to 40,000 effectives, with no single unit at anywhere near full strength. The XI Corps, in particular, was scarcely stronger than a division at fewer than 10,000 men. Turkish "battalions" now comprised about 350 men, as against 1,000 in a Russian equivalent. In practice, this meant that Abdul Kerim Pasha could not have covered his entire defensive line even if he wanted to. Even if many of the mountain ridges and passes were guarded by forts or field guns, others were not, as the Russians discovered when carrying out a simple reconnaissance probe on the night of January 27–28, 1916, near the village of Kornes. Several Turkish-speaking Russian soldiers more or less talked their way across enemy lines, whereupon they "captured the 38th Infantry Division commander, eight staff officers, the division veterinarian, the division artillery commander and three of his staff." To crown their audacious victory, on their way back to their own lines the Russians seized three guns and captured two hundred prisoners. Yudenich concluded from the affair that "extremely large gaps existed at the front." Were he to find them and pour enough men through, many Ottoman fortified positions could be captured from behind.[9]

Yudenich's plan for storming Erzurum, like the one at Köprüköy, combined serious-enough offensive feints with an overwhelming mustering of strength at the enemy's weak point. This time, though, the sequence was to unfold more quickly, with a series of cascading attacks occurring more or less simultaneously, so as to frustrate any Ottoman effort to reinforce the critical sector. In a slightly different twist, the main feint, on the Deve-Boyun ridge, was in the center, with a small supporting diversionary attack on the far northeastern corner of Palandöken at Uzunahmet; there would be no major feint on the right. Once more, though, Yudenich intended to break through at a key hinge between the center and right sections of the Ottoman lines, through the Gürcü-Boğaz defile, guarded only by the forts of Karagöbek (at the Turkish front lines) and Tafet (closer to the city gates). By thrusting three full rifle divisions into this (comparatively) lightly defended gap, Yudenich could outflank all the fortifications on the heights of Deve-Boyun, just south; Palandöken, southwest; and Dumla Dağı, to the north and west, and reach the open, low-lying plain of Kara-Su, which fed down toward the eastern (Kars) gate of Erzurum.[10]

Speed was essential to Yudenich's conception, and his men, encouraged by the recent victory at Köprüköy, did not disappoint. At 2:00 p.m. on February 11, 1916, the Russian guns—nearly 250 of them—opened fire against the two main Ottoman forts on Deve-Boyun, Çoban-Dede and Dalangöz. The Turks returned fire on the attackers, with a contribution from the fort of Uzunahmet, just south on the outer ridge of the Palandöken. The Russian artillery effected little damage on the Turkish forts, though the furious barrage does seem to have put heart into the 153rd Bakinski Regiment, commanded by an Armenian colonel, Pirumyan, who surprised the defenders at Dalangöz by scaling the fortress walls in the dead of night. After hours of "wild bayonet fighting," the fortress fell to the Bakinskis at dawn. Just southeast of Çoban-Dede, the 156th Elizavetpolski Regiment scored a similar success by winning the heights of Küçüktöy. With two signature victories in the first night, Yudenich seemed to signal that his main thrust would come soon here, right into the teeth of the Ottoman fortified position on Deve-Boyun. Understandably, Mehmed Kâmil Pasha (who had returned from Constantinople just in time for the battle) directed his troops to recapture Dalangöz and clear the Russians from Deve-Boyun with a series of attacks the next day.

In doing so, he played into Yudenich's hands. Covered by the furious action on Deve-Boyun, the strongest Russian divisions—the Fourth and Fifth

Turkestan Rifles, commanded by the formidable General Przevalski, and the Fourth Caucasian Rifles—opened the main assault, into the Gürcü-Boğaz defile, on the morning of February 12. The overmatched Turks of X Corps withdrew almost immediately from Karagöbek after destroying the fort's guns, falling back to the rear position surrounding Fort Tafek. Once entrenched there, the Turks resisted fiercely, with both the Thirty-First and Thirty-Second Divisions launching successful counterattacks on February 13. On February 14, 1916, the Russians stormed Fort Tafet, taking heavy losses but capturing 1,500 prisoners and twenty guns. As if to confirm that the battle gods were in Yudenich's favor, a Turkish officer now deserted, carrying a map of the city's defenses, including placement of artillery; it was put to immediate use on day five, as the Russians rained down fire on the enemy gun emplacements.* While sporadic fighting continued on all fronts, especially on the southern slopes of Palandöken where the Russian assault had been weakest, by late afternoon on February 15, Russian airplanes were reporting that a general evacuation was under way, with fires raging across the city. At about 7:00 a.m. on February 16, a regiment of Terek Cossacks entered Erzurum from the Kars gate. Fortress Erzurum had fallen.[11]

It was a signature victory in the First World War. The Russians had captured 327 enemy guns, comprising nearly the entire store of the Ottoman Third Army. Of the forty thousand or so soldiers defending the city, the Turks had suffered at least ten thousand casualties and a similar number of prisoners and deserters, with surviving units fleeing west toward Sivas. The Russians had lost another thousand killed and eight thousand wounded and frostbitten themselves, but then these men, along with the ten thousand or so casualties of Köprüköy, had stormed a reputedly impregnable fortress city and all but destroyed the Ottoman Third Army as a fighting force. Yudenich's triumph would resound through the region, sending Russian prestige soaring.

Hoping to capitalize on his victory while the enemy was still in disarray, Yudenich insisted that the pursuit be carried out more vigorously than after

---

* In *Greenmantle*, John Buchan has a South African hunter-adventurer cross over to Russian lines with a staff map pilfered from a German officer. Improbable though his dramatization may be, Russian sources suggest that an Ottoman staff map was turned over to Yudenich during the battle—even if Erzurum might have fallen anyway.

Köprüköy. Already by the afternoon of February 16, two Cossack regiments had set off for Ilica, the nearest town west of Erzurum, which they captured by nightfall, taking three thousand more prisoners and thirty guns. Mehmed Kâmil Pasha, trying to salvage something on the retreat, ordered six rearguard battalions of battle-hardened frontiersmen to take a stand at Bayburt, while pulling back the rest of his officers and men to Erzincan, nearly 200 kilometers (120 miles) farther west. Once the crown jewel of the Ottoman Third Army, Erzurum was now a secure Russian forward base, from which Yudenich could launch probes and assaults toward the heart of Anatolia.

To cover the flanks of his advancing army, while preempting the arrival of serious Ottoman reinforcements from Gallipoli, Yudenich had meanwhile ordered offensives to proceed simultaneously on both his left (Urmia-Van-Bitlis) and right (from Ajaria along the Black Sea coast) flanks. Although the provisioning of the central thrust meant that Tiflis command could spare only the Sixth Caucasian Rifle Division for the left wing, this proved to be more than enough once news of the disaster at Köprüköy trickled down to the 106th and 107th Ottoman infantry regiments defending the approaches to Muş and Bitlis. After some desultory skirmishing in early February, an advance guard of Cossacks simply marched into Muş on the sixteenth—the same day Erzurum fell—and met no opposition. After pausing to allow the new division of riflemen to catch up to the Cossacks, the Russians resumed their advance at the end of February, reaching the outskirts of Bitlis on the night of March 2, 1916, where the Turks had fortified the mountain walls encasing the city, still covered in snowdrifts. This time it was the Sixth Caucasian Rifles who won the day—without firing their weapons. In a heroic feat of arms, the Russians crept quietly up to the Turkish positions in dead of night, stood bayonets ready, then defeated the enemy after "several hours of fierce hand-to-hand fighting," taking a thousand prisoners and twenty guns in the process. Turkish survivors, as if giving up on stemming the Russian advance, fled not west but south, to Siirt.[12]

The Russian advance was no less rapid on the right wing, despite the formidable obstacles posed by the terrain. Along the mountainous and densely wooded Black Sea coast of Luristan, enemy strongpoints could only be attacked from the water, requiring close coordination with the navy. It helped

ROMANIA
Bucharest •

ROMANIA

• Constanta

Danube

Sevastopol •

proposed lines of Russian naval communications

BULGARIA

• Varna

Black Sea

Adrianople
(Edirne) • Midia

Enos •

R Constantinople

Izmit •

Kastamonu •

Sinop •

Samsun

planned French railway Diarbakır – Sivas – Samsun

GREECE

Aegean Sea

Edremit •

Bursa •

Sakarya

Eskişehir •

Ankara •

planned Russian railway Trabzon–Sivas–Ankara

Giresun •

O T T O M A N

Kızılırmak

Sivas •

Afyon •

Smyrna
(Izmir) •

E M P I R E

Kayseri •

Malatya •

F1

Konya •

Zeytun •
Maraş •

CILICIA

Adana •

Taurus Mountains

Alexandretta •

Amanus Mtns.

Aleppo •

Cyprus
(British)

SYRIA

Mediterranean

Sea

Beirut •

Damascus •

I

B1 Red Zone: Area of direct British Control

B2 "B" Zone: Area of indirect British Control

F1 Blue Zone: Area of direct French Control

F2 "A" Zone: Area of indirect French Control

R Areas of direct Russian Control

I "A" Zone: International Zone control to be determined

Alexandria •

Gaza •
• Jerusalem

EGYPT
(under direct British rule)

⊙ Cairo

0 ————————— 250 miles

The Partition of the Ottoman Empire by Sazonov, Sykes, and Picot, 1916

RUSSIAN EMPIRE

Caucasus Mountains

Caspian Sea

Batum
Artvin
Rize
Trabzon
Olty
Ardahan
Sarıkamış
Kars
Gizman (Kağızman)
Yerevan
Igdyr (Iğdir)
Tiflis
Kura
Baku
Erzincan
Erzurum
Araks
"TURKISH ARMENIA"
R
Muş
L. Van
Van
Hoy
Bitlis
/Dilman
Kharput
Siirt
"KURDISTAN"
L. Urmia
Tabriz
Diarbakır
PERSIAN AZERBAIJAN
Jrfa
Ras ul-Ain
Mosul
Tehran
Der Zor
F2
Euphrates
Tigris
B2
PERSIA
MESOPOTAMIA
Baghdad
Isfahan
B1
Basra
Persian Gulf

that front commander General Lyakhov was already experienced at this sort of operation, having captured the port of Hopa and advanced farther west to Arhavi in February 1915 during the general mopping up after Sarıkamış, before being halted when the Turks dug in on the high western bank of the Arhavi River. When Lyakhov, to cover Yudenich's flank, renewed the offensive on February 5, 1916, it took only a push—two days of shelling by the Russian naval squadron, based at Batum—to dislodge the Turks from their trenches, where they left behind five hundred dead before pulling back to Vice. There, ten days later, the Russian squadron dished out similar punishment, forcing yet another tactical withdrawal on February 16—the day both Erzurum and Muş fell, in a sign of just how well coordinated Yudenich's overall strategic conception was. Still, Lyakhov made his own contribution, bringing up special, back-heavy Black Sea cargo tugs called *elpidiphores*, designed for tacking upstream into the numerous coastal rivers. These were now loaded with troops, and a landing was effected behind Ottoman lines near Atina, which cut off the main body of the Turkish defense from Rize, the largest port city between Batum and Trabzon—the latter city serving as the primary seaborne supply depot for the Ottoman Third Army. On March 8, 1916, the Russians occupied Rize. They were now just thirty miles from Trabzon.[13]

As if to crown Grand Duke Nicholas (in reality, Yudenich) the conqueror of the Ottomans, the very next day negotiations opened in Petrograd over the terms of the empire's partition among Russia's foreign minister, Sergei Sazonov, Britain's delegated expert, Sir Mark Sykes, and France's Georges Picot. It would, indeed, have made very little sense to open these negotiations in the months before March 1916, which had seen the Franco-British forces withdraw in humiliation from Gallipoli, even as Townshend's expeditionary force was defeated at Ctesiphon and now lay surrounded, under siege, at Kut. Now that Russia, always the prime mover in Ottoman affairs, had at last thrown her weight into the battlefield after all the prevarication of 1915, the carcass could be carved up in deadly earnest.

Sazonov, having played a weak hand well during the preliminary negotiations in March 1915, could now negotiate from a position of strength. Considering that he had wrested a postwar claim on Constantinople and the Straits despite Russia having contributed next to nothing at the Dardanelles or

Gallipoli, it is not surprising that he went much further now. Sykes and Picot had already come to a tentative bilateral understanding before coming to Petrograd, demarcating the British red from the French blue zone, with Britain laying claim to Arabia, Palestine, and much of Mesopotamia, and the French claiming Syria (including Lebanon), Cilicia, and much of "Turkish Armenia" and "Kurdistan" stretching from Cilicia through northern Mesopotamia into Urmia. As Sazonov knew, Sykes and the British had no real interest in upholding French claims on her frontier with Russia, beyond ensuring that the French zone constitute a buffer region between Britain and Russia (the assumption of strategists in both London and St. Petersburg being that these old Great Game antagonists would resume their rivalry as soon as the Germans were defeated). And so Sazonov insisted, in a private meeting with Sykes and British ambassador Sir George Buchanan on March 11, 1916, that Sykes personally cross out French "blue" on a draft map across "Turkish Armenia" and "Kurdistan," reassigning them to Russia, along with Persian Azerbaijan and northeastern Turkey. As Sazonov stipulated in a formal aide-mémoire on March 13, 1916, "The entire territory between the Black Sea and a line beginning at Urmia province . . . below Van, through Bitlis, Muş, and Kharput [Elâzığ], up to the mountain range of Tavra and Antitavra [near Sivas] must be placed at Russia's disposal." Sykes did as he was told.[14]

Sykes, a diplomatic amateur if there ever was one, was in over his head.* But the Russians were deadly serious. Parallel to the ongoing, rather one-sided negotiations with Sykes and Picot, Sazonov had convened the army and naval service chiefs to iron out Russia's ideal borders in postwar Asia Minor. Grigorevich and the navy wanted not only Trabzon (not yet conquered) but also the strategic peninsula of Sinop, where the Russians had famously destroyed the Ottoman fleet in 1853 in the opening act of the Crimean War.† This would allow Russia's Black Sea Fleet to dominate a strategic triangle of Sevastopol-Constantinople-Sinop, cutting off any future naval threat from Romania or Bulgaria to the western half of the Black Sea. Sazonov, in a rare

---

* In exchange for redrawing a diplomatic map he had personally promised France to uphold, all Sykes asked for was for Russia to "take a serious approach" to the Zionist question in Palestine. This cheap promise, costing Sazonov nothing, was easy for the Russian to give.

† More recently, Sinop was a listening post for U.S. intelligence during the Cold War.

display of diplomatic caution, overruled his admirals on the grounds that the rump of postwar Turkey would have to be put *somewhere*. His final, "compromise" proposal, offered to the French on April 26, 1916 (Sykes having already given Britain's approval), was that "Russia will annex the provinces of Erzurum, Trabzon, Van and Bitlis up to a point along the Black Sea coast to the west of Trabzon" (this last city having now conveniently fallen to Russian arms ten days previously, lending muscle to Sazonov's claim). Farther south, Sazonov proposed, Russia would rule over "the province of Kurdistan, lying south of Van and Bitlis, between Muş, Siirt [still unconquered, though under threat from now-Russian Bitlis] . . . and the line of the mountains." As a sop, France was given Sivas, Kharput, and Diarbakır, although all three cities would now be frontier towns on the border of postwar Russia, and likely to fall under her influence (plans were already under way to build a Russian railway from Trabzon to Ankara, by way of Sivas). Picot, abandoned by Sykes and with no French troops on the ground in Asiatic Turkey, could do little but comply. In this way the notorious Sykes-Picot (much more accurately *Sazonov-Sykes-Picot*) Agreement partitioning the Ottoman Empire was hashed out, in Russia's capital city and under heavy Russian pressure and influence, pursuant to Russia's ongoing battlefield victories against the Turks.[15]

At this critical and still little understood juncture of the First World War, the only thing keeping the tottering Ottoman Empire together was the friction between the Entente powers greedily carving her up. For nearly a century, Turkey's fate had arguably depended on the failure of Britain and Russia to agree on partition plans. The very phrase "Sick Man" was first used by Tsar Nicholas I in conversation with the British ambassador, Sir George Hamilton Seymour, in March 1853, the tsar's idea being to broach plans for a general Ottoman partition (his remarks instead were used as justification for the hotheads, like Stratford Canning, urging Britain into fighting the Crimean War).* It was Disraeli's summoning of the fleet that had forced the Russians to stand down at San Stefano in 1878. Now that Britain and Russia, in 1916, were wartime allies alongside France, the empire's death knell seemed to have

---

* Although he did *not* say "Sick Man *of Europe*," as is commonly supposed.

rung at last—except that the British and Russians kept failing to coordinate strategy in the Ottoman theater.

It was not that the British were not trying. Had the Russians delivered the troops they had promised Kitchener during the Dardanelles and Gallipoli campaigns, the Ottoman war might have been over by spring 1915. In their own cynical way, the Russians had capitalized on the Franco-British failure at Gallipoli—by launching Yudenich's crushing Köprüköy offensive on January 10, 1916, the day after the last Allied soldier was evacuated from Cape Helles! This was coordination of a sort, but it was one-sided coordination, with Yudenich concluding (sensibly, if self-interestedly, enough) that his offensive stood a better chance of success if he launched it before Enver could move troops from Gallipoli to Erzurum. Had it been launched the previous spring or summer, of course, it might have diverted Turkish strength away from Gallipoli, allowing the Allies a fighting chance in the Krithia battles of May or at Anafarta in August. But their struggle was not Yudenich's problem (even if the Dardanelles campaign had supposedly been launched in the first place to divert Ottoman strength from the Caucasus). Nor was the plight of poor Townshend and the British-Indian expeditionary force under siege in the mud-walled town of Kut Russia's problem, which helps explain why Yudenich and Grand Duke Nicholas threw all their strength against Erzurum in January–February 1916, rather than south into Mesopotamia, where the British were frantically trying to break off the siege, in a series of bloody engagements waged in almost uncanny chronological parallel to the Russian Köprüköy offensive. The new Tigris Army Corps, comprising nineteen thousand troops under Lieutenant General Sir Fenton Aylmer, opened a general attack on Ottoman trench lines at Hannah, south of Kut, on January 7, 1916, capturing some eight hundred prisoners and two guns before nightfall. But the assault bogged down quickly for the usual reasons. The men were too fatigued to throw themselves into the trenches again the next day; then the rains came and turned everything to mud. The Ottoman defensive position was found, in any case, to be "extremely strong," with some trenches dug nine feet deep. Over the next two weeks, assault after assault failed to break the Turkish resistance. On January 23, 1916, Aylmer called off the attack and beat a retreat down the Tigris, having suffered 2,700 casualties in all. Needless to say, no Russian help was forthcoming.[16]

Tiflis, to be sure, was hundreds of miles north of Baghdad. It would have been difficult for Yudenich to send troops to draw off Ottoman strength from Kut, even had he wanted to do so. And yet Baratov's expeditionary force in Persia was only about 250 miles away—closer than was the British rear base at Basra. When Baratov, on February 26, 1916, captured Kermanshah, his Cossacks were only 120 miles from the border town of Hanekin, with Baghdad just 80 miles farther. Understandably, General Nixon now requested that Grand Duke Nicholas lean on Baratov to relieve Townshend at Kut, where the Turks, under the guidance of Goltz Pasha and dozens of German officers and engineers arriving from Gallipoli, had erected nearly impregnable siege works, crowned by 150 German machine guns "of the latest type."* But, although direct radio communication was established between Baratov and Townshend, the grand duke balked at doing more to force Baratov's hand (as it was, the chain of command was slightly awkward—northern Persian affairs were the purview of the viceroy in Tiflis, Vorontsov-Dashkov, not the regular army command). Nixon undercut his own leverage by ordering Aylmer to mount another relief expedition in March, before any promises had been wrung out of Baratov. Part of the reason for Aylmer's haste was that Townshend's food supplies were expected to run out by around April 15; there was also the danger that spring flooding would soon make the entire area south of Kut virtually impassable. Aiming to turn the Ottoman right, or southern, flank, Aylmer ordered his men to launch a surprise attack on the fort at Dujaila, covered by a feint in the center at Hannah, where the last attack had come. The new British offensive commenced on March 7–8, 1916, just as Sykes and Picot were arriving in Petrograd. Once again, to Aylmer's chagrin, the "positions were found to be strongly held by the enemy, who were pouring in reinforcements." Briefly, men from the Thirty-Seventh Brigade gained a foothold in the Dujaila redoubt, only to be beaten back by a ferocious Turkish counterattack. This time the battle was over in a matter of hours, with the

---

* This last detail, gleaned from a Russian intelligence report, may have dissuaded Baratov from challenging the Turco-Germans, much as the greatly superior Russian intelligence on Ottoman shore batteries likely helped stay Eberhart's hand at the Bosphorus. The Russians might have been self-serving, but they were not stupid.

British suffering almost four thousand casualties in a futile attempt to storm the town's citadel. Aylmer, utterly discredited by his failures at Hannah and Dujaila, resigned his command in favor of his chief of staff, Major General Sir George Gorringe.[17]

Meanwhile, inside mud-walled, malarial Kut, food supplies were running out. Even on subsistence rations, they could not possibly last into May. In March the garrison was forced to slaughter its pack animals along with Kut's "skinny cats and dogs." As one soldier recalled of the effects of hunger, "The soles of your feet hurt if you walked or stood, the shoulders and back if you lay down, and the seat if you sat." By April, another man was noting in his diary, "My legs are shockingly thin, less than my arms were, and I can fold my skin round my legs." Compounding the misery of the men, temperatures were already unbearable, often topping 120 degrees Fahrenheit (49 degrees Celsius). Thus far, Baratov and his Russian expeditionary force in Persia had yet to make so much as a feint toward the border.[18]

On April 1, 1916, Grand Duke Nicholas finally roused himself into action, requesting, via his chief of staff, General Bolkhovitinov, that Baratov do what he could to draw off Ottoman strength by marching toward Baghdad. It was such an obvious move to make that Goltz Pasha had already anticipated Baratov, sending four Ottoman battalions and twelve guns toward Hanekin on the Persian frontier. In a sign of the (possibly inflated) importance he gave to the Russian threat, Goltz Pasha entrusted the Hanekin command to a German officer, Major Bopp. Bopp would be disappointed. In the same manner Eberhart had found endless excuses not to show up at the Bosphorus in spring 1915, Baratov said that to mount a proper diversionary strike against Baghdad would require "a long space of time and first of all proper forces and means." Until these were forthcoming, Baratov refused to proceed beyond Kermanshah.

Feeling, perhaps, a slight twinge of shame, Grand Duke Nicholas—the same man whose whining had goaded Russia's allies into the sanguinary tragedies of the Dardanelles and Gallipoli—now asked Baratov to get his act together, as he had no reinforcements to send. And so Baratov, on April 20, 1916, at last marched his Cossacks west toward the Ottoman border, reaching the outskirts of the border town of Hanekin on April 25, 1916. He was now,

Baratov reported to Townshend, "only 5 days' march from Baghdad." His diversion, it appeared, would be joined by around April 30—one day, as it turned out, after Townshend's food supplies ran out, and he was forced to surrender his entire expeditionary force to the Turks. The Russians had arrived late to the British funeral again.[19]

And in fact this time, unlike with Eberhart's halfhearted sorties at the Bosphorus, they never arrived at all. Having lost five hundred men to heat-stroke, malaria, and cholera on the march from Kermanshah to Hanekin, and learning of Townshend's surrender over the radio, Baratov decided not to march on Baghdad after all. His horses were having difficulty finding forage, and it seemed best to salvage what he could of his Cossacks, inter-Allied diversion be damned. After the British finally lodged a complaint with Tiflis command at the unchivalrous behavior of their ally, in late May 1916 Grand Duke Nicholas ordered Baratov, one last time, to "relieve the [British Indian force], operating along the Tigris river below Kut-al-Amara." This time Bara-tov did not even pretend to obey, pulling his Cossacks and cavalry back into the cooler mountains of Luristan instead. In what could only have struck Townshend and his men as a sick joke, had they learned of the remark, in July 1916 Grand Duke Nicholas nonetheless saluted Baratov for the "supreme valor" he had displayed in Persia (if not, evidently, in Mesopotamia).[20]

Once more, the Ottoman Empire had been saved by the failure of its two most dangerous enemies to coordinate their strategy against it. With no Rus-sian cavalry riding to the rescue, Townshend's men were left to slowly starve to death in the malarial mud of Kut as the spring floods began to inundate the valley. Making one last desperate attempt at a breakthrough in mid-April, Gorringe tried to outflank the Ottoman lines on the left, west of the Tigris near Sannaiyat. His men did their best, but the Turks had by now brought down so many troops from Baghdad that a breakthrough was well-nigh impossible. In a series of brutal attacks and counterattacks waged on April 15–16 and again on April 20–22, both sides suffered thousands of casualties, though neither could pierce the other's line. The Turks, one British officer noted with reluctant admiration, "came on magnificently," in such strength that even the fearsome Gurkhas fell back. By now there were only six days' rations left in Kut, with Townshend's emaciated soldiers reduced to a stupor.

Gorringe's men, in the relief force, were scarcely better off, unable to muster energy for more futile assaults. In all, the British Indian Army had suffered 23,000 casualties in its efforts to rescue Townshend since January. Kut, it was clear to Gorringe, "was doomed," with the only question being the terms of Townshend's surrender, now being negotiated "with starvation at the gate."[21]

On April 30, 1916, Townshend ordered the destruction of his remaining artillery and munitions stores and ran up a white flag in place of the Union Jack. He then handed over his sword and pistol to Halil (now "Kut") Pasha. It was a signature victory for Enver, whose uncle now took into custody some thirteen thousand British (mostly Indian) subjects—the most surrendered by any British army since Yorktown—the bulk of whom were sent to labor on the Baghdad Railway.[22] Adding to the frisson of this great propaganda triumph was the fact that a special detachment of Arabic-speaking British intelligence officers, spearheaded by T. E. Lawrence, had unsuccessfully offered Halil a bribe of £1 million in gold to let Townshend and his men go (there was even talk of doubling the bribe to £2 million).[23] True, the news from eastern Turkey, where the Russians were racing from one victory to another, was awful. Still, coming on the heels of Gallipoli, the colossal victory of Enver's uncle in Mesopotamia was almost too good to be true. If the Turks could defeat the world-beating British twice in a row, there must be life in the Ottoman Sick Man yet.

Unfortunately for Enver, there was life in the enemy too. The British Empire had, in this as most of its wars, been slow to muster its strength in a decisive way on the battlefield. But it had considerable reserves to draw on, and its global network of spies and paid clients gave it many different gambits to play. Scarcely had Enver had time to enjoy his uncle's triumph at Kut than he was confronted with a rebellion in the very heartland of Islam, which called into question the entire Ottoman claim to rule its Muslim subjects.

CHAPTER 13

DOUBLE BLUFF:
OTTOMAN HOLY WAR
AND ARAB REVOLT

The killing of the infidels who rule over the Islamic
lands has become a sacred duty.

—Translation of German-produced Arabic-language
holy war pamphlet, ca. November 1914[1]

Then the [Young Turks] rejected God's word, "A Man shall have twice
a woman's share," and made them equal . . . They made weak the person of the
Sultan . . . forbidding him to choose for himself the chief of his personal Cabinet.
Other like things did they to sap the foundation of the Caliphate.

—SHERIF HUSSEIN OF MECCA,
calling Arab Muslims to revolt against the impious Ottoman government,
June 1916[2]

THE CLAIM OF THE OTTOMAN SULTAN to be caliph, or supreme ruler of
the Sunni Islamic *umma* of believers, had always rested ultimately on his tem-
poral power—the strength of his armies. Since the Turkish conquest of the
Islamic holy places of Arabia (Mecca and Medina) in 1517, the title had been
more or less undisputed, but its use had largely fallen into abeyance in the
years of imperial expansion. As long as the empire was strong, it was not necessary to continually remind lesser Muslim princes of the sultan's superiority,

which was taken for granted. The Hamidian revival of the empire's pan-Islamic credentials had been, in this sense, an unwitting recognition of declining Ottoman prestige in the modern era, a last-ditch effort to rally Muslims to the cause before the empire split apart along national or confessional lines. In similar fashion, the Young Turks' invocation of the power of the sultan-caliph to declare a jihad, or "holy war," against Russia and the Entente powers in November 1914 reflected the shaky nature of Turkey's *casus belli* as an ally of "infidel" powers like Germany in a war against her European rivals. Had the war's purpose truly been well understood by Enver's predominantly Muslim conscripts, there would have been no need to propagandize them about it.

Despite the failure of large-scale Islamic uprisings to materialize in British Egypt or India, the holy war had not been a total bust. In the Raj, there were signs the Turks and Germans were winning the propaganda war, with evidence mounting that the sultan's claim to be caliph of global Islam was taken more seriously in the far-off Indian subcontinent than it was closer to home. By summer 1915, Persia had turned into a hotbed of jihadist intrigue, with fiery holy war sermons against Britain and Russia read out in mosques across the country. En route for Afghanistan, Oskar von Niedermayer had helped organize attacks sabotaging bridges and roads used by the Russians in Azerbaijan, along with a series of terrifying Robin Hood–style bank heists to fund anti-Entente terrorism. Near Bushire, a German agent, Wilhelm Wasmuss, had enlisted the Muslim Tangistani tribesmen to sabotage the British position on the Persian Gulf (famously, this "German Lawrence" used a phony wireless set to pretend to commune with "Hajji" Wilhelm). By fall 1915—when Ahmad Shah was mulling over whether to perform a *hejira* from Teheran to Qom and declare holy war against Britain and Russia—Kermanshah, Isfahan, and Shiraz had already gone over to the Turco-Germans, with their Entente consuls put to flight. True, Baratov's Cossacks had then laid down the law and restored Entente (or at least Russian) prestige, but the very size of his expeditionary force of fourteen thousand provided evidence of the success jihad agents had enjoyed in destabilizing the country.[3]

Turco-German efforts to unleash a holy war in North Africa had been still more frightening to the British. During the Tripolitanian war of 1911–12,

Enver had established contact with Sheikh al-Sharif of the fanatical Sanussi order, leaving his brother Nuri behind to maintain an Ottoman presence even after Turkey was forced to surrender to Italy. After the world war was joined, both Enver and the Germans sent envoys to the Sanussi camp in the Libyan desert, bearing weapons, gifts, bribe money, and other cajolements to declare a jihad against England. In November 1915, the Sanussi raided the British outpost at Sidi Barrani, inspiring some 135 Egyptian Muslim soldiers to desert the British. In December and January, the Sanussi overran Sollum, Baqbaq, and Sidi Barrani, reaching as far east as Mersa Matruh, only 175 miles from Alexandria, while capturing three Egyptian desert oases "within easy reach of the Nile." It was enough to put fear in Kitchener, an old Egypt hand, who warned that further Sanussi incursions would lead to "serious unrest and disturbances throughout Egypt and the Sudan." Although the Sanussi offensive sputtered out in February 1916, it cost Maxwell's Egyptian army some 45 killed and 350 wounded and a good deal of worry.[4]

Compared with the overall scale of fighting on the Ottoman fronts, these episodes represented mere pinpricks. And yet in another sense, the impact of the "holy war" was felt more broadly across these fronts in the way it kept the Ottoman army together as a fighting force in spite of periodic disasters on the battlefield. Whether or not the German-produced jihad pamphlets inspired Muslim civilians to take up arms against "the infidels who rule over Islamic lands" (i.e., French, British, and Russian Christians), the idea that they were fighting for their faith surely put heart into Ottoman Muslim soldiers facing the formidable armies of the Entente. "Those who watched the Turkish gunners at Kilid Bahr," noted Gallipoli historian Alan Moorehead, "say that they fought with a wild fanaticism, an Imam chanting prayers to them as they ran to their work on the gun emplacements." Whatever was motivating the Turks to resist the British infidels, it was working. Between the onset of the Dardanelles campaign and the mass surrender at Kut, the British armed forces had suffered 350,000 casualties in the Ottoman theater, against a supposedly moribund opponent that Asquith, Churchill, and many others believed would not put up serious resistance.[5]

Whether or not Turco-German holy war propaganda made a difference in the field, the British certainly took the threat it posed seriously, which gave the whole business the air of a self-fulfilling prophecy. It was the fear of German-sponsored pan-Islam engulfing the Suez Canal and Cairo, for example, that had prompted Kitchener, in January 1915, to pen his notorious letter to Gilbert Clayton, forwarded to Sherif Hussein of Mecca, suggesting that "it may be that an Arab of true race [e.g., a Hashemite like Hussein, supposedly descended from the Prophet] will assume the [C]alifate at Mecca or Medina." Believing the caliphate to be a spiritual office akin to the papacy, Kitchener did not fully understand the implications of what he was offering Hussein—to supplant the Ottoman sultan as supreme ruler of the Islamic world, or at least the kingdom of the Arab-speaking portions of Asiatic Turkey, which is what the sherif himself asked Cairo to give him in summer 1915 in the so-called Damascus Protocol.[6] But Kitchener and his Cairo advisers did understand—or thought they understood—what was at stake following the sultan's declaration of holy war against the British Empire in November 1914: the loyalties of Britain's hundred-million-odd Muslim subjects, spread across the Indian subcontinent, the Persian Gulf States, Egypt, and Anglo-Egyptian Sudan. By seeking to "move" the caliphate from Constantinople to Mecca, Kitchener was effectively playing the Turco-German holy war game, reinforcing the importance of this office for the Islamic world (not least for Hussein himself, who gradually became attached to the idea of becoming caliph).*

It was entirely possible, of course, that *neither* Mehmed Reshad V, the Young Turks' puppet sultan, nor Kitchener's putative candidate, Sherif Hussein, could really summon anything resembling obedience from the world's 300 million Muslims (certainly not from the minority Shiites, who recognized neither man as caliph).† The Turks and Germans had already risked the sultan's credibility by invoking his religious authority to beatify the Ottoman war, with mixed results (in part because the sherif of Mecca, guardian of the holy cities of Islam, had not yet publicly endorsed the Ottoman holy war). Were Hussein, pursuing the chimera of a British-sponsored caliphate, to

---

* After Mustafa Kemal abolished the caliphate in 1924, Hussein would indeed declare himself caliph—although by then the world paid him little attention.

† The Germans did win endorsement of the Ottoman Holy War from the Shia grand mufti of Karbala, for a retainer of $12,000. But this proved as hollow as the pledge Niedermayer won from Emir Habibullah of Afghanistan to invade British India.

assert his own claim to the office by summoning Muslims to revolt against Ottoman authority, he might discover that his own power was just as limited as the sultan's—if not more so.

There were good reasons, therefore, for Sherif Hussein to avoid an open breach with the Sublime Porte, however tempting the idea of a British-sponsored bid to supplant the sultan may have seemed to him in theory, and however profitable in practice (Hussein had been receiving tribute from the Cairo residency ever since attaining his office in 1908, though the amount would surely shoot up dramatically if he rebelled openly against Turkey). Moreover, even if the Hashemites had better bloodlines, the Ottomans still had a much larger army—an army that could easily be turned on Mecca. Nor was Hussein the only Hashemite with a claim to the office. His predecessor, Ali Abdullah Pasha, had been forcibly deposed during the upheaval of 1908, and Enver had already threatened to appoint Ali Haidar Pasha of the dispossessed Zaid branch of the Hashemites if Hussein ever got out of line. Hussein, moreover, was receiving regular shipments of gold and arms from the Ottoman government, even as he pocketed British subsidies—and there was a chance the Germans, if approached the right way, might chip in too. As Emir Habibullah discovered in Afghanistan, "holy war" bidding could be extremely lucrative if played with both sides (the Afghan emir was, by 1916, receiving £400,000 a year from the Raj; he demanded 10 million British pounds from the Germans to launch a jihadist army into India).[7] If the sherif could somehow keep both Enver and the British happy, he could become a very rich man without ever having to call his spiritual authority into question by summoning his followers to arms.

For the first year of the war, this is exactly what Hussein did. At Suez, the sherif split the difference as elegantly as possible, refusing to send troops or camels to support Djemal—although he did send a sixty-five-year-old surrogate to carry the sacred green banner of Mecca (the elderly flag bearer died in Jerusalem on Christmas Eve 1914, the holy war excitement having aggravated his heart condition). Even while sending his second-eldest son, Abdullah, to Cairo to wheedle what he could out of the British in the wake of Kitchener's offer, Hussein dispatched his third-eldest son, Feisal, to Constantinople to sound out the Young Turks.

En route for the Ottoman capital, Feisal paid a long visit to Damascus in March 1915. While no record has ever emerged of precisely who said what to whom, it appears that Feisal's aim was to canvass opinion among the secret, CUP-style societies of educated Arab military officers (*al-'Ahd* and *al-Fatat*) about the prospect of launching a pro-Entente Arab mutiny-cum-rebellion against Turkey. Although flattered to have the attention of the Hashemite sherif of Mecca, the Arab conspirators remained cool to the idea. They seem to have advised Feisal that he and his father should stand pat, promising to help Britain topple the Ottomans only if she promised outright independence for Arabic-speaking areas after the war. It could not hurt, everyone was agreed, to play both sides off each other, to see who would promise the Arabs the most. After examining what passed for "Arab opinion" in Damascus, Feisal then proceeded on to the Ottoman capital to hear out the Young Turks.

The reception in Constantinople was less warm. Enver and Said Halim Pasha, already well informed about Hashemite dealings with British Cairo, refused initially even to meet Feisal. Stepping in as mediator was Baron Max Oppenheim, the Arabist archaeologist-explorer who had conceived the kaiser's holy war strategy to bring down the British Empire, and who had known Feisal's father in his Constantinople days (i.e., before Hussein became sherif). Oppenheim had been gravely disappointed that Hussein, a man he revered, had not yet blessed the cause. Feisal, knowing Oppenheim's enthusiasm for his father, was game for a charm offensive. Paying the German Orientalist a visit at his suite in the Pera Palace Hotel on April 24, 1915 (the day before the Gallipoli landings), Feisal told Oppenheim that he "thanked God that the interests of Islam are entirely identical with those of Germany." Laying it on a bit thick, Feisal then claimed that, when his father, Hussein, had heard of the Ottoman jihad *fetvas* (decrees) in November 1914, he had told his son that "if I die now I will not have a single regret" (curiously, Hussein had not been quite moved enough to publicly endorse the holy war against Britain—lest she stop subsidizing him).[8]

Much of this was humbug, of course. And yet there was an interesting tension in the German-Ottoman relationship Feisal was exploiting here, which reveals something of Hussein's thinking behind the façade of Oriental flattery. Islamic holy war, as Hussein and Feisal both knew, had been a pet

German cause ever since "Hajji" Wilhelm had made his strange pilgrimage to the Damascus tomb of Saladin in 1898, where he had declared himself the "friend for all time" of the world's 300 million Muslims. Enver and the Young Turks had gone along with the idea for their own reasons in November 1914, more as a gesture to shore up Muslim support in Turkey than out of any romantic idea of a global jihad to destroy the British Empire. From the perspective of Arab Mecca, Enver's embrace of holy war appeared even more cynical than the Germans'. For had not the Young Turks forcibly deposed the last true sultan, Abdul Hamid II—the kaiser's friend, no less—and installed a powerless puppet in his place? Had they not ended the Hamidian practice of appointing Arabs to high imperial positions out of pan-Islamic solidarity? Had they not embraced all manner of un-Islamic notions, from the civic equality of non-Muslims to women's rights? Had they not, as Feisal pointedly reminded Oppenheim in the Pera Palace, introduced secular schools in the holy cities of Mecca and Medina, where "infidel" (i.e., European) languages were taught?[9]

There was already a great deal of bad blood between Mecca and the Young Turks before the semi-breach over the holy war declaration of November 1914. Hussein had pointedly refused to lend even rhetorical support to Turkey during the Italian war, let alone muster troops. Ostensibly this was out of resentment at the impious nature of the new Young Turk regime in Constantinople, although the breach over Tripoli suggested that Hussein was also loath to antagonize any of the European powers, least of all the British residency in Cairo, which not only sent him gold but oversaw an ever-growing portion of the pilgrim traffic to Mecca, which was the real basis of the economy of the Hejaz. The precipitous decline in Hajj traffic brought by the world war in 1914, along with Ottoman army requisitions and the Syrian locust plague of 1915, meant that the Hashemites were more dependent on outside subsidies—especially British food shipments—than ever before.[10] It would take far more than Islamic solidarity to convince Hussein to toss the lucrative British connection away by throwing in his lot with Enver, whom he did not trust anyway.

Nevertheless, Feisal did his best to reassure Constantinople that his father would play along. Turning the tables on the Young Turks, Hussein's son suggested that Oppenheim ask them to close down the regime's secular schools in Mecca and Medina and proselytize young Arabs about the jihad against the Entente powers instead. The holy war message, Feisal added, could be hammered into the thousands of British subjects who lived in Mecca and the thousands more who made the Hajj each year. Mischievously, he suggested that the Turks and Germans could help spread stories of mass starvation in the Hejaz and blame the hunger on the Raj—notwithstanding the fact (which Feisal freely admitted) that the British had docked four huge grain ships permanently on the Red Sea coast since the beginning of the war and were almost single-handedly feeding the local population. More speciously, Feisal suggested that his father send holy war emissaries to both Anglo-Egyptian Sudan and India on British vessels, disguised as "adherents of various reform societies." Asked how serious this promise to raise holy war against Hussein's own patron was, Feisal replied that "we will do our duty and will then leave to Allah's will the question of our success."[11]

These were cheap promises, easily made, easily broken. What Enver really wanted to know was what Hussein would do to help Djemal's renewed assault on the Suez Canal, planned for spring 1916. The sherif had wriggled out the first time, but neither Djemal nor Enver would let this happen again. Suez would provide a perfect touchstone for Hussein's loyalty: if he did not contribute something tangible to this vital campaign—something more than a flag, with a man barely strong enough to carry it—then he was clearly Britain's man. Putting Hussein's word on the line, Feisal did promise Enver (via Oppenheim) that his father was prepared to "raise an army of Arab cavalry and other Bedouins to participate in a [future] assault on the Suez Canal," although he was careful, as ever, not to give specifics. Enver, when he heard this, called in Feisal and demanded that Hussein second at least one of his sons to Djemal's army in Damascus—suggesting, helpfully, that Feisal himself would do fine.[12]

Damascus, home to Ottoman Fourth Army headquarters, was, as Enver knew, a dangerous city for Feisal to stay in for very long. If Mecca was the spiritual capital of the Muslim world, Damascus (especially after Cairo was occupied by the British in 1882) was the unofficial capital of Arab political intrigue. Syria, then as now, was home to a bewildering variety of ethno-religious factions—Sunni and Shia Muslims, Alawites, Maronite Christians, Greek Orthodox, Armenians and Assyrian Christians, Druze, indigenous Mizrahi and Sephardic Jews. France, with imperial pretensions in Lebanon and Syria ostensibly dating back to the Crusades, had long been cultivating ties with local Arabs, predominantly (though not exclusively) Christians. One of the first things Djemal had done after taking up his Fourth Army command in Damascus in December 1914 was to sack the French consulate, where he discovered voluminous evidence of seditious Arab contacts with the Entente. To his horror, Djemal discovered that it was not only Christians who had been intriguing with the enemy, but Syrian Muslims, too, especially officers in the army. By the time Feisal returned to Damascus in late May 1915 after his visit with Oppenheim, Djemal had already broken up the three Arab-only divisions in the Fourth Army and arrested dozens of soldiers and civilians suspected of intriguing with the Entente enemy (including several who had met with Feisal). Surprising many foreign observers, Djemal seemed to be singling out Arab Muslims for exemplary treatment, despite more plentiful evidence of disloyalty in the Christian population (Syria's Jews fell somewhere in between, not particularly loyal to the Ottoman government, but more cautious than the Christians about intriguing with Entente agents). Of the eleven Arab traitors executed on Djemal's orders in Beirut in August 1915, ten were Muslims and only one Christian. Another forty-five traitors were condemned to death *in absentia*—many of whom were known associates of Feisal and Hussein. There was little subtlety in Enver's request that Feisal be seconded to Djemal. He was a hostage, and would be closely watched.[13]

Enver's and Djemal's suspicions of Feisal were entirely justified, even if they did not know every detail of his doings. By the time the first executions rocked Ottoman Syria, the Hashemites were up to their necks in treason, on a truly epic scale. To be sure, there had always been an element of fantasy in the dealings between Cairo and Mecca, from Kitchener's promise of a "holy Arabian Koreishite Khalifate" (something that had never existed before), to Hussein's vague and scarcely credible assurances that 100,000 Arab troops in the Ottoman armies (or maybe 250,000?) would desert to his banner. Then there were the ill-fated negotiations between Hussein and Sir Henry

McMahon (Kitchener's handpicked successor as high commissioner in Cairo) over the future disposition of Palestine, Syria, and Mesopotamia, in which McMahon so elegantly sidestepped making direct promises that diplomatic historians (and some politicians) still argue today about who, exactly, the British promised would get to rule each area after the war. With France staking her own claims to Palestine and Syria in the ongoing Sazonov-Sykes-Picot negotiations, and British opinion in London divided, it is understandable that McMahon failed to give Hussein what he wanted. Only in retrospect was the "McMahon-Hussein correspondence," conducted in equally bad faith on both sides, invested with earnestness and epochal significance. At the time, Hussein was simply seeing what he could cajole out of Cairo, even as the British were promising him and his would-be Arab rebel conspiracy what Sir Edward Grey, in an uncharacteristic moment of clarity, called "castle[s] in the air which would never materialize."[14]

By 1916, with a new Suez offensive in the works, the clock was running out on Sherif Hussein's game of playing both sides. With Cairo, the Hashemites could probably have continued to procrastinate more or less indefinitely. While the British wanted them to rebel, the only leverage they really had over Hussein was his retainer; and if they cut this off, he could probably have responded just by squeezing the Turks and Germans harder. Enver and Djemal, by contrast, could hit the Hashemites hard, whether by arresting men closer and closer to Feisal, through armed intimidation of Mecca, or via actual deposition. Trying to lever the Young Turks one last time before Djemal would call his bluff at Suez, Hussein sent a formal request to Enver early in 1916, asking that the Ottoman authorities, to assure his loyalty, end the ongoing trial of some five dozen Arab conspirators in Syria and guarantee "my independence in the whole of the Hejaz and create me a hereditary prince." In essence, the sherif was asking the Young Turks to offer him the same thing Kitchener and McMahon had promised him—an independent Arab kingdom (minus only the title of caliph, which the Ottomans, for obvious reasons, could not offer). It was worth a try.[15]

The reply was not encouraging. Summoning Feisal to his office in early April 1916, Djemal showed him Hussein's presumptuous request and demanded an explanation. All Feisal could do was to protest that his father had been misunderstood, or that there had been some kind of mistake translating his message from Arabic into Ottoman Turkish. Djemal was having none of it. "Let us assume," he told the flustered Feisal, "that the [Ottoman] government complied with your request solely because they wanted to keep you from being troublesome in the troubled times through which we are passing. If the war came to a victorious conclusion, what could prevent the government from dealing with you with the greatest severity once it was over?" To ensure that Mecca got the message, Djemal then announced a new wave of arrests of Arab nationalists in Syria, and informed Hussein that he was dispatching 3,500 troops through the Hejaz—ostensibly to help a German major, Othmar von Stotzingen, set up a new jihad propaganda center for Oppenheim in Yemen.[16]

In May 1916, matters came to a head. The Stotzingen mission had arrived in Damascus and was making ostentatious preparations for its march into the Hejaz (these included a shotgun wedding between Oppenheim's German Islam expert, Karl Neufeld, and his eighteen-year-old Kurdish concubine, to formalize Neufeld's conversion to Islam before he entered the holy cities of Mecca and Medina).* With just weeks remaining before the second Suez offensive was scheduled to begin, Djemal dispatched 50,000 pounds of gold to Mecca, along with weapons (about 1,500 rifles) to equip Hussein's promised battalion of Bedouins. On May 5, he signed the execution orders for twenty-one Arab conspirators, and had them publicly hanged the next day in Damascus and Beirut. When Feisal, who knew some of the victims personally, objected, Djemal showed him the written evidence of guilt. Suppressing his horror, Feisal (according to Djemal's recollection) was made to agree that the sentences had been just. Hussein's son then requested leave from Damascus—to organize the striking force of Hejazi Bedouins for Suez, he said. His suspicions now all but confirmed, Djemal gave Feisal 5,000 gold pounds and 5,000 Maria Theresa silver thalers (these latter had been prized in the Arab world ever since they were minted in 1780) and wished him luck—though he insisted that Feisal be accompanied by a small detachment of Ottoman troops.[17]

---

* The same Karl Neufeld who had famously been held prisoner by the Mahdi in Sudan for 18 years, before being freed by Kitchener at Omdurman in 1898. Neufeld does not appear to have been grateful to the British for his freedom.

The first act of the Arab revolt was both predictable and sordid. As soon as he reached the Hejaz, Feisal dumped his Turkish escort and absconded with Djemal's cash, as if to compensate himself for his own treason. Sometime on or around June 5, 1916, Sherif Hussein then, according to legend, fired a single musket shot into the Ottoman military barracks in Mecca (unless it was at Medina), the traditional gesture of revolt. Part of the reason there remains some dispute as to the date is that, according to Hussein's most recent promise to Cairo, he had planned to launch his rebellion on June 16, only for Djemal's threats to force his hand (unless it was Feisal's robbery of his Turkish hosts that forced it). Our source as to it having begun on June 5 is a chance comment during a meeting in Jedda on the sixth between Hussein's fourth-eldest son, Zeid, and the British Oriental secretary in Cairo, Ronald Storrs. Asked by Storrs what, exactly, Hussein promised to do in exchange for all the money Britain was paying him (the latest demand was for £70,000), Zeid had blurted out that he was "happy to be able to announce to you that [the Arab revolt] began yesterday at Medina." Whether or not it actually had begun the day before at Medina (or at Mecca?), Zeid's revelation convinced Storrs to give him another £10,000, along with five cartons of cigarettes for Feisal and Abdullah (a Maxim machine gun was also promised, though it would not arrive in Jedda for another week). Whenever it actually began, Hussein's revolt seems to have been up and running by the second week of June 1916. By month's end, Hussein's forces had overpowered the small Turkish detachments in Mecca (though not the much larger garrison in Medina, supplied by rail from Damascus) and Taif (in the mountains south of Mecca), along with the Red Sea port cities of Jedda and Yenbo, where the Royal Navy was able to scare off the enemy.[18]

These early successes were misleading. The real worth of any putative Arab rebellion against Ottoman authority, as Hussein had himself maintained all along in his promises to Cairo, lay in its ability to wreck the Turkish armies with mass desertions. It was clearly with such mutinies in mind that Hussein, in his own Arabic-language press release announcing the event (this was not the version sold to Cairo), cloaked his rebellion in the pious garb of Islam, reminding true Arab soldiers of Allah that the government of "union and progress" rejected

God's word, "A Man shall have twice a woman's share," and made them equal. They went further and removed one of the five corner-stones of the Faith . . . by causing the soldiers in garrison in Mecca, Medina and Damascus to break their [Ramadan] fast for new and foolish reasons . . . They made weak the person of the Sultan, and robbed him of his honour, forbidding him to choose for himself the chief of his personal Cabinet. Other like things did they to sap the foundation of the Caliphate.

As propaganda, it was well conceived. Hussein's charges of impiety against the Young Turk regime were largely true, and they easily gave the lie to the regime's own holy war propaganda. And yet his summons fell flat, if we are to judge by the fact that not a single Arab unit in the Ottoman armies defected to the British side intact, nor more than a small handful of officers. Like the Ottoman holy war, Hussein's own holy war failed to ignite.[19]

This is not to say, however, that it was without effect. One of the first serious consequences of Hussein's rebellion was, ironically, to disturb the repose of the British Raj. Cairo may have been flooding the Hejaz with messages promising that "not a single scrap of territory on the Arabian peninsula, which contains the holy places of Islam, will be annexed by us or by any other government," but Britain's own Muslim subjects were not fooled about who was really behind the revolt in Mecca. Judging by the hand-wringing reports filed from Delhi, Britain's own holy war coup in summer 1916 seemed to galvanize more Muslim resentment in the Indian subcontinent than had Germany's attempt to export jihad there the previous winter. Indian Muslims, having "no sympathy for the Arab," were not simply unimpressed by the news from Mecca: many were loudly condemning Hussein for his treachery.[20]

Another indirect result of the revolt in Mecca, more promising to the Entente cause, was to exacerbate tensions between Turks and *Germans*. To begin with, there had been serious friction in the Ottoman high command about sending the Stotzingen-Neufeld military mission across the Hejaz to Yemen—the very mission that, because reputedly it was to be accompanied by a menacing escort of Turkish troops, had given Hussein the spur to rebel. Djemal had been annoyed by Neufeld's ridiculous public conversion ceremony in Damascus, and by the drumbeat of German-sponsored holy war propaganda more generally. News had reached Enver that Major Fritz Klein, who had headed the German mission to win over the Shia grand mufti, had tried to pass himself off as a Muslim in Karbala—the upshot being that local Shia Muslims had been forced to undergo a three-step ritual cleansing of their hands once they learned that the men who had kissed them in greeting were not really Muslims. Enver had only reluctantly approved the Stotzingen mission to Yemen (one of Oppenheim's bright ideas) after warning the German military attaché that for a "party of Germans to travel through Medina and Mecca even under Turkish escort, would be impossible. No one could possibly give a guarantee that they would not be killed on the way." As if to prove Enver's point, after Hussein's revolt broke out in June the Stotzingen mission was assaulted by Bedouins near Yenbo, with most of their Turkish escorts killed in the ambush (curiously, both of the Germans survived this raid, although another group of German agents was massacred that same month north of Jedda). Shaken, Stotzingen confessed that Enver had been right about guaranteeing his safety in the Hejaz, though he blamed this on Enver's inability to subdue the Hashemite rebellion.[21]

Although the Ottoman press initially refused even to mention Hussein's treason, by late summer the story, spread gleefully across the globe by the British and French propaganda machines, was impossible to suppress. So far from convincing Arab soldiers to desert, however, news of the British-sponsored revolt in the Hejaz was taken by most Turkish soldiers as yet another sign of the perfidy of Europeans in general—and of Germans in particular, who had now brought not only Russian conquest but Arab sedition to the empire. It did not help matters that there were more Germans serving in the Ottoman army than ever before—nearly ten thousand by 1916—at a time when that army seemed to be falling apart. An anti-German pamphlet was making its way around the ranks, exhorting Turkish soldiers not to sacrifice their lives "in order to turn the country into a German colony." In the first six months of 1916, twenty-four Turkish officers were court-martialed for having assaulted or molested German nationals. When news of the fall of Trabzon reached Constantinople in April, Enver Pasha himself, seen as Germany's man, was assaulted by a fanatical Muslim who blamed him for dragging Turkey into Germany's war (he survived).[22] In June 1916, the month of Hussein's revolt, Russian agents reported that the German embassy and other buildings where Germans were known to live and work in Pera were defended from the wrath of the mob by German machine-gun units. In August, German civilians were issued hand grenades to defend themselves, and German officers in Sivas were warned by their Turkish counterparts that they should leave Turkey immediately or face a "frightful massacre."[23]

The Germans were not the only target of popular resentment in Turkey that terrible year. Along the line of the Russian advance in Lazistan, a number of retaliatory killings of Pontic Greeks was reported (supposedly because they had aided the invaders), followed by the expulsion of Greeks from Trabzon province in May, shortly after the port fell to the Russians (they were sent inland to Kastamonu and Sivas, both cities believed to be safe—for now— from the Russians). Once rumors began circulating in September that Greece was finally going to enter the war, a larger-scale Greek deportation campaign began, focused on western areas such as Thrace and Smyrna (Izmir). While Ottoman Greeks never suffered anything on the scale of what Armenians went through in 1915, at least 150,000 were forced from their homes in 1915 and 1916, in addition to a similar number displaced between the Balkan Wars and 1914.[24]

Not surprisingly, Ottoman Armenians did not escape persecution during the troubles of 1916. Although Talât had, in theory, ended the Armenian deportation campaign in fall 1915 (he reaffirmed this in a message to all regional governors on March 15, 1916), a sort of loophole was still being used by some officials for "dangerous individuals." On this open-ended pretext, thousands of Armenians were expelled from their homes in 1916 from Konya, Ankara, Antep (Gaziantep), and Maraş. Following the discovery of a weapons cache in a nearby cemetery in November 1916, some three hundred Armenians were deported from Smyrna (Izmir)—although, in a rare instance of forceful German intervention, Liman von Sanders (who was in town on an inspection tour) stepped in to stop further expulsions. Showing that they did not discriminate only on the basis of religion, the Young Turk government also had thousands of Kurds removed from frontline areas near the Russian advance in 1916.[25]

No foreigner or minority was truly immune from the wave of xenophobia sweeping through the Ottoman Empire in 1916. Pera, the beating heart of the cosmopolitan community in Constantinople, saw its street signs purged of all foreign languages (along with Greek and Armenian). German, Austrian, and Hungarian officers were told to wear only Ottoman uniforms, so as not to draw attention to themselves. German professor-doctors teaching at universities in the capital were ordered to teach in Turkish, and to wear the fez in the classroom. When Enver and Talât began pressuring Berlin and Vienna to recognize the final abolition of the Capitulations (finally granted, under duress, in January 1917), it was taken by many German and Austrian nationals as a sign that the time had come to leave Turkey. The Baghdad Railway was being "Turkified," as most of its foreign engineers were leaving. In October 1916, the German bankers financing it requested to pull out before they lost everything (as the railway was not finished yet, the request was denied). As Enver's friend Hans Humann wrote to the Orientalist Ernst Jäckh in November 1916, "Germany and Turkey do not understand each other at all anymore, I believe, neither the statesmen, nor the people."[26]

In a sense, the xenophobic mood sweeping through Turkey in 1916 was born of simple exhaustion with the world war, coming as it did after three years of war against Italy and the Balkan League. By summer 1916, the Turks had already suffered at least 500,000 casualties. With the draft netting only 90,000 conscripts per year, the Ottoman army might have literally run out of soldiers by 1918 or 1919 if losses had continued at this pace. So hungry was the army for bodies that Enver eliminated the last remaining draft exemptions for non-Muslims in April 1915—although the effort to rouse up loyal Christian soldiers was undermined, to put it mildly, by the regime's ongoing persecution of its large Greek and Armenian populations. By June 1916, the month of Hussein's Arab revolt, Ottoman army recruiters were enlisting men as old as fifty-five, in a visible sign of desperation reported gleefully by British and Russian spies.[27] As Enver told Humann in November, by way of explaining burgeoning xenophobia and anti-German sentiments in Turkey, "We have lost seven provinces, hecatombs of our people have been sacrificed, and our economy has been utterly ruined."[28]

Of course, Enver's own policies had much to do with the empire's manpower predicament, not least his curious decision, already mentioned, to send seven crack divisions from Gallipoli to reinforce the Austro-Hungarian fronts in 1916—divisions that were therefore unavailable to stave off the Russian advance, to reinforce Djemal's second Suez offensive, or to crush Hussein's rebellion in the Hejaz. Following the fall of Erzurum, the Third Army was badly broken, by some estimates having lost fifty thousand men to desertion alone.[29] Scrambling to shore up the Caucasian front against the Russians, Enver had to create a new army almost from scratch, assembling it out of bits and pieces of the Second Army in Thrace and the newly formed XVI Corps under Mustafa Kemal, the latter composed largely of Gallipoli veterans. These troops were dispatched to Diarbakır with the aim of attacking the Russian southern flank at Bitlis before Yudenich had destroyed what remained of the Third Army. If all went well, Enver hoped, the Second and Third Armies could link up on the Erzincan plain and then retake Trabzon and Erzurum. Alas, the Second Army's offensive, launched on August 2, 1916, came about a week too late for the Third Army, which had surrendered Erzincan on July 25. Kemal's corps of veterans did succeed in recapturing Bitlis and Muş, but with the Third Army already beaten, these were Pyrrhic victories. By the end of September, with the first snows falling in the mountains, the Turks had fallen back again, with the Russians holding a solid line from Trabzon through Erzincan and Muş into the mountains above Bitlis (where the Ottoman Second Army was holding on for dear life).[30]

Even as Enver was throwing his last strategic reserve against the Russians in the Caucasus, two other reckless Turkish offensives were being launched simultaneously in the first week of August 1916. Following the outbreak of rebellion in the Hejaz, Enver and Djemal might have simply called off the second Suez Canal offensive. Instead, Hussein's effrontery seemed only to make it more urgent to turn the tables on his British patrons. But it would prove much tougher going the second time around, now that the first Suez attack had alerted Cairo to Turco-German intentions—and the British withdrawal from Gallipoli had freed up four divisions to reinforce the Egyptian Expeditionary Force (EEF), now commanded by General Archibald Murray. Murray, a former deputy chief of the Imperial General Staff, had decided on a policy of forward defense, constructing a new single-track railway into the Sinai desert from Kantara to Qatia, twenty-eight miles east of the canal, which allowed the British to fortify nearby Romani, the main oasis town between El-Arish and the canal. Although Kress von Kressenstein, catching wind of these plans, mounted an advance raid on the new British railhead on April 23, 1916, he was unable to capture Qatia or cut the British off from Romani. By the time Kress returned for the main assault in early August, the British had established a forward defensive line at Qatia-Romani, nearly thirty miles east of the Suez Canal.

Still, Kress did his best. Using the El-Arish oasis once again—he did beat the British there, at least—Kress led twelve battalions from the Fourth Army's Third Infantry Division across the Sinai desert, accompanied by several German machine-gun companies, four Austrian and German 10 cm howitzer batteries, trench mortar battalions, and special detachments of German commandos. Sherif or no sherif, it was still a formidable Ottoman force that reached Romani on the night of August 3–4, 1916, comprising 11,873 troops carrying 3,293 rifles, 56 machine guns, and 30 field guns. After canvassing British lines at Romani for a weak spot and not finding one, Kress finally threw caution aside and launched an assault on the morning of August 4, only to be beaten back by a savage British cavalry counterthrust led by the First and Second Australian Light Horse Brigades and the New Zealand Mounted Brigade. The British claim to have taken four thousand prisoners and inflicted nine thousand casualties on the enemy (out of a force they believed to have numbered eighteen thousand, although this is at least 50 percent higher than the real numbers). Kress himself claims to have lost only about a thousand casualties, although he did not deny that his men had been beaten soundly. By August 7, 1916, the Turks, Austrians, and Germans were retreating east across the Sinai desert toward El-Arish, having failed, in the second Suez offensive, even to come within sight of the canal.[31]

Stranger still were Enver's decisions in summer 1916 to capitalize on his uncle's triumph in Mesopotamia by invading Persia, and to approve the dispatch of XV Corps—thirty thousand troops strong—to Austrian Galicia. In May 1916, Enver traveled to Baghdad personally and ordered XIII Corps, commanded by Ali Ihsan Pasha, to mount a large-scale offensive into the heart of Russian-held Persian Azerbaijan. In the first week of August 1916, XIII Corps reached the outskirts of Hamadan. After several days of skirmishing, Baratov ordered his Cossacks to withdraw from the town on the night of August 9–10, pulling his main force back to Kazvin. Ali Ihsan Pasha then ordered his men, exhausted from the long march from Baghdad and weakened by illness, to rest—a rest that lasted plain into the winter. With this curious offensive, Enver had succeeded in mildly inconveniencing Baratov's expeditionary force in Persia—and mortally weakening the defenses of Baghdad whenever the British resumed the offensive in Mesopotamia. Simultaneously, XV Corps arrived in Galicia between August 5 and August 22, 1916, just in time to shore up defenses in Galicia after General Aleksei Brusilov had broken Austro-Hungarian lines in June. In fierce fighting with the Russians that September, the beleaguered Ottoman army lost another seven thousand casualties defending the Dual Monarchy of Austria-Hungary.[32]

The year 1916, which had begun so promisingly for the Ottomans against the British at Gallipoli and Kut, had turned into a litany of strategic woe from the Black Sea to the Suez Canal, interrupted only by quixotic victories in peripheral theaters like Persia and Galicia. To be sure, it had not been a great year for the war's other belligerents either. The German offensive at Verdun (February–December) and the Franco-British one at the Somme (July–November) have become bywords for carnage and horror on the western front, with each side seemingly trying to outdo the other in sanguinary futility. The Somme, coming on the heels of Gallipoli and Kut, finally put a stake through the heart of Asquith's Liberal government, with Lloyd George taking over as prime minister. In Germany, Falkenhayn took the fall for Verdun, making way for the ruthless new regime of Paul von Hindenburg and Erich Ludendorff, which then pushed aside the civilian chancellor, Theobald von Bethmann Hollweg, as well. Even Russia, which had done so well at Erzurum and with Brusilov's breakthrough in Galicia in June, was reeling. Brusilov's offensive, like Hussein's Arab revolt, turned out in the end to be a kind of mutual suicide pact, devastating both the Austro-Hungarian army it was designed to break and the army that launched it, with the Russians themselves suffering more than a million casualties.[33]

Still, if any belligerent was poised to gain something from the wreckage of the war's third terrible year of 1916, it was surely Russia. Battered though her armies in Europe may have been, they were in better shape than the

Austro-Hungarian forces, and the Russians still had huge reserves of unused peasant manpower to draw on. Russian war production, after numerous hiccups early in the war, had finally cranked into gear by 1916, with factories in Moscow, Petrograd, and Tula now producing four times as many shells as Austria-Hungary, and achieving near parity even with the Germans (who had to send the bulk of their own output to the western front). Russian production was augmented by a burgeoning flood of arms imports from the Allies, delivered to the northern port of Murmansk. As they contemplated the prospects for 1917 at inter-Allied conferences in Chantilly and Petrograd, the Entente generals were "full of fight"—not surprising, considering that they now enjoyed "superiority of at least 60 percent in men and guns" on both the western and eastern fronts—and the Russians were planning to outfit twenty-four new divisions by summer 1917. In Turkey, Yudenich's advantage in matériel and manpower was at least two to one and probably greater. In morale, the Russians' superiority over the Turks was all but unassailable as they prepared to renew the offensive in 1917, pushing on from Erzincan toward Sivas and Ankara. In Lazistan, the Russians were building a new rail line along the coast from Batum to Trabzon, with the latter city now an important forward base. The new commander of the Black Sea Fleet, Admiral A. V. Kolchak, was overseeing furious preparations for a large-scale amphibious landing at the Bosphorus, which included the creation of a special Tsargradskii Regiment to spearhead the conquest of Constantinople. Russia's long-awaited Black Sea dreadnought, the *Empress Catherine II*, became fully operational on November 30, 1916, soon to be followed by the *Emperor Alexander III*, expected to be completed in spring 1917.* With SMS *Goeben* down for serious repairs, Russia now had unquestioned naval superiority on the Black Sea for the first time since July 1914. After watching her Allies try, but fail, to win her great prize at Gallipoli, Russia was now poised to seize Constantinople for herself.[34]

---

* The *Imperatritsa Maria* had actually been floated the previous winter and seen some action, but she suffered an internal explosion in October 1916 and sank.

CHAPTER 14

RUSSIA'S MOMENT

It would be absurd and criminal to renounce the biggest prize of the war . . .
in the name of some humanitarian and cosmopolitan idea
of international socialism.

—PAVEL MILYUKOV,
founder of the liberal Kadet Party and first foreign minister
of Russia's Provisional Government, March 1917[1]

THERE HAD NEVER BEEN A GREAT DEAL of mystery about Russian war aims against the Ottoman Empire. For centuries the tsars had coveted Constantinople as the Second Rome of the Orthodox tradition, with Russian strategists christening the city "Tsargrad" in anticipation. Catherine the Great had first broached the idea in a serious way after defeating the Ottomans in the war of 1768–74 and laying claim to Crimea. In the nineteenth century, Russia's lust for Constantinople had become something of a cliché, so common an idea that English music-hall tunes were composed around it. Of course, the British refrain that "the Russians shall not have Constantinople" had served to check tsarist ambitions in 1829, 1853–56, and most recently in 1878. But now things were different. In March 1915, and again with the inking of the final Sazonov-Sykes-Picot Agreement of May 1916, His Majesty's government had endorsed by solemn treaty Russia's long-vexatious claim on Constantinople. The only thing standing in the way of the realization of this age-old dream of the tsars was Russia's own hesitation about landing troops at the Bosphorus to claim her prize.

In winter 1916–17, the auguries for such an amphibious strike were more favorable than ever before, beginning with the withdrawal of SMS *Goeben* (aka the *Yavuz Sultan Selim*, although no one but the Turks referred to her by this name) from active operations. Souchon's German dreadnought had been the thorn in the side of the Entente powers ever since it had miraculously escaped British pursuit in 1914, acquiring a well-earned reputation in a series of violent engagements with the Russians as "the unsinkable battleship" of the Ottoman navy. As a reluctant British admirer told readers of the London *Morning Post* toward the end of the Gallipoli campaign:

> It is again reported that the *Goeben* has appeared again in the Black Sea and has been attacked and injured by a submarine. This German cruiser, whether by the exercise of extreme discretion or good luck bordering on the fabulous, seems to bear a charmed life. Ever since she ran away from the plucky little *Gloucester* at the opening of the war she has been torpedoed, struck one of her own mines, hammered in open fight at sea, with consequent explosions aboard, has been disarmed to provide big guns for shore use, has had a false bottom of cement and other capital repairs effected where no dry docks of sufficient capacity were known to exist.[2]

The *Goeben* had played a role in the engagements of 1916, even if it had not been enough to stem the Russian advance. In February 1916, the *Goeben* had carried Ottoman supplies into Trabzon, including artillery and machine-gun detachments, nearly (though not quite) helping to save Erzurum. But now this indestructible battleship was reported to have made her last voyage. Having sustained serious damage to her hull and propellers, and with a crippling coal shortage in Constantinople making it impossible to fuel her anyway, the *Goeben* had been stripped of her guns and now anchored all but naked in the Bosphorus. Admiral Kolchak would be luckier than Churchill at Gallipoli when he sent in the Tsargradskii Regiment, as this great scourge of the Allies was apparently down for the count.*

---

* Showing that there was truth to the legend, the *Goeben/Yavuz* would survive the war to become the flagship of the Turkish Republican Navy. After briefly standing down the Russians again in the early Cold War, *Yavuz* was

More broadly speaking, the campaigns of 1916 had seen the Russians establish thoroughgoing naval command of the Black Sea, even before the *Goeben* was forced out of the picture. Although she had sunk in Sevastopol harbor in October, Russia's first Black Sea dreadnought, the *Imperatritsa Maria*, had put a serious scare into Souchon back in January 1916 when she fired off ninety-six 305 mm (12-inch) rounds at the *Goeben* before the latter could reply with five of her own (before the Russian warship pulled out of range). It was an inconclusive encounter, with no serious damage sustained by either ship. And yet strategically, the *Maria* had sent an important message: the *Goeben* was no longer boss of the Black Sea. Although the Russian dreadnought was slower than Souchon's flagship, she outgunned her.[3]

The eclipse of the *Goeben*'s superiority mattered greatly, because the Russians had already enjoyed a healthy advantage over the Ottomans in destroyers, cruisers, torpedo boats, and other surface warships. Even when she was at her best, the *Goeben* could never be everywhere at once in such a huge expanse of sea, and the Russian fleet had had considerable success all through the war harassing Turkish troop and coal transports up and down the Black Sea coast. It is indicative of the imbalance that the role played by Souchon's two German warships in the decisive Köprüköy-Erzurum battles of early 1916 was that of armored convoys—the *Goeben* and *Breslau* literally carried men and war matériel in their hulls, as not enough Ottoman warships were available to escort actual transports. The results were meager. The *Goeben* ferried 429 officers and men to Trabzon along with artillery, machine guns, and 300 cases of munitions; the *Breslau* carried only 71 troops and their weapons. The Russians, by contrast, were able to send significant reinforcements to Yudenich by sea after capturing Rize and Trabzon, including two Plastun brigades of Cossacks, two artillery brigades, and two regular infantry divisions. In May and June 1916 alone, the Russian fleet transported some 35,000 men along with their horses, arms, and equipment across the Black Sea to occupied Turkey.[4]

Farther west, the Russians had also seized the upper hand in a long-running

finally decommissioned in 1950, and towed away for scrapping only in 1973—thus outliving Churchill and most of her other enemies.

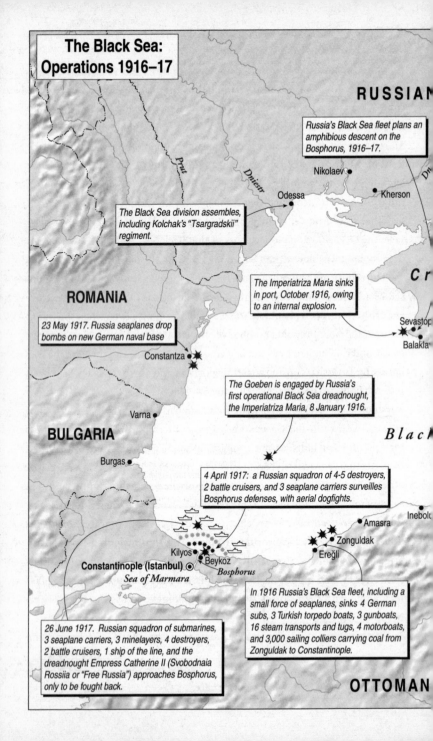

The Black Sea: Operations 1916–17

RUSSIAN

Russia's Black Sea fleet plans an amphibious descent on the Bosphorus, 1916–17.

Nikolaev ●

Odessa ●

● Kherson

The Black Sea division assembles, including Kolchak's "Tsargradskii" regiment.

ROMANIA

The Imperiatriza Maria sinks in port, October 1916, owing to an internal explosion.

Cr

Sevastopol ✹ ●
Balakla ●

23 May 1917. Russia seaplanes drop bombs on new German naval base

Constantza ● ✹✹

Varna ●

BULGARIA

Burgas ●

The Goeben is engaged by Russia's first operational Black Sea dreadnought, the Imperiatriza Maria, 8 January 1916.

Blac

✹

4 April 1917: a Russian squadron of 4-5 destroyers, 2 battle cruisers, and 3 seaplane carriers surveilles Bosphorus defenses, with aerial dogfights.

Amasra ●
Inebol

✹✹ Zonguldak
Kilyos ✹ Beykoz Ereğli ●
Constantinople (Istanbul) ◉ *Bosphorus*
Sea of Marmara

In 1916 Russia's Black Sea fleet, including a small force of seaplanes, sinks 4 German subs, 3 Turkish torpedo boats, 3 gunboats, 16 steam transports and tugs, 4 motorboats, and 3,000 sailing colliers carrying coal from Zonguldak to Constantinople.

26 June 1917. Russian squadron of submarines, 3 seaplane carriers, 3 minelayers, 4 destroyers, 2 battle cruisers, 1 ship of the line, and the dreadnought Empress Catherine II (Svobodnaia Rossiia or "Free Russia") approaches Bosphorus, only to be fought back.

OTTOMAN

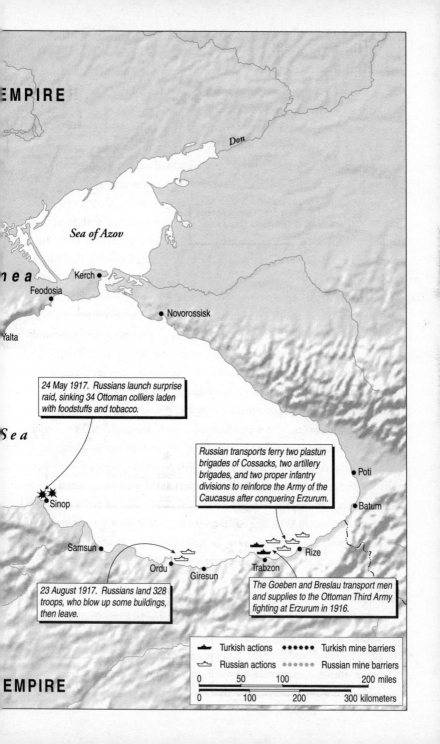

EMPIRE

Don

Sea of Azov

Kerch

Feodosia

Novorossisk

n e a

Yalta

S e a

24 May 1917. Russians launch surprise raid, sinking 34 Ottoman colliers laden with foodstuffs and tobacco.

Russian transports ferry two plastun brigades of Cossacks, two artillery brigades, and two proper infantry divisions to reinforce the Army of the Caucasus after conquering Erzurum.

Poti

Sinop

Batum

Samsun

Ordu

Giresun

Rize

Trabzon

23 August 1917. Russians land 328 troops, who blow up some buildings, then leave.

The Goeben and Breslau transport men and supplies to the Ottoman Third Army fighting at Erzurum in 1916.

EMPIRE

⬥ Turkish actions	✶✶✶✶✶✶	Turkish mine barriers
⬦ Russian actions	⬤⬤⬤⬤⬤⬤	Russian mine barriers

0	50	100		200 miles
0		100	200	300 kilometers

tit-for-tat struggle to control the waters surrounding Zonguldak and Ereğli, 150 miles to the east of the capital, whence came the bulk of Constantinople's coal supply. While the layers of Turkish mines guarding the Bosphorus had helped keep the Russian fleet out, a bit farther out to sea, on the eastern approach, the Russians had begun laying their own mines to harass Souchon's communications. The *Goeben* and *Breslau* had both run over Russian mines, although they had also escorted coal transports to the capital on numerous occasions. Summer 1915 had seen an escalation, with the Germans sending submarines into the Black Sea, and the Russians countering with their own, including the world's first submarine minelayer, the aptly named *Krab*. But it was Russia's surface warships that did the most damage, sinking Turkish colliers regularly—even, on occasion, when they were escorted by the *Goeben*. As a German naval captain observed, "These Russian destroyers with their artillery and speed are the real masters of the sea and need fear no one." In February 1916, the Russians added a fleet of primitive first-generation aircraft carriers (converted ocean liners) to the action near Zonguldak, launching seaplanes that dropped bombs on the harbor and sank a collier. In the course of 1916, Russia's Black Sea Fleet sank four German submarines, three Turkish torpedo boats, three gunboats, sixteen steam transports and tugs, four motorboats, and something like three thousand sailing colliers (although this total might have been inflated, as Turkish captains often scuttled them temporarily in shallow waters, only to refloat them after the Russians left the area). Things got so bad at sea that the Turks organized a new inland supply route via the Sakarya River. After Souchon had arrived in Constantinople in August 1914, he had assured Tirpitz that there was enough coal in Constantinople, but by the end of 1916, the Germans were sending 14,000 tons of coal each month to Turkey along the Baghdad Railway (with the Serbian connection now secure) to cover the growing supply gaps from Zonguldak.

It was not enough. In a kind of vicious spiral, the lack of sufficient coal to power his warships meant that Souchon could not contest the waters near Zonguldak—which reduced his coal supplies still further. By January 1917, the pinch was so acute that *none* of the Ottoman Empire's remaining battleships—not the *Goeben*, not the *Breslau*, nor the *Turgut Reis* or the

Hamidiye—could so much as stage maneuvers. As if to give up on contesting the Black Sea, Souchon had stripped these proud vessels of their guns, mounting them on the shore batteries of the Bosphorus and Dardanelles for a final stand against the Entente assault he imagined was soon coming from both directions.*[5]

As Souchon knew, the Ottoman armies were in no condition to offer much resistance whenever the final Russian push began. The Third Army had fallen to a strength of thirty thousand at best, with its constituent units all but downsized into oblivion: its corps were now divisions, its divisions regiments, its regiments barely battalion strength, with some as small as companies. Recognizing the problem, Enver and his new theater commander, Vehip Pasha, eliminated all the old corps commands in September 1916, forcing what remained of the Third Army into two new corps, styled optimistically "Caucasian I and II" (although their prospects of reaching the Transcaucasus in 1917 were close to zero). Eight entire army divisions simply disappeared from the rolls, in a crude approximation of the fighting power the Third Army had lost in 1916. The new Ottoman Second Army was a bit stronger at something like 64,000 effectives, but even so, it was in a parlous condition after the exhausting battles of late summer—especially after the first snows came, weeks earlier than usual, on September 26, 1916. Ironically, it was on the Turkish right (i.e., southern) flank where the cold bit the hardest: the Third Army had retreated so far west from Erzurum that it was now encamped in the lowlands, whereas the Second Army was stretched out across the heights near Bitlis (elevation 1,400 meters, or 4,500 feet) and the mountain valleys near Dersim (1,500–1,700 meters, about a mile above sea level) and Bingöl (where the peaks rose to 3,000 meters, or 10,000 feet). Whatever élan remained on this front was in Mustafa Kemal's XVI Corps at Bitlis—and it was now grounded in the snows, its men just trying to hold on during the worst and longest winter in living memory. By March 1917, the Second Army would have lost half its strength—over thirty thousand men—to frostbite,

---

* Souchon must not have been very well informed about British parliamentary politics, for he threw great energy into planning for a renewed British amphibious assault on the Dardanelles in winter 1916–17, as if in lockstep with the ever more baroque self-flagellation of the Dardanelles Commission. Had he seen Churchill squirming in the dock under weeks of hostile cross-interrogation, Souchon would surely have shifted shore guns north from the Dardanelles to the Bosphorus in 1917, reversing the direction he shifted them in spring 1915.

typhus and other epidemic diseases, malnutrition or starvation, or simple exhaustion. The Ottoman Sixth Army in Mesopotamia, likewise, was down to scarcely thirty thousand effectives by early 1917.[6]

More promising still, from Russia's perspective, was the situation in the Ottoman capital itself. After the Allied withdrawal from Gallipoli, Enver had stripped the Ottoman Fifth Army of all but two divisions, which now guarded the southern approaches to Constantinople. The First Army still guarded Thrace, but it had been so weakened by the earlier peeling off of strength to Gallipoli that it now consisted of only one fully intact infantry division, the Forty-Ninth, along with a single cavalry brigade. Estimating that it would take at least two weeks for Enver to route reinforcements north from Gallipoli, Kolchak informed the tsar (by way of his army chief of staff, Alekseev) that any Russian troops landed at or near the Bosphorus would face resistance from only one Thracian division. While Alekseev himself was dubious about diverting substantial numbers of troops from the European theater for a chancy amphibious strike, which he thought would require several dozen divisions, Kolchak was confident that five Russian infantry divisions would suffice to secure both the Asian and European shores of the Bosphorus and win Russia her great prize of Tsargrad.[7]

Of course, the tsar's own *muzhiks* were exhausted, too, and the weather was just as harsh for them as for their enemies. The third war winter was the worst yet everywhere in Europe, with the bitter cold punctuated by biting hunger. Germans labeled 1916–17 the "turnip winter," with the food crisis so severe that Ludendorff famously unleashed the U-boats ("unrestricted submarine warfare") in January to starve out England in retaliation for the suffering that Germans blamed on the British blockade. Compounding Turkey's other maladies, the bread ration in Constantinople was cut from the already miserly 250 grams a day to the near-starvation level of 180 grams (about ⅓ pound). Across Russia, meanwhile, blizzards blanketed the rail lines with snow, disabling locomotives and causing terrible supply bottlenecks. Shortages in Petrograd caused huge price spikes in heating oil and bread, which fueled, in turn, the spread of poisonous rumors of pro-German treason in high places.

The story of Russia's February Revolution of 1917 is too well known to require retelling here, but there are important elements that repay closer attention. War weariness was certainly an important component of the popular mood on the front lines, especially in Europe, but it was not antiwar sentiment that drove events in the capital, at least in the early stages of the political crisis. In the critical Duma debate of November 1/14, 1916, when the respected liberal politician Pavel Milyukov, founder of the Kadet Party, famously lit into the tsar's latest chairman of the Council of Ministers, Boris Stürmer ("Is it stupidity or is it treason?"), his theme was not that the government should end the war, but that it was not prosecuting it vigorously enough. Even the Socialist Revolutionary Alexander Kerensky, who pounded the "treason" theme still more shrilly that day in the Duma, denounced the tsar's ministers not as warmongers but as "fratricides and cowards." The poisonous rumors surrounding the peasant faith healer Rasputin and Tsarina Alexandra were likewise based on the idea that the pair was in cahoots with the Germans (as the tsar spent most of his time at the front, it was the tsarina who was believed to have elevated Stürmer earlier that year). After Stürmer, with his unfortunately Germanic name, was forced out to appease the mob, it was the turn of A. P. Trepov to face the Duma on December 2, 1916. To silence the hecklers, Trepov revealed in public, for the first time, that Britain and France had promised Russia Constantinople and the Straits after the war. It was not the last time a Russian statesman would invoke Tsargrad to steady the public. As the French ambassador Paléologue noted in a dispatch to Paris, an increasingly popular refrain heard in Petrograd that winter was "What is the point of this war if it will not give us Constantinople?"[8]

The idea was gradually gaining currency at Russian military headquarters at Mogilev, too, despite Alekseev's skepticism. Nikolai Bazili, chief of the tsar's diplomatic staff at Stavka, had been advocating an amphibious strike at the Bosphorus ever since drawing up Russia's annexation plans for Sazonov in 1915, though his ideas had long been discounted by the generals for reasons of personal bias.* Carried along by the enthusiasm of Kolchak and Bazili, on December 24, 1916, Tsar Nicholas II authorized the creation of a special

---

* Bazili was descended from Greek Phanariots. His aptly named grandfather Constantine was born in Constantinople, and fought at Navarino in 1827—the battle that destroyed Ottoman naval power in the Mediterranean and ensured Greek independence.

amphibious Black Sea division, crowned by Kolchak's Tsargradskii Regiment, although it boasted only about three thousand active soldiers, and Alekseev insisted that it should land not at the Bosphorus, but at Zonguldak to secure the coal mines and move up the Sakarya River.

On February 21/March 6, 1917, the last foreign minister of tsarist Russia, N. N. Pokrovskii, submitted a memorandum to Stavka recommending a Bosphorus strike be carried out as soon as possible, to ensure that Russia not be deprived of her prize by her allies if the war ended that year.

Before Stavka's reply was sent back, revolution broke out in Petrograd, with striking workers joining the women demonstrating on International Women's Day on the twenty-third, the Pavlovskii guard regiment firing into the crowds at Znamenskii Square on the twenty-fifth, and a mutiny spreading through the Petrograd garrison once soldiers from the Pavlovskii barracks vowed not to fire again at the protesters. On February 26/March 11, 1917, Alekseev called in Bazili along with two retired old-regime statesmen visiting Stavka—Sazonov and Stürmer—to discuss Pokrovskii's request in light of the disturbing news from Petrograd. Stürmer, who had learned all about popular mobs, expressly advocated that the seizure of Constantinople was now "essential in order to calm public opinion in Russia." Alekseev objected that he could not spare troops from Europe, but he did concede that the three battalions now guarding Trabzon might join an amphibious force. But Alekseev's own chief of staff, Anton Denikin, was keen on the Bosphorus idea, as was Admiral Bubnov, the navy's representative at Stavka. Together with Kolchak, they began organizing transports for a Bosphorus descent for whenever Alekseev could be made to cough up troops. As it was, weather conditions on the Black Sea ruled out a major amphibious undertaking before June, so there was still time.[9]

Even as these plans were being set in motion, revolution was tearing through Petrograd with astonishing rapidity. On February 26 and 27/March 11 and 12, 1917, mutinous soldiers fanned out across the city, commandeering cars and looting arsenals, shops, restaurants, and rich estates. Tsarist policemen were lynched; mobs sacked the Interior Ministry and Secret Police (Okhrana) headquarters. On February 28/March 13, 1917, the red flag flew over the Winter Palace, and a self-styled "soviet," or council of workers and soldiers, assumed what remained of authority in Petrograd. Next day, the Petrograd Soviet issued "Order No. 1" to Russia's armed forces, which subordinated the army to the soviet and turned over control of military equipment and arms to soldiers' and sailors' committees. Although couched in the flowery language of the Russian socialist intelligentsia, ordinary *muzhiks* had no trouble figuring out what Order No. 1 meant: "Disarm the officers." Next to follow was an amnesty for all tsarist political prisoners, and the dissolution of the police organs. On March 3/16, 1917, the day after Tsar Nicholas II (under pressure from Alekseev and the generals) abdicated his throne, the Petrograd Soviet ordered the arrest of all members of the Romanov family, including Grand Duke Nicholas, commander of the Army of the Caucasus.

One might think that the collapse of the tsarist regime in the capital would have put paid to the ambitious plans being drawn up at Stavka for the conquest of Constantinople. Instead, the chaos in Petrograd gave them new life. Behind the scenes of the drama, a surprisingly seamless transition was under way in the regime actually governing Russia. Parallel to the formation of the Petrograd Soviet, a Provisional Committee of the State Duma was established on February 27/March 12, 1917, which assumed the duties of a ruling cabinet even as the soviet dominated the public sphere. The men making the running in the new cabinet were establishment liberals, with Milyukov, the Kadet leader, taking the reins from Pokrovskii as foreign minister, and Alexander Guchkov, a founder of the Progressive Bloc and head of the Duma's Military-Industrial Committee overseeing war production, named the minister of defense. All through March, Guchkov put his extensive business contacts to use procuring colliers and merchant vessels for Kolchak's planned descent on the Bosphorus.[10] The new liberal foreign minister picked up right where Pokrovskii left off with Bazili, planning to win back the public by seizing Tsargrad. As Milyukov told a liberal friend, "It would be absurd and criminal to renounce the biggest prize of the war . . . in the name of some humanitarian and cosmopolitan idea of international socialism."[11] On March 23/April 5, 1917, Bazili informed Milyukov that two full divisions would be ready to sail for the Bosphorus by mid-May, and hopefully a third by later that summer.[12] Kolchak, meanwhile, reported that, through Guchkov's heroic efforts and the commandeering of Romania's fleet and merchant marine (which had taken refuge at Kherson after the Austro-Germans had routed Romania following her ill-judged entry into the war on August 27, 1916), there were now enough transports available.[13] Although Alekseev continued dragging his heels, Denikin was more enthusiastic than ever, as Bazili wrote hopefully to Milyukov on April 8/21, 1917.[14]

These were not idle communications. All winter and spring, preparations had been under way for a major Bosphorus expedition. In Odessa, where the Black Sea division was assembling, troops were arriving every day by train from the mainland. Every available vessel on the Black Sea, from Danubian river barges to Greek sailing colliers to oil-fired oceangoing steamers, was being outfitted for amphibious operations. Four Romanian passenger liners, the *Regele Carol I*, *Dacia*, *Imperator Trajan*, and *Romania*, which had escaped into the Black Sea before the Germans secured the Danubian basin, had been converted into seaplane carriers, to complement Russia's own *Almaz*, *Imperator Alexander I*, and *Imperator Nikolai I*; each could carry between four and seven seaplanes. Although the effects of Order No. 1 were felt in Odessa, Sevastopol, Kerch, and Novorossisk in March just as through all Russia's urban centers, the initial impact was muted. "Of course there are extremists here as well as in other parts," G. W. Le Page, a British naval liaison officer, reported from Sevastopol on April 29, 1917, "but the general feeling is that the war must be pushed on until the military power of the Central Powers is crushed." On the Ottoman front, if not on Russia's European fronts, tensions between officers and men were tempered by the fellow feeling of a cause everyone believed in. As Le Page observed in an arresting turn of phrase, "The war has . . . without doubt, saved much bloodshed." In mid-April, Admiral Kolchak had received an offer to take over the command of the more powerful Baltic fleet, but he had declined because "he wished to remain here," plotting the conquest of Constantinople and commanding men who shared his objective.[15]

One way or another, with or without Alekseev's cooperation, Kolchak was going to send the Tsargradskii Regiment into action. And so in the last week of March 1917, as the Petrograd Soviet was outlining its goal of a peace without "imperialist" annexations, Russia's Black Sea Fleet launched its first serious probe of the Bosphorus defenses. On March 26, 1917, three of

Kolchak's seaplane carriers arrived on the Turkish Thracian coast just west of the Bosphorus, escorted by a pair of destroyers. It appears to have been a preliminary reconnaissance operation, with the planes doing overflights and dropping a few desultory bombs on coastal targets; two torpedoes were fired off without effect.[16] On April 4, 1917—the very day Milyukov got into hot water with the Petrograd Soviet by announcing at a press conference that Russia had not renounced her war aim of conquering Constantinople and the Straits—the Russians returned to the Bosphorus in "grand style" (as Admiral Usedom noted in his report to the kaiser), sending an entire squadron comprised of "five or six destroyers," two battle cruisers, and no fewer than three seaplane carriers, to a stretch of the Black Sea coast just on the Asian side of the Bosphorus at Beykoz. This time there were real dogfights in the air, as the Germans and Turks scrambled seven of their own seaplanes into action to send the Russian pilots back to their carriers before they could surveille the city's defenses.[17]

Kolchak's sorties to the Bosphorus in spring 1917, though little remembered today, were important salvos in a battle for the soul of Russian foreign policy raging in Petrograd. The issue of war aims was arguably *the* political question opened up by the February Revolution, even if it had been obscured at first in the general popular euphoria over the fall of the tsar and his secret police. For what, after all, were all those millions of wretched *muzhiks* fighting and dying for on a front stretching for thousands of miles from the Gulf of Finland down to the Siret River in Bessarabia, across the Black Sea into Asia Minor, Turkish Armenia, and Persian Azerbaijan? Even as Order No. 1 was transmitted to the army in mid-March 1917, Baratov's Cossacks were sweeping into northern Mesopotamia. If you asked Baratov what his men were fighting for, his answer was "[To] lead Russia in the historical path of Alexander the Great."[18] If you asked Yudenich, architect of the great victories over Turkey in 1916 and now (owing to the fall of the grand duke) commander of the Caucasian Army, the answer was much the same. As Yudenich reported after his men had discussed Order No. 1, "The membership of the soldiers' committees" had resolved "to conduct the war to a victorious end."[19] Kolchak and Denikin, working together to plot the amphibious descent on the Bosphorus, wholeheartedly agreed—indeed it was no accident that the three men most committed to conquering the Ottoman Empire in 1917 would later emerge as leaders of the anti-Bolshevik White Armies. In Petrograd, Guch-kov and Milyukov were wholly on board with Russia's expansionist war aims, even if Milyukov tried to appease the soviet by watering down his position in an April 10, 1917, statement that Russia sought "lasting peace" based on the "self-determination of nations." If you asked the socialist politicians Milyu-kov was trying to appease, the answer was that Russia's *muzhiks* were being "bled white and ruined by this monstrous war"—the implication being (though they refused to spell this out openly) that Russia's expansionist war aims were unjust and should be jettisoned. If you asked the men actually fighting the war, the answer depended on which front they were on (muti-nous sentiment was indeed far lower on the Turkish and Persian fronts, where the Russians were winning, than in Europe, where they faced Germans) and on who, exactly, was commanding them (the vast majority of lynchings in spring 1917 were of officers with German names, suggesting that the men did not want to be conquered by the kaiser's army, even if they weren't quite clear on why the war was being fought).[20]

The burgeoning battle over war aims ratcheted up higher after Lenin arrived in Petrograd on April 3/16, 1917, at 11:10 p.m. If there was one man who was absolutely certain on the matter, it was the Bolsheviks' exiled leader, who had been issuing manifestos denouncing the "imperialist war" from neutral Switzerland ever since 1914.* Not for Lenin the mealymouthed com-promises of the soviet, far less the forthright patriotism of Milyukov, Guch-kov, and the liberals. After arriving at the Finland Station—by way of Stockholm, having been sent thither from Zurich under German military escort—Lenin immediately launched into a fiery speech denouncing the Pro-visional Government for continuing the war and demanded its overthrow ("all power to the Soviets"). Lenin's unequivocal antiwar stance—laid out in his April Theses, though arousing considerable opposition from Bolsheviks who had already been toiling away inside Russia while he was safe abroad—was published in *Pravda* on April 7/20, 1917, laying down the gauntlet for

---

* Lenin had been in Vienna when the war broke out. He was given a visa to travel to Switzerland by the Austro-Hungarian government once it learned that he had endorsed separatism for Russian Ukraine.

Russian socialists on the war question. Were they genuine revolutionaries or mere tools of the imperialist ruling classes?

As foreign minister of the Provisional Government, Milyukov was at the center of the political storm. Though doing his best to appease the radicals of the Petrograd Soviet, the Kadet leader was also at pains to reassure Russia's Western allies, now (after April 6, 1917) including the United States, that she would not abandon the common cause and make a separate peace with the Germans. To square the circle, Milyukov sought counsel from the leaders of the peasant-backed Socialist Revolutionary (SR) Party, which still dominated the soviet, particularly Alexander Kerensky, who had already emerged as the mediator between the radicals and the government (Kerensky, as minister of justice, was the only member of the soviet's executive committee also to hold cabinet office). But Kerensky himself was under pressure from Viktor Chernov, the SR Party leader who, like Lenin, had spent the war in exile and was in no mood to parley: Chernov wanted Milyukov's head, and a replacement who would renounce Russia's imperialist war aims. Seeing a chance to stake his own claim to foreign policy, Kerensky engineered a sort of poison pill compromise, which saw Milyukov affix his signature to a note to Russia's allies affirming her commitment to "carry out [her] obligations"—effectively re-endorsing her war aims, even if this was not spelled out as such.

On April 20/May 3, 1917, the text of this "Milyukov note" was published in the Russian press, causing a sensation among the socialist opposition. The Petrograd Soviet issued a resolution opposing it on the grounds that "revolutionary democracy will not permit the spilling of blood for . . . aggressive objectives." A regiment of Finnish guards, led by a socialist officer called Theodore Linde, marched to the Mariinski Palace (where the Provisional Government usually met, although this day it had convened at Guchkov's office at the Ministry of War) to protest. With the Provisional Government facing the first serious street disorders since the February Revolution, the commander of the Petrograd Military District, General Lavr Kornilov, asked its permission to put down the burgeoning mutiny in the ranks. The cabinet, following Kerensky, denied the request. Smelling blood, Lenin convened the Bolshevik Central Committee and drafted a resolution condemning the Provisional Government as "thoroughly imperialist." Bolshevik demonstrators then marched through the streets with banners proclaiming "Down with the Provisional Government" and "All Power to the Soviets." To provide muscle, the head of the Bolshevik military organization, N. I. Podvoiskii, summoned pro-Bolshevik sailors from the Kronstadt naval base in the Gulf of Finland— notorious brawlers—to the city. By the afternoon of April 21/May 4, 1917, violence had broken out on Nevsky Prospect between government supporters and the Bolsheviks, which cost the lives of three protesters. Kornilov again asked permission to restore order with loyal troops, and was again refused, this time with a note of open defiance from the soviet, which instructed troops not to obey orders from superior officers (like Kornilov) who did not provide orders countersigned by the soviet's executive committee. Kornilov, disgusted, asked to be relieved of his now-emasculated position in Petrograd, and was given command of the Eighth Army facing Galicia.[21]

Lenin, who had remained behind the scenes, later disavowed any intention of overthrowing the government. But his hand was clearly visible in the "April Days" rioting. In his April Theses, Lenin had drawn clear political lines, disavowing both the war and the Provisional Government. While the Bolsheviks did not succeed in toppling the government, they had done it serious damage, exposing the breach between Kerensky's SRs and the Guchkov-Milyukov liberals over the war, and destroying what little independence the army still had from the Petrograd Soviet. Guchkov, realizing this, offered his resignation on April 30/May 13, 1917, followed by Milyukov four days later. The immediate beneficiary of the twilight of Russia's liberals was Kerensky, who took over from Guchkov as minister of war (the new foreign minister, M. I. Tereshchenko, was a nonentity who would operate largely under Kerensky's thumb). In a new declaration of war aims dated May 5/18, 1917, the revamped cabinet vowed to "democratize the army" and disowned imperialist war aims, while also asserting, a bit less convincingly, that "a defeat of Russia and her Allies would be a great misfortune for all peoples, and would delay or make impossible a universal peace."

With Milyukov out of the picture, it was now Kerensky's turn to explain the war to the disgruntled and increasingly mutinous troops who were fighting it. It was a tough sell, but there was no one in Russia better suited to the task. Even before coming to fame with his venomous speeches denouncing tsarism and treason in the Duma, Kerensky had been a wildly successful trial lawyer, and he knew how to make a case. Setting out on a barnstorming tour of the front, he displayed unflagging energy stirring up the troops behind the idea that they were the vanguard of a new Russia, fighting no longer for the wretched tsar but for democracy and the Allies, socialism and the people. One witness likened Kerensky's passage through the front to that of a "cyclone"; another compared him to "a volcano hurling forth sheaves of all-consuming fire."

So long as the great Socialist Revolutionary orator was present, the mood among the men perked up and began to seem ebullient, patriotic, enthusiastic. But, as more critical observers noted, the impact of these speeches "evaporated as soon as Kerensky left the scene." As soon as the men had time to think things over, many of them concluded that Kerensky's pitch did not, quite, pass the smell test. For why, exactly, was it better for *muzhiks* to fight for Russia's allies—Britain, France, and the United States (Serbia herself, Russia's original *casus belli*, having fallen in 1915)—than for Constantinople and the Straits, or even (as Kerensky was in fact proposing in between rhetorical flourishes) Austrian Galicia? No matter how fine Kerensky's talk about democracy and common ideals, what he was really asking was for frontline soldiers to die for war aims dreamed up in distant capitals, whether Petrograd, Paris, or London. "We now have freedom and we are going to get the land," a popular refrain went; "so why should we go and get ourselves crippled?"*22

There was a great deal of humbug in Kerensky's foreign policy, however sincere he may have been in selling it. It was true that his hands were tied, up to a point, by the London Convention of September 1914 (which forbade any of the Entente powers from signing a separate peace with Germany), by the inter-Allied summits the previous winter at Petrograd and Chantilly (which required a Russian diversionary strike on the eastern front in 1917 to ease the burden in the west), and by the moral-material factors such as the Allied war

---

* There is a brilliantly imagined scene in the David Lean epic *Doctor Zhivago*, where a Kerensky-like commissar stands atop a beer barrel exhorting the men to defend their home, their women—not to shamefully surrender to the Germans. The men cheer—until the barrel gives way and the commissar falls into the beer. The men laugh, and shoot him.

matériel pouring into Murmansk all year, not to mention the mutinies that began spreading through the French army at Chemin des Dames in May 1917. It is hard not to sympathize with the pressure Kerensky was under to do *something* to relieve Russia's beleaguered allies, to prevent the Germans from simply turning their armies around from eastern Europe to crush France—even while the people he spoke for in the soviet and in the streets increasingly wanted out of the war. Kerensky's dilemma was Russia's own dilemma. Like him, most Russians wanted it both ways: they did not want to continue the war, but they did not want to surrender dishonorably to the Germans either. In this sense, Kerensky was an ideal democratic politician, channeling the public mood in both his speeches and his policies.

He was not, however, proving himself to be much of a statesman. The problem with the popular mood in Russia was that it was inchoate and incoherent, requiring much firmer guidance than Kerensky was willing to give it. Had he wanted to reestablish law and order in the streets and discipline in the armies, he could have given Kornilov his head to suppress the April riots and then get the frontline troops in line for the planned Galicia offensive promised to the Western allies. Conversely, had Kerensky wished truly to end an "imperialist war" and "democratize the army," he should have disowned the offensive against Austrian Galicia—which was, after all, just the sort of imperial aggression the Petrograd Soviet had repeatedly denounced. The General Staff had planned the invasion of Austrian Galicia in 1914 in order to reach the Carpathian Mountains and consolidate Russia's defensive lines in Europe. Brusilov, in 1916, had re-invaded Galicia in order to break Austria-Hungary. As if in thrall to these old-regime generals, Kerensky even appointed Brusilov the new commander in chief of the army, hoping that he would work some of his magic on the same front as he had made his name the previous summer. The appointment of Brusilov was tacit acknowledgment that Kerensky had no real idea why he was asking his men to invade Galicia, as they did on June 16/29, 1917. It was the last gasp of a dying army. As soon as German reinforcements arrived on July 6, 1917, the Russian troops pitched back into headlong flight, showing how little ice Kerensky's speeches had really cut with them.

The same contradiction was at work with Russia's war aims against the Ottoman Empire. On May 15/28, 1917, the new, post-Milyukov Foreign

Ministry tried to reconcile the terms of Sazonov-Sykes-Picot with the soviet's "peace without annexations" declaration of April. As if to confirm that the ghosts of Russian imperialism were not easily buried, the new statement of revolutionary Russia's war aims referred to "provinces of Asiatic Turkey taken by right of war" before asserting, in an apparent contradiction, that the former Ottoman vilayets of Van, Bitlis, and Erzurum would be "forever Armenian." Trying to blend together the old imperialist paternalism with the new, enlightened humanitarianism, the policy memorandum stipulated, awkwardly, that these "Armenian" provinces would be administered by Russian officials, who would help repatriate Armenian, Kurdish, and Turkish refugees.[23]

There was a revealing omission from this revised statement of Russia's war aims against Turkey. The elephant in the room was, of course, Constantinople and the Straits. Because these had not yet been taken "by right of war," Kerensky's "reformed" Russian Foreign Ministry could elide the matter, as if it had not obsessed Russian statesmen many decades and helped to determine the contours of the first political crisis of the new regime. But the fact was that Russia's admirals were still plotting the conquest of the Ottoman capital, with or without authorization from the Petrograd Soviet. While mutiny had spread through the ranks of even the Black Sea Fleet after the proclamation of Order No. 1, costing the lives of about twenty naval officers in all, Kolchak claimed to have restored discipline by the end of April.* In mid-May, the sailors' soviet of Sevastopol debated the question of whether to invite Lenin—already notorious for his advocacy of ending the war immediately—to town. The vote was 342–20 against.[24] While a more egalitarian ethos prevailed onshore, with the saluting of "bluejackets" frowned upon, once on board most men obeyed orders. Even as Kerensky was touring the front to whip up patriotism before the Galician offensive, Russian warships continued operating with perfect impunity up and down the Black Sea littoral, all but snuffing out Constantinople's coal supplies from Zonguldak. On May 23, Kolchak's fleet carried out

---

* Bad as this sounds, mutinies in the Baltic fleet in spring 1917 were far more serious, costing at least 150 lives. Most of the officers targeted in the Black Sea Fleet were, moreover, those with German names (like the former commander in chief Eberhart), suggesting that a kind of residual patriotism may have been at play on this front where Russia had been so dominant in 1916.

a surprise attack on the (now German controlled) Danube Delta in Romania, with seaplanes dropping bombs on Constanța. Next day, Kolchak launched a surprise raid on Sinop, sinking 34 Ottoman colliers laden with foodstuffs and tobacco. As Britain's naval attaché noted with satisfaction, "The Turks evidently thought the Russians were too intent on their own internal affairs to put to sea." On May 25, a Russian squadron appeared off the Bosphorus again, though it was only a minelaying expedition. Souchon, spooked, reported next day a phantom sighting of a Russian battle cruiser off Kilyos, west of the Bosphorus. The Russian Black Sea Fleet, so far from laying down its arms after the revolution, seemed more active than ever.[25]

Back on shore, however, morale was beginning to crack. "There is no sympathy between officers and men," Le Page had reported in early April, when the effects of Order No. 1 were first being felt: "The officers take no interest in the welfare of their men, no attempt to institute games to occupy their spare time."* Although Kolchak was respected, his position remained precarious: there was a poisonous rumor going round the fleet that he had put the fleet to sea during the February Revolution expressly to avoid a putsch in port. While most sailors, as evidenced by the continuing activity along the Turkish coast, were willing to do their duty on board, soldiers recruited into the Black Sea division felt no such compunction. The Sinop operation on May 24, 1917, for example, was supposed to include a landing of two thousand soldiers to fire the port, except that not a single infantryman agreed to go. Even Kolchak was now having cold feet about a Tsargrad landing. "References in the papers to the iron discipline of the Black Sea fleet," he told Le Page, "were all rot." Disgusted, Kolchak requested to be relieved of his command. A temporary replacement was found in Vice Admiral Lukin, although Kolchak remained under close watch by the sailors' committee.[26]

On June 21, even as the army was rushing reinforcements to Galicia, another mutiny rocked Odessa, with four "objectionable" officers arrested by their men. This one escalated quickly, with a sailors' committee declaring Kolchak's deposition (rather than give mutineers the satisfaction of disarm-

---

* Showing that he was a man ahead of his time, Le Page had suggested teaching the men association football (soccer), only to be told by his Russian fellow officers that "such barbaric and brutal pastimes could not be encouraged."

ing him, the proud admiral threw his sword overboard). Somehow, despite chaos reigning in port, the largest Russian squadron yet assembled steamed to the Bosphorus on June 26, 1917—just three days before the Galician offensive began—consisting of submarines, three seaplane carriers, three minelayers, four destroyers, two battle cruisers and a ship of the line, and, in a crowning touch, the dreadnought *Empress Catherine II* (now renamed *Svobodnaia Rossiia*, or "Free Russia") making her first appearance in combat. At 2:15 p.m., the crew of the *Svobodnaia Rossiia*, catching sight of smoke puffed by the *Breslau*, opened fire from her forward turret, firing off nine salvos, though each missed. Several Russian destroyers then chased the *Breslau* back toward the Bosphorus, before losing her in the minefields. A brief aerial dogfight ensued, in which a Turkish plane succeeded in strafing one of the seaplane carriers, whereupon the Russians broke off the attack and pulled back.[27]

The Tsargrad dream refused to die. But the sting was out of the beast. There was a scare in Constantinople on the night of July 9–10, 1917, when an enemy warplane circled over the airfield at San Stefano (Yeşilköy), more or less on the grounds of today's Istanbul Atatürk Airport, before dropping ten bombs into the Golden Horn aimed at the *Goeben* and the *General*, and then another two on the Ottoman War Ministry (Harbiye Nezareti). All salvos missed their targets, although a few torpedo boats anchored near the *Goeben* sustained damage, and one bomb took out the War Ministry's horse stables. So far as Souchon and Usedom could tell, however, these bombers came from the Aegean and were thus not Russian. (It was in fact a British pilot flying a Handley Page 0/100 3124 from Mudros.)[28] On August 23, a Russian squadron did appear off the Turkish coast to cover an amphibious landing of some 328 troops at Ordu, roughly halfway between Trabzon and Samsun. Showing less than great élan, the *muzhiks* blew up a few buildings in the harbor but failed to fire the main hangar they had been ordered to destroy, before re-embarking and heading home. Four days later, the Russians tried another halfhearted landing nearby at Vona (today called Perşembe, or "Thursday"), only to break off the attempt as soon as the Turks opened fire from shore. Right into October 1917, up to the eve of the Bolshevik seizure of power, what remained of an officer corps at Black Sea command continued planning for a major amphibious landing at Sinop, originally slated to involve a full army corps, until this was whittled down to a "surprise raid" of eight infantry and eight cavalry battalions, then whittled down to nothing at all.[29] But the crowning symbolic moment of the campaign had come back on July 26, 1917, following yet another mutiny in Odessa, when a single Russian motorboat wound its way through the Bosphorus minefields, until it reached close enough to shore for its crew to toss over a message in a bottle. This "Proclamation from the Russian Revolutionary Fleet to the Turkish Nation" declared that

> the Germans should take their hands off Russia and Turkey. The enemy of the Turks and our enemy is the same. It is Germany. For this reason all German soldiers, officers and officials should be chased out of Turkey together. Then we could live together with you as good neighbors. The only despotisms left in the world [i.e., after the Russian Revolution] are the German and the Austrian regimes.

In this way Russia's age-old Tsargrad dream foundered on the shoals of revolution.[30]

Or did it? Read closely, the message-in-a-bottle of the Russian revolutionary fleet betrays more than a passing resemblance to old-regime policy memoranda on the Ottoman Straits. Like Kerensky, the revolutionary sailors of Sevastopol and Odessa wanted to have it both ways. As Russian patriots, they remained livid that "Turkey closed the Straits during the Italian and Balkan wars" (they were mistaken on the latter conflict, which is itself suggestive about popular Russian opinion on the subject), in an undeclared act of war "which caused monstrous damage to Russia." Though proudly informing the "Turkish Nation" that their revolutionary brethren in Petrograd had "renounced Constantinople," these Red sailors still wanted it to be known that "we can under no circumstances allow that the Bosphorus and Dardanelles fall into the hands of the Germans, because then Russia would fall under German influence." Sounding like Churchill and his British cabinet colleagues in asserting that "Germany forced Turkey into this war" out of her own imperial interests in the Near East, the authors betrayed a willfully naive understanding of Ottoman politics to match their lack of self-awareness. For how, aside from the renunciation of Sazonov's negotiated claim on Constantinople, did the demands of these revolutionaries (the expulsion of German personnel from Turkey, and a guarantee of unfettered Russian Straits access) differ from traditional tsarist foreign policy in their essentially bullying tone toward the Ottoman Empire?[31]

There was a confusion of ends and means here, typical of all revolutionary movements but no less interesting for that. For if the Black Sea sailor-revolutionaries, like Kerensky and his colleagues in the soviet, truly wanted to win the war, why had they fired Kolchak and emasculated the naval command structure? Having weakened Russia's hitherto dominant Black Sea Fleet to the point where it could barely function, what position were these sailors in to be making demands of the Ottoman government? By blaming the war on German imperialist aims in Turkey, meanwhile, these benighted ideologues were merely reprising themes first cooked up by Russian army intelligence to undermine Turkish fighting morale so that Yudenich could conquer the country. Now, the aim of the revolutionaries' similar Ottoman agitprop was—what exactly? To convince the Young Turks to declare war on Germany, their own benefactor and paymaster? As the message in the bottle concluded its pitch to the Turks, democratic nations everywhere, "above all free America," were now taking the war to Germany, so a free Turkey should too. Here was a dream even less realistic than that of conquering Tsargrad.[32]

Alone among the political factions competing for power in revolutionary Russia, the Bolsheviks avoided such confusion over foreign policy. Not for Lenin the tortuous twists and turns required of Kerensky, to beatify a war plainly waged by Russia for imperial gain as some kind of crusade for democracy and against German autocracy and imperialism. Lenin's promise of peace, land, and bread may have been two-thirds cynical (he had no bread to give, and no intention of letting peasants keep their land, which he wished to nationalize), but the "peace" part was real: Lenin really did want to end the war, even if it meant surrendering to the Germans. If this meant giving up on Russia's juicier war aims ("We don't want the Dardanelles!" was one Bolshevik slogan), so be it. If it meant no more pretense of standing side-by-side with "democratic" allies such as Britain, France, and "free America," fine—they were all imperialists anyway. If asking the enemy for a ceasefire meant exposing oneself to the charge of being a German agent, that was a small price to pay for ending an "imperialist war" and beginning the world revolution. Alone among Russia's revolutionaries, that is, Lenin wanted a revolution in foreign policy, a true break with the policies of the old regime.

By fall 1917, things were moving Lenin's way in Russia. A feud between Kerensky and the latest commander in chief, Kornilov, which broke out in late August, led to a fatal breach between the government and the army. On August 30/September 12, those few Bolsheviks still stewing in prison after a second failed Bolshevik putsch in July were released in a general amnesty (Lenin, having fled to Finland, had been spared imprisonment). This allowed the party to throw its full energy into elections to the soviet in Moscow and Petrograd on September 19 and 25/October 2 and 8, 1917, attaining majorities in both for the first time. True, with the Socialist Revolutionaries dominant in the countryside, the Bolsheviks stood no chance in the nationwide parliamentary poll scheduled for November. But Lenin cared little for such niceties. With Kerensky and the Socialist Revolutionaries floundering, with the Mensheviks hamstrung by their own principles, which required the revolution to pass a "bourgeois-parliamentary" stage before the proletarian dictatorship could commence, the Bolsheviks were the one party with a plan: end the war now. As a political platform, it might not have won the assent of a majority of Russians, the bulk of whom still hoped for victory over Germany. But it was more than enough cause for overthrowing Kerensky's government.

In October 1917, the Germans, having followed Sun Tzu's advice for most of the year—failing to interfere with the Russian armies as they destroyed themselves—resumed their advance along the Baltic coast, seizing several islands in the Gulf of Riga and then Riga itself. The Russians evacuated Tallinn too—the last armed stronghold between the Germans and Petrograd. Kerensky, still minister of war, ordered reinforcements sent to the front on October 9/22, only to be ignored by garrison committees, which blamed him for sacking Kornilov, among other sins. Isolated, despised by Russian patriots and antiwar revolutionaries alike, Kerensky hunkered down in the Winter Palace, preparing for the Bolshevik putsch he and everyone else in Petrograd knew was coming. Lenin had, by now, returned from Finland (to this day no one knows when and how); on October 10/23 he convened the Bolshevik Central Committee to vote on whether or not to strike. To Lenin's chagrin,

Trotsky tabled a motion to delay the revolution for two weeks, until the convening of a new Congress of Soviets could furnish a plausible pretext for a putsch. Trotsky's motion carried, 10–2. And so it was not until October 25/ November 6, 1917, that armed Bolshevik loyalists fanned out across Petrograd, occupying key choke points one by one in a putsch so quietly conducted that few Russians even knew it was happening. With the army having no remaining interest in backing Kerensky, the only resistance came from Guards of the Winter Palace, where the Provisional Government was still sitting (Kerensky himself, pleased to finally have a pretext to crush the Bolsheviks by force, had slipped out of town in a car borrowed from an American diplomat, hoping to raise a loyal army at the front).* Just past 2:00 a.m. on October 26/ November 7, 1917, the cabinet was taken under arrest, with a Red Guard stopping the clock to mark the moment (the clock still reads 2:10 to this day).

It took several more weeks for the Bolsheviks to secure Moscow and the other urban centers of European Russia, and five more years for them to reconquer the rest of the tsarist domains. But the revolution in Russian foreign policy was immediate. On November 8/21, 1917, the Second Congress of Soviets passed a Decree on Peace, written up on Lenin's instructions, a kind of declaration of universal ceasefire in the world war (the idea being that, following popular revolutions, all the other belligerents would lay down their arms too). Transmitted to diplomatic envoys on November 9/22, 1917, Lenin's Decree on Peace was declared dead on arrival by the Entente powers, which viewed Lenin as a German agent. Three days later, Lenin transmitted his peace decree to German military headquarters on the eastern front (Germany having no diplomats in Russia to give it to), where his request for a unilateral ceasefire (as it was there interpreted) met with a far friendlier reception. The German Foreign Office, after all, had sent Lenin to Russia in April with precisely this outcome in mind. It was almost too perfect: next day, Kurt Riezler, Berlin's liaison to the Bolshevik Foreign Mission in Stockholm, sent a circular to all German diplomats abroad asking them to "conceal their glee" at public

---

* Failing utterly to galvanize support at the front for a counterrevolutionary strike to topple the Bolsheviks, Kerensky left Russia; he would never see Petrograd again. Fifty years later, he was invited to give lectures at Stanford University—on the Russian Revolution. He expressed no regrets about his own role in it.

receptions.[33] For Germany, Lenin's seizure of power was the best news since the war began in 1914.

For the Sublime Porte, the news was hardly less momentous. After a year in which Russia's Black Sea Fleet had given the Turks one scare after another, Constantinople was finally safe, and the Army of the Caucasus, threatening in the spring to crash down into central Anatolia, would now be lucky to survive the winter intact. But even as the age-old threat from the north was receding, the empire's southern defenses were under greater pressure than ever before. With the Ottoman high command mesmerized by the drama in Russia, it was time for Britain to make its move.

CHAPTER 15

TURNING THE ARABS

He would like British troops to help him, but he did not want any help
from the French or anything to do with them.

—FEISAL BIN AL-HUSSEIN,

son of the sherif of Mecca, remarks as reported by a British agent,

January 30, 1917[1]

NINETEEN SEVENTEEN WAS A CURIOUS YEAR in Ottoman military history. The Caucasian front, arguably the most active single theater in the entire world war in 1916, was so quiet that, to this day, scarcely anything is known about it. The Ottoman Third Army, after being all but destroyed in the campaigning of spring and summer 1916, was content to rest and regroup as revolution tore through Russia. On the Russian side, the mutinous sentiment so prominent on the European front was mostly absent among the troops occupying northeastern Turkey, owing to resilient morale in the still-undefeated Army of the Caucasus. Yudenich did order the evacuation of Muş in May 1917, but this was a political gesture to please the Tiflis Soviet and unrelated to anything the Turks did. In the official history of the war published by the Turkish General Staff, the entirety of 1917 merits all of 20 pages out of 1,660, and in these the Russians are hardly mentioned.[2]

It was not only Russia's strategic meltdown, however, that explains the reticence of the Turkish official history to discuss 1917. On the southern fronts, the year was marked by a reversal of fortune just as dramatic as the turnabout in the north. The years 1915 and 1916 had seen the Ottoman Empire summon unexpected reserves of strength as Liman and Kemal saw off the Allied thrust at the Dardanelles and Gallipoli, and then captured the entirety of Townshend's expeditionary force at Kut. Even as Enver was celebrating his uncle's triumph in Mesopotamia, however, the seeds of Britain's eventual victory were being sown.

In retrospect, it is not hard to see the decisive turning point in the British-Ottoman war: the second Suez offensive of August 1916. Although Kress had once again been able to perform a logistical miracle in crossing the Sinai desert with a large force including both machine-gun and artillery batteries, the Turks were checked nearly thirty miles short of the canal the second time around, and would not get a sniff at Suez again. In December 1916, the Egyptian Expeditionary Force captured El-Arish and Rafa, establishing firm British control of Sinai, which meant the railway from Kantara could now be extended eastward across the desert. In a symbolic changing of the guard, by early 1917 the British-built Sinai railway passed right on by the single-track line the Germans and Turks, under head engineer Heinrich August Meissner Pasha (the same who had built the Hejaz railway), had been building southwest from Jenin and Beersheba. It would now be Cairo threatening Ottoman Palestine, with British Egypt safe from attack.[3]

Meanwhile, Hussein's nationalist-cum-Islamist rebellion at Mecca, though failing to catch fire behind Ottoman lines, was beginning to threaten Ottoman communications in the northern Hejaz, on the right flank of the British forces advancing toward Palestine. Because the so-called Arab revolt left such a powerful political residue in the postwar Middle East, it is worth pausing for a moment to disentangle exactly what it was, and was not. First, as noted already, Hussein's call to arms failed utterly to galvanize Arab opinion in the Ottoman Empire as a whole, as the vast majority of Arab Muslim soldiers continued serving the sultan loyally. There was no more than a handful of defections in the officer corps, and not a single Arab regiment deserted to the enemy. Led by Hussein's second-eldest son, Abdullah, Arab warriors loyal to the sherif did quickly overpower the small Ottoman garrison in Mecca, along with Taif, the "summer capital" in the mountains nearby. With the aid of British naval gunnery, Abdullah's men were able to seize the Red Sea port of Jedda, which became the main logistical hub of the budding military alliance between British Cairo and Mecca. But, so far, this was it. Medina, the largest city in the Hejaz and supplied by rail from Damascus, had held firm. The final Arab attempt to storm Medina, led by Hussein's third son, Feisal, in early October 1916, was "pummeled" by the Turks, whereupon the remnants of Feisal's force withdrew into the mountains near Rabegh. As against the crushing Russian advance in eastern Anatolia in 1916, the Arab revolt had amounted to a mere pinprick, a minor distraction.

Then, at the very moment when the Arab revolt was poised to collapse, T. E. Lawrence took a hand—at least, so goes the legend. While correct about the timing of the key moment, the traditional story (most famously told in the David Lean epic *Lawrence of Arabia*) conceals the nature of the critical decisions then taken. In fact, Lawrence was a mere twenty-eight-year-old army captain when he first visited Jedda on October 16, 1916. Although he was a perceptive intelligence officer, he was a man of little importance in either Cairo or the Hejaz, attached while on army leave to a mission led by Ronald Storrs, the Oriental secretary in Cairo, more because Storrs liked his company than for any other reason. (Storrs referred to him as "little Lawrence," knowing that his friend had been turned down for regular army service as too short.) It was thus largely by accident that Lawrence first met both Abdullah, who had come to Jedda to plead with the British for more war matériel, and Colonel Eduard Brémond, head of a large French military mission to Jedda and the Hejaz—larger than anything the British had contributed—consisting of 42 officers and 983 men. Hussein was apparently taken with the detailed knowledge, gleaned from his keen map-reading in the Hotel Savoy in Cairo, that Lawrence displayed in a quick verbal résumé of the regional order of battle ("Is this man God, to know everything?" Abdullah was said to ask in wonderment). Impressed, Abdullah accepted Lawrence's self-invitation to visit the Hejaz as his personal guest, so as to be able to provide the British authorities in Cairo with a firsthand report on the military situation there. This was a real career coup for Lawrence, though the resulting visit to Feisal's camp near Rabegh—lasting all of twenty-six hours—would not have mattered much in the end were it not for his second encounter in Jedda, which had even more far-reaching consequences.[4]

This was with Brémond, though the Frenchman himself seems not to have taken notice of Lawrence. Off the record and out of Abdullah's hearing, the Frenchman let slip a chance remark while he was hosting his British counterparts for dinner, to the effect that "the Arabs must not be allowed to take Medina." Believing France's allies, not unreasonably in view of the Sazonov-Sykes-Picot Agreement negotiated earlier that year on the partition of the Ottoman Empire, to share her basic approach to the Arab question, Brémond inadvertently revealed here French concerns that the "Arab revolt," if it ever spread north of the Hejaz, might prejudice British or (especially) French territorial claims on Palestine, Syria, and Mesopotamia. As a matter of policy, this meant that Brémond wanted to send regular French and British troops, as many as ten thousand, into the Hejaz, both to bail out Hussein's floundering "revolt" and to ensure that there was no ambiguity about who was really in charge of it. Without knowing it, Brémond had blundered right into a trap, offering up what we would today call a perfect "sound bite" for anyone listening in who was unscrupulous enough to betray his confidence.[5]

Lawrence was such a man. The real genius of this young intelligence officer, contrary to his later reputation as a field man par excellence, lay in his ability to read and master the British imperial bureaucracy. As Storrs had informed Lawrence on the trip over from Cairo, Henry McMahon, the high commissioner in Egypt, was opposed to sending British troops into the Hejaz for fear of political fallout with Arabs and Muslims more generally. The Koran made perfectly clear that Mecca and Medina, the two holiest cities of Islam, were off-limits to infidels. Perhaps more important, Lawrence knew that McMahon's view was shared by his good friend Gilbert Clayton, director of intelligence in Cairo and founder of the Arab Bureau, whose influence reached into both the Egyptian Expeditionary Force (Clayton was McMahon's liaison officer to General Murray) and the Egyptian Army in the Sudan (he was also liaison to Sir Reginald Wingate—sirdar, or governor-general, of Khartoum). Of the three men running Britain's Ottoman war on the Syrian-Palestine front—Murray, McMahon, and Wingate—only Wingate favored sending ground troops into Arabia, though both Storrs and Clayton thought he could be worked on, in part because of the general wave of anti-French sentiment overwhelming the British in the wake of the Somme offensive, launched by General Haig in July to draw off pressure from the French at Verdun (the battle was just now drawing to its bitter end, having cost Britain nearly 500,000 casualties). Leveraging his brief intelligence trip for all it was worth, Lawrence reported first to Wingate in Khartoum on November 7, 1916, that all Feisal's men really needed was "moral and material support," and that any French advisers Brémond might wish to send inland to the Hejaz would have to do without a British military escort. Although Wingate was not entirely convinced, he agreed to limit his own contribution to a brigade and to hold it offshore, to be deployed only in case of emergency.

Back in Cairo, Lawrence and Clayton upped the ante. Having learned that Wingate had been named to replace McMahon as high commissioner, the two men agreed to scuttle Wingate's plans to send a brigade to reinforce the French military mission at Jedda by blackening Brémond's name. In a soon-to-be-famous policy memorandum penned shortly after he met with Clayton on November 16, 1916, Lawrence played the naive idealist, declaring that the Arabs were "deeply grateful" for British support and would remain "very good friends while we respect their independence," but warned that "if the British with or without the Sherif's support landed at Rabegh an armed force strong enough to" threaten Medina, Feisal's Arab army "would, I am convinced, say 'we are betrayed' and scatter to their tents." He then went in for the kill, informing British policymakers that Brémond had insisted that "the Arabs must not take Medina," thus showing that the French had no real desire for the Arab revolt to succeed. Shrewdly, Clayton submitted Lawrence's manipulative memo to General Murray, knowing that the EEF commander would be pleased to see his own views confirmed so eloquently by an officer in the field, while *not* sending it to Wingate, who might have objected. Murray promptly forwarded Lawrence's memo on to General William Robertson, the chief of the Imperial General Staff in London, noting in his own gloss that Feisal and Lawrence were implacably opposed to the "dispatch of white troops to Arabia" favored by the French. Over the next few days, the name of Lawrence was on the lips of everyone in the War Council in London, his rising influence as oracle of the Arabs so apparent that Wingate began denying that he had proposed something so objectionable as sending troops to support Brémond, and personally advocated entrusting the new, low-footprint military liaison mission to Rabegh to—Lawrence! Thoroughly defeated by a man he did not even know to be an opponent, poor Colonel Brémond, after

Lawrence's leak was passed on to the high command on the western front, found himself being rebuked in a brutal telegram sent by France's commander in chief, Marshal Joseph Joffre, for suggesting that France did not desire that the Arabs conquer Medina from the Turks.[6]

In this way T. E. Lawrence (or rather Gilbert Clayton, probably the real mastermind of the affair) adumbrated, in the course of a few decisive weeks in November 1916, the political approach Britain would take to the post-Ottoman settlement vis-à-vis France, namely, that an autonomously generated "Arab revolt," led by Feisal on behalf of the sherif of Mecca, was contributing materially to the Allied war effort and must therefore be granted due deference in the peace settlement to come (at least in territories claimed by France in the Sazonov-Sykes-Picot Agreement). This, and not some innate capacity for reading the Arab mind or knack for guerrilla warfare, is what catapulted Lawrence to the top of the British policymaking firmament.

Lawrence exploited his newfound influence to the fullest, helped along by a series of fortuitous accidents on the way. Feisal, praised to the skies by Lawrence ("he is magnificent"; "a real ripper"), almost immediately fell on his face, getting trapped on the wrong side of a Turkish mounted patrol in November 1916, whereupon his Arab soldiers fled in panic from their mountain lair down toward the coast at Yenbo, where Feisal hoped the British could send the fleet to rescue him. In an ironic turnabout, Lawrence found himself meeting with none other than Brémond in Yenbo, who promptly fired off a cable to Wingate in Cairo asking for British and French troops to land so as to "save Sherif and his Arabs in spite of themselves." But the Frenchman's apparent revenge was short-lived, as the pursuing Turks turned back from Yenbo as soon as they saw the British warships in port, obviating the need for reinforcements. With the Turks having retreated back inland to Medina, the British were able to land a small contingent of armed Arabs (not including Feisal) ashore at Wejh, a port town north of Yenbo, demonstrating yet again that British naval power dwarfed anything the Hashemites of Mecca had to offer. In a slightly embarrassing illustration of this fact, Feisal had pointedly insisted on sleeping on board a British warship docked in the port for much of December 1916 until the Turkish threat to Yenbo had passed. Lawrence, who had standing orders to return to Cairo, could have been ruined by

Feisal's debacle. Instead, Feisal was so grateful for his friend's indulgence and flattery that he sent off a cable to Cairo (by way of Jedda) demanding that Lawrence not be allowed to leave him. For good measure Feisal, clearly coached by his friend, told a British interlocutor in January 1917 that, while

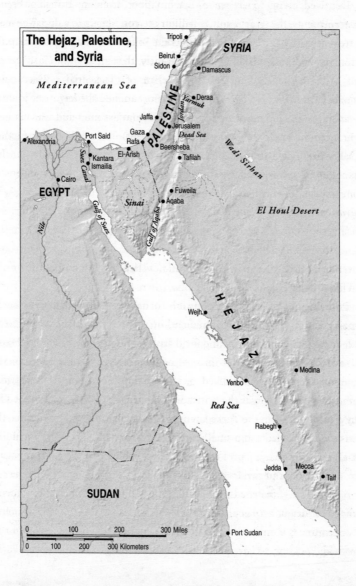

The Hejaz, Palestine, and Syria

"he would like British troops to help him . . . he did not want any help from the French or to have anything to do with them." Lawrence had charmed this Hashemite prince so thoroughly that abject failure seemed only to bind them closer together.[7]

Deprived, owing to Lawrence's machinations, from any British or French reinforcements, the Arab revolt, in military terms, remained a dud. The main strategic priority in Cairo for 1917 was the invasion of Palestine, where the Ottomans had pulled back to a defensive line stretching from Gaza, on the coast, to Beersheba, about thirty miles inland. The Sinai railway, being extended from Kantara by British engineers, reached the key oasis town of El-Arish in January, allowing Murray's EEF to mass men and war matériel right up to the border of Ottoman Palestine. By now the EEF had more than 200,000 troops massing in the theater, a real achievement considering that this required upward of 1.2 million gallons of water a day to be transported from the canal, which required the use of thousands of camels along with railway wagons. After they had crossed the Sinai desert, motivation for conquering the watered oases of Gaza and/or Beersheba was not hard to come by. As one British lieutenant noted after catching his first glimpse of cultivated Palestine, seeing this "delightful country" was a revelation after "the miles and miles of bare sand."[8]

If morale on the British side was robust, however, it was equally so in the opposite camp. Having passed from the offensive to the defensive, the Ottoman army was now fighting to defend an integral part of the empire, and a particularly strategic area at that. Although there were only about eleven thousand infantrymen stretched out along the thirty-mile front between Gaza and Beersheba against an invading force at least three times that size, they had dug trenches and prepared a strong defensive position under the ever-competent leadership of Kress von Kressenstein. The Turks had 150 guns, achieving rough parity with the EEF (although the British had poison gas), and a thousand cavalrymen, allowing Kress some mobility if he needed to reinforce a threatened area. Choosing to ignore Beersheba, Murray launched a furious artillery barrage against Gaza on March 26, 1917, which to all appearances stunned the Turks into silence. Believing the enemy to be beaten and possibly to have pulled back northward up the coast toward Jaffa,

Murray sent in his cavalry to reconnoiter the town, only to learn that the defenders had not given an inch. Over the next two days, EEF infantrymen attacked in waves, only to be beaten back. The fighting was brutal. As one German officer recalled, "Every hedge, every house was fought for." In all, Murray's side suffered some four thousand casualties—about twice as many as the Turks—including fifteen hundred dead left behind to be buried by the enemy. Strangely, Murray composed a cable to the War Office in London claiming victory in the battle, despite the fact that Gaza had not fallen.*[9]

In a curious coincidence, Lawrence got his first taste of combat on the first day of the Gaza battle, about five hundred miles away to the southeast. This was at Aba el Naam, a station of the Hejaz railway about forty miles north of Medina. Having effectively (though not publicly) given up on Feisal, in mid-March 1917 Lawrence had trekked inland to the camp of Abdullah, Hussein's second-eldest son, at Wadi Ais. The purpose of his mission was to convince Abdullah's Arab guerrillas to attack the Hejaz railway, so as to prevent the Turks from using it to bring troops up from Medina to reinforce Kress in Palestine. Back in February, British intelligence had intercepted a telegram from Djemal, in Damascus, to Medina, ordering the evacuation of this second-holiest city of Islam (and largest city in the Hejaz). What Lawrence did not know was that Djemal, strongly rebuked for the idea of abandoning the holy places by Ali Haidar Pasha, the Hashemite prince the CUP had chosen to replace Hussein as sherif, had sent a second telegram rescinding the first order. Still, the Hejaz railway junction at Aba el Naam was a good target, an important test of the strategic potential of Lawrence's guerrilla warfare strategy, and not least of his skill at cajoling the Hashemites into actually fighting. If they succeeded in cutting off the railway, then maybe there was something in the "Arab revolt" after all.

The results were mixed. Abdullah, like Feisal, proved a disappointment: he refused to take part. Still, on March 25, 1917, Lawrence was able, by politicking among the other sheikhs, to convince about eight hundred Arabs to promise to join him (although only three hundred actually followed him

---

* Catching wind of this, the Turks dropped a leaflet behind enemy lines, taunting Murray that "you beat us at communiqués, but we beat you at Gaza."

when it counted the next day). Trained by a far less famous British officer, Major Herbert Garland, in the art of laying explosives under rail track in such a way as to detonate when a train came through, Lawrence was able to mine the southern approach to the junction at a strategic spot covered by two machine guns, while sending a team of Arabs to mine the northern side too (with less success). He then prepared an ambush, with Arab gunners hidden in the hills on all sides opening fire simultaneously. It worked, up to a point. The main water tank was blown up, and the Turks, taken by surprise, lost seventy casualties and thirty prisoners, out of a garrison of about four hundred. But the Turks held the junction. Although Lawrence's own mine detonated as planned, the Arab machine gunners covering it fled, allowing the Turks to repair the tracks, unmolested. As Lawrence reported with uncharacteristic modesty, "We did not wholly fail."[10]

Even had Lawrence succeeded in blowing a hole in the Hejaz line, it would not have had much impact on the simultaneous invasion of Palestine. True, it was not his fault that Djemal had changed his mind about evacuating from Medina, or that the British had failed to take Gaza even though he had not reinforced it with troops from the Hejaz. Nor was it Lawrence's fault that Murray's EEF failed *again* to break through in the Second Battle of Gaza, waged April 17–19, 1917, despite deploying poison gas for the first time in the Ottoman theater, and deploying a flotilla of warships along the coast to give naval covering fire to the attackers. If the Turks were not going to buckle against the best that Britain's regular troops had to offer on land and sea—as, indeed, they had not done at Gallipoli or Kut—then it was hard to imagine that Lawrence's on-again, off-again coalitions of Arab guerrillas were going to put much of a scare into Djemal or Kress.

Nonetheless, developments elsewhere in the war were finally turning in Britain's favor in spring 1917, and these would soon be felt in Palestine and Arabia. The February Revolution would, by the end of the year, wreak havoc with the Russian war effort, but in the short run it actually helped the Entente cause in one potentially decisive way: easing the entry of the United States into the war, by removing the tsarist autocracy and thereby enabling the argument that the Allies fought for shared democratic ideals (Russia was now, as President Woodrow Wilson put it, a "fit partner for a League of Honor"). The

Germans had brought this one on themselves, of course, by unleashing "unrestricted submarine warfare" and then foolishly seeking to sabotage any possible U.S. intervention before it even happened by wiring to Mexico City on January 16, 1917—via a U.S. embassy cable!—with a promise that, if Mexico declared war on the United States, she would receive Texas, Arizona, and New Mexico in the postwar settlement. This soon-notorious "Zimmermann telegram," coupled with the advent of "democracy" in Russia, finally gave Wilson the political cover he needed to get a declaration of war on Germany (although not yet her co-belligerents) out of the U.S. Congress on April 6, 1917.[11]

Compounding the effect of the U.S. entry into the war, at least in propaganda terms, was an Allied public relations coup that occurred almost simultaneously. After the first British assault on Gaza had been—barely—repulsed on March 28, 1917, Djemal Pasha ordered the evacuation of Jaffa, forty miles north along the coast, for security reasons. There was nothing unusual about this decision in and of itself: Gaza too had been evacuated back in February prior to the British assault on it, as indeed commanders have always done with population centers located near active military fronts to clear a line of retreat for the defending army in case a breakthrough occurs. The trouble in Jaffa began with the timing, during Passover, which inevitably raised the hackles of the city's large Jewish population, concentrated in the northern district known as Tel Aviv. Jews were not singled out in Djemal's evacuation order: most of the city's Arabs (Muslims and Christians alike) were deported too. In fact, protests from local Jewish leaders were strong enough that Djemal actually gave Jews an extra week to get their affairs in order before leaving on April 6—the same day, as it turned out, that the United States entered the First World War. In the event, some ten thousand Ottoman subjects were deported from Jaffa into inland, desert Syria in April 1917, of which about one-third were Jewish.* It was not the finest hour for Djemal or the Ottomans, but in the context of deportations in the empire or elsewhere during the war, it was rather a minor affair.

This is not, however, what the world would be told about Jaffa. Little noticed or reported at the time, Djemal's deportations from this small yet

---

* Some 750 Russian Jews had been deported from Jaffa back in 1914 as potential security risks.

strategic town on the coast of Palestine were transformed, in the course of May 1917, into a *cause célèbre* of the world Zionist cause. The key figure in the transformation was Sir Mark Sykes—the same who had teamed up with Georges Picot and Sergei Sazonov in 1916 to partition the Ottoman Empire. On April 27, 1917, Sykes, in Cairo to adjudicate the conflicting claims on Syria between France and the Hashemite Arabs, met with Aaron Aaronsohn, an Ottoman Jewish agronomist who, in addition to consulting for Djemal on the Syrian locust plague and matters to do with lubricating oils, ran a spy network for the Allies in Palestine. Informed by Aaronsohn that "Televiv has been sacked" and that "10,000 Palestinian Jews are now without home or food," Sykes passed on the story to the *Jewish Chronicle*, a Zionist newspaper in London, and to leading Zionists in New York whose names were given him by Aaronsohn. Within days the story, suitably amplified in the retelling, was on the cover of the *New York Times* ("Cruelties to Jews Deported in Jaffa"). By summer most Western Zionists, previously divided in their loyalties between the two wartime coalitions—Berlin was still home to the World Zionist Executive, and Russia had long been seen as the greatest enemy of world Jewry and Zionism—were beginning to shift decisively toward the Entente powers, which now, buttressed by the United States and a Russia hopefully reinvigorated by democratic rule, seemed poised to win the war.[12]

Reinforcing these trends was the advent of a stronger coalition government in London that was not only ferociously committed to winning the war, but wanted to do so by shifting its focus eastward—and was more than willing to embrace the Zionist cause as part of the package. With the Liberals discredited in no small part by the disasters at Gallipoli and Kut, Prime Minister Asquith resigned along with his entire cabinet in December 1916—except Secretary of State for War David Lloyd George, who promptly put together a coalition with the Unionist-Conservative Party, with Arthur Balfour, a former prime minister, taking office as foreign secretary. With Grey and Asquith gone, Churchill in political exile following his scapegoating for Gallipoli, and Kitchener dead,* the deck was cleared for a new approach to

---

* In a curious coincidence, Kitchener perished at sea while on a mission to Russia when his ship ran over a mine in the North Sea on June 5, 1916—nearly simultaneous to the outbreak of the Arab revolt, which his own scheming had helped bring to fruition.

the war, and Lloyd George made no secret of his own preference: an Eastern strategy focused on conquering the Ottoman Empire. By spring 1917, as Maurice Hankey noted, everyone in the cabinet had "come completely round to Ll[oyd] G[eorge]'s view ... that it is necessary to devote our main efforts against Turkey." The prime minister's embrace of Zionism, manifest in the Balfour Declaration issued by the new foreign secretary on November 2, 1917, pointing the way to "the establishment in Palestine of a national home for the Jewish people" (while also promising to protect "the civil and religious rights of existing non-Jewish communities in Palestine") was an important part of this new strategic emphasis on the Ottoman theater—although not necessarily more important than Britain's possibly contradictory promises to France, Sherif Hussein, and the Arabs.[13]

Of course, before Lloyd George's Eastern strategy could amount to anything, there was still the nagging problem that Britain had, to date, mostly been humiliated in the Ottoman theater. Gallipoli and Kut remained bylines for incompetence, and First and Second Gaza did not seem to portend much better for the Palestinian front. In the wake of British military performance so far, one could certainly understand the hesitation of Arab tribesmen— including, notably, Hussein's sons Abdullah and Feisal—to tie their own fates to that of their paymasters in Cairo by actually risking their lives in battle.

Just when all hope seemed to have been lost, however, news came in from Mesopotamia that did a great deal to restore British prestige with Arabs and across the greater Near East more generally. After the humiliation at Kut, the reorganized Tigris Corps (III Indian Army Corps) had gone back to essentials, focusing for most of the rest of 1916 on logistics and supply. With Townshend a prisoner of the Turks and Aylmer and Gorringe having displayed only incompetence, the high command brought in an outsider, Lieutenant General Sir Frederick Stanley Maude, to right the ship. Son of a Crimean War hero and veteran of campaigns stretching from the Boer War to the western front and Gallipoli, Maude was a military man through and through. Paying little attention to the politics of Sykes-Picot and British intentions toward the

---

Churchill reacted to his (short-lived) political eclipse by going to fight on the western front in 1916, taking a commission to command the 6th Battalion of Royal Scots Fusiliers. Characteristically bold to the point of recklessness, he made thirty-six personal forays into no-man's-land before tiring of the slog and returning to London.

Arab world, Maude simply got on with the job at hand, modernizing the port of Basra, overseeing the construction of hospitals and ship repair facilities, and quickly setting his engineers to work building roads up the Tigris toward Amara—including one raised aboveground for thirty-six miles to hedge against flooding—along with seventy new bridges, and even a rail line to Nasiriyah. The roads and bridges would not only be used for walking, either: Maude had ordered a thousand Ford vans from the United States, of which seven hundred arrived by winter. Survivors of the Kut campaign were given time to recover their health, and reinforcements began to pour in from India. By December 1916, the Tigris Corps counted more than 100,000 active-duty troops, with 45,000 infantry, 3,500 cavalry, and 174 field guns available for the main Tigris front targeting Kut and Baghdad. Facing them was an Ottoman force, Halil "Kut" Pasha's XVIII Corps, which numbered only about 11,000 effectives.[14]

The Turks were, however, extremely well dug in below Kut, as Aylmer and Gorringe had discovered the previous spring, and Maude would now learn in turn. One fortified position at the Khaidiri bend in the Tigris took the Thirteenth Division nearly ten days of "strenuous fighting," January 9–19, 1917, to reduce. Another bend, the Dahra, likewise took ten days for the entire III Corps to seize in mid-February, despite enjoying a 20–1 advantage over the Turks in guns. As one British soldier wrote of the Turks at Dahra, "Although they are our enemies we cannot but admire them for the magnificent show they put up." The trenches at Sannaiyat were almost up to German standards on the western front, such that Seventh Division troops spent three days rehearsing with a mock-up constructed from aerial reconnaissance before storming them (they failed anyway). The Third Battle of Kut proved to be just as brutal and drawn-out as the Second, lasting, through fits and starts related to the weather, from mid-December 1916 to February 22, 1917, when Maude's men at last bridged the Tigris above Kut only to find that Halil Pasha had retreated toward Baghdad, some hundred miles upriver.[15]

Based on recent form in the theater, there was no reason to expect that the battle of Baghdad would be any less brutally difficult. And yet this time, British pursuit was swift enough to obviate much chance of organizing a proper defense. Halil Pasha, it turned out, had thrown all his cards into Kut, failing

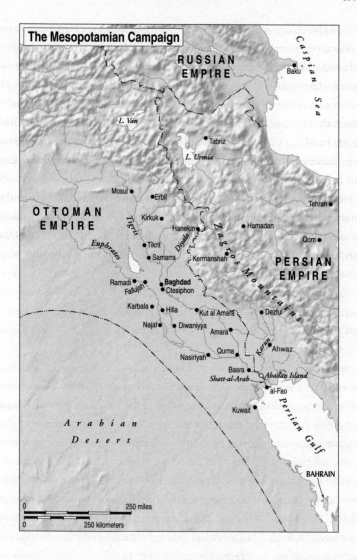

The Mesopotamian Campaign

to prepare any serious fortifications outside Baghdad. Surprisingly, he had even abandoned the old lines at Ctesiphon (Salman Pak), meaning that Kut had been, effectively, the last prepared defensive position before Baghdad. The Turks had also lost nearly seven thousand men taken prisoner alone at Kut, leaving behind only the skeleton of an army (although the British may not have been sure of this, having overestimated the size of the Ottoman force at Kut at twenty thousand). Meanwhile, the Ottoman XIII Corps, sent by Enver on a fool's errand into Persia back in summer 1916, was still kicking its heels at Hamadan, with word of the Kut debacle reaching Ali Ihsan Pasha too late for him to relieve Halil. Reaching Baghdad on February 26, 1917, with the British—using their riverine fleet on the Tigris as a kind of "super cavalry"— in hot pursuit, Halil concluded that the city was indefensible. Thinking in terms of strategy and prestige, Enver overruled him and ordered that Baghdad be held. Halil did his best, ordering the digging of trenches along an eight-mile front along the banks of the Diyala River, a tributary that meets the Tigris south of Baghdad. But he had little time: the gun emplacements were not even finished by the time the British arrived on March 7, 1917. Three days later, the East Lancashires of the Thirty-Eighth Brigade bridged the Diyala under heavy fire. With British cavalry patrols already circling the railway station—terminus of the famed (though not yet finished) railway from Constantinople and Berlin—Halil gave up the ghost, ordering what remained of XVIII Corps to abandon the city at 8:00 p.m. on March 10, 1917. Baghdad had fallen.[16]

In military terms, the battle of Baghdad was something of an anticlimax after all the drama at Kut. The actual British conquest, indeed, was rather a sordid affair, marked by hours of looting and arson, with most of Maude's men—though happy to find fresh fruit, which they had not seen in months— generally disappointed that this fabled city of the Orient was in reality a jumble of "narrow, filthy, evil-smelling streets . . . blocked in places by tumble-down houses and heaps of garbage." Even the large buildings taken over by the occupiers for administration were found to be "indescribably dirty and verminous." The bad impression was, moreover, mutual, as Maude, a man with little patience for ritual, entered the city with little ceremony and made no grand public pronouncement.*

Still, the symbolism of Maude's triumph was powerful. Baghdad was not only the seat of the Abbasid Caliphate from 750 to 1258 in the glory years of

---

* A statue of Maude was erected, and stood in downtown Baghdad until it was destroyed in the revolution of 1958. His fame lived on: after the 2003 war, the British headquarters in Baghdad's Green Zone was called Maude House.

Islam, but more recently the focal point of German strategy as the terminus of the kaiser's dream railway from the North Sea to the Persian Gulf. In the hands of Sir Mark Sykes, a man of more imagination (and with fewer scruples) than Maude, who was asked to draft the official policy communiqué to the Arab people, the fall of Baghdad began to sound almost biblical. After reciting the litany of woe that had ensued following the city's sack by the Mongols in 1258, especially during the Ottoman centuries when "many noble Arabs have perished in the cause of Arab freedom, at the hands of those alien rulers, the Turks," Sykes declared it "the wish, not only of my King and his peoples, but also of the great Nations with whom he is in alliance, that you should prosper even as in the past, when your lands were fertile . . . and Baghdad was one of the wonders of the world."[17]

Florid rhetoric aside, the fall of Baghdad in March 1917 was an important milestone in the collapse of the Ottoman Empire, which gave Britain desperately needed credibility at a time when the Allied cause was at low ebb in Russia and France—and in Palestine, where the EEF was just then being routed in the First Battle of Gaza. For a brief moment it even seemed that British and Russian troops might join together to finish off what remained of the Ottoman Sixth Army. In what might have been a critical strategic moment, British cavalry officers met with their Russian counterparts for the first time at Kizilrobat, on the Diyala River northeast of Baghdad, after just barely failing to encircle the Turkish XIII Corps retreating from Persia. Baratov, finally getting his act together, had ordered his Cossacks across the Mesopotamian border near Hamadan in March 1917. As if obeying some hidden geopolitical law forbidding genuine British-Russian cooperation against the Ottomans, however, Baratov's offensive ground to a halt as soon as it began, for reasons equally mysterious to the British and the Turks. Order No. 1, it turned out, had been transmitted from the Petrograd Soviet, whereupon even Baratov's hardy Kuban and Terek Cossacks formed soviets and held "endless meetings" to discuss "not only matters of supply" but what Baratov, disgusted, called "issues of a most general character." In the absence of a Russian threat that once again failed to materialize, the Turkish XIII and XVIII Corps were able to regroup between Samara and Tikrit, forming a solid defensive line below Mosul, even while the main British force was stalled in the Sunni triangle northwest of Baghdad. Although Fallujah, the next Ottoman fort on the Euphrates, and Ramadi, the Baghdad Railway station upriver from Fallujah, were both taken in late March 1917, thereafter Maude decided to hunker down at Baghdad in the torrid summer heat while he planned his next move.[18]

The momentum in the Ottoman theater now returned to Palestine, helped along by a feat of derring-do by Lawrence. Setting out into the Arabian desert from the Red Sea port of Wejh on May 9, 1917, the young British liaison officer displayed considerable courage by crossing the notoriously barren desert known to the Arabs as El Houl (the Terror) accompanied by only forty-five Arab tribesmen—not including Feisal, who trekked inland only a mile or two to say a ceremonial goodbye before returning to his politicking with the British on the coast. The party's objective was the valley of Wadi Sirhan in southern Syria, about three weeks' march away, where Lawrence hoped to enlist the Howeitat tribesmen led by Auda Abu Tayi in the war. Despite suffering all the familiar horrors of sandstorms, dehydration, and fatigue, they made it. Having—more or less—won over a pledge from Abu Tayi to join him, in early June 1917 Lawrence set out north into the Syrian desert to canvass opinion in the main oasis towns. In Azraq, he met An-Nuri Ibn Shal'an, sheikh of the camel-breeding Rwala, the most powerful Bedouin tribe in the desert region between Damascus, lower Mesopotamia, and north Arabia (Ibn Shal'an was also a ferocious warrior, rumored to have "killed with his own hands no less than 120 men"—among them two of his own brothers). Although Ibn Shal'an was less committal than Abu Tayi, the mere fact that this eccentric young Englishman had ventured so far north into enemy territory impressed him,* as it would Lawrence's superior officers in Cairo, who would later award him the Distinguished Service Order for his Syrian desert mission.[19]

Now began the third and most critical leg of Lawrence's mystery mission. A whiff of legend has always surrounded the Aqaba offensive, beginning with its origins. To begin with, seizing Aqaba was not an original idea of Lawrence's. This small port town, sited just where the Red Sea meets the Sinai peninsula to the north, was so strategic that Britain and the Ottoman Empire

---

* Unless it was the 6,000 gold sovereigns Lawrence reportedly gave him.

had nearly gone to war over it in 1906 in the so-called Aqaba crisis.* Because there was no railhead closer than Ma'an (seventy-five miles inland), it was also thinly held, with the Ottoman garrison numbering 150 in peacetime and not much larger in wartime. It was an obvious military target, obvious enough that the British had sought Sherif Hussein's approval for taking it in October 1916. As an amphibious operation, it would be a breeze compared with Gallipoli, a mere baby step up in difficulty from the seizure of Jedda, Yenbo, and Wejh on the Red Sea—indeed it was the logical next step, and widely discussed as such in Cairo all through winter 1916–17.

The reason this was *not* done was entirely owing to politics, with Lawrence, once again, playing his cards just right. In January 1917, Colonel Brémond, after first clearing the idea with the French high command, proposed a Franco-British amphibious strike on Aqaba to the new high commissioner in Cairo. Wingate was positive, but he was opposed by General Murray, then still aglow with the anti-French fervor Lawrence had whipped up (and not as yet discredited by his failures-to-come in Gaza). Helping seal the case against Brémond's proposal was Lawrence, who objected that Feisal had made clear that he wanted no help from the French. In this way Brémond's eminently sensible idea of taking Aqaba from the sea was shelved indefinitely.[†20]

Aqaba was thus still free for the taking when Lawrence set out from Wadi Sirhan on June 18, 1917, accompanied by about five hundred tribal warriors (mostly Howeitat). At Bair, the main oasis en route to Ma'an, Lawrence's party discovered that the Turks had blown three wells, failing to detonate the fourth merely because the charge had failed to go off. Realizing that the enemy was expecting his advance, Lawrence ordered a feint northward, toward the railhead at Amman, capital of present-day Jordan. The Turks responded by dispatching a relief column, 550 strong, from Ma'an. For ten days the two forces, almost equally matched, kept missing each other. Finally, at dawn on

---

* In 1905, the German engineer Heinrich August Meissner Pasha, then building the Hejaz railway, proposed to build a branch line westward to Aqaba, which would have allowed the Turks to reinforce this critical port whenever it was threatened, rather than relying on camels past the railhead at Ma'an, 118 kilometers away. Both Britain and Turkey sent troops into Sinai in 1906, and the Aqaba crisis nearly blew up into a war.

† It is true that the Turks had 12-inch guns at Aqaba pointing out toward the sea, which, in the David Lean epic film, gives Lawrence his cue for a landward operation. But there were all of two of them, which could have easily been silenced by British or French naval guns outranging them. Compared with the Dardanelles, Aqaba would have been an amphibious cakewalk.

July 2, 1917, the Arabs ambushed the Turks as they slept at Fuweila, a key pass on the road from Ma'an just forty miles from Aqaba. A hundred or so Turks escaped, with the rest killed, taken prisoner, or left for dead along a small stream bank near the battlefield. Compared with this slaughter, the actual seizure of Aqaba was "anti-climactic": the Ottoman garrison commander simply surrendered on July 6, 1917, with "barely a shot fired." To crown the victory, Lawrence now famously walked (with two Arab guides) across 150 miles of the Sinai desert, reaching Port Suez, where he reported the taking of Aqaba in time to allow the British to land troops and supplies there before the Turks returned to retake it.[21]

Although the strategic importance of the seizure of Aqaba was much smaller than chroniclers have sometimes claimed, it was still a signature achievement in guerrilla warfare, helped along (as with so much else in Lawrence's career) by exquisite timing. Since the fall of Baghdad in March, the British had lost two painful battles at Gaza; the French army had mutinied at Chemin des Dames during the Nivelle offensive on the western front; and Russia's revolution had careened from euphoria to despair, with the twilight of the liberals in May followed by the disastrous Kerensky offensive of June. When word of Lawrence's exploit at Aqaba reached Cairo and the British high command on July 9–10, 1917, the Allies were desperate for a scrap of good news, and now here it was. Compounding the effect was the recent arrival in Cairo of Sir Edmund Allenby, a formidable personality known to his troops as "Bloody Bull," to assume command of the EEF in late June following Murray's epic failures at Gaza. Invited in to brief the new commander in chief on July 12, 1917, Lawrence summoned all his eloquence to stump for the Arab cause, proposing an elaborate guerrilla campaign behind Turkish lines, on the right flank of Allenby's EEF—which, he suggested, should now resume the offensive in Palestine. Allenby, pleased to hear that someone had actually done something right in the Ottoman theater, agreed with surprising alacrity, all but gushing as he reported to London that "the advantages offered by Arab co-operation on lines proposed by Captain Lawrence are, in my opinion, of such importance that no effort should be spared to reap full benefit therefrom."[22]

These were not idle words. British subsidies for Sherif Hussein and his sons, never stingy, now ramped up dramatically. Initially put on a retainer of £50,000 a month after the revolt was declared in June 1916, Hussein had, by winter 1917, lobbied this up to £125,000; then £200,000. After Lawrence captured Allenby's imagination, British subvention of the Arab revolt would reach the astonishing total of £500,000 a month in fall 1917, the equivalent of over $20 million annually in 1917 dollars, akin to $2 billion a year today—all paid in physical gold sovereigns, the only kind of money Arabs trusted. By the end of the war, Ronald Storrs later estimated, Britain had spent some £11 million in gold on the "Arab revolt," at a time when the *entire gold reserve* of the government in Cairo totaled only £2.6 million (meaning that Hussein's retainer was ultimately paid by way of the Exchequer in London, i.e., the British taxpayer—and the American bond buyer). Little wonder that a Bedouin sheikh, asked fifty years later, after the David Lean film, whether he remembered "Lawrence of Arabia," replied crisply, "He was the man with the gold."[23]

Whether the money was wisely invested was another matter. Feisal and his thousand-odd Bedouin tribal warriors, after they were shipped to Aqaba, were given proper training for the first time by a new liaison officer, Lieutenant Colonel Pierce Charles Joyce, who, though less glamorous than Lawrence, seems to have known his business. Nonetheless, this vaunted "Arab army corps," even after being augmented by 2,500 Ottoman army veterans freed from prisoner-of-war camps, never amounted to more than a small subsidiary wing on the right flank of Allenby's EEF, and was never trusted enough by Allenby to be used in the front lines. Lawrence, sent eastward into the southern Syrian desert to raise local Bedouins to revolt, failed utterly in his main operational object, assigned by Allenby, to destroy a high-arched railway viaduct near the Yarmuk gorge, some fifteen miles west of Deraa, in order to harass Ottoman communications. Many of the Bedouin volunteers, as usual, disappeared along the way to the target. In the end, though, Lawrence's failure owed to bad luck: someone dropped a rifle, making enough noise to alert a Turkish sentry. The Arabs bolted, and Lawrence followed them.[24]

Even had Lawrence succeeded in his sabotage mission, the strategic impact would have been mooted by the fact that, by the time he reached Yarmuk in early November, the Third Battle of Gaza had already been joined—and won. Though willing to humor Lawrence's pretensions, Allenby had no intention of waiting for news from the desert before launching his Palestinian offensive (his haste may also have owed to Lloyd George's request that he take Jerusalem before Christmas as a "gift" to the war-weary British public). On October 31, the guns of the EEF opened yet another crushing artillery barrage against Gaza. This time it was a feint, as the real British thrust came inland at Beersheba, where the Australian Fourth Light Horse Brigade led a brilliant charge and captured fifteen of the seventeen wells intact, ensuring an adequate drinking supply for the EEF as it advanced into Palestine. The inland road, from Beersheba to Jerusalem, was now open for Allenby, though the bulk of Kress's force (now reorganized into a new Eighth Army) remained intact at Gaza. To be sure of his flank, Allenby had his XVI Corps double back to the coast and storm Gaza on November 2, 1917. The final Ottoman positions were overwhelmed on November 7, 1917—the same day Lawrence tried, but failed, to blow the Yarmuk bridges. With their confidence—and trust in General Kress von Kressenstein—now shaken, the Turks beat a hasty retreat north toward Jerusalem. Jaffa fell on November 16, 1917. But the Turks made a strong stand in the Judean Hills, inflicting heavy casualties on the advancing EEF in a series of fierce engagements in the second half of November. At last, on December 9, Jerusalem surrendered, allowing Allenby to make a ceremonial entry into the holy city through the Jaffa Gate—accompanied by Lawrence, who had temporarily abandoned his Arab friends to join the conqueror's suite (Allenby having apparently forgiven him for the failure at Yarmuk).[25]

In symbolic terms, the fall of Jerusalem in December 1917 was even grander, for Christians at least, than that of Baghdad in March. Crowning Allenby's triumph was the fact that, nominally at least, the Ottoman army he had defeated was now commanded by Erich von Falkenhayn, the former chief of the German General Staff, who had been sent to Turkey to assume command of a new *Yildirim* ("Lightning Bolt") Ottoman army group (called Group F by the Germans) in May. Originally intended, in Enver's conception, to reconquer Baghdad, after Allenby struck in the fall the new army group had been routed instead to Palestine, only for its three German infantry battalions and nine Turkish divisions (composed of troops returning from

Enver's deployment to Galicia) to arrive too late to affect the outcome. Falkenhayn himself reached Jerusalem only on November 6, 1917, just in time to oversee the retreat from Gaza and to surrender the city to Allenby. In a year that had seen the Entente powers endure yet more charnel-house horrors on the western front at Passchendaele, French mutinies at Chemin des Dames, the ongoing Russian collapse, and (in November 1917) the Germano-Austrian rout of Italy at Caporetto, "Jerusalem for Christmas" was the miracle Lloyd George had been hoping for, celebrated by the ringing of church bells across England.

In truth the fall of Jerusalem, no less nor more than Baghdad, was of little military significance in itself. Just as at Baghdad, the real battles had been joined and won earlier, at Beersheba and Gaza. As in Mesopotamia, the Turks had escaped with their army still intact, with no encirclement, no mass taking of prisoners. Excellent news though it was for Cairo, London, and the Entente powers more generally, the conquest of Jerusalem was far from a decisive blow against the Ottoman Empire. Indeed, just as the news came in to Constantinople, Enver was already plotting new conquests elsewhere.

CHAPTER 16

BREST-LITOVSK:
THE POISONED CHALICE

In the Ukrainian capital, where milk and honey were supposed to be
flowing freely, we cannot even get bread.

—WILHELM GROENER
to Erich Ludendorff, March 23, 1918[1]

LENIN'S SEIZURE OF POWER CAME just in time for the Ottoman Empire.
First transmitted to the Ottoman Third Army on December 3, 1917, the Russian ceasefire request became active across all Ottoman fronts on the night of
December 17–18. During the two weeks in between, the bread ration in Constantinople was cut in half from the already inadequate 180 grams a day,
which brought the peril of mass starvation that winter. Before the Bolshevik
putsch, the "revolutionary sailors" of Sevastopol were conducting regular raids
along the Turkish coastline, regular enough to scare colliers off from Zonguldak. In a flash, Lenin's ceasefire opened the prospect that coal deliveries to
Constantinople could resume, even as grain could (hopefully) be shipped
across the Black Sea from Ukraine. Turks—at least those lucky enough to
reside in the capital—might not have to starve or freeze that winter after all.[2]

The opening of the Black Sea also nipped off a burgeoning crisis in
German-Turkish relations before it reached dangerous levels. From German
headquarters, Ludendorff had warned in early December 1917, shortly before
the Russian ceasefire, that Germany could no longer spare coal for Turkey,
which added the specter of fuel shortages to the bread pinch. The Germans
had been widely blamed for the fall of Baghdad in March, with a story

making the rounds that German officers had left shortly before Halil "Kut" Pasha abandoned the city to the British. It was in part to scotch the rumor and shore up the Ottoman Empire's southern defenses that Ludendorff had sent Falkenhayn to assume command of the new Yildirim Army Group, only for the former chief of the German General Staff to endure the humiliation of surrendering Jerusalem to Allenby. Now the rumor was that Falkenhayn had allowed Allenby into the city to prevent the Christian holy places from being disturbed.[3] On top of this, Germans were being routinely blamed in the popular press for food and fuel shortages. On September 6, 1917, the greatest symbol of Germany's investment in the Ottoman Empire—Haydarpasha, the flagship station of the Berlin-Baghdad Railway—suffered a fire that engulfed ammunition, fuel, and explosives dumps and produced an explosion so colossal that it "blew out homes in Pera" on the other side of the water. Arson was widely suspected, even if no culprit was ever arrested. There was no telling what German asset might next be the target of Turkish mob rage, were shortages to persist into the winter. Now, thanks to Lenin, the increasingly unpopular Germans might be able to ship desperately needed food supplies to Constantinople by sea, whether from a friendly postwar Ukraine or from the Danube Delta in occupied Romania, where the German Admiralty established its new Black Sea naval command.[4]

On the Ottoman front lines, the news from Petrograd was no less welcome. If the food ration in the capital was inadequate, so much the worse at the front, where, as Liman observed after taking over the Yildirim command in Syria from the swiftly discredited Falkenhayn, the men "were half-starved, or starved to death, and dressed in rags."[5] The revolutionary upheavals of spring and summer 1917 had been enough to upend Russian plans to land troops at the Bosphorus, and to cut the legs out of any offensive Yudenich was planning at Erzincan. Muş had been evacuated in May, as part of a defensive consolidation of Russian lines in eastern Turkey. Even so, Russian troops were still encamped at Erzincan, Trabzon, Erzurum, and the shores of Lake Van, though the lines were thinly held.[6] Order No. 1 had been transmitted to the Caucasus and eastern Turkey, too, but mutinous sentiment was lower there than on any other front, for the obvious reason that the Russian Caucasian Army had been unambiguously victorious in 1916. At a soldiers' soviet convened in Tiflis in April 1917, a ranking general was even elected chairman, showing that the men retained residual respect for their officers. The Bolsheviks tried all summer to create radical cells in the Caucasian Army, but made little headway, except in the Second Grenadier Division and several regiments of the First Caucasian Division. The Tiflis Soviet was dominated by prowar Mensheviks and Kerensky's SRs, with a sprinkling of Dashnaks and other Armenian socialists who were ferociously committed to defeating the Turks to avenge the massacres of 1915. The Bolshevik coup was denounced as illegitimate by the Tiflis Soviet on November 8, 1917, suggesting that the men there wanted to carry on the fight against Turkey. But the ceasefire ended all this. For why should even the most gung-ho *muzhik* man his post in far-off Anatolia, when the war was over and the great peasant land-grab was beginning back home?[7]

It is important to emphasize the consequences of the Bolshevik ceasefire order, for it was *the* key plank of Lenin's "peace, land, and bread" slogan, the one that distinguished the Bolsheviks from all the other factions competing for power in Russia. In their own way, the Mensheviks, the SRs, the Kadets and conservatives and monarchists had all wanted to win the war with Germany and Turkey. Judging by the November 1917 elections, in which Kerensky's party won 40.4 percent of the vote compared with 24 percent for the already-in-power Bolsheviks and 1 percent for "Left SRs" aligned with them, Lenin's "peace" policy commanded support from, at best, a quarter of the Russian people. As if to crown its controversial nature, the Bolshevik ceasefire order was transmitted to the front with the mischievous instruction that troops begin "fraternizing" with the enemy. When the commander in chief, General Dukhonin, received these orders, he refused to obey. So Lenin broadcast a message to the troops, denouncing their commander as a "counterrevolutionary." Catching the hint, a mob of radical soldiers promptly lynched Dukhonin. The mutiny at Russian military headquarters, like the melting away of the Caucasian Army, was born of deliberate Bolshevik policy, not the general revolutionary upheaval of 1917. It was Lenin—not Kerensky or the soviets or the Russian people—who ended Russia's war against Turkey.[8]

Moreover, Lenin's surrender on all fronts did not simply mean that the Ottoman Empire could *survive*. In a sense, the February Revolution had already made this possible, by halting the advance of the Russian armies past Erzincan and complicating Kolchak's efforts to organize a Bosphorus descent. The upshot was to improve the Ottoman strategic posture on the Russian fronts from one of desperate defense to something like stalemate-by-mutual-exhaustion. But now, after the October Revolution, the enemy forces were disintegrating. Russia's still superior Black Sea Fleet, pursuant to the armistice terms, limped back to port, when ships were not summarily scuttled by mutineers. In Anatolia, the armistice commission set up shop at Kilkit, about 45 kilometers (28 miles) north of Erzincan, theoretically to cement the Russo-Turkish front lines currently in place. But troops on the Russian side of the line began going home immediately, and not in a particularly orderly fashion. Vehip Pasha, commander of the now surprisingly victorious Ottoman Third Army, protested vigorously at the brutal behavior of the departing Russians, who were plundering and robbing everywhere they went.[9]

Of all the deathbed miracles that had saved the Ottoman Empire in the modern era, Lenin's revolution was surely the greatest. The previous winter had seen Turkey on its last legs, its broken armies trying desperately to hold on as soon as the final Russian push for Constantinople began, with Britain and France poised to claim what remained of the Ottoman carcass. Now, with Russia's armies melting away, Talât Pasha, now grand vizier, thought that Lenin's coup had "opened the doors to the realization of Turkey's eastern empire." Sober Ottoman newspapers like *Sabah* and *Tasvir-i-Efkar* were discussing "the immediate recovery of lands in eastern Anatolia and Transcaucasia." Translated into policy, this meant that Ottoman diplomats sent to the armistice negotiations at Brest-Litovsk could demand not simply the restoration of Turkey's 1914 borders with Russia, but the 1877 ones—including *Elviye-i-Selâse*—the "three provinces" of Kars, Ardahan, and Batum seized by Russia after the last Russo-Ottoman war. Even Baku, hub of the Russian oil industry and gateway to the Caspian and Turkic Central Asia, might now be in play—although here the Turks would have to compete with their own German allies, who wanted the oil too. After a horrible run in 1916, Enver now looked set to go down in history as the greatest living Turk, the man who had defeated the empire's archenemy to the north.[10]

Of course, turning Enver Pasha into a *ghazi* hero was not really what the

Bolsheviks had set out to do in seizing power. From Lenin's perspective, it was all well and good that the ceasefire had accelerated the disintegration of the tsarist armies, thus eliminating the most dangerous weapon of the counterrevolution. But this did not mean that he wished to enable Russia's enemies to build their own empires at her expense. Opportunist he may have been, but Lenin was not really, as Kerensky and the Allied governments believed, a German agent. When Trotsky, the Bolsheviks' foreign minister, gleefully released the terms of the Sazonov-Sykes-Picot Agreement to the *Manchester Guardian* in November 1917, he meant to embarrass all the belligerents by exposing their naked imperialism, not just the Entente powers whose correspondence he happened to discover in the archives. Likewise, Lenin's strategy in agreeing to the ceasefire and sending representatives to Brest-Litovsk was not to give the Germans what they wanted, but to win enough time for copycat revolutions to break out across Europe before Russia had to ink what were sure to be onerous surrender terms. As Trotsky later explained, "We began peace negotiations in the hope of arousing the workmen's parties of Germany and Austria-Hungary as well as those of the Entente countries. For this reason we were obliged to delay the negotiations as long as possible to give the European workmen time to understand the Soviet revolution."[11]

The first session of the Brest-Litovsk armistice negotiations, held between December 22 and 28, 1917, was something of a farce. The two leading Bolshevik delegates, Adolf Joffe (a trusted friend of Trotsky, like Joffe an ex-Menshevik) and Lev Kamenev, an old Bolshevik confidant of Lenin's, were serious enough. But Kamenev and Joffe were accompanied by a motley collection of bohemians and criminals, such as Madame Anastasia Bitsenko, released from a Siberian prison (her offense had been assassinating a governor-general), and Roman Stashkov, a peasant who had been literally plucked from the street in Petrograd by Joffe, who had realized after motoring off that he did not have a "representative of the peasantry."* With the Germans and

---

* "Where are you going, comrade?" Joffe's aides assailed Stashkov. "Come with us to Brest-Litovsk and make peace with the Germans." To vet this "representative of the Russian peasantry," they then asked what Stashkov's politics were. Informed that he (like most peasants) was a Socialist Revolutionary, Joffe then asked Stashkov: left or right? "Left, comrade!" the peasant replied quickly. "The very leftest." It was the correct answer.

Austrians still hoping that the Christmas spirit might nudge the Entente governments into sending delegations, no one was in a particular hurry, and a good time was had by all. Stashkov was seen shoving food into his mouth with both hands "through his enormous untrimmed beard." Asked, by his German hosts, whether he preferred red or white wine with his meal, Stashkov happily replied, "Which is the stronger?"[12]

Underneath the bonhomie, however, considerable tensions were building on both sides of the negotiating table. Austria-Hungary's position in the war had been, if anything, even more desperate than Turkey's after the Brusilov offensive of 1916. Following the death of Emperor Franz Josef I in November of that year, everyone had expected the empire to fracture along national lines in 1917, and it very nearly had. The Russian Revolution had saved the Habsburg empire no less dramatically than it had the Ottoman; and the food situation was no better in Vienna than in Constantinople. The lead Austrian negotiator at Brest-Litovsk, Count Ottokar Czernin, had been warned that the Dual Monarchy would fall if the negotiations dragged out too long. Czernin surprised everyone when, as if carried away by the Christmas spirit (or the Bolsheviks' peace propaganda), he announced that Austria-Hungary would renounce all territories conquered during the war if the Entente powers would come to Brest-Litovsk and negotiate (viewing Lenin's as a German puppet government, the Allies refused to humor the idea that this was a real peace conference). Czernin's suggestion infuriated the German generals present, along with press hardliners in Berlin, who denounced Germany's lead negotiator, State Secretary Richard von Kühlmann, for allowing Czernin to suggest surrendering land "bought with the blood and lives of hundreds of thousands." The small Bulgarian delegation, too, was livid at the idea they might have to give back occupied Serbia and parts of upper Dobruja and lower Bessarabia keenly coveted in Sofia (or the area in western Thrace given up by the Ottomans in 1915, which the Turks now wanted back). Turkey's position, as stated by Foreign Minister Ahmed Nesimî, was subtler but no less clear: before Turkey would consider abandoning her territorial claims, Russia must complete her withdrawal from all Ottoman territories she had occupied. With friction growing among the victors, the conference adjourned on December 28, 1917, for everyone to think things over.[13]

Trotsky and Lenin were not the only ones who believed that time was on their side. The Bolsheviks may have entertained hopes that revolution would break out in Central Europe, cutting the legs off Germany's plans to absorb Russian territory. But the Germans could play this game, too, and in a more serious way, by inviting to Brest-Litovsk separatist factions keen to split off from Russia, such as three delegates from the Council, or Rada, of Ukraine, which had proclaimed independence in December. The Turks, meanwhile, had conjured up popular proclamations in formerly Ottoman Kars, Ardahan, and Batum, in favor of rejoining the empire. On December 22, 1917, Enver established a "Caucasus committee" to negotiate with Turkey's co-belligerents the reincorporation of *Elviye-i-Selâse*. Germany's ambassador to the Ottoman Empire, Count Johann Heinrich von Bernstorff, was opposed to Enver's claim, which he dismissed as "Oriental haggling."[14] But Kühlmann, as Enver knew, was much friendlier to Turkish aspirations (a former ambassador to Turkey himself, Kühlmann had actually been born in Constantinople). Kühlmann, favoring the Ukrainian Rada-style approach, suggested that Turkey hold plebiscites in the former Ottoman provinces to justify their annexation. With Germany's state secretary endorsing Turkey's claims on *Elviye-i-Selâse*, and the tsarist Army of the Caucasus a shadow of its former self, it seemed only a matter of time before Enver would succeed in restoring Turkey's 1877 borders.[15]

Nevertheless, the Bolsheviks still had cards to play. The Commissariat of Nationality Affairs, first established under the Provisional Government to keep Russian minorities in the fold, was entrusted to Stalin after the October Revolution. In December, Stalin began arming Armenian veterans of the Caucasian Army, with an eye to resisting Turkish penetration. By month's end, the Armenian Corps—embryo of what Armenians hoped would be a national army—consisted of some twenty-four battalions of infantry riflemen, eight militia battalions, and about a thousand cavalrymen—some twenty thousand strong.[16] On January 11, 1918, Lenin and Stalin cosigned a special Decree on Armenia updating the ambiguous declaration of May 28, 1917, this time openly endorsing the principle of "self-determination" for "Turkish Armenia." On January 20, 1918, Talât Pasha submitted a formal protest against the Bolsheviks' arming of Armenian legions.[17] Despite all the

Bolsheviks' peace propaganda, Talât complained, "the Russian leopard has not changed its spots."[18] Scarcely had the war ended than battle lines began forming anew, with Bolsheviks and Armenians taking the place of Yudenich's mostly Russian-Cossack army. For all the happy talk at Brest-Litovsk over Christmas, the stage was being set for another Caucasian bloodletting.

When negotiations resumed at Brest-Litovsk on January 9, 1918, with no sign of Entente participation, there was a sense of pretense being abandoned as the real business began. The Bolsheviks now knew that the Germans planned to detach Ukraine from Russia, and that Turkey was preparing to fight her way back into the Caucasus. Small wonder that Lenin enjoined Trotsky himself to take over the negotiations. The holiday fun came to a screeching halt, as Trotsky forced his team (including Stashkov) to sleep and dine in separate quarters from the Germans, so as not to be corrupted by free wine and champagne. The Bolshevik orator then showed impressive stamina as he dueled with Kühlmann for days over the precise meaning of "national self-determination," an idea given sudden urgency by U.S. president Woodrow Wilson's announcement, on January 8, 1918, of the Fourteen Points.* Curiously, the Germans allowed transcripts of the proceedings to be released to the world press, which gave the megaphone to Trotsky as he railed against German imperialism and hypocrisy. Kühlmann, though annoyed by his interlocutor's antics, was game, directing the discussion in a more and more abstract direction as he tried to pin Trotsky down on the justice of popular sovereignty (the German idea being to use democratic plebiscites to justify detaching Ukraine and the Baltic provinces from Russia). But not everyone was a match for Trotsky. Czernin, who had difficulty getting a word in edgewise, wrote in his diary at one point that, fed up with the "endless spiritual wrestling matches with this wild beast," he hoped a Charlotte Corday would show up to assassinate the goateed Bolshevik in his bathtub.[19]

Tiring of the academic debate over sovereignty and self-determination, on January 18, 1918, General Max Hoffman, representing the German high

---

* Intended to regain the moral high ground from Lenin after the Bolsheviks had the "secret treaties" of the Entente published in the *Manchester Guardian*, Wilson's rhetoric about the need to adjust colonial claims in accord with the view of "the peoples concerned" (later simplified to the principle of "self-determination") proved useful for the Central Powers as a cudgel with which to browbeat the Bolsheviks at Brest-Litovsk, though this was far from Wilson's intention (point 6 directed that German troops must "evacuate Russian territory").

command at Brest-Litovsk, presented Trotsky with a draft map of the proposed borders of postwar Russia, which detached all territories already occupied by German troops, including Poland and most of the Baltic area. Hoffman also let slip, in remarks immediately regretted by both Kühlmann and Czernin, that Germany had absolutely no intentions of withdrawing troops from formerly Russian territories "even a year after the conclusion of the peace." Powerless to oppose this brutal *fait accompli* of German arms, all Trotsky could do was sputter about how "a referendum is the best means of expressing the will of the people," before requesting an adjournment to receive further instructions from Petrograd.

The Bolshevik foreign minister was in a difficult position. Back in Petrograd during the break between the second and third sessions, Trotsky found himself mediating between the Leninist and oppositionist wings of the Bolsheviks over the question of whether to sign a humiliating peace treaty or unleash "revolutionary war" against a grasping imperialist Germany. After word reached the Russian capital that the Germans had no intention of giving up their gains in eastern Europe, Lenin convened a Petrograd conference of party leaders from the main Bolshevik strongholds—Moscow, the Urals, and the capital itself. On January 21, 1918, the delegates voted on three possible policies on the war. Lenin's proposal, to sign a peace treaty with Germany immediately, despite its harsh terms, won 15 of 63 votes. The Bukharin proposal to resume the war against the Central Powers, in the hope that revolution would break out behind German lines,* won a slim majority of 32 votes. Trotsky, arguing that it was "crystal clear" that Russia would lose if she chose to prolong the war with Germany, came up with another ingenious compromise, reminiscent of the one he had engineered in October over timing the Bolshevik putsch. As he explained to his somewhat dumbfounded Bolshevik colleagues, what they should do was "declare that the war is over, but that we refuse to sign off on an annexationist peace treaty forced upon us by Germany." The Bolsheviks could thus make a kind of "pedagogical demonstration"

---

* Interestingly, a massive series of strikes indeed rocked Germany's industrial centers exactly a week after this, motivated by the idea of a "peace without annexations," suggesting some prescience on the part of Bukharin—although the swiftness with which the strikes were put down suggests that Trotsky was right on the strength of German morale in January 1918.

at Brest-Litovsk. By suspending hostilities and demobilizing Russia's army in a grand propaganda gesture, they could accomplish two things at once: destroy the widespread belief that they were "agents of the Hohenzollern crown," and make clear to the "working classes of the entire world" that the treaty had no legitimacy, but was being foisted upon Russia "by German bayonets." Trotsky's novel proposal, reduced to the catchphrase "neither peace nor war," won only 16 votes of 63 before the conference of party leaders. But the real power was held by the Central Committee, and here Trotsky's compromise pulled more weight, passing 9–7. With this curious mandate in hand, Trotsky returned to Brest-Litovsk.[20]

The session that followed was the most dramatic yet. In a sense, all that came before was a prelude to the supreme postwar issue: Ukraine. Poland and most of the Baltic area had been lost to the Germans in 1915, after all; Trotsky's protest at their detachment from Russia was thus a bit like spitting in the historical wind. Ukraine, with its rich "black earth" farmland, coal mines, and industrial centers, was a far greater prize, and its loss would be catastrophic for any Russian government. In strategic terms, control of Ukraine, and particularly the Crimean Peninsula, annexed in 1783, had been central to the rise of Russia in the modern era—and the decline of Ottoman power. As long as the tsars had dominated the Black Sea, neither Turkey's northern coastline nor Constantinople itself had ever been secure. Conversely, if Ukraine were neutralized, Ottoman leaders, with their capital safe, could begin throwing their weight around again even as Russia was reduced to the second rank of the powers. Moreover, Ukraine, unlike the Transcaucasus, was a subject on which the Central Powers were in agreement. Bulgaria had no pretensions there, nor did Turkey. Austria-Hungary, to be sure, had plausible fears that Ukrainian independence would set a precedent for her own Slavic minorities. But the desperate food situation in Vienna easily overrode such concerns: what the Austrians really wanted was grain, potatoes, and coal, which the Rada of an independent Ukraine (along with the Germano-Austro-Hungarian occupying armies) could ostensibly give them. Most of all, each of the Central Powers shared a basic interest in undermining Russian power, and detaching Ukraine was the obvious way to do this. On February 1, 1918, the day the third sitting of the armistice negotiations began, Talât wrote to Enver that the Bolsheviks, no less imperialist than the tsars, were aiming to create a "United Russian Republic" incorporating Ukraine. To forestall any such restoration of the traditional threat from the north, the grand vizier promised Enver that he would work with the Germans and Austrians to detach Ukraine by offering her recognition at Brest-Litovsk.[21]

Seeking to corner Trotsky, Kühlmann and Czernin let the Ukrainian Rada delegates take the floor as the session opened. These idealistic young socialists let forth a blistering harangue against the Bolsheviks for betraying the spirit of the revolution, assaulting an elected parliament, and oppressing Ukrainians and other minorities itching for their freedom. Trotsky retorted that the Rada represented a territory no greater than the hotel rooms the Germans had rented for it. As General Hoffman noted, there was merit in Trotsky's cynical remark. In fact, the Rada in Kiev was tottering and armed Bolsheviks were gaining in strength (they would seize the city, expelling the Rada, a week later, on February 8). Bolshevism had taken hold of the Black Sea Fleet as well, spilling over onto port cities such as Odessa, where a local Rada had declared loyalty to Lenin's party.[22] Bolshevism was making headway even in the German armies. Under cover of armistice negotiations, as Kaiser Wilhelm II pointedly complained in a telegram to Brest-Litovsk on February 9, 1918, "the Bolshevik Government has addressed my troops *en clair* by radio, and urged them to rise and openly disobey their military superiors."[*23] Infuriated by the Bolsheviks' double-dealing, the Germans signed a separate peace with the Ukrainian Rada, backed by Austria-Hungary and Turkey. Kühlmann informed Trotsky that he would have to sign the treaty within twenty-four hours or face the resumption of hostilities. Playing his trump, Trotsky now announced that Russia was leaving the war and demobilizing her armies, though she refused to sign a "peace of landlords and capitalists": Germany and her allies must now explain to their war-weary publics why they were still fighting a country without an army. General Hoffman, hearing this, could only stammer, "*Unerhört!* [Unheard-of!]." Satisfied with his propaganda coup, Trotsky returned to Petrograd. It was likely with this exchange in mind that Colonel Raymond Robins, the U.S. liaison to Lenin's still

---

* Trotsky himself had been witnessed throwing "peace" leaflets from the train as it pulled into Brest-Litovsk.

unrecognized government, called Trotsky "a four-kind son of a bitch, but the greatest Jew since Jesus."[24]

Flummoxed by Trotsky's unprecedented maneuver, the Germans now had the debate they probably should have conducted weeks earlier, at a crown council on February 13, 1918. Speaking for the high command, Ludendorff said that he was fed up with Trotsky's delaying tactics. Hoping to finish off Allied resistance in France with a crushing spring offensive before American troops could bring their weight to bear, Ludendorff wanted a swift resolution in the east so as to free up troops for the western front. If the Bolsheviks continued to resist signing the treaty, then the Germans should march into Petrograd and overthrow them. Although similarly frustrated with Trotsky, Kühlmann, on behalf of the Foreign Office, argued against being drawn too deeply into the "center of revolutionary contagion," proposing instead that the Germans revert to their Sun Tzu-esque policy of 1917, doing nothing on the eastern front so as not to provoke a patriotic counterrevolution against the Bolsheviks.[25]

Kühlmann had logic on his side, but the emotion in the crown council went the other way. Kaiser Wilhelm II was personally offended that the Bolsheviks were inciting his troops to mutiny, despite all the support Germany had given them; he had also begun receiving the first reports of the "madness reigning" in Bolshevized Petrograd (e.g., government decrees "expropriating" private bank accounts). The elderly chief of the General Staff, Field Marshal Hindenburg, contributing his own pfennigs to the ideas Ludendorff usually thought up for him, said that Germany could not risk losing Ukraine, and its grain, to the Bolsheviks; far better to crush them instead. Count Georg von Hertling, Bethmann Hollweg's defanged successor as chancellor, tried gamely to mediate, but was bulldozed by the kaiser and the generals. While the question of an occupation of Petrograd was left unresolved for now, a firm decision was taken to resume the offensive in the east on February 18, 1918.[26]

Although sometimes taken for granted as the inevitable outcome of the October Revolution, Ludendorff's calling of Trotsky's Brest-Litovsk bluff was just as contingent, and bizarre, a decision as was the bluff itself. There was nothing foreordained about Trotsky's inspired "neither peace nor war" policy: it won a very close vote in the Bolshevik Central Committee after losing decisively in a larger party conference, a vote that might have gone Bukharin's way had it been held a week later, when Germany was rocked by strikes. Nor was there a clear precedent in all history for the "voluntary" demobilization of the Russian army ordered on January 29, 1918.[27] Likewise, Ludendorff's proposal of invading a prostrate Russia in late February 1918 was almost shockingly illogical, both in the sense that the government he wished to topple had been more or less installed by the German Foreign Office, and in that every man he was devoting to it could not be used for the western offensive he was planning to launch the very next month.* It might have made sense to send troops to root out the Bolshevik disease Germany herself had planted in Russia, or to devote every resource instead to a great offensive in France before the mass of American doughboys was thrown into battle. But to do both simultaneously was a species of madness.[28]

Nonetheless, the initial results were impressive. On the Baltic front, Dvinsk fell without a fight on February 17, 1918, and the Germans pressed on into Latvia and Estonia. By month's end, German warplanes were dropping bombs on Petrograd. In the center, the Germans moved into White Russia, seizing Minsk and Pskov with ease. Farther south, German, Austrian, and Hungarian troops moved swiftly into Ukraine. Kiev, the "capital," fell on March 1, 1918, allowing the Germans to begin drawing up terms with the Rada for the transfer of Ukrainian grain to Berlin, Vienna, and Constantinople. Austro-Hungarian troops, deliberately kept out of Kiev by the German high command, targeted Odessa instead. Meanwhile, the German advance guard, under General Wilhelm Groener, raced on to Kharkov and Donetsk, even as a southern army group, led by the redoubtable General Mackensen, swept down into the Crimean Peninsula. By May 8, 1918, the Germans were at Rostov-on-Don and Taganrog, with advance scouting teams being sent east to Tsaritsyn (later Stalingrad) on the Volga and south into the Caucasus. In just over ten weeks, the Germans had conquered a swathe of territory larger

---

* The German official history claims that 38 divisions were freed up from the eastern front in winter 1917–18 for Ludendorff's western offensive, including the most formidable—Guards, Jäger battalions, the best Prussian, Schwabian, and Bavarian divisions. Theoretically, only second-rate units were left behind, stripped of men under thirty-five and losing most of their horses. Nevertheless, even on the most favorable calculation to Ludendorff's purposes, it remains true that *nearly fifty* German divisions remained deployed on the eastern front, and over a million men, as of March 21, 1918, when Ludendorff struck in the west.

than (prewar) Germany itself. As General Hoffman, overall commander on the eastern front, gloated with a hint of *Schadenfreude*, "This is the most comic war I have ever experienced—it is waged almost exclusively in trains and automobiles. One puts on the train a few infantry with machine guns and one artillery piece, and proceeds on to the next railroad station, seizes it, arrests the Bolsheviks, entrains another detachment, and moves on." Unable to resist twisting in the knife, Hoffman added, "Trotsky's theories could not resist facts."[29]

On the Ottoman front, progress was nearly as rapid. In mutually shared disgust over Trotsky's antics, the Germans had abandoned their earlier opposition to Turkish encroachment into the Caucasus, stipulating in the final draft of the Brest-Litovsk Treaty that "the districts of Ardahan, Kars, and Batum will . . . be cleared of Russian troops." The reorganized Ottoman Third Army (which now incorporated divisions from the disbanded Second), commanded by Vehip Pasha, took Trabzon on February 24, 1918, though not without bloodshed (nearly 600 were killed and 700 wounded in an explosion in an ammunitions depot that may or may not have been an accident; the casualties

included 1,050 Russians and 250 Greeks).[30] On the Erzincan-Erzurum front, the newly formed First Caucasian Army, under Musa Kâzim Karabekir Pasha, took Mana Hatun on February 24, and Erzincan a few days later. Erzurum fell on March 12. With the terrible verdict of 1916 thus overturned, Karabekir and Vehip Pasha now pushed back to the 1914 borders. On April 4, 1918, as if to exorcise Enver's demons from 1914, Ottoman troops marched into Sarıkamış. Next it was time to turn the clock back to the 1870s, as the Turks marched into the three lost provinces. After rolling up Ardahan province in a few days, on April 12, 1918, Vehip Pasha took the surrender of Batum (after a few hours' desultory resistance). On April 25, the First Ottoman Caucasian Army marched unopposed into Kars, thus completing a reversal that had seen the Ottoman Empire recoup forty years of territorial losses in two months.[31]

Of course, the triumphant march of the Germans and Turks into Bolshevized Russia was a good deal messier on the ground than it appeared on staff maps back at headquarters. Hoping to harness the resources of Ukraine, the Germans and their allies discovered a country all but put to the torch. Odessa and Sevastopol, as the Germans approached them in early March 1918, had turned into "Bolshevik robber-nests," plagued by "terrorist incidents" of all kinds as "armed bands roamed across the cit[ies], plundering, stealing, murdering, arresting bourgeois citizens and officers, unleashing full-on anarchy."[32] After the Germans arrived in Odessa on March 13, they were horrified to learn that no oil was available, as the tanks had all been set on fire. Coal could not be bought at any price, and there was no prospect of a grain surplus, as the city did not have enough food on hand to feed its own population, now expanded by around 200,000 refugees from the countryside.[33] Nikolaev, home to the greatest dockyards on the Black Sea (it was here that Russia had built her dreadnoughts), had been fully Bolshevized. This port saw brutal fighting as the Germans and Austrians tried to secure the dockyards and the telegraph station; twelve were killed, forty wounded, and another seventy were missing.[34] At Kherson, four German companies were ambushed by "Bolshevik bands." Out at sea, a strange stalemate prevailed, with German submarines circling Ukrainian ports, though unable to come in safely because Bolshevik mutineers had taken over most of the warships, with uncertain intentions. The situation was serious enough that the German army requested help from Souchon at Okmeidan, who promptly sent the newly repaired *Goe-ben* to show the German flag at Sevastopol, Odessa, and Kherson.[35]

Russia's Black Sea Fleet was a valuable asset that the Germans had hoped to seize intact. The Brest-Litovsk Treaty, ratified by Lenin's government on March 3, 1918, stipulated that Russian warships be "detained" in port "until the conclusion of a general peace"—after which the Germans hoped to take them. By the time the Germans had reached the coastal ports of Ukraine, however, it became clear that not much was left of the Russian fleet. The dreadnought *Imperatritsa Maria*, for example, had been undergoing repairs for most of 1917, and had been expected to resume her role as the Russian flagship. Soon after the Bolshevik seizure of power, the repairs had been halted. The *Maria* began taking on water again, and promptly sank, this time for good. What remained of Russia's Black Sea Fleet—two (considerably below-strength) dreadnoughts, the *Volya* and the *Svobodnaia Rossiia*, five destroyers, some transports and torpedo boats, and a few submarines—was sent to anchor at Sevastopol. By the time the first German scouts arrived, even these had been rendered all but useless, as any officers opposed to Bolshevism had been lynched. There were, a German captain reported in mid-March 1918, no admirals left, nor any officer of a rank experienced enough to command a fleet. Even if there had been, there was not enough coal or oil to fuel the ships, nor ammunition to fire from the turrets (most shells and other ordnance had been tossed overboard in various onboard mutinies). Whereas, after the February Revolution, Russia's fleet had continued operating more or less as normal, maintaining command of the Black Sea and menacing Turkey's coastline until well into fall 1917, German intelligence estimated in early April 1918 that its striking power had been reduced by 99 percent.[36] This estimate, moreover, was registered *before* the greatest naval scuttling yet took place on April 30, 1918, just as the first German field batteries were sighted in the heights above Sevastopol: Russia's last two Black Sea dreadnoughts were sunk by their own crews, along with twenty torpedo boats, destroyers, and transport ships.[37]

In the face of disappointments like this, the German romance with the Ukrainian Rada soured even more quickly than that with the Bolsheviks. Trotsky's gibe was telling: the student socialists of Kiev proved incapable of governing their own capital, let alone Ukraine. In the countryside outside those railway towns where the Germans stationed troops, chaos reigned, as farmers took up arms to defend their produce against robber bands of all varieties—including German and Austro-Hungarian troops. In a pattern soon to become painfully familiar across the Bolshevized lands of the former tsarist empire, peasants had adopted a "pox on all your houses" approach to the roaming armies, hiding their produce in underground storage dugouts rather than bringing it to market. Whatever agreements the German army signed with the Rada, there was simply no grain to be had. As Groener wrote Ludendorff, in the Ukrainian capital where Germans had so naively assumed that "milk and honey" would flow freely, "we cannot even get bread." And so, on April 23, 1918, Ludendorff authorized Groener to overthrow the Rada if food shipments were not forthcoming and set up a law-and-order regime respecting private property in order to coax the peasants into parting with their grain. On April 28, German soldiers occupied the Rada and arrested its deputies. In an inspired touch, Groener had a Cossack tsarist army veteran, Pavlo Skoropadskyi, descendant of a chief of the Hetmanate, or Zaporizhian Host of Cossacks who had ruled central Ukraine between 1649 and 1764, acclaimed as hetman. Having helped empower bohemian Bolsheviks like Trotsky and Ukraine's student radicals in the Rada, and then jousting with Trotsky over Wilsonian self-determination, the Germans had now defrosted a form of Cossack strongman governance not seen since the seventeenth century.[38]

On the Caucasian front, the story was no more edifying. Van, changing hands for the fourth time in the war, saw bitter fighting as the Armenians who had stayed behind to contest the city after the Russians left, about a thousand strong, sold their lives dearly.[39] When Karabekir's forces arrived in Erzincan in late February, they reported that "all the wells were stuffed with corpses," most of them Muslims. Vehip Pasha, witnessing similar scenes of horror along the Trabzon-Batum front, wrote an urgent dispatch to Russian headquarters in Tiflis that something be done to hold back the Armenians, who appeared "resolved to destroy and annihilate Ottoman Muslims."[40] The Armenian National Council in the Caucasus, for its part, sent appeals to the German high command to hold back the Turks, who were subjecting them to another round of oppression in their march into Ardahan and Kars, which had left "Armenians swimming in blood"—not just Ottoman Armenians, but now (former) Russian subjects too. The salvation of the Armenian nation and people, the council declared not without reason, "lay with Germany."[41] It is clear that the fighting on the Caucasian front during the Ottoman offensive of spring 1918 was just as savage as ever.

Control of the Transcaucasus was still up in the air. In the chaos following Lenin's seizure of power, non-Bolshevik socialists of various stripes (mostly Georgian Mensheviks and Armenian Dashnaks, though a few Azeri Tatars got in on the act) had joined together in Tiflis to form a proto-parliament akin to the Ukrainian Rada, called the Seim. Again following the Ukrainian lead, the Seim declared itself authorized to negotiate a peace treaty with the Central Powers, though stopping short of proclaiming formal independence. Unable to put together a delegation in time to reach Brest-Litovsk, the Seim instead sent representatives to Trabzon, hoping to win recognition from the Turks in a bilateral peace treaty. The embryonic pseudo-state of Transcaucasia thus found itself in the curious position of negotiating with its own conqueror as the Ottoman armies moved into Ardahan, Kars, and Batum. It was, in fact, the Ottoman generals who wanted the Seim to declare independence, so that they could impose peace terms on it, just as the Germans had done on the Rada (before it had proved too weak to enforce them). In what can only be described as an inauspicious beginning, the Seim declared the independence of the Transcaucasian Democratic Federative Republic on April 22, 1918, immediately following the surrender of Batum to Vehip Pasha. The Turks now had their own "Rada" to push around, and they wasted no time imposing peace terms on it, which included "the free use by the Turks of all Transcaucasian railways." The hint was clear: the Ottoman armies planned to take Baku.[42]

Tiflis, like Kiev, saw its bright shining dawn of independence pass quickly. No sooner had "Transcaucasia" been recognized by the Ottoman Empire than it began to break apart into national factions in a desperate scramble for survival. Georgians, giving up the temporary alliance of convenience with Armenians, petitioned the Germans for a protectorate. Colonel Kress von Kressenstein, fresh in from Syria, was promptly accredited to Tiflis as military plenipotentiary. After securing generous mineral concessions for Berlin, Kress authorized the proclamation of Georgian independence at the town hall in Tiflis on May 27, 1918, which in effect ended the brief existence of the Transcaucasian Democratic Federative Republic (the Seim was accordingly dissolved). Abandoned by their fellow Christian Georgians, the Armenians moved their own National Council from Tiflis to Yerevan, which would be the capital of the new Armenian Republic. Inevitably, the third main national group of the Transcaucasus, Azeri Tatars—or Azerbaijanis, as we call them today—now moved to declare independence too—although under protection of the Ottomans, who promised to "provide military support to the Azerbaijani Government if this is seen as necessary by the latter for domestic stability and national security." Implied, though not stated, was that the Azeri Tatars wanted the Turks to win them Baku (just as the Germans had retaken Kiev for the Rada), a city now controlled by a radical "Commune" cobbled together by local Bolsheviks and Armenian Dashnaks (most of the Muslim population had taken to the hills after bloody street fighting at Shamkhor in early April, which had seen an armed Bolshevik-Dashnak force massacre several thousand Azeri Tatar Muslims).[43]

Of the three new nations of the Transcaucasus, only Armenia would fight for its independence. At the end of May, after falling back from Alexandropol, the Armenians made a furious stand at Karakilise and Sardarabad outside Yerevan, inflicting the first real defeat of 1918 on the advancing Ottoman army. It was not the Armenians' first choice for a capital: Tiflis was, despite being the former capital of the kingdom of Georgia, a far more important center of Armenian culture: Armenians comprised 40 percent of the prewar population, larger than the Georgian share of 35 percent; moreover, Armenians dominated the local economy and had the most widely read newspapers. Yerevan, by contrast, was a dull provincial town distant from the main strategic artery of the Transcaucasus running from Batum through Tiflis to Baku, along which ran a railway and an oil pipeline. Still, partly for this very reason, Vehip Pasha now agreed to cede Yerevan to Turkey's archenemy. Armenia would live—for now.[44]

The most contentious prize of the Transcaucasus was the oil fields of Baku. In theory, the Ottomans had already been invited into the city by the embryonic government of Azerbaijan, which, however, did not control it. The Germans, already in possession of the middle leg of the pipeline through Georgia (though not its terminus at Batum), were hoping to reach the city first, or to have the Bolsheviks give it to them. With German soldiers and marines pouring into Georgia by way of Sukhum and Poti, and the Turks landing reinforcements at Batum, the race for Baku was on. At the end of May, the German liaison general at Batum, General Otto von Lossow, left in protest at Turkish encroachment into the Transcaucasus, heading straight for Berlin to make his case, which included the rather harsh judgment that the Turks were "incapable of administering [Azerbaijan] and regulating petroleum production [at Baku]." On June 9, 1918, Ludendorff, from German headquarters, asked Enver to withdraw his forces to the line agreed to at Brest-Litovsk. Vehip Pasha, for his part, informed Enver that German soldiers had been spotted fighting alongside the Armenians at Karakilise. Refusing to give in, Vehip Pasha routed his forces northward into Georgia, where they encountered several of Kress's makeshift German companies on the Alexandropol-Tiflis road near a town called Vorontsovka. Here, on June 10, 1918, occurred the first hostile exchange of fire between Turks and Germans in the world war. The Turks routed the vastly outnumbered Germans, taking "a considerable number of prisoners." Ludendorff was livid: he warned Enver that if Vehip Pasha did not return the prisoners to Kress, Germany would recall all of its troops—numbering some twenty thousand—from the Ottoman Empire. Reluctantly, Enver agreed, and ordered Vehip Pasha to withdraw back to the south.[45]

Enver's climbdown was only tactical. Conceding Georgia to Kress and the Germans, he ordered Vehip Pasha to reorient his offensive south and east, through Armenia toward Elizavetpol, where the Azeri Tatars had established their capital after fleeing Baku. In a sign of the priority Enver gave to capturing Baku, he recalled his uncle Halil "Kut" Pasha from Mesopotamia to assume overall command of the front, and appointed his younger brother Nuri Pasha (who had been overseeing relations with the Sanussi in Libya) commander of a new Army of Islam, which combined Turkish regulars from the Fifth Caucasian Division with Azeri Tatar and other Muslim volunteers. The Army of Islam was meant to give point to the operation, to embody the aspirations of all Transcaucasian Muslims to statehood (though under an Ottoman security umbrella, of course). Setting up shop in Elizavetpol to recruit volunteers on May 25, 1918, Nuri Pasha was disappointed by the turnout,* and ended up having to rely on Vehip Pasha's regulars, who began arriving via Armenia on June 20. By mid-July, Nuri's Army of Islam, though smaller than he and Enver had hoped—comprising ten thousand actives—had advanced within fifty miles of Baku, striking such terror into the Armenians of Baku that they invited a British force of a thousand troops encamped in northern Persia, commanded by General Dunsterville, to come across the Caspian and save them.[46]

Georgia, meanwhile, had turned into a booby prize for the Germans. Rather than an advance base for projecting Teutonic power, Tiflis turned out to be more of a way station for those fleeing the brutal fighting in Armenia and Azerbaijan, including German and Austro-Hungarian subjects. By August 1918, Kress was spending most of his time requesting aid from the German naval command in evacuating refugees by way of Poti, and grain shipments for his men from Ukraine (which, owing to the inability of the Germans to requisition enough grain for Berlin, Vienna, or Constantinople, were predictably not forthcoming). The Turks were doing nothing to help, as processing refugees would clog up their supply lines to Nuri Pasha's forces. Nearly all spare troops in the Ottoman Empire, the Germans complained, were now being sent to Batum to strengthen the Army of Islam, rather than reinforce the empire's precarious defenses in Mesopotamia, Syria, Thrace, and the Dardanelles.[47]

The Turks could have said the same thing, of course, about Germany diverting essential manpower east to occupied Russia even after Ludendorff's great spring offensive, following the Second Battle of the Marne in July 1918, swung into reverse. German troops had been dispatched to locations as far afield as Finland in order to secure that province's independence from Russia, and there was even talk (beginning in August) of sending as many as fifty thousand troops at Murmansk by invitation of the Bolsheviks to expel the

---

* Amusingly, one of Nuri's beleaguered recruiters, encountering an elderly *hoca* volunteer, was heard to remark that "the Army of Islam has no place for men of religion."

Allied forces there. Much as the Western allies would have loved to take credit for thus "re-activating the eastern front" (the strategic aim of their intervention in north Russia), in truth it was the Germans' own folly that lay behind these deployments, above all in occupied Ukraine. Having themselves unleashed the furies of Bolshevism into tsarist Russia, the Germans were receiving a painful education in the economics of Communism. The upending of private property had led to a war of all against all, with the Germans now ruling (via their hetman) over a country in which "robbery, murder, manslaughter, bloody revolts, bandit battles, fires, explosions, declarations of martial law and so on are daily occurrences." Rather than export a coal surplus, German Ukraine had to import coal from Germany to get the trains to run. Because no grain was coming to market, German troops had to begin requisitioning foodstuffs from peasants at gunpoint, which meant, in turn, that more troops were needed daily. By September–October 1918, the maw of revolutionary Ukraine had sucked in 600,000 German occupying troops—at a time when the war was being decided on the western front. True, these may not have been "first-line" troops, but they were certainly doing active combat duty, often skirmishing with peasant partisans over the food supply. By diverting the equivalent of two or three entire armies into Ukraine alone, Ludendorff and the high command were able to requisition all of 35,000 wagonloads of foodstuffs by November 1918, of which Austria-Hungary received 20,000, Germany 14,000, and Bulgaria and Turkey fewer than 200 each.[48]

As if dissatisfied with his eastern overextension to date, Ludendorff schemed to send even more troops into Russia in fall 1918. However sour Germany's fortunes were looking in the west, the possibilities in the east still seemed endless. By one count, tsarist Russia had given birth to thirty different governments, with Lenin's at best a kind of *primus inter pares* (though it did control Moscow and Petrograd). In May, a legion of 40,000 freed pro-Entente Czechoslovak prisoners of war, after skirmishing with pro-German Hungarians at Cheliabinsk, had taken over western Siberia (including the gold reserves at Kazan). Trotsky, now minister of war, had ordered the legion disarmed, only to discover that it had more men under arms than he did. The episode poisoned trust between Trotsky and the Entente missions, which had taken the Czechoslovak side. The smart money was now betting on the

Bolsheviks' overthrow—indeed Britain's envoy to Lenin's regime, Bruce Lockhart, gave ten million rubles to General Alekseev, commander of the anti-Bolshevik Volunteer Army, in late July, shortly before the Bolsheviks arrested two hundred English and French nationals in Moscow. On August 1, 1918, Lenin requested that the Germans send troops to expel Allied forces from Murmansk—and (he hoped) to help smother the Volunteer Army, operating under protection of the Kuban Cossacks in the north Caucasus. As the Germans were then negotiating deals with both the Kuban and Don Cossacks (sending no less than 15 million rubles to the latter, even more than the British spent on the Volunteers), this last was out of the question—although Ludendorff did see merit in the idea of a north Russia deployment, *if* it could be routed by way of Petrograd. And so it came about that, on August 6, 1918, Ludendorff issued orders that "six or seven" German divisions should be sent to Petrograd, with their objective left open-ended (Ludendorff's own aim, to overthrow the Bolsheviks, was still running into furious opposition from Kühlmann and the Foreign Office, who had, after all, helped put them in power in the first place). Alas, we will never know what the result of Ludendorff's "Operation Schlußstein" would have been, for it was called off on September 27, 1918.[49]

Meanwhile, the struggle for Baku was heating up. Here, if not in the Kuban and Don regions where the Germans were cutting deals with the Cossacks, the interests of Bolshevik Moscow and Berlin aligned well—against those of Enver and the Ottoman government. As Trotsky argued in the Central Committee, Baku was, strategically speaking, more important than Moscow; without its oil much of Russia's rail network, along with shipping on the Volga, would grind to a halt.* In a supplement to the Treaty of Brest-Litovsk ratified on August 27, 1918, Germany agreed to "prevent the military forces of any third power [i.e., Turkey] in the Caucasus from overstepping" military lines comprising most of Azerbaijan, including Baku. In exchange for this pledge to keep the Turks away from the Caspian, the Bolsheviks agreed to give Berlin a permanent quota of 25 percent of the "crude oil products produced in the Baku district." The Bolsheviks also agreed, at German

---

* As in fact they did do, before the Reds finally recaptured Baku in April 1920.

insistence, to recognize an independent Georgia. The government in Tiflis, in turn, promised to supply Germany with refined oil from Maikop and Grozny once these North Caucasian cities were secured. With an eye toward contesting Azerbaijan if Enver did not call off the Army of Islam under diplomatic pressure, Kress had ordered up two more German batteries and three field artillery batteries, which arrived in Tiflis, by way of Poti, in July. By August 1918, Kress had something like five thousand German troops in Georgia, which was all to the good, as the pro-German Bolsheviks had been ousted from the Baku Soviet on July 31 (although Lenin's government, not trusting the Germans, did not inform them of this).[50]

The dispute over Baku had poisoned what little trust there still remained between Berlin and Constantinople. On August 4, 1918 (the day Dunsterville and his British force arrived in Baku), Ludendorff, via General von Seeckt, issued a pointed threat to recall all German officers from the Ottoman Empire if the Army of Islam marched on Baku. On August 14, Seeckt, recalled to German headquarters at Spa in Belgium, agreed with Ludendorff that the Germans would resist a Turkish entry into Baku "with all available means," up to and including sabotaging the railways Nuri Pasha was using to supply his army. Ludendorff's plans to conquer Petrograd were now running up against the possible need to send several army divisions to the Caucasus to contest Baku. On August 22, Ludendorff authorized the dispatch of a full infantry division and a cavalry brigade to Georgia, to strengthen Kress's force and hopefully scare Enver off from his Baku offensive. Meanwhile, Nuri Pasha complained to Enver that the Bolshevik-dominated Commune of Baku had been delivering oil to the Germans in Ukraine by way of Caspian and Volga steamers (at least until the Bolsheviks had been ousted from the Commune on July 31). To sabotage the Army of Islam, the Germans burned down a railway bridge linking Azerbaijan to Georgia and Batum. Nuri Pasha avenged this hostile act by blowing up a road bridge nearby, to prevent the Germans from sending troops into Azerbaijan. Despite his reputation as a Germanophile, Enver was so personally committed now to the conquest of Baku that he expressly authorized his brother to engage German units in battle if any stood in his way before the Caspian.[51]

Considering what we now know of German plans, these were not idle instructions. On September 13, 1918, Ludendorff issued Kress "top secret" orders (to be delivered only "hand to hand") to begin preparations for the imminent storming of Baku.* Two days later, Nuri Pasha's Army of Islam launched a furious artillery barrage at Baku's western Wolf's Gate. The battle pitted some 7,500 Turks and roughly the same number of Azeri Tatar irregulars against a rapidly overwhelmed Armenian-British force of about 8,000. By afternoon, Turkish shells had reached across town to the main Caspian harbor, and a general evacuation was under way. With painful inevitability, Baku's now-swollen population of Armenians was cleansed from the city in ostensible retaliation for the massacre of Muslims in early April (even if that massacre had been perpetrated as much by the now-departed Bolsheviks as by Armenian Dashnaks), with at least 9,000 or 10,000 Armenians killed, mostly by Azeri Tatar militiamen, and another 50,000 or 60,000 escaping with Dunsterville and his British force on boats across the Caspian.[52]

Considering the amount of blood that had been shed to acquire this greatest prize of the Caucasian war, the fall of Baku on September 15, 1918, should have been the occasion for wild rejoicing in Constantinople. And yet there was little celebration. Drawn deep into Russia by the temptations of Brest-Litovsk, Enver and the Turks had paid nowhere near enough attention to the forces gathering on the empire's southern and western frontiers. Nor were the Germans able to long enjoy the fruits of their great victory in the East. For all the titanic drama taking place in Russia, the outcome of the war was being decided elsewhere.

---

* Two weeks after the Turkish conquest of Baku on September 15, 1918 (news of which reached Europe slowly), orders were still being sent from Spa for the Germans to seize the city and "plant the German flag on the Caspian."

PART III

DEATH

AND

REBIRTH

MUDROS

---

*It would not be possible for the British to go on fighting the Turks simply because
the French wanted Syria or Armenia or the Italians wanted Adalia [Antalya].*

—DAVID LLOYD GEORGE[1]

IN RETROSPECT IT IS EASY to see the folly of the Turco-German thrust into
Bolshevized Russia in 1918, especially the jousting over Baku in September,
the very month that saw the Allies begin to break through on one front after
another. And yet it is unfair to judge Enver and Ludendorff in hindsight for
failing to foresee the *Götterdämmerung*, for almost no one realized at the
time that the war was coming to an end. As late as September 3, 1918, a British
government memorandum predicted that, once U.S. military strength was
fully brought to bear, the "supreme military effort" would be made by July
1919. Five days after this, Philippe Pétain, commander of the French armies,
seconded the British judgment. The supreme Allied commander, Ferdinand
Foch, was more optimistic about the possibility of breaking enemy resistance,
but even so, he continued planning right into September 1918 on the assumption that the war would be decided the following summer. Right into the last
week of September, the Allies had still not broken the Siegfried, or Hindenburg, line, believed to constitute "five miles of the most formidable defensive
position in the history of warfare." Lenin, an astute analyst of the balance of
forces, believed the Germans would win, as evidenced not only by his request
for German troops, but also by the fact that the Bolsheviks dutifully fulfilled their obligations under Brest-Litovsk and sent the first two of five

installments of reparations to Germany on September 10 and 30, 1918, including 93 metric tons of gold. Even if the Germans were pushed back from the Hindenburg line, meanwhile, they could withdraw to the Rhine and blow the bridgeheads. With an empire in the East won with German blood, there was every reason for the Germans to fight on.[2]

In the end it was a little-expected twist on one of the war's quietest fronts— Macedonia—that was the real catalyst of defeat for the Central Powers. Almost forgotten in the drama of Gallipoli, then lodged still further back in everyone's mind by the Russian Revolution and the quarreling over the spoils at Brest-Litovsk, the Franco-British landing at Salonica, originally limited to four divisions, had metastasized almost by accident into a multinational deployment large enough to tip the balance on the war's eastern front. Arriving in late October 1915, the Allies had come a few weeks too late to prevent Serbia from being overrun by the combined forces of Germany, Austria-Hungary, and Bulgaria, which meant, in turn, that they had failed in their secondary object of bringing Greece into the war on the Allied side. In a process eerily similar to the ever-galloping commitment to Gallipoli, the very futility of the Macedonian deployment argued in favor of its reinforcement, as only by sending thousands more troops to Salonica could anything (such as Greek intervention) possibly be salvaged by it. By the end of April 1917, the Allies—including Italy, the rump of the Serbian army, and even a few Russian divisions—had a force of nearly 250,000 troops in Macedonia, with another 150,000 or so support personnel. At this dire time of the war for the Allies, with Russia in revolution and the French armies in quasi-mutiny, the British Admiralty, which was responsible for provisioning and feeding the Allies in Macedonia, not unnaturally requested that they be evacuated to a more active front. After studying the matter, however, the British War Office concluded in May 1917 that withdrawal would put even more strain on the overstretched British fleet than simply maintaining the status quo. And so the Allies stayed on, basically to wait on events.[3]

The Allied non-withdrawal from formerly Ottoman Macedonia turned out to be one of the most critical decisions (or non-decisions) of the entire war. To begin with, it kept alive the possibility that Greece would enter the conflict. The French had frequently mooted the idea of sending the

Macedonian army south into Greece to depose the Germanophile King Constantine and give the pro-Entente Venizelists their head. Although British diplomats in Athens advised strongly against a full-on invasion, a compromise was finally adopted, which saw the British fleet blockade Greek ports in early June prior to a French landing at Piraeus, the port southeast of Athens. On June 11, 1917, the Allies simply handed the king an ultimatum. Constantine, getting the message, invited Venizelos back from his exile on Crete, paving the way for Greece's declaration of war on the Central Powers on July 2, 1917. Although the initial impact was fairly limited on a front where conditions approximating the entrenched stalemate in France still prevailed, by 1918 the Greeks had contributed nine divisions, giving the Allies clear local numerical superiority over the enemy whenever a breakthrough became possible.

In the end, however, it was not anything the Allies did that disturbed the strategic equilibrium in Macedonia, but rather the rupturing of the enemy coalition over the spoils of Brest-Litovsk. Despite Bulgaria's decisive contribution to the crushing of Serbia in 1915, which had given the Central Powers firm control of the Balkans, her diplomats had been bit players in the armistice talks with Russia, and this was deeply resented in Sofia. The flip side of the oversized Allied deployment in Macedonia was that Bulgaria had to do the lion's share of the duty defending against any potential Balkan breakout, which duty kept more than 200,000 of her troops pinned down in the south, unable to participate in the great carve-up of the Russian empire in 1918. For this, the Bulgarians blamed the Germans, who never came through with enough reinforcements for Macedonia, or enough provisions generally (it will be recalled that Bulgaria received fewer than two hundred wagonloads of foodstuffs from occupied Ukraine in 1918). As if to confirm the worst suspicions in Sofia, the German high command peeled off six infantry battalions and six field batteries from the Macedonian front in May–June 1918.[4] Bulgaria was, anyhow, a Slavic country created under Russian sponsorship, and Russophile sympathies remained strong in the general population. Germans and Austrians in Constantinople were under no illusions, estimating that "at least two-thirds" of the Bulgarian public, if not more, was secretly pro-Entente. Only faith in the supremacy of German arms kept the Bulgarians in the fold, and this might not survive a run of defeats.[5]

As for Bulgaria's relations with the Sublime Porte, there had never been more than a grudging acceptance of the Turks—battlefield enemies as recently as 1913—as alliance partners of convenience. Bulgarian diplomats still eyed Ottoman Adrianople, which Sofia had ruled between the two Balkan Wars, and had insisted on Turkey's cession of a western Thracian territory as the price of her alliance in 1915. When Bulgarian diplomats put forward claims on upper Dobruja and lower Bessarabia at Brest-Litovsk, the Turks had insisted that Sofia give back what it had taken from Turkey in 1915. In the final settlement of the question signed at Bucharest on May 7, 1918, Bulgaria was given only the southern half of upper Dobruja, with the rest under joint administration of the Central Powers.* In June 1918, the same month the Turks and Germans first came to blows at Vorontsovka over the spoils of Transcaucasia, Bulgarian frustrations with her allies came to a boil, resulting in the toppling of the Vasil Radoslavov cabinet and the installation of a moderate prime minister, Alexandar Malinov, who quietly opened secret talks with the Entente powers.[6]

The fight was seeping out of the Bulgarians, who now held one of the war's key defensive positions for the Central Powers, for whose common interests they had tired of bleeding and dying (in all Bulgaria lost 266,000 casualties in the First World War, the vast majority of them on the Macedonian front).† Well informed of the sagging morale of his opponent, the new Allied commander at Salonica, the wonderfully named Louis-Félix-Marie-François Franchet d'Esperey, launched a series of probes in early September 1918, before ordering a general attack all along the front on the fifteenth. Within hours the Allies had blown a hole in the enemy line nearly 11 kilometers long. By the next day, the breakthrough had expanded to 25 kilometers wide; by September 17, to 35 kilometers wide and 15 deep. By September 20, the breakout was 50 kilometers wide and just as far forward.[7]

---

* The Treaty of Bucharest, a kind of tack-on to Brest-Litovsk, was signed between the Central Powers and Romania, forced to give up the ghost following Russia's collapse.

† Most of these casualties were incurred, to be sure, after the battle in Macedonia was finally joined in September 1918. Still, Bulgaria's losses were not negligible, amounting to some 40,000 or 50,000 casualties on the Macedonian front up to that point. Easy as it would be to malign Bulgarian statesmen for opportunism in joining the Central Powers in 1915, one can understand their motivation to avenge the Second Balkan War, following the ganging-up of Greece and Serbia against her after the First. Of course, all this availed Sofia was to relive the same agony in 1918, as the fruits of her victories seemed yet again to have been stolen away by her co-belligerents.

Even as the Entente armies still faced the reputedly impregnable Siegfried line on the western front, in the east they had punctured a hole wide enough for an entire army to march through—whether north, into the Balkans and Central Europe, or east, where the right wing of Franchet d'Esperey's army, under British general George Francis Milne, could race across Thrace to Constantinople. It was the strategic breakout Churchill and Kitchener had dreamed of in vain at the Dardanelles. Ludendorff threw up his hands as he told his closest aides confidentially after he heard the news that the loss of Bulgaria meant that the war was lost for the Central Powers.[8] Though battered and bruised, with their morale beginning to crack under a series of escalating Allied attacks, what remained of Germany's first-line troops could make a final stand at the Siegfried line in the west, or redeploy east to defend the vast, totally unmanned expanses of Central Europe against Franchet d'Esperey's army. They could not do both.

It was fitting that the war's center of strategic gravity returned in 1918 to the Balkans, where the great conflagration had begun. The precise impact of the Macedonian breakthrough on the decisive battles at the Siegfried line, which began on September 26, 1918, is hard to measure. As we have seen, it certainly crushed Ludendorff's morale, if not also that of his men, who began surrendering in huge numbers.[9] On the Ottoman fronts, in any case, the impact was inarguably immediate and drastic. Grand Vizier Talât Pasha, returning from a diplomatic mission to Berlin on the Orient Express railway (shortly before it fell under Allied control), witnessed the Bulgarian collapse firsthand. After being told by top Bulgarian officials that they were about to surrender (as they did on September 29, 1918), Talât turned to one of his Turkish aides and remarked simply, "We're done" (*Boku yedik*, or literally, "We've eaten shit").[10]

Just four days after the Bulgarian front collapsed, Allenby resumed the offensive in Palestine. The Palestine/Syria front had been quiet for most of 1918 as both sides withdrew men and matériel to other theaters, the British to shore up the western front after the Ludendorff offensive, the Turks to enable Enver's Transcaucasian adventure. The EEF did take Jericho in March, but failed to seize Amman, across the Jordan River, in two small-scale offensives conducted in March and May. Ironically, it was actually in this quiet period, when nearly everyone forgot about Palestine, that Lawrence's Arab irregulars came into their own, terrorizing the Turks with ambush-style raids behind front lines in southern Syria. At Tafilah, near the Dead Sea in present-day Jordan, on or around January 15, 1918, Lawrence stormed the Turkish garrison with five hundred warriors from Feisal's Arab Legion (although Feisal was apparently not present), flanked by Bedouins on camels. It was a real battle, with the Arabs firing shrapnel rounds from British Vickers and Hotchkiss guns, while the Turks replied with Maxim machine guns. Losses seem actually to have been heavier on the Arab side, with twenty-five killed and forty wounded, although they chased the garrison from Tafilah and took two hundred prisoners. But Lawrence failed, once again, in his actual objective, which was to link up with Allenby's EEF at Jericho. His field report from Tafilah, filed on January 26, 1918, provides a fascinating glimpse of the "Arab revolt" as it looked on the ground:

> Affairs are in rather a curious state here. The place surrendered (after two false reports and a little fighting at the last) on the 15th. The local people are divided up into two bitterly opposed factions, and are therefore terrified of each other and us. There is shooting up and down the streets every night, and a general tension. The conflict of ideas, local feuds, and party interests are so wild (this being the moment of anarchy the whole district has been longing for for years) that hardly anyone could straighten them out in a hurry.[11]

With their strength bled away as Enver routed his best troops to the Caucasian front, with the ranks decimated further by desertion, the Turks were in no condition to offer more than token resistance when Allenby's assault began in September 1918. Theoretically there were still three Ottoman armies deployed across Syria, the Seventh and Eighth along the coast, the Fourth (remnants of Djemal's original army) inland near Amman. And yet these were mere skeletons. As Liman noted, his men were suffering from "munitions shortages, malnutrition, were dressed in rags and mostly barefoot." His thirsty pack animals, fed barely a kilogram of barley a day, were "so powerless, that they can no longer carry weapons and equipment." The men had begun deserting "in heaps," such that all that remained in the main Yildirim Army Group, when the storm broke, was about 29,000 men, barely as strong as a corps. Mustafa Kemal, commanding the Seventh Army holding the central sector of the front, could rely on only about 7,000 frontline troops. "We are like a cotton thread," he wrote about a week before Allenby's offensive began, "drawn across [the enemy's] path."[12]

At 4:30 a.m. on September 19, 1918, Allenby's forces opened a crushing artillery barrage against the Ottoman Eighth Army on the whole line between the Mediterranean coast and the mountains near Megiddo (the biblical Armageddon). At first light, British warplanes began flying over Turkish lines, dropping bombs on a number of Ottoman command and control posts and severing the telephone lines. Liman and Kemal did not therefore learn until about 9:00 a.m. that a breakthrough had occurred on the coast, although in fact the line had been punctured shortly before 7:00 a.m. (it helped the attackers immeasurably that little barbed wire was to hand in Palestine to slow them down). After mopping up what little resistance was offered by the Eighth Army on the coast, Allenby then swung east to attack Kemal's Seventh Army, which began retreating east toward the Jordan River. Although the crossing was achieved, the retreating Turks were harried and harassed by local Arabs and Bedouins, who sensed their day as rulers was done. In a flourish symbolizing the transfer of sovereignty, an entire Arab regiment of the Ottoman Eighth Army threw down its arms and went over to the British. Realizing that they did not have the men to hold Palestine, Liman and Kemal fell back to Damascus, then farther north to Baalbek, in the Bekaa Valley in Lebanon. The rout was on.[13]

Piling on where it hurt, Soviet foreign minister Georgii Chicherin informed the Ottoman ambassador the very next day that the Bolsheviks now viewed the terms of Brest-Litovsk relating to Turkey as a dead letter. There had always been something illusory about the Ottoman "victory" over Russia, dependent as it so clearly had been on the Germans. With Enver's regime now reeling under the impact of two simultaneous military catastrophes, the Bolsheviks were in no mood to keep up pretenses.* And so the Ottoman high

---

* Nor would they be several weeks later, once it became clear that the Germans, too, were going down. In addition to voiding the terms of Brest-Litovsk, the Bolsheviks took particular pleasure in looting the German consulate in Petrograd, where they found 250 million rubles stuffed away in thirty extremely heavy diplomatic mailbags.

command was now faced not only with the prospect of a general collapse in Palestine and Syria, on top of the opening of the Thracian front guarding the capital, but with the reactivation of Russian military activity in the Caucasus and along Turkey's Black Sea coast. With the world crumbling around him, Enver at last took the advice Liman (and Kemal, though he never listened to the latter) had been trying to give him since 1914 and pulled back his troops to shore up the empire's defenses. On October 2, 1918, Enver ordered the evacuation of the Transcaucasus, freeing up (in theory) four divisions to defend the capital.* The Ninth Division of the Ottoman Sixth Army, still spread out along the Persian front, was ordered back to Mosul, to defend against the British Indian Army advancing north from Baghdad.[14]

It was far too little, and at least a year too late. So spent had Turkey's fighting power been by the end of 1917, so overstretched her limited supplies of war matériel and lines of communication, that Liman had advised Enver, on the eve of Brest-Litovsk, that she could muster only enough strength "for a vigorous campaign on *one* front." Instead the Ottoman generalissimo had wagered the Ottoman Empire on a mad gamble to expand to the Caspian. While the extent of Enver's romantic attachment to "pan-Turkism," or the idea of uniting the Turkic peoples of Central Asia, Afghanistan, Persia, and the Caucasus in a Turkified Ottoman Empire, has sometimes been exaggerated, it is undeniable that Enver devoted a great deal of the empire's waning strength to the Transcaucasian offensive of 1918, including its best divisions— command of which he gave to his brother and uncle, in a clear sign of the real priority he accorded the conquest of Baku. First-line units freed up from the Romanian front, as the Germans had complained, were sent not to Thrace or Palestine, but to Batum and Azerbaijan. Even as the British were mustering their forces for Allenby's offensive in Palestine, Joseph Pomiankowski, the Austro-Hungarian military attaché, observed that "on the Turkish side . . . all available reserves and reinforcements of personnel and war materiél were sent to the Caucasus." Hearing venomous criticism from Liman all spring, Enver had at last agreed, in June, to second the Ottoman Thirty-Seventh and

---

* Tellingly, this was fully a week after Ludendorff himself requested urgently that Enver pull back all available troops to fend off the unfolding catastrophe in Thrace, offering for Germany's part to send the 16th Landwehr Division from the Crimea to Adrianople.

Forty-Seventh Divisions from the Caucasian Army Corps to Liman in Palestine, but it took them so long to get there that only the first eight battalions were able to participate in the September battles. In spring 1918, Liman's Yildirim Army Group had been strong enough to deflect Allenby's attempted raids across the Jordan. By September, it had been pared down to 26,000 rifles, 1,200 cavalry, and 250 guns, facing Allenby's 57,000 infantry, 12,000 cavalry, and 550 guns.* With his eyes on Baku, Enver had all but ceded Arab Palestine and Syria to the enemy—possibly by political design. It is a testament to the generalissimo's misplaced priorities that Damascus, capital of inland Syria and longtime headquarters of the Ottoman Fourth Army, was conquered, unopposed, by units of Australian light cavalry on October 1, 1918, the Turks having no troops left to defend it.[15]

The story in Mesopotamia was similar, not least in that Baghdad, like Damascus, had been abandoned without a fight. The Ottoman Sixth Army in Mosul under Ismail Hakki Bey, reduced to something like 30,000 effectives by the end of 1917, was further decimated by hunger and disease by September 1918, losing another 17,000 men despite the fact that it had seen little action of any kind since a bit of skirmishing near Tikrit in late March.[16] The Mesopotamian front was such a backwater by 1918 that it might not have seen any more fighting at all, but for the news from Macedonia and Syria, which suggested that the war might end before William Marshall, Maude's successor as commander of the British-Indian expeditionary force (Maude had died of cholera in November 1917), had conquered Mosul. In one of the more transparently political directives of the entire conflict, on October 2, 1918, the War Council instructed Marshall to "occupy as large a portion of the oil-bearing regions as possible."[17]

Marshall duly obliged, although with a bit less alacrity than was desired in London. After breaking through Ottoman lines at Sharqat on October 28, 1918, Marshall accepted Hakki Bey's surrender, taking 11,322 prisoners, at 7:30 a.m. on October 30—the same day an armistice was signed between

---

* In Enver's defense, it was not entirely his fault that the Yildirim Army Group was this weak. Ludendorff had demanded in June that German troops serving under Liman's command be recalled to Europe (this was the proximate cause of Enver's reluctant decision to rout reinforcements from the Caucasus to Palestine). Not all went, but Liman did lose eight battalions. The Palestinian front thus fell victim to both Enver's Caucasian gambit and the general German crisis in France.

Britain and Turkey, effective at noon on the thirty-first. In a painful reminder, for the Turks, of the shady way Churchill and Britain had begun the war in the Persian Gulf prematurely four years before (to the day), Marshall pushed on *after* the armistice was signed, reaching Mosul on November 2, 1918, in clear violation of the armistice terms. The reason is not hard to grasp: Mosul had been promised to France, but His Majesty's government no longer wished her to have it. In a process eerily similar to the falling-out of the Central Powers at Brest-Litovsk, Britain and France (the Russians having forfeited their own claims by signing a separate peace with Germany) were already squabbling over the Ottoman carcass.[18]

Still, important as the British advance in Palestine, Syria, and Mesopotamia was to the postwar future of the Middle East, in truth it had little to do with the outcome of the Ottoman war. The real price of Enver's foolish Caucasian gambit was paid in European Turkey, where the Ottoman "force pool" had been all but emptied, leaving Constantinople effectively undefended. The First Army there had been whittled down to fewer than two full divisions in 1917, and then stripped in summer 1918 down to almost nothing at all. Following the September disasters in Macedonia and Palestine, Enver ordered the Tenth Caucasian Infantry Division back to Thrace, but it had still not arrived by the time the armistice was signed, leaving all of about 7,500 troops in place to resist the advance of General Milne's British force of seven whole divisions, given clearance to advance on Constantinople after Franchet d'Esperey had forced an armistice on Bulgaria on September 28 (the main Salonica force was itself advancing north, helping Serbia reconquer Belgrade, and reaching the Danube by the end of October). The Ottoman Fifth Army, which had so ably repulsed the Allies at Gallipoli in 1915, had been pared down to a mere two well-below-strength divisions (the Forty-Ninth and Fifty-Seventh) by summer 1918, scarcely enough to defend the shore batteries. Here, too, Enver ordered reinforcements in from the Caucasus, but they would arrive far too late to affect the final act of the war.[19]

With no prospect of defending the capital, Talât Pasha petitioned the Entente powers for an armistice in the first week of October 1918, the same time as Ludendorff did (indeed it was precisely because he learned that Berlin had sued for peace that Talât was able to convince the Ottoman cabinet to give up). Talât even used the same diplomatic gambit as the Germans, petitioning President Wilson to mediate on the basis of the Fourteen Points, which seemed to offer a way to avoid the worst territorial losses. As a sweetener for the Americans, Talât proposed (again following Ludendorff's lead) that he and his fellow Young Turk triumvirs Enver and Djemal resign, to allow a more Entente-friendly government to ameliorate the armistice terms. In July, Mehmed Reshad V had died, so there was already a new sultan on the throne, his younger brother, Mehmed VI (Vahdettin). Asserting authority his brother never had, Vahdettin suggested that Talât hand over authority to Ahmet Tevfik Pasha, the old Hamidian stalwart who had served as foreign minister from 1899 to 1909 (before ascending to the office of grand vizier in the short-lived counterrevolutionary period following the "March 31 incident," which episode had crowned his position as symbolic head of the anti-CUP opposition). Not surprisingly, in view of his history, Tevfik Pasha insisted on a full purge of CUP men from the cabinet, a condition Talât refused to grant. And so, after a week of haggling, a compromise government was put together including a few CUP members (such as Djavid Bey, who had always opposed the German alliance) under Ahmed Izzet Pasha, the general who had been Kemal's commanding officer on the Caucasian front in 1916 (Izzet Pasha also shared Kemal's view that joining Germany had been a mistake). The key appointment, from the diplomatic perspective, was the installation of Captain Hüseyin Rauf (Orbay), a known Anglophile who had notoriously quarreled with the Germans during the war, as naval minister.* After Enver, Djemal, and Talât resigned on October 13, 1918, it was these men who would bear the ignominy of surrender, just as Friedrich Ebert and the Social Democrats would do in Berlin.[20]

Alas, like Ludendorff, the Turks were somewhat ill-informed about what the Fourteen Points actually said. Contrary to popular belief, Wilson had not really stipulated in either these points or the Four Particulars following them that there would be no gains of territory by the victors; rather he had qualified such annexations according to certain general principles ("every territorial

---

* In January 1915, Rauf had confiscated the kit of Oskar von Niedermayer, head of the German diplomatic mission to Afghanistan, including most of Niedermayer's weapons. Deeply unpopular with the Germans, Rauf would end his career as Turkish ambassador in London during the Second World War.

settlement . . . must be made in the interest and for the benefit of the populations concerned"). The Germans would soon discover that Wilson had no objection to the French reconquest of Alsace-Lorraine so long as it was made to accord with the inchoate notion of "self-determination" (indeed Wilson assured the French of this privately on October 16, 1918, although of course he did not inform Berlin). The Turks, for their part, would learn that the idea of "autonomous development" for national minorities in the Ottoman Empire, laid out by Wilson in point 12, was not at all incompatible with their forcible dismemberment from that empire by Britain and France. At any rate, it made even less sense for Talât to put his trust in Wilson than it did for Ludendorff. The United States was not at war with the Ottoman Empire, nor a party to any of the treaties related to its dismemberment.[21]

The fact was that the Allied breakthrough in Macedonia, and the German collapse coming in its wake, had undermined any possible negotiating leverage the Sublime Porte still had, whether on the Americans or anyone else. On October 12, 1918, Franchet d'Esperey's forces cut the Balkan rail link between Berlin and Constantinople, rendering a defense of the capital effectively impossible, even had the Young Turks wanted to fight to the bitter end. To be sure, there were still battle-hardened Ottoman divisions occupying the Transcaucasus, and in northern Syria, what remained of the Yildirim Army Group was waging a fighting retreat. As late as October 25, 1918, Kemal's rump "army," now down to 5,500 actives, defended Aleppo against Feisal's Arab irregulars, with Kemal taking a page from Lawrence's playbook and bribing the Bedouins into leaving town.*[22] After (briefly) restoring order in Aleppo, Kemal retreated northwest to Katma, a town on the lower slopes of the Amanus (Nur) mountain range guarding the Anatolian heartland, where, according to legend, he established "the border drawn by Turkish bayonets."†
In an act of symbolic political importance that *could* have altered the course

---

* Lawrence himself was nowhere to be seen at Aleppo. Two days after the fall of Damascus, to which his only contribution was to be chauffeured into town afterwards in a Rolls-Royce sedan (the Blue Mist), Lawrence asked Allenby for permission to return to England, whence he returned to begin composing his own legend.

† But we should give this legend no more credence than those of Lawrence. In fact Kemal returned to Constantinople after the armistice and began politicking along with all the other unemployed ex-army officers flooding into the capital.

of the war had it continued on into the winter, Liman Pasha turned over his Syrian command on October 31, 1918, to none other than Mustafa Kemal, whom he saluted personally for having proved himself "in many a glorious battle." Praising Kemal's fellow officers and men for the "devoted bravery" with which they had resisted Allenby's "far superior" forces, Liman signed off graciously. But there was little Kemal could do once the armistice was declared. The Sazonov-Sykes-Picot Agreement was not set in stone—especially now that the Russians had dropped out—but the British and French were now in a position to draw up more or less any armistice terms they wished to, limited only by their lack of trust for each other as they did so, and by their need to throw enough morsels to Italy and Greece to satisfy their opportunistic co-belligerents.[23]

Abandoned by the men who had pushed Turkey into the war, Izzet Pasha and Rauf (Orbay) did their best to maneuver with the empire's (mostly) British conquerors. But it was tough sledding, made tougher than it needed to be by their own inexperience. Their first mistake was trusting the word of General Charles Townshend, the man who had surrendered at Kut-al-Amara. Even while his mostly Indian soldiers had been detailed to hard labor on the Baghdad Railway, Townshend had been curiously indulged by the Young Turks ever since 1916, given a luxurious villa on Prinkipo island (Büyükada) in the Sea of Marmara and allowed to move about city society freely, which allowed him to become acquainted with both Izzet Pasha and Rauf Bey.* On October 17, 1918, Townshend offered to mediate on their behalf with the British. His suggestion, which would have been regarded with skepticism by more seasoned officials (Townshend had, after all, been deprived of contact with his own government for two and a half years), was to ask London to grant a peace that would allow the Ottomans to hold on to the Transcaucasus (still in Turkish hands) and even now-British-occupied Syria and Mesopotamia by giving these regions autonomy inside the empire, along the lines suggested in the Fourteen Points. Townshend would further assure the British, based on

---

* Not that Townshend was grateful for this indulgence. Among other "tortures" he suffered in his villa, he complained that he was forced to pay for his own groceries.

the evidence of his own generous treatment, that "Turkey desires above all things to be friendly with England" and ask, in return, that London step in with financial aid to alleviate shortages once German subsidies ceased at the end of the war. Looking Townshend's gift horse straight in the mouth, Rauf and Izzet Pasha agreed to let him contact the Admiralty on their behalf. On October 20, 1918, the self-appointed go-between was taken aboard a British vessel off the coast of Mytilene, and brought quickly to see Admiral Somerset Calthorpe, commander of Britain's Mediterranean fleet, aboard the *Agamemnon* in Mudros Harbor on Lemnos island. The Turks would now learn what fate Britain really had in store for them.[24]

British intentions toward the Ottoman Empire were still in flux. The last major German fortification, the Hermann line, was breached on October 20—the very day Townshend made contact with Calthorpe—and a German request for a ceasefire had been lodged. Even so, the German armies were still resisting, inflicting fierce casualties on the Allies as they retreated in good order toward the Rhine. There was a feeling in the War Cabinet that Britain needed an Ottoman armistice almost as badly as the Turks did, to free up the Straits and send forces into the Black Sea to menace the Central Powers from the rear. True, Britain wished to seize Mosul and Aleppo before the war ended (orders to this effect were issued on October 24, 1918). But the grasping claims of her allies, who had done so little fighting in Asiatic Turkey, were another matter. "It would not be possible," Lloyd George had told the cabinet on October 3, "for the British to go on fighting the Turks simply because the French wanted Syria or Armenia or the Italians wanted Adalia [Antalya]."[25] Lloyd George had even mooted the idea of jettisoning Sykes-Picot to speed things along with Turkey, although in the end his Conservative colleagues, Foreign Secretary Arthur Balfour and Chancellor of the Exchequer Andrew Bonar Law, had forced him to back down. At an inter-Allied summit held at Versailles on October 6–8, Lloyd George had won grudging acceptance from France and Italy of a draft Ottoman armistice, including the stipulation that whichever power Turkey approached first (which he assumed would be Britain) could open peace talks. The price was to add in a number of harsh clauses at French and Italian insistence giving Allied troops the right to occupy "any part of the Armenian vilayets" or, more broadly still, "any strategic point"—neither France nor Italy having yet succeeded, as the British had, in wresting control of the parts of the Ottoman Empire they coveted.

After hearing from Townshend and Calthorpe, the War Cabinet reconvened on October 21. By now there was broad agreement with Lloyd George's position that Britain should go it alone in forcing an armistice on Turkey (it helped that Franchet d'Esperey, to save time and free up forces to move into Serbia, had imposed the Bulgarian armistice unilaterally for France, thus establishing a regional precedent). In diplomatic practice, this meant that Calthorpe would insist on Britain's own armistice terms but not necessarily those of her allies. Although George Curzon, Lord President of the Council, who viewed the Turks as a "badly beaten enemy," believed that Britain should insist on full compliance, Lloyd George won over the military chiefs, who— still unsure about German intentions—wanted to open up the Straits before winter.* The War Cabinet thus agreed to allow Admiral Calthorpe considerable leeway in jettisoning any of the French and Italian terms the Turks considered objectionable. The French and Italian governments were duly informed that Calthorpe was opening armistice negotiations with the Ottoman Empire on their behalf, hoping to get acceptance of all twenty-four draft terms but insisting only on the first four, which broadly guaranteed "the condition of complete free and secure access to Constantinople and the Black Sea."[26]

Had experienced diplomats been sent to Mudros, Turkey might have secured a relatively lenient armistice by playing Britain's desire to settle things quickly off against the grasping goals of her allies. The British War Cabinet, especially Lloyd George, viewed French and Italian designs on Turkey with distaste, as neither power had fought for them directly, and by insisting on the right of occupation, they might prolong the war. Instead, Izzet Pasha sent Rauf (Orbay), the very Anglophile who had trusted Townshend. Having been trained by English naval officers, Rauf had taken fully on board notions of British "gentlemanliness" and "fair play." Admiral Calthorpe, after receiving the Turkish naval minister aboard the *Agamemnon* at 9:30 a.m. on

---

* British haste to open the Straits was strategically sound. The passage of the fleet through the Straits would immediately undermine German control of Ukraine and the Black Sea, greatly weakening Berlin's bargaining position at any peace conference.

October 27, 1918, gave Rauf "the impression of being an honest and open-minded man." Even Calthorpe's second-in-command, Aegean squadron commander Rear Admiral Seymour, who played something like "bad cop" to Calthorpe's "good cop" at Mudros, "did not appear" to Rauf "to be moved by a spirit of revenge." What made these judgments of character still more puzzling was that they were made *after* Rauf had already signed away the store to Calthorpe, agreeing to even the most onerous French and Italian demands with only minor reservations.[27]

What Rauf seems not to have understood was that English "gentlemanliness," whatever else it was, was a very shrewd negotiating strategy. Not for nothing had the Germans plied the bohemian Bolsheviks with food and drink at Brest-Litovsk; with equally good reason Trotsky had cut off the flow and quarantined his negotiators to restore Russian pride and diplomatic initiative. With no Trotsky to spoil the party, all accounts agree that the armistice talks carried out aboard the *Agamemnon* were extremely amicable, with no flashes of temper on either side. Acting as if there were no rush, Calthorpe proceeded through the terms so gingerly that it was late afternoon by the time he reached the explosive clause 16, which demanded the "surrender of all [Ottoman] garrisons in Hejaz, Asir, Yemen, Syria, Mesopotamia and Cilicia to the nearest Allied Commander or Arab representative." Clause 7, which granted the Allies the vague, ominously open-ended "right to occupy any strategic points" (this had been put in at Italian insistence), was passed over by Calthorpe as if insignificant; he simply said he would consult London to ask what it meant. As for France's poison pill, it was nightfall by the time Calthorpe reached clause 24, which stipulated that "in case of disorder in the Armenian vilayets, the Allies reserve to themselves the right to occupy any part of them." By this point Rauf was too exhausted to object. He had put up piecemeal objections all day, but the only concession he was able to win from Calthorpe was a promise not to let Italian or Greek troops occupy any of the Straits forts.

In fairness to Rauf, he was up against a masterly negotiator. Somehow Calthorpe was able to persuade the Ottoman naval minister that clause 7 could not possibly mean that the Allies could send troops *anywhere* in the Ottoman Empire—only to "some strategic points," which he hoped Britain's allies would define a bit more clearly; that the "use of Constantinople as a naval base" meant merely control of her dockyards, which would be stipulated expressly; that clause 24 only gave the Allies [e.g., France] the right to send troops to "Armenian" areas "in the event of threatened disorder," which would really apply only in exceptional circumstances (e.g., a new massacre or change of government in Turkey); and finally, that Calthorpe would personally recommend (though he could not put this in the armistice) that Greek warships would not dock in Smyrna (Izmir) or Constantinople. Turkey's own counter-request for financial aid to replace German subsidies was rejected out of hand. Finally, to force his opponent's hand, Calthorpe rejected Rauf's request that he be permitted time to telegraph Constantinople to see if the sultan and grand vizier would sign off on clause 7, huffing that "the longer the armistice proceedings took, the more chance there was of the whole thing being broken off." So Rauf had to decide alone whether or not to sign the draconian draft armistice before Calthorpe's stated deadline of 9:00 p.m. on October 30, 1918. He signed.[28]

Turkey now reaped what Enver had sown in his foolish push to the Caspian.* Individually, the clauses of the Mudros armistice might have sounded reasonable. Collectively, they amounted to a thoroughgoing dismemberment of the Ottoman Empire. "Allied occupation of the Dardanelles and Bosphorus forts" and the "opening of the Dardanelles and Bosphorus to secure access to the Black Sea" (clause 1) did not necessarily mean occupation of the capital, but this was implied in clause 9, even in Calthorpe's softened form demanding the "use of all ship repair facilities at all Turkish ports and arsenals." By stipulating the withdrawal and/or surrender of Ottoman garrisons from Persia and Transcaucasia (clause 11), the Hejaz, Assir, Yemen, Syria, and Mesopotamia (clause 16), and Tripoli and Cyrenaica (clause 17), and giving the Allies control over the "Taurus tunnel system" of the Baghdad Railway (built by the Germans and finally completed in 1918, these tunnels effectively divided the empire from the Arab provinces), Mudros effectively reduced the Ottoman

---

* This push was not over, either. With news of the armistice traveling slowly to the Caucasus, the Army of Islam continued rolling up the Transcaucasus, pivoting north into Daghestan after the fall of Baku. The Daghestani capital of Petrovsk (today's Makhachkala) fell on November 8, 1918, whereupon its conquering army learned that it had lost the war and would have to return this along with all its other Caucasian prizes.

Empire to its Anatolian rump, even if this was not yet enshrined in a formal treaty. Two major port cities still under firm Turkish control, Batum and Baku, were not only to be evacuated: the armistice expressly stipulated that the Allies would occupy them (clause 15), along with all trans-Caucasian railways. Moreover, by using antique geographic terms ("Palestine," "Mesopotamia," and "Cilicia") that corresponded to no known Ottoman administrative divisions, the British had deliberately left considerable leeway for interpretation. With the demobilization of the Ottoman armies required by clause 5, the only thing that would limit the final carve-up of the Ottoman carcass was the notion of British fair play that Rauf had unfortunately banked on.[29]

Worse was to come, and soon. One of the very few concessions Rauf was able to cajole out of Calthorpe was the modification of clause 16 so as to allow Turkey to maintain enough troops in "Cilicia" to "maintain order," while withdrawing the rest. The idea was that these troops, unlike those in Mesopotamia and the other Arab provinces, would not have to surrender. A corollary, implied though unstated, was that Allenby's troops, pursuant to the very idea of a "ceasefire," would not advance farther than the armistice lines. As early as November 5, 1918—shortly after Marshall (in clear violation of the armistice terms) seized Mosul—the British notified Mustafa Kemal that they intended to occupy Alexandretta (Iskenderun), as if daring him to do something about it.

He was the wrong man to cross. Two days previously, Kemal had asked Izzet Pasha for clarification of the rather nebulous armistice terms applying to his sector: what exactly was this "Cilicia" from which he was to withdraw some (though not all) of his troops? The ostensible pretext of the British request for Alexandretta was that, having already occupied Aleppo, they needed a port nearby to supply their forces and evacuate their wounded. Kemal, less trusting of British gentlemanliness than Rauf, believed the real reason was to cut off his army and force it to surrender. On November 6, 1918, Kemal sent off a wire informing the grand vizier that he had authorized his troops to fire on any troops landing at Alexandretta.* "My innate disposi-

---

* It is emblematic of Britain's peculiar choices in the Ottoman war that she did not get around to occupying Alexandretta until the war was over—only to find that the city's defenses, owing to the influx of Kemal and the rump

tion," Kemal explained to Izzet Pasha, "does not allow me to apply faithfully orders which justify the deceptive practices of the British, more eloquently than the latter do themselves. I therefore request you to appoint speedily a successor to whom I can . . . hand over my command."[30]

Kemal's instincts, and his reading of British and Allied intentions, were sound. But his timing was poor. The proud commander of what remained of the Yildirim Army Group was soundly rebuked for insubordination by Izzet Pasha, and forced to rescind his orders to resist the British at Alexandretta. On November 7, 1918, the Yildirim armies were formally disbanded by order of the sultan, and Kemal was recalled to the War Ministry. After four years of world war, and three years of regional war before that, the fight was out of the Turks—even out of the country's greatest general, who would now return to the Ottoman capital stripped of his new command before he could make anything of it. Before he left, however, Kemal issued secret orders to ship military stores north into Anatolia before the Allies seized the Taurus tunnels, and to distribute arms to militia groups forming in Antep (Gaziantep). Mustafa Kemal would be heard from again.

---

of his Syrian army, were now stiffer than they had been during the war, when she could have taken the city with ease.

CHAPTER 18

SÈVRES

From such knowledge of the East as I possess, I cannot help thinking
that this great pack of cards which is being reared will, almost at the first blow,
tumble in fragments towards the ground.

—GEORGE CURZON,

Lord President of the Council, former Viceroy of India,
and shortly to be named Secretary of State for Foreign Affairs[1]

DESPITE THE GREAT SKILL with which Calthorpe had induced Turkey to accept nearly every clause of the draft armistice, not everyone on the Allied side was happy with it. Victors in war are rarely magnanimous, after all, especially after fighting as savage as that seen in Europe and the Middle East between 1914 and 1918. What had seemed to Calthorpe like selfless indulgence to French interests was perceived as anything but in Paris. The French were furious after news was received that Calthorpe had expressly refused to allow a French negotiator aboard the *Agamemnon* on behalf of Admiral Dominique Gauchet, Calthorpe's superior officer (France having been given the Mediterranean command by inter-Allied agreement in 1914, although this had been honored in the breach ever since). France's powerful premier, Georges Clemenceau, protested the snub vigorously when he met with Lloyd George at the Quai d'Orsay on October 30, 1918, just as the armistice was being signed at Mudros. As Colonel E. M. House, President Wilson's liaison to the Supreme Command, recalled of the hostile encounter, "They bandied like fish-wives, at least Lloyd George did." Against Clemenceau's complaint that France had been excluded from armistice talks, the British prime minister retorted that Britain had "captured three or four Turkish armies and had incurred hundreds of thousands of casualties in the war with Turkey. The other governments had only put in a few nigger policemen to see that we did not steal the Holy Sepulchre!" Besides, as Foreign Secretary Arthur Balfour reminded Clemenceau a bit more diplomatically, Franchet d'Esperey had imposed his own armistice on Bulgaria, so Calthorpe was only following French precedent. Although Clemenceau went along, he did so under evident duress. Lloyd George's bullying tone suggested that he had no intention of honoring the Sykes-Picot Agreement now that Britain had Turkey in her power.[2]

In the Arab provinces, the battle over the Ottoman inheritance had already been joined. With British troops occupying most of Mesopotamia and Palestine, there was little France could do to make good her claims there, as Clemenceau tacitly admitted when he signed off (verbally) on British control of both in December 1918—including Mosul, which had been expressly placed in the French zone in 1916 to form a buffer against now-Bolshevized Russia. To stake her claims to Syrian Lebanon and Cilicia under the open-ended terms of Mudros, France could and did land troops at Beirut, Alexandretta, and Mersin (near Adana). But inland Syria, conquered in 1918 and now occupied by Allenby's army, was another matter. During the Sazonov-Sykes-Picot negotiations of 1916, the British had agreed to cede most of greater Ottoman Syria to the French zone of influence, although only the coastal area (i.e., today's Lebanon) was supposed to be under direct French rule, with the inland portions under "independent" Arab administration, which in practice meant Feisal and Hussein's other sons. Theoretically there was to be a kind of border between the two zones stretching along a line drawn through Damascus, Homs, Hama, and Aleppo, each allotted to the Arab side—though these cities were still squarely in the French "zone of influence." But how was France to exert predominance over areas now occupied by British troops?

Complicating these questions further was the Woodrow Wilson factor. Because of the possibly decisive contribution of American troops to the collapse of German morale on the western front, along with the financial leverage U.S. banking institutions now enjoyed vis-à-vis the Allies indebted to them, the American president was believed to be nearly all-powerful on the eve of the peace talks that would open in Paris in January. As we saw in the German and Ottoman pleas for peace, the Wilsonian ideal of national "self-determination" had acquired the properties of an all-purpose diplomatic and political talisman in the course of 1918, suggesting that both Britain and France would have to pay it lip service, at least, as they proceeded to carve up the Ottoman Empire.

In the strange new diplomatic game of appeasing American sensitivities on the Ottoman settlement (even though the United States had not gone to war with Turkey!), Lloyd George and the British believed that, in Feisal and his Arab irregulars, they had an ace in the hole, a façade to rule behind. Indeed it was precisely to cloak the British conquest of Syria in the garb of Arab self-determination that Allenby had tried to stage-manage the conquest of Damascus as Feisal's doing, only for the Turks to withdraw from the city (along with most Ottoman government officials) while Feisal's Arabs were still miles away. Feisal himself had only arrived on October 3, 1918, two days after the fall of Damascus, after a small pro-Hashemite clique had been cynically installed in city government by the British. Allenby himself was game enough to inform Feisal that he would have to rule inland Syria "under French guidance and financial backing," but the fact remained that it had been British (actually Australian) troops who had taken Damascus, and they were not going anywhere.[3]

The British, Australian, and Indian conquerors of Ottoman Syria would now be transformed, through a kind of diplomatic alchemy, into Arabs. Anticipating this very tack, the French press sought to undermine Feisal's Arabs by playing up Lawrence's role in leading them. Astonishingly, in light of his later rise to world fame, Lawrence was entirely unknown to the Western public before the end of the war, largely by design. Both Allenby and his chief political officer, Gilbert Clayton, had concealed Lawrence's role in public communiqués so as not to compromise Feisal's political prospects. As late as December 30, 1918, Lawrence was unmentioned in the account of the fall of Damascus published in the *London Gazette*.[4] It was actually a French newspaper that first broke Lawrence's "cover," expressly to belittle Feisal's Arabs. Colonel Lawrence, the *Echo de Paris* reported in late September 1918, riding at the head of a cavalry force of "Bedouins and Druze," had "sever[ed] enemy communications between Damascus and Haifa by cutting the Hejaz railway near Deraa," thereby playing "a part of the greatest importance in the Palestine victory."[5]

By introducing T. E. Lawrence to the world, the French scored an own goal of the most self-destructive kind. Seeking to undermine Feisal, the *Echo de Paris* had instead glorified Feisal's greatest champion, a man born for the role of mythmaker. Rather than deny his role in the Arab revolt, Lawrence shrewdly manipulated his newfound fame, presenting himself not as an effective liaison officer who had helped Arab guerrillas blow up some railway junctions but as a witness to an Arab national awakening. At first subtly, then with more and more brazen confidence, Lawrence began to lie outright about the Arab contribution in Syria, claiming that 4,000 Arab troops led by Feisal had entered Damascus first, thereby staking an unshakable claim to the Syrian capital. Lloyd George then inflated this figure further, inducing Feisal to issue a public statement claiming that no fewer than 100,000 Arabs had fought under him. With British subsidies to Feisal now running at £150,000 a *month*, the British were doubling down on their investment.[6]

Falling for their own propaganda, the British even used Feisal to beatify the Zionist cause. Calling the bluff of Britain's Balfour Declaration, Vladimir Jabotinsky had raised a special Jewish Legion to fight alongside Allenby, which had reached the front in February 1918, in time to participate in the push to Damascus (if not the conquest of Palestine itself, as Jaffa and Jerusalem had already fallen). But, in the course of occupying Palestine, the British government had belatedly discovered that encouraging further Jewish settlement—let alone creating a Zionist state there—was not terrifically popular with the local Arab Christians and (especially) Muslims.* British foreign secretary Arthur Balfour therefore urged Feisal, while he was visiting London in December 1918, to come to some kind of agreement with Chaim Weizmann, president of the World Zionist Organization. The resulting Feisal-Weizmann Agreement, signed by both men on January 3, 1919, was a

---

* As Lloyd George wrote with revealing bitterness in his memoirs, "We could not get in touch with the Palestinian Arabs, as they were fighting with us" (i.e., serving loyally in the Ottoman armies, rather than joining Feisal).

wonderfully cynical brainstorm of the British Foreign Office, in which Zionists agreed to recognize Feisal's claim on Syria in exchange for "Arab" endorsement of Zionism up to and including the proviso that "all necessary measures shall be taken to encourage and stimulate immigration of Jews into Palestine on a large scale." The entire improbable edifice, however, was made conditional on Syrian Arab independence being achieved on the principle of self-determination, a principle Feisal himself had just symbolically repudiated by signing off on Zionist claims on Palestine, where Jews constituted nowhere near a majority. By so doing, Feisal had also, perhaps inadvertently, forfeited his own claim to coastal Palestine, although his brother Abdullah was later given a kingdom in the large desert area split off from it (Transjordan, or today's Jordan). Moreover, by swallowing Balfour's poison pill, Feisal had gravely undermined his family's claim to speak for the Arabs, as the vast majority of Arabs was vociferously opposed to Zionism.[7]

By the time Feisal himself arrived in Paris on February 6, 1919, to present the case for Arab "self-government" in Syria, Lawrence and the British had assembled an entire public relations team for him, pumping gullible journalists (especially American ones) with tales of derring-do by the Hashemite prince. Embracing his part, Feisal showed up to address the Supreme Council wearing "white robes embroidered with gold," with "a scimitar at his side," thus inaugurating the curious twentieth-century tradition of Arab leaders addressing diplomatic assemblies while fully armed. In an inspired touch, Lawrence "interpreted" Feisal's remarks to the Supreme Allied Council himself (in fact Lawrence's Arabic was rather poor, so that what he was really doing was making Feisal's arguments for him; the rumor was that Feisal was merely reciting the Koran). Speaking for Feisal, Lawrence said that the Arabs wanted, above all, self-determination. The Lawrence-Feisal show, judging by the effusions of Colonel House (in whom Feisal "inspired a kindly feeling for the Arabs") and U.S. secretary of state Robert Lansing (Feisal "seemed to breathe the perfume of frankincense"), thoroughly bamboozled the Americans. The French, outmaneuvered, denounced the infuriating Feisal as "British imperialism with Arab headgear."[8]

The bad faith being displayed by both sides here was breathtaking. With an eye to appeasing Wilson and the Americans, Lloyd George and

Clemenceau had issued a joint "Anglo-French declaration" on November 9, 1918, ostensibly endorsing Arab self-determination ("the setting up of national governments and administrations deriving their authority from the free exercise of the initiative and choice of the indigenous populations"). Neither man really intended to honor any such principle, although Lloyd George wanted to pledge Clemenceau to do so, so as to scuttle any French claim to Syria. No fool, Clemenceau had therefore conditioned the declaration with a promise that the Allies would provide "such support and efficacious help as will ensure the smooth working of the governments." Confronted with Feisal's dubious claim to represent the people of Syria, the French had first tried to woo him away from Britain, going so far as to award him the *Légion d'honneur*. When this failed, they had tried to sideline him by erasing his name from the list of accredited delegates in Paris.* After Feisal's command performance in February 1919, Clemenceau summoned an Arab, Shukri Ganem, who purported to speak for a "Central Syrian Committee," to remind everyone (especially the Americans) that the Hashemites of Mecca had no prior connection to his country, which, of course, they did not. The British quietly slipped a note to President Wilson pointing out that Ganem had lived in Paris for the past thirty-five years (it turned out he did not even remember his Arabic).[9]

Tiring of the charade, on February 15, 1919, Clemenceau simply proposed a quid pro quo to Lloyd George. France would agree to scrap Sykes-Picot and formally cede both Mosul and Palestine, so long as Britain would give France the mandate for greater Syria and a quarter of the oil production of Mosul, which would be brought to market via pipelines to be constructed in French Syria. Lloyd George, unwilling to give up the Feisal card, refused to budge.[10]

Woodrow Wilson, for whose benefit Feisal's floor show had been performed, was not impressed. After a brief return trip to Washington, the president returned to Paris in March, determined to stick to his guns. On March 20, 1919, the president was called in to mediate between Clemenceau and

---

* The French were apparently unaware of the enormous size of the subsidy Britain was paying Feisal. The British, for their part, were equally unaware that Feisal's retainer had not purchased sufficient loyalty to prevent him from promising the Young Turks to spread tales through the bazaars of Mecca blaming them for deliberately mass-starving Muslims. Truly, if devious diplomatic dance partners ever deserved each other, it was these three.

Lloyd George. After enduring more histrionics over Syria, Wilson called the Briton's bluff. If the "consent of the governed" was the basis on which the postwar Arab world would be organized, then why not, Wilson suggested, send a fact-finding commission to "discover the desires of the population in these regions" so as to provide "the most scientific basis possible for a settlement"? Now it was Clemenceau's turn to bluff. Certainly, he agreed, we must see if Syrians wished to be ruled by France—but only as long as the inhabitants of Palestine and Mesopotamia, too, were asked whether they desired to be British subjects. Calling Clemenceau's bluff in turn, Wilson enjoined the Supreme Council of the Allies to send "neutral" committees to canvass opinion in "certain areas comprising . . . Palestine, Syria, the Arab countries to the east of Palestine and Syria, Mesopotamia, Armenian, Cilicia, and perhaps additional areas in Asia Minor [Anatolia]," to ensure that any governments there created would rule "with approval of the inhabitants."[*11]

The U.S. government was in a peculiar position vis-à-vis the Ottoman question, analogous in some ways to the sudden emergence of Wilhelmine Germany in the 1890s as the least threatening power for Abdul Hamid II. Precisely because they had not gone to war with Turkey, the Americans were viewed by nearly all post-Ottoman factions as the ideal postwar patrons, being untainted by imperial ambition in the region. The Wilsonian commission sent to canvass opinion in Asiatic Turkey, headed by the Americans Charles Crane and Henry C. King (neither Clemenceau nor Lloyd George wishing to humor its importance by appointing their own people), reported nearly unanimous sentiment in favor of an American mandate in Palestine and Syria, because the United States was seen as the power most likely to accept Arab independence.[12] Even Feisal, despite his friendship with Lawrence and his colossal British retainer, endorsed the idea of a U.S. mandate for Syria in February 1919, rather startling the Americans when they heard this. At times even British officials, such as Maurice Hankey, the secretary of the war cabinet, toyed with the idea of giving Washington the mandate for Palestine, "with the object of creating a buffer state to cover Egypt."[13]

---

* Feisal, when he learned this, was said to have drunk champagne to celebrate, thus casting (for anyone who heard the story) yet more doubt on his claim to faithfully represent the Arab Muslim cause.

Above all, it was the Armenian delegation in Paris, represented by Boghos Nubar Pasha (speaking for the large global diaspora) and Avedis Aharonian (a Dashnak veteran representing the new Republic of Armenia), that looked to Wilson for salvation. American missionaries had borne witness to the suffering of Ottoman Armenians for decades, and their testimony about the massacres of 1915 had been especially valuable in shaping opinion in Western capitals. In the United States itself, there were dozens of activist groups advocating the Armenian cause, crowned by the American Committee for the Independence of Armenia, headed by the former U.S. ambassador, James Gerard, and adorned by luminaries such as former secretary of state William Jennings Bryan, Supreme Court justice and future secretary of state Charles Evans Hughes, the governor of New York, and the presidents of Harvard and Columbia. Before he headed to Paris, Woodrow Wilson's White House had been flooded with petitions demanding that he "help Armenia to establish adequate reparation for the terrible losses the Armenian people have suffered during the war."[14]

There was indeed much to be said for an American mandate over Turkish Armenia, or more broadly for Asia Minor (Anatolia) as a whole. Despite his own sympathies with the Armenian cause, President Wilson had consistently insisted that Turks, too, must have self-determination, implying that the American officials would do everything they could to broker things as fairly as possible. Alone of all the powers, the United States had the financial wherewithal and available manpower to invest in a long-term occupation of Anatolia of the kind probably necessary to protect Armenians and other minorities, which, some believed, might require as many as 100,000 troops. If she did so, she could count on British and even (though more reluctantly) French support. When Colonel House told Lloyd George and Clemenceau on March 7, 1919, that the United States would accept a mandate after all, the Briton was "delighted" to hear that the Americans were finally taking up this "noble duty." Of course, like all Lloyd George's effusions, there was likely a hidden motive to this one, which is not hard to fathom (the Americans, once installed, would presumably keep the French out of Asia Minor). Still, there is no question that a U.S. mandate for "Armenia," however broadly defined, would have been welcomed by the Supreme Allied Council in Paris.[15]

Even the Turks, once they learned of the proposals circulating around Paris for a U.S. mandate, embraced the idea. A special government committee in Constantinople, headed by now-former grand vizier Izzet Pasha, was established to encourage the Americans to take over a mandate for the *entirety* of the Ottoman Empire (or whatever was left of it), more or less in order "to save it from the Greeks and Armenians." Nearly all the leading Ottoman newspapers were on board, along with the educated classes of Constantinople. As Ahmed Emin Bey (Yalman), editor of *Vakit*, argued, the choice was really "between an American mandate and chaos." Even Turkish nationalists who had fled to the interior liked the idea. Rıza Nur, a military surgeon who would become one of the founding members of the Turkish Grand National Assembly in Ankara, believed that "if America were to accept the mandate and behave in a just and honest manner, it could within twenty years bring us a degree of development which Turks, left to themselves, would not be able to achieve in a century." Showing that this was not an isolated opinion, the proposed U.S. mandate was accepted at a nationalist congress in Sivas in September 1919, on the condition that the Americans not violate the country's independence and integrity. So alluring was the idea of an American mandate for Armenia that Woodrow Wilson himself, after months of hemming and hawing, endorsed it in Paris on May 14, 1919, subject only to approval from the U.S. Senate. In this way one of the most tangled and morally vexatious of Ottoman succession controversies seemed to have been settled to the satisfaction of all parties.[16]

The problem with U.S. mandates for Armenia, Anatolia, Syria, Palestine, or Ottoman Turkey writ large was, of course, that the Americans themselves wanted no part of them. It was one thing to advocate for Ottoman Armenians, and to support the rights of other former Ottoman subject peoples to self-determination. It was quite another to send young men into harm's way, in a deeply unfamiliar land, to enforce a difficult settlement on fractious peoples who had good reason not to trust one another. Before his nerves began to crack in May, Wilson had repeatedly told the Supreme Council not to count on the United States to police the Ottoman settlement. As the president put it in a moment of unusual frankness, he "could think of nothing the people of the United States would be less inclined to accept than military responsibility in Asia." By the time the King-Crane Commission submitted its findings on August 28, 1919, advocating a tripartite U.S. mandate for Constantinople and environs, "Armenia," and the rest of Anatolian Turkey,* the Americanophile sentiments it reported were already moot, as Wilson had left Paris and the treaty negotiated there was being roundly criticized in the American press, with ratification destined to go down to a famous defeat in the U.S. Senate. What might have become a historic record of public opinion in the Ottoman Empire at the very moment of its dissolution was instead shelved as irrelevant (the King-Crane report was published only in 1922, and remains almost unknown today).[17]

Disappointing as the rapid American withdrawal from the Ottoman settlement was for so many, it should not have been terribly surprising. The very reason such disparate groups as Armenians, Arabs, and Turks favored a U.S. mandate over British or French ones—American disinterest and lack of ambition in the region—was sufficient explanation for why the United States would not stick around to take one. Americans, as a people, simply had no interest in taking up new burdens of empire in 1919, especially not in a troubled and violent part of the world where they had little experience beyond the missionary colleges in Constantinople and Beirut.[†] It is easy to see why this American unworldliness appealed to peoples who wished to escape the clutches of European imperialists, and no less easy to see why it proved a mirage.

Where Americans feared to tread, others proved more than willing. The Greeks, parvenus to the world war, wasted little time capitalizing on the good fortune that had seen them join the Allies at Salonica shortly before Franchet d'Esperey's breakthrough.[‡] Shortly following the Mudros armistice, Greek

---

* The King-Crane Commission did grudgingly accept British mandates for Mesopotamia and Palestine, and France's for Syria, but the latter in particular was recommended only as "frankly based, not on the primary desires of the people but on the international need of preserving friendly relations between France and Great Britain."

† Judging by the anti-interventionist reaction that followed the recent wars in Afghanistan and Iraq, one could say the same thing today. From Rudyard Kipling ("take up the white man's burden"), to Hankey and Lloyd George in 1919, Churchill in 1946 (the "Iron Curtain" speech), to Niall Ferguson in recent years, there is a long and venerable tradition of Britons trying to sell Americans on the imperial vocation. It remains a tough ask.

‡ Although Greece had mobilized 230,000 troops, she lost only some 5,000 dead and about 26,000 casualties, the lowest share suffered by any belligerent other than Japan and the United States.

troops seized the Aegean port of Dedeagatch (Alexandroupoli) from Bulgaria, along with the remainder of Bulgarian Thrace. In early January, the Greeks pushed on into the Ottoman sections of western Thrace, meeting little resistance as they distributed arms to local Greeks and put Turkish Muslims to flight. By April the Greeks had (with first tacit, then explicit, Allied approval) advanced as far as Tekirdağ, leaving little but a rump Turkish hinterland guarding the capital.[18]

Anxious to prevent perfidious Albion from taking all the Ottoman spoils for herself, the French had moved nearly as fast as the Greeks. Although inland Syria remained out of reach so long as Allenby's army was there, the French began landing troops along the coast as early as December 11, 1918, fanning out into the Hatay and taking Antioch (Antakya). Farther north, the French landed a small force at Mersin on December 18, which swept north to occupy Adana, the largest city and ostensible capital of "Cilicia" (a geographic term still awaiting definition). Back in Ottoman Europe, French troops seized the key railway junctions of the Orient Express railway between Macedonia and Thrace, and dispatched a brigade by train to occupy Constantinople alongside the British, who were ferrying troops in via the Aegean. By early 1919 the Allies had 3,500 troops occupying the capital, few of them pretending to an interest in the dockyards—thus giving the lie to Calthorpe's modified clause 9 of the Mudros armistice. Instead the occupiers appropriated all the prime real estate in the capital, taking over the military barracks in Taksim, the Bosphorus forts at Rumeli Kavak, and other strategic points. The British set up their command headquarters at the military school at Harbiye, the French in the Sixth District municipal building on the heights of Tünel above the Galata Tower, and the Italians in grand style in a luxurious pasha's villa in Nişantaşı, the Soho of modern Istanbul. More broadly, the Italian occupation zone comprised the Asian parts of the city, including Üsküdar, Kadıköy, and most of the Marmara islands. The British took the northern European districts extending from Pera (Beyoğlu) up to the Black Sea. The French helped themselves to what was supposed to have been Russia's zone: the old city of Byzantium, including the Orient Express railway terminus of Sirkeci station.[19] Still, the French were not satisfied. Invoking clause 7, which granted the right of occupation "in the event of a situation arising which threatens the security of the Allies," the French, following an outbreak of (mostly Greek) partisan banditry near Zonguldak, landed troops there in March 1919 to secure the coal mines.[20]

No less quick off the mark were the Italians. In the Treaty of London, under which the country had entered the war in May 1915, Italy had been promised a "just share in the Mediterranean region adjacent to the province of Adalia [Antalya]." With excellent timing, Italy's foreign minister, Baron Sidney Sonnino, had pressed for a clarification of the Italian claim in the Ottoman carve-up in April 1917, at the nadir of Allied fortunes in the war—and, crucially, before Greece had entered the war. Concerned that, with mutinies spreading through the armies of revolutionary Russia, the whole Allied position in the East was falling apart, Lloyd George had reluctantly agreed, in the St.-Jean-de-Maurienne agreement of April 26, 1917, to expand the Italian zone westward to the Aegean, taking in the Kaş/Kalkan area, Fethiye, and even Aydin and Smyrna. (Awkwardly, the Greeks had then been induced to enter the war two months later, largely on the understanding that Smyrna would be given to them, although this had not been put in writing.) As early as December 1918, small advance contingents of Greek and Italian troops landed in Smyrna to stake their countries' respective claims, in a standoff soon to have historic consequences. But the real move came at the end of March 1919, when the Italians, seizing on the same clause 7 the French used to justify their move into Zonguldak, landed troops in Antalya, Kaş, and Silifke (between Antalya and Mersin), who quickly fanned out along Turkey's Mediterranean coast.[21]

So far, the Turks had proved uncharacteristically docile in the face of these abuses of the Mudros armistice. The French move into coastal Syria and Cilicia had been expected, as had the British push beyond the armistice lines to Mosul and Aleppo. The Italian move into Antalya and environs was somewhat absurd (the only "historic justification" the Italians came up with was that Rome had ruled the area two millennia ago). Still, the very tenuousness of the Italian claim to southern Turkey, or the French to Zonguldak, made these moves less threatening than, say, a Greek or Armenian occupation might have been. It was not always such a bad thing to have troops in areas plagued by banditry, and in some places, such as Fethiye, the Italians seem to have met a friendly reception. According to multiple sources, Mustafa Kemal himself, during his days kicking around occupied Constantinople, got in touch with the Italian high commissioner, Count Carlo Sforza, possibly in order to leverage the Italians against the more threatening British.[22] Even the Greek push into Thrace, although accompanied by a wave of ethnic cleansing, was accepted in Constantinople as a kind of *fait accompli*, brought on by Enver's foolish degrading of the force pool defending the capital.

Likewise, the Allied occupation of Constantinople itself, though a bitter pill for proud Turks to swallow, was impossible for them to resist in any effective way now that the Allied fleet, after being granted free passage through a Dardanelles now cleared of mines, was anchored in the Bosphorus. While small groups of conspirators began meeting and plotting in secret, the Ottoman government offered full compliance with the Allied occupation authorities. On November 11, 1918, the cabinet had been purged of its last CUP elements, with Izzet Pasha making way for Tevfik Pasha, the old, now half-senile Hamidian, as grand vizier. In December, Tevfik Pasha agreed to let the Allies set up a war crimes tribunal to try CUP officials guilty of crimes against humanity, particularly those who had participated in the Armenian massacres of 1915. The sultan agreed, although Vahdettin, fearing a popular backlash if the government was seen too obviously to be toadying to the Allies, asked that Britain also consider crimes committed against Turkish Muslims during the war. This request, along with a plea that representatives from four neutral governments (Denmark, Spain, Sweden, and the Netherlands) participate in the process, was submitted to the Allied high commissioners on February 12, 1919. Both requests were denied.[23]

Whether out of a genuine desire for justice or (as cynics suspected) in order to deflect blame onto the now-disgraced CUP, the Ottoman government duly convened an Istanbul Court-Martial (*Divan-i Harb-i Örfi*) under Allied supervision, followed shortly by war crimes tribunals set up in provincial cities, notably in Yozgat (near Ankara), Trabzon, Erzincan, and Bayburt. Some thirty senior CUP officials were arrested in the capital at the end of January 1919, shortly to be followed by a hundred lesser lights. Seven leading figures who had fled (such as Enver, Djemal, Talât, and Dr. Nazım) were put on trial *in absentia* for war crimes. Enver's notorious Special Organization

(*Teşkilat-ı -Mahsusa*) was also implicated in offenses related to the deportation and massacre of Armenian civilians. While some sixty-seven prisoners—about half of the original arrestees—were released in May, a few serious indictments were handed down in July 1919, notably death sentences pronounced on Talât, Enver, Djemal, and Dr. Nazım. Although the pace slowed considerably after the first trial of the CUP leadership, the tribunal continued handing down verdicts until 1922.

The nature and importance of the Istanbul tribunal have been debated ever since. Ottoman jurisprudence was never particularly transparent, and these trials proved no exception. For reasons of expediency, witnesses were not called to corroborate the government's claims against defendants, which rested instead on written documents or depositions taken elsewhere. Moreover, defendants—even those actually present—were not allowed the right of cross-examination. Some of this may have been by design, as the Ottoman government may have been subtly trying to undermine its own verdicts, so as not to anger critics who believed the tribunal represented "victor's justice." Admiral Calthorpe, who, after signing the Mudros armistice, took over as British high commissioner in occupied Constantinople, warned London in August 1919 that the trials were "proving to be a farce and injurious to our own prestige and to that of the Turkish government." Trial records were poorly kept, and most have disappeared. Historians trying to reconstruct the evidence have had to rely on the running chronicle in the Ottoman government gazette, the *Takvim-i Vekayi*, and popular press reports of the proceedings. These sources have furnished ammunition to genocide scholars, although they are problematic. Taner Akçam, who has analyzed the postwar tribunals thoroughly, bases much of his own "genocide" case against the CUP (and Enver's Special Organization in particular) on testimony related to documents the prosecution was *unable* to produce, because these had been allegedly "carried off" (*aşırılmış*) by the departing leadership. Akçam has even found surviving Ottoman government orders to destroy documents, which suggests that many materials relating to the deportation campaign of 1915 had indeed disappeared by 1919, as government prosecutors complained. The evidence of document tampering discussed during the postwar trials is suggestive, but suggestive of exactly what, we simply do not know.[24]

In the end the postwar war crimes tribunals satisfied almost no one. They provided some, but not nearly enough, documentation of CUP crimes and human rights abuses to please either the Armenians or the Allies who wanted justice for them; and of course the death sentences against the CUP ringleaders were not carried out, thus depriving victims of closure.* Nor were any Greeks or Armenians tried for crimes committed against Muslims during the war, which undermined the credibility of the tribunal with Turkish nationalists and Ottoman Muslims more generally. During the war, the Ottoman government, with no motivation to curry favor with outside powers, had itself convened more than a thousand courts-martial against officials "found guilty of organizing or failing to prevent [attacks]" against (mostly Armenian) civilians. By contrast, the much-vaunted postwar tribunals produced only a handful of convictions. Little wonder Admiral de Robeck, one of Calthorpe's commissioners, concluded that their "findings cannot be held of any account at all."[25]

The war crimes tribunals were probably never going to be accepted as fully legitimate by Ottoman Muslims, who believed themselves to have suffered as much during the war as anyone else. Had the government's requests that neutral powers participate, and that crimes against Muslims also be prosecuted, been honored, it is possible that the trials would have acquired more gravity and caused more serious soul-searching among Turks about the wartime persecution of Armenians and other Christians. Even so, there were limits to Turkish forbearance, and these limits were being sorely tested. French, Italian, and British occupation, the Greeks in Thrace—all this was bad enough. But when Turks learned that the French had invited an "Armenian Legion" to participate in the occupation of Cilicia, this was something else. The *Légion arménienne*, comprising three of the four battalions of the so-called *Légion d'Orient*, had been trained on Cyprus, and then participated in a supporting role in Allenby's campaign in Palestine and Syria in 1918, attached to the British XXI Army Corps. The bulk of its volunteers were Ottoman subjects from the heights above Antioch (Antakya), who had taken

---

* Although they *were* arguably later carried out by Armenian vengeance-seekers, who assassinated Talât in Berlin in March 1921 and Djemal in Tiflis in August 1922. Enver himself died, weapon in hand, fighting alongside the Turkic Basmachi (Muslim guerrilla) rebels against the Red Army near Dushanbe, in present-day Tajikistan.

up arms after the deportation campaign began and then fled aboard a French warship, which had appeared off the coast near Alexandretta in early August 1915. Recovering at Port Said, the Armenian refugees asked France to arm them in order "to continue their fight against the Turks."[26]

Now, they did so. In part because the French did not have other forces in the region, it was primarily the Armenian Legion that carried out the Cilician occupation, securing the Baghdad Railway from Pozantı to Dörtyol, from Islahiye and Adana. Along the way, they went on a rampage. As General Hamelin, commander of the Legion, reported to the French high commissioner on February 2, 1919, his Armenian soldiers were "burning with a desire to take vengeance for the exactions which they had experienced for so many years"; it would thus have required "discipline of iron to force them to act as French soldiers." Clearly they did not so act, as Hamelin lamented that "since their arrival in Cilicia, there has not been a day when I have not been apprised by the local Ottoman authorities or by the British authorities of complaints, unhappily most often very well founded, against the Armenians' excesses of all kinds toward the local populations (thefts, armed attacks, pillages, murders)." By the time the first significant detachments of actual French troops began arriving in Cilicia in July 1919, it was too late to erase the bad impression created by the Armenian Legion among local Muslims.[27]

The most serious mistake made by the Allies in 1919 was the decision to allow the Greeks to occupy Smyrna. If there was a single place in the empire crying out for a careful approach, for occupation by some kind of multinational gendarmerie on the precedent of Crete in 1897 or Macedonia in 1903, it was here. Although the population figures were ferociously contested, there is no doubt that the Greek population of the city was substantial, half or more of nearly 300,000 in 1919, or that Greek merchants and businessmen dominated the local culture and the economy, too, from manufacturing to foreign trade. Of some 4,600 factories and artisanal shops in Aydin province, more than 4,000 were owned by native Ottoman Greeks, which caused no little resentment among Ottoman Muslims.[28] Adding fuel to the demographic polemics, there had been a huge influx of foreign Greeks from the "mainland" as Smyrna's economy boomed in the nineteenth century, in part owing to the propagation of the "Megali Idea" of a restored Greek-Byzantine empire, in which Smyrna figured so prominently. The city had become even more Greek as it prospered, with Greeks peaking at nearly 50 percent of the population by the turn of the twentieth century, which lent ammunition to the irredentist claims on it pressed by expansionists like Venizelos in Athens. This influx had, however, swung sharply into reverse in the wake of the Balkan Wars, which had seen the forced exodus of at least 150,000 ethnic Greeks from the Aegean coast, including tens of thousands from the Smyrna area (though more from nearby towns such as Soke, Sevdiyeköy, and Çeşme than from the city itself), even as Muslim refugees flooded in from Europe to replace them.[29] It was this inter-ethnic chaos that had nearly led to a Third Balkan War between Turkey and Greece in summer 1914, only for the Sarajevo incident to preempt the carnage—or postpone it. The dry kindling was there, and the dangers of lighting it should have been painfully aware to the Supreme Council in Paris.

In the end, it may have been the odd man out who tipped the balance in favor of a Greek move into Smyrna: Woodrow Wilson. David Lloyd George, after all, had never made a secret of his passion for the Greek cause. The British prime minister, a Welshman, had close ties to the Greek business community in London, above all Basil Zaharoff, an Ottoman Greek arms dealer who had been instrumental in organizing the Venizelos coup of 1917 and who would soon spend a large portion of his considerable fortune supporting the Greek incursion into Asia Minor. Lloyd George and Venizelos had been good friends since 1912, so it was not surprising that the Briton threw his weight behind the Greek prime minister in Paris. Precisely because these two men were so close, Clemenceau and the French had been much cooler toward Venizelos, quietly encouraging the Italian move into Antalya as a counterweight to Greek ambitions. But the Italians overplayed their hand, and began making trouble in the Adriatic, too, insisting on control of the ports of Fiume and Trieste (which the Allies wished to give to the new Serb-dominated state of Yugoslavia). On April 24, 1919, the Italian delegation left Paris in protest, thus isolating Rome even as the question of Smyrna was being taken up (reducing the Big Four to the Big Three of Clemenceau, Lloyd George, and Wilson). Venizelos pounced quickly, warning the Big Three that the Italians were advancing from Fethiye and about to send warships to Smyrna. For added effect, petitions from the Greek population on Italian-occupied Rhodes were addressed to Wilson, complaining of mistreatment. "Italy is a menace to peace," the president fumed, concluding that the best way to rectify Italy's egregious violations of the self-determination principle was to assign "Greek" areas of the Ottoman Empire to Greece. With the Italians expected to rejoin the Supreme Council on May 7, the Big Three met the day before to beat them to the pass. When the Hellenophile Welshman simply proposed "that we should tell Mr. Venizelos to send troops to Smyrna," the president, fully coached, replied, "Why not tell them to land as of now?" Venizelos, called in to hear the pleasing verdict, responded simply, "We are ready."[30]

At around 2:00 a.m. on May 15, 1919, a veritable armada of Greek war-ships, eighteen in all including a British escort, HMS *Iron Duke*, arrived in the harbor of Smyrna, carrying an amphibious force of 13,000 infantrymen, 4,000 pack animals, and 750 guns. Reaction in the city was predictably polarized, with ecstatic Greeks waving the blue-and-white flag of the home-land, lighting torches, and massing in the streets to welcome their would-be liberators, even as the muezzin summoned Muslims to resist. All night the war drums were beating in the Turkish quarters while town criers went around to rouse the faithful to the terrible news that the city was being occu-pied by the Greeks. It was rumored that several hundred Turkish prisoners were let out of prison, with the complicity of an Italian army major keen to stop the Greeks. With painful inevitability, fighting began as soon as Greek troops neared an Ottoman army barracks and a fateful shot was fired, felling the Greek flag bearer of the elite *Evzones* brigades (to this day no one knows for certain by whom, although Greek soldiers at the scene blamed a Turkish nationalist journalist, Hasan Tahsin Recep, and promptly beat him to death). The Greek soldiers responded with fury, firing into the barracks and (accord-ing to some reports) into the mostly civilian crowd surrounding it, which prompted the Muslims, in turn, to form mobs (if these had not already been formed) and roam around the city brawling with Greeks. Turkish soldiers from the offending barracks, after being arrested, were force-marched through town, with stragglers and others who ran afoul of the Greeks "knocked down, bayoneted or shot, stripped of valuables, and thrown into the sea." By nightfall between three hundred and four hundred Turks had been killed, and about a hundred Greeks.[31]

Mustafa Kemal was paying a farewell call on the grand vizier when all this happened, about to board a steamer en route for Samsun—and the Turkish interior. The two events were not unrelated. The Black Sea coast, like Smyrna, still had a large Pontic Greek population, despite the wartime deportations, and the Samsun-Giresun area remained heavily Greek, especially in the towns. As part of the price for his desired Smyrna occupation, Venizelos had reassured the Supreme Council that he would press no claims in the Black Sea, as his "hands" were already "quite full with Thrace and Anatolia." To quell burgeoning tensions between Pontic Greeks and Muslims, the British had been forced to land two hundred troops of their own in Samsun in March 1919, only to discover that they were vastly outnumbered by remnants of the supposedly demobilizing Ottoman army in Sivas and Erzurum, which was now coalescing into a new Ninth Army. In a decision almost as short-sighted as the green-lighting of the Greek move into Smyrna, the British high commissioner agreed to the appointment of Mustafa Kemal as inspector of the Ninth Army—ostensibly to oversee collection of its weapons and investigate reports that "soviets" were being formed in the ranks (the British then believing the spread of Bolshevism a greater threat than Turkish nationalist resistance).

On May 19, 1919, Mustafa Kemal docked in Samsun.* Whether or not he had made up his mind in advance on a course of action, it did not take long for Kemal to sense a groundswell of popular sentiment in favor of resistance. As Kemal later recalled, if "the enemy had not stupidly come [to Smyrna], the whole country might have slept on heedlessly." Mass meetings to protest the Greek occupation were spreading across the country, from Bursa to the Black Sea coast to Erzurum. By the end of May, the protests had reached the capital itself, where a mass meeting in the old, largely Muslim quarter of Sultanahmet, unusually, brought out large numbers of women, including Halidé Edib, who roused her fellow Turks to join "the just revolt of our hearts" against the

---

* Since 1935, this date has been a national holiday in Turkey.

"European armies of conquest." In early June, Admiral Calthorpe, for the High Commission, warned London that "opposition to the Greeks" had become so "universal, that it seems to me hopeless to endeavor to stop it." To their chagrin, the British command in Samsun discovered that Kemal had "practically monopolized the telegraph" to communicate with surrounding towns, rousing up resistance. Under pressure from the high commissioners, War Minister Shevket Turgut Pasha issued orders on June 8, 1919, for Kemal to return to the capital. But Kemal had already slipped out of British-controlled Samsun with a handful of followers, setting up shop fifty miles inland at Havza. Defiantly, Kemal asked on what grounds he was being recalled, and refused to come.[32]

In summoning Ottoman army officers to resist an Allied occupation already careening out of control, Kemal was pushing on an open door. Refet (Bele), an old friend of Kemal's from Salonica who had most recently served as commander of the Constantinople gendarmerie, had accompanied Kemal to Samsun and now served him loyally as a kind of unofficial chief of staff. Several other resistance-minded generals had arrived in the interior even earlier. Kâzim Karabekir, who had taken command of the XV Army Corps headquartered at Erzurum in April, had proposed setting up a new government in the east to Kemal while they were still in Constantinople; he was pleased to see that Kemal had now come around, too, and offered his full cooperation.[*] Ali Fuat Cebesoy, who had served under Kemal in the Yildirim Army Group in Syria and helped smuggle its weapons north of the Taurus, was in Ankara, commanding the XX Army Corps, when Kemal arrived at Samsun. Crowning the resistance was Rauf, *signator* of Mudros, who was now determined to avenge his humiliation. Together, Ali Fuat, Refet, Rauf, and Kemal met in Amasya between June 19 and June 22, 1919, to draw up the principles of national resistance. The conspirators then proceeded to Erzurum, where Karabekir offered the support of his 13,000-strong army corps (July 23–August 7), and then to Sivas for a national congress (September 4–11). The result was a National Pact, or *Mısak-i-Milli*. Its key terms involved the cessation of

---

[*] Inevitably, there were later polemics about who began what where, and first. In the case of Karabekir and Kemal, the two most powerful Turkish resistance leaders, it seems most fair to say that they both got going about the same time, with equal determination.

demobilization, the "indivisibility of the Turkish nation" in areas believed to
have Turkish majorities (with the corollary that no separate Kurdish or Armenian state would be allowed in the southeast nor an outpost of Greece in the
Pontic Black Sea, Thrace, or the Aegean area; by contrast, Arab provinces
south of the Taurus and Amanus Mountains would be permitted to separate
via national referenda), and the creation of a Representative Committee
(*Heyeti Temsiliye*), separate from the government in the capital, headed by
Kemal. As a symbolic act of defiance, Kemal resigned his army commission,
thus inaugurating one of the great political careers of the twentieth century.[33]

The Allies were slow to awaken to the importance of what was brewing in
Anatolia. Theoretically, the whole region was still to fall under the aegis of an
American mandate. It was not until after Wilson's stroke in early October,
and the rejection of the Versailles Treaty by the U.S. Senate in November, that
the Allies realized the U.S. mandate was a dead letter. Meanwhile, the Anglo-
French feud over Syria occupied most of Lloyd George's attention. In the end
it was more the growing political pressure to demobilize and curtail expenditure than any sense of remorse that forced the stubborn Welshman to back
down on September 13, 1919, when he informed Clemenceau that Britain
would withdraw her troops from Syria in November. No sooner had Allenby's
army departed than French troops, under General Henri Gouraud, clashed
with Feisal's Arabs in the Bekaa Valley and seized Baalbek by force. Before
long, the French had a genuine war on their hands in Syria, even while Kemal's
nationalists, spurred on by the aggressive disposition of the Armenian Legion,
were harassing the French in Cilicia. On January 21, 1920, the Turks surrounded French-Armenian-occupied Maraş, commencing a three-week
siege, which would see some of the most brutal inter-ethnic bloodletting since
Van in 1915. By the time a French relief force arrived from Adana around
February 10, there was little left of the town, and the surviving Armenian and
French soldiers could only stage a fighting retreat south into Syria, harried by
Muslim guerrillas all the way. Thousands of Armenian civilians reportedly
died on the march, even while the departing legionnaires committed all man-
ner of atrocities against Muslims in the villages through which they passed.
Realizing that the costs of holding both Cilicia and Syria would be prohibi-
tive, Gouraud sent peace feelers to Kemal (by now in Ankara), opening the

most serious breach yet in the Allied occupation of Turkey. It would not be the last.[34]

Lloyd George's unleashing of the Greeks at Smyrna had backfired. Evidence was mounting that the Turkish Muslim masses would never willingly accept rule by outside powers, especially if those powers were relying on Greek and Armenian auxiliaries with irredentist claims on contested regions. A great deal had changed since the Sazonov-Sykes-Picot negotiations of 1916, beginning with the cutting off of the Russians from their promised share of the Ottoman carve-up.* Without the old Russian Army of the Caucasus serving as a battering ram, the Allies had no real force capable of dominating the Turkish heartland. Instead of Russians and Cossacks, Lloyd George had Italians, who were no one's idea of reliable (indeed the Italians, seeking a way to undermine their rivals, had begun negotiating with Kemal even before the French had). Suspicious of Italian motives, Lloyd George had turned to Venizelos and the Greeks to do Britain's dirty work—a people who, as occupiers, were just as unacceptable to Turks as Russians, only far less formidable.

The winter of 1919–20 should have offered the perfect time for a rethink of British policy in Turkey. While the fighting in Cilicia continued, in most of the rest of the country it was too cold for serious military operations. Instead, there was a pause, of sorts, for elections across most of the rump Ottoman Empire. These returned a parliament with a Kemalist-nationalist majority, which convened in Constantinople on January 16, 1920 (Kemal himself, by now regarded as an outlaw by the Sublime Porte, stayed behind in Ankara), and promptly ratified the National Pact. Woodrow Wilson, on whom so many had placed their hopes, was now an invalid (though he refused to be declared incompetent). After the entire Versailles settlement, including U.S. membership in the League of Nations, had gone down to defeat in the Senate, Wilson's foreign policy was in tatters: it was clear no U.S. mandate for Armenia, Constantinople, or Anatolia writ large was in prospect. The French had gone their own way in Syria, and were about to go their own way with Kemal.

---

* Not that the Russians were happy about this, at least not the patriotic imperialists on the White side. Kolchak's Provisional All-Russian Government sent delegates to Paris in July 1919 who demanded Russian participation in the new Ottoman Straits regime, along with the mandate for Armenia. With the Russian Civil War still raging, these pleas were ignored.

While British intelligence on Kemal and his nationalists remained patchy, enough news had reached London to suggest that something serious was afoot. Trouble was spreading across the new British Empire in the Middle East, with Arab-Jewish tensions boiling over in Palestine and signs of serious popular discontent in Mesopotamia. Winston Churchill, whom Lloyd George had brought back into the cabinet in January 1919 as secretary of state for war (and for air), had the unenviable task of arranging for the defense of an empire now larger than ever before, even as Parliament was demanding drastic cuts in military expenditure and a thoroughgoing demobilization. All this was in addition to the explosion of domestic unrest, with a wave of industrial strikes and Irish troubles. "The delays in demobilisation caused by the delay in reaching peace with Germany and Turkey," Churchill complained to Lloyd George as early as August 1919, "have already added more than 60 millions to the Army Estimates, for which no Parliamentary sanction have been obtained." With his characteristic blend of foresight and imagination, Churchill asked in October 1919

whether the European Powers should not, jointly and simultaneously, renounce all separate interests in the Turkish Empire other than those which existed before the war. That is to say, the Greeks should quit Smyrna, the French should give up Syria, we should give up Palestine and Mesopotamia, and the Italians should give up their sphere. Instead of dividing up the Empire into separate territorial spheres of exploitation, we should combine to preserve the integrity of the Turkish Empire as it existed before the war but should subject that Empire to a strict form of international control, treating it as a whole and directing it from Constantinople.

Realizing that his proposal ran up against Lloyd George's increasingly grandiose visions of empire, Churchill gently reminded the prime minister that Britain already had "far more territory . . . than we shall be able to develop for many generations." The strategic imperative should have been obvious: "We ought to . . . concentrate our resources on developing our existing Empire instead of dissipating them in new enlargements."[35]

It was sound advice. But Lloyd George was having none of it. Rather than cut his losses in Turkey before things went really sour, he doubled down. Doubtless he had long been thinking about making a decisive move against the nationalists, but the Ottoman parliament's ratification of the Kemalist National Pact on February 12, 1920, and the news of the new round of Armenian massacres at Maraş, which arrived in Paris almost simultaneously, gave him the pretext he needed (Maraş also gave Lloyd George political cover with the French, before they decided against further provoking Kemal). And so on March 5, 1920, the Supreme Council hashed out the final terms of the diktat peace later to be imposed on Turkey at Sèvres, which included such explosive clauses as the formal cession of Smyrna and Thrace (up to the Çatalca lines) to Greece and a fully independent Armenia and autonomous Kurdistan. Knowing full well what ferocious resistance such terms would summon forth from the nationalist camp, Lloyd George decided, with the logic of the self-fulfilling prophecy, to meet force with force, hoping that the Allies could crush the inevitable resistance before it engulfed them. And so Calthorpe and the other high commissioners were enjoined to occupy Constantinople (i.e., with more troops than previously) and impose martial law, up to and including the suppression of the new Ottoman parliament (or at least the purging of nationalist deputies). As added insurance, Lloyd George promised the commissioners that if their own forces proved inadequate to the task, Venizelos had generously promised to contribute up to 100,000 Greek troops to subdue the capital. On March 10, 1920, the three Allied high commissioners (including also Calthorpe's French and Italian counterparts) unanimously protested the new policy of imposing a draconian peace by force, which was certain to provoke "the flight of Parliament to Anatolia" and throw Kemal into the arms of the Bolsheviks. But Lloyd George was even less interested in their opinion than in Churchill's. The orders went ahead.[36]

On the night of March 15–16, 1920, the British fleet blockaded the Bosphorus and then began landing troops at strategic points around the city. At around 5:30 a.m., British marines fired into the military barracks of the Tenth Caucasus Division, killing four Turks (some accounts claim six) and wounding another ten. Other units fanned out across the city, arresting government ministers and army officers known to be sympathetic to the nationalists.

Armored cars rumbled through the streets. At 10:00 a.m. British troops took over the Army and Navy Ministries, while French troops spread out across old Stambul, occupying the imperial storehouses at Saraçhane along with, for some reason, the archaeological museum next to Topkapı Palace. Allied detachments mounted machine guns at key strongpoints to overawe any mobs of resisters, including a French one placed menacingly in front of Hagia Sofia. All of the main Turkish newspapers were taken in hand, with strict censorship imposed, and the death penalty was decreed for anyone harboring Turkish nationalist rebels. Even the Turkish Red Crescent office was "raided by thirty soldiers." Everywhere in the city was chaos and terror. As Halidé Edib recalled, "English soldiers were searching houses and digging out the old tombs in search of bombs and arms." Toward midday, the telegraph office was occupied, although not before news of the ongoing operation had reached Kemal in Ankara.[37]

The "Second Occupation" of the Ottoman capital was a fateful step. A diktat peace, imposed on a proud warrior people like the Turks, was never fated to last. Overriding the counsel of his own advisers, including those obliged to carry out his controversial policies, Lloyd George now got the war he wanted. He should have been more careful what he wished for.

CHAPTER 19

SAKARYA

[The enemy] will be throttled in the inner sanctuary of the fatherland.

—Mustafa Kemal[1]

The Sèvres Treaty, handed over to Ottoman representatives at Versailles on May 11, 1920, was the best possible recruiting poster for Mustafa Kemal's nationalist army. As if intentionally wishing to enrage as many Turks as possible, Lloyd George's terms pressed all of their most sensitive buttons. The hated Capitulations abolished in September 1914 were restored in full, up to and including Western oversight over all Ottoman government revenue-gathering and expenditure, in part to ensure the payment of reparations to the Allied governments that had fought Turkey in the war. That Britain and France wrested mandatory control of the Arab provinces, and Italy the south-central coastal sector of Anatolia between Antalya and Afyon (Afyon-karahisar),* was expected, but the decisions regarding eastern Anatolia were as explosive as possible. With the United States declining the mandate, then-independent Armenia was assigned not only the territories she had already won under arms but also the former Ottoman vilayets of Van, Erzurum (including Erzincan), Bitlis, and Trabzon, with (as an added insult) now-invalid Armenophile President Woodrow Wilson invited to draw the final

---

* The -*karahisar* suffix refers to the "black fortress" perched on a towering rock above the city. Although Afyon-karahisar is still the official name of the city today, most Turks then and now have called it Afyon for short.

boundary lines. Although the treaty did not, technically, create an independent Kurdistan, it did give Kurds the right to hold a plebiscite, under the auspices of the League of Nations, in favor of autonomy broadly defined. Greece was handed sovereign control of eastern Thrace, all contested islands in the Aegean, and—following a plebiscite to be held after five years—Smyrna, already under Greek military occupation. Constantinople and the Straits, promised to Russia in the wartime treaties, were left under nominal Turkish sovereignty but would be governed by an international commission. What remained of the Ottoman "empire" was reduced to an Anatolian rump on the other side of the Sakarya River, with its only major urban centers of note Ankara, Eskişehir, Kütahya, Samsun, and Sivas.[2]

With the logic of the self-fulfilling prophecy, Lloyd George's diktat peace drained all remaining political legitimacy from the sultan's government expected to sign it in Constantinople, transferring sovereignty to that very territorial rump to which it reduced the empire. With astonishing rapidity, Mustafa Kemal called for national elections to a new Grand National Assembly with Extraordinary Powers on March 17, 1920, the day after Allied troops

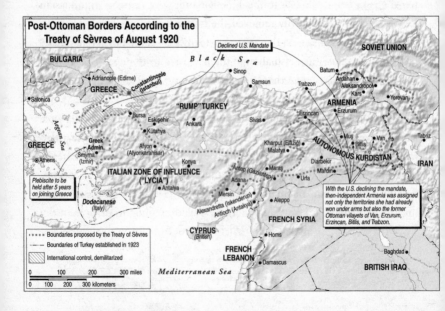

had dispersed the Ottoman parliament in the capital. Unsurprisingly, many of the deputies elected to the new assembly had been deputies in Constantinople who had escaped the Allied cordon set up to ensnare them (posters had been placarded around Constantinople threatening with "DEATH" anyone who harbored nationalists). On April 23, 1920, the Turkish Grand National Assembly convened in Ankara, a date now celebrated in Turkey as National Sovereignty and Children's Day.* Next day, Kemal was elected president of the assembly. Although Kemal, in order not to violate Ottoman or Islamic tradition, declared that the Grand National Assembly was acting to defend a sultan-caliph now held "captive" by the Allied occupiers in Constantinople, he also made clear that it now represented the highest authority in the land and must be obeyed. *De facto* if not yet *de jure*, the transfer of sovereignty from Constantinople to Ankara was now complete.

Although Sèvres helped clear the political decks for Kemal and his nationalists, the strategic picture facing Ankara was less favorable. Britain, France, and Italy now had upward of 50,000 soldiers occupying Turkey, enough to outnumber what remained of the Ottoman army. The Greeks had already poured more than 100,000 troops into the bridgehead at Smyrna, and they were "champing at the bit" to break out inland.[3] The chaos of the Russian Revolution had temporarily removed the traditional threat from the north and east, but it—along with the Mudros armistice forcing Turkey to evacuate the Transcaucasus—had also allowed the new Armenian Republic to flex its muscles. By February 1919, the Ottomans had completed, under Allied supervision, the mandated withdrawal in the east behind the 1914 borders. Once the small British force left in April, Kars was occupied by Armenian troops, who quickly secured the Alexandropol-Kars-Sarıkamış rail line while also fanning out north into Ardahan province and south toward Kağızman. On the weekend of May 10–11, 1919—the same week that saw the Greek occupation of Smyrna—the Armenian Dashnak premier, Alexandre Khatisian, rode through Kars in a military parade before attending Sunday services in the "historic Church of the Apostles," where he proclaimed that the Armenian

---

* The body was to have met on Thursday, April 22, only for Kemal's Representative Committee to wait until after Friday prayers to give it greater legitimacy among Muslims.

armies would soon sweep down into the plains of Alashkert to secure the rest of historic Armenia.[4]

Symbolically important though the Armenian conquest of Kars was to both Armenians and Turks, in truth the Armenian nationalist cause was only as strong as Russia was weak. Like all wars, civil wars make for strange bed-fellows, and Khatisian's ruling Dashnak Party in Yerevan, despite its origins as a socialist party opposed to tsarist as well as Ottoman oppression, found itself rooting for the Whites in the Russian Civil War so as to stave off a Red conquest of the Transcaucasus.[*] Kemal's Turkish nationalists were mean-while trying to open diplomatic relations with the Bolsheviks, as both sides shared enmity with the Entente powers, which were (though with varying levels of enthusiasm) backing the Whites—and the Armenians. The embry-onic Republic of Armenia thus found itself in a precarious position when, for his own idiosyncratic reasons of state, Lloyd George abandoned the White cause in winter 1919–20, jettisoning the Baltic blockade of Petrograd and cutting off British aid to the White armies. After the disastrous White evac-uation from Novorossisk in February 1920, which bottled up the Volunteer Army (now commanded, following Denikin's resignation, by Baron P. N. Wrangel) in the Crimea, it was only a matter of time before the Red Army wheeled south to snuff out the independent republics of the Transcaucasus.[5]

In April 1920, the Red Army swept down along the Caspian coast, captur-ing Petrovsk (the Daghestani capital briefly occupied by the Turks after the armistice) and Derbent before crossing the frontier of independent Azerbai-jan. Shortly before dawn on April 28, 1920, the Red Army marched unop-posed into Baku, invited in by a Bolshevik revolutionary committee that now proclaimed the Azerbaijan Soviet Socialist Republic. On May 7, Georgia signed a treaty with Soviet Russia, recognized as an independent republic though under obvious military pressure and—in a clear signal to the Dash-naks in Yerevan—with borders encompassing the province of Batum, includ-ing the Chorokhi (Çoruh) Valley and other areas claimed by Armenia. On May 10, pro-Bolshevik uprisings rocked Kars and Sarıkamış, both cities

---

[*] Not idly, either. Yerevan sent diplomatic envoys to both Admiral Kolchak's Siberian People's Army and Anton Denikin's Volunteer Army in 1919. Kolchak even authorized the Dashnak envoy, Grigor Dsamoev, to raise the Armenian flag over his headquarters and issue Armenian passports and visas.

recent acquisitions of the Republic of Armenia. Next day, the Red Army marched into Karabagh, an ethnically mixed area violently contested between Armenia and Azerbaijan (as it is even today). Although the Dashnaks held out for independence, by the end of May 1920 the Republic of Armenia was slowly being strangled in all directions by pro-Bolshevik forces.[6]

The budding tactical alliance between Kemalist Turkey and Bolshevik Russia, about which the Allied high commissioners in Constantinople had tried in vain to warn Lloyd George, now bloomed in earnest. Mutual interest, based on shared enmity with Britain and the Entente, had long been present. But until the two pariah states shared a border, it was difficult to organize anything properly. Even sending a diplomatic envoy to Moscow had been hazardous while fighting continued in the Russian Civil War, which created confusion as negotiations proceeded among multiple parties through back channels (including between Enver Pasha and the Bolsheviks, by way of Berlin). After the Red Army's push into the Transcaucasus in April–May 1920, all that separated Kemal and the Bolsheviks was the beleaguered Republic of Armenia.* The Dashnaks had banked on British and French support, and invested political capital in the White cause. While this policy had seemed sensible enough at the end of the world war, and on into fall 1919 (which had seen Denikin push north toward Moscow, even as the Northwestern Army of Yudenich had threatened Petrograd), by 1920 it was out of date. The White moment in Russia had come and gone, and the last British and French troops in the region were leaving via Batum (although the Allied Supreme Council had agreed to supply arms to the Armenian Republic, at least in theory).[7]

Despite Armenia's isolation, it was not a foregone conclusion that the republic would go under. The Armenian national army had earned its spurs against Nuri Pasha's Army of Islam in 1918, had (more or less) beaten the Georgians that December, and had subdued majority Muslim areas in Karabagh and Kars in 1919. By most reckonings the Armenian army was superior to Karabekir's XV Corps in Erzurum, the only fully intact Ottoman

---

* The logical regional partner Armenia might have turned to was, of course, Christian Georgia. And yet, owing to conflicting claims over Tiflis and Batum, Armenia had invaded Georgia in December 1918—a short but bloody war that had reached its climax on Christmas Day, when horrified Allied representatives in Tiflis brokered a truce.

army corps to have survived the Mudros-mandated demobilization. Even the Red Army, which dwarfed the Armenian forces in size, had hesitated before taking them on directly, in part because the Bolsheviks wanted to absorb the republic in the same relatively bloodless manner they had annexed Azerbaijan. Nor was Karabekir in any hurry to take on the Armenians, at least not until he had mustered enough troops to ensure victory. On June 8, 1920, Karabekir, now given the title of Commander of the Eastern Front, ordered partial mobilization, although it proceeded slowly. An Armenian incursion into the contested frontier district of Oltu on June 18–22, though opposed by Tatar and Turkish irregulars and protested vigorously in Erzurum, drew no stronger response from Karabekir, who did not have Kemal's authorization to open hostilities with Armenia (in part because the Greek advance beyond Smyrna, authorized by the Allies, began that very week). So far from bringing a renewal of Armeno-Turkish bloodletting, the Oltu operation inspired the first exchange of diplomatic notes between Yerevan and Ankara. Although the exchange was inconclusive, it showed that a certain wary respect was growing between two bitter enemies.[8]

So long as negotiations with Soviet Russia were under way, there were good reasons for caution in both Yerevan and Ankara. The summer of 1920 was something of a coming-out party for the Bolsheviks. Although the Polish invasion of Ukraine in April 1920 (targeting Kiev) put the Red Army temporarily on its heels, allowing Wrangel's Whites to survive in the Crimea until November, by August things were going Moscow's way, with the Red Army approaching Warsaw. That month saw the first real Congress of the Communist International, with delegates from across Europe taken on jaw-dropping tours of Red Petrograd and the Moscow Kremlin, with special VIPs then taken on a victory tour of areas of Ukraine recently reconquered from the Whites and Poles. On September 1, 1920, the soon-to-be-legendary Congress of the Peoples of the East convened in Baku, and broadcast the message that Soviet Russia stood with the world's oppressed against European imperialism.* With the Communist world revolution—or at least, the Red Army—

---

* Striking a discordant note in Baku was the presence of Enver Pasha, denounced by the Turkish Communist delegation as an imperialist and war criminal.

seeming to advance from triumph to triumph, the focus of regional diplomacy shifted naturally to Moscow.[9]

The Bolsheviks themselves, meanwhile, were still working out their own policy vis-à-vis Turkey and the Transcaucasus. In the euphoria of summer, when the Red Army was advancing into Poland, a treaty of cooperation with Kemal's nationalist regime was inked in Moscow between Kemal's envoy, the Circassian Bekir Sami (Kunduh), and the Soviet foreign minister, Georgii Chicherin: the idea was for the Bolsheviks to begin supplying Ankara with arms in exchange for Turkey ceding parts of Van and Bitlis provinces to Armenia. By the time this message reached Kemal by courier, however, events on the ground had considerably weakened both the Russian and Armenian position. After defeating the Red Army at Warsaw in August, the Poles had regained the strategic initiative in September, pushing the Russians back across the Niemen and well into Ukraine. With exquisite timing, Kemal authorized Karabekir to advance into Kars on September 20, 1920, just as Moscow was suing for peace with Warsaw. Nine days later, Ottoman troops captured Sarıkamış, meeting only desultory resistance as the Armenians pulled back toward Kars.

Negotiating now from strength, Kemal issued his formal reply to Chicherin on October 16, 1920: Turkey would not cede any territory already conquered. By now the Armenian side had all but lost hope for independence, petitioning Moscow for a protectorate that would allow Yerevan to control Kars and Ardahan, at least, if not all the other territories promised her by the Western allies at Sèvres. Pressing on while he had the initiative (and before the Red Army, then mopping up Wrangel's rump White Army in Crimea, could reach the Caucasus in full strength), on October 24, 1920, Kemal ordered Karabekir to advance on Kars. In a revealing sequence of events, a Soviet plenipotentiary to Yerevan, Boris Legran, signed a treaty recognizing Kars as part of the Armenian Republic on October 28—two days before Karabekir conquered the Kars citadel, capturing more than two thousand Armenian soldiers. In November, Karabekir pressed on to the eastern boundary of Kars, forcing Yerevan to sue for peace. On December 2, 1920, the Armenian Republic signed the punitive Treaty of Gümrü with the Grand National Assembly in Ankara, the first of any kind signed by Kemal's government.

Four days later, the Red Army marched into Yerevan, to annex an Armenian Republic that had proved too moribund to resist the Turkish advance. Working in a curious sort of half-hostile, half-friendly partnership, Karabekir's XV Corps and the Red Army then proceeded to carve up what remained of the Transcaucasus, with the Reds absorbing most of Georgia and winning the race to Batum, even while the Turks rolled up most of Ardahan province and Artvin. On March 16, 1921, Kemalist Turkey and Soviet Russia signed a treaty in Moscow recognizing the new borders forged by arms, with the Turks regaining two-thirds of *Elviye-i-Selâse* (Kars and Ardahan) and the Russians taking Batum. Karabekir's feat of arms in Kars ensured that Turkey's eastern front was now secure, as it has remained ever since.[10]

This was all to the good for Ankara, for there were a number of other fronts to worry about. With the French increasingly busy in Syria, a temporary truce was signed following the Turkish capture of Pozantı in Cilicia in June 1920, although fighting continued in the Taurus Mountains on through the winter, with the Turks storming the French-Armenian stronghold of Haçin (Saimbeyli) in October, though losing Antep (Gaziantep) to the French in February 1921 after a ten-month siege. The Italians, enjoying the discomfiture of their rivals, gave no trouble to the Turkish nationalists in 1920. Even so, central Anatolia remained a war zone, with various Circassian and Kurdish bandit chieftains contesting Kemal's authority wherever the nationalists were weak, such as in the area inland from Smyrna, the shores of Izmit, the mountains around Kütahya and near Bolu, and even the western approaches to Ankara itself. Whenever the nationalists could throw regulars in, they dispersed the rebels with ease. But it was difficult to put out fires in all directions with the limited forces at Kemal's disposal, which numbered ten thousand or fifteen thousand at best, and these were ill-equipped and short of spare ammunition. Kemal's real achievement, at this stage, was in limiting the war to small battles he could win, while keeping his many enemies—the Armenian Republic, the Franco-Armenian occupiers of Cilicia, the Italians, the Greeks, and the British—from uniting against him. So long as Greece's rivals did not allow her to advance beyond Smyrna, Kemal could continue to pick his battles against forces inferior, or at least not greatly superior, to his own.

In the end it was a rather minor operation that tipped the balance. In early June 1920, a small Turkish nationalist force pursued rebels down the western slopes of the Bolu Mountains toward Izmit, where the British had posted a battalion to guard the Asian approaches to Constantinople. While covering fire from Allied warships in the Gulf of Izmit prevented the Turks from over-running the British outpost, the local commander, realizing he was outnum-bered, ordered his stores to be blown up and prepared to hold out under siege. It was the first direct military confrontation between Kemal's nationalists and the British occupiers, and it was a serious one. With only 4,469 rifles in Constantinople, and another 2,272 guarding the railway between Izmit and Afyon (to the south), Britain had nowhere enough troops to defend the capital if Kemal mounted a serious offensive, nor reinforcements available nearby (other than 657 soldiers guarding the Dardanelles shore batteries). Of course, had a different sort of man been in power in London, these facts might have led to a reconsideration of the wisdom of imposing a diktat peace so obvi-ously unacceptable to the Turks, without enough occupying troops to enforce it. But Lloyd George, unlike his allies and even most of his own advisers, was fully committed to Sèvres—to the policy of forcibly dismembering Turkey. As soon as he learned that British forces would not suffice for the purpose, the prime minister summoned Venizelos to London on June 14, 1920, to ask if Greek troops could do the job for him.[11]

In this backhanded way began the second stage of the Greek invasion of Turkey. In order to keep the French, and British cabinet critics, on board, Lloyd George did agree to limit the Greek advance to the area immediately east and north of Smyrna, up to Panderma (Bandırma); meanwhile, the Greeks were to second a division to General Milne's British forces at Izmit. At first, the operation proceeded according to plan. Under Venizelos's hand-picked commander, General Leonidas Paraskevopoulos, Greek troops fanned out inland from Smyrna on June 22, 1920, in a three-pronged advance, with the spearhead "Archipelago division" racing up the railway toward Panderma, which fell on July 7, along with Balikesir. The Greeks then pivoted east, taking Bursa on July 8. Although strategically insignificant, Bursa was the original capital of the Ottoman (*Osmanli*) Empire: the founder, Osman, is buried there, and to this day it remains an important religio-cultural center for

Turkish Muslims. Unsurprisingly, the fall of Bursa touched off a wave of mourning in Ankara, where black banners were hung from the windows; many deputies in the Grand National Assembly were said to be in tears, too benumbed to speak.[12]

In theory, the Greek offensive was now done. Although Paraskevopoulos wanted to go on, Venizelos was wary of abusing Lloyd George's confidence and so informed the Allied Supreme Council at Spa, on July 7, 1920, that Greek troops would stay where they were until the Sèvres Treaty was signed by the sultan. Quietly, however, the Greek advance continued. In a clever bit of camouflage, Paraskevopoulos peeled off an infantry regiment from Panderma, and a division from Smyrna, to strengthen Greek forces in Thrace. On July 26, 1920, the Greeks entered Adrianople—the second Ottoman capital after Bursa—in force, prompting yet another round of teeth-gnashing and wailing in Ankara. In late August, the Greeks moved into Uşak and then, in early September, into Gediz and Kandira. On September 5, Greek troops marched into Yalova, the most important port city on the southeastern shore of the Sea of Marmara where it feeds into the Gulf of Izmit (whence depart, to this day, most of the Marmara ferries to old Stambul). These incursions were egregious violations of Venizelos's promises to the Supreme Council, and of the terms Lloyd George had set down in the spring, and they were carried out with impunity. As an Inter-Allied Investigating Commission observed of the summer 1920 offensive:

> The advancing Greek army burned hundreds of villages and towns and assaulted their inhabitants as it went along, without the systematic massacres that had accompanied its initial occupation of Aydin province, but with enough brutality to cause thousands of Turks to flee to refuge behind the Turkish lines.[13]

With rampaging Greek troops serving as Lloyd George's battering ram, delegates sent by the Allies' puppet sultan, Mehmed VI (Vahdettin), signed the Sèvres Treaty on August 10, 1920.

After all the theatrics leading up to its imposition, the actual ratification of the Allies' diktat peace treaty came as something of an anticlimax. Another round of mourning descended on Ankara, shared this time in Constantinople itself, with shops closed, black banners draped across buildings, and street traffic halted. In time the Grand National Assembly roused itself to declare a kind of anathema ("treason to the nation") on those members of the sultan's government who had supported signing the treaty, but in August not even this much was done. In a certain sense, the treaty remained unratified, or at least unresolved, as it had not been run past the Ottoman parliament, now meeting out of the reach of the Allies, in Ankara. Viewing Sèvres as obviously invalid, Kemal and the nationalists were in no mood to humor the treaty by debating it. Aside from the Greek move into Yalova in early September, there was a lull in fighting on most fronts, which lasted until Karabekir began his advance into Kars.

In Greece, too, the public had grown weary of the Turkish war, and Venizelos was forced to call for new parliamentary elections in September. Sensing that his historic moment of opportunity might be passing, Venizelos resolved to push on into Anatolia before the winter snows came—even before, ideally, the Greek elections took place in November. On October 5, 1920, the embattled Greek prime minister sent Lloyd George a long telegram proposing an ambitious offensive "with the object of destroying definitively the nationalist forces around [Ankara] and the Pontus" and establishing a new Greek super-state along the Black Sea coast contiguous with the greater Armenia the Allies had created—on paper, at least—in the Sèvres Treaty. To cover his flank, Venizelos requested that British troops advance from Izmit to secure the Sakarya River basin. Britain was also asked to supply the Greeks with arms, woolen uniforms, and a monthly subsidy of £3 million. As added inducement, Venizelos issued an implied threat to withdraw his troops from Anatolia if these terms were not met, leaving the British exposed to Kemal's nationalists. In late October 1920, Venizelos authorized a limited advance, with Greek troops moving up the slopes east of Bursa, occupying Inegöl, Karamürsel, and Larissa (Yenişehir).[14]

This time, Venizelos had gone too far. Not even the arch-Hellenist Lloyd George was reckless enough to sanction a Greek advance from the Aegean to the Black Sea on such a tight timetable, with both France and Italy—and the bulk of his own cabinet—wary about provoking Kemal still further. While

Lloyd George was mulling over how to handle Venizelos's explosive proposal, fate intervened in Athens. On September 30, the young "Venizelist" King Alexander—he who had replaced the Germanophile King Constantine after the pro-Entente coup in 1917—went for a walk in the gardens of Tatoi Palace. Chasing his dog into a clump of bushes, the king was bitten in the calf by a monkey. It was not clear at first that the wound was serious, but Alexander soon succumbed to a terrible fever and died, of blood poisoning, on October 25, 1920—just as Venizelos's new offensive was beginning in Anatolia. To allow for a period of mourning, the Greek elections were postponed until November 14. With a restoration suddenly thinkable, the opposition rallied around King Constantine, turning the election into something like a referendum on Venizelos and his entire foreign policy. To general (though not universal) surprise, the Venizelists were crushed at the polls, winning only 118 out of 369 seats in the parliament. So sweeping was the repudiation that Venizelos resigned before facing the inevitable no-confidence vote, and a referendum was swiftly scheduled for early December to return Constantine to his throne.

The political fallout from the monkey's bite seemed, at first glance, to portend a Greek climbdown in Turkey. The Germanophile King Constantine remained *persona non grata* in London and Paris. As early as December 4, 1920—the day *before* the Greek referendum on Constantine's return was scheduled—the Supreme Allied Council issued a communiqué condemning the king's "disloyal attitude and conduct toward the Allies during the war," stating that a vote for his return would be regarded as "a ratification of his hostile acts," and cutting the Allies loose from any commitment to Greece, including further financial support, if he returned to his throne. No matter: Constantine received a broad popular mandate (about 60 percent) in the referendum held on Sunday, December 5, 1920, and returned to Athens in triumph two weeks later. With the flow of Allied funds to Athens and Smyrna cut off and a purge of the Venizelists in both the Greek civil service and army expected to follow in short order, it seemed the clock was about to run out on the Greek occupation of Anatolia.

It did not turn out that way. Showing that the idea of Greater Greece ran deeper than any partisan sentiments for or against Venizelos, the new Greek government of Dimitrios Rallis issued a defiant statement on December 29, 1920, reminding the Allies that Greek soldiers were "fight[ing] on the front of Asia Minor for the common interests of the Powers," and declaring that Greece would carry out this task "with more enthusiasm than ever following the restoration of liberty and the return of the King."[15] General Anastasios Papoulas, a Constantinist exiled to Crete, replaced Paraskevopoulos as commander in chief.

To digest the political revolution in Athens and figure out what it portended for the Sèvres Treaty, Lloyd George convened another conference in February 1921, grudgingly agreeing for the first time to receive a Kemalist delegation from Ankara led by Bekir Sami (Kunduh). As if to prove the new regime's nationalist bona fides, Papoulas ordered an immediate advance from Bursa toward Eskişehir even before the conference convened. On January 6, 1921, the advancing Greeks ran into a nationalist force entrenched near the railway station at Inönü. After several days of savage fighting, the Turks, under General Ismet, began to withdraw, only to be surprised to learn that the Greeks, too, had pulled back. Although inconclusive and smallish by the standards of the world war—the Turks lost some 95 killed and 183 wounded—this First Battle of Inönü, as it came to be called, had outsized strategic consequences. Simply by proving that they could resist the superior forces of the Greek invaders, the Turkish nationalists had shown enough for France and Italy. French troops had already experienced the bitter taste of defeat against the Turks in Cilicia. The May 1920 truce with Kemal had allowed General Gouraud to crush Feisal's Arabs without worrying about his northern flank that summer, conquering Damascus with ease and forcing Feisal to accept Britain's "consolation prize" as king of Iraq.* By contrast, as French premier Aristide Briand observed in London in February 1921, French troops north of the Taurus

had been facing the Turks in that theatre of war for over a year and as a result he personally had come to have a decided respect for this so-called

---

* Taking a page from the playbook of Kaiser Wilhelm II, Gouraud visited the tomb of Saladin, though with less humility. "Saladin," he told the medieval Muslim warrior-hero who had helped to push back the Frankish Christian Crusaders, "we're back."

rabble band which the Greek prime minister [i.e., Venizelos] despised. The experience gained by the French forces went to prove that the Turkish army did not disperse as easily as the conference had to-day been led to believe. These forces had inflicted cruel losses on the French soldiers. For a month the French army had invested Aintab [Antep] which had been fiercely defended. In a word the French had found the Turkish troops to be full of pluck, to fight savagely and defend every inch of ground.[16]

On March 9, 1921, Briand signed a sweeping ceasefire with Bekir Sami (Kunduh), promising that French troops would evacuate all Cilicia above the Taurus Mountains, remaining only in the district of Alexandretta (Iskenderun), known today as the Hatay, in exchange for economic concessions (along with extensive through rights for the Turkish portions of the Baghdad Railway) and provisions for disarming the population meant to protect Armenians and other minorities. Three days later, the Italians signed an accord, promising to withdraw all troops from Anatolia and to support the Turkish claims in Smyrna and along the Black Sea coast—that is, against those of Greece—in exchange for economic concessions and a promise to respect Italy's claims on Rhodes and the other Dodecanese islands. On March 16, 1921, Kemal's man in Moscow, Ali Fuat Pasha, signed the agreement provisionally fixing Turkey's eastern borders with Soviet Russia. In an appendix to this Moscow agreement, Soviet foreign minister Chicherin promised to remit 10 million gold rubles to Turkey for "economic development," while also promising to speed up arms deliveries across the Black Sea—including rifles, machine guns, and field artillery. In this way Kemal's government was given *de facto*, if not quite *de jure*, recognition, even as the new Greek government under King Constantine was becoming estranged from the alliance it had joined on his deposition in 1917.

Britain remained the holdout, but in London there were signs of a policy shift in the making. Lloyd George, although still personally committed to the Greek occupiers in Anatolia, could no longer command support from his own cabinet, nor wheedle funds for them out of the Commons. The prime minister was even forced to lean on Greece to accept modifications in the Sèvres Treaty limiting her claims in Smyrna province—although, to win this concession, he quietly agreed, on March 7, 1921, to lift the Supreme Council's restrictions on the movements of Greek troops in Anatolia, in a decision that enraged his advisers when they learned of it. Sir Henry Wilson, chief of the Imperial General Staff, summed up the attitude of the cabinet when he remarked that "the whole thing is disgusting. In my opinion, the end of this will be the total ruin of the Greeks—the friends of Lloyd George." In the prime minister's defense, although he had given Papoulas a kind of green light, the upshot of the London conference was also a kind of formal disownment of the Greek armies. Officially, the Allied high commissioners in Constantinople were now neutral in the Greco-Turkish war, and would no longer allow the Greek army or navy access to facilities in the capital, or permit them to transport war matériel through the Straits. The Greeks were on their own.[17]

On March 23, 1921, Papoulas resumed the Greek offensive. On the southern front, progress was rapid, with Afyon falling to the invader on March 27. But along the main front at İnönü, the Turks held the line once again, pushing the Greeks back with a blistering counterattack on March 31, which made the name of the commander, who now took the name Ismet İnönü. Encouraged

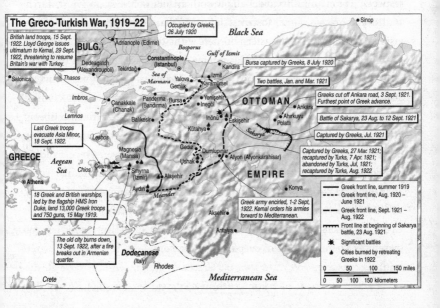

The Greco-Turkish War, 1919–22

British land troops, 15 Sept. 1922. Lloyd George issues ultimatum to Kemal, 29 Sept. 1922, threatening to resume Britain's war with Turkey.

Occupied by Greeks, 26 July 1920

Bursa captured by Greeks, 8 July 1920

Two battles, Jan. and Mar. 1921

Greeks cut off Ankara road, 3 Sept. 1921. Furthest point of Greek advance.

Battle of Sakarya, 23 Aug. to 12 Sept. 1921

Captured by Greeks, Jul. 1921

Last Greek troops evacuate Asia Minor, 18 Sept. 1922.

Captured by Greeks, 27 Mar. 1921; recaptured by Turks, 7 Apr. 1921; abandoned by Turks, Jul. 1921; recaptured by Turks, Aug. 1921

18 Greek and British warships, led by the flagship HMS Iron Duke, land 13,000 Greek troops and 750 guns, 15 May 1919.

Greek army encircled, 1–2 Sept. 1922. Kemal orders his armies forward to Mediterranean.

The old city burns down, 13 Sept. 1922, after a fire breaks out in Armenian quarter.

Black Sea
Sea of Marmara
Aegean Sea
Mediterranean Sea

OTTOMAN EMPIRE
GREECE
BULG.
Dodecanese (Italy)
Rhodes
Crete

Sinop · Adrianople (Edirne) · Bosporus · Gulf of Izmit · Constantinople (Istanbul) · Salonica · Dedeagatch (Alexandroupoli) · Tekirdağ · Thasos · Imbros · Çanakkale (Chanak) · Lemnos · Panderma (Bandırma) · Bursa · İnegöl · Yalova · Gemlik · Karamürsel · Kandira · İzmit · Yenişehir · Ahirkuyu · Ankara · Polatlı · Eskişehir · İnönü · Kütahya · Sakarya · Balıkesir · Gediz · Dumlupınar · Uşak · Afyon (Afyonkarahisar) · Magnesia (Manisa) · Çeşme · Chios · Smyrna (İzmir) · Alaşehir · Aydın · Meander · Konya · Akşehir · Antalya · Athens

Greek front line, summer 1919
Greek front line, Aug. 1920 – June 1921
Greek front line, Sept. 1921 – Aug. 1922
Front line at beginning of Sakarya battle, 23 Aug. 1921
Significant battles
Cities burned by retreating Greeks in 1922

0   50   100   150 miles
0 50 100 150 kilometers

by Ismet's success, Refet, the commander of the southern front, retook Afyon on April 7. Once again, there was a lull in the fighting, which suggested to Allied military attachés that the invaders might pull back to consolidate their gains. In fact, Papoulas was waging a tactical scorched-earth retreat, securing his flanks by burning out hundreds of Turkish villages straddling his supply lines, as a number of foreign observers, most famously Arnold Toynbee in a series of dispatches for the *Manchester Guardian*, would soon reveal to the world. Papoulas was also frantically calling up reserves, bringing the size of the Greek occupying army to more than 200,000 men as he prepared for the final push. King Constantine himself, who had commanded Greek forces against Turkey in both the 1897 Cretan war and the two Balkan Wars, arrived in Smyrna on June 12, 1921, to beatify the cause. "You are fighting here," the king assured his troops, "for the Hellenic idea which produced in this very place that incomparable civilization which will never cease to merit the admiration of the whole world." After two years of probes and preliminary skirmishing, the Third Balkan War—the fourth war in as many decades between Turkey and Greece—would now erupt in earnest.[18]

On July 10, 1921, the Greek armies struck hard at the Turkish center between Afyon and Kütahya. By now both armies were peaking in strength, with some 126,000 Greeks against some 122,000 Turks (though the Greeks were much better armed, with 410 field guns to 160, 4,000 machine guns to 700, and 20 warplanes to 4). Here, on the baked-out plain on the western Anatolian plateau in high summer, was ideal ground for flanking maneuvers—except that there was little for men and horses to drink, which amplified the need for speed. Once the Greeks broke through Turkish lines at Kütahya, Papoulas ordered an advance guard to wheel north and east toward Eskişehir, even while his right wing cut the rail line above Afyon. To avoid envelopment, the Turks were forced to abandon Eskişehir and Afyon, retreating to the far banks of the Sakarya River near the railway station at Polatlı, about 75 kilometers (50 miles) west of Ankara itself. Turkish battlefield losses already stood at 40,000, with as many having deserted. In the Grand National Assembly, there was talk of evacuating Ankara and pulling back to Kayseri or Sivas.

It was a moment of truth for the Turks, and for Mustafa Kemal. The president of the Assembly, although no longer an active military officer, had quietly supervised the army's retreat toward Ankara and was already under political fire for abandoning so much territory to the enemy. Now that the capital itself was in danger, there was a growing chorus of deputies who wanted Kemal to take up the army command himself. On August 5, 1921, Kemal accepted the challenge, assuming full responsibility as commander in chief for a period of three months. Although his command could, in theory, be revoked by the Grand National Assembly, in practice it amounted to a kind of conditional military dictatorship—conditional, of course, on the outcome of the coming clash with the Greeks. To shore up civilian morale, Kemal issued a proclamation vowing that the invaders would be "throttled in the inner sanctuary of the fatherland."

In private, Kemal doubted that he could hold the Greeks west of the Sakarya River. Papoulas had both numerical superiority in theater and far greater firepower. In strictly military terms, Kemal believed the survival of his army as a fighting force was more important than either the Sakarya River or Ankara; but he knew that opinion in the Grand National Assembly, and among Ankara civilians, required that the capital be defended. Even so, the archives were sent off to Kayseri, with standing orders for a full-on government evacuation should the Greeks break through. Kemal's mood was not improved when, on August 12, he fell from his horse while inspecting troops, breaking a rib, which caused him considerable pain and made it difficult to sleep. To supply and feed his army, Kemal issued a new round of onerous requisitions of everything from foodstuffs and fuel to horses and pack animals, knowing how deeply these were resented by peasant toilers who had just barely recovered from the depredations of the world war. Like his men, Kemal had no lack of patriotic motivation to resist the Greek invaders, but after a decade of near-continous warfare, there was no élan, no enthusiasm, just a resignation to the fate of battle.

There were second thoughts on the Greek side too. Supply lines back to Smyrna were already stretched and precariously held, with bandits and Turkish irregulars, often mounted on cavalry, harassing the Greeks wherever they could. Despite the brutal scorched-earth tactics designed to root out "banditry" behind the lines, the Greeks were grossly outnumbered in western

Anatolia, and they knew it. The farther east they went from the Smyrna bridgehead and the Marmara coast, the more emphatically Muslim was the population. As Prince Andrew, heir to Constantine's throne and a voice of caution in the Greek camp, put the problem of defeating Kemal: "How far would we be able to pursue him? Could we follow him through the immense expanses of Asia Minor to Kurdistan and the frontiers of Persia?" At the crucial planning conference held in Kütahya on July 28, 1921, Papoulas's staff advisers were all but unanimous in urging against venturing deeper into the arid plains of central Anatolia, across a largely uninhabited salt desert, without a clear endgame in mind. Even if the nationalist capital was captured, moreover, could it be occupied securely in the face of a hostile population? Now that the Allies had cut off the aid spigot, how long could Athens pay for the war anyway? In the end the only real argument in favor of going on was political: to finish off Turkish nationalism and create a greater Greek empire, and this is the one Papoulas adopted. And so a forward march to the Sakarya River was ordered, with a further advance from Polatlı to Ankara left conditional on the destruction of Turkish resistance. But these seemingly aggressive orders also included a fallback clause, whereby if "circumstances" were "not favorable," the Greeks would sabotage the railway and retreat to Eskişehir. In this way the Greek armies were urged forward into Kemal's trap, kicking up more than enough sand as they crossed the salt desert as if to alert the enemy long in advance of their arrival.[19]

Although little known today outside Greece and Turkey, the Battle of Sakarya, waged between August 23 and September 12, 1921, was of historic significance. In a sense it was the last real battle of the First World War. Pitting some 100,000 Greeks against about 90,000 Turks along a front 60 miles (100 kilometers) wide, Sakarya did not compare in scale to the Somme, or Verdun, or even Gallipoli. Casualty figures were likewise compressed by world war standards, with both sides losing about 4,000 dead and 18,000 or 19,000 wounded. But the stakes could not have been any higher, with two evenly matched historical enemies staking claims to the same territory. True, not even the most chauvinistic pan-Hellenist on the Greek side was claiming that there was a Greek ethnic majority in the Sakarya basin itself, but the invaders did claim this for large swathes of Anatolia along the Aegean and

Black Sea coasts—lands for which the Greeks were now bleeding and dying, even as the Turks were fighting to deny them to Athens. The stakes were fully appreciated by everyone, with eyewitness accounts testifying to the nerve-racking atmosphere at headquarters on both sides.

The outcome was in doubt until the very end. All summer the Greeks had won victories, taking territory from the Turks—and they continued to do so at Sakarya. Although the defenders held the higher ground on the eastern banks of the river, raining fire down from various raised escarpments and hilltops, the Greeks succeeded in crossing the river in force anyway on the night of August 23, 1921, before the Turks could blow the third and last bridge. One by one the Greeks captured key elevated strongpoints on the eastern side of the river, with place-names now famous: Mangal Dağı, Kara Ilyas, Kartal Tepe. On September 2, 1921, the Greeks stormed the highest peak in the area, Çaldağı (Mount Çal). From this "giant hill of ink-black earth," the invaders caught their first glimpse of the lights of Ankara glimmering in the distance. Next day, a Greek advance guard cut the main Ankara-Polatlı highway at Ahırkuyu, cutting Kemal's forces in two. The boom of the guns could now be heard in the capital, and a kind of terror set in, with prayers read out in all the mosques and sheep sacrificed for deliverance. Receiving the latest news from the battlefield, Dimitrios Gounaris, leader of the new Constantinist parliamentary majority in Athens, told the British ambassador that "Turkey might be considered dead."[20]

The judgment was premature. Having learned what the world war had to teach, Kemal worked out a sensible, if unheroic, principle of "defense in depth," with multiple lines of trenches allowing his men to stage tactical retreats during the battle. Although the Greeks broke through the first two defensive lines, seized most of the heights, and even split the Turkish armies in two, the supreme offensive effort exhausted Papoulas's frontline troops, even while Kemal was slowly bringing in fresh reserves called up in Ankara and points east. In a sense, his task was relatively simple: the Turks needed only to survive the initial battles until the Greeks wore themselves out. Papoula recognized this, and as soon as September 2–3, his nerves began to break: despite winning ground on both days, the Greek commander in chief wired Athens requesting if he could ask Kemal for a ceasefire. The request was refused. On the seventeenth day of the battle, September 8, 1921, Kemal at last ordered a blistering counterattack, which had a devastating impact on Greek morale. On September 11, 1921, Papoulas sounded the retreat, conceding defeat to a reporter from the London *Times* ("The battle is over"). Next day, Mount Çal was recaptured by the Turks, and shortly afterward all the other heights recently lost to the invader were also retaken. Halidé Edib, who witnessed the Turkish storming of Mount Çal, later recalled above all the vision of "a single Turk standing all alone against the setting sun, his water bottle glistening against the blue-gold sky."*[21]

Owing to Papoulas's success in sabotaging the railway, and the power of Greek covering fire, Kemal was unable to pursue in force. And so the Greek occupying army survived the debacle. Nevertheless, Sakarya was a clear Turkish victory delineating the high-water mark of the Greek invasion of Turkey, and of the idea of greater Greece more generally. The Kemalist government in Ankara, having proved itself in battle, was here to stay.

---

* A similar vision greets travelers on the road to Ankara today just west of Polatlı, where a giant statue shows a Turkish soldier holding his arm up, asking the invader to halt.

CHAPTER 20

SMYRNA

The oppressive and arrogant army of the enemy has been defeated.
Armies! Your first goal is the Mediterranean! Forward!

—MUSTAFA KEMAL
to his troops, September 1, 1922[1]

THE WAR FOR ANATOLIA now entered a strange lull. Despite losing every engagement but the last, the Turks had defeated the Greeks soundly at Sakarya, taking fourteen thousand prisoners while losing only eight hundred themselves. Still, before resigning his command, Papoulas had retreated in time to save his army, and destroyed enough of the railway, along with the principal roads and bridges west of Ankara, to make pursuit by the Turks nearly impossible. Regrouping in Eskişehir and Afyon, the Greeks dug in, without much of a plan other than to survive the winter and make things as tough as possible for Kemal whenever he went on the offensive. As Harry Lamb, the British consul at Smyrna, reported to London of Papoulas's scorched-earth retreat:

> The Greeks have realised that they have got to go, but they are decided to leave a desert behind them, no matter whose interests may suffer thereby. Everything which they have time and means to move will be carried off to Greece; the Turks will be plundered and burnt out of house and home. The fate of Anatolia will be settled by blood and fire alone. Nothing will be spared.[2]

With the dream of Greater Greece dashed, there was little left to motivate Greek soldiers in Anatolia. After resigning his command of II Army Corps in October 1921, Prince Andrew wrote home from Smyrna that "something must be done quickly to remove us from the nightmare of Asia Minor. I don't know what, but we must stop bluffing and face the situation as it really is. Because finally which is better?—to fall into the sea or to escape before we are ducked [into it]?" Morale in the Greek camp was abysmal. Many officers, granted holiday leave to return to mainland Greece, simply never came back. Common soldiers took solace in antiquities and other loot they hoped to bring home, only to discover that after they had burned down Turkish villages, there was not much left worth stealing. The Greek high commissioner in Smyrna, Aristides Sterghiades, was shocked to see the state of Greek deserters who began pouring into Smyrna in 1922. "Here are men," he told the U.S. consul, George Horton,

> who burn, kill and plunder and then fill their sacks with heavy loads of absolutely worthless materials which they carry for days on foot through the hot sun. On opening the sacks we find in them stones, bricks, worthless pieces of common clay jugs ... old shoes which are seldom even in pairs ... when we turn these out and ask them why they have carried these worthless objects so far, they simply stare at us like idiots and make no reply. After they have been fed and rested a day or two, all this passes away like a dream and they become docile and reasonable again and express their desire to return and resume fighting.[3]

The only real hope for Papoulas and what remained of his army of occupation was that Lloyd George would bail him out somehow, conjuring up enough British funds and war matériel to allow him to resume the initiative against Kemal. On January 12, 1922, the Greek premier, Dimitrios Gounaris, met with Lloyd George and His Majesty's foreign secretary George Curzon in Rome. This time, the Hellenophile prime minister, hamstrung by the opposition of Curzon and the rest of his cabinet to any further involvement in the Greco-Turkish war, had little to offer. Gounaris proceeded on to London in February, presenting a long report on the sorry state of Papoulas's army in a

Sir Edward Grey,
His Majesty's foreign secretary,
1905–1916

Mustafa Kemal
at Gallipoli, 1915

Turkish soldiers at Gallipoli, 1915

General Sir Ian Standish Monteith Hamilton, commander of British Mediterranean Expeditionary Force at Gallipoli

Rafael de Nogales, Venezuelan soldier of fortune, in Ottoman military uniform

Lieutenant general (later field marshal) Sir William Riddell Birdwood, commander of the Australian and New Zealand Army Corps (ANZAC) at Gallipoli, 1915

Armenian partisans during the Van uprising of April–May 1915

Armenian expellees being escorted by Ottoman troops near Kharput, 1915

Armenian victims, 1915. Photo originally reproduced in
Henry Morgenthau's memoirs. Location unknown.

An Armenian woman refugee kneeling beside
child believed dead near Aleppo, 1915

Kut-al-Amara on the Tigris, ca. 1914

Grand Duke Nicholas, commander in chief of the Russian Army of the Caucasus, 1915–1917

Russians pose next to Turkish guns captured at
Mecidiye Fort, Erzurum, 1916

Sergei Sazonov,
foreign minister of tsarist
Russia, 1910–1916

British trenches at Gaza, 1917

General Erich von Falkenhayn, chief of German General Staff, 1914–1916, and commander of Army Group F in Palestine, 1917

letter to Curzon and threatening, if no British aid were forthcoming, to withdraw from Turkey and leave the British to face Kemal alone. Curzon was not
impressed, and Lloyd George, finally getting the hint from his cabinet,
refused to grant Gounaris one last audience before he returned to Athens.
Instead the Greeks were advised to hold on, pursuant to a final evacuation,
which, the British hoped, would be carried out in an orderly fashion as part of
a final peace settlement.[4]

It was not only the decisive defeat at Sakarya that had weakened the Greek
negotiating position in London. After years of hearing only one side of the
story regarding atrocities in Asia Minor, British public opinion was being
rocked by stories of the murderous behavior of Greek troops and irregular
chete bands in western Turkey. Lending added credence to the tales of Greek
human rights abuses in Turkey was the source: the reports filed by Arnold
Toynbee—a professor of medieval and modern Greek history at University
College London whose chair had been endowed by Greek shipowners—in the
Manchester Guardian, a liberal newspaper traditionally pro-Hellenic (and
anti-Turkish) in the Gladstonian tradition. Upon landing in Yalova on a ferry
from Constantinople in May 1921, after the Yalova-Gemlik peninsula had
fallen to the Greeks, Toynbee informed readers of the *Guardian* that every
Muslim village in the district but two had been burned out by either the
Greek army or by irregular *chete* bands (he was not sure which). Out of seven
thousand Turks resident in Yalova six weeks previously, there were fewer than
seven hundred survivors, and "the whole Muslim population is terrorized
and in daily danger of death." Proceeding eastward toward Izmit in June,
Toynbee then "caught the Greek army red-handed burning Turkish villages"—regular soldiers, he emphasized, in uniform, who were "burning in
cold blood, villages as well as boats moored off the coast." On Toynbee went,
touring the areas conquered by Greece, witnessing everywhere "charred
human bodies under the cinders" of burned houses. All in all, he concluded
that the Greek campaign was marked by a "deliberate effort—largely
successful—to ruin and destroy the Turkish population in the area marked
on the map." For such courageous reporting, Toynbee was sacked from his
Greek history chair in London.[5]

Toynbee was not the only witness to such brutality. His reports were widely corroborated by others, beginning with his wife, Rosalind, who reported almost identical scenes in her letters home to her mother.[6] Rear Admiral Mark Bristol, the U.S. high commissioner, filed numerous reports with the State Department in summer 1921 of Greek atrocities on the Yalova-Gemlik peninsula.[7] Maurice Gehri, a Red Cross representative from Switzerland who headed up an inter-Allied observation commission visiting a devastated village in the area, saw "here and there among the smoking ruins, a few inhabitants. The rest had fled into the mountains. Eight corpses, four being those of women . . . some had been mutilated." A Greek officer attached to the commission, contesting survivors' claims that regular troops from mainland Greece were the culprits, summoned a "little girl," on the idea that "in the mouths of children the truth is found." "The child," Gehri noted, "declared quietly and categorically that the criminals had been Greek soldiers."[8]

There were atrocities committed on the Turkish side of the war, too, of course. But, in sharp contrast to the pattern prevailing during the world war, these remained little known in the West. In summer 1921, while the Greeks were still advancing, a Greek warship bombed Inebolu, the main Black Sea port used to supply Ankara with the gold and arms coming from Bolshevik Russia. In retaliation, the local Turkish commander, "Bearded" Nureddin (now) Pasha (hero of the Mesopotamian campaign), ordered Greek males between the ages of fifteen and fifty to be deported to the interior. At least 25,000 Greeks were uprooted, of which a substantial number must have perished en route, although reports were few. An Independence Tribunal set up in Samsun to try traitors to the nationalist cause promulgated 485 death sentences in the second half of 1921 alone, most against Greek or Armenian irregulars.[9]

So far from galvanizing Western opinion against the Turks, the spread of the brutal Greco-Turkish war to the Pontic coast was generally blamed, for once, on the Greeks, who had violated the Allied prohibition on using the Straits for military purposes by sending warships through the Straits into the Black Sea. Inebolu was only the beginning, as Greek warships also bombarded Samsun, Sinop, and Trabzon in summer 1921, causing hundreds of civilian casualties onshore, while also ostentatiously boarding a number of vessels believed (not always incorrectly) to be carrying arms sent by the Bolsheviks to Kemal. Sir Horace Rumbold, the new British high commissioner in Constantinople, reported these Greek violations to Curzon on July 30 and August 4, 1921, thus helping to further sour opinion in the British Foreign Office regarding the Greek cause.[10] Little wonder Curzon threw cold water on Lloyd George's pleas to bail out the Greeks that winter. "I am not quite certain," Curzon wrote to Sir Francis Lindley, the British ambassador in Athens, in February 1922, "that it would not be better to get Greece out of Asia Minor before she is beaten and before she gets a loan (if she does) than for us to incur the odium of the loan and her the ignominy of defeat."[11]

Long the darling of London, Greece was now left out in the cold. So far had Athens fallen in Western esteem that, at a Franco-Italian-British summit held in Paris from March 22 to 26, 1922, none of the three powers proposed allowing Greece to hold on to Smyrna, let alone Anatolian territories farther east that she was then still occupying. Curzon did insist that a Greek evacuation be made conditional on the Turks accepting a peace settlement based on Sèvres. But even this was too much for the French and Italians, who had begun making their own arrangements with Kemal. Raymond Poincaré, the former French president who was now premier, repudiated Sèvres as illegitimate and insisted on a prior Greek withdrawal as a prerequisite for a Greco-Turkish armistice—not a consequence of one. Remarkably, in view of France's own role in arming the Armenian Legion in Cilicia, Poincaré even disavowed Curzon's proposal to return Cilicia, Kars, and Ardahan to (now Soviet) Armenia and to send an international gendarmerie to protect Turkish Armenians. Kemal's bilateral treaties with both Armenia and Soviet Russia, Poincaré argued, were *faits accomplis*, backed by force of arms and accepted by all interested parties; were the Allies to try to reverse them, it would require them to go to war with Kemal. Even Curzon's watered-down version of the Sèvres Treaty, which stripped the Greeks and Armenians of most of what had been promised to them in the original draft, Curzon informed the London cabinet, was now viewed with "complete indifference amounting almost to open hostility by French and with only tepid support by Italians." The final armistice proposal agreed on in Paris required Greece to evacuate Anatolia entirely, although she would be allowed to hold on to western Thrace, including Adrianople and Gallipoli (which the British wished to keep out of Turkish hands). The Turks would also be required to restore the Capitulations to protect Westerners in general (if not Greeks in particular). Realizing that this was probably the best Greece, deprived of British financial support for her war effort, could get, the Greek parliament accepted the terms, on condition that an international gendarmerie be sent to protect Greek Christians in Anatolia.[12]

The response from the Turkish Grand National Assembly was less obliging, beginning with a firm rejection of any restoration of the Capitulations. Reasoning, logically enough, that the powers were asking for an armistice only because "after Sakarya the Greek army is unfit for an offensive," Kemal had no desire to let the enemy off the hook. "This is no time for peace talks," he informed a British envoy off the record. "We are now in a position to force our own terms upon the Greeks and Allies." Although Ankara's formal response to the Allied armistice proposal, lodged with the high commissioners on April 22, 1922, was polite, Kemal insisted on an immediate and unconditional Greek withdrawal from Anatolia, and that no foreign gendarmerie be sent to replace them. As he must have predicted, these terms proved unacceptable for Curzon and—especially—for Lloyd George, who had insisted all winter that he wanted the Greek army to remain in Anatolia as long as possible precisely in order to force Kemal to accept the harshest peace settlement possible.[13]

There were solid, material reasons for Kemal's refusal to give in. In a sign of the diplomatic turnabout wrought by the battles of Inönü and Sakarya, the Ankara government was less isolated now than Greece. Italy had always been hostile to Greek claims in Turkey, but France had changed course nearly 180 degrees from her policy in 1919–20, going so far as to turn over surplus weapons and uniforms to the Turks after French forces evacuated Cilicia, including at least 10,000 rifles and 500 crates of ammunition. Meanwhile, just as the Allied high commissioners had foreseen, Lloyd George's aggressive Hellenophile policy had pushed the Turkish nationalists into a *de facto* alliance with Moscow, and Kemal was reaping its fruits. Quietly, the Bolsheviks had been shipping gold to Ankara for months, including hundreds of ingots looted by the Red Army after it conquered Bukhara in September 1920, and this gold allowed Kemal to pay his troops.[14] Following the final evacuation of the White armies from the Crimea in November 1920, the Bolsheviks also felt secure enough at home to send substantial quantities of weaponry and ammunition to Ankara, amounting, by spring 1922, to some 37,812 rifles, 324 machine guns, nearly 45,000 crates full of ammunition, 66 cannons, and 200,000 shells. By the time he was informed of the Allied armistice terms in April 1922, Kemal was confident enough of Moscow's support that he lodged a special request for 10 million rubles to support a summer offensive. If the Greek invaders were not going to withdraw voluntarily, or be required to by their backers in London, then the Turks would have to make them leave. As Kemal explained to the Russian ambassador, in terms the Bolsheviks, having expelled foreign armies during their own civil war, could appreciate:

> Very well, we shall have to prove by force of arms that we have a right to exist. It won't be recognized until we clear our land of interventionists. A nation, like an individual, will seek attention and justice in vain, until it shows its worth in action and displays its strength and capabilities.[15]

Kemal's decision to fight on in summer 1922 was a gamble, but a very well-calculated one. The Greek military position in western Anatolia grew more precarious every day, even as the Turkish army gathered strength. The only real strategic risk for Ankara was that Lloyd George, to rescue the Greeks along with his own tottering policy, would resume Britain's war against Turkey. But the odds of this were low for many reasons. By 1922, it had begun to dawn on many policymakers in London that if hostilities resumed, Kemal could do far more damage to British interests in the region than vice versa, simply by contesting the oil-bearing region near Mosul. Mesopotamia, so far from the prize imperial planners had hoped for, had turned into a hornet's nest, with armed resistance to British rule by local Arabs and Bedouins costing the occupiers at least two thousand casualties in 1920 and 1921.[16]

Sitting on a human volcano like this, and learning of Kemal's crushing victory at Sakarya, the British high commissioner in Mesopotamia, Sir Percy Cox, not unnaturally requested that London endeavor "to secure if possible friendly state on borders of Iraq." Churchill, now secretary of state for the colonies, submitted a memorandum to the cabinet warning that "a few thousand Turkish troops sent into the Mosul Vilayet" would force Britain either to evacuate the oil fields, or to bring in massive reinforcements. Speaking more forthrightly still, Colonel Richard Meinertzhagen, head of British military intelligence in Cairo, summed up the opinion among British officers and diplomats in the field that "we must make friends with the Turk and drop our pro-Greek policy; or we must run the risk of being driven out of Constantinople and Mosul, if not Baghdad . . . we shall never get peace with Turkey so long as a single Greek soldier remains on Turkish territory."[17]

By insisting, against the advice of his advisers from the field, that the Greek army remain in Anatolia, Lloyd George was unwittingly playing into Kemal's hands. Rather than meet the Turks halfway, he had staked the Allied negotiating position on a battered army of occupation surrounded by a hostile civilian population, most of whose officers and enlisted men simply wanted to go home. It did not help matters that General George Hatzianestis, Papoulas's successor as commander in chief of the Anatolian army, was widely believed by his fellow officers to be psychologically unbalanced. Touring the front in June 1922, Hatzianestis evinced an uncharacteristic calm, though this may not have been a good sign, as his conclusion was that the front would hold easily if Kemal attacked. It is true that the Greeks still had some 225,000 men in Anatolia, who remained better equipped in machine guns, field guns, and motorized vehicles than the Turks. But fighting morale was another matter. The Greeks held a front nearly 400 miles long comprising a kind of gigantic triangular salient from Gemlik, on the Sea of Marmara, southeast to Afyon, and then forking back southwest along the Meander (Menderes) River valley to the Aegean and Mediterranean. And all of this land, according to an armistice agreement proposed by the Allies and accepted by the Greek parliament, had already been promised back to Turkey! Little wonder the men were listless and apathetic. Hatzianestis also failed to notice, on his tour of the front, the rapid spread of Communist influence through the Greek army, helped along by the distribution of Bolshevik propaganda leaflets by the Turks—another benefit of Kemal's tactical alliance with Moscow—"exhorting the Greeks in stilted Greek to go home and leave their Turkish comrades in place." For many exhausted and demoralized Greek soldiers, Communist rhetoric blaming the war on "British imperialism" offered an easy rationalization for quitting. "By the summer of 1922," writes Michael Llewellyn-Smith in *The Ionian Vision*, "the Greek army was like an apple eaten out inside by insects or disease, superficially whole and apparently firm, but ready to disintegrate at the first sharp blow."[18]

As if taking pity on an enemy he knew to be beaten, Kemal waited all through June, July, and August to see if the Greeks might wise up and decide to leave on their own. Even if they did, evacuation would not have been easy, and it grew less easy with each passing week. Much of the railway linking Afyon and Eskişehir with the coast was single-track, limiting carrying capacity severely (and leaving any evacuation vulnerable to a simple act of sabotage on the line). Because the Greeks would have to use roads, too, this meant that any serious evacuation would have to begin before the rainy season began in September. As if to test the infrastructure for a proper evacuation, Hatzianestis withdrew two battalions and three infantry regiments to the Thracian front in July, but all that this accomplished was to weaken his main force facing Kemal and to isolate Greece still further, as it appeared to the Allies that he was making a play for Constantinople. On July 29, 1922, the high commissioners warned Hatzianestis that any violation of the neutral zone in the capital by Greek troops would be met with force. In a speech to the Commons on August 4, 1922, Lloyd George more or less disavowed this warning when he complained that the Allies "were not allowing the Greeks to wage war with their full strength," and saluted the Greeks for the "daring and reckless military enterprise" that had seen them "march through impenetrable defiles hundreds of miles into [Anatolia]." But, although Lloyd George's pep talk was well received in Athens (where many newspapers led with his speech), for Greek soldiers on the front lines in Turkey it was pretty weak tea, backed by not so much as a hint of material aid from the Allies. The Greeks, notwithstanding Lloyd George's rhetoric, were on their own.[19]

All year, Kemal had been methodically preparing for a major offensive. A new conscription law passed in February called up older Turks, born between 1881 and 1901, to join the younger cohort already serving. A partial amnesty for deserters netted yet more men, by lifting punishment if their families could replace them with fresh recruits. Hundreds of experienced former

Ottoman officers, taken prisoner by the tsarist army during the world war, were handed back by the Bolsheviks, helping to replace the large cohort of Turkish officers who had fallen at Sakarya. The agreements with the Bolsheviks over the new Caucasian borders and with France, over Cilicia, freed up most of the men on those fronts for service against the Greeks. By summer 1922 Kemal had mustered an army numbering some 200,000 men and 8,568 officers against the Greeks, supported by nearly 80,000 horses and pack animals. Though deficient in trucks and inferior in machine guns and artillery, the Turkish army was superior in cavalry and, more important, in morale.

By the end of July, it was clear that the moment for a Greek evacuation had passed. Rather than save his army, Hatzianestis had weakened it with his feint toward Constantinople, which, to Turkish officers in a fighting mood, was like waving a red flag before a bull. On the night of July 28, Kemal met with his field commanders near the front at Akşehir, the cover story for his presence being his desire to watch a football game between two teams of officers. The decision was made that night to prepare an offensive for mid-August, in which the First Army, led by Nureddin Pasha, would target the Greek salient in the heights above Afyon, while the Second Army launched a feint toward Bursa. On August 17, Kemal left Ankara again in strictest secrecy. To camouflage his intentions, a rumor was spread that Kemal had invited leading officers to his house in Çankaya for a tea party on the twenty-first (for added effect, Kemal even lied to his own mother, Zübeyde, that he was off to a reception the night he left for the front).* Over the next few nights, the First Army was reinforced by units from the Second Army, moving under cover of darkness. On August 25, 1922, Kemal arrived at First Army headquarters to assume command of the coming battle.

As dawn broke on the Anatolian plateau, the guns of the Turkish First Army boomed all along the line. Most of the enemy observation posts were knocked out, which made it difficult for the Greek gunners to return fire. Nonetheless, the Greeks put up staunch resistance when the Turkish infantry

---

* No fool, Zübeyde *hanım*, observing her son in field uniform, replied cheekily that he was not properly dressed for a tea party.

tried to storm their positions. All day a seesaw battle raged along a front twenty-five miles long, with a number of hilltop positions changing hands multiple times. One Turkish commander, Colonel Resat, promised Kemal he would capture his target—the peak of Ciğiltepe—within a half hour. Failing to do so, he committed suicide. By nightfall, although the Turks had made a few gains, it was clear that the Greek lines had held.

The Turkish breakthrough was, however, not long in coming. On the morning of the second day of the battle, August 27, 1922, IV Corps, under Colonel Kemalettin Sami, punctured Greek lines and captured the heights of Erkmentepe, one of the key positions southwest of Afyon. A Turkish cavalry corps then raced through a gap in the Greek lines and reached open ground in the enemy's rear. Fearing encirclement, the commander of the Greek I Corps, General Trikoupis, sounded the retreat, abandoning huge military stores in Afyon, where Kemal established his new headquarters. The breakthrough was so sudden that Trikoupis lost wireless contact with his divisional commanders, leading to considerable confusion as the Greeks fell back from the salient.[20]

This time, unlike in the aftermath of Sakarya, pursuit was swift and unrelenting. Giving Trikoupis no time to recover, the Turks scarcely paused to digest their victory before marching on his heels. With advanced cavalry reconnaissance suggesting that what remained of Trikoupis's First Corps was trying to rejoin the Greek Second Corps, commanded by General Dighenis, near Dumlupınar—thirty miles west of Afyon en route for Smyrna—on August 31 Kemal ordered that the Turkish Second Army wheel down to cut off Dumlupınar from the northern side even while Nureddin Pasha wheeled around it from the south. While this would leave the Greek Third Corps free to escape on the northern flank toward the Sea of Marmara, Kemal insisted that the main objective was to envelop and thereby neutralize the main Greek force in the south so as to open the roads to the Aegean and Mediterranean. On September 1, 1922, Kemal issued an order from a house above Dumlupınar, which became almost instantly famous: "Armies! The Mediterranean is your immediate objective. Forward!" The Turks did not disappoint, advancing so quickly that they passed right on by whole Greek units, taking the surrender of Trikoupis and Dighenis on September 2 almost as afterthoughts. So sudden was this coup that Trikoupis was appointed the new commander in chief in Anatolia over the disgraced Hatzianestis two days *after* he was captured by the Turks, the news evidently not having yet reached Athens. Kemal, taking Trikoupis prisoner, offered him coffee and cigarettes and consoled his defeated adversary that war was a game of chance in which "the very best is often worsted." It was a rare moment of humanity in a brutal war.[21]

Not everyone was so magnanimous. Surveying the burning wreckage at Dumlupınar, Halidé Edib, accompanying Kemal on campaign, observed "amidst it all corpses—of men and animals—lay as they had fallen." No longer taking the time to loot or steal pottery or antiquities, the retreating Greeks simply burned every town in their path toward the ocean. En route to Smyrna, Rumbold reported to Curzon after reading the reports from Consul Sir Harry Lamb, Greeks "went to pieces altogether," looting, killing, torching villages, and generally compiling "a sickening record of bestiality and brutality." Not to be outdone, Lamb himself described the conduct of the retreating Greek army as "indescribably disgusting."[22] Although he furnished no details, Lamb might have been referring to rumors that Greek soldiers and *chete* bands had abducted, raped, and often mutilated thousands of Muslim girls in towns like Alaşehir and Manısa—rumors initially discounted by many Allied officials, only to be confirmed in the main later, when fact-finding missions were sent to towns devastated during the Greek retreat.[23] The humanitarian situation almost everywhere in western Turkey, U.S. Consul Horton reported from Smyrna as early as September 2, 1922—the day Kemal received the defeated Greek corps commanders at Dumlupınar—was already

extremely grave owing to exhaustion and low morale of Greek forces. Uşak and Kuta[h]ya were evacuated and burned yesterday . . . Third [Greek] Army Corps at Eskişehir but will probably soon evacuate and burn the town . . . panic spreading among Christian population foreigners as well as Greeks and many are trying to leave. When demoralized Greek army reaches Smyrna serious trouble more than possible and threats to burn the town are freely heard.

Five days later, Horton informed Washington that "the main towns of the district Eskişehir, Kutahya, Uşak, Magnesia [Manısa], Alaşehir, Aydın and Nazli have been burned or largely destroyed. These are cities of between 35,000 and 100,000 inhabitants." Both Allied and Turkish investigatory commissions confirmed the veracity of Horton's reports, adding that Kasaba, too, an important trade center of twenty thousand people that lay at the terminus of the inland railway from Smyrna, had been turned into "a smoking ruin of ashes and stones," with only eight thousand survivors left after the Greeks torched the town. At Uşak, the Greeks had even burned down the apple orchards. With nowhere else for civilian refugees to go, Smyrna, like Constantinople during the Balkan Wars, had turned into a refugee camp. "Fully fifty thousand of these wretched persons," Horton reported, "of whom are not a few Turks," were "now sleeping in the courtyards of the churches, in mosques, and even on the sidewalks."[24]

As the backwash of the defeated Greek army poured into the city alongside Ottoman Greeks who feared reprisals for its terrible conduct, the Allied consuls and the foreign and Christian communities of Smyrna braced for the worst. The Allied powers all docked warships in port—eleven British, five French, three American, and two Italian—and landed small detachments of marines ashore to protect Western subjects and property. J. G. Ware, a U.S. naval intelligence officer who had gone inland to gauge the temperature of the Greeks, said that he heard "repeated threats by Greek officers to burn the city." Not unnaturally, citing these threats along with the precedent set by the Greeks' scorched-earth retreat across western Turkey, the U.S., French, and British consuls telegraphed to the Greek minister of war, Nikolaus Theotokis, on September 6, 1922, demanding his written assurance that Smyrna not be burned or pillaged by the Greek army. Theotokis, in view of the fact that no one was entirely certain who was actually commanding what was left of the Greek army in Anatolia—he was just now being informed that his new choice for the position was now a prisoner of war—confessed that he was "not able to give assurances to that effect." Theotokis might have leaned instead on the Greek high commissioner in Smyrna, Aristides Sterghiades, an ornery Venizelist who had come under fire from the local Ottoman Greek community for his periodic crackdowns on nationalist and anti-Muslim excesses, except that Sterghiades left Smyrna himself on Friday night, September 8, 1922, under British protection—boarding, in a symbolic flourish, the same HMS *Iron Duke* that had accompanied the Greek occupying flotilla in May 1919.* In part to avoid the bottleneck at Smyrna, an order was given that Greek soldiers should try to evacuate instead via Çeşme, a port some fifty miles to the west and south, directly across from the Greek-controlled island of Chios. With no Greek authorities left to protect Smyrna or to surrender it to the Turks, the Allied consuls took the unusual step of proposing to travel inland to Kasaba themselves to negotiate the city's surrender and demand assurances that the Christian population would be protected, as if to confess that the Greek occupation of Smyrna had been a Western-controlled affair all along. Having remained relatively unperturbed at the often-atrocious Greek behavior through the campaign so far, it was when he heard this that Kemal finally lost his temper, thundering, "Whose city are they giving to whom?"[25]

The Allies need not have bothered sending messengers to Kasaba. So swift was the Turkish advance that the first cavalry regiment, four hundred strong, rode into Smyrna at around 11:00 a.m. on Saturday morning, September 9, 1922. When Kemal recovered his composure after an aide brought him the news, his mood changed to one of pity for the man who had launched the disastrous Greek invasion of Anatolia: "Poor Lloyd George! What's going to happen to him tomorrow? He'll be destroyed." The initial impression the Turks made on the locals of Smyrna was a positive one, as the troops appeared "well dressed and under good discipline," and notably "well-fed and fresh" compared with the "filthy, untidy, slouching" Greek soldiers who had recently passed through, not to mention the bedraggled civilian refugees underfoot. A proclamation had been published in all the papers, signed by Kemal, ordering the summary execution of any Turkish officer who molested noncombatants. One English nurse wrote home that "everyone [was] inwardly delighted to have the Turks back again." On Sunday, September 10, Kemal himself drove

---

* Afraid to face the inevitable court-martial—or popular lynching—in Greece, Sterghiadis went to France instead, by way of Romania.

into Smyrna at 4:00 p.m. "at the head of a procession of open cars, decked with olive branches," meant to symbolize the conqueror's peaceful intentions. Turkish Muslims sacrificed an ox to Kemal, though he did not stay to enjoy the ceremony. Strolling into the bar of the Kraemer hotel along the quay as if incognito, Kemal ordered a raki and asked the predominantly Greek patrons if King Constantine had ever raised his glass with them there. Informed that the sovereign had not done so, Kemal replied quizzically, "Why did he bother to take Smyrna, then?"[26]

It was a good beginning for Turkish Smyrna. But after a war lasting three years, each one more savage than the last, and with recent Greek atrocities nearby in mind, the forbearance of the Turkish occupiers was not fated to last. Even foreigners impressed by the Turks' "extraordinarily good" discipline observed "wholesale looting of bazaars however by soldiers with connivance or at least assent of their officers." Already on Saturday afternoon, violent incidents were reported here and there, which mushroomed through the night as screams were heard across the city. A Turkish cavalryman, riding along the waterfront, was shot from his horse, provoking reprisals. A British captain saw Turkish soldiers shoot dead a Greek man who failed to obey their commands. Five corpses were found near the Aydin railway station. More significantly, Chrysostom, the Greek metropolitan of Smyrna who had, unlike Sterghiades, stayed on with his flock, was lynched by a mob of Muslims shortly after being received by Nureddin Pasha at the Governor's Konak, by most accounts on Nureddin's express encouragement. Other "traitors," including Turks who had worked for or prominently collaborated with the Greek occupation authorities, were court-martialed and shot. Because most (though not all) Greeks had either fled already or had resigned themselves to evacuation as soon as they could get onto a boat in the harbor, the violence was most serious in the Armenian quarter, where armed Christians were actually fighting back. Slowly but steadily, the death toll climbed, reaching some four hundred in the first three days. As the U.S. high commissioner in Constantinople, Admiral Bristol, reported somewhat equivocally on Wednesday after reading all the reports from Smyrna, despite "considerable killing especially in Armenian quarter by local rowdies, nothing whatever in the nature of a massacre has occurred in spite of the fact that Turkish troops on entry into town were fired upon and bombed three times by Greek and Armenian civilians."[27]

Then all hell broke loose. On September 13, 1922, the day Bristol was filing this report with the U.S. State Department, a terrible fire broke out in the Armenian quarter of Smyrna. Spreading rapidly through the wooden buildings of the old city, the fire consumed many of the most beautiful areas along the waterfront, including the shops of "Frank street" (the trading colony of the old Frankish, i.e., European, merchants), the cinema houses and cafés, the British, French, American, Danish, Dutch, and Russian consulates, the Smyrna Theater, churches, synagogues, mosques, and even the Kraemer hotel, where Kemal had just drunk his raki. From the safety of the deck of HMS *Iron Duke*, the British correspondent for the *Daily Mail*, Ward Price, observed onshore "an unbroken wall of fire, two miles long, in which twenty distinct volcanoes of raging flames are throwing up jagged, writhing tongues to a height of a hundred feet." All of the old city's "warehouses, business buildings, and European residences," he observed, "burned like furious torches." The scene at the quay was out of Dante's *Inferno*—similar in its impact on those who saw it from the harbor to that on those who witnessed the carnage of 9/11—beginning with the "nauseous smell" of charred and burning bodies, even while desperate screams were heard from those seeking to escape the deadly fumes. From aboard the *George V*, an English captain thought that "many people were shoved into the sea, simply by the crowds nearest the houses trying to get further away from the fire . . . many did undoubtedly jump into the sea, from sheer panic." Compounding the horror, for those unable to reach the water or to swim once they did, was the fact that most boats in the harbor, already overflowing with refugees, refused, at first, to take more passengers on board for fear of capsizing. At last, toward nightfall, many of the Allied warships pulled in closer to shore and lowered cutters to save the drowning—although many still insisted on checking the nationality of the victims (those able to pronounce "*J'ai perdu mes papiers*" correctly were said to have found French vessels more welcoming). By the time the terrible fire burned itself out on Friday, September 15, the Greek, Armenian, and Frankish quarters, closest to the water, lay in ruins, and untold thousands had perished in the fire or drowned in the harbor.[28]

Just as with the burning of Moscow in 1812, the question of who lit the fire, and why, has raged ever since. Nearly all accounts agree that the flames first rose in the Armenian quarter, which suggests that Armenian nationals would have had no motive for starting it. Greek officials and politicians, predictably, blamed the Turks for torching "Greek" Smyrna, who retorted in turn that it made little sense for them to burn a city they had just conquered. Sense or no sense, two pieces of circumstantial evidence do point more in the Turkish direction than otherwise. First, by September 13, 1922, the Turkish army was clearly in control of the city, which it had taken virtually without resistance; most Greek soldiers who had not evacuated already were avoiding the city and heading to Çeşme instead. Second, the fire never did spread to the main Muslim-Turkish quarter, which was located in the hills south of and above the waterfront area, nor, interestingly, to the Jewish quarter, which was likewise inland in the same general direction. In part this was because the wind, unusually, was blowing north and out to sea that fateful Wednesday (which, some foreign observers suggested, may have provided a pretext for arsonists to go to work when they did—and there were many who did claim to have seen Turkish arsonists at work). There were further reports that trenches were quickly dug around both the Turkish and Jewish quarters to prevent the fire spreading there, with fire brigades standing by to ensure these areas were spared.[29]

None of this constitutes proof of intentional arson, of course. As if to ward off the inevitable accusations that his troops were responsible, as early as September 15, 1922, in conversation with Michel Graillet, the French consul, Kemal accused armed Greeks and Armenians of setting the fire, a claim he put in writing two days later in an official report sent to Ankara, in which he added that Turkish soldiers had "worked with everything that they have to put out the fires." Yet according to Latife Hanım, the woman who hosted Kemal in Smyrna and would soon become the most famous of all his lovers (he married her in 1923), the conqueror of Smyrna remarked even as the fire was still raging, "Let it burn, let it crash down. We can replace everything."*

---

* Latife herself lost considerable property in the fire, and in fact it was her own equanimity about these losses ("I don't care; it can all be burnt") which seems to have prompted Kemal's own remark, rather than any spontaneous exultation.

One of the most famous contemporary Turkish journalistic accounts of the fire, published by Falih Rifki (Atay) in *Aksam*, noted that "the fire destroyed a great deal of the wealth of Muslims in the city"; Atay further insisted that he saw "thousands of [Turkish] soldiers . . . fighting fiercely to put out the fire." Yet this same Atay, in the first, uncensored version of his memoirs, later wrote that "Gavur [infidel] Izmir burned and came to an end with its flames in the darkness and its smoke in daylight. Were those responsible for the fire really the Armenian arsonists as we were told in those days?" Citing his diary from September 1922, Atay confessed to writing at the time, "The plunderers helped spread the fire . . . why were we burning down Izmir? Were we afraid that if the waterfront konaks, hotels and taverns stayed in place, we would never be able to get rid of the minorities?" No less interesting was the reflection of Ismet Inönü in his memoirs on the conflagration of Smyrna, alongside the Greek-lit fires that destroyed towns across western Turkey. "The cause of these fires," Ismet wrote, "should be sought in the great events of history. Subordinates say they carried out orders; senior figures say there was a breakdown in discipline." Whoever actually started the great fire of Smyrna, it seems clear that many Turks saw it as poetic justice for the dozens of cities and towns the Greeks had put to the flames farther inland. For the fact remains that, even if many Turks lost property and a few mosques in the old city were burned, it was the Christians of Smyrna, Ottoman and European alike, who lost everything.[30]

What perished alongside the old city of Smyrna in September 1922 was the very idea that Greeks and Turks, Christians and Muslims, could live together peacefully in Asia Minor—or in mainland Greece, for that matter. If the brutal Greek scorched-earth campaigns of 1920, 1921, and 1922 had begun the project of ethnic separation, the Smyrna fire brought this to its dramatic conclusion. To forestall further outbreaks of intercommunal violence, Nureddin Pasha gave Smyrna Christians who wished to leave a grace period to, in effect, forfeit Ottoman citizenship, though it was not a long one (the initial deadline of September 30 was, owing to the continued bottleneck in port, later extended to October 15). By October 2, 1922, according to U.S. naval sources, no fewer than 200,000 predominantly Greek refugees had been evacuated aboard Greek or Allied ships from Smyrna to mainland Greece, where they hoped to be accepted as citizens; other Allied sources suggest the number was as high as 300,000. But these Greeks were the lucky ones—mostly women, children, and the elderly. Any male Ottoman Armenian or Greek subject between eighteen and forty-five who had taken up arms or collaborated with the occupation authorities—which meant in practice, just about all of them, as many as 100,000 or 120,000—was sent to prisoner-of-war camps in the Anatolian interior or impressed into labor gangs "sent to rebuild the villages and roads which the Greek army had destroyed during its flight." We must treat all these suspiciously round numbers with caution. Nevertheless, it is abundantly clear that nearly the entire Greek community of Smyrna and environs, alongside those Greek civilian refugees who had fled westward with the retreating army, in all perhaps 350,000 souls, were uprooted from their ancestral homes, which most would never see again. A precedent was thus set for what would soon become the largest mutual population exchange ever recorded between two sovereign states, as Greek Muslim subjects would be expelled to Turkey to "replace" Ottoman Christians sent to Greece.[31]

In the meantime, the war was still on. For Kemal, the fall of Smyrna was not the end but merely an important victory in his campaign to realize the principles of the National Pact. Turkey's eastern border with Soviet Russia was now clearly established; her southeastern boundary with French Syria agreed, if not—quite—also that with British Mesopotamia (Iraq); and the Greeks were expelled from western Anatolia. But there were still Greek troops in eastern Thrace and Allied troops in Constantinople, along the Gulf of Izmit, and in some of the Straits batteries abutting the Dardanelles: for Kemal to fulfill the National Pact would require that they either leave voluntarily, or be expelled by force of arms. In a sense the Ottoman Empire, reborn under Kemal, now stood roughly where it had in the early fourteenth century when Bursa had been the capital and the Turks had not yet crossed into Europe. Would Kemal now follow the path of the conquerors in retaking Adrianople and Constantinople by the sword? Or would the Allies and the Greeks withdraw in peace to forestall another year of bloodshed?

The answer to this question, like so many others since the end of the world war, depended on Lloyd George. Although the Greek army had not yet abandoned eastern Thrace, by September 18, 1922, the last intact unit of the Greek army had left Asia Minor via Çeşme, which meant there were no more Greek troops between Kemal's forces and the Allied troops at the Straits and Izmit. In Smyrna, Kemal received British consul general Sir Harry Lamb, in part to ascertain British intentions. Informed that the consul represented the interests of the high commissioner in Constantinople, Kemal replied that his government "considered itself in a state of war with Great Britain and therefore did not recognize [the] High Commissioner." As such Kemal believed that he would have been "justified in interning all British subjects," although he assured Lamb that he had no plans to do so and that Britons in Turkey "were free to leave if [they] liked." Asked to clarify whether he was sincere in viewing himself as in a state of war with Britain, Kemal climbed down slightly, noting that no relations existed between Ankara and London. In effect, Kemal was inviting—or daring—Lloyd George to offer his government diplomatic recognition as a way of demonstrating his lack of hostility toward Turkey. If it was not offered, then his troops would march on to secure Turkey's borders in accordance with the National Pact.[32]

The first signs coming from the British side were not encouraging. As early as September 7, even before the Turks took Smyrna, the British cabinet—without consulting either Parliament or Britain's allies—authorized General Charles Harington, commander in chief of British occupation forces in Turkey and the Black Sea, to send troops to occupy the Gallipoli Peninsula, so as to forestall a possible Turkish landing there en route for Thrace. Strongly backing this move to hold on to Gallipoli, in part for personal reasons not difficult to fathom, was Winston Churchill. Though long sour on the Greek cause, Churchill saw things very differently now that the issue was Turkish or British control of the Straits: his imagination was aroused and his blood was up. "The line of deep water separating Asia from Europe," he argued, "was a line of great significance, and we must make that line secure by every means within our power. If the Turks take the Gallipoli Peninsula and Constantinople, we shall have lost the whole fruits of our victory." Emboldened by Churchill's about-face on the Turkish war and believing the Greeks to be not yet finished, Lloyd George went further still, informing the cabinet that if the

Turks proposed to cross the Straits in force, "we should fight to prevent their doing so." In order that the Britons buried at Gallipoli not have died in vain, Lloyd George and Churchill proposed that more of them bleed and die there again. In one sense, they proposed to go even further than in 1915: on September 12, 1922, Harington landed troops at Chanak (Çanakkale), on the Asian side of the Straits, as if daring Kemal to dislodge them. The battle to control the Straits, on hiatus since 1918, was heating up again.

The anti-Kemal coalition, however, was fracturing badly. Although they won over the cabinet—grudgingly—Lloyd George and Churchill had less luck with Britain's allies. France and Italy initially agreed to send small contingents to the European (Gallipoli) side of the Straits, but they refused to follow Harington into Asia. Quietly Poincaré assured Kemal, via the French high commissioner, General Pellé, that France would not participate in any British campaign at the Straits. On September 15, 1922, Churchill sent a telegram to the prime ministers of Australia, New Zealand, South Africa, and Canada, asking them to reprise the heroic epic of Gallipoli in order to secure the "vital Imperial and world-wide interests involved in the freedom of the Straits." This time, the appeal fell flat. New Zealand offered a battalion, Australia and Canada politely declined, and South Africa did not deign to reply. Granted a sort of diplomatic equality when they were offered seats at the Paris Peace Conference, the Dominions now astonished the mother country by refusing to follow her into war. Even the usually belligerent *Daily Mail* refused to get on board, running a sensational cover: "STOP THIS NEW WAR!" Poincaré, piling on the increasingly isolated Lloyd George, ordered all French troops withdrawn from Gallipoli on September 18, 1922. With French abandonment of the Straits now clear, the cabinet authorized Curzon to go to Paris almost as a supplicant, begging for French help. On September 23, 1922, Poincaré, berating this former viceroy of India so brutally that Curzon broke down in tears, insisted that Britain cede all of Kemal's territorial demands, including Constantinople, the Straits, and eastern Thrace. Kemal had not only conquered "Greek" Smyrna and expelled the Greeks from Asia; he had rent the British Empire into its constituent parts, and destroyed the last remaining diplomatic comity between Paris and London.[33]

This was not all. As if not satisfied with the scale of his humiliation so far, Lloyd George insisted that Harington stand his ground and fight if the Turks threatened Çanakkale. Curzon may already have signed away the Straits in Paris, but the prime minister wanted to make clear that he was *giving* them to Kemal as part of a negotiated settlement, not surrendering them to force. Meanwhile, if it did come to war, Lloyd George believed, Britain could win. He rested this belief on the assumption that the Greek armies had not really been fairly beaten but rather betrayed by the treachery of King Constantine and the incompetence of mad Hatzianestis.* Now that the Venizelists, following Constantine's abdication on September 27, 1922, were back in power, Lloyd George was certain that a reenergized Greece would reenter the war. Warming to his theme, the prime minister explained to the cabinet upon hearing of the revolution in Athens, "In Thrace the Turks would come up, not against Constantine's tired, ill-commanded and dispirited army, but against a national [Greek] resistance, inspired by Venizelos and the revolution, invigorated by having the British Empire at its back, and with its old Generals restored." Staking his credibility as clearly as he could on the clash at Çanakkale, Lloyd George promised that "by the time Musta[f]a Kemal is beaten and held we shall be strong enough to move up from Chanak to Izmi[t], where with a relatively small force we shall cut his communications and compel a humiliating surrender." Showing that this was no bluff, on Friday, September 29, 1922, Lloyd George drew up an ultimatum for Harington to hand to Kemal stipulating that "*unless his troops are withdrawn* by a time to be fixed by you at which time our combined forces will be in their proper positions *all the forces at our disposal, naval military and air will open fire on the Turks.*"[34]

Things did not turn out quite as Lloyd George hoped. According to Maurice Hankey, Churchill, Lloyd George, and the entire cabinet "all Saturday waited breathless to know whether the guns had gone off or whether the Turks had withdrawn." But no news came. Harington, it turned out, had

---

* On the same soothing yet implausible theory, eight leading Constantinists, including Prime Minister Gounaris and army commander in chief Hatzianestis, were put on trial in Athens on November 13, 1922, for high treason, convicted two weeks later, and executed (except for the two least important men, who were merely sentenced to life in prison, which is why the affair is often referred to, inaccurately, as the "trial of the six").

sought the counsel of Sir Horace Rumbold, the British high commissioner in Constantinople, and they had both decided not to risk war by delivering the ultimatum to Kemal. Lloyd George was deprived of the war he desperately wanted by his own subordinates in the field,* and the rout of his Hellenophile policy in Turkey finally broke the coalition government he had been leading since 1916, with the Conservatives bolting. In elections held on November 15, 1922, Lloyd George and his Liberal Party were so thoroughly vanquished that he did not even get to be leader of the Opposition, as Labour passed the Liberals into second place for the first time, never to look back. After weathering dozens of international crises in the last two years of the world war and the first four years of the peace, Lloyd George was thereby ushered into political oblivion, along with his entire political party, by Mustafa Kemal.

The Allies' puppet sultan, Mehmed VI (Vahdettin), was the next victim of Kemal's triumphant army. On November 1, 1922, the Turkish Grand National Assembly abolished the Ottoman sultanate, making official the transfer of sovereignty from the Sublime Porte to the government in Ankara. Two weeks later Vahdettin, now a private citizen, left the city aboard (appropriately enough) a British warship bound for Malta, never to return. Implied by the sultan's forced departure, although not yet confirmed by diplomacy, was the abolition of all previous treaties and agreements signed by the Ottoman sultans, up to and including the hated Capitulations. Kemal could now negotiate a final peace settlement with the Western powers as a sovereign equal.

After surviving more than six centuries, the Ottoman Empire had perished under the strains of the First World War. Like a phoenix rising from the ashes, the empire would be reborn as the Republic of Turkey.

---

* Although frequently dishonest in his memoirs, Lloyd George pulled no punches on Çanakkale. "I certainly meant to fight," he wrote, "and I was certain we would win."

LAUSANNE AND THE OTTOMAN LEGACY

---

*To unmix the populations of the Near East will tend to secure
[the] true pacification of the Near East.*

—FRIDTJOF NANSEN,
League of Nations high commissioner for refugees,
addressing the Lausanne peace conference on December 1, 1922.[1]

AFTER MORE THAN ELEVEN YEARS OF CARNAGE, peace now came at last to the Ottoman Empire. It was not a moment too soon. In the absence of precise record-keeping we can only surmise the number of victims across all fronts of the various conflicts (and the home front) between 1911 and 1923. Perhaps 400,000 or 500,000 Ottoman soldiers died in the First World War, but this is only a small fraction of total casualties for the broader conflict we might call the War of the Ottoman Succession. The best estimates suggest that the population inhabiting the territory of the Ottoman Empire prior to 1911 (about 21 million) dropped to less than 17 million by 1923, of which no more than 13 million now resided in the truncated borders of Kemalist Turkey. While all of these numbers are gross approximations—and it is not clear how many were lost to emigration as compared with disease, malnutrition, and other more directly war-related causes—there is broad agreement that mortality rates for the empire as a whole approached 20 percent, a shocking number when compared with the worst per capita figure on the western front, which saw France lose 3.5 percent. Something of the apocalyptic impact of the war in Asiatic Turkey is captured in the stunning casualty rates seen even in the comparatively well-supplied and cared-for British expeditionary force in Mesopotamia, which recorded 207,000 casualties from sickness in 1916 alone. The Four Horsemen of the Apocalypse—war, famine, pestilence, and death—had ridden roughshod over the Ottoman lands, with the totality of their conquest staved off only by Kemal's heroics after 1919.

The raw numbers of dead and wounded tell, of course, only a small part of the terrible story of the Ottoman war. Entire peoples, in some cases entire nations, were uprooted from homes they had inhabited for centuries, along with their entire way of life. The Armenian catastrophe of 1915 is well known, but by no means unique in a decade-long conflict that saw hundreds of thousands of Balkan Muslims displaced in the Balkan Wars, hundreds of thousands of Greek Christians expelled from Anatolia in 1913–14, 1916, and again in 1921–22, thousands of Tatar and other Circassian Muslims deported on the Caucasian front in 1914–15, the locust plague devastation of Palestine and Syria in 1915, countless Turkish Muslims burned out of their villages and homes in the Greco-Turkish war, thousands more Greeks deported yet again from Smyrna and its hinterland in winter 1922–23, and on and on.

To make sense of all this human loss, to find meaning in the plight of millions of forced refugees, and in nearly as many painful and agonizing military and civilian deaths, is surely impossible. At the least, after the passage of a century we can begin to reckon with the geopolitical consequences. The Ottoman Empire had limped into the twentieth century still standing—if not tall, then as some passable facsimile of its earlier fearsome self. Despite European encroachment into his empire in the form of the Capitulations and financial oversight, Abdul Hamid II was still recognized as sultan by millions of Ottoman subjects, Muslim, Christian, and Jew alike, and millions more Muslims farther afield looked upon him as caliph of the Islamic world. True, the upheaval of 1908–9 had toppled the Hamidian regime and shaken the sultanate to its foundations, but, judging from reports filed from as far away as the Raj in India, some kind of homage was still paid by global Muslims even to the Young Turks' puppet sultan Mehmed V (Reshad) until 1918, and then to Mehmed VI (Vahdettin) until he was deposed by Kemal on

November 1, 1922—to be replaced, as caliph if not sultan, by Abdul Mecid II, until Turkey abolished the caliphate itself in March 1924. Of all the enduring changes brought about by the wars of the Ottoman Succession, this must rank as among the most important. For the abolition of the caliphate, Mustafa Kemal has often been given the credit—or the blame (in the latter case notably by, among many others, Osama bin Laden). But in truth it was the empire's crushing defeat in 1918 that had destroyed the prestige of the Ottomans, no less than defeat put paid to the Hohenzollerns, Habsburgs, and Romanovs in Europe. The difference, in the Turkish case, is that the fall of the dynasty also destroyed the last institution uniting the world's (Sunni) Muslims—and linking them by extension to the caliphs of Islam's classical age. As if to give the point emphasis, King Hussein proclaimed himself caliph of all Muslims upon hearing the news from Turkey in March 1924—only to lose control of Mecca to the Wahhabi Ikhwan warriors of Ibn Saud scarcely six months later. Because Ibn Saud himself had no claim to legitimacy other than his own puritanical ferocity, since 1924 there has been no caliph to unite the world's Muslims. The Islamic world has never been the same.

It was not only the Ottoman sultanate and caliphate that disappeared from the earth. The empire itself, after surviving one assault after another over the centuries, was finally smashed into pieces, never to be reassembled. This was true of all the belligerent countries that lost the First World War, of course, including Russia, carved up by the Central Powers at Brest-Litovsk, and the other Central Powers—Germany, Austria-Hungary, and (on a smaller scale) Bulgaria. But the Ottoman case was still unique in several respects. Turkey's wartime allies Germany and Austria, united by Hitler in the Anschluss in 1938, did make a run at restoring the old borders and, with Operation Barbarossa in 1941, at re-creating the eastern empire glimpsed at Brest-Litovsk. But Hitler's gambits were short-lived, and modern Germany and Austria are both considerably truncated from their pre-1914 boundaries. Soviet Russia was more successful in recapturing nearly all the lands of the former tsarist empire and even (in a few places such as Galicia and Kaliningrad) expanding them further still. But, despite serial laments across the Muslim world over the collapse of the caliphate, there has been no real attempt

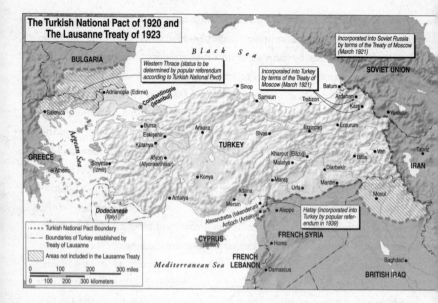

to restore the Ottoman Empire or the caliphate until very recently.* Nor, owing to the completeness of Kemal's military victory in 1922, did outside powers ever seriously contest Turkey's new borders (with the exception of Stalin demanding Kars and Ardahan in the full afterglow of his triumph in the Second World War—and even he failed).

In all the cartographical havoc wreaked by the First World War, it is a curious fact that both the most stable and the least stable boundaries were drawn in the former Ottoman Empire. The fragility of the postwar settlement in the Arab Middle East has become a well-worn cliché in recent years, with the recent emergence of the Islamic State in the lands defined as "Syria" and "Iraq" only the latest (though perhaps most serious) perturbation. And yet the borders of Kemal's Turkish Republic, forged by blood in the field—not on paper by faraway diplomats—have proved to be just as solid as those of Turkey's southeastern neighbors are porous. It is testimony to Kemal's success as

---

* The neo-Ottoman revival of Turkish influence in the Middle East in the era of Recep Tayyip Erdoğan seems, by this writing, to have petered out. More serious was the announcement by Abu Bakr Al-Bagdadi of the Islamic State, after the fall of Mosul in June 2014, of the creation of a global caliphate (with himself as Caliph Ibrahim).

a statesman that the borders drawn at Lausanne in 1923 have endured until today with no modification other than the addition of the Hatay in 1939, absorbed from French Syria in a popular referendum that filled out the last territory claimed in the Turkish National Pact of 1919–20.* Pursuant to the earlier, *de facto* agreements with France and Italy, Kemal accepted Italian control of the Dodecanese islands, and French rule in Syria as a whole. Nor did he dispute the British claim on Mosul, even though it was included in the National Pact owing to its large Turkish ("Turkmen") population, and he might easily have defeated the inferior British forces in Iraq. In exchange for his forbearance in victory, Kemal demanded the abolition of the hated Capitulations in perpetuity: and he got it.

In view of its lasting success in its main object—delineating the postwar boundaries between Turkey and her wartime enemies—it is curious that the Treaty of Lausanne, signed on July 24, 1923, does not have a better reputation. If it is remembered at all today, Lausanne stands for one thing above all: the population exchange between Greece and Turkey. Already adumbrated in the evacuation and expulsion of Greek Orthodox Christians from Smyrna after it fell to the Turks, the "Convention Concerning the Exchange of Greek and Turkish Populations," signed on January 30, 1923, completed the work begun during the war with selective deportations from frontline areas in Gallipoli and the Pontic areas of the Greek coast. The only new development was that now Muslim subjects of Greece, too, would be forced to flee in the other direction. In all some 1.2 million Ottoman subjects of Greek Orthodox faith or origin, counting those who had already fled or been forced out (perhaps as many as three-quarters), were deported westward to Greece, as against some 400,000 Muslims expelled eastward into Turkey. To this day the abandoned churches of Anatolia bear mute but eloquent witness to this Christian exodus, just as the emptied mosques, bathhouses, and *tekkes* of formerly Ottoman Rumeli (including, though it is often forgotten because of the city's prominence in Jewish history, Salonica) remind visitors of its banished Islamic civilization. "If you were trying to work out the history of Europe's southeastern edge

---

* The two maps were not quite identical, with Kemal agreeing at Lausanne to cede western Thrace to Greece, and Mosul to Britain. The Hatay was also not yet included in Turkey's borders in 1923, although it would be incorporated sixteen years later. Otherwise the borders match perfectly.

from architectural evidence alone," writes Bruce Clark in *Twice a Stranger*, "you might well conclude that some terrible catastrophe, either natural or manmade, had struck both sides of the Aegean . . . and that the region had not fully recovered." The principle of "collective population transfer" decreed at Lausanne redounded on through the twentieth century, most notoriously in the population exchanges negotiated by Hitler and Stalin between 1939 and 1941, Stalin's deportation of Crimean Tatars and of Chechen and other Circassian Muslims in 1944, the mass expulsions of German nationals by Czechoslovakia, Hungary, Poland, and Romania after the Second World War (expulsions justified by U.S. president Franklin Delano Roosevelt as early as 1943 by explicit reference to Lausanne), the India/Pakistan partition of 1948, and the mutual mass exodus/expulsion of Arabs from Israel, and Jews from Arab countries, which followed the Arab-Israeli War that same year. More recently, the "Lausanne precedent" has been applied (though often without explicit acknowledgment) in the expulsion of Turkish Muslims from Bulgaria in 1989, the ethnic sorting-out following the wars in the former Yugoslavia, Armenia's cleansing of Azeri Muslims from Nagorno-Karabagh in 1994, and even, arguably, in the ongoing partition of formerly independent Ukraine.[2]

There are plenty of other good reasons to lament the Lausanne legacy. Despite the fact that it was a treaty marking Turkey's recognition after a victorious war of independence, Turks today often lambaste Lausanne more strongly than do the Greeks they had defeated on the battlefield. In terms of human capital, Turkey undeniably lost far more than Greece in the exchange, both in the aggregate (about three times as many people left than arrived) and in the qualitative sense that Greek Christians leaving tended to be more educated and more prosperous than the Muslim peasants who did not come close to replacing them. For decades, the Turkish Republic was short of everything from merchants to apothecaries to engineers to skilled craftsmen. An economy ravaged by a decade-long war, in dire need of all hands on deck for recovery, was crippled at the outset by a shortage of skilled labor. In terms of growth and industrial development, the Turkish economy did not really roar back to life until the reforms of Turgut Özal in the 1980s. In cultural terms, Turkey has arguably still not recovered. Although tourists now descend on Istanbul in larger numbers than ever and the old European quarter of Pera (today's

Beyoğlu) has recovered some of its old cosmopolitan flavor, almost nothing remains today of the old Greek, Armenian, and Jewish communities that so enriched the city's cultural and economic life. Nor can many Turks, owing to the Latinization of the Turkish language, read Ottoman-era literature, poetry, or documents, cutting them off from their own history.

All this is true, and there is good reason to cast a wary eye on the Lausanne settlement and the hard majoritarian ethno-nationalism it represents. Prior to the upheaval of 1911–23, few of the peoples involved in the population exchange would even have defined themselves in national terms as Greeks and Turks, but rather as Christians or Muslims. Although many thousands—particularly Greek Christians resident in Anatolia—had been uprooted from their communities or forced into work-gangs already, those still living in their homes in 1923 were never consulted, and most of them appear to have been understandably bewildered when they were told they had to pack up and leave. If they had been asked their opinion, it seems clear that few of the expellees would have willingly agreed to leave homes they and their ancestors had lived in for as long as they and their ancestors could remember, on terms almost shockingly dismissive of their freedom of movement (the Lausanne convention decreed a "compulsory exchange" of populations and stipulated that "these persons shall not return to live in Turkey or Greece without the authorization of the Turkish government or the Greek government respectively.") Even those few groups initially expected to be spared, such as the 50,000-odd Greek Christians of Cappadocia, an area that had seen virtually no intercommunal tensions during the entire period 1911–23, ended up being forced onto the refugee trail.*

Deeply offensive as all this is to modern sensibilities, we must nevertheless be careful about judging the statesmen involved without understanding the problems they were trying to solve. It was not simply that Greek and Turkish and Western diplomats were trying to bring an end to a brutal war. They were also managing a serious refugee crisis, with thousands of civilians

---

* Two exceptions of note were, in the end, allowed. The patriarchate of the Orthodox Church in Constantinople, which Turkish delegates wished to expel, was permitted to remain, though its old political functions (as in tax collecting) were eliminated; likewise enough Greeks were permitted to remain in the city so as to allow it to function (the final exodus of most Greeks did not occur until 1955). In exchange, 100,000 Muslims were allowed to remain in western Thrace, partly to reconcile Turkish hardliners with the cession of this territory to Greece.

fleeing war zones in both directions, all of whom needed to be settled in new homes. Cruel and unfair though these decisions were to those who wished to stay where they were, it made a backhanded kind of humanitarian sense to "open" homes for incoming refugees by enjoining their current occupants to leave. Mutual separation of Greeks and Turks seemed, to the men of Lausanne, to be the "humanitarian solution": it was indeed proposed as such by none other than Fridtjof Nansen, the Norwegian explorer-diplomat named the first League of Nations high commissioner for refugees. "To unmix the populations of the Near East," Nansen proposed as the Lausanne conference opened on December 1, 1922, "will tend to secure [the] true pacification of the Near East." Despite the inevitable petty cruelties and injustices suffered by the victims, the fact remains that the actual population exchange was conducted relatively peacefully, with few reports of violence. Although many liberal Western newspapers cried foul, with critics suggesting that Nansen had allowed himself to be used by the Turkish and Greek governments to beatify their worst intentions, the fact remains that there was a broad consensus at Lausanne in favor of ethno-religious separation. For helping to broker the population exchange, Nansen was even awarded the Nobel Peace Prize for 1922 (although the prize reflected his earlier activities in Europe, it expressly mentioned his "present work for the refugees in Asia Minor and Thrace").[3]

We should not forget that all empires produce chaos and misery on a grand scale when they collapse, along with the accompanying laments for a lost golden age of cosmopolitanism, an imagined tolerance. But in an Anatolia torn apart by a decade of conflict, by a war that had, between 1919 and 1922, turned into the most savage kind of inter-ethnic bloodletting pitting neighbors against one another, there was no cosmopolitanism left and very little tolerance. For the abrupt decline in Greco-Turkish comity, the wars of 1912–13, 1917–18, and 1919–22, all fought over classic, old-fashioned claims over territory between two peoples with a history of enmity, were clearly responsible, and it makes little sense to blame the peace treaty that ended them.

As for the Arabic-speaking countries in the formerly Ottoman Middle East, one can certainly understand the lament for the fall of the Ottomans. Unloved though the Turks may have been as conquerors and administrators, ramshackle though Ottoman administration was in practice, the empire had provided both a nonsectarian unifying principle and a common identity for millions. Unequal though the status of non-Muslims was in Sharia law, most Levantine Christians and Jews had done well for themselves under the Ottomans, and by modern times enjoyed even a kind of special status owing to their role in trade and relations with the Western powers. True, the very prosperity of these minority peoples often marked them out for resentment and persecution, but so long as Ottoman prestige—along with the corresponding pride of Muslim subjects in their place at the top of the social order—remained intact, there was a rough equilibrium protecting most Christians and Jews from the worst. Just as the fall of the Habsburg and Hohenzollern empires produced an age of intolerance and anti-Semitism in central Europe, the fall of the Ottomans ushered in a time of troubles in the Middle East. The Arab-Israeli war of 1948, and its aftermath, produced a mass exodus of Arab Muslims and Christians (from Palestine) and Jews (from Arab countries including Syria and Iraq), with upward of 500,000 people uprooted on both sides. Baghdad's once thriving Jewish population is today reduced almost to zero. The ancient Christian communities of Iraq and Egypt have been reduced to a fraction of their numbers from Ottoman times, a fraction which gets smaller every year.* Lebanon's civil war displaced nearly a million residents. No one knows how the horrendous civil war in Syria will end, but it seems a safe bet on past regional precedent that its Druze and Christian minorities will fare poorly, as will, of course, whichever of the main belligerent factions (Sunni or Shia/Alawite) loses. And all this may be mere prelude to the upheavals to come, with pan-Islamic movements such as al-Qaeda and, especially, Islamic State destroying what remains of the old national borders, even as a broader Shia-Sunni war spreads outward from Syria and Iraq, which may well embroil not only the Islamic State but the two leading outside sponsors, Iran and Saudi Arabia, in a battle to the death for the soul of Islam.

Still, no matter how messy and violent the history of the Middle East has

---

* In the case of Iraq, the fraction was down to 5 percent a decade ago, and has dropped to 1 percent or less since with the death or departure of more than a million Christians since the 2003 war. The Copts of Egypt, who constituted a majority of the population well into medieval times, are today believed to have dropped below 10 percent, with numbers plunging in the wake of persecution since the oddly misnamed "Arab Spring" of 2011.

undeniably been since the fall of the empire, we should not romanticize the Ottoman past. Just because the Western world did not hear a great deal about what went on in Arabia, Syria, Mesopotamia, or Palestine does not mean that the Middle East was a peaceful idyll before the rude interruption of the First World War. The Arabian peninsula was already in the midst of a multitiered civil war in 1914, and its outcome was only obliquely affected by the military verdict elsewhere. If European influence had truly been decisive, then surely Hussein of Mecca would have emerged as king of all Arabia (or, conversely, an Ottoman victory in the world war would have secured that title for Ibn Rashid, Enver's man). Instead the Wahhabist Ikhwan warriors of Ibn Saud, though just as willing to pocket British subsidies as the Hashemites, essentially made their own history in Arabia, history that would not have looked terribly different absent the war of 1914–18.

Syria was far more directly embroiled in the world war than Arabia, of course. Nevertheless, the explosive charge of its post-Ottoman future was already being laid long before 1914, with Arab secret societies intriguing with French diplomats in Damascus and Zionists petitioning everyone from Sultan Abdul Hamid II to Kaiser Wilhelm II for an audience. The world war brought these conspiracies into the open, exposing the deep ethno-religious fractures in the Levantine world and giving motivation to outside powers to exploit them. The Entente victory allowed France to stake its claim to Syria, and Britain to champion the notoriously conflicting causes of Arab nationalism and Zionism. In the sense that a Turco-German victory would have put the brakes on all three of these imperial (or quasi-imperial) projects, one can argue that the First World War laid the seeds of the lasting strife between Israel and the Arabs. And yet those tensions were already long simmering in Palestine, if they had not yet reached white-hot temperatures. In summer 1917, the German ambassador had asked Talât Pasha, then grand vizier, if Germany could endorse Zionism to beat the British to the punch. Talât, who had been interior minister during the Armenian deportation-massacres of 1915 and thus had not inconsiderable experience of Ottoman minority issues, replied, "I would be happy to establish a national home for the Jews [in Palestine]," except that, in his view, there would be little point to the exercise, as "the Arabs will only kill the Jews."[4]

Those who blame Britain and France for the endless strife in Palestine, Lebanon, and Syria have a plausible case in the sense that the age-old imperial policy of "divide and rule," applied to an already fractious region, helped to exacerbate existing tensions between Arabs and Jews, Christians and Muslims, Sunnis and Shiite Muslims, and so on. They should also recall, however, that these occupying powers withdrew their last troops from the region in 1946 and 1947, before the first Arab-Israeli war broke out.

After two Gulf wars and now a third pitting the United States and its allies against the Islamic State, Iraq has arguably become an even greater geopolitical sore point than Israel/Palestine. Clearly the borders established by British diplomats after the First World War, such as the "line in the sand" drawn by Sir Percy Cox separating Iraq from Kuwait that was notoriously crossed by the armies of Saddam Hussein in 1990, have not held up well. Ottoman Mosul and the other Kurdish (and Turkish) areas of the north were never meant to be yoked together with the predominantly Arab Ottoman vilayets of Baghdad and Basra in the south. Owing to the close proximity of the Sunni triangle near Baghdad and the Shiite holy cities of Najaf and Karbala, the Sunni-Shiite divide in Iraq is more volatile in Iraq than anywhere else in the Islamic world, leading to dangerous centrifugal tendencies among Shiites looking east to Iran and Sunni Muslims looking south into Arabia for succor and sponsorship. In the sectarian warfare between these groups, as in the ethnic struggle between Iraq's Kurds, Arabs, and Turkmen, Iraq's smaller minorities of Christians and Jews have mostly tried to keep their heads down and avoid the crossfire. The horrendous violence in Iraq, which followed the toppling of Saddam Hussein's Baathist regime in 2003, has taught the world, among other bitter lessons, that it had taken one of history's most brutal dictators to keep a lid on seething tribal, inter-ethnic and interfaith tensions of this fragile country cobbled together by British imperialists. Serious civil violence in post-Ottoman Iraq began as soon as 1920 and continues to this day.

All this is true. But it is equally true that Ottoman Mesopotamia was a violent place before 1914, too, if the violence was not quite as spectacular (and visible to most Westerners). An architectural curiosity noted by European visitors of the time was that local houses—despite being located in one of the hottest countries on earth—tended to have no windows, so as to prevent their residents from being shot through them. Bedouin raids on villages, towns, and even Ottoman garrisons were common, and it was a foolish man who traveled about Mesopotamia unarmed. The British consul in Baghdad was no fool, traveling up and down the Tigris on a specially armored yacht. The Germans' Baghdad Railway Company, Karl Figdor reported for the *Vossische Zeitung* in May 1914, had been forced to erect elaborate fortified camps to protect its workers. "A continuous barbed wire fence encircled the compound," Figdor observed. "Only the windows and doors facing the protected interior courtyard could be opened . . . the stations situated in the most dangerous areas had no windows at all, only angled slits in the walls to protect the station against Bedouin bullets." Even Muslim employees had to be "escorted daily to the work sites under armed guard."[5] During the war, British, Ottoman, and German soldiers alike were horrified by the treatment accorded wounded and dying men by Bedouin warriors, who circled every battlefield like vultures to loot the fallen and stragglers separated from their units. "The Arabs," wrote the German veteran Hans Lührs, "stripped those fallen in action completely, leaving them naked and unburied, often desecrating their victims as well."[6] However its borders were defined and by whom, Iraq was never going to be an easy country to govern.

If there was a virtue in Ottoman administration lost in the transition to the postwar Hashemite (read: British) regime, it lay in its relatively light hand. It was not so much that the Ottomans misruled Mesopotamia as that they scarcely tried to rule it at all. At the height of the Iraqi uprising in summer 1920, Lawrence wrote ruefully in the *Sunday Times* that "our government is worse than the old Turkish system. They kept fourteen thousand local conscripts embodied, and killed a yearly average of two hundred Arabs in maintaining peace. We keep ninety thousand men, with aeroplanes, armoured cars, gunboats and armoured trains. We have killed about ten thousand Arabs in this rising this summer. We cannot hope to maintain such an average."[7] Whatever the accuracy of Lawrence's figures, he was getting at an important problem faced by the British in Iraq—and later the Americans. While tribe feuded with tribe, Sunni with Shia, Kurd with Arab, almost none of the warring factions (except the Turkmen minority) loved the Turks. But at least they were Muslims, with some claim to legitimacy via the Ottoman caliphate. Other than the small Jewish and Christian minorities, few Iraqis had any desire whatsoever to be ruled by Europeans (or Americans). In retrospect, one can understand why Mustafa Kemal decided not to contest Mosul against Britain, despite its abundant and well-known oil deposits. After 1918, Iraq was no longer Turkey's nightmare.

The prewar Ottoman-Arab world may have been a less violent place overall than the postwar version under British and French tutelage, but it was not necessarily a more stable one. In places such as Mesopotamia, Ottoman sovereignty was largely a fiction by 1914, though possibly a useful and constructive one. The encroachment of European diplomats, engineers, and businessmen into the region was long since under way and would likely have wrenched Palestine, Syria, and Mesopotamia into the Western orbit even without a Great Power war, just as Russia was gradually taking over eastern Turkey and northern Persia. The Ottoman Empire had already lost Africa in the Italian war and most of European Rumeli in the Balkan Wars, along with most of the Aegean and Dodecanese islands. The decision by Turkish statesmen to enter the war in 1914 is best understood as a last gasp effort to stave off decline and partition by harnessing German might against the more dangerous powers with designs on Ottoman territory— Russia, Britain, and France (in roughly that order). Even had the Central Powers won the war—as they thought they had done at Brest-Litovsk—a victorious Germany would likely have ended up in a kind of mandatory position overseeing Turkey's administration and economy. Even then, a semivictorious Britain may still have picked off Ottoman Palestine, Mesopotamia, and Syria in exchange for accepting the German position in Russia and Ukraine. Given the security problems facing the empire in 1914, there was no realistic scenario in which it could have endured indefinitely on some kind of status quo ante, only bad and worse options. In the end Kemal and the Turkish nationalists, following the failure of Enver's Caucasian gambit in 1918, chose triage, abandoning the ungovernable empire—and its troublesome minorities—in favor of an exclusionary nation-state they could govern with a firm hand. In this project, they succeeded beyond expectations. Outside Turkey's borders, the War of the Ottoman Succession rages on, with no end in sight.

ACKNOWLEDGMENTS

I have incurred many debts in the writing of this book. When I began researching the subject, I was still employed by Bilkent University in Ankara, and I owe much to Ali Doğramaci, who gave me my first real job in academe and stuck with me to the end. The bulk of the book was written, however, after I had moved to Koç University in Istanbul, where I must thank President Umran Inan and Dean Sami Gülgöz for their kind support, along with that of my colleagues in history, Dilek Barlas, Yonca Köksal, Can Nacar, Aslı Niyazoğlu, Mark Baker, and Alexis Rappas. I was also given the warmest possible encouragement in this project by Nur Yalman and Ömer Koç of Koç University's Board of Trustees. It was no fault of any of these esteemed friends and colleagues that I fell afoul of the byzantine Turkish academic bureaucracy, which prompted my recent move to Bard College in Annandale-on-Hudson, New York. For arranging my exciting new position as professor of history at Bard, I am grateful to President Leon Botstein and Dean Michèle Dominy, as well as my new history colleagues, Greg Moynahan, Richard Aldous, Mark Lytle, Omar Cheta, Miles Rodriguez, Tabetha Ewing, Christian Crouch, Carolyn Dewald, Myra Armstead, Alice Stroup, Drew Thomson, and Gennady Shkliarevsky. Greg in particular has gone well beyond the call of duty in answering my endless questions and helping—among other vital matters— find decent daycare for my children. Mark and Richard have shared their accumulated wisdom and made me feel right at home. Although only the last few chapters of this book were written here in Annandale, I have already found Bard to be an extremely pleasant place to teach and to write.

While working on this project, I have often felt that I was standing on the shoulders of giants. In addition to inviting me to Turkey in the first place back in 2002 to join his Turco-Russian Centre, Norman Stone has taught me a good deal of what I know about Turkey and Russia, and much else besides. One cannot begin to understand the Turkish army without drawing on Ed Erickson's expertise in Ottoman military history, as I have done now for years. Ed has often gone out of his way to answer queries, and I am grateful to him for his time. Mustafa

Aksakal's *Ottoman Road to War* is the best introduction I know to the controversies surrounding Turkey's entry into the war in 1914, and Mike Reynolds's *Shattering Empires* is the place to begin studying the geostrategic dimensions of the Russo-Ottoman clash. Mike has always been generous with his time, never hesitating to answer questions, of which I have bombarded him with many. I have also learned a great deal about Ottoman history from Justin McCarthy, not simply from his books but also from a spectacular lecture he delivered several years ago in Sarajevo on Britain's path not taken in 1915 at Alexandretta and Cilicia (my own map of this alternative landing site to Gallipoli is inspired by his own versions). McCarthy is known, both to his admirers and critics, primarily as a social historian and demographer, but I have found him to be exceptionally learned on all matters pertaining to late Ottoman affairs, including military affairs and strategy. For the period between the Mudros armistice and Lausanne, I would have been lost without the pioneering multivolume history *From Empire to Republic* of the late Stanford Shaw, a former colleague at Bilkent. This slightly eccentric study has the useful merit of collating together long original document citations from archives far and wide. Thanks to Shaw, one can peruse these at ease in the comfort of home or office, and draw one's own conclusions, whether or not they always match Shaw's. Outdated though it is in some respects, the old classic *Caucasian Battlefields*, by William Allen and Paul Muratoff, remains essential reading on the Russo-Ottoman wars, and I could not have done without it. Although I have not met him, I would also like to pay tribute to Scott Anderson for his wonderfully wry new study *Lawrence in Arabia*, on which I drew heavily in my account of the Arab side of the war. Needless to say, I am alone responsible for any errors or miscues in the text.

Eugene Rogan has just come out with his own ambitious history of the Middle Eastern theater of the First World War. I regret only that I was unable to obtain a copy until we had gone to print. Let us hope that both books help to restore the Ottoman Empire to the central role it should merit in the history of that war.

It was Scott Moyers of Penguin USA who first suggested that I tackle this huge and important subject, and he guided it expertly to completion. My agent Andrew Lownie helped whip the project into shape, and I am grateful as always for his time and sharp critical eye. Simon Winder, for Penguin in London, gave the text a very close reading and the final result has benefitted enormously from his helpful suggestions.

The archivists and librarians who have helped me over the years I was working on this project in a half dozen countries are too numerous to count, although I would like to make special mention of Paul Friedman of the New York Public Library, who devoted a whole dog day afternoon scanning materials for me on a tight deadline last summer.

I could not have written this, nor any of my books, without the patient forbearance of my wife, Nesrin, along with my adorable children, Ayla and Errol. It is for them that I write, even if they are not yet at an age when they might read this kind of book. Someday, I fervently hope, they will do so. I hope they will enjoy it.

NOTES

INTRODUCTION: THE SYKES-PICOT MYTH AND THE MODERN MIDDLE EAST

1 Cockburn, "Is It the End of Sykes-Picot?" *London Review of Books*, vol. 35, no. 11 (6 June 2013).
2 From the closed-captioned script of David Lean's *Lawrence of Arabia*. http://www.angelfire.com/movies/closedcaptioned/lawrence_of_arabia.txt.

PROLOGUE: SEPTEMBER 7, 1876

1 Details in Haslip, *The Sultan: The Life of Abdul Hamid II*, 84–85. For the bridge and cable car omens, Davison, *Reform in the Ottoman Empire, 1856–1876*, 355.
2 Gladstone, *Bulgarian Horrors*. For Edwin Pears, Gladstone's sourcing, and Disraeli, "coffee-house babble," see R. W. Seton-Watson, *Disraeli, Gladstone, and the Eastern Question*, 52–53 (and notes). For the best summary of differing casualty figures, see Sumner, *Russia and the Balkans, 1870–1880*, 171, n.1; and for the Russian translation of Gladstone, see 187, n. 1.
3 Haslip, *The Sultan: The Life of Abdul Hamid II*, 63, 78–79.
4 Sumner, *Russia and the Balkans*, 199 and n. 3.

CHAPTER 1: THE SICK PATIENT

1 Gibbon, "General Observations on the Fall of the Roman Empire," in *The History of the Decline and Fall of the Roman Empire*, 509.
2 Mansel, *Constantinople*, 272; Davison, *Reform in the Ottoman Empire*, 4.
3 Cited in Figes, *Crimea*, 483.
4 Sumner, *Russia and the Balkans*, 220–21, 228; William Fuller, *Strategy and Power*, 314.
5 Davison, *Reform in the Ottoman Empire*, 386–87. For Gladstone, "Turkish Constitution!!!": Hanioğlu, *Brief History of the Late Ottoman Empire*, 118.
6 Cited in Sumner, *Russia and the Balkans*, 237.
7 Cited in Roberts, *Salisbury*, 160.
8 Sumner, *Russia and the Balkans*, 299–300.
9 Cited in ibid., 302. See also Mansel, *Constantinople*, 304–5.
10 Fuller, *Strategy and Power*, 323, 326.
11 Cited in Mansel, *Constantinople*, 306.
12 Sumner, *Russia and the Balkans*, 359; Mansel, *Constantinople*, 307. On Aya Stefanos (footnoted): see Mutlu, "The Russian Monument at *Ayastefanos* (San Stefano): Between Defeat and Revenge, Remembering and Forgetting," in *Middle Eastern Studies*, vol. 43, no. 1 (Jan. 2007): 75–86; and "Ghost Buildings of Istanbul." http://www.hayal-et.org/i.php/site/building/ayastefanos_ant.
13 Terms in Sumner, *Russia and the Balkans*, 401–5.
14 Cited in Geiss, *Der Berliner Kongress 1878*, xxiii, n. 68. For the original French-language treaty, Sumner, *Russia and the Balkans*, appendix 10, 658–69. On the financial side, see also Palmer, *Decline and Fall of the Ottoman Empire*, 160–61.
15 Stanford and Ezel Kural Shaw, *History of the Ottoman Empire and Modern Turkey*, vol. 2, 221–25.
16 Erickson, *Defeat in Detail*, 13–14.

17 McMeekin, *Berlin-Baghdad Express*, 9.
18 Dündar, *Crime of Numbers*, 141–45. For another useful overview of the clashing figures, see Lewy, *Armenian Massacres*, 20–26, and compare with Bloxham, *Great Game of Genocide*, 51 (Bloxham gives a figure of "80–100,000" for the period overall from 1894 to 1896, although he does not provide a source for it).
19 McMeekin, *Berlin-Baghdad Express*, 11.
20 Erickson, *Defeat in Detail*, 14–15; Gardiner, *Conway's All the World's Fighting Ships, 1860–1905*, 387–92.
21 Palmer, *Decline and Fall*, 184–85.
22 Wilhelm II, "Tischrede in Damaskus (8 November 1898)," in Ernst Johann (ed.), *Reden des Kaisers*, 81.
23 Tevfik Pasha to Bernhard von Bülow, 23 June 1899, in PAAA, R 14155; for the excavation rights, Oppenheim to Bülow, 12 May 1903, in PAAA, R 14559.
24 For the initial concession, see "The Baghdad Railway," in the London *Times*, 3 January 1900, clipped in QO, Corr. Pol. Nouvelle Série. Turquie, vol. 334. On supplementary terms, see McMeekin, *Berlin-Baghdad Express*, 46.
25 See McKale, *War by Revolution*, 19, 239, n. 5.
26 Hanioğlu, *Brief History of the Late Ottoman Empire*, 128–30; and Mansel, *Constantinople*, 320 and *passim*.
27 Census figures in Karpat, *Ottoman Population*, 148–49; and for Constantinople, 104. See also Stanford and Ezel Kural Shaw, *History of the Ottoman Empire and Modern Turkey*, vol. 2, 241.
28 Ibid.; Palmer, *Decline and Fall*, 158; McMeekin, *Berlin-Baghdad Express*, 55.
29 The phrase is that of Stanford and Ezel Kural Shaw, *History of the Ottoman Empire and Modern Turkey*, vol. 2, chap. 3; on education, see especially 112–13, 249–53; on economic developments, 230–35. See also Zürcher, *Unionist Factor*, 12–13.
30 On all this, see especially Hanioğlu, *Brief History of the Late Ottoman Empire*, 133–35.

CHAPTER 2: RADICAL SURGERY: THE YOUNG TURKS

1   Edib, *Memoirs*, 272.
2   Marschall to Berlin from Therapia, 7 October 1909, in PAAA, R 14160.
3   Mansel, *Constantinople*, 355–56.
4   Citations in Ramsaur, *Young Turks*, 37, 42.
5   *Le Matin*, 16 January 1900; "Mahmoud Pacha and the Sultan," in the *Standard*, 22 January 1900, clipped and filed in PAAA, R 14156.
6   "Ausland," in *Der Bund*, 14 August 1900, clipped and filed in PAAA, R 14157.
7   Hanioğlu, *Young Turks in Opposition*, 84–86.
8   Citations in Ramsaur, *Young Turks*, 67–72.
9   Prince Sabahaddin to Sir Edward Grey, in the London *Times*, 13 August 1906, clipped in PAAA, R 14158.
10 Lewis, *Emergence of Modern Turkey*, 202.
11 Haslip, *Sultan*, 254–55.
12 Stanford and Ezel Kural Shaw, *History of the Ottoman Empire and Modern Turkey*, 263–64; Ramsaur, *Young Turks*, 116–17.
13 For the best casualty figures, see Erickson, *Defeat in Detail*, 43. See also Jelavich, *History of the Balkans*, 94–95; and "More Desperate Fighting. Turks Repulsed with Heavy Loss," in *Fielding Star*, vol. 25, issue 53 (17 August 1903), 2.
14 Ramsaur, *Young Turks*, 130–31.
15 Ibid., 102–3.
16 For an amusing account, see Mango, *Atatürk*, 67–68.
17 Cited in ibid., 74.
18 Cited in Turfan, *Rise of the Young Turks*, 65–66.
19 The accounts are numerous. I have mostly followed here Ramsaur, *Young Turks*, 132–36; Mango, *Atatürk*, 76–78; and Stanford and Ezel Kural Shaw, *History of the Ottoman Empire*, 266–67.
20 Ibid., and Hanioğlu, *Brief History*, 149.
21 Citations in Edib, *Memoirs*, 259–60.

22 Cited in Turfan, *Rise of the Young Turks*, 144.

23 Hanioğlu, *Brief History*, 149; Shaw, *History of the Ottoman Empire*, 274–77.

24 Edib, *Memoirs*, 271–72.

25 Mansel, *Constantinople*, 348–49.

26 On the army element in the protests, see Erickson, *Defeat in Detail*, 23–24.

27 Baron Marschall from Pera to Berlin, 13 April 1909, in PAAA, R 14160; Ahmad, "The Young Turk Revolution," in *Journal of Contemporary History* 3 (3) (July 1968), 29; and Shaw, *History of the Ottoman Empire*, 280–81.

28 Lewis, *Emergence of Modern Turkey*, 211–12; Lewy, *Armenian Massacres in Ottoman Turkey*, 33; McMurray, *Distant Ties*, 49. For analysis of casualty estimates in the Adana riots, see Dündar, *Crime of Numbers*, 144–45.

29 See McMeekin, *Berlin-Baghdad Express*, 69, 73.

30 Mansel, *Constantinople*, 352.

31 Shaw, *History of the Ottoman Empire*, 282.

32 Cited in Lewis, *Emergence of Modern Turkey*, 213.

33 Marschall from Therapia, 7 October 1909, in PAAA, R 14160.

34 Marschall from Pera, 22 and 23 April 1911, in PAAA, R 14160.

35 Erickson, *Defeat in Detail*, 24–30.

36 Aide-mémoire from the German Chancellor's Office, forwarded to the Porte by the German embassy in Pera, 11 January 1914, in BOA, HR-H 329; and notes verbales dated 7 May 1915 and 9 May 1916, in BOA, HR-H 336.

CHAPTER 3: THE JACKALS POUNCE

1 "The Powers' Note," in *Sydney Morning Herald*, 10 October 1912.

2 Treaty of Peace Between Turkey and the Balkan Allies, signed at London, 30 May 1913, no. 190 in Hurst, *Key Treaties for the Great Powers*, 853.

3 Tuchman, *Guns of August*, chap. 1; McMeekin, *Russian Origins*, 14–15.

4 Albertini, *Origins of the War of 1914*, vol. 1, 201, 306–11, 341.

5 McMeekin, *Russian Origins*, chap. 1.

6 "Secret Annex to Treaty of Friendship and Alliance Between Bulgaria and Serbia," Sofia, 29 February, 1912; Military Convention of 29 April 1912; Treaty of Defensive Alliance Between Bulgaria and Greece, 16/29 May 1912; Alliance Between Serbia and Montenegro, 6 October 1912, all in Hurst, *Key Treaties for the Great Powers*, 819–29. See also Jelavich, *History of the Balkans*, vol. 2, 97 and *passim*; and Albertini, *Origins of the War of 1914*, 366, 376–77.

7 Cited in Albertini, *Origins of the War of 1914*, 381.

8 Stanford and Ezel Kural Shaw, *History of the Ottoman Empire and Modern Turkey*, 289–91.

9 *Op. cit.*, and Albertini, *Origins of the War of 1914*, 376–77.

10 The figures seem to clash hopelessly in most of the literature on the conflict. For the best Ottoman estimates, see Erickson, *Defeat in Detail*, 67–72, 169–70, and compare with Hall, *The Balkan Wars 1912-1913*, 22 and 46. For Ottoman estimates of enemy forces, see also Mango, *Atatürk*, 112; and Jelavich, *History of the Balkans*, vol. 2, 97.

11 Mango, *Atatürk*, 106, 110–11.

12 For details and figures, see Erickson, *Defeat in Detail*, 86–122; Hall, *Balkan Wars*, 22–32.

13 Notes verbales dated 7 May 1915 and 9 June 1916, in BOA, HR-H 336.

14 Erickson, *Defeat in Detail*, 171 and *passim* (terms of the Salonica Surrender Protocol are reproduced on 225).

15 Cited in McCarthy, *Ottoman Peoples and the End of Empire*, 79.

16 Mansel, *Constantinople*, 364–66.

17 *Livre Noir*, 17 November 1912, 345–46.

18 McMeekin, *Berlin-Baghdad Express*, 102.

19 Cited in Albertini, *Origins of the War of 1914*, vol. 2, 394.

20 McMeekin, *Russian Origins*, 23–25.

21 Cited in Hull, *Entourage*, 263.

22 Cited in Fay, *Origins of the World War*, vol. 2, 207.

23 Cited in Hall, *Balkan Wars*, 71.

24 Stanford and Ezel Kural Shaw, *History of the Ottoman Empire and Modern Turkey*, 294–95; Erickson, *Defeat in Detail*, 244–45; and Mansel, *Constantinople*, 367–68.

25 Erickson, *Gallipoli: The Ottoman Campaign*, 5–6.

26 On Thrace and Adrianople: Ibid., and Erickson, *Defeat in Detail*, 251–82. On Scutari: Hall, *Balkan Wars*, 91–97.

27 Cited in Hall, *Balkan Wars*, 104. On Sazonov, the Bulgarians, and the Straits question, see McMeekin, *Russian Origins*, chap. 1.

28 Citation and figures in Erickson, *Defeat in Detail*, 322–39.

29 Aksakal, *Ottoman Road to War in 1914*, 23, 44.

CHAPTER 4: SEARCHING FOR AN ALLY

1   Cited in Aksakal, *Ottoman Road to War in 1914*, 34.

2   On the Saud-Wahhabi conquest, see Rogan, *The Arabs*, 177. Russians and Kurds: see McMeekin, *Russian Origins of the First World War*, chap. 6, and chap. 10 below. Arab secret societies: see chap. 13 below.

3   Citations in Aksakal, *Ottoman Road to War in 1914*, 29–30.

4   Cited in ibid., 27.

5   Ottoman navy instruction manual, translated into Russian, dated 5/18 December 1911, in AVPRI, fond 138, opis' 467, del' 461/480, list' 4 (and back), 5; and Grigorevich to Sazonov, 6/19 January 1914, in AVPRI, fond 138, opis' 467, del' 462/481, 2–4 (and backs). On the Greek panic, see Aksakal, *Ottoman Road to War in 1914*, chap. 2; and on the Russians more generally, see McMeekin, *Russian Origins*, chap. 1.

6   On the British efforts to oust Djavid, see Marschall from Pera, 1 and 5 May 1911, in PAAA, R 14560. On Fitzmaurice, see McMeekin, *Berlin-Baghdad Express*, 76–78.

7   The original 8/21 February 1914 Russian naval planning conference transcript is in AVPRI, fond 138, opis' 467.

8   *Op. cit.*

9   "Secret telegram" from Ambassador Girs to Alexander Izvolsky, Imperial Russian ambassador to Paris, copied to S. D. Sazonov, 4/17 October 1913, in AVPRI, fond 172, opis' 514–2, del' 633, list' 19. On the failure to mention "Armenia" or "Armenian provinces" and Russian/Armenian reactions, see Hovannisian, "The Armenian Question in the Ottoman Empire," in *The Armenian People from Ancient to Modern Times*, 237.

10 Citations in Wolf, *Gallipoli 1915*, 19–20.

11 Sazonov to Tsar Nicholas II, 6 January 1914, reproduced in the *Krasnyi Arkhiv*, vol. 6, 41 and passim. On Russia's response to the Liman appointment, see also Reynolds, *Shattering Empires*, 76, and McMeekin, *Russian Origins*, chap. 1.

12 Pokrovskii, *Drei Konferenzen*, 40–42.

13 Turhan Pasha forwarding Sazonov to the Sublime Porte, 15 January 1914, cited in Reynolds, "The Ottoman-Russian Struggle for Eastern Anatolia and the Caucasus, 1908–1918," 125, n. 114.

14 Erickson, *Defeat in Detail*, 338–41. Liman objected to this purge, but could do little about it. See Liman, *Five Years in Turkey*, 7–9.

15 Erickson, *Defeat in Detail*, 338–41; and Erickson, *Ordered to Die*, 37.

16 Agiropulo to Girs, 15 June 1914, no. 244 in IBZI, vol. 3; and Girs to Sazonov, 18 June 1914, no. 304 in IBZI, vol. 3. For analysis, see Aksakal, *Ottoman Road to War in 1914*, chap. 2 and esp. 45–50.

CHAPTER 5: MANNA FROM MARS: THE ARRIVAL OF SMS *GOEBEN*

1   Cited (from Souchon's memoirs) in Tuchman, *Guns of August*, 177. Souchon may have embellished his thoughts. In his operational report sent to Kaiser Wilhelm II from Constantinople on 21 September 1914, he said something similar about his reaction to the rescinded orders on 6 August ("I decided not to waver from my duty to break out into the eastern Mediterranean . . . [so as] to reach Constantinople and thereby be able to bring the war into the Black Sea") before noting that several days later, he decided

to make for the Black Sea "even against the Turks' will" (although he did not say his objective was to force Turkey into the war). In BA/MA, RM 40/457, 402 and 403 (back). As literary embellishments go, this is, in any case, a very good one. Whether or not it expresses precisely what Souchon *intended* to do on 6 or 8–9 August 1914, it captures the essence of what he *actually did do* that October.

2   McMeekin, *July 1914: Countdown to War.*
3   Original transcript of 21 February 1914 planning conference, in AVPRI, fond 138, opis' 467, del' 462; Sazonov to Grigorevich, 30 June 1914, no. 24 in IBZI, vol. 4. For Girs, "immediate counter measures," see Girs to Sazonov, 15 June 1914, no. 265 in IBZI, vol. 3. For "offensive against Constantinople inevitable": Sazonov, *Fateful Years*, 126–27.
4   Cited in Trumpener, *Germany and the Ottoman Empire*, 15–16.
5   Bethmann to Wangenheim, 1 August 1914 (2:30 p.m.), no. 547 in DD, vol. 3.
6   Yanushkevitch to Yudenich at Tiflis command, 14/27 July 1914, in RGVIA, fond 2000, opis' 1, del' 3796, list' 13.
7   Girs to Sazonov, 14/27 July 1914, reproduced in Pokrovskii, *Tsarskaia Rossiia v mirovoi voine*, vol. 1, 4–5, and as document 154 in IBZI, vol. 5, 125–26.
8   Yanushkevitch to Yudenich, 16/29 July 1914, in RGVIA, fond 2000, opis' 1, del' 3796, list' 19.
9   Sazonov to Benckendorff, 17/30 July 1914, document 281 in IBZI, vol. 5, 195. On the handover, see also McLaughlin, *The Escape of "The Goeben,"* 40–41.
10 On Churchill's action and its immediate context, see especially Fromkin, *Peace to End All Peace*, 52 and *passim.*
11 Wangenheim to Wilhelmstrasse, 2 August 1914, as cited in Trumpener, *Germany and the Ottoman Empire*, 24 and 24, fn. 7. For Enver's prior knowledge of the *de facto* British seizure of the *Sultan Osman I* (which Trumpener missed), see Fromkin, *Peace to End All Peace*, 61.
12 The alliance treaty is reproduced as no. 733 in DD, vol. 3.
13 Wangenheim to Wilhelmstrasse, 2 August 1914, as cited in Aksakal, 103–4.
14 Ibid., 104–7.
15 Moltke to Wilhelmstrasse, 2 August 1914, no. 662 in DD, vol. 3. See also Trumpener, *Germany and the Ottoman Empire*, 26.
16 Admiralty to Souchon, 2:35 a.m. on 4 August 1914, as cited in Trumpener, 26 (but see DD, ref above). The order was apparently deciphered aboard the *Goeben* at 3:15 a.m. on 4 August 1914, as cited in Wolf, *Gallipoli 1915.*
17 Aksakal, *Ottoman Road to War in 1914*, 35 and fn. 67. For "spit in the soup": cited from Souchon's memoirs in Tuchman, *Guns of August*, 167.
18 Wolf, *Gallipoli 1915*, 35, and, for Souchon's own postmortem account, Souchon to Admiralty from Haydar Pasha, 21 September 1914, in BA/MA, RM 40/457, 400. For "taste that moment of fire . . .": cited in Tuchman, *Guns of August*, 173.
19 McLaughlin, *Escape of "The Goeben,"* 58–59.
20 Ibid., and see also Tuchman, 170 and *passim.*
21 Souchon, 21 September postmortem, *op. cit.*, 400 (back); and *Escape of "The Goeben,"* 58–59.
22 Souchon, 21 September postmortem, *op. cit.*, 401 (back). See also Miller, *Superior Force*, chap. 4 (citations in fn. 53 and fn. 54).
23 Souchon, 21 September postmortem, *op. cit.*, 400 (back); and for details McLaughlin, *Escape of "The Goeben,"* 67–68, and Tuchman, *Guns of August*, 177.
24 Souchon, 21 September postmortem, *op. cit.*, 401 (back), 402.
25 Citations (including the Souchon quote footnoted) in McLaughlin, *Escape of "The Goeben,"* 69–70.
26 Miller, *Superior Force*, chap. 6 ("Admiral Troubridge Changes His Mind").
27 Ibid., chap. 7. Miller claims that Kelly erroneously believed the *Goeben* to have opened fire; "in fact she had not." According to Souchon's 21 September postmortem in the German Admiralty files, *op. cit.*, she had (although he admitted that he was not sure whether his torpedoes had scored hits, which they seem not to have done).
28 Citations in Aksakal, *Ottoman Road to War in 1914*, 116; and Trumpener, *Germany and the Ottoman Empire*, 28.
29 Souchon postmortem, *op. cit.*, 404.
30 Girs to Sazonov, 23 July/5 August 1914, and follow-up note of same date, original in AVPRI, fond 151, opis' 482, del' 4068, list' 10 and 13.

31 Girs to Sazonov, 9 August 1914 (twice), nos. 48 and 49 in IBZI, vol. 6/1. For context and analysis, see Aksakal, 127–30.

32 Ibid., and Yanushkevitch to Sazonov, 27 July/9 August 1914, in AVPRI, fond 151, opis' 482, del' 4068, list' 29 (and back). Wangenheim to Bethmann, 9 August 1914, is cited in Trumpener, 29–30. On Milne: see Miller, *Superior Force*, chap. 7, and Tuchman, *Guns of August*, 181.

33 Souchon postmortem to Kaiser, *op. cit.*, 404 and back.

34 Ibid., and, for the Kress-Enver exchange, cited in Wolf, *Gallipoli 1915*, 38.

35 Cited in Tuchman, *Guns of August*, 184 (which also has the Churchill quote). For Djemal (in the footnote): *Memories of a Turkish Statesman*, 126; for Morgenthau, *Ambassador Morgenthau's Story*, 71.

36 Asquith to Venetia Stanley, 12 August 1914, no. 122 in *Asquith, Letters*, 168.

37 Wolf, in *Gallipoli 1915* (40 and *passim*), takes up Miller's interesting proposition, noting many curious instances when the British failed to pursue or fire (e.g., on the *General* or the *Rodosto* on 11 August). I remain, however, unconvinced. Intriguing though it is, Miller's theory breaks down at the most basic level. British intelligence on the *Goeben*'s movements, gleaned in Athens, may well have allowed far more competent pursuit—but it is not hard at all to explain how and why these reports did not reach Churchill or Milne in time, and in accurate enough form, to make a difference. Even granting that a British rear admiral may have been in on a "conspiracy" to help coal Souchon's ships, this does not prove that the conspiracy reached up into the British War Council. In his careful and well-documented narrative, Miller is more honest about what his evidence does and does not prove than is suggested by his own arresting jacket copy.

38 Cited in Wolf, *Gallipoli 1915*, 40.

CHAPTER 6: THE BATTLE FOR OTTOMAN BELLIGERENCE

1 Wilhelm Souchon, ms note on Bronsart to Souchon (passing on Enver), 25 October 1914, in BA/MA, N 156–2, 2.

2 Beaumont to Grey, 11 August 1914, in the "Correspondence Respecting Events Leading to the Rupture of Relations with Turkey" (henceforth "Turkey Correspondence").

3 Wangenheim to Wilhelmstrasse, 14 August 1914, cited in Trumpener, *Germany and the Ottoman Empire*, 31–32.

4 Beaumont to Grey, 6 and 10 August 1914, and, for the quote footnoted, Churchill's minute on Grey-Beaumont correspondence, 8 August 1914, all in FO 371/2137.

5 "Abschrift aus dem Kriegstagebuch der Mittelmeer-Division Souchon vom 2. VIII.14–31.V.15," entries for 15 and 16 August, in BA/MA, RM 40/184.

6 Pavlovich, *Fleet in the First World War*, 281.

7 Souchon to Tirpitz and replies, 15–19 August 1914, cited in Wolf, *Gallipoli 1915*, 42; and in Aksakal, *Ottoman Road to War in 1914*, 135–36.

8 Asquith to Venetia Stanley, 17 August 1914, in *Asquith, Letters*, 171.

9 Sazonov to Girs, 27 July/9 August 1914, document 38 in IBZI, vol. 6, 35.

10 Citations in Aksakal, *Ottoman Road to War in 1914*, 136–37.

11 "Abschrift aus dem Kriegstagebuch der Mittelmeer-Division Souchon vom 2. VIII.14–31.V.15," entry for 17 August, in BA/MA, RM 40/184.

12 Mallet to Grey, 20 August 1914, in the "Turkey Correspondence," *op. cit.*

13 Wangenheim to Wilhelmstrasse, and Liman to Kaiser Wilhelm II, both on 19 August 1914, cited in Trumpener, *Germany and the Ottoman Empire*, 33 and n. 25.

14 Citations in Aksakal, *Ottoman Road to War in 1914*, 138, and Trumpener, *Germany and the Ottoman Empire*, 33–34.

15 Morgenthau, *Ambassador Morgenthau's Story*, 79.

16 Bethmann to Wangenheim, 7 September 1914 in PAAA, R 21124. For Moltke to Liman, 4 September 1914 (passed on to Souchon), and Souchon's reply, in BA/MA, RM 40/454, 346–48.

17 Wangenheim to Wilhelmstrasse, 8 September 1914 (twice), in PAAA, R 21124; and Zimmermann to Jagow, 10 September 1914, cited in Aksakal, 150.

18 See Trumpener, *Germany and the Ottoman Empire*, 37–38.

19   "Abschrift aus dem Kriegstagebuch der Mittelmeer-Division Souchon vom 2. VIII.14–31.V.15," entry for 14 September 1914, in BA/MA, RM 40/184. Emphasis added.

20   "Aus Unterredungen mit türkischen Vertrauensleuten," 15 September 1914, in BA/MA, RM 40/4.

21   See Aksakal, *Ottoman Road to War in 1914*, 162.

22   "Abschrift aus dem Kriegstagebuch der Mittelmeer-Division Souchon vom 2. VIII.14–31.V.15," entry for 17 September 1914, in BA/MA, RM 40/4.

23   Wolf, *Gallipoli 1915*, 48–49.

24   Ibid., and German spy's report dated 23 September 1914, in BA/MA, RM 40/4 (116–18).

25   "Mitteilungen vom 21. 9. 1914," in BA/MA, RM 40/4, 127–28, and Trumpener, *Germany and the Ottoman Empire*, 42–43.

26   "Around the end of September and beginning of October," the Russian Admiralty log reports, "the Turko-German navy started showing up in the waters of the Black Sea more and more frequently." Pavlovich, *Fleet in the First World War*, 282.

27   Izvolsky to Sazonov, 11 August 1914, reproduced in Pokrovskii, *Tsarskaia Rossiia*, vol. 1, 17.

28   Girs to Sazonov, 27 July 1914, in Pokrovskii, *Tsarskaia Rossiia*, vol. 1, 4–5; Girs to G. N. Trubetskoi, 28 September/11 October 1914, in AVPRI, fond 151, opis' 482, del' 4068, 224. For Krivoshein: cited in McMeekin, *Berlin-Baghdad Express*, 117.

29   See McMeekin, *Russian Origins of the First World War*, chap. 3.

30   Cited in Aksakal, *Ottoman Road to War in 1914*, 165.

31   Cited in Miller, *Straits*, chap. 19 ("The Forward Policy of Winston Churchill"), n. 24.

32   Fromkin, *Peace to End All Peace*, 67; McMeekin, *Berlin-Baghdad Express*, 117; and Trumpener, *Germany and the Ottoman Empire*.

33   See Asquith, 17 August 1914, *op. cit.*, and Fromkin, 66–67.

34   Girs to Sazonov, 19 September/2 October 1914, and 27 September/10 October 1914, in AVPRI, fond 151, opis' 482, del' 4068, list' 184 and 215. For analysis, see McMeekin, *Russian Origins*, chap. 4.

35   Girs to Sazonov, 21 September/4 October 1914, in AVPRI, fond 151, opis' 482, del' 4068, list' 187.

36   Girs to Sazonov, 19 September/2 October 1914, *op. cit.*

37   Girs to Sazonov, 17 and 19 October 1914, in AVPRI, fond 151, opis' 482, del' 4068, list' 230 and 233.

38   Humann, "Besprechung mit Enver am 3. Oktober 1914," in BA/MA, RM 40/4, 91–92.

39   Zimmermann to Jagow and Jagow to Zimmermann, 1 October 1914, cited in Aksakal, *Ottoman Road to War in 1914*, 167.

40   "Vertrauliche Mitteilungen vom 5. Oktober 1914," in BA/MA, RM 40/4, 82.

41   Cited in Aksakal, *Ottoman Road to War in 1914*, 172. For further details on the negotiations: "Besprechung mit Enver Pascha am 9. Oktober 1914," in BA/MA, RM 40/4, 70–72; "Bericht über die Beratung beim Botschafter am 11.10.1914," in BA/MA, RM 40/4, 61–63.

42   Girs to Sazonov, 19, 20, and 25 October 1914, and Ketlinskii to Sazonov, 21 October 1914, in AVPRI, fond 151, opis' 482, del' 4068, list' 233, 234, and 235. The instructions to Black Sea port officers are cited in Airapetov, "Sud'ba Bosforskoi ekspeditsii," 191.

43   Souchon, "Besprechung mit Enver Pascha am 23. Oktober 1914," in BA/MA, RM 40/4, 31–33.

44   Wilhelm Souchon, ms note on Bronsart to Souchon (passing on Enver), 25 October 1914, in BA/MA, N 156–2, 2. For instructions to destroy orders: Aksakal, *Ottoman Road to War*, 176.

45   The most thorough sources are Pavlovich, *Fleet in the First World War*, 284–91, and Greger, *Russische Flotte im Ersten Weltkrieg*, 45. For a Turkish-sourced account, see Erickson, *Ordered to Die*, 35.

46   Citations in Aksakal, *Ottoman Road to War in 1914*, 180–81.

47   Cited in ibid., 183.

48   Churchill, citing himself, in *World Crisis*, vol. 1, 540.

49   Proclamation of war on the Ottoman empire signed by Tsar Nicholas II, 20 October/2 November 1914, in leaflet form, in RGVIA, fond 2000, opis' 1, del' 3796, list' 192.

50   Cited in Yasamee, "Ottoman Empire," 257–58.

CHAPTER 7: BASRA, SARIKAMIŞ, AND SUEZ

1   Enver Pasha "Suret" from Ahbisor, 20–21 Aralık 1914, reproduced in *Askerî Tarih Belgeleri Dergisi, 30'Uncu Tümen Sarıkamış Harekati Ceridesi* (Muharebe Safhası: 20 Aralık–10 Ocak 1915), 6–7.

2   Ottoman deployment details in Erickson, *Ordered to Die*, 32–47 and (for Mesopotamia) 66–67.

3   Churchill, *World Crisis*, vol. 1, 541.

4   For dates of the dispatch of the expeditionary force to Bahrain, see Pomiankowski, *Zusammenbruch des Ottomanischen Reiches*, 105. On Delamain's sealed orders: Townshend, *When God Made Hell*, 3–4.

5   Cited in Ulrichsen, *The First World War in the Middle East*, 23.

6   "Report on Naval Cooperation with the Expeditionary Force in Mesopotamia," by Commander Wilfrid Nunn (henceforth "Mesopotamia Expedition Report"), in PRO, ADM 137/204, 16–22. On the grand mufti and the Shia pilgrim traffic, see McMeekin, *Berlin-Baghdad Express*, 207.

7   "Mesopotamia Expedition Report," 22–25.

8   Ibid., 26 and *passim*. On the hunt for the *Emden*, see Churchill, *World Crisis*, vol. 1, 542–43, and also Knight, *British Army in Mesopotamia*, 14.

9   "Mesopotamia Expedition Report," 47–53.

10 Ibid., 56–57; and, on the sinking of the *Ekbatana* and the view from Basra generally, see Mrs. Christine Bennett, *Basra Diary*, entries for 4–22 November 1914. http://paperspast.natlib.govt.nz/cgi-bin/paperspast?a=d&d=OSWCC19160222.2.15 (accessed May 2015).

11 "Mesopotamia Expedition Report," 59–67.

12 Ibid., 68–79.

13 Ibid.

14 McMeekin, *Berlin-Baghdad Express*, 204, 278.

15 Cited in Strachan, *The First World War. Volume One: To Arms*, 722–23. For the point about wood for fires, see Pomiankowski, *Zusammenbruch*, 102–3.

16 Details in Erickson, *Ordered to Die*, 54; Pomiankowski, *Zusammenbruch*, 103.

17 Shaw, *Ottoman Empire in World War I*, 773.

18 Kirsanov to Girs from Mosul, 7 March 1913, in AVPRI, fond 180, opis' 517/2, del' 3573, list' 38–39 (and backs); and, for explication, McMeekin, *Russian Origins*, 148–49.

19 Yudenich to Yanushkevitch at Stavka, 18/31 August 1914, in RGVIA, fond 2000, opis' 1, del' 3851, list' 12 (and back), 13.

20 Adamov report on leaving Erzurum, 19 October/1 November 1914, in RGVIA, fond 2000, opis' 1, del' 3860, list' 613–14.

21 Ottoman figures in Erickson, *Ordered to Die*, 57; Russian figures in Strachan, *To Arms*, 715.

22 Enver Pasha "Suret" from Ahbisor, 20–21 Aralık 1914, *op. cit.*

23 Staff Colonel Hafız Hakkı, "23 Aralık 1914 Tarihi İçin Taaruz Emri," reproduced in *Askeri Tarih Belgeleri Dergisi, 30'Uncu Tümen Sarıkamış Harekati Ceridesi* (Muharebe Safhası: 20 Aralık–10 Ocak 1915), 24.

24 Stolitsa from Tiflis command, 3:35 p.m. on 17/30 December 1914 (twice) and again at 3:31 p.m. on 19 December/1 January 1915, in AVPRI, fond 151, opis' 482, del' 4113, 12–14. For Myshlayevskii's capture of the staff report and his reaction: Allen and Muratoff, *Caucasian Battlefields*, 267–68.

25 Ulrichsen, *First World War in the Middle East*, 58.

26 In addition to the Russian and Ottoman documents cited above, I have compiled this narrative of Sarıkamış from a number of accounts, including Erickson, *Ordered to Die*, 52–60; Strachan, *To Arms*, 722–28; Pomiankowski, *Zusammenbruch*, 103–4; Allen and Muratoff, *Caucasian Battlefields*, 249–77; and the two-part series "L'opération de Sarakamych" by General Inostrantsev in *Revue militaire française*, vol. 105, nos. 164–65, February–March 1935. (A copy of this article is preserved in box 1 of the Nikolai N. Baratov collection at the Hoover Institution Archives, Stanford, CA.)

As far as interpretation, there is broad agreement on most individual episodes in the campaign, although less so for the overall result and consequences. Erickson, working mostly from Ottoman sources, tends to downplay the negative sides, seeing in the long marches to Sarıkamış and beyond a "remarkable accomplishment" (p. 60), despite the heavy losses. He concludes, "The fact that the Turkish envelopment came within a hair's breadth of snapping shut as planned validates their basic operational concept."

Strachan, who has drawn on Russian sources in translation (notably the Inostrantsev article) is less impressed, noting (724) that the Ottoman campaign bore traces of flawed German thinking, putting "the weight on planning and timetabling, not on flexibility and improvisation." Enver's final plan "set a march programme that took little account of human frailty or of supply problems." And of course, it took far too little cognizance of the constraints posed by "the terrain and the weather." While Erickson's sympathetic account does help to balance out the sharply negative evaluations of Sarıkamış that still dominate the Western literature, it is hard not to see wisdom in Strachan's critique (focused as much on German doctrine as on Enver personally).

27 Figures in Erickson, *Ordered to Die*, 69–70.

28 Clayton: cited in Strachan, 737. For Cheetham: Cheetham to Grey, 7 December 1914, cited in McGuirk, *Sanusi's Little War*, 63. For Mannesmann and Frobenius: McMeekin, *Berlin-Baghdad Express*, 87–90 and chap. 7.

29 Kress, *Mit den Türken zum Suezkanal*, 78–80, 88.

30 Ibid., 90.

31 Commander in chief, East Indies, to Admiralty, 2 February 1915, and Maxwell to Kitchener, 2 February 1915 (5:00 p.m.), both in PRO, WO 33/731. Erickson, incidentally, insists in *Ordered to Die* that the "Turks had achieved complete surprise at all levels." British sources suggest otherwise.

32 Maxwell to Kitchener, 3 and 4 February 1915, in PRO, WO 33/731. "Grouse drive": cited in McGuirk, *Sanusi's Little War*, 84.

33 Maxwell to Kitchener, 4 February 1915, in PRO, WO 33/731.

34 Figures in Erickson, *Ordered to Die*, 71. Camels lost: Strachan, *To Arms*, 742.

35 Maxwell to Kitchener, 18 February 1915, in PRO, WO 33/731.

36 Asquith to Venetia Stanley, 3 February 1915 (midnight), no. 288 in *Asquith, Letters*, 414. Herbert to Sykes: cited in Fromkin, *Peace to End All Peace*, 121–22.

CHAPTER 8: DARDANELLES

1   Minutes of the 7 January 1915 British War Council, cited in Miller, *Straits*, chap. 23, n. 49.

2   Kudashev aide-mémoire, 31 December 1914, reproduced as no. 11 in *Konstantinopol i prolivyi*, vol. 2, 128–29. For "reports could be spread at the same time that Constantinople was threatened": see immediately below.

3   Kitchener to Churchill, 2 January 1915, cited in Miller, *Straits*, chap. 22, n. 54. Emphasis added.

4   Hanbury-Williams to Kitchener, 3 January 1915, cited in Miller, *Straits*, chap. 22, n. 56.

5   Citations in ibid., nn. 26, 40, 41.

6   Demidov to Petersburg from Athens, 7/20 January 1915, in AVPRI, fond 151, opis' 482, del' 4113, 22; and Stavka report of same date cited in Airapetov, "Sud'ba Bosforskoi ekspeditsii," 202.

7   Plan cited in Airapetov, "Sud'ba Bosforskoi ekspeditsii," 202. Miller, in *Straits*, calls this one of Churchill's "bizarre schemes." In fact the grand duke proposed it himself, honorably, as the only way Russia could help at the Dardanelles.

8   Cited in Airapetov, "Sud'ba Bosforskoi ekspeditsii," 204.

9   For details, see Wolf, *Gallipoli*, 77–81 (and map on p. 192); and Erickson, *Gallipoli*, 11–14, 28–29.

10 Usedom to Kaiser Wilhelm II from "Chanak in den Dardanellen," 18 December 1914, in BA/MA, RM 40–1.

11 Morgenthau, *Ambassador Morgenthau's Story*, 210.

12 Citations in Miller, *Straits*, chap. 23, n. 36 (Jackson), and chap. 24, n. 27 (Fisher). Miller's account provides the most thorough examination of the British records surrounding the Dardanelles campaign and subsequent postmortems: he is unable to find any evidence that Churchill or his admirals had any idea what they were up against in the revamped Ottoman shore batteries.

13 Maurice Hankey cabinet minutes, 13 January 1915, cited in Churchill, *World Crisis*, vol. 2, 103–4. On Churchill's learning about the *Goeben*: Miller, *Straits*, chap. 23, nn. 44–47. Emphasis added.

14 Wolf, *Gallipoli 1915*, 85 (citing an excellent German eyewitness account).

15 Miller, *Straits*, chap. 22, n. 17.

16 Ibid., nn. 21–22; and, for details about the hostages, McMeekin, *Berlin-Baghdad Express*, 130–32.

17 Asquith, midnight on 3–4 February 1915, no. 288 in Asquith, *Letters to Venetia Stanley*, 414.

18 From the War Council minutes of 7 January 1915, cited in Miller, *Straits*, chap. 23, nn. 49 and 51. On Kitchener's idea being merely hypothetical ("theoretic"), see also Churchill, *World Crisis*, vol. 2, 93.

19 Cited in Lewy, *Armenian Massacres in Ottoman Turkey*, 104–5.

20 Hankey to Balfour, 17 February 1915, cited in Miller, *Straits*, chap. 26, n. 30.

21 Citations in Miller, *Straits*, chap. 25, nn. 9 and 10. Kitchener: *op. cit.*

22 Cited in ibid., chap. 24, n. 10.

23 "The Dardanelles Commission. Statements of evidence and documents concerning period 2/7/15–5/9/17" (henceforth "Dardanelles Commission"), Grey interrogation, in PRO, ADM 116/1437B.

24 Citations in Airapetov, "Sud'ba Bosforskoi ekspeditsii," 205, 210. For the grand duke to Hanbury-Williams: cited in Miller, *Straits*, chap. 25, n. 14. For repeated requests, see McMeekin, *Russian Origins*, 131–34. For secret orders from the Russian Admiralty on 17 February: cited in Pavlovich, *Fleet in the First World War*, 316.

25 Churchill to Stavka, by way of Buchanan and Sazonov, 7/20 January 1915, in KP, vol. 2, 129–30.

26 Cited in Fromkin, *Peace to End All Peace*, 133. For "we should never forgive ourselves": Minutes of the 19 February 1915 War Council, cited in Miller, *Straits*, chap. 26, n. 36.

27 Minutes of the 19 February 1915 War Council, *op. cit.*

28 Morgenthau, *Ambassador Morgenthau's Story*, 185, 187, and, for corroboration, Pallavicini from Pera, 4 January 1915, in HHSA, Liasse Krieg 21a. Türkei, box 943. Still, while Pallavicini's report lends credence to his claim about the atmosphere among civilian leaders and diplomats in Constantinople, Morgenthau was wrong when he asserted that "nearly all of the German military and naval forces not only regarded the forcing of the Dardanelles as possible, but they believed it to be inevitable." This was not true of Liman, and certainly not of Usedom.

29 Grey, quoted by Hankey, in "Dardanelles Operations. Papers collected in Secretary's Office," in PRO, ADM 116/3491. The date given here is 13 January 1915, but according to Miller, in *Straits* (chap. 26, nn. 27 and 28), the line was uttered at the 28 January War Council instead.

30 Dardanelles Commission Report, Grey interrogation, de Robeck interrogation, and (second) Churchill interrogation, in PRO, ADM 116/1437B. For John French: Miller, *Straits*, chap. 30, n. 14.

31 Miller, *Straits*, chap. 30, nn. 1–3.

32 "Dardanelles Commission," second Churchill interrogation (Hall sub-interrogation—i.e., Hall being questioned as a witness by Churchill, acting as his own "defense" barrister), in PRO, ADM 116/1437B.

33 "Dardanelles Commission," first Churchill interrogation, in PRO, ADM 116/1437B.

34 Usedom to Kaiser Wilhelm II from "Chanak in den Dardanellen," 21 February 1915, in BA/MA, RM 40–1. Further details in Wolf, *Gallipoli 1915*, 87–88.

35 Izvolsky to Sazonov, 10/23 February 1915; Benckendorff to Sazonov, 12/25 February 1915, and Sazonov passing on these messages to Kudashev at Stavka, 15/28 February and 28 February/1 March 1915, in AVPRI, fond 138, opis' 467, del' 472/492, list' 2, 5, 7, 10–11. For grand duke and Eberhart: Airapetov, "Sud'ba Bosforskoi ekspeditsii," 212–13.

36 Elliott to Grey, 28 February, 1 and 3 March 1915, cited in Miller, *Straits*, chap. 30, nn. 19, 28, 32.

37 Cited in Airapetov, "Sud'ba Bosforskoi ekspeditsii," 213. For Buchanan to Grey, 3 March 1915: cited in Miller, *Straits*, chap. 30, n. 40.

38 Churchill to Grey, 6 March 1915 (drafted but unsent), reproduced in Churchill, *World Crisis*, vol. 2, 205.

39 Asquith, 6 March 1915, in Asquith, *Letters to Venetia Stanley*, 460.

40 Paléologue to Delcassé, 4, 5, and 6 March 1915, copied (in original handwriting) in the Nicholas de Basily collection, Hoover Institution Archives (Stanford, CA), box 9.

41 Usedom to Kaiser Wilhelm II from "Chanak in den Dardanellen," 17 March 1915, in BA/MA, RM 40–1.

42 Churchill, *World Crisis*, vol. 2, 206–8; Timothy Travers, *Gallipoli 1915*, 25–27; and Wolf, *Gallipoli 1915*, 89.

43 For the Russian intelligence footnoted: Russian Foreign Office intercept from Sofia, forwarded to Sazonov on 20 February/5 March 1915, and Neratov to Kudashev, 3/16 March 1915, in AVPRI, fond 138, opis' 467, del' 476/496, list' 46, 58.

44 Sazonov to Kudashev, 1 and 5 March 1915, in AVPRI, fond 138, opis' 467, del' 476/496, list' 32 (and back), 38.

45 Sazonov aide-mémoire, 17 February/2 March 1915, and Sazonov to Yanushkevitch, 18 February/3 March 1915, in AVPRI, fond 138, opis' 467, del' 477, list' 3 and 4.

46 Sazonov aide-mémoire for ambassadors, 4 March 1915, no. XVI in RAT, 118–19.

47 Paléologue to Delcassé, 5 and 6 March 1915, *op. cit.*

48 Sazonov to Kudashev, 22 February/7 March 1915, in AVPRI, fond 138, opis' 467, del' 477, list' 6.

49 Paléologue aide-mémoire, 8 March 1915, no. XX in RAT, 122–23.

50 Paléologue aide-mémoire, 27 February/12 March 1915, Sazonov's response to same, 28 February/13 March 1915, in AVPRI, fond 138, opis' 467, del' 477, list' 7 and 8. Final French acceptance: Paléologue "note verbale" to Sazonov, 10 April 1915, no. XXXVII in RAT, 134. Grey to War Council (in footnote): cited Fromkin, *Peace to End All Peace*, 138. Asquith (in footnote): 10 March 1915, in Asquith, *Letters to Venetia Stanley*, 469.

51 Carden and Churchill, 11, 14, 15 March 1915: reproduced in Churchill, *World Crisis*, vol. 2, 220–21. De Robeck: cited in Travers, *Gallipoli 1915*, 28.

52 Kitchener to Churchill and Hamilton to Churchill, 12 March 1915, reproduced in Churchill, *World Crisis*, vol. 2, 209–10. On 10 March 1915 War Council and 47,600 Russians: "Dardanelles Commission," Hankey interrogation, in PRO, ADM 116/1437B. Emphasis added.

53 "Dardanelles Commission," Hamilton interrogation, in PRO, ADM 116/1437B.

54 Miller, *Straits*, chap. 30, n. 16.

55 Churchill to Carden, 13 March 1915, reproduced in "Dardanelles Operations. Papers collected in Secretary's Office. Correspondence by First Lord. (Churchill), also Colonel M. P. A. Hankey," in ADM 116/3491.

56 "Dardanelles Commission," Hankey interrogation, in PRO, ADM 116/1437B. On Morgenthau and Enver: see Pomiankowski, *Zusammenbruch*, 120.

57 Correspondence cited in Churchill, *World Crisis*, vol. 2, 223–24.

58 Usedom to Kaiser Wilhelm II from "Chanak in den Dardanellen," 17 March 1915, in BA/MA, RM 40-1.

59 George Schreiner letter to Frederic Roy Martin, 19 March 1915 (intercepted by British intelligence), in PRO, WO 106/1465.

60 Ibid. For operational details on British side: de Robeck to Churchill, 18 March 1915, cited in Churchill, *World Crisis*, vol. 2, 233–34; Moorehead, *Gallipoli*, 64–69. For Turco-German side: Usedom to Kaiser Wilhelm II, 23 March 1915, in BA/MA, RM 40-1; Erickson (with the story about Seyit), *Gallipoli: the Ottoman Campaign*, 19–21.

61 De Robeck to Churchill, 18 March 1915, and Churchill to de Robeck, 20 and 23 March 1915, reproduced in Churchill, *World Crisis*, vol. 2, 233–38. Keyes: cited in Moorehead, *Gallipoli*, 69. For more details on the showdown: Fromkin, *Peace to End All Peace*, 152–53. For Churchill's likely source for his claim that the Germans and Turks were running out of ammunition (footnoted): see Travers, *Gallipoli 1915*, 320, n. 28.

62 Usedom to Kaiser Wilhelm II from "Chanak in den Dardanellen," 23 March 1915, in BA/MA, RM 40-1; Wolf, *Gallipoli 1915*, 94; and, for the figures on the small-caliber guns (using Ottoman military sources), Erickson, *Gallipoli: The Ottoman Campaign*, 26–27, and Travers, *Gallipoli 1915*, 36–37.

63 Cited in Wolf, *Gallipoli 1915*, 93. For Schreiner: letter to Frederic Roy Martin, 19 March 1915, *op. cit.*

CHAPTER 9: GALLIPOLI

1 "Landing of Army on the Gallipoli Peninsula, April 25–26 1915. By Vice-Admiral John M. de Robeck," in PRO, ADM 116/3491.

2 Cited in Mango, *Atatürk*, 146.

3 For details, see Usedom to Kaiser Wilhelm II, 23 April 1915, in BA/MA, RM 40-1; and Wolf, *Gallipoli 1915*, 95.

4 For the meeting of 22 March 1915 aboard the *Queen Elizabeth*: Travers, *Gallipoli 1915*, 39–42. Liman's appointment: Liman, *Five Years in Turkey*, 57.

5 See Pomiankowski, *Zusammenbruch*, 125.

6 Cited in Airapetov, *Sud'ba bosforskoi operatsii*, 216.

7 Usedom to Kaiser Wilhelm II, 23 April 1915, *op. cit.*

8 Pomiankowski, *Zusammenbruch*, 127.

9 Eberhart to Sazonov et al., 26 March/8 April 1915, in AVPRI, fond 138, opis' 467, del' 472, 53. For the *Goeben*'s movements in early April 1915: Airapetov, *Sud'ba bosforskoi operatsii*, 218.

10 Liman, *Five Years in Turkey*, 61–62; and for more details on logistics, Wolf, *Gallipoli 1915*, 102.

11 Djevad Bey to Enver, 20 April 1915, cited in Travers, *Gallipoli*, 48–49; and Usedom to Kaiser Wilhelm II, 23 April 1915, *op. cit.*

12 On Liman's focus on Bulair see, in particular, Travers (citing Mühlmann), *Gallipoli*, 49–51. For the details on 27th Regiment at Gaba Tepe, see Erickson, *Gallipoli: The Ottoman Campaign*, 48–49.

13 Liman, *Five Years in Turkey*, 60.

14 "Dardanelles Commission," Hamilton interrogation, in PRO, ADM 116/1437B.

15 Moorehead, *Gallipoli*, 123.

16 Liman, *Five Years in Turkey*, 63.

17 Sazonov passing on de Robeck to Eberhart through Kudashev, 5/18 and 7/20 April 1915, in AVPRI, fond 138, opis' 467, del' 472, list' 57 and 59.

18 Hamilton, "Report on operations in the Gallipoli Peninsula," in PRO, WO 32/5118.

19 Ibid., and "Landing of Army on the Gallipoli Peninsula, April 25–26 1915. By Vice-Admiral John M. de Robeck," in PRO, ADM 116/3491.

20 Cited in Travers, *Gallipoli 1915*, 65.

21 Moorehead, *Gallipoli*, 142.

22 "Landing of Army on the Gallipoli Peninsula, April 25–26 1915. By Vice-Admiral John M. de Robeck," in PRO, ADM 116/3491.

23 Cited in Liman, *Five Years in Turkey*, 70.

24 "Invasion of the Bay of Teke (W)" and "Invasion of the Bay of Ertugrul (V)," in *Birinci Dunya Savaşı'nda Çanakkale Cephesi* (25 Nisan 1915–04 Hazıran 1915), vol. 5, 150–54.

25 "Invasion of the region in the Bay of Ikiz (V)," in ibid., 155.

26 Erickson, *Gallipoli: The Ottoman Campaign*, 76.

27 Moorehead, *Gallipoli*, 145–46.

28 Travers, *Gallipoli 1915*, 75–78. On the Menderes bridge, see Wolf, *Gallipoli 1915*, 110–11.

29 See Travers, *Gallipoli 1915*, 85.

30 Erickson, *Gallipoli: The Ottoman Campaign*, 49.

31 Cited in ibid., 56; see also Travers, *Gallipoli 1915*, 101. For the Kemal quotes and their exegesis: Mango, *Atatürk*, 146–47.

32 On Halil Sami, see Erickson, 71–73; for general postmortems, see Travers, *Gallipoli 1915*, chap. 3.

33 Enver to Souchon, 31 March 1915, and accompanying Souchon operation reports dated 3 February, 4 March, and 16 March 1915, all in BA/MA, RM 40/454.

34 Souchon operational reports, 29 March, 31 March, and 11 April 1915, in BA/MA, RM 40/454. For the Russian side, see Airapetov, "Sud'ba Bosforskoi ekspeditsii," 218. For orders from Stavka forbidding troops from being dispatched by sea from Batum footnoted: cited in Pavlovich, *Fleet in the First World War*, 319.

35 Serafimov, passing on Eberhart from Dedeagatch, 12/25 April 1915, in AVPRI, fond 138, opis' 467, del' 472, list' 60. That this message was sent directly through Dedeagatch, the nearest "neutral" town on the Greek side of the Turkish border, shows the importance Eberhart gave it. But the Turks and Germans were not impressed. Admiralty files do not even register this halfhearted attack. The Russians don't seem to have put much stock in Eberhart's claims either: the 25 April attack is not mentioned in Pavlovich's semi-official Soviet history, *The Fleet in the First World War*. René Greger's slightly more detailed daily chronicle *Die Russische Flotte im Ersten Weltkrieg* repeats (49) Eberhart's claim to have opened fire on the coastal forts, but gives no figures as to shells fired or damage caused.

36 Man'kovskii, passing on Eberhart, 20 April/3 May 1915, in AVPRI, fond 138, opis' 467, del' 472, list' 61. On shells fired: Airapetov, "Sud'ba Bosforskoi ekspeditsii," 218. Pavlovich's account *The Fleet in the First World War* (326) gives the same figures for 3 May. For 2 May, both Pavlovich and Greger, in *Russische Flotte im Ersten Weltkrieg*, report hundreds more shells discharged, although they appear to have been fired in open sea to little effect (likely panic fire in the general direction of the *Goeben*).

37 Souchon operations reports, 4 and 6 May 1915, in BA/MA, RM 40/454. For "only a few houses were destroyed," see Usedom to Kaiser from Chanak, 23 May 1915, in BA/MA, RM 40/1.

38 Kudashev, passing on Eberhart via Sazonov, 2/15 May 1915, in AVPRI, fond 138, opis' 467, del' 472, list' 67.

39 Sazonov to Kudashev, 30 April/13 May 1915, in AVPRI, fond 138, opis' 467, del' 472.

40 Cited in Moorehead, *Gallipoli*, 153–54.

41 De Robeck to Churchill, 10 May 1915, as cited in Churchill, *World Crisis*, vol. 2, 350–51.

42 Moorehead, *Gallipoli*, 225, and, for a more technical analysis of the problem, see Hikmet Özdemir, "Unburied Corpses," in *The Ottoman Army 1914–1918: Disease & Death on the Battlefield*. Some of the

best descriptions of life in the Gallipoli trenches I have found, especially on the Turkish side, are in Louis de Bernières's underrated work of fiction, *Birds Without Wings*, chap. 63 ("Karatavuk at Gallipoli: Karatavuk Remembers").

CHAPTER 10: MASSACRE IN TURKISH ARMENIA

1 Nogales, *Memoirs of a Soldier of Fortune*, 269.

2 Townley to Grey, 8 October 1914, telegram no. 269, in PRO, FO 438/3; and Stolitsa to Stavka, 24 December 1914/6 January 1915, in AVPRI, fond 151, opis' 482, del' 4113, list' 18.

3 Goltz to Zimmermann, 30 January 1915, in PAAA, R 21035. For operational details, see Allen and Muratoff, *Caucasian Battlefields*, 289, 296–97.

4 Ibid., 298–99.

5 Olferiev to Girs from Van, 18/31 March and 25 March/7 April 1913, in AVPRI, fond 180, opis' 517-2, del' 3573, list' 53–55, 85.

6 Smith to Mallet, 10 January 1914, cited in McCarthy et al., *Armenian Rebellion at Van*, 184–85.

7 Allen and Muratoff, *Caucasian Battlefields*, 299 and n. 1.

8 Summary of rebel activity by Şükrü, in Van, for the Ottoman Third Army, circa April 1915, in ATASE, 528–2061, 21 (1–18). Also reproduced in TCGB, *Arşiv Belgeleriyle Ermeni Faaliyetleri 1914–1918*, vol. 1 (cited passages on 114).

9 Ibid.

10 Adamov report upon leaving Erzurum, 19 October/1 November 1914, in RGVIA, fond 2000, opis' 1, del' 3860, list' 613–14. I have also reproduced a photostat scan of this document in my own *Russian Origins*, 162–63.

11 Gul'kevich (for Sazonov) to Tiflis command by way of Vorontsov-Dashkov, 4/17 December 1914, in RGVIA, fond 2000, opis' 1, del' 3851, list' 24.

12 Vorontsov-Dashkov to Stavka from Tiflis, 7/20 February 1915, in RGVIA, fond 2000, opis' 1, del' 3851, list' 82.

13 Erickson, *Ottomans and Armenians*, 164. Lewy, in *Armenian Massacres* (1040) gives a figure of 500 deaths for Ottoman sources in the Zeytun clash, but this seems high.

14 Neratov to Benckendorff (passing on Tiflis command), 28 March/10 April 1915, and Stolitsa to Sazonov from Tiflis command, 3/16 April 1915, in RGVIA, fond 2000, opis' 1, del' 3851, list' 93–94.

15 Erickson, *Ottomans and Armenians*, 162–66 and 179–81, and McCarthy et al., *Armenian Rebellion at Van*, 194–97.

16 Cited in McCarthy et al., *Armenian Rebellion at Van*, 196–97.

17 Stolitsa to Stavka, passed on to Sazonov at the Foreign Ministry, 23 April/6 May 1915, in AVPRI, fond 151, opis' 482, del' 3505, list' 2.

18 Nogales, *Memoirs of a Soldier of Fortune*, 269–70.

19 Nogales, *Four Years Beneath the Crescent*, as cited in McCarthy et al., *Armenian Rebellion at Van*, 209.

20 "Vozstanie v' Vane," in *Russkoe Slovo*, no. 141 (20 June/3 July 1915), clipped in AVPRI, fond 151, opis' 482, del' 3505, list' 7–8.

21 Telegram from Aram (Manukian) Pasha and "the Armenians of Van" to His Imperial Viceroy Vorontsov-Dashkov, sent to Tiflis by way of Begri-Kala, 7/20 May 1915, in AVPRI, fond 151, opis' 482, del' 3505, list' 6.

22 *Mshak* cover story, 30 September 1915, as translated (into Russian) and clipped by Tiflis command and forwarded to Sazonov and Grand Duke Nicholas, in AVPRI, fond 151, opis' 482, del' 3480, list' 20.

23 Morgenthau to U.S. secretary of state, 25 May 1915, widely (though by no means universally) cited: Lewy, *Armenian Massacres*, 92, and Erickson, *Ottomans and Armenians*, 166–67. That this quote goes against the grain of what Morgenthau says in his memoirs is an understatement (the only mention of armed Armenians in the memoirs [299] is of "1,500 men" who fought the Turks at Van). Needless to say, the memoirs are better known. Emphasis added.

24 This is the essential argument made by Erickson in *Ottomans and Armenians: A Study in Counterinsurgency*. One can obviously debate the point, beginning with the term "counterinsurgency"—which, as Erickson himself admits, is anachronistic for 1915 (even if the concept may have predated the actual

term). Still, whether or not the Ottoman "threat perception" was, for Enver and Talât, more of a cynical smokescreen for preconceived anti-Armenian malice than a genuinely reasoned response to ongoing events, historians trying to impute genocidal "premeditation" can no sooner wish away documents from April–May 1915, which display evolving logistic/security concerns at Ottoman army command, than those trying to exculpate the Turks can wish away evidence from later that summer pertaining to systematic expropriation, persecution, deportation, and massacres of Armenian civilians.

25 Citations in Akçam, *The Young Turks' Crime Against Humanity*, 185–89. The original text of Talât's 24 April instructions to Enver is in ATASE, BDH 401–1580, 1–3, also reproduced in TCGB, *Arşiv Belgeleriyle Ermeni Faaliyetleri 1914–1918*, vol. 1, 127–29. On the Greek deportations, see McMeekin, *Berlin-Baghdad Express*, 251 and n. 50.

26 Cited in Akçam, *The Young Turks' Crime Against Humanity*, 189.

27 Cited in Erickson, *Ottomans and Armenians*, 189.

28 Decree by "Minister of Internal Affairs" Talât Pasha, on the "Coercive political circumstances necessitating the relocation and transfer of the Armenians," 31 May 1915, ATASE, BDH 361–1445, 1–4; also reproduced in TCGB, *Arşiv Belgeleriyle Ermeni Faaliyetleri 1914–1918*, vol. 1, 131–37. On the issue of Der Zor and Talât's intentions regarding the final fate of the Armenian deportees, see especially Reynolds, *Shattering Empires*, 152, and discussion of the Akçam-Dündar-et-al. polemic below.

29 Citation in Shaw, *Ottoman Empire in World War I*, vol. 2, 1061–62. For more on the extension of the campaign, exemptions, and how they were disregarded, see especially Bloxham, *Great Game of Genocide*, 89 and 124–25. On the specific provisions regarding Baghdad Railway employees, see McMeekin, *Berlin-Baghdad Express*, 254–58.

30 On the disposition of Armenian property, see especially Akçam, *A Shameful Act*, 272–73. See also Hovannisian, "The Allies and Armenia, 1915–18," 163.

31 Shaw, *From Empire to Republic*, vol. 1, 58–59.

32 See the reports filed by a Baghdad Railway Company engineer, Dr. Winkler, from Kushchular, outside Adana, 16 September 1915, in PAAA, R 13531. For more on friction between the Adana vali and Talât, see also Lewy, *Armenian Massacres*, 184.

33 Nogales, *Memoirs of a Soldier of Fortune*, 287.

34 Reynolds, *Shattering Empires*, 152.

35 Until fairly recently the general "consensus" number that commonly appeared in print was 1.5 million Armenian deaths, but in light of new research, few scholars subscribe to this figure anymore. In 2005, Guenter Lewy, crunching all the conflicting numbers, estimated 642,000 Armenian lives lost out of a prewar population of 1.75 million, or 37 percent. In 2010 Fuat Dündar, following a thorough statistical analysis of all census and casualty figures, came up with a slightly higher figure of 664,000 deaths in *Crime of Numbers* (151) out of a prewar population of about 1.5 million, or a mortality rate of 45 percent. Neither estimate is without critics, but they are considered more plausible than earlier, suspiciously rounded numbers, not least because, with a prewar population of some 1.5 million Ottoman Armenians, a death figure that high would have left no survivors, which is obviously untrue. Although more sympathetic to the traditional genocide narrative, both Donald Bloxham (in *The Great Game of Genocide*, 141) and Taner Akçam (in *A Shameful Act*, 183) favor a figure closer to 800,000 (at the low end), not going above one million. The Ottoman army registry of the deportations, with figures of those Armenians who "either died in the clashes or ran away," was published in TCGB, *Arşiv Belgeleriyle Ermeni Faaliyetleri 1914–1918*, vol. 1, 159.

Of course, there remains bitter argument over interpretation and the issue of genocidal "intent." Interestingly, in recent years it is Turkish scholars such as Taner Akçam who have dominated the public discussion, in large part because they have done the most thorough research in Ottoman archives. Akçam's work has come in for criticism from Erman Şahin and Fuat Dündar for his selective interpretation and translations of critical documents (e.g., translating "pillage and plunder" as massacre; ascribing intent to "annihilate" without documentation). For an overview, see Şahin, "A Scrutiny of Akçam's Version of History and the Armenian Genocide," in the *Journal of Muslim Minority Affairs* 28 (2), August 2008. Akçam struck back at Dündar (though not at Şahin, to whom he had, as of this writing, not yet responded) in his new book *The Young Turks' Crime Against Humanity* (243, n. 56), saying that Dündar "uncritically accept[s] some denialist arguments of the Turkish state." For Dündar's own view on "intent," see his essay "Pouring a People into the Desert: The 'Definitive Solution' to the Armenian Question," in Suny et al., eds., *A Question of Genocide*.

One can see why this war over terminology has created a stir. Definitions matter, as does intent. Still, one regrets that scholars cannot, at the very least, agree that the suffering and mortality of Armenian refugees was terrible whether it was deliberately ("genocidally") intended or was "merely" a matter of malicious indifference to the well-being and lives of forced civilian refugees on the part of the Ottoman government.

In a further coda, many historians have pointed out that death rates among *Muslim* civilians in frontline areas during the war were comparable. As Reynolds observes in *Shattering Empires* (154–55), overall mortality rates in Van, Erzurum, and Bitlis provinces averaged 40 percent between 1914 and 1921 (in Van as many as 62 percent may have died), against an Armenian mortality rate of 45 percent (the mortality rate for Assyrian Christians was similar). An Armenian priest, Grigoris Balakian, observed of uprooted Kurds and Muslims that "there was no visible difference at all between these refugees and Armenian exiles in the deserts of Der Zor." Still, as Reynolds sensibly notes, this does not excuse the Ottoman government for failing to provide protection and nourishment for Armenians *deliberately* uprooted from their communities, as opposed to Muslim civilians buffeted about by the pressures of war (although some of the latter were killed by Armenian partisans). There was clearly malicious intent toward Armenian deportees on the part of many Ottoman officials (who often abused the letter of Talât's decrees), even if the government's aim may not have been to "exterminate" them deliberately in the premeditated, Holocaust-style manner often implied in the literature.

36 Allen and Muratoff, *Caucasian Battlefields*, 302–10.

37 Cited in McMeekin, *The Berlin-Baghdad Express*, 248.

38 Akçam, *A Shameful Act*, 140.

39 The Ottoman army registry of the deportations, *op. cit.*, 159.

40 Vorontsov-Dashkov to Stavka from Tiflis, 7/20 February 1915, *op. cit.*

41 Citation in Lewy, *Armenian Massacres*, 105.

42 Citation in ibid., 105.

43 Sykes to Callwell, 14 and 16 July 1915, cited in Erickson, *Ottomans and Armenians*, 201 and nn. 94 and 95.

44 Armenian National Defense Committee to Sir John Maxwell, 24 July 1915, reproduced as no. 119 in *Boghos Nubar Papers*, as cited in Lewy, *Armenian Massacres*, 105.

45 McMahon to Foreign Office, 24 September 1915, cited in Erickson, *Ottomans and Armenians*, 201.

46 See Scott Anderson, *Lawrence in Arabia*, 95–99. Anderson suggests that a 3 January 1915 Intelligence Department "note" in the Foreign Office archives, outlining the advantages of an Alexandretta landing, was authored by Lawrence, citing a follow-up letter from Lawrence to his mentor, David Hogarth, which alludes to Alexandretta in code.

CHAPTER 11: A COLD WINTER FOR THE BRITISH EMPIRE

1 Hamilton to Kitchener, 17 August 1915, in PRO, WO 32/5119.

2 Churchill, "A Further Note on the General Military Situation," 18 June 1915, reproduced in *World Crisis*, vol. 2, 420–28.

3 Ibid.

4 War Office to Hamilton, 11 and 12 June 1915, Hamilton to War Office, 12 June 1915, and Churchill to Kitchener, 15 June 1915, reproduced in ibid., 416–19. For Turco-German expectation of a new landing: Usedom from Chanak to Kaiser Wilhelm II, 25 July 1915, in RM 40–1, 94; and Liman, *Five Years in Turkey*, 79.

5 Hamilton to Kitchener, 17 August 1915, in PRO, WO 32/5119. "Disturbed ants": the phrase is Moorehead's, from *Gallipoli*, 248.

6 Cited in Churchill, *World Crisis*, 444–47.

7 Liman, *Five Years in Turkey*, 89.

8 Details in Erickson, *Gallipoli: The Ottoman Campaign*, 139–66.

9 Hamilton to Kitchener, 17 August 1915, *op. cit.*, and Stopford Memorandum, 18 August 1915, in PRO, WO 32/5119. Gibson: cited in Travers, *Gallipoli 1915*, 189.

10 Cited in ibid., 172–73.

11 Erickson, 166; Wolf, 161.

12 Falkenhayn, *General Headquarters and Its Critical Decisions*, 159–61.

13 As Churchill recalled learning on those dates, in *World Crisis*, vol. 2, 498.

14 Falkenhayn, *General Headquarters and Its Critical Decisions*, 175–92.

15 Citations in Moorehead, *Gallipoli*, 297, 302.

16 Churchill to War Council, 5 October 1915, reproduced in *World Crisis*, 507–10.

17 Kitchener to Birdwood, 3 November 1915, reproduced in *World Crisis*, 517–18.

18 On the evacuation I have followed mostly Moorehead's superb account in *Gallipoli*, chap. 17.

19 Liman, *Five Years in Turkey*, 103. "God be praised": cited in Erickson, *Gallipoli*, 180. For casualty estimates, see Özdemir, *Ottoman Army 1914–1918*, 114–15.

20 McMeekin, *Berlin-Baghdad Express*, 225–29.

21 For details, see Hopkirk, *On Secret Service East of Constantinople*, chap. 12 ("The Christmas Day Plot").

22 Captain Nunn, "Report on Naval Co-Operation with the Expeditionary Force in Mesopotamia," *op. cit.*, vol. 2; and Erickson, *Ordered to Die*, 110. On Ahwaz, see also Hans Lührs, *Gegenspieler des Obersten Lawrence*, 95–103.

23 Cited in Townshend, *When God Made Hell*, 107. For more details on Amara: Lührs, *Gegenspieler des Obersten Lawrence*, 123–24; and Captain Nunn, "Report on Naval Co-Operation with the Expeditionary Force in Mesopotamia," *op. cit.*, vol. 2.

24 Cited in Townshend, *When God Made Hell*, 97. Lührs: *Gegenspieler des Obersten Lawrence*, 81–82.

25 Captain Nunn, "Report on Naval Co-Operation with the Expeditionary Force in Mesopotamia," *op. cit.*, vol. 2. Citations in Townshend, *When God Made Hell*, 109–19.

26 Ibid., 123–25.

27 Captain Nunn, "Report on Naval Co-Operation with the Expeditionary Force in Mesopotamia," *op. cit.*, vol. 2; and Townshend, *When God Made Hell*, 125–30.

28 Citations in Townshend, *When God Made Hell*, 133, 137, 143.

29 Captain Nunn, "Report on Naval Co-Operation with the Expeditionary Force in Mesopotamia," *op. cit.*, vol. 2; and Townshend, *When God Made Hell*, 157–66.

30 Ibid.; Captain Nunn, "Report on Naval Co-Operation with the Expeditionary Force in Mesopotamia," *op. cit.*, vol. 2; and (for casualty figures and "dubious refuge") Erickson, *Ordered to Die*, 112–14.

CHAPTER 12: ERZURUM AND KUT

1 "Enver Paşa şöyle düşünüyordu," in section "Dördüncü Konferans" (January 1916), in *Birinci Dünya Savaşın'da Doğu Cephesi*, ed. Mareşal Fevzi Çakmak, 112.

2 McMeekin, *Russian Origins of the First World War*, chap. 7.

3 Details in Allen and Muratoff, *Caucasian Battlefields*, 322–29; Nik Cornish, *The Russian Army and the First World War*, 88–89.

4 "Enver Paşa şöyle düşünüyordu," *op. cit.*

5 Erickson, *Ordered to Die*, 121.

6 This detail in "Azap Yarmasi (Kroki-29)," entry for 12 January 1916, in section "1915 Yili Sonunda Genel Durum," in *Birinci Dünya Savaşın'da Doğu Cephesi*, *op. cit.*, 116.

7 For the battle I have mostly followed Allen and Muratoff, 330–43, with certain details gleaned from the Ottoman-sourced account in *Birinci Dünya Savaşın'da Doğu Cephesi*, *op. cit.*, entries for 12–16 January 1916, 116–17.

8 "Azap Yarmasi (Kroki-29)," entry for 16 January 1916, in section "1915 Yili Sonunda Genel Durum," in *Birinci Dünya Savaşın'da Doğu Cephesi*, *op. cit.*, 118.

9 Erickson, *Ordered to Die*, 124–25.

10 Allen and Muratoff, *Caucasian Battlefields*, 355–57.

11 Ibid., 357–63. For details of the Turkish defense, and the firing of the city's ammunition stores: "Ruslarin Erzurum'a Taarruzu Erzurum Müstahkem Mevkii (Kroki-31)," in section "1915 Yili Sonunda Genel Durum," in *Birinci Dünya Savaşın'da Doğu Cephesi*, *op. cit.*, 124. For Russian sources on the Turkish deserter turning over the map: Airapetov, "Sud'ba Bosforskoi ekspeditsii," 232.

12 Allen and Muratoff, *Caucasian Battlefields*, 364–68.

13 Ibid., 368–72.

14 Buchanan aide-mémoire, reporting on Sir Mark Sykes's presentation of the map modified according to Sazonov's instructions, 11 March 1916, and Sazonov aide-mémoire, 29 February/13 March

1916, signed by Tsar Nicholas II on 1/14 March 1916, nos. LXXV and LXXVII in *Razdel aziatskoi Turtsii*, 157, 160–61.

15 Sazonov aide-mémoire drafted for Paléologue, 13/26 April 1916, and Paléologue "Note" to Sazonov, 26 April 1916, nos. CLLL and CIV in *Razdel aziatskoi Turtsii*, 185–87. For the final Franco-British arrangement, see Cambon to Grey, 15 May 1916, and Grey to Cambon, 16 May 1916, in Butler and Woodward, eds., *Documents on British Foreign Policy 1919–1939*, 1st series, vol. 4, 244–47.

16 Captain Nunn, "Report on Naval Co-Operation with the Expeditionary Force in Mesopotamia," *op. cit.*, vol. 4.

17 Ibid.

18 Citations in Townshend, *When God Made Hell*, 243. For the bit footnoted about German machine guns from Russian intelligence: Strelianov, *Korpus generala Baratova*, 24. "Skinny cats and dogs": Hopkirk, *On Secret Service East of Constantinople*, 213.

19 Baratov, "Extract from the Order to Russian Expeditionary Corps in Persia," 10 June 1918, in Hoover Institution Archives, Baratov collection (Stanford, CA), box 3.

20 Strelianov, *Korpus generala Baratova*, 41–46.

21 Citations in Townshend, *When God Made Hell*, 237–48, and in Captain Nunn, "Report on Naval Co-Operation with the Expeditionary Force in Mesopotamia," *op. cit.*, vol. 4.

22 As noted by Erickson, in *Ordered to Die*, 151.

23 Townshend, *When God Made Hell*, 252.

CHAPTER 13: DOUBLE BLUFF: OTTOMAN HOLY WAR AND ARAB REVOLT

1 Pamphlet submitted by J. B. Jackson, U.S. consul in Aleppo, to Ambassador Morgenthau, 8 April 1915, in National Archives of the United States in the U.S. embassy in Ankara, M 353, roll 6.

2 Cited by Snouck Hurgronje, in *Revolt in Arabia*, 43 and *passim*.

3 See McMeekin, *Berlin-Baghdad Express*, chaps. 13 and 16.

4 McMeekin, *Berlin-Baghdad Express*, chap. 15.

5 Anderson, *Lawrence in Arabia*, 182; and Moorehead, *Gallipoli*, 76.

6 Fromkin, *Peace to End All Peace*, 103–4, 174.

7 Seidt, *Berlin Kabul Moskau*, 81.

8 As recounted in the *Compte rendu d'une séance politique* between Oppenheim and Feisal on 24 April 1915 in the Pera Palace Hotel, in MvO 1/19, folder labeled "Algerien, Afrika und Vorderer Orient. 1886–1941."

9 Ibid.

10 On the locust plague and its regional impact, see Tamari, *Year of the Locust: A Soldier's Diary and the Erasure of Palestine's Ottoman Past*.

11 Oppenheim-Feisal *Compte rendu*; and Oppenheim, "Besuch be idem Scherifen Fessal [Feisal] in Bujuk-dere am 30. April 1915," in MvO 1/19, folder labeled "Algerien, Afrika und Vorderer Orient. 1886–1941."

12 "Texte des instructions au Grand Chérif de Mecque remis à son fils Chérif Faïsal Bey par son Excellence Enver Pacha le 9 mai 1915," and Oppenheim, "Besuch be idem Scherifen Fessal [Feisal] in Bujukdere am 30. April 1915," both in MvO 1/19, folder labeled "Algerien, Afrika und Vorderer Orient. 1886–1941."

13 Enver was quite clear about this in conversation with German colleagues such as Humann. See Humann report, 12 July 1916, in EJP, 1/35.

14 Cited in Fromkin, *Peace to End All Peace*, 185.

15 Oppenheim reproduces a copy of this telegram in MvO, 1/19, section of memoirs labeled "Personalien . . . Stammbaum der Scherifen vol. Mekka. Fesal. Aufstand im Hedjaz."

16 McMeekin, *Berlin-Baghdad Express*, 293.

17 Wolff-Metternich from Pera, passing on Mecklenburg from Baghdad, June 1916, in PAAA, R 13571.

18 Details in Anderson, *Lawrence in Arabia*, 188–89.

19 Cited by Snouck Hurgronje, in *Revolt in Arabia*, 43 and *passim*.

20 See citations in Will, *Kein Griff nach der Weltmacht*, 223 and 297. For the British pledge not to dismember Arabia, see French-language translation of English-language pamphlet intercepted by Ottoman intelligence, ca. summer 1916, in BOA, HR.SYS 2318-6.

21 Stotzingen from El-Ula, 5 May 1916, and from Damascus, 16 July 1918, both in PAAA, R 21142. See also McKale, *War by Revolution*, 178.

22 Khogopian dispatch intercepted by Russian army intelligence, 1/14 June 1916; and (for 24 officers) Bakheralt to Sazonov from Bern, passing on Russian spy Mandel'shtam's report, 15/28 June 1916, both in AVPRI, fond 151, opis' 482, del' 4073, 99–100, 114.

23 Werth from Sivas, 14 August 1916, in PAAA, R 13753.

24 Akçam, *Young Turks' Crime Against Humanity*, 105–11 and, for estimates of overall numbers of Greeks deported, 87–89. For the First World War as a whole, Akçam gives a figure of 481,109, of which 129,727 were deported from Thrace and the remainder from Asia Minor. His source is a Turkish reprint of a Greek press report dating to February 1919—the immediate postwar period, when all manner of exaggerated claims were flying in the rush to impress the Allied powers deliberating at Versailles over the fates of nations. Bloxham's slightly lower estimates in *Great Game of Genocide*, 98–99, seem more plausible, although those, too, are not really based on what we might call hard evidence. Demographic research into the Greek population of Asia Minor before and during the war still lags behind that on the Armenians, so we must probably settle for rather general estimates until our knowledge improves. At any rate, the number of Greeks expelled from their homes during the First World War was not negligible, and there seem to have been two main peaks: during the Gallipoli campaign, and then again in fall-winter 1916–17.

25 Lewy, *Armenian Massacres in Ottoman Turkey*, 205–8; and Bloxham, *Great Game of Genocide*, 98–99.

26 Humann to Jäckh, 15 November 1916, in PAAA, R 13753.

27 British spy report of agent in Constantinople from 3 to 27 June 1916, forwarded from Alexandria on 11 July 1916, in RGVIA, fond 2000, opis' 1, del' 3888, 168.

28 Humann to Jäckh, 15 November 1916, *op. cit.*

29 Pomiankowski, *Zusammenbruch*, 225.

30 "Altinci Konferans," entries for August and September 1916, in *Birinci Dünya Savaşı'nda Doğu Cephesi*, 215–18. For summaries, see also Erickson, *Ordered to Die*, 127–33; and Allen and Muratoff, *Caucasian Battlefields*, 422–28, 440.

31 Kress to Tirpitz, 24 August 1916, in BA/MA, RM 40/215. For more see also Pomiankowski, *Zusammenbruch*, 227; Erickson, *Ordered to Die*, 153–55; and Ulrichsen, *First World War in the Middle East*, 107–8. Ulrichsen, using British sources, is more detailed on that side of the battle, though he wildly overestimates the size of Kress's striking force.

32 Allen and Muratoff, *Caucasian Battlefields*, 430–35. For the Galician deployment, see Erickson, *Ordered to Die*, 137–41.

33 On the Habsburg side, see especially Tunstall, "Austria-Hungary and the Brusilov Offensive of 1916," in *Historian* 70 (1): 30–53. On the fallout for Russia, see Timothy Dowling, *The Brusilov Offensive*.

34 Details in McMeekin, *Russian Origins*, chap. 9; and (for *Imperatriza Maria*), see German naval intelligence report filed from Bucharest, 29 March 1917 (based on the report of a captured Russian naval officer), in RM 40/192. On the *Alexander III*: Airapetov, "*Sud'ba Bosforskoi ekspeditsii*," 245. Twenty-four new divisions by summer 1917: see dispatch signed by Grand Duke Nicholas, 26 December 1916, in the Nicholas de Basily collection, Hoover Institution Archives (Stanford, CA), box 1.

CHAPTER 14: RUSSIA'S MOMENT

1 Cited by Stites in "Miliukov and the Russian Revolution," foreword to Miliukov, *The Russian Revolution*, xii.

2 "Turkish Gunboats Sunk. Russian Exploits in the Black Sea," *Morning Post*, London, 28 December 1915 (clipped with glee by the German Admiralty and preserved in BA/MA, RM 40/223).

3 Halpern, *Naval History of World War I*, 237. Relying on secondary sources, Halpern misidentifies the *Maria* as the *Catherine*, but otherwise the details in his account check out.

4 Airapetov, "*Sud'ba Bosforskoi ekspeditsii*," 236.

5 Ibid., 237–43; and Halpern, *Naval History of World War I*, 234–44. The Soviet historian Pavlovich, in *Fleet in the First World War* (446), confirms that "for the period in question the Russian navy practically achieved supremacy at sea."

6 Erickson, *Ordered to Die*, 135–37; Allen and Muratoff, *Caucasian Battlefields*, 438. See also Pomiankowski, *Zusammenbruch*, 225–26.

7 Airapetov, "*Sud'ba Bosforskoi ekspeditsii*," 246.

8 Paléologue to Briand, 31 October 1916, in the Nicholas de Basily collection, Hoover Institution Archives (Stanford, CA), box 9. Trepov: Pipes, *Russian Revolution*, 257–58.

9 Bazili to N. N. Pokrovskii, from Stavka, 26 February/11 March 1917, in AVPRI, fond 138, opis' 467, del' 493/515, list' 1 (and back).

10 Guchkov telegram to Stavka, 19 March/1 April 1917, in the Nicholas de Basili collection, Hoover Institution Archives (Stanford, CA), box 11.

11 *Op. cit.*

12 Bazili to Milyukov, 23 March/5 April 1917, in AVPRI, fond 138, opis' 467, del' 493/515, list' 4-6 (and backs).

13 Kolchak to Russian Naval Command, 23 March/5 April 1917, in AVPRI, fond 138, opis' 467, del' 493/515, list' 11.

14 Bazili to Milyukov from Stavka, 8/21 April 1917, in AVPRI, fond 138, opis' 467, del' 493/515, list' 12–16. On Romanian vessels: see G. W. Le Page to Captain H. G. Grenfell, 4 January 1917, in PRO, ADM 137/940.

15 G. W. Le Page to Captain H. G. Grenfell from aboard the *Almaz* at Sevastopol, 29 April 1917, in PRO, ADM 137/940.

16 Le Page to Grenfell from Petrograd, 3 April 1917, in PRO, ADM 137/940.

17 Usedom to Kaiser Wilhelm II, 16 April 1917, in BA/MA, RM 40-4. Seven seaplanes: Greger, *Russische Flotte im Ersten Weltkrieg*, 61.

18 Baratov, "Prikaz' zakluchitel'nyi voiskam' Otdelnago Kavkazkago Kavaleriiskago Korpusa . . . Generala ot' Kavalerii Baratova," 10 June 1918, in the Hoover Institution Archives (Stanford, CA), box 3, folder 3–5 ("Russian Expeditionary Force. Farewell to Troops").

19 Cited in Kazemzadeh, *Struggle for Transcaucasia*, 61. See also Wildman, *End of the Russian Imperial Army*, vol. 2, 141.

20 Citations in Pipes, *Russian Revolution*, 329, 399–400. For more on mutinies targeting officers with German names, see Airapetov, "*Sud'ba Bosforskoi ekspeditsii*," 248 and *passim*.

21 Citations in Pipes, *Russian Revolution*, 399–403.

22 Cited in ibid., 413.

23 "Rukovodiashchiia ukazaniia General'Komissaru oblasti Turtsii, zanyatyikh' po pravu voinyi," adjusted to comply with the "peace without annexations" declaration by the Petrograd Soviet, 15/28 May 1917, in AVPRI, fond 151, opis' 482, del' 3481, list' 81–82.

24 G. W. Le Page to Captain H. G. Grenfell from aboard the *Almaz* at Sevastopol, 23 May 1917, in PRO, ADM 137/940.

25 Usedom to Kaiser Wilhelm II, 24 September 1917, in BA/MA, RM 40-4; Le Page to Grenfell from the *Almaz* off Sevastopol, 23 and 30 May 1917, in PRO, ADM 137/940; and German intelligence report dated 4 July 1917, in BA/MA, RM 40-192. For more details on Russian operations on 25–26 May 1917: Greger, *Russische Flotte im Ersten Weltkrieg*, 61–62.

26 Le Page to Grenfell from the *Almaz* off Sevastopol, 3 April and 30 May 1917, in PRO, ADM 137/940. On rumors surrounding Kolchak sending the fleet out during the February Revolution: *Novoe Vremya* article dated 20 April/3 May 1917, clipped in BA/MA, RM 40-192.

27 Le Page to Grenfell from the *Almaz* off Sevastopol, 23 June 1917, in PRO, ADM 137/940. See also Halpern, *A Naval History of World War I*, 252–53, and Pavlovich, *Fleet in the First World War*, 460–63.

28 Usedom to Kaiser Wilhelm II, 24 September 1917, in BA/MA, RM 40-4. Several of Usedom's details are, however, incorrect. The British warplane did not actually drop any bombs on the Yeşilköy airfield, and Usedom believed all the Golden Horn bombs to have targeted the *General*, not the *Goeben* (although this does not speak well for the British bomber's accuracy). For a more detailed account of this raid, see Harvey, "Bombs on Constantinople," in *Cross and Cockade International Journal*, vol. 38 (no. 3): 165–67.

29 Greger, *Russische Flotte im Ersten Weltkrieg*, 63.

30 "Proklamation der revolutionaeren russischen Flotte um die tuerkische Nation," tossed overboard from a Russian motorboat near the entrance to the Bosphorus, 26 April 1917, and attached to Usedom's report to Kaiser Wilhelm II, 24 September 1917, in BA/MA, RM 40-4.

31 Ibid. On the Odessa mutiny (which occurred on 19–20 July), see German agent's report from Constantinople, 2 September 1917, in BA/MA, RM 40-193.

32 "Proklamation der revolutionaeren russischen Flotte um die tuerkische Nation," *op. cit.*

33 Telegram from Kurt von Lersner at Gr. Hauptquartier to the Foreign Office in Berlin, 25 November 1917, in PAAA, R 10085; and Riezler telegram from Stockholm to the Foreign Office in Berlin, 26 November 1917, in PAAA, R 2000.

CHAPTER 15: TURNING THE ARABS

1 T. E. Lawrence to Gilbert Clayton, 22 January 1918, in PRO, WO 158/634.

2 As noted by Erickson in *Ordered to Die*, 160–61. On Muş and the reasons for Yudenich's move, see Allen and Muratoff, *Caucasian Battlefields*, 449; and Reynolds, *Shattering Empires*, 168–69.

3 See McMeekin, *Berlin-Baghdad Express*, 270–71 and 271n.

4 Cited in Anderson, *Lawrence in Arabia*, 199–200. "Little Lawrence": cited in Fromkin, *Peace to End All Peace*, 226.

5 Cited in Anderson, *Lawrence in Arabia*, 198.

6 As noted by Anderson in ibid., 233.

7 Ibid., 235–43, 257–58, and 264.

8 Cited in Ulrichsen, *First World War in the Middle East*, 109. For details on the Ottoman order of battle: Pomiankowski, *Zusammenbruch*, 274–75.

9 Liman, *Five Years in Turkey*, 164–65.

10 Cited in Anderson, *Lawrence in Arabia*, 283.

11 The best account remains Tuchman's *Zimmermann Telegram*.

12 On German Zionism and its role in the war, see McMeekin, *Berlin-Baghdad Express*, epilogue. The *New York Times* headline is cited in Anderson, *Lawrence in Arabia*, 303.

13 Citation in Fromkin, *Peace to End All Peace*, 236. On the Balfour Declaration: see also chap. 18 below.

14 Captain Nunn, "Report on Naval Co-Operation with the Expeditionary Force in Mesopotamia," *op. cit.*, vol. 4; and Townshend, *When God Made Hell*, 337–42. For 11,000 effectives: Pomiankowski, *Zusammenbruch*, 273.

15 Captain Nunn, "Report on Naval Co-Operation with the Expeditionary Force in Mesopotamia," *op. cit.*, vol. 4; and Townshend, *When God Made Hell*, 343–59.

16 Liman, *Five Years in Turkey*, 161–63.

17 Cited in Townshend, *When God Made Hell*, 373.

18 Baratov, "Bor'ba v' Persii vo vremenii Revoliutsii," in the Baratov collection, Hoover Institution Archives (Stanford, CA), box 3. For more operational detail, see Pomiankowski, *Zusammenbruch*, 273; and Liman, *Five Years in Turkey*, 163–64, 181–82.

19 Anderson, *Lawrence in Arabia*, 311–23. For the Aqaba crisis: see McMeekin, *Berlin-Baghdad Express*, 26–27 and n. 26.

20 Cited in Anderson, *Lawrence in Arabia*, 264.

21 Ibid., 328–38.

22 Chief, Egyptforce to C-in-Chief, London, 19 July 1917, in PRO, WO 158/634.

23 Cited in Fromkin, *Peace to End All Peace*, 312; for the total figure estimated by Storrs, see 223. For interim figures and the size of the gold reserve in Cairo: Wingate from Cairo, 29 January 1917; Wingate from Ramleh, 18 July 1917; and Wingate from Cairo, 15 November 1917, in PRO, FO 371/3048.

24 Anderson, *Lawrence in Arabia*, 389–90.

25 Details in Pomiankowski, *Zusammenbruch*, 292–93; Ulrichsen, *First World War in the Middle East*, 111–13; and (for the bit about Jerusalem for Christmas) Fromkin, *Peace to End All Peace*, 308.

CHAPTER 16: BREST-LITOVSK: THE POISONED CHALICE

1 Cited, with a slight paraphrase, in Baumgart, *Deutsche Ostpolitik*, 125–26.

2 The Russo-Ottoman armistice terms are reproduced in Kurat, *Brest-Litovsk Müzakereleri ve Barışı*, 378–79. For details of its enactment along the Russo-Ottoman fronts and at sea, see also Halpern, *A Naval History of World War I*, 255; and Airapetov, "Sud'ba Bosforskoi expeditsii," 252.

3 Mango, *Atatürk*, 167.

4 Usedom to Kaiser Wilhelm II, 24 September 1917 in BA-MA, RM 40-4. On Turkish-German tensions in 1916–17 generally, see McMeekin, *Berlin-Baghdad Express*, chap. 18. See also Halpern, *A Naval History of World War I*, 257.

5 Liman, *Five Years in Turkey*, 189–91, 195.

6 Pomiankowski, *Zusammenbruch*, 329.

7 Kazemzadeh, *Struggle for Transcaucasia*, 43–44, 61; Wildman, *End of the Russian Imperial Army*, vol. 2, 135.

8 Wheeler-Bennett, *Brest-Litovsk: The Forgotten Peace*, 70–73.

9 Pomiankowski, *Zusammenbruch*, 330. For more on atrocities committed by the departing Russians, see also "Nouvelles alarmantes," in *Ribal*, 8 February 1918, as clipped by the German Admiralty and preserved in BA/MA, RM 40/215.

10 Citations in Gökay, *Clash of Empires*, 17–18.

11 Cited in Wheeler-Bennett, *Brest-Litovsk: The Forgotten Peace*, 115.

12 Ibid., 85–87, 114.

13 Ibid., 118–19; and Reynolds, *Shattering Empires*, 174–75.

14 Bernstorff to Kühlmann, 17 December 1917, in PAAA, R 13755.

15 Reynolds, *Shattering Empires*, 175–76.

16 Allen and Muratoff, *Caucasian Battlefields*, 458–59.

17 This decree is reproduced (in Turkish translation) in Kurat, *Brest-Litovsk Müzakereleri ve Barışı*, 385–86. Talât's protest: 390.

18 Cited in Reynolds, "The Ottoman-Russian Struggle for Eastern Anatolia and the Caucasus, 1908–1918," 333.

19 Wheeler-Bennett, *Brest-Litovsk: The Forgotten Peace*, 165–66. See also Baumgart, *Deutsche Ostpolitik*, 20.

20 Baumgart, *Deutsche Ostpolitik*, 21; and Pipes, *Russian Revolution*, 582–83.

21 Cited in Reynolds, *Shattering Empires*, 183.

22 Hoffman report from Brailia for NATEKO, 28 March 1915, in BA/MA, RM 40-251.

23 Cited in Pipes, *Russian Revolution*, 584.

24 Citations in Wheeler-Bennett, *Brest-Litovsk: The Forgotten Peace*, 152, 226–28.

25 Citations in Baumgart, *Deutsche Ostpolitik*, 23–25.

26 Ibid., 25–26. On the expropriation of private bank accounts, see McMeekin, *History's Greatest Heist*, chap. 1.

27 Keegan, *The First World War*, 382.

28 For figures and analysis of German troop deployments prior to the Ludendorff offensive, see Stevenson, *Cataclysm*, 398–99.

29 Baumgart, *Deutsche Ostpolitik*, 119–27. For Hoffman citation, Pipes, *Russian Revolution*, 586–87.

30 Humann from Constantinople, 9 March 1918, in BA/MA, RM 40-251.

31 "Augenblicklichen Lage im Kaukasus," 6 April 1918, in BA/MA, RM 40/215; and Pomiankowski, *Zusammenbruch*, 335.

32 Hoffman passing on Romanian admiral Balescu, 8/9 March 1918, in BA/MA, RM 40-251.

33 Hoffman from Braila, 28 March 1918, *op. cit.*

34 Ibid., and Generalkommando passing on Bene from the field, 23/24 March 1918, in BA/MA, RM 40-251.

35 Hoffman from Braila, 23 March 1918; and Bene from the field, 26 March 1918, both in BA/MA, RM 40-251.

36 Report of Captain-Lieutenant Nusret from Constantinople after his tour of Russia's Black Sea ports, 14 April 1918, in BA/MA, RM 40-252.

37 Baumgart, *Deutsche Ostpolitik*, 162.

38 Ibid., 124–29.

39 "Augenblickliche Lage im Kaukasus," 6 April 1918, *op. cit.*

40 Reynolds, "The Ottoman-Russian Struggle for Eastern Anatolia and the Caucasus," 372.

41 German Army Abschrift dated 13 April 1918, in BA/MA, RM 40-251.

42 Reynolds, "The Ottoman-Russian Struggle for Eastern Anatolia and the Caucasus," 467; and Gökay, *Clash of Empires*, 26.

43 "Augenblickliche Lage im Kaukasus," 6 April 1918, *op. cit.*; Reynolds, *Shattering Empires*, 200; and Allen and Muratoff, *Caucasian Battlefields*, 495, n. 1.

44　Reynolds, *Shattering Empires*, 206–15.

45　Pomiankowski, *Zusammenbruch*, 361–63; Erickson, *Ordered to Die*, 186–87; and Allen and Muratoff, *Caucasian Battlefields*, 476–78.

46　Reynolds, *Shattering Empires*, 227; Pomiankowski, *Zusammenbruch*, 365.

47　Kress to Oberste Heerestleitung and Reichskanzler Hertling, 6 August 1918, and reply dated 24 August 1918, in BA/MA, RM 40-254. On the Turkish troops being routed to Batum, see German agent's report on his "Rundreise im Asow-Meer," dated 19 August 1918, in BA/MA, RM 40-254.

48　Baumgart, *Deutsche Ostpolitik*, 132–33, 147, 150, n. 166.

49　Ibid., 109–17 and (for subsidy to Don Cossacks) 142. For the agreement with the Kuban Cossacks, over matters such as the turning over of German prisoners of war on their territory and German rights of navigation on the Sea of Azov, see "Niederschrift der Besprechung am 15. August zu Jeisk," in BA/MA, RM 40-254.

50　Baumgart, *Deutsche Ostpolitik*, 194, n. 80, On the agreement with Georgia on Maikop and Grozny, see German agent's report on his "Rundreise im Asow-Meer," dated 19 August 1918, in BA/MA, RM 40-254.

51　Reynolds, "The Ottoman-Russian Struggle for Eastern Anatolia and the Caucasus, 1908–1918," 468–69; and Baumgart, *Deutsche Ostpolitik*, 200.

52　Allen and Muratoff, *Caucasian Battlefields*, 494–95. Orders to storm Baku, "plant the German flag on the Caspian": citations in Baumgart, *Deutsche Ostpolitik*, 204–5. On contested casualty figures in the "Shamkhor" and Baku massacres, see Kazemzadeh, *Struggle for Transcaucasia*, 70–73, 83–84; Pipes, *Formation of the Soviet Union*, 103; and Gökay, *Clash of Empires*, 23. Initial Turkish claims that 12,000 Azeris were killed at Shamkhor were almost certainly exaggerated, though at least 3,000 or so seems a reasonable estimate. Likewise, talk of as many as 70,000 Armenians being killed at Baku in September is usually dismissed, on the grounds that a general evacuation was conducted in reasonably good order. Nevertheless, there was clearly a brutal settling of accounts by Azeris with local Armenians after the city fell to the Army of Islam, with a body count numbering well into the thousands.

CHAPTER 17: MUDROS

1　Cited in Dyer, "Turkish Armistice," 316.

2　Citations in Lloyd, *Hundred Days*, 139–40. On the gold shipments, see McMeekin, *History's Greatest Heist*, chap. 5.

3　See the extensive "Correspondence in the Event of a Withdrawal from Salonika," in PRO, WO 106/1359.

4　Mühlmann, *Oberste Heeresleitung und Balkan im Weltkrieg*, 212–13.

5　Pomiankowski, *Zusammenbruch*, 379.

6　Mühlmann, *Oberste Heeresleitung und Balkan im Weltkrieg*, 225 and *passim*.

7　Ibid., 229; and Pomiankowski, *Zusammenbruch*, 380–81.

8　Cited in Stevenson, *Cataclysm*, 468.

9　For recent discussions, see Lloyd, *Hundred Days*, and Stevenson, *With Our Backs to the Wall: Victory and Defeat in 1918*.

10　Cited in Mango, *Atatürk*, 185.

11　T. E. Lawrence to Gilbert Clayton from Tafilah, 22 January 1918, in PRO, WO 158/634.

12　Citations in Liman, *Five Years in Turkey*, 269; Pomiankowski, *Zusammenbruch*, 383–84; and Mango, *Atatürk*, 179.

13　Details in Erickson, *Ordered to Die*, 197–99; Mango, *Atatürk*, 179–80; and Fromkin, *Peace to End All Peace*, 333.

14　Pomiankowski, *Zusammenbruch*, 384–85; and Mühlmann, *Oberste Heeresleitung und Balkan im Weltkrieg*, 250–51.

15　Ibid., and Liman, *Five Years in Turkey*, 196.

16　Ibid., 243.

17　Citation in Fromkin, *Peace to End All Peace*, 364.

18　On the Mesopotamian finale: Townshend, *When God Made Hell*, 432–35.

19 See Erickson, *Ordered to Die*, 188, 197, 202 (tables 7.3, 7.4, 7.5). For Franchet d'Esperey and Milne: Stevenson, *Cataclysm*, 483–84.

20 Details in Mango, *Atatürk*, 185–86. On Rauf: see Wangenheim (passing on Niedermayer) to Berlin, 18 January 1915, in PAAA, R 21034, and Sarre to Nadolny, 20 April 1915, in PAAA, R 21042. For Rauf's side of the story, see Keleşyılmaz, *Teşkilat-i-Mahsûsa'nın Hindistan Misyonu (1914–1918)*, 91–94.

21 As noted by Fromkin in *Peace to End All Peace*, 258–59.

22 On Lawrence in October 1918: Anderson, *Lawrence in Arabia*, 473–74, 484. See also Allenby's report for the *London Gazette*, preserved in PRO, WO 32/5128.

23 Liman, *Five Years in Turkey*, 320. Kemal's "border drawn by Turkish bayonets": Akşin, *Ana Çizgileriyle Türkiye'nin Yakın Tarihi 1789–1980*, 114. For the fall of Petrovsk, see Reynolds, *Shattering Empires*, 251.

24 Townshend, *When God Made Hell*, 432–33. For Townshend's proposed terms, see also Dyer, "Turkish Armistice," 319.

25 Cited in Dyer, "Turkish Armistice," 316.

26 Citations in ibid., 316, 321–22. See also Fromkin, *Peace to End All Peace*, 364–65, 370–71.

27 Cited in Dyer, "Turkish Armistice," 335.

28 Ibid.

29 The final armistice terms, with rolling modifications and Ottoman comments on individual clauses, are reproduced in Shaw, *From Empire to Republic*, vol. 1, 81–93.

30 Cited in Mango, *Atatürk*, 192.

CHAPTER 18: SÈVRES

1 Cited in Shaw, *From Empire to Republic*, vol. 2, 400.

2 Cited in Fromkin, *Peace to End All Peace*, 373.

3 Cited in ibid., 341.

4 Not mentioned in the *London Gazette*: see both censored and uncensored versions of Allenby's report for the *London Gazette*, preserved in PRO, WO 32/5128.

5 Cited in Barr, *A Line in the Sand*, 61–62.

6 Cited in Fromkin, *Peace to End All Peace*, 377.

7 As noted by Anderson, in *Lawrence in Arabia*, 485–86.

8 Barr, *A Line in the Sand*, 75–76.

9 MacMillan, *Paris 1919*, 390–91.

10 Barr, *A Line in the Sand*, 77; and "Anglo-French Declaration of 7 November 1918." http://www.balfourproject.org/anglo-french-declaration/

11 Cited in Shaw, *From Empire to Republic*, vol. 2, 425.

12 Ibid., 429.

13 Cited in Fromkin, *Peace to End All Peace*, 374.

14 Cited in Shaw, *From Empire to Republic*, vol. 2, 378–79.

15 Citations in MacMillan, *Paris 1919*, 379.

16 Mango, *Atatürk*, 246–47; and Shaw, *From Empire to Republic*, vol. 2, 426, 430–31.

17 The King-Crane Commission report is reproduced in Shaw, *From Empire to Republic*, 448–50. "Nothing the people of the United States": cited in MacMillan, *Paris 1919*, 379.

18 Shaw, *From Empire to Republic*, vol. 2, 463 and *passim*.

19 Ibid., vol. 1, 144–45.

20 Mango, *Atatürk*, 196–97.

21 Shaw, *From Empire to Republic*, vol. 2, 603–4.

22 See Mango, *Atatürk*, 204–5. The surprising and short-lived Italian occupation of Fethiye is amusingly reconstructed in Bernières, *Birds Without Wings*.

23 Lewy, *Armenian Massacres*, 77.

24 Akçam, *Young Turks' Crime Against Humanity*, 10–17 and *passim*. Of course, Akçam himself is confident about what the evidence of missing documents suggests: a deliberate campaign to suppress evidence relating to the genocidal intentions of the Ottoman government in 1915. By buttressing this

claim with some *actual* documentation from 1915, he makes a strong evidentiary case for "intentionality," much stronger than other accounts, which rely only on hearsay about what Turkish officials supposedly said they were doing that year. It must be said, however, that claims based on what Akçam admits is the "incomplete" trial record of the Istanbul Tribunal are problematic. In some ways the Turkish government's own wartime courts-martial against officials who had committed crimes against civilians are more reliable, as these verdicts were reached without outside political pressure from an occupying army, and most of the sentences handed down were actually carried out. On the wartime courts-martial, see Shaw, *From Empire to Republic*, vol. 1, 58–59.

25 Cited in Lewy, *Armenian Massacres*, 81.

26 "Les réfugiés Arméniens de Port Said," 25 September 1916, in folder marked "Armement des contingents irréguliers," in VSHD, 7 N 2150 ("Section d'Afrique. 1915–1918. Subventions aux corps de partisans d'Orient . . . Irréguliers, Arméniens, etc.").

27 Cited in Shaw, *From Empire to Republic*, vol. 2, 878–79. See also Kerr, *The Lions of Maraş: Personal Experiences with American Near Eastern Relief*, 33–34.

28 Shaw, *From Empire to Republic*, vol. 2, 469–70.

29 See Mansel, *Levant*, 190–91.

30 Citations in Llewellyn-Smith, *Ionian Vision*, 77–78, and MacMillan, *Paris 1919*, 431–32.

31 Citations in Llewellyn-Smith, *Ionian Vision*, 89–90, and Shaw, *Empire to Republic*, vol. 2, 516–19.

32 Citations in Mansel, *Levant*, and Mango, *Atatürk*, 225–26.

33 Ibid., and Kinross, *Atatürk: The Rebirth of a Nation*, "The Start of the Struggle" and *passim*.

34 Barr, *A Line in the Sand*, 101–2; Shaw, *From Empire to Republic*, vol. 2, 901 and *passim*.

35 Churchill to Balfour, 23 August 1919, and Churchill Memorandum dated 25 October 1919, cited in ibid., 404–6.

36 Citations in Shaw, *From Empire to Republic*, vol. 2, 808–11.

37 Ibid., 824–27; and Kinross, *Atatürk: The Rebirth of a Nation*, 206–7.

CHAPTER 19: SAKARYA

1 Cited in Mango, *Atatürk*, 318.

2 Terms of the Treaty of Sèvres, widely available, as at http://www.hri.org/docs/sevres/part1.html (and part 2, 3, 4, etc.).

3 The phrase is Llewellyn-Smith's, from *Ionian Vision*, 123.

4 Hovannisian, "The Annexation of Kars," in *The Republic of Armenia*, vol. 1.

5 On Lloyd George's abandonment of the Whites, see McMeekin, *History's Greatest Heist*, 132–36. For the Armenian perspective on all this, see Hovannisian, "The Russian Crisis and Transcaucasia," in *The Republic of Armenia*, vol. 2.

6 Hovannisian, "Bolshevik Movements in Transcaucasia," and "The May Uprising in Armenia," in *The Republic of Armenia*, vol. 3.

7 Mango, *Atatürk*, 240–45. On the Armeno-Georgian war of December 1918 see Hovannisian, "The Armeno-Georgian Entanglement," in *The Republic of Armenia*, vol. 1.

8 Ibid., "The Summer Campaigns of 1920," in vol. 3, esp. 298–305.

9 On the strategic picture, the Comintern Congress and the general euphoria in Moscow in August 1920, see McMeekin, *The Red Millionaire*, chap. 5 ("Moscow").

10 Reynolds, *Shattering Empires* 255–59; Mango, *Atatürk*, 290–95; and Kinross, *Atatürk: The Rebirth of a Nation*, 244–45.

11 Llewellyn-Smith, *Ionian Vision*, 123–25.

12 Shaw, *From Empire to Republic*, vol. 3, pt. 1, 1181–83.

13 Cited in ibid., 1180. See also Llewellyn-Smith, *Ionian Vision*, 126–30.

14 Shaw, *From Empire to Republic*, vol. 3, pt. 1, 1186–88. For Venizelos to Lloyd George: cited in Llewellyn-Smith, *Ionian Vision*, 131.

15 Cited in Shaw, *From Empire to Republic*, vol. 3, pt. 1, 1191–92.

16 Cited in ibid., 1125–26.

17 Llewellyn-Smith, *Ionian Vision*, 183–97; Mango, *Atatürk*, 308–11. Wilson: cited in Shaw, *From Empire to Republic*, vol. 3, pt. 1, 1254–55.

18 Cited in Mansel, *Levant*, 209. On Toynbee's dispatches and their effect on Western, particularly British, opinion, see chap. 20 below.

19 Citations in Llewellyn-Smith, *Ionian Vision*, 227–331, and (for Prince Andrew) in Giles Milton, *Paradise Lost*, 210.

20 Citations and details in Shaw, *From Empire to Republic*, vol. 3, pt. 1, 1346–49.

21 Citations in ibid., 1350–52, and (for Halidé Edib) in Giles Milton, *Paradise Lost*, 214–15.

CHAPTER 20: SMYRNA

1 Cited in Shaw, *From Empire to Republic*, vol. 4, 1692–93.

2 Cited in ibid., vol. 3, pt. 1, 1352.

3 Horton to Secretary of State, Washington, DC, from Smyrna, 7 September 1922, reproduced in *American Documents on Greek Occupation of Anatolia*.

4 Llewellyn-Smith, *Ionian Vision*, 249–52.

5 Passages from Toynbee's dispatches cited in Shaw, *From Empire to Republic*, vol. 3, pt. 1, 1265–70. For details on Toynbee's sacking, see also Mango, *Atatürk*, 329.

6 Shaw, *From Empire to Republic*, vol. 3, pt. 1, 1272–73.

7 See, e.g., Bristol to Secretary of State, 2 July 1921, document 31 in *American Documents on Greek Occupation of Anatolia*.

8 Cited in Llewellyn-Smith, *Ionian Vision*, 213–14.

9 Mango, *Atatürk*, 329–31.

10 Cited in Shaw, *From Empire to Republic*, vol. 3, pt. 1, 1335.

11 Cited in Llewellyn-Smith, *Ionian Vision*, 251.

12 Citations in Shaw, *From Empire to Republic*, vol. 3, pt. 2, 1608–12.

13 Citation in ibid., 1639. On Lloyd George insisting the Greek army stay on as a bargaining lever with Kemal, see Llewellyn-Smith, *Ionian Vision*, 256.

14 On the Bukharan gold, see McMeekin, *History's Greatest Heist*, 67–68.

15 Citations in Shaw, *From Empire to Republic*, vol. 3, pt. 2, 1620, 1675.

16 Fromkin, *Peace to End All Peace*, 497.

17 Citations in Shaw, *From Empire to Republic*, 1643–45.

18 Llewellyn-Smith, *Ionian Vision*, 276.

19 Cited in Kinross, *Atatürk: The Rebirth of a Nation*, 306–7.

20 Ibid., 309–14; and Mango, *Atatürk*, 341–42.

21 Cited in Kinross, *Atatürk: The Rebirth of a Nation*, 316.

22 Rumbold to Curzon, 19 September 1922, cited in Shaw, *From Empire to Republic*, vol. 4, 1700. Halidé Edib: cited in Kinross, *Atatürk: The Rebirth of a Nation*.

23 Confirmed by, for example, Lieutenant Barry of USS *Edsall* on 3 October 1922 after touring a number of cities in western Turkey, and Henry Franklin-Bouillon, a French parliamentary deputy who visited Manısa at the same time. Cited in Shaw, *From Empire to Republic*, vol. 4, 1710–16.

24 Horton from Smyrna, 2 and 7 September 1922, reproduced in *American Documents on Greek Occupation of Anatolia*. Turkish investigatory commission: cited in Shaw, *From Empire to Republic*, vol. 4, 1704–6.

25 Intelligence report filed by J. G. Ware from USS *Scorpion* to U.S. high commissioner in Constantinople Admiral Mark Bristol, 9 September 1922, reproduced in *American Documents on Greek Occupation of Anatolia*. On Sterghiades's checkered reputation with the local Greek community of Smyrna, see Llewellyn-Smith, *Ionian Vision*, esp. 91–101 and *passim*. "Whose city are they giving to whom?": cited in Kinross, *Atatürk: The Birth of a Nation*, 318.

26 Ware to Bristol, *op. cit.*, and Kinross, *Atatürk: The Birth of a Nation*, 321–22. "Well-fed and fresh": cited in Llewellyn-Smith, *Ionian Vision*, 306. "Filthy, untidy, slouching"; "inwardly delighted to have the Turks back again": citations in Mansel, *Levant*, 213–14.

27 Details in Llewellyn-Smith, *Ionian Vision*, 306–8; Mansel, *Levant*, 214–15.

28 Llewellyn-Smith, *Ionian Vision*, 308–11; Mansel, *Levant*, 215–18.

29 Both Llewellyn-Smith, in *Ionian Vision*, and Mansel, in *Levant*, insist on these points, and they make a very strong case. Shaw, in *From Empire to Republic*, argues conversely that the Turks lost a great deal

of property in Smyrna, too, and he writes (vol. 4, 1734) that it "is difficult to accept the claims that the Turks burned their own city after reconquering it and celebrating their victory in the streets." A bit more weakly, Shaw concludes that the "final determination of who or which group, if any, in fact set the fire . . . probably will never be reached." Considering the vigor with which Shaw pursues each and every claim of Greek atrocities in Anatolia, his reticence here is out of character. Before we simply dismiss Shaw's account because of pro-Turkish bias, however, it should be remembered that most popular accounts of the burning of Smyrna are one-sided in the other direction, passing quickly over stories of the Greeks burning down Anatolian cities en route for the coast even while luxuriating in the horrors on the waterfront of Smyrna. What Shaw is really doing is trying to restore balance and context to the broader story of the Greco-Turkish war, even if he may sometimes go too far in his own direction.

30   See Kemal and Atay citations in Mango, *Atatürk*, 346, and, for a longer Atay citation, Mansel, *Levant*, 223–24. Shaw, in *From Empire to Republic*, notably cites Atay's lengthy article in *Aksam*—but not his diary entry or memoir.

31   Shaw, *From Empire to Republic*, vol. 4, 1740–41. In *Levant* (220), Mansel cites a figure of 125,000 deported, of which 15,000 returned, although this is from a Greek source that likely exaggerates the numbers involved. Still, there is no reason to doubt that the deportees were generally abused and treated badly. Many of those who survived the winter were later sent to Greece as part of the population exchange mandated by the Lausanne Treaty. See below, and more generally Bruce Clark's study *Twice a Stranger: How Mass Expulsion Forged Modern Greece and Turkey*.

32   Cited in Shaw, *From Empire to Republic*, vol. 4, 1749.

33   Cited in ibid., 1754. For Dominions and *Daily Mail*: Fromkin, *Peace to End All Peace*, 550.

34   Citations in Shaw, *From Empire to Republic*, vol. 4, 1766 and 1778. Emphasis added.

EPILOGUE: LAUSANNE AND THE OTTOMAN LEGACY

1   Cited in Rainer Munz and Rainer Ohliger, *Diasporas and Ethnic Migrants*, 93.

2   Clark, *Twice a Stranger*, 2 and *passim*.

3   Cited in ibid., 95.

4   Cited by Zechlin, *Deutsche Politik und die Juden im Ersten Weltkrieg*, 371, n. 116.

5   As paraphrased from Figdor's report by Jonathan McMurray, in *Distant Ties*, 99.

6   Lührs, *Gegenspieler des Obersten Lawrence*, 81–82.

7   Cited in Fromkin, *Peace to End All Peace*, 497.

BIBLIOGRAPHY

LIST OF ARCHIVES AND PRINCIPAL COLLECTIONS CONSULTED, WITH THE ABBREVIATIONS USED FOR THEM IN THE SOURCE NOTES

Arkhiv Vneshnei Politiki Rossiiskoi Imperii (AVPRI). Moscow, Russia.

Fond 138, Opis' 467. Sekretnyi Arkhiv Ministra.

Del' 461/480. Correspondence with the Black Sea Fleet, pertaining to amphibious operations against Constantinople. February 1912–December 1913.

Del' 462/481. Correspondence relating to plans for amphibious operations against Constantinople, 8/21 February 1914–13/26 June 1914.

Del' 467/486. Correspondence on the Straits and Gallipoli, 13/26 February–4 September 1915.

Del' 472/492. More correspondence on the Straits and Gallipoli, 10/23 February–12/25 August 1915.

Del' 476/496. Correspondence with Paris and London on Constantinople and the Straits.

Fond 151, Opis' 482. Politicheskii Arkhiv.

Del' 3505. "Vozstanie armyan' v Vane, vyizvannyim turetskimi zhestokami." 1915.

Del' 3480–81. "Armyane. Budushchee ustroistvo Armyanii." 1915–.

Del' 4068. "Politicheskie i vnutrenyie polozhenie Turtsii do razryiva. Peregovoryi s Turtsiei."

Del' 4073. "Polozhenie vnutri Turtsii vo vremya voinyi s neyu." 1914–17.

Del' 4113. "Turtsiya." 1914–16.

Del' 4116. "Russko-turetskie voennyie deistvie." 1914.

Fond 172, opis' 514/2. Posol'stvo v Vene.

Del' 633. "Turtsiya. Armeniya." 1913–14.

Fond 149, opis' 502b. Turetskii stol. Opis' 502b. Miscellaneous.

Askeri Tarih ve Stratejik Etüt Başkanlığı Arşivi (ATASE). Ankara, Turkey.

BDH (First World War Collection).

Bundesarchiv Militärabteilung (BA/MA). Freiburg, Germany.

N 56. Nachlass of Wilhelm Souchon.

RM 40/1. Sonderkommandos der Marine in der Türkei. Abschriften der Immidiat-berichte an S.M. und Adm. Stab. September 1914–September 1917.

RM 40–4. Sonderkommandos der Marine in der Türkei. Politische Nachrichten und allgemeine Nachrichten über den Kriegsverlauf.

RM 40/54. Mittelmeerdivision u. Flotte. Sonderkommandos der Marine in der Türkei. August 1914–April 1915.

RM 40/130. Sonderkommando d. Marine in der Turkei. O-Akten.

RM 40/191. Akten der Mittelmeerdivision. N.-Akten. Russische Flotte und ihre Aktionen im Schwarzen Meer. January 1916–August 1916.

RM 40/192. Continuation of previous, July 1916–July 1917.

RM 40/193. Continuation of previous, June 1917–July 1918.

RM 40/211. N. Akten of Mittelmeerdivision. Nachrichten über Ägypten und Senussi. December 1915–February 1918.

RM 40/212. Nachrichten von der türk. IV. Armee in Syrien, von Djemal Pasha und von der syrischen Küste. January 1916–October 1917.

RM 40/213. Continuation of previous, October 1917–October 1918.

RM 40/214. More N.-Akten. Nachrichten von der türk. Armee Gen. Feldm.Von d. Goltz, Irakflotille, Persien, Afghanistan, Indien und Kaukasus. January 1916–September 1917.

RM 40/215. Continuation of same, February 1918–October 1918.

RM 40/216. Akten der Mittelmeerdivision. N.-Akten. Nachrichten von der Kleinasiatischen Küste. January 1916–September 1918.

RM 40/223. Press accounts of Turkish fleet and German U-boat actions in German and foreign press, December 1915–October 1916.

RM 40/251. Akten der Mittelmeerdivision. N.-Akten. Vorgänge in Schwarzen Meer nach dem Waffenstillstand. December 1917–April 1918.

RM 40/252. Continuation of previous, March 1918–October 1918.

RM 40/254. Akten etc. Nachrichten aus der Ukraine. July 1918–November 1918.

RM 40/262. Akten der Mittelmeerdivision. N.-Akten. Operationen Ägypten. January 1916–October 1918.

RM 40/329. Vorgänge im Kaukasus.

RM 40/457. Politisches. August 1914–February 1916.

RM 40/622. Kriegsnachrichten. N.d. Ganz geheim.

RM 40/671. Politisches. Vom 6.8.14–13.10.14.

Başbakanlık Osmanlı Arşivleri (BOA). Istanbul, Turkey.

  Hariciye Nezareti Hukuk Kismi (HR-H). Sublime Porte Correspondence.

    Box 329. "Almanya. Muhtelif Yazişmalar." 1914–18.

    Box 425. "Fransa. Muhtelif Yazişmalar." March–October 1914.

    Box 579. "Rusya. Muhtelif Yazişmalar." 13 April 1912–28 October 1914.

  Dahiliye Nezareti. Şifre Kalemi (DH-ŞFR). Ottoman government telegrams.

    Boxes 47–48. Wartime communiqués. 1914–16.

Gosudarstvennyi Arkhiv Rossiiskoi Federatsii (GARF). Moscow, Russia.

  Fond 529, opis' 1. "Byuro zaveduyushchego zagranichnoi agenturoi departmenta politsii v Konstantinopole." (Okhrana files.) 1911–14.

Haus-, Hof- und Straatsarchiv (HHSA). Vienna, Austria.

  Politisches Archiv I, Liasse Krieg 21a. Türkei und Krieg 22–4.

    Kartons 942–8. Turkey wartime correspondence, 1914–18.

    Karton 841. Deutschland 1918.

    Karton 467. Türkei (misc.).

Kriegsarchiv Wien (KW). Vienna, Austria.

  Generalstab. Militärattachees Konstantinopel.

  Evidenzbüro. Türkei.

    Karton 3502. 1914. Telegramme, Berichte v. Jänner-August.

    Karton 3506. 1914. Resumes d. Vertraulichen Nachrichten-Italien, Russland, Balkan.

Max von Oppenheim Stiftung (MvO), Sal. Oppenheim Jr. & Cie KGaA, Cologne, Germany.

  Nachlass Max von Oppenheim. Lebenserinnerungen.

    1/19. "Erster Weltkrieg. 1914–18. Politisches."

      "Compte rendu d'une séance politique. A Pera Palace Hotel. Constantinople Samedi 24 Avril 1915."

National Archives of the United Kingdom (PRO). Kew Gardens, London, UK.

  ADM (Admiralty Office Correspondence).

    File 137/940. Russia. Black Sea Fleet Reports. September 1916–June 1917.

    File 116/3491. Dardanelles Operations. Papers collected in Secretary's Office. Correspondence by First Lord (Churchill), also Colonel M. P. A. Hankey.

    File 116/1437B. The Dardanelles Commission. Statements of evidence and documents concerning period 2/7/15–5/9/17.

    File 137/38. Dardanelles Operations. 19 February–17 March.

    File 137/39. Dardanelles Operations. 1915 (18 March–24 April).

    File 137/40. Dardanelles Operations. 1915. April 25–26.

    File 137/204. Mesopotamia. River Operations. 1914–17. Report compiled in 1919 by Capt. W. Nunn, CB, CSI, CMG, DSO, RN.

  FO 371. Foreign Office Correspondence.

    Boxes 2135–41. Turkey Files, 1914 (up to Turkey's entry into war).

    Boxes 2445–50. Russia (War) correspondence, 1914–.

Boxes 2147, 2481–92, 2769–72, 2781, 3046–60, 3391–99.
Turkey (War) Files and Correspondence, 1914–18.
WO (War Office Corrrespondence).
File 106/1464. Secret. Russian troops available for Dardanelles.
File 106/1465. Bombardment of Dardanelles on March 19th [sic] 1915.
File 107/44. Private letters from Dardanelles.
File 32/5118. Report on operations in the Gallipoli Peninsula.
File 32/5119. Orders & instructions issued for recent operations. 31/8/15.
File 158/611. Report on siege of Kut by Lt. H. S. D. McNeal.
File 32/5206. Lt. Gen F. S. Maude's report on operations carried out in Mesopotamia from 28/8/16 to 31/3/17.
File 32/5128. Allenby's official communiqué for *London Gazette* on the conquest of Syria, 31 December 1918.
File 158/611. Appreciation of the Situation in Palestine from 1st July 1917.
File 158/634. Operation of Arab Forces in Hejaz & Syria.
File 158/635. Arab Cooperation in Syria. Aircraft Operations.
File 106/ 1357. Bulgaria. Intelligence Notes. Military Situation. 23 December 1916.
File 106/1359. Correspondence in the Event of Withdrawal of Salonika. 1917 May.
File 158/756. History of the British Salonica Force.
File 158/465. Colonel J. G. Heywood. Report of Special Mission to Bulgaria 6 October 1918.
Politisches Archiv des Auswärtigen Amtes (PAAA), Berlin, Germany.
Krieg 1914. Unternehmungen und Aufwiegelungen gegen unserer Feinde.
-R 29050. (Ukraine).
-R 21008–21025. (Kaukasus.)
-R 21028–21062. (Afghanistan und Persien.)
-R 21283. ("Die Senussi.")
Das Verhaeltnis der Tuerkei zu Deutschland. (Tuerkei 152.)
-R 13742–13760. 1898–1918.
Quai d'Orsay Archives (QO), Paris, France.
Guerre 1914–1918. Affaires Musulmanes. I. Panislamisme. Guerre Sainte. La Turquie dans la Guerre Européenne. Files 1650, 1654, 1655, 1658, 1662.
Guerre 1914–1918. Turquie. Files 845–48.
Guerre 1914–1918. Turquie. Notes Journalières. Files 896–99.
Rossiiskii Gosudarstvennyi Voenno-Istoricheskii Arkhiv (RGVIA). Moscow, Russia.
Fond 450. Opis' 1. Turtsiia.
Del' 118–131. Correspondence with "voennyi agent" in Constantinople, 1897–1906.
Fond 2000. Opis' 1. Glavnoe upravlenie General'nago Shtaba. (Stavka.)
Del' 2219. Materialyi o podgotovke i provedenii desantnyikh operatsii na Chernom more v sluchae voinyi s Turtsiei. 6 July 1909–12 November 1911.
Del' 2220. Desantnaya Ekspeditsia. 18 April 1912–15 November 1912.
Del' 2221. To zhe. Dessantnaya ekspedits. Podgotovka ekspeditsii snabzheniya i drug. 25 September 1912–15 September 1913.
Del' 2222. To zhe. Dessantnaya ekspeditsiya. O dessantnyikh operatsiyakh v Chernom more na 1914 g. 31 January 1914–31 May 1914.
Del' 2247. Zapiska N. A. Bazili: "O tselyakh Rossii na prolivakh."
Del' 3796. Dokladyi po GUGSh, perepiska so shtabom Kavkazskogo voennago okruga i spravochnyie materialyi o voennyikh' prigotovleniyakh i sostave voiskovyikh chastei okruga; mobilizatsii turetskoi armii, ee sostave, sosredotochenii i boevyikh deistviyakh' na Kavkazskom fronte; opisanie ukreplenii Bosfora i Dardanell.
Del' 3846. Svodki svedenii shtaba Kavkazskogo voennogo okruga a vnutripoliticheskom polozhenii Turtsii; kompletovanii i boevoi gotovnosti ee armii i stroitel'stve Bagdadskoi xh.d. 23 September 1913–21 September 1914.
Del' 3848. Perepiska so shtabom Kavkazskom voennogo okruga i russkim voennyim agentom v Turtsii o planakh razpolozheniya turetskoi armii v 1914 g. 1 November 1913–8 September 1914.

Del' 3851. Perepiska s Mob. Otdelom, shtabom Kavkazskogo voennogo okruga i russkim diploma-ticheskimi predstavitelyami v Turtsii i Persii o podgotovke k vooruzhennomu vosstaniyu turetskikh armyan, aiserov i kurdov protiv turok. 31 July 1914–9 Apr. 1915.

Del' 3852. Doneseniya shtabov Verkhovnogo glavnokomanduyushchego, 7 i Kavkazskoi armii, russkikh diplomaticheskikh predstavitelei v Egipte i Frantsii i voennyikh agentov v Bolgarii, Gretsii, Rumyinii, o vnutripolitcheskom polozhenii Turtsii, Gretsii i Egipta i dislokatsii turetskoi armii. 6 February–25 April 1915.

Del' 3860. Doneseniya shtaba Kavkazskoi armii, russkikh diplomaticheskikh predstavitelei i voennyikh agentov v Turtsii, Persii, Balkanskikh gosudarstvakh i Frantsii o vnutripolitiches-kom polozhenii v Turtsii i Persii, vstuplenii Turtsii v mirovuyu voinu, mobilizatsii armii i khode boevyikh deistvii. 15 October 1914–17 January 1915.

Del' 3861. Svodki svedenii shtabov Kavkazskoi I 7 armii o sostave i gruppirovke turetskoi armii. 5 November 1914–8 June 1915.

Del' 3888. Razvedyivatel'nyie materialyi o sostoyanii turetskoi armii, voennom politicheskom i ekonomicheskom polozhenii Turtsii, Germanii, Bolgarii i Palestinyi. 1915–16.

Del' 3890. Perepiska so shtabom Kavkazskoi armii i doneseniya shtaba Turkestanskogo voennogo okruga i russkogo voennogo agenta v Gretsii o formirovanii i dislokatsii turetskoi armii, voennom polozhenii na persidskom fronte i deistviyakh germanskikh otryadov v Afganis-tane. 9 January 1916–9 July 1917.

Vincennes. Service Historique de la Défense (VSHD). Vincennes, Paris, France.

7 N 1559. Attachés militaires. Russie. 1917–1919. Mission au Caucase. Corr. Arménie.

7 N 1649. Attachés militaires. Turquie. 1917–1919. Caucase et Arménie.

7 N 2150. Section d'Afrique. 1915–1918. Subventions aux corps de partisans d'Orient . . . Irréguliers, Arméniens, etc.

PRINTED AND ONLINE WORKS CITED, INCLUDING MEMOIRS

Adamov, E. A., ed. *Konstantinopol i prolivyi*. 2 vols. Moscow: Izdanie Litizdata NKID, 1925–26.

——. *Razdel aziatskoi Turtsii. Po sekretnyim dokumentam b. Ministerstva inostrannyikh del*. Moscow: Izdanie Litizdata NKID, 1924.

Ahmad, Feroz. "The Young Turk Revolution." *Journal of Contemporary History*, vol. 3, no. 3 (July 1968): 19–36.

Airapetov, O. R., ed. "Na Vostochnom napravlenii. Sud'ba Bosforskoi ekspeditsii v pravlenie imperatora Nikolaia II." In Airapetov, ed., *Poslednaia voina imperatorskoi Rossii: sbornik statei*, 158–252. Mos-cow: Tri kvadrata, 2002.

Akçam, Taner. *A Shameful Act: The Armenian Genocide and the Question of Turkish Responsibility*, trans. Paul Bessemer. New York: Metropolitan Books, 2006.

——. *The Young Turks' Crime Against Humanity: The Armenian Genocide and Ethnic Cleansing in the Ottoman Empire*. Princeton: Princeton University Press, 2012.

Aksakal, Mustafa. *The Ottoman Road to War in 1914: The Ottoman Empire and the First World War*. Cam-bridge: Cambridge University Press, 2008.

Akşin, Sina. *Ana Çizgileriyle Türkiye'nin Yakın Tarihi 1789–1980*. Istanbul: Yenigün Haber Ajansi, n.d.

Albertini, Luigi. *The Origins of the War of 1914*. New York: Oxford University Press, 1952–57. 3 vols.

Allen, Roger. *Spies, Scandals, and Sultans: Istanbul in the Twilight of the Ottoman Empire*. New York: Row-man & Littlefield, 2008.

Allen, W. E. D., and Paul Muratoff. *Caucasian Battlefields: A History of the Wars on the Turco-Caucasian Border, 1828–1921*. Cambridge: Cambridge University Press, 1953.

Anderson, Scott. *Lawrence in Arabia: War, Deceit, Imperial Folly and the Making of the Modern Middle East*. London: Atlantic Books, 2014.

Anglo-French Declaration of 7 November 1918. http://www.balfourproject.org/anglo-french-declaration/.

Askerî Tarih Belgeleri Dergisi, 30'Uncu Tümen Sarıkamış Harekatî Ceridesi. No. 122 (2 Auğustos–20 Aralık 1914) and No. 123 (20 Aralık 1914–10 Ocak 1915. Ankara: Genelkurmay Basimevi, 2009.

Asquith, H. H. *Letters to Venetia Stanley*. Eds. Michael and Eleanor Brock. Oxford: Oxford University Press, 1982.

Barr, James. *A Line in the Sand: Britain, France and the Struggle That Shaped the Middle East.* London: Simon & Schuster, 2011.

Baumgart, Winfried. *Deutsche Ostpolitik 1918: Von Brest-Litovsk bis zum Ende des Ersten Weltkrieges.* Vienna: R. Oldenbourg Verlag, 1966.

Bayur, Yusuf Hikmet. *Türk İnkılabı Tarihi.* 3 vols. Ankara: Türk Tarih Kurumu Basimevi, 1940–67.

Bennett, Christine. *Basra Diary.* http://paperspast.natlib.govt.nz/cgi-bin/paperspast?a=d&d=OSWCC 19160222.2.15 (accessed May 2015).

Bernières, Louis de. *Birds Without Wings.* London: Random House, 2005.

Bloxham, Donald. *The Great Game of Genocide: Imperialism, Nationalism, and the Destruction of the Ottoman Armenians.* Oxford: Oxford University Press, 2005.

Bobroff, Ronald Park. *Roads to Glory: Late Imperial Russia and the Turkish Straits.* London: I. B. Tauris, 2006.

Bodger, Alan. "Russia and the End of the Ottoman Empire." In Marian Kent, ed., *The Great Powers and the End of the Ottoman Empire.* London: Frank Cass, 1984.

Buchan, John. *Greenmantle.* London: Penguin, 2001.

Butler, Rohan, and E. L. Woodward, eds. *Documents on British Foreign Policy 1919–1939.* 65 vols. London: HMSO, 1946–1989.

Çakmak, Mareşal Fevzi. *Birinci Dünya Savaşın'da Doğu Cephesi.* Ankara: Genelkurmay Basım Evi, 2005.

Chalabian, Antranig. *General Andranik and the Armenian Revolutionary Movement.* Southfield, MI: Antranig Chalabian, 1988.

Churchill, Winston. *The Unknown War: The Eastern Front.* New York: Scribner, 1931.

———. *The World Crisis.* 4 vols. 1923–1929. New York: Scribner.

Clark, Bruce. *Twice a Stranger: How Mass Expulsion Forged Modern Greece and Turkey.* London: Granta Books, 2006.

Cockburn, Patrick. "Is It the End of Sykes-Picot?" *London Review of Books,* vol. 35, no. 11 (6 June 2013).

Cornish, Nik. *The Russian Army and the First World War.* Stroud, Gloucestershire: Spellmount, 2006.

"Correspondence Respecting Events Leading to the Rupture of Relations with Turkey." Printed by Harrison & Sons for His Majesty's Stationery Office, November 1914.

Dadrian, Vahakn N. *The History of the Armenian Genocide: Ethnic Conflict from the Balkans to Anatolia to the Caucasus.* New York: Berghahn Books, 1995.

Davison, Roderic. *Reform in the Ottoman Empire, 1856–1876.* New York: Gordian Press, 1973.

Demirel, Muammer. *Birinci dünya harbinde Erzurum ve çevresinde Ermeni hareketleri (1914–1918).* Ankara, 1996.

Die deutschen Dokumente zum Kriegsausbruch. Eds. Karl Kautsky, Max Montgelas, and Prof. Walter Schücking. 4 vols. Charlottenburg, Berlin: Deutsche Verlagsgesellschaft für Politik und Geschichte, 1919.

Dowling, Timothy C. *The Brusilov Offensive.* Bloomington: Indiana University Press, 2009.

Djemal Pasha. *Memories of a Turkish Statesman, 1913–1919.* New York: George H. Doran, 1922.

Dündar, Fuat. *Crime of Numbers: The Role of Statistics in the Armenian Question (1878–1918).* New Brunswick, NJ: Transaction, 2010.

———. "Pouring a People into the Desert: The 'Definitive Solution' to the Armenian Question," in Ronald Suny et al., eds., *A Question of Genocide.*

Dyer, Gwinne. "The Turkish Armistice of 1918." *Middle Eastern Studies,* vol. 8, no. 2 (1972): 143–78.

Edib, Halidé. *Memoirs of Halidé Edib.* Piscataway, NJ: Gorgias Press, 2005 (reprint).

Erhan, Çağrı. *American Documents on Greek Occupation of Anatolia.* Ankara: Center for Strategic Research (SAM), 1999.

Erickson, Edward. "Armenian Massacres: New Records Undercut Old Blame." *Middle East Quarterly,* vol. 11, no. 3 (Summer 2006): 67–75.

———. "The Armenians and Ottoman Military Policy, 1915." *War in History,* vol. 15, no. 2 (2008): 141–67.

———. *Defeat in Detail: The Ottoman Army in the Balkans, 1912–1913.* Westport, CT: Praeger, 2003.

———. *Gallipoli: The Ottoman Campaign.* South Yorkshire: Pen & Sword Military, 2010.

———. *Ordered to Die: A History of the Ottoman Army in the First World War.* Westport, CT: Greenwood Press, 2001.

———. *Ottomans and Armenians: A Study in Counterinsurgency.* New York: Palgrave Macmillan, 2013.

Falkenhayn, General Erich von. *General Headquarters and Its Critical Decisions, 1914–1916.* New York: Dodd, Mead, 1920.

Fay, Sidney Bradshaw. *The Origins of the World War.* 2 vols. New York: Macmillan, 1935.

Figes, Orlando. *Crimea.* London: Penguin, 2010.

Fromkin, David. *A Peace to End All Peace: The Fall of the Ottoman Empire and the Creation of the Modern Middle East.* New York: Henry Holt, 1989.

Fuller, William C., Jr. *Strategy and Power in Russia 1600–1914.* New York: Free Press, 1992.

Gardiner, Robert, ed. *Conway's All the World's Fighting Ships 1860–1905.* London: Conway Maritime, 1979.

Geiss, Immanuel. *Der Berliner Kongress 1878: Protokolle und Materialien.* Boppard am Rhein: Boldt, 1978.

"Ghost Buildings of Istanbul." http://www.hayal-et.org/i.php/site/building/ayastefanos_ant

Gibbon, Edward. *The History of the Decline and Fall of the Roman Empire*, Volume the Third (1781). London: Penguin Press/Allen Lane Edition, 1994.

Gladstone, William Ewart. *The Bulgarian Horrors and the Question of the East.* London: J. Murray, 1876.

Gökay, Bülent. *A Clash of Empires: Turkey Between Russian Bolshevism and British Imperialism, 1918–1923.* London: I. B. Tauris, 1997.

Greger, René. *Die Russische Flotte im Ersten Weltkrieg, 1914–1917.* Munich: J. F. Lehmann, 1970.

Hall, Richard C. *The Balkan Wars, 1912–1913: Prelude to the Great War.* London: Routledge, 2000.

Halpern, Paul G. *A Naval History of World War I.* Annapolis, MD: Naval Institute Press, 1994.

Hanioğlu, M. Şükrü: *A Brief History of the Late Ottoman Empire.* Princeton: Princeton University Press, 2008.

———. *The Young Turks in Opposition.* New York: Oxford University Press, 1995.

Harvey, A. D. "Bombs on Constantinople." *Cross and Cockade International Journal*, vol. 38, no. 3: 165–67.

Haslip, Joan. *The Sultan: The Life of Abdul Hamid II.* New York: Holt, Rinehart and Winston, 1973.

Hopkirk, Peter. *On Secret Service East of Constantinople: The Plot to Bring Down the British Empire.* London: John Murray, 1994.

Hovannisian, Richard G. "The Allies and Armenia, 1915–18." *Journal of Contemporary History*, vol. 3, no. 1 (January 1968): 145–68.

———, ed. *The Armenian Genocide: History, Politics, Ethics.* New York: Macmillan, 1992.

———, ed. *The Armenian Genocide in Perspective.* New Brunswick, NJ: Transaction Books, 1986.

———. "The Armenian Question in the Ottoman Empire." In Hovannisian, ed., *The Armenian People from Ancient to Modern Times.* 2 vols. New York: Macmillan, 1997.

———. *The Republic of Armenia.* 4 vols. Berkeley: University of California Press, 1971–96.

Hull, Isabel V. *The Entourage of Kaiser Wilhelm II, 1888–1918.* New York: Cambridge University Press, 1982.

Hurst, Michael, ed. *Key Treaties for the Great Powers, 1814–1914.* New York: St. Martin's, 1972.

Internationale Beziehungen in Zeitalter des Imperialismus. Edited by M. N. Pokrovskii. 8+ vols. Berlin: R. Hobbing, 1931–.

Inostrantsev, Michael A. "L'opération de Sarakamych" by General Inostrantsev. *Revue militaire française*, vol. 105, nos. 164–65, February–March 1935.

Jelavich, Barbara. *History of the Balkans.* 2 vols. New York: Cambridge University Press, 1983.

Karpat, Kemal. *Ottoman Population 1830–1914: Demographic and Social Characteristics.* Madison: University of Wisconsin Press, 1985.

Karsh, Efraim, and Inari Karsh. *Empires of the Sand: The Struggle for Mastery in the Middle East 1789–1923.* Cambridge: Harvard University Press, 1999.

Kazemzadeh, Firuz. *The Struggle for Transcaucasia, 1917–1921.* New York: Philosophical Library, 1951.

Keegan, John. *The First World War.* London: Hutchinson, 1998.

Keleşyılmaz, Vahdet. *Teşkilat-i-Mahsûsa'nın Hindistan Misyonu (1914–1918).* Ankara: AKDTYK Atatürk Araştırma Merkezi, 1999.

Kerr, Stanley. *The Lions of Maraş: Personal Experiences with American Near Eastern Relief.* State University of New York Press, 1973.

Khalidi, Rashid. *Resurrecting Empire: Western Footprints and America's Perilous Path in the Middle East.* Boston: Beacon Press, 2004.

Kinross, Patrick. *Atatürk: The Rebirth of a Nation.* London: Phoenix, 2001 (orig. 1964).

Knight, Paul. *British Army in Mesopotamia, 1914–1918.* Jefferson, NC: MacFarland, 2013.

Krasnyi Arkhiv: Istoricheskii zhurnal. 106 vols. Moscow: Gospolitizdat, 1922–41.

Kress von Kressenstein, Friedrich. *Mit den Türken zum Suezkanal*. Berlin: Vorhut-Verlag, 1938.

Kurat, Akdes Nimet, Dr. *Brest-Litovsk Müzakereleri ve Barışı*. Ankara: n.p., n.d.

———. *Türkiye ve Rusya*. Ankara: Kültür Bakanlığı, 1990.

Larcher, Maurice. *La guerre turque dans la guerre mondiale*. Paris: E. Chiron, 1926.

Lazarev, M. S. *Kurdskii vopros (1891–1917)*. Moscow: Izdatel'stvo "Nauka," 1972.

Lewis, Bernard. *The Emergence of Modern Turkey*. London: Oxford University Press, 1961.

Lewy, Guenter. *The Armenian Massacres in Ottoman Turkey: A Disputed Genocide*. Salt Lake City: University of Utah Press, 2005.

Liman von Sanders, Otto. *Five Years in Turkey*, trans. U.S. Naval Institute. East Sussex: Naval & Military Press, n.d.

Un Livre noir. Diplomatie d'avant-guerre d'après les documents des archive russes, Novembre 1910–Juillet 1914. Preface by René Marchand. Paris: Librarie dutravail, 1922.

Llewellyn-Smith, Michael. *Ionian Vision: Greece in Asia Minor 1919–1922*. London: Hurst, 1998 (orig. 1973).

Lloyd, Nick. *Hundred Days: The Campaign That Ended World War I*. New York: Basic Books, 2014.

Lohr, Eric. "The Russian Army and the Jews: Mass Deportation, Hostages, and Violence During World War I." *Russian Review* 60 (July 2001): 404–19.

Lührs, Hans. *Gegenspieler des Obersten Lawrence*. Berlin: Otto Schlegel, 1936.

MacMillan, Margaret. *Paris 1919: Six Months That Changed the World*. New York: Random House, 2002.

Mango, Andrew. *Atatürk*. London: John Murray, 1999.

Mansel, Philip. *Constantinople: City of the World's Desire, 1453–1924*. London: Penguin, 1997.

———. *Levant: Splendour and Catastrophe on the Mediterranean*. London: Murray, 2010.

Mazower, Mark. *Salonica, City of Ghosts: Christians, Muslims, and Jews, 1430–1950*. New York: Knopf, 2005.

McCarthy, Justin, et al. *The Armenian Rebellion at Van*. Salt Lake City: University of Utah Press, 2006.

———. *Death and Exile: The Ethnic Cleansing of Ottoman Muslims, 1821–1922*. Princeton: Darwin Press, 1995.

———. *The Ottoman Peoples and the End of Empire*. London: Oxford University Press, 2001.

McGuirk, Russell. *The Sanusi's Little War: The Amazing Story of a Forgotten Conflict in the Western Desert, 1915–1917*. London: Arabian Publishing, 2007.

McKale, Donald. *War by Revolution: Germany and Great Britain in the Middle East in the Era of World War I*. Kent, OH: Kent State University Press, 1988.

McLaughlin, Redmond. *The Escape of "The Goeben": Prelude to Gallipoli*. New York: Scribner, 1974.

McMeekin, Sean. *The Berlin-Baghdad Express: The Ottoman Empire and Germany's Bid for World Power, 1898–1918*. London: Penguin/Allen Lane, 2010.

———. *History's Greatest Heist: The Bolshevik Looting of Russia*. New Haven: Yale University Press, 2008.

———. *July 1914: Countdown to War*. New York: Basic Books, 2013.

———. *The Red Millionaire: A Political Biography of Willi Münzenberg, Moscow's Secret Propaganda Tsar in the West*. New Haven: Yale University Press, 2004.

———. *The Russian Origins of the First World War*. Cambridge, MA: Harvard University Press, 2011.

McMurray, Jonathan S. *Distant Ties: Germany, the Ottoman Empire, and the Construction of the Baghdad Railway*. Westport, CT: Praeger, 2001.

Miller, Geoffrey. *Straits: British Policy Towards the Ottoman Empire and the Origins of the Dardanelles Campaign*. Hull: University of Hull Press, 1997.

———. *Superior Force: The Conspiracy Behind the Escape of Goeben and Breslau*. Hull: University of Hull Press, 1996.

Milton, Giles. *Paradise Lost: Smyrna 1922: The Destruction of a Christian City in the Islamic World*. New York: Basic Books, 2008.

Moorehead, Alan. *Gallipoli*. London: H. Hamilton, 1956.

Morgenthau, Henry. *Ambassador Morgenthau's Story*. New York: Doubleday, 1918.

———. *Secrets of the Bosphorus*. London: Hutchinson, 1918.

Mühlmann, Carl. *Oberste Heeresleitung und Balkan im Weltkrieg 1914–1918*. Berlin: W. Limpert, 1942.

Münz, Rainer, and Rainer Ohliger. *Diasporas and Ethnic Migrants: German, Israel, and Post-Soviet Successor States in Comparative Perspective*. London: Frank Cass, 2003.

Mutlu, Dilek Kaya. "The Russian Monument at *Ayastefanos* (San Stefano): Between Defeat and Revenge, Remembering and Forgetting." *Middle Eastern Studies*, vol. 43, no. 1 (January 2007): 75–86.

Nalbandian, Louise. *The Armenian Revolutionary Movement: The Development of Armenian Political Parties Through the Nineteenth Century*. Berkeley: University of California Press, 1963.

Nogales, Rafael de. *Memoirs of a Soldier of Fortune*. New York: Harrison Smith, 1932 (reprint edition by J. F. Tapley).

Özdemir, Hikmet. *The Ottoman Army 1914–1918: Disease and Death on the Battlefield*. Salt Lake City: University of Utah Press, 2008.

Palmer, Alan Warwick. *The Decline and Fall of the Ottoman Empire*. London: J. Murray, 1992.

Pavlovich, N. B. *The Fleet in the First World War*, trans. C. M. Rao. New Delhi: Amerind, 1979.

Pipes, Richard. *The Formation of the Soviet Union: Communism and Nationalism, 1917–1923*. Cambridge: Harvard University Press, 1954.

———. *The Russian Revolution*. New York: Knopf, 1990.

Pokrovskii, M. N., ed. *Drei Konferenzen (zur Vorgeschichte des Krieges)*. Berlin: Arbeiterbuchhandlung, 1920.

———. *Internationale Beziehungen im Zeitalter des Imperialismus*. 8+ vols. Berlin: R. Hobbing, 1931–.

———. *Tsarskaia Rossiia v mirovoi voine*. Vol 1. Leningrad, 1926.

Pomiankowski, Joseph. *Der Zusammenbruch des Ottomanischen Reiches: Erinnerungen an die Türkei aus der Zeit des Weltkrieges*. Zurich: Amalthea, 1928.

"The Powers' Note." *Sydney Morning Herald*, 10 October 1912.

Ramsaur, Ernest Edmondson. *The Young Turks: Prelude to the Revolution of 1908*. Princeton: Princeton University Press, 1957.

Rogan, Eugene. *The Arabs: A History*. New York: Basic Books, 2009.

Reynolds, Michael A. "The Ottoman-Russian Struggle for Eastern Anatolia and the Caucasus, 1908–1918." Unpublished Ph.D. dissertation, Princeton University, 2003.

———. *Shattering Empires: The Clash and Collapse of the Ottoman and Russian Empires*. New York: Cambridge University Press, 2011.

Roberts, Andrew. *Salisbury: Victorian Titan*. London: Phoenix, 2000.

Şahin, Erman. "A Scrutiny of Akçam's Version of History and the Armenian Genocide." *Journal of Muslim Minority Affairs*, vol. 28, no. 2 (August 2008).

Sazonov, S. D. *Fateful Years, 1909–1916: The Reminiscences of Serge Sazonov, Russia's Minister for Foreign Affairs: 1914*. London: J. Cape, 1928.

Seidt, Hans-Ulrich. *Berlin, Kabul, Moskau: Oskar Ritter von Niedermayer und Deutschlands Ostpolitik*. Munich: Universitas, 2002.

Seton-Watson, R. W. *Disraeli, Gladstone, and the Eastern Question*. London: Frank Cass, 1962.

Shaw, Stanford. *From Empire to Republic: The Turkish War of National Liberation 1918–1923: A Documentary Study*. 5 vols. Ankara: Türk Tarih Kurumu, 2000.

———. *The Ottoman Empire in World War I*. Ankara: Turkish Historical Society, 2006.

Shaw, Stanford J., and Ezel Kural. *History of the Ottoman Empire and Modern Turkey*. 2 vols. Cambridge: Cambridge University Press, 1976–77.

Siegel, Jennifer. *Endgame: Britain, Russia, and the Final Struggle for Central Asia*. London: I. B. Tauris, 2002.

Snouck Hurgronje, Dr. C. *The Holy War "Made in Germany."* New York: G. P. Putnam's Sons, 1915.

Stevenson, David. *Cataclysm: The First World War as Political Tragedy*. New York: Basic Books, 2004.

———. *With Our Backs to the Wall: Victory and Defeat in 1918*. London: Allen Lane, 2011.

Stites, Richard. "Miliukov and the Russian Revolution." In Paul N. Miliukov, *The Russian Revolution*, ed. Richard Stites.

Stone, Norman. *The Eastern Front 1914–1917*. New York: Charles Scribner's Sons, 1975.

———. *World War One: A Short History*. London: Allen Lane, 2007.

Strachan, Hew. *The First World War*. New York: Viking, 2004.

Strelianov, P. N. *Korpus generala Baratova, 1915–1918 gg*. Moscow: s.n., 2002.

Sumner, B. H. *Russia and the Balkans, 1870–1880*. Hamden, CT: Archer Books, 1962.

Suny, Ronald. *Armenia in the Twentieth Century*. Chico, CA: Scholars Press, 1983.

———. "Empire and Nation: Armenians, Turks, and the End of the Ottoman Empire." *Armenian Forum*, vol. 1, no. 2 (1998): 17–51.

Suny, Ronald, Fatma Müge Goçek, and Norman Naimark. *A Question of Genocide: Armenians and Turks at the End of the Ottoman Empire*. New York: Oxford University Press, 2011.

Tamari, Salim. *Year of the Locust: A Soldier's Diary and the Erasure of Palestine's Ottoman Past*. Berkeley: University of California Press, 2011.

TCGB (T. C. GenelKurmay Başkanlığı). *Arşiv Belgeleriyle Ermeni Faaliyetleri 1914–1918*. 4 vols. Ankara: Genelkurmay Basim Evi, 2005.

"Terms of the Treaty of Sèvres." http://www.hri.org/docs/sevres/part1.html.

Townshend, Charles. *When God Made Hell: The British Invasion of Mesopotamia and the Creation of Iraq, 1914–1921*. London: Faber & Faber, 2010.

Travers, Timothy. *Gallipoli 1915*. Stroud: Tempus, 2001.

Trumpener, Ulrich. *Germany and the Ottoman Empire, 1914–1918*. Princeton: Princeton University Press, 1968.

Tuchman, Barbara Wertheim. *The Guns of August*. New York: Macmillan, 1962.

———. *The Zimmermann Telegram*. New York: Viking, 1958.

Tunstall, Graydon. "Austria-Hungary and the Brusilov Offensive of 1916." *Historian*, vol. 70, no. 1:30–53.

Turfan, M. Naim. *Rise of the Young Turks: Politics, the Military, and the Ottoman Collapse*. New York: I. B. Tauris, 2000.

Ulrichsen, Kristian Coates. *The First World War in the Middle East*. London: Hurst, 2014.

"Vozstanie v' Vane." In *Russkoe Slovo* no. 141, 20 June/3 July 1915.

Weber, Frank G. *Eagles on the Crescent: Germany, Austria, and the Diplomacy of the Turkish Alliance, 1914–1918*. Ithaca: Cornell University Press, 1970.

Wheeler-Bennett, John W. *Brest-Litovsk: The Forgotten Peace*. London: Macmillan, 1956 (orig. 1938).

Wildman, Allan K. *The End of the Russian Imperial Army*. 2 vols. Princeton: Princeton University Press, 1980/1987.

Wilhelm II (Emperor of Germany). *Reden des Kaisers: Ansprachen, Predigten, und Trinksprüche*. Ed. Ernst Johann. Munich: Deutscher Taschenbuch-Verlag, 1966.

Will, Alexander. *Kein Griff nach der Weltmacht: Geheime Dienste und Propaganda im Deutsch-österreichisch-türkischen Bündnis 1914–1918*. Cologne: Böhlau, 2012.

Wolf, Klaus. *Gallipoli 1915: Das deutsch-türkische Militärbündnis im Ersten Weltkrieg*. Bonn: Report Verlag, 2008.

Wynn, Antony. *Persia in the Great Game*. London: John Murray, 2004.

Yasamee, F. A. K. "Ottoman Empire." In Keith Wilson, ed., *Decisions for War, 1914*, 229–68. New York: St. Martin's, 1995.

Zechlin, Egmont. *Die deutsche Politik und die Juden im Ersten Weltkrieg*. Göttingen: Vandenhoeck und Ruprecht, 1969.

Zürcher, Erik. *The Unionist Factor: The Role of the Committee of Union and Progress in the Turkish National Movement, 1905–1926*. Leiden: E. J. Brill, 1984.